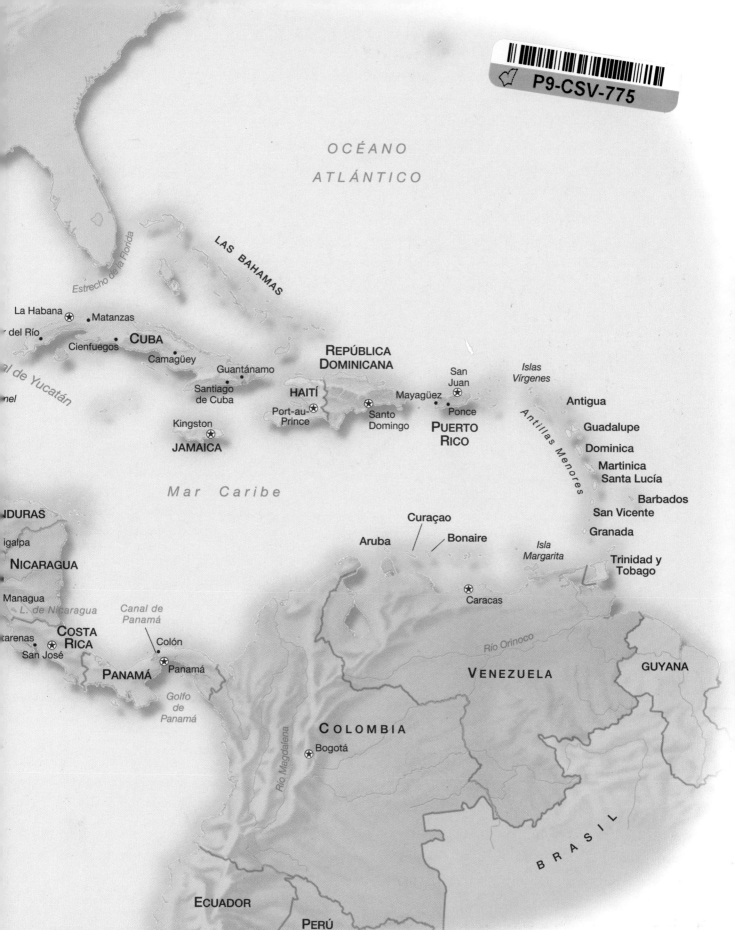

OCÉANO

ATLÁNTICO

P9-CSV-775

LAS BAHAMAS

Estrecho de la Florida

La Habana ✪  • Matanzas
del Río •
Cienfuegos •    **CUBA**
              Camagüey •
al de Yucatán              Guantánamo •
                    Santiago
el •                de Cuba •      **HAITÍ**
                              Port-au-
                Kingston •      Prince ✪
              **JAMAICA** ✪

Mar   Caribe

**REPÚBLICA
DOMINICANA**
                    San
                    Juan
          Santo         Ponce •
          Domingo    **PUERTO
                     RICO**

Islas
Vírgenes

Antigua

Guadalupe

Dominica

Martinica
Santa Lucía

Barbados
San Vicente

Granada

Isla
Margarita

Trinidad y
Tobago

Mayagüez •

Antillas Menores

Curaçao

Aruba          Bonaire

DURAS
igalpa •
**NICARAGUA**

Managua •
L. de Nicaragua

arenas •  **COSTA
           RICA** ✪
San José •

Canal de
Panamá

Colón •

**PANAMÁ**    Panamá •

Golfo
de
Panamá

Caracas ✪

Río Orinoco

**VENEZUELA**

**GUYANA**

Río Magdalena

**COLOMBIA**
  Bogotá ✪

**ECUADOR**

**PERÚ**

B R A S I L

*Fifth Edition*

# MOSAICOS

Spanish as a World Language

## Matilde Olivella de Castells (Late)

Emerita, California State University, Los Angeles

## Elizabeth E. Guzmán

University of Iowa

## Paloma Lapuerta

Central Connecticut State University

## Judith E. Liskin-Gasparro

University of Iowa

**Prentice Hall**

Upper Saddle River   London   Singapore   Toronto
Tokyo   Sydney   Hong Kong   Mexico City

*Dedicamos esta edición de Mosaicos a Matilde Castells, quien puso juntas, una a una, las piezas de este libro con un talento y profesionalismo admirables.*

*Executive Editor:* Julia Caballero
*Development Editors:* Elizabeth Lantz, Celia Meana
*Executive Marketing Manager:* Kris Ellis-Levy
*Senior Marketing Manager:* Denise Miller
*Marketing Coordinator:* William J. Bliss
*Senior Managing Editor:* Mary Rottino
*Associate Managing Editor:* Janice Stangel
*Project Manager:* Manuel Echevarria
*Development Editor for Assessment:* Melissa Marolla Brown
*Media Editor:* Meriel Martínez
*Senior Media Editor:* Samantha Alducin
*Art Manager:* Gail Cocker
*Illustrator:* Andrew Lange Illustration
*Cartographer:* Peter Bull Studio
*Assistant Editor/EditorialCoordinator:* Jennifer Murphy
*Manufacturing Buyer:* Cathleen Petersen

*Manager, Print Production:* Brian Mackey
*Manager, Rights and Permissions:* Zina Arabia
*Manager, Visual Research:* Beth Brenzel
*Manager, Cover Visual Research & Permissions:* Karen Sanatar
*Image Permission Coordinator:* Fran Toepfer
*Cover Image:* Ferran Traite Soler/IStockphoto.com
*Photo Researcher:* Diane Austin
*Designer:* Ximena Tamvakopoulos
*Creative Design Director:* Leslie Osher
*Art Director, Interior:* John Christiana
*Editorial Assistant:* Katie Spiegel
*Publisher:* Phil Miller
*Composition/Full-Service Project Management:* Macmillan Publishing Solutions
*Printer/Binder:* Courier Kendallville, Inc.

This book was set in 10/12.5 Sabon.

Credits and acknowledgments borrowed from other sources and reproduced, with permission, in this textbook appear on pages A54–A55.

**Library of Congress Cataloging-in-Publication Data**

Mosaicos : Spanish as a world language / Matilde Olivella de Castells ... [et al.]. — 5th ed.
    p. cm.
  English and Spanish.
  Includes bibliographical references and index.
  ISBN-13: 978-0-13-500153-0 (hardbound : alk. paper)
  ISBN-10: 0-13-500153-6 (hardbound : alk. paper)
  1.  Spanish language—Textbooks for foreign speakers—English.  I. Castells, Matilde Olivella de.

PC4129.E5M69 2008
468.2'421—dc22

      2008046837

10 9 8 7 6 5 4 3 2 1

| | |
|---|---|
| Student Edition ISBN - 10: | 0-13-500153-6 |
| Student Edition ISBN - 13: | 978-0-13-500153-0 |
| Annotated Instructor's Edition ISBN - 10: | 0-205-66392-3 |
| Annotated Instructor's Edition ISBN - 13: | 978-0-205-66392-7 |
| Volume 1 ISBN - 10: | 0-205-63609-8 |
| Volume 1 ISBN - 13: | 978-0-205-63609-9 |
| Volume 2 ISBN - 10: | 0-205-63608-X |
| Volume 2 ISBN - 13: | 978-0-205-63608-2 |
| Volume 3 ISBN - 10: | 0-205-63607-1 |
| Volume 3 ISBN - 13: | 978-0-205-63607-5 |
| A la carte ISBN - 10: | 0-205-73042-6 |
| A la carte ISBN - 13: | 978-0-205-73042-1 |

**Prentice Hall**
is an imprint of

www.pearsonhighered.com

# BRIEF CONTENTS

# SCOPE AND SEQUENCE

| Capítulo | Communicative objectives | A primera vista |
|---|---|---|

| Capítulo | Communicative objectives | A primera vista |
|---|---|---|

vii

| Capítulo | Communicative objectives | A primera vista |
|---|---|---|

### De compras  188

Talk about clothing, prices, and shopping
Talk about past events
Express likes and dislikes

### Los deportes  222

Talk about sports and physical activities
Ask and answer questions about weather
Discuss past events

### Nuestras tradiciones  256

Talk about holidays, traditions, and celebrations
Express ongoing actions in the past
Narrate past events
Make comparisons

| Capítulo | Communicative objectives | A primera vista |
|---|---|---|

| Capítulo | Communicative objectives | A primera vista |
|---|---|---|

# PREFACE

## Welcome to the Fifth Edition of *Mosaicos*

Since the publication of its first edition more than a decade ago, *Mosaicos* has been widely acclaimed for its practical, communicative, culturally based approach to first-year Spanish. The approach has been refined over the course of several editions, and for this fifth edition we have been especially thorough in examining all aspects of the Student Text and all components of the *Mosaicos* program. The result is a fresh, twenty-first-century perspective on language teaching and learning in the context of a dynamic introduction to the Hispanic world and its people. We hope that both veteran users and those new to *Mosaicos* will discover a text that is richly contextualized, cognitively engaging, visually attractive, and readily accessible, accompanied by a wide array of resources that support student learning and make each class period valuable and enjoyable.

One of the hallmarks of the *Mosaicos* approach—and the rationale for the title—is the emphasis on the integration of the many different instructional strands that comprise a beginning Spanish course. We have made a special effort to ensure that this fifth edition effectively integrates elements that other programs often treat in isolation. We have gone farther than ever before in our effort to synthesize linguistic content with appropriate cultural contexts. We have refined and improved the open-ended *Situaciones* activities, in which students are asked to integrate their knowledge of grammatical structures and functions with thematically relevant vocabulary. Finally, we have made major revisions to the *Mosaicos* section of each chapter, in which students put linguistic and cultural knowledge together as they develop and practice their listening, speaking, reading, and writing skills.

*Mosaicos* reflects the wisdom and experience of the many expert language instructors who have used the program and have provided helpful suggestions over the years. But at a deeper level, it is grounded in current theories of language learning and in pedagogical principles embraced by most language instructors today. It presents vocabulary within communicative and cultural contexts. Its grammar sections move from meaning to form, providing an understanding of the language that is both functional and structural. It emphasizes the social aspects of language use by providing an abundance of carefully sequenced pair and group activities. It fosters awareness of the diversity of the Spanish-speaking world through photos, realia, maps, readings, and activities, as well as a new video program. By engaging students in the linguistic, cognitive, and social aspects of language learning, the distinctive *Mosaicos* approach draws on current knowledge about language learning to prepare first-year students to continue their study of Spanish language and culture at the intermediate level.

## Highlights of the Fifth Edition

While building on the strengths of earlier editions, the fifth edition of *Mosaicos* incorporates many new and remarkable features. With its focus on learning strategies and communicative functions, it provides students and instructors with more tools than ever before to enhance and enrich the learning experience.

### Vocabulary in Context

The *Mosaicos* program features a culturally and communicatively rich format for presenting and practicing new vocabulary. Through the two-page spread at the beginning of each chapter and in the *A primera vista* section that follows, students encounter new words in appropriate linguistic and cultural contexts.

The chapter-opening pages have been completely redesigned to provide a stimulating introduction both to the chapter theme and to the country or region that the chapter targets. New chapter titles highlight the text's active, functional approach to language learning, and abundant annotations on the chapter-opening pages guide instructors in introducing and recycling relevant vocabulary.

In the *A primera vista* section, new vocabulary is presented in contexts that reflect the chapter theme in various ways. Language samples, photos, line drawings, and realia are used to present new material, rather than word lists and translations. The activities that follow foster the use of new and previously learned vocabulary in natural, thematically relevant contexts. Special features include the following:

- Boldface type is used within the language samples to highlight new words and phrases that students will need to learn to use actively. (A convenient list of these words and phrases is provided at the end of each chapter.)

- Audio icons remind students that recorded versions of the language samples are available in the *Mosaicos* audio program.

- *Cultura* boxes (many new to this edition) raise awareness of the cultural contexts in which the language is used and help students learn the skills of close observation and interpretation of cultural products.

- *En otras palabras* boxes (all new to this edition) give examples of regional variations in the language.

## Grammar as Function and Meaning

In the newly renamed *Funciones y formas* section of each chapter, grammar is presented as a means to effective communication. The bulleted explanations—clear, concise, and easy to understand—are designed to be studied at home, although their integration into the main body of the text enables students to use them for quick reference as they practice communication in class.

- Visuals and brief language samples are now used consistently to introduce new structures in meaningful contexts. The new structures are highlighted in boldface type.

- Short comprehension-based activities (all new to this edition) draw students' attention to the connection between meaning and linguistic form, providing a bridge from *función* to *forma*. These *Piénselo* activities are designed to help students develop their ability to think about how each structure communicates meaning by means of particular forms.

- A carefully designed sequence of communicative activities (many new or revised for this edition) follow the bulleted grammatical explanations. These activities focus attention on the communicative purpose of the linguistic structures while invoking culturally relevant contexts. All activities require students to process meaning as well as form so that they develop confidence in speaking and skill in using their linguistic knowledge to gather information, answer questions, and resolve problems.

- A large number of open-ended *Situaciones* activities (many new or revised for this edition) prompt students to integrate relevant grammatical structures with contexts drawn from the chapter theme. Two *Situaciones* role-plays are now provided for each grammar topic, and the format of these activities has been standardized so that there are always two roles (Role A and Role B). *En directo* boxes introduce colloquial expressions and encourage students to use them in the *Situaciones* and other communicative activities.

- Strategically placed *Lengua* boxes offer succinct grammatical information when it is needed to support self-expression.

- The grammatical scope and sequence has been modified in order to meet the communicative needs of beginning students more effectively. The *Algo más* boxes used in the fourth edition to present new structures have been eliminated; all essential structures are now given the full range of explanation and activities. Major topics, such as the preterit and imperfect, **ser/estar**, and object pronouns, are recycled to enhance learning, and basic topics such as regular verbs and **gustar** are presented earlier to spread essential structures more evenly over the book's fifteen chapters.

## Integrated Culture

The fifth edition of *Mosaicos* builds on the successful integration of culture and language of previous editions. Each chapter focuses on a specific country or region, and numerous references to that country or region appear in the chapter's language samples, photos, maps, and realia. Related cultural content is interwoven throughout the activities and readings.

- A newly designed two-page chapter opener highlights the country or region that is the focus of the chapter. It includes a relevant work of art as well as maps and photos. A new warm-up activity (called *A vista de pájaro*) encourages students to process the visually presented information while accessing relevant prior knowledge. Numerous annotations offer instructors factual, conversational, and linguistic suggestions to pique students' interest and ease them into the chapter.

- The *Enfoque cultural* section of each chapter has new readings and accompanying activities. The first set of activities is available online as well as in the textbook. A final activity asks students to use the reading as a point of departure for expanding and sharing their knowledge. The standardized format of this section makes it possible for students to work with the readings independently so that class time may be devoted to the cultural content.

- Brief *Cultura* boxes found throughout each chapter explain cultural products, practices, and perspectives, making the cultural contexts of the vocabulary and grammatical activities meaningful and accessible to students.

## Engaging New Video

A completely new video, entitled *Diarios de bicicleta*, has been scripted and filmed specifically to accompany the fifth edition of *Mosaicos*. Each episode of this engaging, often humorous video reflects the corresponding chapter's communicative objectives, recycling vocabulary and previewing functions and forms. The story line revolves around four recurring characters, but each episode is self-contained and independent of other episodes.

- The video segment for each chapter includes short excerpts that highlight the language functions introduced in the *Funciones y formas* section of the text.

- Pre-viewing, viewing, and post-viewing activities (all new to this edition) are provided in the Student Text in a special section of each chapter entitled *En acción*. Additional activities may be found in the Student Activities Manual.

## A Four-Skills Synthesis

Like its predecessors, the fifth edition devotes a prominent section of each chapter to the development and practice of communication skills. These newly streamlined *Mosaicos* sections provide students with a unique opportunity to bring together the chapter's thematic content and vocabulary with its linguistic structures and cultural focus. New features, texts, and activities enhance the effectiveness of this aspect of the program.

- Specific strategies are now presented in each chapter for each of the four skills (listening, speaking, reading, and writing). The strategies build on each other within and across chapters. Activities are designed so that students systematically practice implementing the strategies presented.

- New listening activities have been created for the *A escuchar* sections. The content and genre of the listening texts, as well as the accompanying strategies, consistently support the chapter theme.

- In the *A conversar* sections, specific strategies are now provided for speaking as they are for other skill areas. The speaking activities that follow encourage structured pair interaction and help students develop interpersonal speaking skills.

- The streamlined *A leer* sections now include only one reading each. The reading selections (many new to this edition) are drawn largely from authentic texts. They reflect a variety of discourse types, ranging from expository to journalistic to literary. Activities linked to the reading strategy boost students' comprehension and reading skills.

- The process writing activities in the *A escribir* sections have been revised so that the pre- and post-writing activities now guide students through critical steps in the writing process. Where possible, these activities refer students back to the immediately preceding reading, deepening students' comprehension and awareness of text structure.

## Informed by National Standards

The *Standards for Foreign Language Learning: Preparing for the 21st Century*, whose five goal areas have served as an organizing principle for language instruction for more than a decade, inform the pedagogy of the fifth edition of *Mosaicos*. Marginal notes throughout the Annotated Instructor's Edition draw attention to the way specific activities or other elements of the program help students develop proficiency in the five goal areas. A number of general strategies have been followed.

Communication.    Students are prompted to engage in meaningful conversations throughout the text, providing and obtaining information, expressing their opinions and preferences, and sharing their experiences. Readings and listening activities invite them to interpret language on a variety of topics, while *presentaciones* and writing assignments call on them to present information and ideas in both written and oral modes.

Cultures.    Many features of the text, including the maps, photos, *Cultura* boxes, and the readings in the *Mosaicos* and *Enfoque cultural* sections of each chapter, give students an understanding of the relationship between culture and language throughout the Spanish-speaking world.

Connections.    Realia, readings, the *Enfoque cultural* application activities, and conversation activities throughout the text provide opportunities to make connections with other disciplines. Students gain information and insight into the distinctive viewpoints of Spanish speakers and their cultures.

**Comparisons.** *Lengua* and *En otras palabras* boxes often provide students with points of comparison between English and Spanish (and among the varieties of Spanish spoken in different parts of the world). Readings and activities frequently juxtapose U.S. and Hispanic cultural products, practices, and perspectives.

**Communities.** The text encourages students to extend their learning through guided research on the Internet and/or other sources, and many of the topics explored in *Mosaicos* can stimulate exploration, personal enjoyment, and enrichment beyond the confines of formal language instruction. Instructors are reminded to encourage students to become acquainted with Spanish-speaking communities in their areas.

## The Complete Program

*Mosaicos* is a complete teaching and learning program that includes a variety of resources for students and instructors, including an innovative offering of online resources.

## For the student

### Student Text

The *Mosaicos* Student Text is available in a complete, hardbound version, consisting of a preliminary chapter followed by Chapters 1 through 15. New to this edition is the option of three paperback volumes rather than the single hardcover version. Volume 1 of the paperback series contains the preliminary chapter plus Chapters 1 to 5; Volume 2, Chapters 5 to 10; and Volume 3, Chapters 10 to 15. All three volumes include the complete front and back matter.

### Student Activities Manual

The Student Activities Manual (SAM), thoroughly revised for this edition, includes workbook activities together with audio- and video-based activities, all designed to provide extensive practice of the vocabulary, grammar, culture, and skills introduced in each chapter. The organization of these materials now parallels that of the student text, with an *A primera vista* section followed by *En acción* video activities, *Funciones y formas*, *Mosaicos*, and *Enfoque cultural*. A new section in each chapter (entitled *Repaso*) provides additional activities designed to help students review the material of the chapter as well as to prepare for tests.

The printed Student Activities Manual is available both in a single volume and in a series of separate volumes, paralleling the paperback volumes of the student text. The contents of the Student Activities Manual and MySpanishLab are also available online.

### Answer Key to Accompany Student Activities Manual

An Answer Key to the Student Activities Manual is available separately, giving instructors the option of allowing students to check their homework. The Answer Key now includes answers to all SAM activities.

### Supplementary Activities Book

Also available is a Supplementary Activities Book consisting of a range of fun, engaging activities that complement the vocabulary and grammar themes of each chapter. It offers instructors additional materials that can serve to energize and enrich their students' classroom experience.

### Audio CDs to Accompany Student Text

A set of audio CDs contains recordings of the *A primera vista* language samples and the end-of-chapter vocabulary lists. It also contains audio material for listening activities included in the student text. These recordings are also available online.

### Audio CDs to Accompany Student Activities Manual

A second set of audio CDs contains audio material for the listening activities in the Student Activities Manual. These recordings are also available online.

### Video on DVD

*Diarios de bicicleta* is an original video filmed to accompany the fifth edition of *Mosaicos*. Students see the vocabulary and grammar structures of each chapter in use in realistic situations while gaining a deeper understanding of Hispanic cultures. The video also includes segments highlighting the communicative functions of each chapter. Pre-viewing, viewing, and post-viewing activities are found in the *En acción* sections of the textbook and the Student Activities Manual. The video is available for student purchase on DVD, and it is also available within MySpanishLab.

### Meet the Cast

Here are the main characters of *Diarios de bicicleta*, who you will get to know when you watch the video:

Javier

Luciana

Daniel

Gaby

In addition to *Diarios de bicicleta*, two other videos are available for use in conjunction with the *Mosaicos* program. *Entrevistas* consists of interviews in which native speakers use authentic Spanish to address topics related to each chapter's theme. *Vistas culturales* contains nineteen 10–minute vignettes with footage from every Spanish-speaking country. Each of the accompanying narrations, which employ vocabulary and grammar designed for first-year language learners, was written by a native of the featured country or region. All three videos are also available online.

## For the instructor

### Annotated Instructor's Edition

The Annotated Instructor's Edition contains an abundance of marginal annotations (many newly written or revised for this edition) designed especially for novice instructors, instructors who are new to the *Mosaicos* program, or instructors who have limited time for class preparation. A new format allows ample space for annotations alongside full-size pages of the student text. Marginal annotations suggest warm-up and expansion exercises and activities and provide teaching tips, additional cultural information, and audioscripts for the in-text listening activities. Answers to discrete-point activities are printed in blue type for the instructor's convenience. *Resources* boxes (new to this edition) offer cross-references to related material in other components of the *Mosaicos* program, enabling instructors to see at a glance what material is available for student homework and additional practice, as well as for use in the classroom.

### Instructor's Resource Manual

The Instructor's Resource Manual (IRM) now contains complete lesson plans for all chapters, integrated syllabi for regular and hybrid courses, as well as helpful suggestions for new and experienced instructors alike. It also provides additional oral practice activities (similar to the *Situaciones* activities in the student text), videoscripts for all episodes of the *Diarios de bicicleta* video, audioscripts for listening activities in the Student Activities Manual, and a complete guide to all *Mosaicos* supplements. The Instructor's Resource Manual is available to instructors online at the *Mosaicos* Instructor Resource Center.

### Testing Program

The Testing Program has been thoroughly revised and expanded for this edition. The testing content correlates with the vocabulary, grammar, culture, and skills material presented in the student text. For each chapter of the text, a bank of testing activities is provided in modular form; instructors can select and combine modules to create customized tests tailored to the needs of their classes. Two complete, ready-to-use tests are also provided for each chapter. The tests and testing modules are available to instructors online at the *Mosaicos* Instructor Resource Center.

### Testing Audio CD

A special set of audio CDs, available to instructors only, contains recordings corresponding to the listening comprehension portions of the Testing Program.

### PowerPoint™ Presentations

A PowerPoint™ Presentation (new to this edition) is available for each chapter of the text. These dynamic, visually engaging presentations allow instructors to enliven class sessions and reinforce key concepts. The presentations are available to instructors online at the *Mosaicos* Instructor Resource Center.

### *Situaciones adicionales*

The *Situaciones adicionales* provide instructors with additional opportunities for reinforcing and assessing students' speaking skills.

**Instructor Resource Center**

Several of the instructor supplements listed above—the Instructor's Resource Manual, the Testing Program, the Power-Point™ Presentations, and the *Situaciones adicionales* as well as the Supplementary Activities Book—are available for download at the access-protected *Mosaicos* Instructor Resource Center (www.pearsonhighered.com/educator). An access code will be provided at no charge to instructors once their faculty status has been verified.

## Online resources

### MySpanishLab™

MySpanishLab is a new, nationally hosted online learning system created for students in college-level language courses. It brings together—in one convenient, easily navigable site—a wide array of language-learning tools and resources, including an interactive version of the *Mosaicos* Student Activities Manual, an electronic version of the *Mosaicos* student text, and all materials from the *Mosaicos* audio and video programs. Readiness checks, chapter tests, and tutorials personalize instruction to meet the unique needs of individual students. Instructors can use the system to make assignments, set grading parameters, listen to student-created audio recordings, and provide feedback on student work. Instructor access is provided at no charge. Students can purchase access codes online or at their local bookstore.

### Companion Website

The open-access Companion Website (www.pearsonhighered.com/mosaicos) includes an array of activities and resources designed to reinforce the vocabulary, grammar, and cultural material introduced in each chapter. It also provides audio recordings for the student text and Student Activities Manual, links for Internet-based activites in the student text, and additional web exploration activities for each chapter. All contents of the Companion Website are also included in MySpanishLab.

## Acknowledgments

*Mosaicos* is the result of a collaborative effort among the authors, our publisher, and our colleagues. We are especially indebted to many members of the Spanish teaching community for their time, candor, and insightful suggestions as they reviewed the drafts of the fifth edition of *Mosaicos*. Their critiques and recommendations helped us to sharpen our pedagogical focus and improve the overall quality of the program. We gratefully acknowledge the contributions of the following reviewers:

Rafael Arias, *Los Angeles Valley College*
Alejandra Balestra, *University of New Mexico*
Aymará Boggiano, *University of Houston*
Amanda Boomershine, *University of North Carolina-Wilmington*
Talia Bugel, *Indiana University-Purdue University Fort Wayne*
José Carrasquel, *Florida International University*
Zoila Clark, *Florida International University*
Daria Cohen, *Rider University*
Alyce Cook, *Columbus State University*
Richard Curry, *Texas A&M University*
Marta de la Caridad Pérez, *Florida International University*
Beatrice DeAngelis, *University of Pittsburgh*
Marisol del Teso Craviotto, *Miami University of Ohio*
Angela Erickson-Grussing, *St. John's University/College of St. Benedict*
Juliet Falce-Robinson, *University of California-Los Angeles*
Gayle Fiedler-Vierma, *University of Southern California*
Óscar Flores, *State University of New York-Plattsburgh*
Ausenda Folch, *Florida International University*
Myriam García, *Florida International University*
Rosa María Gómez García-Bermejo, *Florida International University*

Frozina Goussak, *Collin County Community College*
Dawn Heston, *University of Missouri-Columbia*
Casilde Isabelli, *University of Nevada-Reno*
Keith Johnson, *California State University-Fresno*
Linda Keown, *University of Missouri-Columbia*
Ruth Konopka, *Grossmont College*
Lina Llerena Callahan, *Fullerton College*
Susana Liso, *University of Virginia-Wise*
Leticia López, *San Diego Mesa College*
Libardo Mitchell, *Portland Community College-Sylvania*
Dorothy Moore, *Gettysburg College*
Michelle Orecchio, *University of Michigan*
Teresa Pérez-Gamboa, *University of Georgia*
Ana María Pinzón, *Frederick Community College*
Mónica Prieto, *Florida International University*
Nuria Sagarra, *Pennsylvania State University*
Toni Trives, *Santa Monica College*
Clara Vega, *Almance Community College*
Celinés Villalba, *University of California-Berkeley*
Lisa Volle, *Central Texas College*
Sarah Williams, *University of Pittsburgh*
Loretta Zehngut, *Pennsylvania State University*

We are also grateful for the guidance of Elizabeth Lantz, development editor, for all of her work, suggestions, attention to detail, and dedication to the text. Her support and spirit helped us to achieve the final product. Special thanks are due to Celia Meana, development editor, for helping with the art program, with the final pages, and with many other editorial details. We would also like to thank the contributors who assisted us in the preparation of the fifth edition: Daria Cohen, Marisol del Teso Craviotto, Juliet Falce-Robinson, Linda Keown, Gustavo Mejía, Teresa Pérez-Gamboa, Anne Prucha, and Lilián Uribe. Special thanks to Ninon Larché and Debbie King for their assistance in the preparation of the manuscript. We are very grateful to other colleagues and friends at Prentice Hall: Meriel Martínez, Media Editor, for helping us produce such a great video, audio programs, and Companion Website; Melissa Marolla Brown, Development Editor for Assessment, for the diligent coordination among the text, Student Activities Manual, and Testing Program; Samantha Alducin, Senior Media Editor, for managing the creation of *Mosaicos* materials for My SpanishLab™; and Jenn Murphy, Assistant Editor/Editorial Coordinator, for her work in managing the preparation of the other supplements. Thanks to Katie Spiegel, Editorial Assistant, for her hard work and efficiency in obtaining reviews and attending to many administrative details.

We are very grateful to our marketing team, Kris Ellis-Levy, Denise Miller, and Bill Bliss, for their creativity and efforts in coordinating all marketing and promotion for this edition. Thanks, too, to our production team, Mary Rottino, Janice Stangel, and Manuel Echevarria, who guided *Mosaicos* through the many stages of production; to our partners at Macmillan Publishing Solutions, especially Jill Traut, for her careful and professional editing and production services. We also thank our art team, Gail Cocker, Peter Bull, and Andrew Lange, for their amazing creativity and beautiful maps and illustrations. Special thanks to Leslie Osher, John Christina, and Ximena Tamvakopoulos for the gorgeous interior and cover designs. Finally, we would like to express our sincere thanks to Phil Miller, Publisher, and Julia Caballero, Executive Editor, for their guidance and support through every aspect of this new edition.

# A Guide to *Mosaicos* Icons

| | | |
|---|---|---|
| | *A vista de pájaro* | This icon indicates a panoramic, quick overview. It accompanies the chapter opener activity and reminds students to activate background knowledge about the country or countries featured in the chapter, as well as to use the information presented in the map. |
| | Text Audio Program | This icon indicates that recorded material is available for students in the *Mosaicos* text audio program for students. The audio includes vocabulary and dialogues presented in *A primera vista*, as well as the listening activities presented in the text. |
| | Pair Activity | This icon indicates that the activity is designed to be done by students working in pairs. |
| | Group Activity | This icon indicates that the activity is designed to be done by students working in small groups. |
| | Web Activity | This icon indicates that the activity involves use of the World Wide Web. Helpful links and activities can be found on the *Mosaicos* Companion Website. |

# ABOUT THE AUTHORS

**Elizabeth E. Guzmán** is the Director of the Elementary and Intermediate Spanish Language Program at the University of Iowa. Previously, she served as Language Coordinator at St. John's University/College of St. Benedict, Director of the Spanish Program at Yale University, and Coordinator and Co-Director of the Elementary and Intermediate Language Program at The University of Michigan. In her native Chile, she supervised instructors of English as a Foreign Language. Ms. Guzmán received her B.A. in English from Universidad de Santiago (Chile) and her M.A. in English as a Second Language from West Virginia University, and then pursued doctoral studies at the University of Pittsburgh. She is a co-author of Prentice-Hall's *Identidades* and several earlier editions of *Mosaicos*.

**Paloma Lapuerta** holds the title of Professor of Spanish at Central Connecticut State University, where she teaches courses in Spanish language, culture, and literature. She has over twenty years of teaching experience at higher institutions around the world, including Spain, Switzerland, South Africa, and the United States, where she has taught at the University of Michigan, Dartmouth College, and the Middlebury College Spanish School. She completed her *Licenciatura* in Spanish Philology at the University of Salamanca, and she holds a Ph.D. in Spanish literature from the University of Geneva, Switzerland. She has published numerous articles and a book on Spanish culture and literature. She is a co-author of *Identidades*, *La escritura paso a paso*, and earlier editions of *Mosaicos*, all published by Prentice Hall.

**Judith E. Liskin-Gasparro** is a professor of Spanish at the University of Iowa, where she teaches courses in second language acquisition, pedagogy, and Spanish language. She is the co-director of FLARE (Foreign Language Acquisition Research and Education), which offers an interdisciplinary doctoral program in Second Language Acquisition, and she was formerly the Director of the Elementary and Intermediate Spanish Language Program. Previously, she taught at Middlebury College and worked as a test development consultant at Educational Testing Service. She received her B.A. in Spanish from Bryn Mawr College, her M.A. from Princeton University, and her Ph.D. in Foreign Language Education from the University of Texas at Austin. She has published articles and books on language learning and teaching and has led many workshops for language teachers. She is a co-author of *Identidades*, published by Prentice Hall.

# Bienvenidos

El mundo hispano les da la bienvenida.

# In this chapter you will learn how to:

- introduce yourself, greet others, and say good-bye
- use expressions of courtesy
- spell in Spanish
- identify people and classroom objects
- locate people and things

- use numbers from 0–99
- express dates
- tell time
- use classroom expressions
- comment on the weather

## Personas que hablan español (en millones)

Estados Unidos 35
Cuba 11,4
República Dominicana 9,4
Puerto Rico 3,9
España 40,4
México 108,7
Guatemala 12,7
El Salvador 6,9
Honduras 7,5
Nicaragua 5,7
Venezuela 26
Costa Rica 4,1
Colombia 44,4
Panamá 3,2
Guinea
Ecuatorial 0,7
Ecuador 13,8
Perú 28,7
Bolivia 9,1
Paraguay 6,7
Chile 16,3
Uruguay 3,4
Argentina 40,3
Filipinas 2,9

**A vista de pájaro.** Relying on your knowledge of the world, look at the map and determine whether each statement is true (**Cierto**) or false (**Falso**).

1. _____ Más de (*More than*) 350 millones de personas hablan español en el mundo.
2. _____ En Filipinas no se habla español.
3. _____ En Estados Unidos hablan español más personas que (*more … than*) en Chile.
4. _____ En Guinea Ecuatorial se habla español.
5. _____ En Brasil se habla portugués.
6. _____ El español se habla en 23 países.

3

# Las presentaciones

CD 1
Track 1

ANTONIO: **Me llamo** Antonio Mendoza.
**Y tú, ¿cómo te llamas?**

BENITO: Me llamo Benito Sánchez.

ANTONIO: **Mucho gusto.**

BENITO: **Igualmente.**

PROFESOR: **¿Cómo se llama usted?**

ISABEL: Me llamo Isabel Contreras.

PROFESOR: Mucho gusto.

LAURA: María, **mi amigo** José.

MARÍA: Mucho gusto.

JOSÉ: **Encantado.**

- Spanish has more than one word meaning *you*. Use **tú** when talking to some-one on a first-name basis (a child, close friend, or relative).

  Use **usted** when talking to someone you address in a respectful or formal manner; for example, **doctor/doctora; profesor/profesora; señor/señora**. Also use **usted** to address individuals you do not know well.

- Young people normally use **tú** when speaking to each other.

- **Mucho gusto** is used by both men and women when they are meeting someone for the first time. A man may also say **encantado**, and a woman, **encantada**.

- You may respond to **mucho gusto** with either **encantado/a** or **igualmente**.

**P-1 Presentaciones.** PRIMERA FASE. Complete the following conversation with the appropriate expressions from the box on the right.

ALICIA: Me llamo Alicia. Y tú, ¿cómo te llamas?

ISABEL: Isabel Pérez. _____.

ALICIA: _____.

ALICIA: Isabel, _____.

ISABEL: Mucho gusto.

PEDRO: _____.

> Igualmente
> Mucho gusto
> Encantado
> mi amigo Pedro

SEGUNDA FASE. Move around the classroom, introducing yourself to several classmates and introducing classmates to each other.

4

# Los saludos y las despedidas

## Los saludos

CD 1
Track 2

SEÑOR: **Buenos días, señorita** Rivas.

SEÑORITA: Buenos días. **¿Cómo está usted, señor** Gómez?

SEÑOR: **Bien, gracias.** ¿Y usted?

SEÑORITA: **Muy** bien, gracias.

MARTA: **¡Hola,** Inés! **¿Qué tal? ¿Cómo estás?**

INÉS: **Regular,** ¿y tú?

MARTA: **Bastante** bien, gracias.

SEÑORA: **Buenas tardes,** Felipe. ¿Cómo estás?

FELIPE: Bien, gracias. Y usted, ¿cómo está, **señora**?

SEÑORA: **Mal,** Felipe, mal.

FELIPE: **Lo siento.**

■ Use **buenos días** until lunchtime.

■ Use **buenas tardes** from noon until nightfall. After nightfall, use **buenas noches** (*good evening, good night*).

■ **¿Qué tal?** is a more informal greeting. It is normally used with **tú**, but it may also be used with **usted**.

■ Use **está** with **usted** and **estás** with **tú**.

**P-2 Saludos.** You work as a receptionist in a hotel. Which greeting (**buenos días, buenas tardes, buenas noches**) is appropriate at the following times?

1. 9:00 a.m.
2. 11:00 p.m.
3. 4:00 p.m.
4. 8:00 a.m.
5. 1:00 p.m.
6. 10:00 p.m.

## Las despedidas

CD 1
Track 3

| | |
|---|---|
| **adiós** | *good-bye* |
| **hasta luego** | *see you later* |
| **hasta mañana** | *see you tomorrow* |
| **hasta pronto** | *see you soon* |
| **chao** | *good-bye* |

■ **Adiós** is generally used when you do not expect to see the other person for a while. It is also used as a greeting when people pass each other but have no time to stop and talk.

■ **Chao** (also spelled **chau**) is an informal way of saying good-bye. It is popular in South America.

**P-3 Despedidas.** How would you say good-bye in these situations?
1. You'll see your friend tomorrow.
2. You arrange to meet your classmate at the library in 10 minutes.
3. Your roommate is leaving for a semester abroad.
4. You run into a good friend on campus.

## Expresiones de cortesía

CD 1
Track 4

| | |
|---|---|
| **por favor** | *please* |
| **gracias** | *thanks, thank you* |
| **de nada** | *you're welcome* |
| **lo siento** | *I'm sorry (to hear that)* |
| **con permiso** | *pardon me, excuse me* |
| **perdón** | *pardon me, excuse me* |

■ **Con permiso** and **perdón** may be used before the fact, as when asking a person to allow you to go by or when trying to get someone's attention. Only **perdón** is used after the fact, as when you have stepped on someone's foot or have interrupted a conversation.

**P-4 ¿Perdón o con permiso?** Would you use **perdón** or **con permiso** in these situations?

1.  2.  3.

4.  5.

**P-5 Despedidas y expresiones de cortesía.** Which expression(s) would you use in the following situations?

| | | |
|---|---|---|
| adiós | gracias | lo siento |
| de nada | hasta luego | por favor |

1. Someone thanks you.
2. You say good-bye to a friend you will see later this evening.
3. You ask if you can borrow a classmate's notes.
4. You hear that your friend is sick.
5. You receive a present from your cousin.
6. Your friend is leaving for a vacation in Costa Rica.

**P-6 Encuentros (*Encounters*).** You meet the following people on the street. Greet them, ask how they are, and then say good-bye. Switch roles and role play the encounters again.

1. su (*your*) amigo Miguel
2. su profesor/a

3. su amiga Isabel
4. su doctor/a

# •)) Distinguishing Registers

CD 1
Track 5
When you talk to different people, you use different registers, that is, you address them with various degrees of formality, depending on your level of intimacy and the context of the exchange. For example, when you talk to a professor, you probably use more formal language than when you talk to classmates or friends. In Spanish, one way to mark this difference is by using **tú** (informal) and **usted** (formal).

Now you will hear four brief conversations in which people greet each other. Before you listen, complete the following chart with the pronoun you think you would use in each case.

| WHEN TALKING TO YOUR ... | TÚ | USTED |
|---|---|---|
| 1. brother or sister | | |
| 2. doctor | | |
| 3. coach | | |
| 4. parents | | |

**P-7 Conversaciones.** As you listen to the four conversations, mark (✓) the appropriate column to indicate whether the greetings are formal (with **usted**) or informal (with **tú**). Do not worry if you do not understand every word.

|  | FORMAL | INFORMAL |
|---|---|---|
| 1. | _____ | _____ |
| 2. | _____ | _____ |
| 3. | _____ | _____ |
| 4. | _____ | _____ |

# ◢)) El alfabeto

CD 1
Track 6

| a | a | o | o |
|---|---|---|---|
| b | be | p | pe |
| c | ce | q | cu |
| d | de | r | ere, erre |
| e | e | s | ese |
| f | efe | t | te |
| g | ge | u | u |
| h | hache | v | ve, uve |
| i | i | w | doble ve, doble uve |
| j | jota | | uve doble, ve doble |
| k | ka | x | equis |
| l | ele | y | i griega, ye |
| m | eme | z | zeta |
| n | ene | | |
| ñ | eñe | | |

## En otras palabras

Like English speakers, Spanish speakers have different accents that reflect their region or country of origin. For example, the letter **c** before vowels **e** and **i** and the letter **z** are pronounced like **s**, except in certain regions of Spain, where they are similar to the English *th*.

■ The Spanish alphabet includes ñ, a letter that does not exist in English. Its sound is similar to the pronunciation of *ni* and *ny* in the English words *onion* and *canyon*.

■ The letters **k** and **w** appear mainly in words of foreign origin.

 **P-8 ¿Cómo se escribe?** Ask your classmate how to spell these Spanish last names.

MODELO:     Zamora
        E1:  *¿Cómo se escribe Zamora?*
        E2:  *Con zeta.*

1. Celaya
2. Montalvo
3. Salas

4. Bolaños
5. Henares
6. Velázquez

 **P-9 Los nombres.** You are at the admissions office of a university in a Spanish-speaking country. Spell out your first or last name for the clerk. Take turns.

MODELO:  E1:  *¿Cómo se llama usted?*
        E2:  *Me llamo David Robinson.*
        E1:  *¿Cómo se escribe Robinson?*
        E2:  *ere-o-be-i-ene-ese-o-ene.*

# Identificación y descripción de personas

CD 1
Track 7

CARLOS: **¿Quién es ese chico?**

SANDRA: **Es** Julio.

CARLOS: **¿Cómo es** Julio?

SANDRA: **Es** romántico y sentimental.

LUIS: ¿Quién es **esa chica**?

QUIQUE: Es Carmen.

LUIS: ¿Cómo es Carmen?

QUIQUE: Es activa y muy seria.

■ The verb *ser* is used to identify and describe.

Esa chica **es** Carmen. Ella **es** activa y muy seria.

Rodolfo **es** su amigo. **Es** atractivo.

■ Here are the forms of *ser* you will be using in this chapter.

| SER *(to be)* | | | |
|---|---|---|---|
| yo | **soy** | *I* | *am* |
| tú | **eres** | *you* | *are* |
| usted | **es** | *you* | *are* |
| él, ella | **es** | *he, she* | *is* |

■ To make a sentence negative, place **no** before the appropriate form of **ser**. When responding negatively to a question, say **no** twice.

Ella es inteligente. → Ella **no** es inteligente.

¿Es rebelde? → **No, no** es rebelde.

## Cognados

**Cognados** (*cognates*) are words from two languages that have the same origin and are similar in form and meaning. Since English and Spanish have many cognates, you will discover that you already recognize many Spanish words. Here are some cognates that you may use to describe people.

■ The following cognates use the same form to describe a man or a woman.

| | | | |
|---|---|---|---|
| arrogante | importante | optimista | popular |
| eficiente | independiente | paciente | responsable |
| elegante | inteligente | perfeccionista | sentimental |
| idealista | interesante | pesimista | tradicional |

■ The following cognates have two forms. The **-o** form is used to describe a male, and the **-a** form to describe a female.

| | | | |
|---|---|---|---|
| activo/a | creativo/a | introvertido/a | romántico/a |
| ambicioso/a | dinámico/a | moderno/a | serio/a |
| atlético/a | extrovertido/a | nervioso/a | sincero/a |
| atractivo/a | generoso/a | pasivo/a | tímido/a |
| cómico/a | impulsivo/a | religioso/a | tranquilo/a |

■ Some words appear to be cognates but do not have the same meaning in both languages. These are called false cognates. **Lectura** (*reading*) and **éxito** (*success*) are examples. You will find other examples in future chapters.

 **P-10 ¿Cómo es mi compañero/a?** Choose from the preceding lists of cognates to ask the person next to you about his/her personality.

**MODELO:** E1: *¿Eres pesimista?*
E2: *No, no soy pesimista. O Sí, soy (muy) pesimista.*

Then find out how your classmate describes himself/herself.

**MODELO:** E1: *¿Cómo eres (tú)?*
E2: *Soy activo, optimista y creativo.*

**P-11 Descripciones.** Ask each other about your classmates. Describe them by using cognates from the preceding lists.

**MODELO:** E1: *¿Cómo es... ?*
E2: *Es...*

# ¿Qué hay en el salón de clase?

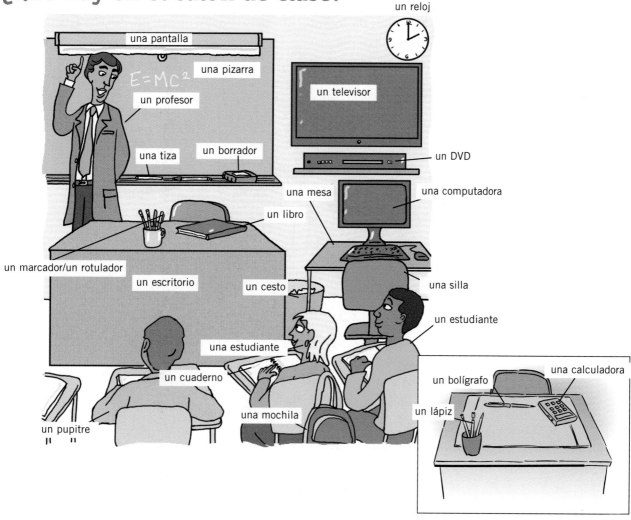

un reloj

una pantalla

una pizarra

un profesor

una tiza

un borrador

un televisor

un DVD

una mesa

una computadora

un libro

un marcador/un rotulador

un escritorio

un cesto

una silla

un estudiante

una estudiante

una calculadora

un bolígrafo

un cuaderno

un lápiz

una mochila

un pupitre

**P-12 Identificación.** With a partner, identify the items on this table.

h.

a.

g.

f.

e.

d.

b.

c.

**P-13 Para la clase de español.** Write down a list of the things you need for this class. Compare your list with that of your partner.

# ¿Dónde está?

■ To ask about the location of a person or an object, use **dónde + está**.

¿**Dónde está** la profesora?    Está en la clase.

¿**Dónde está** el libro?    Está sobre el escritorio.

**P-14 Localización.** PRIMERA FASE. Indicate whether each statement is true (**Cierto**) or false (**Falso**), based on the relative position of people and objects in the drawing.

|  | CIERTO | FALSO |
|---|---|---|
| 1. El televisor está detrás de la profesora. | ____ | ____ |
| 2. Juan está al lado de la profesora. | ____ | ____ |
| 3. El libro está sobre el escritorio. | ____ | ____ |
| 4. María está entre Mercedes y Juan. | ____ | ____ |
| 5. Mercedes está enfrente de la ventana. | ____ | ____ |
| 6. El cesto está debajo de un pupitre. | ____ | ____ |

SEGUNDA FASE. Now complete the following sentences, based on the relative position of people and objects in the drawing. Compare your answers.

1. La pizarra está _____ la profesora.
2. María está _____ la profesora.
3. Mercedes está _____ Juan y María.
4. Juan está _____ Mercedes.
5. El cesto está _____ Juan.
6. El televisor está _____ la pizarra y la puerta.

# ◉)) Listening with Visuals

CD 1
Track 8 When you are talking with someone, paying attention to the pictures or objects that the speaker points to or refers to can help you understand what is being said. These objects may be around you, or they may not, in which case you have only a mental representation of them. For example, when a friend describes his/her Spanish classroom, an image of a classroom comes to your mind based on your experience as a student.

In Spanish, make a list of the people and objects you expect to see in a classroom.

Now, as you listen to the statements about the location of people and objects, look at the drawing of the classroom on page 12 to help you understand what the speakers are saying.

Indicate (✓) whether each statement is true (**Cierto**) or false (**Falso**).

|   | CIERTO | FALSO |
|---|---|---|
| 1. | _____ | _____ |
| 2. | _____ | _____ |
| 3. | _____ | _____ |
| 4. | _____ | _____ |
| 5. | _____ | _____ |
| 6. | _____ | _____ |

**P-15 En la clase.** Look at the seating chart below, and then follow the instructions.

| María | Juan | Ester | | Susana | Pedro |
|---|---|---|---|---|---|
| Carlos | Cristina | Ángeles | | Alberto | Anita |
| Mercedes | Victoria | Roberto | | Rocío | Pablo |
| | | El profesor Gallegos | | | |

ESTUDIANTE 1: Ask where Juan, Pedro, Cristina, Mercedes, Roberto, and Pablo are sitting.

ESTUDIANTE 2: Ask where *María, Ester, Susana, Carlos, Ángeles, Alberto, Anita, Victoria, Rocío,* and *Profesor Gallegos* are sitting.

**P-16 ¿Dónde está?** Take turns asking where several items in your classroom are. Answer by giving their position in relation to a person or another object.

MODELO: E1: *¿Dónde está el libro?*
E2: *Está sobre el escritorio.*

**P-17 ¿Quién es?** Based on what your partner says regarding the location of another student, guess who he/she is.

MODELO: E1: *Está al lado de Juan. ¿Quién es?*
E2: *Es María.*

# ◄)) Los números 0 a 99

CD 1
Track 9

| | | | | | |
|---|---|---|---|---|---|
| 0 | cero | 11 | once | 22 | veintidós |
| 1 | uno | 12 | doce | 23 | veintitrés |
| 2 | dos | 13 | trece | 30 | treinta |
| 3 | tres | 14 | catorce | 31 | treinta y uno |
| 4 | cuatro | 15 | quince | 40 | cuarenta |
| 5 | cinco | 16 | dieciséis | 50 | cincuenta |
| 6 | seis | 17 | diecisiete | 60 | sesenta |
| 7 | siete | 18 | dieciocho | 70 | setenta |
| 8 | ocho | 19 | diecinueve | 80 | ochenta |
| 9 | nueve | 20 | veinte | 90 | noventa |
| 10 | diez | 21 | veintiuno | | |

■ Numbers from sixteen through twenty-nine are usually written as one word. Note the spelling changes and the written accent on some forms.

18: **dieciocho**          22: **veintidós**

■ Beginning with thirty-one, numbers are written as three words.

31: **treinta y uno**          45: **cuarenta y cinco**

■ The number *one* has three forms in Spanish: **uno, un,** and **una.** Use **uno** when counting: **uno, dos, tres…** Use **un** or **una** before nouns: **un borrador, una mochila, veintiún libros, veintiuna mochilas.**

■ Use **hay** for both *there is* and *there are.*

**Hay** un libro sobre la mesa.          *There is one book on the table.*
**Hay** dos libros sobre la mesa.          *There are two books on the table.*

 **P-18 ¿Qué número es?** Your instructor will read a number from each group. Circle the number you hear. Then compare your responses with those of your partner.

a.  8    4    3    5
b.  12    9    16    6
c.  37    59    41    26
d.  54    38    76    95
e.  83    62    72    49
f.  47    14    91    56

**P-19 Para la oficina.** You and your partner are student assistants in the Spanish department. You have to check a shipment of equipment and supplies that just arrived. Choose five items and tell your partner how many of each there are. He/She will take notes. Exchange roles.

MODELO:  4-7 mesas: *Hay cuatro mesas.*

a. 6-10 teléfonos
b. 8-12 escritorios
c. 1-2 silla(s)
d. 6-12 calculadoras
e. 10-20 cestos

f. 90-95 bolígrafos
g. 9-15 computadoras
h. 22-24 computadoras portátiles
i. 1-3 reloj(es)
j. ...

**P-20 Problemas.** Take turns solving the following arithmetic problems. Use **y** (**+**), **menos** (**–**), and **son** (**=**).

MODELO:  2 + 4 =                    12 – 5 =
         Dos y cuatro son seis.     Doce menos cinco son siete.

a. 11 + 4 =
b. 8 + 2 =
c. 13 + 3 =

d. 20 – 6 =
e. 39 + 50 =
f. 80 – 1 =

g. 50 – 25 =
h. 26 + 40 =
i. 90 – 12 =

**P-21 Los números de teléfono y las direcciones (*addresses*).** With your partner, take turns asking each other the phone numbers and addresses of the people listed in the chart below.

| | | |
|---|---|---|
| ● Cárdenas Alfaro, Joaquín | General Páez 40 | 423-4837 |
| ● Cárdenas Villanueva, Sara | Avenida Bolívar 7 | 956-1709 |
| ● Castelar Torres, Adelaida | Paseo del Prado 85 | 218-3642 |
| ● Castellanos Rey, Carlos | Colón 62 | 654-6416 |
| ● Castelli Rivero, Victoria | Chamberí 3 | 615-7359 |
| ● Castillo Montoya, Rafael | Santa Cruz 73 | 956-3382 |

MODELO:       Castellanos Rey, Carlos
         E1:  *¿Cuál es la dirección de Carlos Castellanos Rey?*
         E2:  *Calle Colón, número 62.*
         E1:  *¿Cuál es su teléfono?*
         E2:  *(Es el) 6-54-64-16*

# ◁)) Los meses del año y los días de la semana

CD 1
Track 10

| | | | | | |
|---|---|---|---|---|---|
| **enero** | *January* | **mayo** | *May* | **septiembre** | *September* |
| **febrero** | *February* | **junio** | *June* | **octubre** | *October* |
| **marzo** | *March* | **julio** | *July* | **noviembre** | *November* |
| **abril** | *April* | **agosto** | *August* | **diciembre** | *December* |

Days of the week and months of the year are not generally capitalized in Spanish, but sometimes they are capitalized in advertisements and invitations.

■ Monday (**lunes**) is normally considered the first day of the week.

■ To ask what day it is, use **¿Qué día es hoy?** Answer with **Hoy es...**

■ To ask about the date, use **¿Qué fecha es?** or **¿Cuál es la fecha?** Respond with **Es el (14) de (octubre)**.

■ Express *on + a day of the week* as follows:

| | |
|---|---|
| **el lunes** | *on Monday* |
| **los lunes** | *on Mondays* |
| **el domingo** | *on Sunday* |
| **los domingos** | *on Sundays* |

■ Cardinal numbers are used with dates (e.g., **el dos, el tres**), except for the first day of the month, which is **el primero**. In Spain the first day is also referred to as **el uno**.

## Lengua

When dates are written using only numerals, the day normally precedes the month: *11/8* = **el 11 de agosto**.

**P-22 ¿Qué día de la semana es?** Using the preceding calendar, take turns asking *¿Qué día de la semana es… ?*

| | |
|---|---|
| **1.** el 2 | **5.** el 10 |
| **2.** el 5 | **6.** el 13 |
| **3.** el 22 | **7.** el 28 |
| **4.** el 18 | **8.** el… |

 **P-23 Preguntas.** Take turns asking and answering these questions.

1. ¿Qué día es hoy?
2. Hoy es… ¿Qué día es mañana?
3. Hoy es el… de… ¿Qué fecha es mañana?
4. ¿Hay clase de español los domingos? ¿Y los sábados?
5. ¿Qué días hay clase de español?

**P-24 Fechas importantes.** Working with a partner, tell each other the dates on which these events take place.

MODELO:    la reunión de estudiantes (10/9)
E1:  *¿Cuándo es la reunión de estudiantes?*
E2:  *(Es) el 10 de septiembre.*

1. el concierto de Marc Anthony (12/11)
2. el aniversario de Carlos y María (14/4)
3. el banquete (1/3)
4. la graduación (22/5)
5. la fiesta de bienvenida (24/8)

 **P-25 El cumpleaños (*birthday*).** Find out when your classmates' birthdays are. Write their names and birthdays in the appropriate space in the chart.

MODELO:    E1:  *¿Cuándo es tu cumpleaños?*
E2:  *(Es) el 3 de mayo.*

| CUMPLEAÑOS | | | |
|---|---|---|---|
| enero | febrero | marzo | abril |
| mayo | junio | julio | agosto |
| septiembre | octubre | noviembre | diciembre |

### Lengua

You may have noticed that the word **tú** (meaning *you*) has a written accent mark, and that the word **tu** (meaning *your*) does not. In *Mosaicos*, boxes similar to this one will help you focus on when to use accent marks. You will find a complete set of the rules for accentuation in the appendix.

# La hora

■ Use **¿Qué hora es?** to inquire about the time. To tell time, use **Es la...** from one o'clock to one thirty and **Son las...** with the other hours.

| | |
|---|---|
| **Es la** una. | *It is one o'clock.* |
| **Son las** tres. | *It is three o'clock.* |

■ To express the quarter hour, use **y cuarto** or **y quince**. To express the half hour, use **y media** or **y treinta**.

Es la una **y media.**
Es la una **y treinta.** }    *It is one thirty.*

Son las dos **y cuarto.**
Son las dos **y quince.** }    *It is two fifteen.*

■ To express time after the half hour, subtract minutes from the next hour, using **menos**.

| | |
|---|---|
| Son las cuatro **menos** diez. | *It is ten to four.* |

■ Add **en punto** for the exact time and **más o menos** for approximate time.

| | |
|---|---|
| Es la una **en punto.** | *It is one o'clock on the dot/sharp.* |
| Son las cinco menos cuarto, **más o menos.** | *It is about a quarter to five.* |

■ For *a.m.* and *p.m.*, use the following:

| | |
|---|---|
| **de la mañana** | (from midnight to noon) |
| **de la tarde** | (from noon to nightfall) |
| **de la noche** | (from nightfall to midnight) |

**P-26 ¿Qué hora es en... ?** What time is it in the following cities?

México, p.m.

San Juan, p.m.

Buenos Aires, p.m.

Madrid, p.m.

**P-27 El horario de María.** Take turns asking and answering questions about María's schedule below. Then write down your own Monday schedule, omitting the time each class meets. Exchange schedules with your partner, and find out what time each of his/her classes starts.

**MODELO:**   E1:   *¿A qué hora es la clase de español?*
           E2:   *Es a las nueve.*

| LUNES | | | |
|---|---|---|---|
| 9:00 | la clase de español | 12:30 | el almuerzo |
| 10:00 | la clase de matemáticas | 1:00 | la clase de física |
| 11:00 | la clase de psicología | 5:00 | la clase de tenis |
| 12:00 | el laboratorio | | |

# El tiempo

Hoy hace sol. Hace buen tiempo.

Hoy llueve. Hace mal tiempo.

■ Use **¿Qué tiempo hace?** to inquire about the weather. To answer, you may use the following expressions that start with **hace:**

**Hace** buen tiempo.     *The weather is good.*
**Hace** mal tiempo.      *The weather is bad.*

■ To express that it is sunny or that it is raining use the following:

**Hace sol.**                   *It is sunny.*
**Llueve./Está lloviendo**.   *It is raining.*

**P-29 ¿Qué tiempo hace hoy?** Take turns with your partner asking about the weather in these cities.

**MODELO:**        Miami: ☀
          E1:  *¿Qué tiempo hace en Miami?*
          E2:  *En Miami hace buen tiempo. Hace sol.*

1. Madrid: ☀
2. Quito: 🌧
3. Lima: 🌧
4. Ciudad de México: ☀
5. Bogotá: 🌧
6. Nueva York: ☀

# Expresiones útiles en la clase

CD 1
Track 11

La tarea, por favor.

Vaya a la pizarra.

Conteste.

Repita.

Levante la mano.

Escriba.

Lea.

■ When asking two or more people to do something, the verb form ends in **-n**: **vaya → vayan, conteste → contesten, repita → repitan.**

■ Although you may not have to use all these expressions, it is useful to be able to recognize them and to respond accordingly. Other expressions that you may hear or say in the classroom include the following:

| | |
|---|---|
| **¿Comprende(n)?** | *Do you understand?* |
| **No comprendo.** | *I do not understand.* |
| **No sé.** | *I do not know.* |
| **Más despacio, por favor.** | *More slowly, please.* |
| **Más alto, por favor.** | *Louder, please.* |
| **Otra vez.** | *Again.* |
| **¿Tienen alguna pregunta?** | *Do you have any questions?* |
| **Tengo una pregunta…** | *I have a question.* |
| **¿En qué página?** | *On what page?* |
| **¿Cómo se dice… en español?** | *How do you say … in Spanish?* |
| **¿Cómo se escribe…?** | *How do you spell … ?* |
| **Vaya(n) a la pizarra.** | *Go to the board.* |
| **Conteste(n), por favor.** | *Please answer.* |
| **Presente.** | *Here (present).* |

# VOCABULARIO

CD 1
cks 12-18

## Las presentaciones — Introductions

| | |
|---|---|
| ¿Cómo se llama usted? | *What's your name?* (formal) |
| ¿Cómo te llamas? | *What's your name?* (familiar) |
| encantado/a | *pleased/nice to meet you* |
| igualmente | *likewise* |
| me llamo… | *my name is …* |
| mucho gusto | *pleased/nice to meet you* |

## Los saludos — Greetings

| | |
|---|---|
| bastante | *rather* |
| bien | *well* |
| buenas tardes/buenas noches | *good afternoon/good evening, good night* |
| buenos días | *good morning* |
| ¿Cómo está? | *How are you (formal)?* |
| ¿Cómo estás? | *How are you (informal)?* |
| hola | *hi, hello* |
| mal | *bad* |
| muy | *very* |
| regular | *fair* |
| ¿Qué tal? | *What's up? What's new? (informal)* |

## En el salón de clase — In the classroom

| | |
|---|---|
| el bolígrafo | *ballpoint pen* |
| el borrador | *eraser* |
| la calculadora | *calculator* |
| el cesto | *wastebasket* |
| la computadora | *computer* |
| la computadora portátil | *laptop* |
| el cuaderno | *notebook* |
| el DVD | *DVD; DVD player* |
| el escritorio | *desk* |
| el lápiz | *pencil* |
| el libro | *book* |
| el mapa | *map* |
| el marcador/el rotulador | *marker* |
| la mesa | *table* |
| la mochila | *backpack* |
| la pantalla | *screen* |
| la pizarra | *chalkboard* |
| la puerta | *door* |
| el pupitre | *student desk* |
| el reloj | *clock* |
| la silla | *chair* |
| el televisor | *television set* |
| la tiza | *chalk* |
| la ventana | *window* |

## Las personas — People

| | |
|---|---|
| el amigo/la amiga | *friend* |
| el/chico/la chica | *boy/girl* |
| él | *he* |
| ella | *she* |
| el/la estudiante | *student* |
| el profesor/la profesora | *professor, teacher* |
| el señor (Sr.) | *Mr.* |
| la señora (Sra.) | *Ms., Mrs.* |
| la señorita (Srta.) | *Ms, Miss* |
| tú | *you (familiar)* |
| usted | *you (formal)* |
| yo | *I* |

## La posición — Position

| | |
|---|---|
| al lado (de) | *next to* |
| debajo (de) | *under* |
| detrás (de) | *behind* |
| enfrente (de) | *in front of* |
| entre | *between, among* |
| sobre | *on, above* |

## Verbos — Verbs

| | |
|---|---|
| eres | *you are (familiar)* |
| es | *you are (formal), he/she is* |
| está | *he/she is, you are (formal)* |
| estás | *you are (familiar)* |
| hay | *there is, there are* |
| soy | *I am* |

## Palabras y expresiones útiles — Useful words and expressions

| | |
|---|---|
| a | *at, to* |
| el año | *year* |
| ¿Cómo es? | *What is he/she/it like?* |
| el día | *day* |
| ¿Dónde está… ? | *Where is … ?* |
| en | *in* |
| ese/a | *that (adjective)* |
| hoy | *today* |
| mañana | *tomorrow* |
| la mañana | *morning* |
| más o menos | *more or less* |
| el mes | *month* |
| mi(s) | *my* |
| ¿Quién es… ? | *Who is … ?* |
| la semana | *week* |
| sí | *yes* |
| su(s) | *his/her/their* |
| tu(s) | *your (familiar)* |
| un/una | *a, an* |
| y | *and* |

See page 5 for expressions for leave-taking.
See page 6 for expressions of courtesy.
See page 10 for cognates.
See pages 14 and 16 for numbers, days of the week, and months.
See page 18 for telling time.
See page 19 for weather expressions.
See page 20 for classroom expressions.

CAPÍTULO

1

# *En la universidad*

Un fresco del siglo XVI en la Universidad de Salamanca

# In this chapter you will learn how to:

- exchange information about classes
- identify locations at the university
- talk about academic life and daily occurrences
- ask and answer questions

Museo Guggenheim

FRANCIA

Santiago de Compostela

Bilbao

Universidad de Salamanca

E S P A Ñ A

Barcelona

Salamanca

Segovia

Paella valenciana

OCÉANO ATLÁNTICO

PORTUGAL

Madrid ✪

Valencia

Plaza de toros

Córdoba

Sevilla

Granada

Mar Mediterráneo

La Alhambra

 **A vista de pájaro.** Look at the map and complete the following sentences based on what you know.

1. ___ España está en...
   a. América.
   b. Europa.
   c. Asia.
2. ___ La capital de España es...
   a. Barcelona.
   b. Madrid.
   c. Sevilla.
3. ___ La paella es típica de...
   a. Valencia.
   b. Salamanca.
   c. Madrid.
4. ___ En la universidad hay...
   a. estudiantes.
   b. catedrales.
   c. toros.
5. ___ En la plaza de toros hay espectáculos (*shows*)...
   a. religiosos.
   b. cómicos.
   c. populares.

# A PRIMERA VISTA

## Los estudiantes y los cursos

CD 1
Track 19
Me llamo Rosa Pereda. **Estudio sociología** en la **Facultad de Humanidades** de la **Universidad** de Salamanca. Mis clases son muy temprano. **Llego** a la universidad a las ocho y media. Este semestre mis cursos son **economía, ciencias políticas, psicología, antropología** y **estadística**. La clase de economía es mi **favorita**. La clase de antropología es **difícil**, pero el profesor es muy **bueno**. La clase de psicología es **fácil** y muy **interesante**. Por las tardes **trabajo** en una **oficina**.

CD 1
Track 20
Este chico es mi amigo. Se llama David Thomas. Es **norteamericano** y estudia español en mi universidad. También estudia **literatura, historia** y **geografía**. David es un chico muy responsable y **estudioso**. Generalmente llega a la universidad a las diez. **Habla** español y **practica todos los días** con sus **compañeros** de clase, sus profesores y sus amigos de la universidad. Por la tarde, **escribe** sus **tareas** en la computadora, estudia en el **laboratorio** con uno de sus **compañeros** y **escucha** música o **mira** programas en español en la televisión.

### Cultura

Some of Spain's public universities, such as the Universidad de Salamanca, the Universidad de Santiago, and the Universidad Complutense de Madrid, are among the oldest in Europe, dating back hundreds of years. Most private universities in Spain, which are much newer, have higher tuition. To be accepted to a university students take a competitive comprehensive exam, known as **Selectividad**. Many universities offer Spanish language and culture courses for foreign students.

**1-1 ¿Qué sabe usted de Rosa?** Refer to the information about Rosa to match the information in the right column with the information on the left.

| | |
|---|---|
| 1. ___ nombre completo | a. antropología |
| 2. ___ universidad | b. psicología |
| 3. ___ clase favorita | c. Salamanca |
| 4. ___ clase difícil | d. economía |
| 5. ___ clase fácil | e. Rosa Pereda |

**1-2 ¿Y David?** Indicate whether each statement about David is true (**Cierto**) or false (**Falso**).

1. _____ Es norteamericano.
2. _____ Habla español.
3. _____ Estudia literatura, historia y geografía.
4. _____ Llega a la universidad a las nueve.
5. _____ Practica español con sus amigos.
6. _____ Escucha música por la mañana.

La Universidad de San Marcos, en Lima, Perú, se fundó en 1551.

# David y Carmen hablan de sus clases

**CD 1
Track 21**

DAVID: Hola, Carmen. ¿Cómo estás?

CARMEN: Hola, David. **¿Cómo te va?**

DAVID: Bueno…bastante bien, pero mi clase de historia es muy difícil.

CARMEN: ¿Quién es tu profesor?

DAVID: Se llama Pedro Hernández. Es inteligente y dedicado, pero la clase es **aburrida** y **saco malas notas**.

CARMEN: ¡Vaya! Lo siento. ¿Estudias lo suficiente?

DAVID: Estudio mucho.

CARMEN: **¡Qué lástima!** Mis cinco clases son excelentes. Y tú, **¿cuántas clases tienes?**

DAVID: **Tengo sólo** cuatro.

CARMEN: ¡Uy! Son las once. Tengo un **examen** de economía **ahora**. Hasta luego.

DAVID: Hasta pronto. **¡Buena suerte!**

**1-3 ¿En qué clase…?** Match the words on the left with the appropriate class on the right.

1. ___ *Don Quijote* de Cervantes
2. ___ números
3. ___ mapa digital
4. ___ animales
5. ___ Freud
6. ___ Napoleón

a. geografía
b. biología
c. literatura
d. historia
e. matemáticas
f. psicología

**1-4 Mis clases. PRIMERA FASE.** Make a list of your classes. Indicate the days and time each class meets and whether it is easy or difficult, interesting or boring. You will find some subjects in the list below.

| | | |
|---|---|---|
| economía | comunicaciones | negocios |
| bioquímica | sociología | historia del arte |
| física | cálculo | informática |
| artes plásticas | estadística | seminario de… |
| contabilidad | astronomía | filosofía |

| CLASE | DÍAS | HORA | ¿CÓMO ES? |
|---|---|---|---|
| | | | |
| | | | |
| | | | |
| | | | |
| | | | |

**SEGUNDA FASE.** Tell your partner about your classes. Take turns completing the following ideas.

1. Llego a la universidad a la(s)…
2. Mi clase favorita es…
3. El profesor/La profesora se llama…
4. La clase es muy…
5. Practico español en…
6. En mi clase de español hay…

**1-5 Las clases de mis compañeros/as. PRIMERA FASE.** Use the following questions to interview your partner. Take notes. Then switch roles.

1. ¿Qué estudias este semestre?
2. ¿Cuántas clases tienes?
3. ¿Cuál es tu clase favorita?
4. ¿Qué día y a qué hora es tu clase favorita?
5. Tu clase de español, ¿cómo es? ¿Es fácil o difícil? ¿Es interesante o aburrida?
6. ¿Trabajas con computadoras? ¿Dónde?
7. ¿Sacas buenas notas?
8. ¿Tienes muchos exámenes?

**SEGUNDA FASE.** Introduce your partner to another classmate and state one piece of interesting information about him/her. Your classmate will ask your partner about his/her classes.

**MODELO:**  USTED: *Él es Pedro. Estudia ciencias políticas y tiene cuatro clases este semestre.*

SU COMPAÑERO/A: *Mucho gusto. ¿_____?*

# ·)) La universidad

CD 1
Track 22

Facultad de Arquitectura

Gimnasio

Facultad de Medicina

Cafetería

Plaza

Librería

Facultad de Informática

Facultad de Ciencias

Facultad de Humanidades

Biblioteca

Carmen

Lorena

**1-6 ¿En qué facultad estudian? PRIMERA FASE.** Match the names of the university students pictured at the right with the school where they study.

1. ___ Juan
2. ___ Carmen
3. ___ Lorena
4. ___ Álvaro

a. Facultad de Medicina
b. Facultad de Arquitectura
c. Facultad de Humanidades
d. Facultad de Ciencias

Álvaro

**SEGUNDA FASE.** Exchange the information with a classmate and indicate two classes that each student is probably taking.

MODELO: E1: *¿Dónde estudia Carmen?*
E2: *Carmen estudia en la Facultad de… Probablemente tiene clase de… y de…*

Juan

**1-7 Mapa de la universidad.** Look at the map above and indicate if each statement is true (**Cierto**) or false (**Falso**). If it is **Falso,** correct the information.

1. _____ La plaza está en el centro del campus.
2. _____ La Facultad de Humanidades está junto a (*next to*) la biblioteca.
3. _____ La cafetería está detrás del gimnasio.
4. _____ La Facultad de Ciencias está delante de (*in front of*) la Facultad de Informática.
5. _____ La librería está al lado de la cafetería.
6. _____ La Facultad de Medicina está al lado del gimnasio.

# Las actividades de los estudiantes

 ### En la biblioteca

CD 1
Track 23

Unos **alumnos** estudian en la biblioteca. **Toman apuntes** y trabajan en sus tareas. A veces **buscan** palabras en el **diccionario**. Frecuentemente **conversan** sobre sus clases.

 ### Los fines de semana

CD 1
Track 24

Los estudiantes **toman algo** en un **café**.

**Miran** televisión en **casa**.

**Bailan** en una **discoteca** con amigos.

**Caminan** en la **playa**.

**Montan** en bicicleta.

**1-8 Para escoger.** Look at the illustrations above. Then choose the word or phrase that completes the sentence logically.

1. Los estudiantes ___ en la biblioteca.
   a. toman café          b. estudian          c. hablan
2. Buscan palabras en ___ .
   a. el reloj          b. el diccionario          c. el laboratorio
3. Miran televisión en ___ .
   a. la biblioteca          b. la playa          c. casa
4. Montan en bicicleta ___ .
   a. los fines de semana          b. en el café          c. en una discoteca

# En la librería

CD 1
Track 25

ESTUDIANTE: **Necesito comprar** un diccionario para mi clase de literatura española.

DEPENDIENTE: **¿Grande** o **pequeño?**

ESTUDIANTE: Grande, y todo en español.

DEPENDIENTE: **Este** diccionario es muy bueno.

ESTUDIANTE: **¿Cuánto cuesta?**

DEPENDIENTE: Cuarenta y ocho **euros.**

**1-9 ¿Qué necesita?** Complete the following statements, based on the previous conversation.

1. El estudiante necesita...
2. Es un diccionario...
3. Es para su clase de...
4. El diccionario cuesta...

**1-10 ¿Cuánto cuesta?** During your semester abroad, you go to the university bookstore. Ask the salesclerk how much the following items cost.

> *Cuaderno €1.5*
> HISTORIA
> DICCIONARIO
> *€ 47*
> *€ 38*
> *Psicología*
> Lápices
> CIENCIAS
> *€ 54*
> *€ 87*
> *6 Lápices €5*
> *bolígrafos €1*
> *Calculadora €23*

## Cultura

Since 2002, the euro has been the official monetary unit of the so-called Eurozone, which includes (as of January 2008) Austria, Belgium, Cyprus, Finland, France, Germany, Greece, Ireland, Italy, Luxembourg, Malta, the Netherlands, Portugal, Slovenia, and Spain. In some other European countries and the United Kingdom, the euro, although not official, is accepted in stores. The euro currency sign is € and the banking code is EUR.

**MODELO:**

ESTUDIANTE: *¿Cuánto cuesta el mapa?*
DEPENDIENTE/A: *Cuesta cincuenta euros.*

**1-11 Entrevista (*Interview*).** Ask where and when your classmate does each of the following activities.

MODELO:          practicar baloncesto (*basketball*)
          E1:  *¿Dónde practicas baloncesto? ¿Y cuándo?*
          E2:  *Practico baloncesto en la plaza por las tardes.*

| ACTIVIDAD | DÓNDE | CUÁNDO |
|---|---|---|
| **1.** estudiar para un examen difícil | | |
| **2.** mirar televisión | | |
| **3.** tomar café/chocolate | | |
| **4.** bailar salsa | | |
| **5.** escuchar música | | |
| **6.** comprar un diccionario/CDs/materiales para tus clases | | |

 **1-12 Las actividades de sus compañeros.** PRIMERA FASE.  Go around the classroom and interview three people. Ask two different questions of each of them. Take notes to report later. Answer the questions of classmates who interview you.

1. ¿Qué haces (*do you do*) los fines de semana?
2. ¿Dónde miras televisión?
3. ¿Qué compras en la librería?
4. ¿Dónde estudias normalmente?
5. ¿Trabajas los fines de semana? ¿Dónde trabajas?

SEGUNDA FASE.  Now share your classmates' answers with the rest of the class.

MODELO:  *María estudia normalmente en casa. No trabaja los fines de semana.*

**1-13 ¿Qué hacen? (*What do they do?*)**  You will hear three people talking about their activities during the week and on weekends. Before you listen, list your own activities in the chart.

CD 1
Track 26

| MIS ACTIVIDADES DE TODOS LOS DÍAS | MIS ACTIVIDADES DEL FIN DE SEMANA |
|---|---|
| | |
| | |
| | |

Now pay attention to the general idea of what is said in the recording. As you listen, decide which activities each person is talking about. Then write the number of the speaker (1, 2, 3) next to the appropriate topic.

___ los estudios
___ el tiempo libre (*free time*)
___ el trabajo

# EN ACCIÓN

## Diarios de bicicleta: La chivita

### Antes de ver

**1-14** In this video segment, you will be introduced to four college students, some of whom do not know each other. Write down four expressions you think they may use to greet and introduce each other.

### Mientras ve

**1-15** As you watch, indicate whether the following statements refer to Javier (**J**), Daniel (**D**), Luciana (**L**), or Gabi (**G**).

1. ___ Son sus diarios de bicicleta.
2. ___ Es compañera de Gaby.
3. ___ Viaja en bicicleta.
4. ___ Es puntual, simpático y cómico.
5. ___ Olvida (*forgets*) su teléfono en la cafetería.

### Después de ver

**1-16** Check off the expressions you prepared in *Antes de ver* that were used in this segment.

# FUNCIONES Y FORMAS

## 1. Talking about academic life and daily occurrences: Present tense of regular -ar verbs

Sara     Marta

| | |
|---|---|
| REPORTERO: | Perdón. Soy Pablo Brito del canal 11 de televisión. ¿Su nombre, por favor? |
| SARA: | Yo soy Sara y ella es Marta. |
| REPORTERO: | ¿Tienen ustedes una vida muy activa? |
| MARTA: | Sí, nosotras somos (are) atletas. **Practicamos** muchos deportes. Sara **participa** en maratones y **practica** el tenis. Yo **practico** el fútbol y el baloncesto. |
| SARA: | Y los fines de semana **montamos** en bicicleta. |
| REPORTERO: | ¡Qué interesante! Gracias, señoritas. |

**Piénselo.** Check (✔) all the statements that are true, based on the reporter's interview with Sara and Marta.

1. _____ Pablo es un reportero de radio.
2. _____ Marta y Sara **practican** muchos deportes (*sports*).
3. _____ Marta **participa** en maratones.
4. _____ Marta **practica** el fútbol.
5. _____ Sara **practica** el baloncesto.
6. _____ Sara y Marta **montan** en bicicleta.

■ To talk about actions, feelings, and states of being, you need to use verbs. In both English and Spanish, the infinitive is the base form of the verb that appears in vocabulary lists and dictionaries. In English, infinitives are preceded by *to*: *to speak*. Infinitives in Spanish belong to one of three groups, depending on whether they end in **-ar**, **-er**, or **-ir**. Verbs ending in **-ar** are presented here, and verbs ending in **-er** and **-ir** are presented in the next section.

| HABLAR (*to speak*) | | | |
| --- | --- | --- | --- |
| yo | hab**lo** | nosotros/as | hab**lamos** |
| tú | hab**las** | vosotros/as | hab**láis** |
| él, ella, Ud. | hab**la** | ellos, ellas, Uds. | hab**lan** |

■ Use the present tense to express what you and others generally or habitually do or do not do. You may also use the present tense to express an ongoing action. Context will tell you which meaning is intended.

Ana **trabaja** en la oficina.
{ *Ana works in the office.*
{ *Ana is working in the office.*

Luis **practica** el piano todos los días.   *Luis practices the piano every day.*

■ Here are some expressions you may find useful when talking about the frequency of actions.

| | | | |
| --- | --- | --- | --- |
| **siempre** | *always* | **muchas veces** | *often* |
| **todos los días/meses** | *every day/month* | **a veces** | *sometimes* |
| **todas las semanas** | *every week* | **nunca** | *never* |

■ Some common **-ar** verbs are **bailar, buscar, caminar, comprar, conversar, escuchar, estudiar, llegar, mirar, montar, necesitar, participar, practicar, sacar, tomar,** and **trabajar.**

**1-17 Preferencias. PRIMERA FASE.** Rank these activities from 1 to 9, according to your preferences (1 = most interesting, 9 = least interesting).

_____ bailar en una discoteca
_____ mirar televisión en casa
_____ estudiar otras culturas
_____ comprar DVDs y CDs
_____ caminar en la playa

_____ montar en bicicleta cuando hace sol
_____ escuchar música rock
_____ conversar con los amigos con mensajes de texto
_____ bajar (*download*) música de Internet

**SEGUNDA FASE.** Now compare your answers with those of a classmate. Follow the model.

**MODELO:**   E1: *Para mí, bailar en una discoteca es número 1. ¿Y para ti?*
E2: *Para mí, caminar en la playa es número 1.*

**1-18 Mi rutina.** PRIMERA FASE. Indicate (✓) the activities that are part of your routine at school.

1. _____ Llego a la universidad a las nueve de la mañana.
2. _____ Converso con mis amigos por teléfono.
3. _____ Tomo notas en todas las clases.
4. _____ Hablo con mis compañeros en la cafetería.
5. _____ Estudio en la biblioteca por las mañanas.
6. _____ Trabajo en mis tareas todas las noches.
7. _____ Miro programas cómicos en la televisión.
8. _____ A veces practico un deporte con mis amigos/as.

 SEGUNDA FASE. Now compare your answers with those of a classmate. The expressions in *En directo* will help you react as your classmate tells you about himself/herself. Report your findings to the class.

MODELO:   *Daniel y yo somos (muy) similares. Él y yo miramos programas cómicos en la televisión./Daniel y yo somos (muy) diferentes. Yo estudio por las mañanas; él estudia por las tardes.*

---

**En directo**

To express disbelief:

**¡Qué increíble!**

To show surprise at a coincidence:

**¡Qué casualidad!**

---

**1-19 A preguntar.** PRIMERA FASE. Find four different classmates, each of whom does one of the following activities. Write each name on the appropriate line. The expressions in *En directo* will help you carry on the conversation.

MODELO:       mirar televisión por la noche
        E1: *¡Oye! ¿Miras televisión por la tarde?*
        E2: *Sí, miro televisión por la tarde. O*
            *No, no miro televisión por la tarde.*

---

**En directo**

To get someone's attention:

**¡Oye!** (to someone your age or younger)

**Oiga, por favor.** (to someone unknown to you)

To interrupt to ask a question:

**Perdón, tengo una pregunta.**

To agree to answer:

**Con mucho gusto.**

---

| PERSONA | ACTIVIDAD |
|---|---|
| _____ | estudiar español todos los días |
| _____ | llegar a la universidad a las 9:30 a.m. |
| _____ | escuchar música clásica en casa por la noche |
| _____ | trabajar en una oficina por la tarde |

SEGUNDA FASE. Now report to the class your findings about your classmates' activities.

**1-20 Mis actividades.** PRIMERA FASE. Mark (✓) the space that indicates how often you do the following activities:

| ACTIVIDADES | A VECES | MUCHAS VECES | SIEMPRE | NUNCA |
|---|---|---|---|---|
| estudiar con amigos | | | | |
| sacar buenas notas | | | | |
| montar en bicicleta los fines de semana | | | | |
| mirar televisión por la tarde | | | | |
| bailar los sábados | | | | |
| tomar café | | | | |

**SEGUNDA FASE.** Now tell each other how often you do these activities, and then ask where your partner does them.

MODELO:  E1:  *Yo estudio con amigos a veces, ¿y tú?*
         E2:  *Yo siempre estudio con amigos.*
         E1:  *¿Dónde estudian ustedes?*
         E2:  *Estudiamos en la biblioteca.*

### 1-21 Un día típico en la vida de Luisa. PRIMERA FASE. Describe what Luisa does on a typical day.

MODELO:  *Luisa llega a la oficina a las nueve menos diez.*

1.

2.

3.

4.

**SEGUNDA FASE.** Now, based on a typical day in her life, describe Luisa's personality. Then explain what you normally do on a regular day.

Este bar de Madrid tiene una selección de tapas deliciosas.

## SITUACIONES

1. **Role A.** Your friend works in the afternoon. Ask a) where he/she works; b) the days of the week and the hours that he/she works; and c) if the job (**trabajo**) is interesting/boring/difficult/easy. Then answer your friend's questions about your job.

   **Role B.** Tell your friend that you work in the afternoon. Answer your friend's questions about your job. Then ask three questions about his/her job (**trabajo**).

2. **Role A.** You need to read *Don Quijote de la Mancha* by Miguel de Cervantes for your World Literature class, so you go to the university library. Tell the librarian that you need a book, and answer the librarian's questions about title (**título**) and author (**autor**).

   **Role B.** You are a librarian at the university library. A student tells you that he/she needs a book. Ask the title of the book (**¿cuál es el título?**) and the author (**autor**). Comment on the book.

## 2. Talking about academic life and daily occurrences: Present tense of regular *-er* and *-ir* verbs

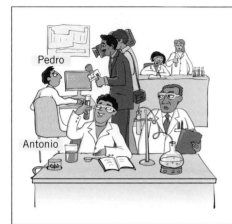

REPORTERO: Y ustedes, ¿qué hacen durante el día?

PEDRO: Antonio estudia ciencias en la universidad. **Asiste** a sus clases y luego **corre** al laboratorio, donde trabaja todos los días. Habla con el profesor y **aprende** mucho. Los estudiantes de ciencias **leen** mucho, **escriben** trabajos de investigación y sacan buenas notas. Yo soy un estudiante de arquitectura, y mis compañeros y yo **leemos** y **escribimos** mucho también. Yo casi (*almost*) **vivo** en la biblioteca cuando estudio para los exámenes.

**Piénselo.** Check (✓) all the statements that are true, based on the reporter's interview with Pedro.

1. _____ Antonio estudia arquitectura.
2. _____ Antonio trabaja en el laboratorio y **aprende** (*learns*) mucho.
3. _____ Los estudiantes **leen** y **escriben** mucho.
4. _____ Antonio no **asiste** (*attends*) a sus clases.
5. _____ Los estudiantes de ciencias sacan buenas notas.
6. _____ Pedro estudia arquitectura.
7. _____ Pedro **vive** (*lives*) en el laboratorio.

■ You have learned in this chapter that the present tense is used to express activities and ongoing actions. You have also learned the present tense forms for verbs whose infinitives end in **-ar**. Now you will learn those forms for verbs whose infinitives end in **-er** and **-ir**.

■ Note that **-er** and **-ir** verbs have the same endings, except for the **nosotros/as** and **vosotros/as** forms.

| APRENDER (*to learn*) | | | |
|---|---|---|---|
| yo | aprend**o** | nosotros/as | aprend**emos** |
| tú | aprend**es** | vosotros/as | aprend**éis** |
| él, ella, Ud. | aprend**e** | ellos, ellas, Uds. | aprend**en** |

| VIVIR (*to live*) | | | |
|---|---|---|---|
| yo | viv**o** | nosotros/as | viv**imos** |
| tú | viv**es** | vosotros/as | viv**ís** |
| él, ella, Ud. | viv**e** | ellos, ellas, Uds. | viv**en** |

■ Other common **-er** and **-ir** verbs are **comer** (*to eat*), **comprender, correr, leer, responder** (*to respond*), **asistir**, and **escribir**.

■ The verb **ver** (*to see*) has an irregular **yo** form: **veo, ves, ve, vemos, veis, ven**.

**Veo** películas los fines de semana.　　*I see movies on weekends.*

■ Use **deber** + *infinitive* to express that you should/must/ought to do something.

Los atletas **deben beber** mucha agua.　　*Athletes should drink lots of water.*

**1-22 Mi profesor/a modelo.** PRIMERA FASE. Indicate which of the activities are part of the routine of an ideal instructor inside and outside the classroom.

|  | SÍ | NO |
|---|---|---|
| 1. Lee el periódico (*newspaper*) en clase. | _____ | _____ |
| 2. Escucha los problemas de los estudiantes. | _____ | _____ |
| 3. Bebe café y come en la clase. | _____ | _____ |
| 4. Escribe buenos ejemplos en la pizarra. | _____ | _____ |
| 5. Nunca prepara sus clases. | _____ | _____ |
| 6. Siempre asiste a clase. | _____ | _____ |
| 7. Responde a las preguntas de los estudiantes. | _____ | _____ |
| 8. Habla con los estudiantes en su oficina. | _____ | _____ |

SEGUNDA FASE. Compare your answers with those of a classmate. Together write two more activities typical of an ideal instructor and ask your instructor if they are part of his/her academic routine.

**1-23 Para pasarlo bien (*To have a good time*).** PRIMERA FASE. Indicate which of the following activities your classmates do to have a good time.

1. _____ Leen libros en español todas las semanas.
2. _____ Escriben mensajes de texto.
3. _____ Practican deportes con los amigos.
4. _____ Asisten a clase a las ocho de la mañana.
5. _____ Corren en el gimnasio y en el parque.
6. _____ Ven películas y programas de televisión en casa.
7. _____ Comen en restaurantes elegantes.
8. _____ Beben sólo Coca-Cola en las fiestas.

SEGUNDA FASE. Compare your answers with those of a classmate. Then exchange information with another pair (**pareja**) about the activities you all do to have a good time. Use the expressions in *En directo* to help you react naturally to your classmates' responses.

MODELO:　PAREJA 1: *Nosotros bailamos en discotecas para pasarlo bien. ¿Y ustedes?*
　　　　　PAREJA 2: *Bebemos café y conversamos con los amigos.*

---

### En directo

To react to what someone has said:

**¡Qué interesante!**

**¡Qué divertido!**
*How funny!*

**¡Qué aburrido!**
*How boring!*

**1-24 Lugares y actividades.** Ask what your classmate does in the following places. He/She will respond with one of the activities listed. Then ask what your classmate does not do in those places.

MODELO: en la clase

E1: *¿Qué haces en la clase?*

E2: *Veo películas en español.*

E1: *¿Qué no haces en la clase?*

E2: *No leo el periódico.*

| LUGARES | ACTIVIDADES |
|---|---|
| en la playa | beber cerveza |
| en un café | tomar el sol |
| en una discoteca | bailar salsa |
| en una fiesta | mirar televisión |
| en el cine | leer el periódico |
| en la casa | ver películas de horror |
| en un restaurante | escuchar música clásica |
| en la biblioteca | comer un sándwich y tomar un café |

**1-25 A preguntar.** PRIMERA FASE. Find four different classmates, each of whom does one of the following activities. Write each name in the chart below.

MODELO: ver películas en casa

E1: *¿Ves películas en casa?*

E2: *Sí, veo películas en casa./ No, no veo películas en casa.*

| PERSONA | ACTIVIDAD |
|---|---|
| _____ | asistir a conciertos de música rock |
| _____ | beber café todos los días |
| _____ | vivir en casa con la familia |
| _____ | escribir mensajes de texto por la noche |

SEGUNDA FASE. Now report to the class your findings about your classmates' activities.

**1-26 ¿Qué deben hacer?** Read the situations in the column on the left and select the best advice from the column on the right.

1. ___ Maricela desea sacar buenas notas.
2. ___ Carlos corre en el parque.
3. ___ Luisa y Jorge están (*are*) muy nerviosos.
4. ___ Los estudiantes desean comer tapas.
5. ___ Óscar desea aprender a bailar.
6. ___ Carolina desea preparar tacos, burritos y enchiladas.

a. Debe trabajar en un restaurante mexicano.
b. Deben visitar España.
c. Debe estudiar todos los días.
d. Debe tomar clases de baile.
e. No deben beber café con cafeína.
f. Debe beber mucha agua.

## SITUACIONES

1. **Role A.** You see a classmate at a coffee shop with laptop and books spread out on the table. Ask if he/she a) drinks coffee every day; b) often studies in the coffee shop; c) reads the newspaper there; and d) writes on the computer in the coffee shop.

   **Role B.** You are sitting at a table with your laptop and books at your favorite coffee shop. A classmate comes in and walks over. Answer your classmate's questions about what you usually do there.

2. **Role A.** On the way to Spanish class you run into a classmate and ask how he/she is. Your classmate confides that he/she isn't getting good grades in Spanish. Suggest that he/she a) should always attend class; b) must read the chapter every week; c) should study in the library; and d) ought to look for a good dictionary.

   **Role B.** In the hallway you run into the person who sits next to you in Spanish class. When he/she asks how you are, say you're so-so. Explain that you are not getting good grades in Spanish and that you are not learning the vocabulary. Listen to your classmate's advice and thank him/her.

## 3. Specifying gender and number: Articles and nouns

MANUEL: Hola, Rocío. Tengo **un** plan. ¿Estudiamos español en **la** universidad esta tarde? Necesito **un** diccionario para **la** tarea.

ROCÍO: ¡Buena idea! ¿En **la** biblioteca? **El** profesor de español es bueno, pero es **una** clase difícil. ¿Invitamos a mi amigo Marcos?

MANUEL: Fenomenal. Usamos **la** pizarra y **el** escritorio **del** salón 12 de **la** biblioteca.

**Piénselo.** Match the words on the right with those on the left. Use the dialogue and the endings of the nouns as clues.

1. ___ clase                          **a.** el
2. ___ diccionario de español        **b.** la
3. ___ pizarra                        **c.** un
4. ___ escritorio                     **d.** una
5. ___ universidad

## Gender

▪ Nouns are words that name a person, place, or thing. In English all nouns use the same definite article, *the*, and all singular nouns use the indefinite articles *a* and *an*. Spanish nouns, whether they refer to people or to things, have either masculine or feminine gender. Masculine singular nouns use **el** or **un** and feminine singular nouns use **la** or **una**.

The terms *masculine* and *feminine* are used in a grammatical sense and have nothing to do with biological gender.

|                              | MASCULINE | FEMININE |       |
|------------------------------|-----------|----------|-------|
| SINGULAR DEFINITE ARTICLES   | el        | la       | *the* |
| SINGULAR INDEFINITE ARTICLES | un        | una      | *a/an* |

■ Generally, nouns that end in **-o** are masculine and require **el** or **un**, and those that end in **-a** are feminine and require **la** or **una**.

| | | |
|---|---|---|
| **el/un** libr**o** | **el/un** cuaderno | **el/un** diccionario |
| **la/una** mesa | **la/una** silla | **la/una** ventana |

■ Nouns that end in **-dad, -ción, -sión** are feminine and require **la** or **una**.

**la/una** universi**dad**     **la/una** lec**ción**     **la/una** televi**sión**

■ Nouns that end in **-ma** are generally masculine.

**el/un** progra**ma**     **el/un** proble**ma**

**el/un** dra**ma**     **el/un** poe**ma**

■ In general, nouns that refer to males are masculine, and nouns that refer to females are feminine. Masculine nouns ending in **-o** change the **-o** to **-a** for the feminine; those ending in a consonant add **-a** for the feminine.

**el/un** amig**o**     **la/una** amig**a**

**el/un** profes**or**     **la/una** profes**ora**

■ Nouns ending in **-ante** and **-ente** may be feminine or masculine. Gender is signaled by the article (**el/la estudiante**).

■ Use definite articles with titles when you are talking about someone. Do not use definite articles when addressing someone directly.

**La** señorita Andrade es **la** secretaria en el Departamento de Lenguas Europeas. **El** profesor Campos es **el** director del departamento.

*Ms. Andrade is the secretary in the Department of European Languages. Professor Campos is the chair of the department.*

Todos los días, el profesor Campos dice "Buenos días, señorita Andrade". Ella contesta, "Buenos días, profesor Campos".

*Every day, Professor Campos says "Good morning, Ms. Andrade." She responds, "Good morning, Professor Campos."*

## Number

| | MASCULINE | FEMININE | |
|---|---|---|---|
| PLURAL DEFINITE ARTICLES | **los** | **las** | *the* |
| PLURAL INDEFINITE ARTICLES | **unos** | **unas** | *some* |

■ Add **-s** to form the plural of nouns that end in a vowel. Add **-es** to nouns ending in a consonant.

| la silla → las silla**s** | el cuaderno → los cuaderno**s** |
|---|---|
| la activida**d** → las activida**des** | el señor → los señor**es** |

■ Nouns that end in **-z** change the **z** to **c** before **-es**.

el lápi**z** → los lápi**ces**

■ To refer to a mixed group, use masculine plural forms.

los chic**os**     *the boys and girls*

**1-27 Conversaciones incompletas.** Complete the dialogues.

1. Supply the definite articles (**el, la, los, las**).
   E1: ¿Dónde está María?
   E2: Está en __ clase de __ profesora Sánchez.
   E1: ¡Qué lástima! Necesito hablar con ella. Es urgente.
   E2: Bueno, ella está en __ salón de clase hasta __ una, y por
       __ tarde trabaja en __ laboratorio.
   E1: ¿Y a qué hora llega?
   E2: Llega a __ dos, más o menos.

2. Supply the indefinite articles (**un, una, unos, unas**).
   E1: Necesito comprar __ calculadora y __ lápices.
   E2: Y yo necesito __ bolígrafo y __ diccionario, pero ¿qué diccionario compro?
   E1: Para el curso de español, __ profesores usan __ diccionario pequeño y otros usan
       __ diccionario grande. ¿Por qué (*Why*) no hablas con tu profesor?

3. Supply the definite or indefinite articles.
   E1: Tengo __ examen de matemáticas mañana y necesito sacar __ buena nota en esa clase.
   E2: ¿Quién es __ profesor?
   E1: Es __ doctora Solís.
   E2: ¡Ah! Es __ profesora excelente.
   E1: Sí, pero __ clase es muy difícil. Estudio y escribo __ tareas todos
       __ días, pero no saco buenas notas.
   E2: ¡Vaya! Lo siento mucho.

**1-28 ¿Qué necesitan?** Take turns saying what these classmates need.

MODELO: Alicia tiene que buscar unas palabras. *Necesita un diccionario.*

1. Mónica tiene que tomar apuntes en la clase de historia.
2. Carlos y Ana deben hacer la tarea de matemáticas.
3. Alfredo tiene que estudiar para el examen de geografía.
4. Isabel tiene que escribir una composición para su clase de inglés.
5. Blanca y Lucía tienen que encontrar (*find*) dónde está Salamanca.
6. David tiene que escuchar una canción (*song*) para su clase de música.

## SITUACIONES

1. **Role A.** You have missed the first day of class. Ask a classmate a) at what time the class meets; b) who the professor is; and c) what you need for the class.

   **Role B.** Tell your classmate a) that the class is at 8:00 in the morning; b) the name of the professor and what he/she is like; and c) at least three items that your classmate needs for the class.

2. **Role A.** You work for the student newspaper at your college and have been asked to interview two students to find out how they typically spend their weekends. After introducing yourself, find out a) if they work, and where; b) what they study; and c) what they do (**hacen**) on Saturdays and Sundays.

   **Roles B, C.** Tell the interviewer a) if you work and, if so, where; b) the classes you take; and c) what you do on weekends, where, and with whom.

## 4. Expressing location and states of being: Present tense of *estar*

Elisa          Humberto

ELISA: ¿Humberto? Te habla Elisa.

HUMBERTO: ¡Elisa! ¡Qué sorpresa! ¿Dónde **estás**?

ELISA: **Estoy** en el aeropuerto de Barajas, en Madrid. ¿Y tú?

HUMBERTO: Mi padre y yo **estamos** de vacaciones en Nueva York. En este momento, mi padre **está** en la tienda *Best Buy*. ¿Y cómo **están** todos en tu familia?

ELISA: Todos **estamos** muy bien. ¡Qué bueno escucharte! Lo siento, Humberto, pero el vuelo (*flight*) sale (*leaves*) pronto. Hablamos más mañana. Adiós.

**Piénselo.** Indicate whether each statement is true (**Cierto**) or false (**Falso**), based on the conversation. If it is **Falso**, correct the information.

1. _____ Humberto **está** en el aeropuerto.
2. _____ Elisa **está** de vacaciones en Nueva York.
3. _____ Humberto **está** en una ciudad grande con una persona de su familia.
4. _____ La tienda *Best Buy* de esta conversación **está** en Madrid.
5. _____ Elisa y Humberto **están** contentos de hablar por teléfono.

■ You have already been using some forms of **estar**. Here are all the present tense forms of this verb.

| ESTAR (*to be*) | | | |
|---|---|---|---|
| yo | **estoy** | nosotros/as | **estamos** |
| tú | **estás** | vosotros/as | **estáis** |
| Ud., él, ella | **está** | Uds., ellos, ellas | **están** |

■ Use **estar** to express the location of persons or objects.

| | |
|---|---|
| ¿Dónde **está** Humberto? | *Where is Humberto?* |
| **Está** en Nueva York. | *He is in New York* |

■ Use **estar** to talk about states of health or being.

| | |
|---|---|
| ¿Cómo **está** la familia de Elisa? | *How is Elisa's family?* |
| **Está** muy bien. | *They are very well.* |

**1-29 En la cafetería.** In the cafeteria, you run across a former classmate. Complete the conversation, using the correct forms of **estar**. Then indicate in the parentheses if **estar** signals location (**L**) or a state of being (**S**).

ROBERTO: Hola, Carlos. ¿Qué tal? ¿Cómo _____?

CARLOS: _____ muy bien. ¿Y tú?

ROBERTO: Muy bien, muy bien. ¿Y cómo _____ tu hermana *(sister)* Ana?

CARLOS: Bien, gracias. Ella y mamá _____ en España ahora.

ROBERTO: ¡Qué suerte! Y nosotros _____ en la universidad, ¡y en la semana de exámenes!

**1-30 Horas y lugares favoritos. PRIMERA FASE.** Ask your classmate his/her favorite time of day or day of the week. Then ask where he/she usually is at that time or on that day.

MODELO: E1: *¿Cuál es tu hora favorita del día?*
E2: *Las 10:00 de la mañana.*
E1: *Generalmente, ¿dónde estás a las 10:00 de la mañana?*
E2: Estoy en... . *¿Y cuál es tu hora favorita?*
E1: ... .
E2: *¿Y dónde estás?*
E1: *Estoy en... .*

**SEGUNDA FASE.** Compare your responses with those of your partner. Identify any similarities and/or differences in your preferences.

**1-31 Conversación.** Ask a classmate where the people in these drawings are, how they feel, and what they are doing.

MODELO: E1: *¿Dónde está María Luisa?*
E2: *Está en la biblioteca.*
E1: *¿Cómo está?*
E2: *Está regular.*
E1: *¿Qué hace?*
E2: *Estudia.*

María Luisa

**1.** Berta    Lorena    **2.** Carlos    el Dr. Núñez    **3.** Marcelo    Eduardo

---

**SITUACIONES**

1. **Role A.** As editor of the new student handbook, you must give the graphic designer directions for drawing the campus map. First draw a rough sketch of the map, including the places below. Then explain their location to the designer.

   la biblioteca
   la cafetería
   la Facultad de Ciencias
   la Facultad de Humanidades

   **Role B.** You are a graphic designer. Ask questions about the location of these buildings as you draw the new map. When you have finished, show the map to the editor to check if you have understood his/her explanations.

2. **Role A.** You are a new student at the university and you do not know where the gym is. Introduce yourself to a classmate. Explain that you want to run in the gym and ask where it is located. Thank your classmate for the help (**Gracias por la ayuda**).

   **Role B.** A new student will greet you and ask questions. Make your answers as complete and specific as possible.

# 5. Asking and answering questions: Interrogative words

Andrea Pérez conversa con su consejera (*advisor*) en la universidad. La consejera necesita rellenar (*fill out*) algunos formularios con información sobre Andrea. Aquí están algunas de las preguntas de la consejera y en la columna de la derecha, las respuestas de Andrea.

| CONSEJERA | ANDREA |
|---|---|
| ¿**Cómo** se llama la residencia estudiantil donde vives? | Se llama Casa Cervantes. |
| ¿**Dónde** está? | Está en la Avenida España. |
| ¿**Cuándo** son tus clases? | Por la mañana y por la tarde. |
| ¿**Cuánto** cuesta tu transporte por mes? | Aproximadamente 35 euros. |
| ¿**Quién** es tu compañera de cuarto? | Cristina Zapatero. |
| ¿**Por qué** deseas (*want to*) estudiar psicología? | Para ayudar (*help*) a otras personas. |

**Piénselo.** Match Andrea's responses in the left column with the questions her advisor asked her in the right column. **OJO:** You will be able to answer some of the advisor's questions with the information from the conversation above.

1. ___ Es el profesor Agustín Reyes-Torres.
2. ___ Se llama Cristina Zapatero.
3. ___ En la Casa Cervantes.
4. ___ 400 euros al mes.
5. ___ Por la tarde.

a. ¿**Dónde** vives?
b. ¿**Cuándo** es tu clase de psicología?
c. ¿**Quién** es tu profesor favorito?
d. ¿**Cómo** se llama tu compañera de cuarto?
e. ¿**Cuánto** cuesta vivir en la residencia?

---

■ Interrogative words are used to ask questions or to obtain specific information. You have already been using many of these words.

| | | | |
|---|---|---|---|
| ¿**cómo**? | *how/what?* | ¿**cuál(es)**? | *which?* |
| ¿**dónde**? | *where?* | ¿**quién(es)**? | *who?* |
| ¿**qué**? | *what?* | ¿**cuánto/a**? | *how much?* |
| ¿**cuándo**? | *when?* | ¿**cuántos/as**? | *how many?* |
| ¿**por qué**? | *why?* | ¿**para qué**? | *why?/what for?* |

■ If a subject is used in a question, it normally follows the verb.

¿**Dónde** trabaja Elsa?     *Where does Elsa work?*

■ Use **por qué** to ask *why* and **porque** to answer *because.*

¿**Por qué** está Pepe en la biblioteca?    *Why is Pepe at the library?*

**Porque** necesita estudiar.    *Because he needs to study.*

■ Use **qué + ser** when you want to ask for a definition or an explanation.

¿**Qué es** la sardana?    *What is the sardana?*

Es un baile típico de Cataluña.    *It is a typical dance of Catalonia.*

## Lengua

All question words have a written accent over the stressed syllable: **cómo**, **dónde**.

When these words are used in a non-interrogative context, they do not have a written accent.

¿**Dónde** está la biblioteca?
*Where is the library?*

Esta es la biblioteca **donde** estudio todos los días.
*This is the library where I study everyday.*

■ Use **cuál(es) + ser** when you want to ask which one(s).

| | |
|---|---|
| ¿**Cuál es** tu mochila? | *Which (one) is your backpack?* |
| ¿**Cuáles son** tus papeles? | *Which (ones) are your papers?* |

■ Questions that may be answered with **sí** or **no** do not use a question word.

| | |
|---|---|
| ¿Trabajan ustedes los sábados? | *Do you work on Saturdays?* |
| No, no trabajamos. | *No, we do not.* |

■ Another way to ask a question is to place an interrogative tag after a declarative statement.

| | |
|---|---|
| Tú hablas inglés, ¿**verdad?** | *You speak English, don't you?* |
| David es norteamericano, ¿**no?** | *David is an American, isn't he?* |

**1-32 Preguntas.** First look at the cues in the right column and then complete the questions with **quién, cuándo, cuántos/as, cuál,** or **por qué,** as logical. Use your questions to interview two people as you walk around the room.

1. ¿ _____ clases tomas?        Tomo…
2. ¿ _____ son tus clases?        Por la…
3. ¿ _____ es tu clase favorita?        La clase de…
4. ¿ _____ es tu profesor/a favorito/a?        El profesor/La profesora…
5. ¿ _____ estudias español?        Porque…
6. ¿ _____ estudiantes hay en tu clase        Hay…
    de español?

**1-33 Entrevista.** Ask your classmate questions to find out the following information. Use the appropriate expressions to show disbelief, coincidence, how interesting the answers are, and so on.

1. número de clases que toma este semestre
2. su clase favorita y razón (y por qué)
3. número de alumnos en la clase favorita
4. nombre del profesor favorito/de la profesora favorita
5. lugar donde estudia generalmente y cuántas horas estudia por (*per*) día
6. lugar donde trabaja

## SITUACIONES

1. **Role A.** You have just run across a friend you have not seen all year. Inquire about your friend's life in college including a) the location and size of his/her college/university; b) courses this semester; and c) his/her activities.

   **Role B.** You are talking with a friend you have not seen in a long time. Answer your friend's questions about your life in college. Then ask your friend some questions to get the same information.

2. **Role A.** It is the beginning of the term, and you need to add a psychology class. One of your friends is in a class that looks promising. Ask a) who the professor is; b) if there is a lot of homework; c) when the class meets; and d) if there is an exam soon. Then ask if you should know (**saber**) anything else (**algo más**) about the class.

   **Role B.** Your friend wants some information about your psychology class. Reply as specifically as possible to all of his/her questions. Then offer some additional information about the class.

# MOSAICOS

## A escuchar

**Listen for the gist**

When you are having a conversation or are listening to other people talking in your native language, you may get the gist of what is said without understanding every word or paying attention to every detail. You do this by relying on what you do understand, your knowledge of the topic, and your subconscious expectations of what happens in a conversational exchange. You will find these techniques helpful when listening to Spanish.

### Antes de escuchar

**1-34 Preparación.** You will hear two students talking about their classes. Before listening to the recording, think about the topics they may talk about and make a list of the things you may expect to hear, based on your experience as a student.

### Escuchar

CD 1
Track 27

**1-35 ¿Comprende usted?** First read the following statements. Then listen to the conversation between Ana and Mario and indicate whether each statement is true (**Cierto**) or false (**Falso**).

1. _____ Mario y Ana estudian en la misma (*same*) universidad este semestre.
2. _____ Mario toma clases de ciencias y de humanidades.
3. _____ Ana lee en la biblioteca para sus clases.
4. _____ Ana toma clases por la tarde.
5. _____ Mario realmente visita otros países en una de sus clases.

### Después de escuchar

**1-36 Ahora usted.** Tell your classmate what you usually do on the following days and times. Your classmate will take notes. Then switch roles. Finally, verify with each other that the notes you took are correct.

| LUNES | MARTES | MIÉRCOLES | JUEVES | VIERNES |
|---|---|---|---|---|
| 8:00 a.m. | 3:00 p.m. | 5:00 p.m. | 9:00 p.m. | 1:00 p.m. |
|  |  |  |  |  |

# A conversar

## Antes de conversar

**1-37 Preparación.** Write the questions answered by the clerk at your campus bookstore.

1. _____    La dirección de la librería es Calle Mayor, número 50.
2. _____    Sí, tengo libros de historia de España en español.
3. _____    Sí, tengo diccionarios en español.
4. _____    El diccionario bilingüe cuesta 40 euros.

## Conversar

**1-38 Entre nosotros.** You are a Spaniard studying in Malaga. Your American friend would like to purchase some gifts to take home: a fancy pen, a book on the history of Spain, a Spanish dictionary, and a map of Spain. Read the following ad and call the bookstore to find out if it has what your friend needs. Your classmate will play the role of the bookstore clerk. Remember to follow the formalities of phone conversations with someone you do not know.

> **En directo**
>
> To answer the phone in Spain:
>    **¿Diga?**
>
> To greet someone formally:
>    **Buenos días./Buenas tardes.**
>
> To ask if they have what you need:
>    **Necesito/Busco un/una...**

# LIBRERÍA CERVANTES

Papelería • Impresos • Artículos para escritorio

Libros de texto • Revistas

Casa especializada en estilógrafos y bolígrafos

**Plaza Constitución, 3**
**29005   Málaga**
**Teléfono  221 19 99**

## Después de conversar

**1-39 Un poco más.** Call your American friend to explain whether the bookstore has each item he/she needs and the price.

# A leer

## Antes de leer

**1-40 Preparación.** Indicate which courses from the list students in the following majors (**carreras**) should take.

anatomía                drogas tóxicas              medicinas alternativas
conflictos sociales     estructura del español     muralistas mexicanos
depresión               fisiología
diseño gráfico          historia de la lengua

| MEDICINA | BELLAS ARTES | FARMACIA | PSICOLOGÍA | FILOLOGÍA |
|----------|--------------|----------|------------|-----------|
|          |              |          |            |           |
|          |              |          |            |           |

## Leer

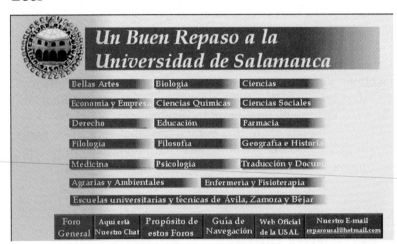

**1-41 Primera mirada.** Circle the letter that completes each statement, based on the information in this web page.

1. Esta es una...                          **a.** página de un libro.   **b.** página web.
2. El logo indica que esta institución es... **a.** muy nueva.           **b.** muy antigua.
3. Esta página web presenta una lista de... **a.** carreras.             **b.** clases.
4. La información de esta página web es...   **a.** muy específica.       **b.** muy general.
5. Esta institución tiene...                 **a.** un campus.            **b.** más de un campus.

**1-42 Segunda mirada.** Answer the following questions, according to the information in the text.

1. Al final (*the bottom*) de esta página web hay varias teclas (*keys*). ¿Qué tecla usan los estudiantes para conversar con personas que trabajan en la Universidad de Salamanca?
2. Imagínese que usted necesita información sobre su carrera en la Universidad de Salamanca. ¿Qué facultad tiene la información que usted necesita?

## Después de leer

**1-43 Ampliación.** Explore the **Servicio Central de Idiomas** page on the Universidad de Salamanca website by following the link on the *Mosaicos* website and answer the questions that accompany the link. Be prepared to share your answers with the rest of the class.

# A escribir

## Antes de escribir

**1-44 Preparación.** As part of course work in your Spanish class, you have been asked to correspond by e-mail with a university student in Spain. Think about and write down the information you would like to include in your first e-mail. Brainstorm…

1. some basic questions that this Spanish student may have about your college life.
2. some words and ideas that will help you answer those questions.
3. the order in which you will organize these ideas.

## Escribir

**1-45 Manos a la obra.** Now write the Spanish student an e-mail about life at your college or university. Use the information you gathered in *Preparación*. Consider including the following points, if you have not already listed them.

1. introducing yourself
2. telling how things are going for you
3. describing your school and your classes: class number and names, when you are taking them, how interesting (or not) your classes and professors are
4. describing your daily routine at school, what you do after classes and on weekends, where and with whom you do these activities, and so on

## Después de escribir

**1-46 Revisión.** After writing your e-mail, you may discuss it with a classmate. Then go over it carefully.

1. Make sure you have provided all the information your Spanish friend may need or any other you deem necessary. Pay attention to the content of your message and to the order in which you presented the information.
2. Revise any errors in language use, spelling, punctuation, accentuation, and so on.
3. Finally, make any changes that will help make your email clear and comprehensible to your e-mail pen pal.

## ESTRATEGIA

**Brainstorm key ideas before writing**

Brainstorming stimulates your creativity and helps you access your ideas. To brainstorm, make a note on a blank paper or computer screen of an idea or perspective you may want to emphasize. List words and ideas that will answer any questions that may arise.

Then organize them in the order in which you will use them in your text.

Thinking ahead and jotting down key words and ideas before you start to write your first draft is useful. It helps you think logically, focus on the topic, and put ideas in your own words.

# ENFOQUE CULTURAL

## Escuelas y universidades en España

El sistema escolar español es diferente del sistema de Estados Unidos y está dividido en cuatro partes: Educación Infantil, Educación Primaria, Educación Superior Obligatoria y, finalmente, el Bachillerato. En España, los niños y niñas hacen la Educación Infantil (que no es obligatoria sino voluntaria) hasta los seis años. Después empiezan la Educación Primaria, que es obligatoria y dura seis cursos, de los seis a los doce años de edad.

Entre los doce y los dieciséis años, los niños y niñas españoles cursan la Escuela Superior Obligatoria (ESO). La ESO completa la escolaridad obligatoria, pero muchos españoles continúan estudiando dos años más para terminar el Bachillerato, que los prepara para continuar con los estudios universitarios.

Rectorado de la Universidad Complutense

### En otras palabras

**Expresiones españolas**

**¡Vamos de tapas!**
*Let's go out for tapas!*

¡Me han **cateado**!
*They've flunked me!*

Ella es muy **maja**.
*She's a very nice person.*

Te llamo luego, **¿vale?**
*I'll call you later, OK?*

¿Dónde está ese **chaval**?
*Where is that kid?*

En España hay muchas universidades. La Universidad de Salamanca es una de las más antiguas del mundo y una de las más importantes de Europa. Esta universidad tiene un excelente programa de español para extranjeros y sus cursos de verano (durante junio, julio y agosto) tienen mucho prestigio.

De otra parte, la Universidad Complutense de Madrid es la más grande de España y también es muy antigua. Tiene un campus muy grande que se llama Ciudad Universitaria. Este nombre es muy apropiado, porque tiene más de 100.000 estudiantes.

El fútbol es un deporte muy popular en España.

En general, en las universidades españolas los estudiantes practican muchos deportes, pero la competencia entre universidades no es tan intensa como en Estados Unidos. Los deportes más populares entre los estudiantes universitarios españoles son el fútbol, el baloncesto y el atletismo, pero muchos estudiantes practican otros deportes también.

Los estudiantes universitarios españoles, como los de Estados Unidos, se divierten bailando en discotecas y clubes. Pero la música que escuchan no es necesariamente igual. A los jóvenes españoles les gusta escuchar música de rock en español. Hay muchos grupos de rock españoles. "El canto del loco" y "Fito y Fitipaldi" son dos grupos de rock español muy populares. A muchos jóvenes también les gusta bailar el flamenco, la música tradicional de Andalucía. En Sevilla, por ejemplo, hay clubes donde sólo tocan sevillanas, una música típica de esta ciudad. Finalmente, en su tiempo libre, muchos estudiantes españoles van de tapas y, por ejemplo, la Ciudad Universitaria está cerca de muchos bares de tapas.

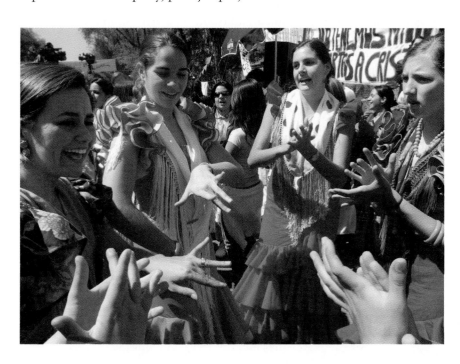

**1-47 Comprensión.** PRIMERA FASE. **Reconocimiento de palabras clave.** Find in the text the Spanish word or phrase that best expresses the meaning of the following concepts:

preschool _____

middle school _____

high school _____

summer school _____

soccer _____

track _____

dance _____

SEGUNDA FASE. **Oraciones importantes.** Underline the statements that contain ideas found in the text. Then indicate where in the text those ideas appear.

1. Some Spanish students finish school at sixteen, while others continue with their education until they are eighteen.
2. Kindergarten is compulsory in Spain at the age of six.
3. Spanish universities are mostly private institutions.
4. The University of Salamanca has a long history.
5. The University of Madrid is so big that it is like a small city in itself.
6. Spanish universities offer their students the opportunity to practice sports.
7. Fito and Fitipaldi are two famous Spanish Formula drivers.
8. Many Spanish students enjoy dancing to traditional Spanish music.

TERCERA FASE. **Ideas principales.** Write a brief paragraph in English summarizing the main ideas expressed in the text.

**1-48 Use la información.** Prepare a poster to present to the class comparing what you have learned about the educational system of Spain to that of your own country. Use visuals to illustrate the different stages of the educational system, a few of the oldest and most important universities, and some of the activities that are popular with students in their free time.

# VOCABULARIO

| Las materias o asignaturas | Subjects |
|---|---|
| la antropología | anthropology |
| las ciencias políticas | political science |
| la economía | economics |
| el español | Spanish |
| la estadística | statistics |
| la geografía | geography |
| la historia | history |
| la informática/ | computer |
| la computación | science |
| la literatura | literature |
| la psicología | psychology |
| la sociología | sociology |

| Los lugares | Places |
|---|---|
| la biblioteca | library |
| el café | cafe, coffee shop |
| la cafetería | cafeteria |
| la casa | house, home |
| la discoteca | dance club |
| el gimnasio | gymnasium |
| el laboratorio | laboratory |
| la librería | bookstore |
| la oficina | office |
| la playa | beach |
| la plaza | plaza, square |
| la universidad | university |

| Las Facultades | Schools, departments |
|---|---|
| de Arquitectura | of Architecture |
| de Ciencias | of Sciences |
| de Humanidades | of Humanities |
| de Informática | of Computer Science |
| de Medicina | of Medicine |

| Las personas | People |
|---|---|
| el alumno/la alumna | student |
| el compañero/ | partner, |
| la compañera | classmate |
| el dependiente/ | |
| la dependienta | salesperson |
| ellos/ellas | they |
| nosotros/nosotras | we |
| ustedes | you (plural) |

| Las descripciones | Descriptions |
|---|---|
| aburrido/a | boring |
| antiguo/a | old |
| bueno/a | good |
| difícil | difficult |
| estudioso/a | studious |
| excelente | excellent |
| fácil | easy |
| favorito/a | favorite |
| grande | big |
| interesante | interesting |
| malo/a | bad |
| norteamericano/a | North American |
| pequeño/a | small |

| Verbos | Verbs |
|---|---|
| aprender | to learn |
| asistir | to attend |
| bailar | to dance |
| beber | to drink |
| buscar | to look for |
| caminar | to walk |
| comer | to eat |
| comprar | to buy |
| comprender | to understand |
| conversar | to talk, to converse |
| correr | to run |
| deber | should |
| escribir | to write |
| escuchar | to listen (to) |
| estar | to be |
| estudiar | to study |
| hablar | to speak |
| leer | to read |
| llegar | to arrive |
| mirar | to look (at) |
| montar (en bicicleta) | to ride (a bicycle) |
| necesitar | to need |
| participar | to participate |
| practicar | to practice |
| sacar buenas/malas notas | to get good/bad grades |
| tomar | to take; to drink |
| tomar apuntes/notas | to take notes |
| trabajar | to work |
| ver | to see |
| vivir | to live |

| Palabras y expresiones útiles | Useful words and expressions |
|---|---|
| ahora | now |
| algo | something |
| ¡Buena suerte! | Good luck! |
| ¿Cómo te va? | How is it going? |
| con | with |
| ¿Cuánto cuesta? | How much is it? |
| el diccionario | dictionary |
| este/a | this |
| el examen | test |
| el fin de semana | weekend |
| para | for, to |
| pero | but |
| ¡Qué lástima! | What a pity! |
| sólo | only (adv.) |
| también | also |
| la tarea | homework |
| tengo/tienes | I have/you have |
| ¿verdad? | right? |

See page 33 for expressions of frequency.
See page 44 for question words.

# Mis amigos y yo

*Yo soy/Myself*, por Cristina Cárdenas, una pintora norteamericana de origen mexicano

# In this chapter you will learn how to:

- describe people, places, and things
- state where and when events take place
- express origin and possession
- express likes and dislikes

**Cultural focus:** **Estados Unidos**

CANADÁ

OCÉANO PACÍFICO

Un rapero latino,
Daddy Yankee

Los actores hispanos
Antonio Banderas y Salma Hayek

San Francisco

ESTADOS
UNIDOS

Chicago

New York
Philadelphia

Los Angeles

Santa Fe

Phoenix

Tucson

Una margarita
con guacamole y chips

Houston

San Antonio

MÉXICO

Golfo de
México

OCÉANO ATLÁNTICO

Calle Ocho, Miami

Miami

El Álamo, San Antonio, Texas

 **A vista de pájaro.** Using the map and photos, as well as what you may already know, provide the following facts about Hispanics.

1. Tres hispanos famosos
2. El grupo hispano más numeroso en Estados Unidos
3. La ciudad (*city*) en Estados Unidos con más puertorriqueños
4. El estado con más mexicanos
5. Un producto hispano
6. Un tipo de música latina

# A PRIMERA VISTA

## Mis amigos y yo

### ¿Quiénes somos?

CD 1
Track 35

Me llamo Mario Quintana. Soy de Puerto Rico y **tengo** veintidós **años. Me gusta** escuchar música y mirar televisión. Estudio en una universidad de Nueva York y **deseo** ser profesor de historia. Los chicos en estas fotografías son mis amigos. Ellos también son **hispanos** y estudian en la universidad. **Todos** somos **bilingües**.

Esta chica es Amanda Martone. Es **alta, delgada** y **morena**. Tiene los **ojos** de color café y el **pelo negro** y muy **largo**. Amanda es una chica muy **agradable**. Estudia **mucho** y desea ser economista. Su familia es dominicana, pero vive en Estados Unidos.

### Cultura

Puerto Rico was a Spanish colony for almost four centuries until it was ceded to the United States following the Spanish-American War in 1898. Puerto Rico is a freely associated commonwealth (*estado libre asociado*) of the United States, and its people have been U.S. citizens since 1917. Most Puerto Ricans on the mainland live in New York; New Jersey, Pennsylvania, and Illinois also have large Puerto Rican communities. However, Puerto Rico remains geographically and culturally part of Latin America and almost all of its residents speak Spanish as their primary language. English is also widely spoken. Being bilingual opens doors to better economic opportunities in Puerto Rico and on the mainland.

Esta chica se llama Ana Villegas. No es alta ni baja. Es de **estatura mediana** y usa **lentes de contacto**. Es **pelirroja** y tiene los ojos **oscuros**. Ana es **callada, trabajadora** y muy inteligente. Sus padres son cubanos.

Este chico se llama Ernesto Fernández. Ernesto es moreno y tiene los ojos **castaños** y el pelo **corto**. Es **bajo, fuerte**, muy **conversador** y **simpático. Le gusta usar** la computadora para conversar con sus amigos de aquí y de México.

Esta chica es Marta Chávez Conde. Es española y tiene veintiún años. Es **rubia**, tiene los ojos **azules** y es muy **divertida**. Este año está en Estados Unidos con su familia.

### *Cultura*

According to the 2000 census, one of every seven people in the United States is of Hispanic origin. With a population of 44,252,278, Hispanics account for 14 percent of the country's inhabitants. The Foundation of the Americas predicts that, by 2015, Hispanics will be the largest minority in the United States, numbering about 62.7 million. Although Hispanics can be found everywhere in the United States, most live in Los Angeles, New York, Miami, San Francisco, and Chicago. Mexicans constitute the largest Hispanic group, followed by Puerto Ricans and Cubans.

**2-1 Asociaciones.** To whom do the descriptions on the left refer?

1. ____ Tiene el pelo largo.
2. ____ Tiene veintidós años.
3. ____ Es de España.
4. ____ Es bajo y fuerte.
5. ____ Usa lentes de contacto.
6. ____ Habla mucho.
7. ____ Tiene los ojos de color café.
8. ____ Tiene el pelo negro y es muy agradable.
9. ____ Tiene los ojos azules y el pelo rubio, es muy divertida.
10. ____ Desea ser profesor de historia.

a. Mario Quintana
b. Amanda Martone
c. Ernesto Fernández
d. Ana Villegas
e. Marta Chávez Conde

**2-2 ¿Quién es?** PRIMERA FASE. Read the texts on pages 56–57 again and write a list of at least eight expressions that you may use to describe people, including physical appearance (*apariencia*) and personality traits (*personalidad*).

SEGUNDA FASE. Now, without mentioning his/her name, describe a classmate in at least three sentences, using the vocabulary from the *Primera fase*, or any other that you may need. The rest of the group will try to guess who this person is. The group can ask questions if more information is needed to guess the student's identity.

MODELO: E1: *Es de estatura mediana y delgado. Tiene el pelo negro. Es fuerte y callado.*
E2: *¿Es… ?*

### *Lengua*

Depending on the region or country, *moreno/a* or *negro/a* may be used to refer to African ancestry and skin color or to hair color. The word *trigueño/a* (from *trigo*, wheat) is used to describe light brown skin color. *Corto/a* generally refers to length (*pelo corto*), while *bajo/a* refers to height (*Ella es baja*).

**2-3 ¿Qué me gusta?** Tell your classmate if you like each of the following activities. Then compare your responses.

comer en restaurantes italianos
escribir correos electrónicos
bailar los sábados por la noche

estudiar español
trabajar los fines de semana
tomar café por la noche

practicar tenis/fútbol/béisbol
tener animales en casa

MODELO: estar en casa por las noches
E1: *¿Te gusta estar en casa por las noches?*
E2: *Sí, me gusta. /No, no me gusta.*

# Las descripciones

CD 1
Track 36 ## ¿Cómo son estas personas?

| fuerte | débil | joven | vieja/mayor | lista | tonto |

| trabajador | perezoso | simpático | antipático | triste | alegre |

| pobre | rica | casado | soltero |

## ))) ¿Cómo son estos animales?

CD 1
Track 37

Este perro es **feo** y **gordo**.

Esta gata es **bonita** y **delgada**.

**2-4 Opuestos.** Complete the following statements about these famous people.

MODELO: *Shakira no es mayor, es joven.*

1. \_\_\_\_ Penélope Cruz no es gorda, es...
2. \_\_\_\_ El presidente de la compañía no es perezoso, es...
3. \_\_\_\_ Jennifer López no es antipática, es...
4. \_\_\_\_ Madonna no es tonta, es...
5. \_\_\_\_ Bill Gates no es pobre, es...
6. \_\_\_\_ Enrique Iglesias no es feo, es...

a. trabajador
b. lista
c. delgada
d. rico
e. guapo
f. simpática

## ))) ¿De qué color son estas cosas?

CD 1
Track 38

Este auto es **rojo** y es muy bueno.

Esta flor es **amarilla** y **blanca**. Es muy bonita.

La silla **azul** es alta.

La silla **verde** es baja.

## ))) Otros colores

CD 1
Track 39

marrón

gris

rosado

morado

anaranjado

negro

**2-5 ¿De qué color son estas banderas (*flags*)?** PRIMERA FASE. Read each description and then write the name of the country under its flag.

1. La bandera de Bolivia es roja, amarilla y verde.
2. La bandera de Estados Unidos es roja, blanca y azul.
3. La bandera de España es roja y amarilla.
4. La bandera de México es verde, blanca y roja.
5. La bandera de Colombia es amarilla, azul y roja.

a. _____      b. _____      c. _____

d. _____      e. _____

**SEGUNDA FASE.** Take turns choosing a color and stating how many objects of that color are in the classroom. Your classmate will guess the color.

MODELO:   E1:   *Hay dos mochilas y ocho pantalones vaqueros (jeans).*
          E2:   *Es el azul.*

 **2-6 Vamos a describir.** Describe the people in these photos.

Eva

Alicia y Raquel

Alejandro

José Luis

**2-7 ¿Quién soy?** Write a brief description of yourself including at least three physical traits, two personality traits, and two activities that you like to do. Do not include your name on the paper. Give the paper to your instructor. He/She will ask each student to pick a description, read it, and try to guess who wrote it.

# El origen

🔊 **¿De dónde son... ?**

CD 1
Track 40

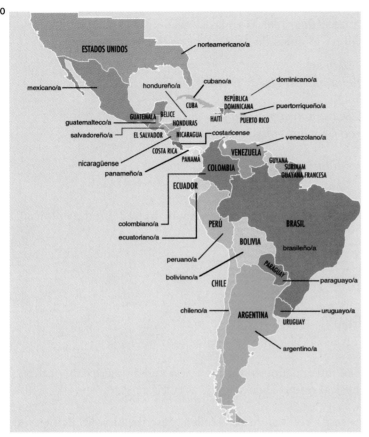

## Lengua

These are other examples of nationalities:

**alemán/alemana** (*German*), **canadiense**, **francés/francesa**, **japonés/japonesa**, **marroquí, nigeriano/a**, **polaco/a, portugués/ portuguesa**.

**2-8 Nacionalidades.** PRIMERA FASE. Indicate the nationalities of the following people.

MODELO: *Carolina Herrera es una diseñadora famosa de Venezuela.*
*Es <u>venezolana</u>.*

1. Albert Pujols es un jugador de béisbol de República Dominicana.
   Es _____ .
2. Salma Hayek es una actriz de México, protagonista de *Frida*. Es _____.
3. Rigoberta Menchú es una activista de Guatemala, Premio Nobel de la Paz, 1992. Es _____.
4. Julio Bocca es un bailarín de Argentina. Es _____.
5. Isabel Allende es escritora, originaria de Chile, autora de *La casa de los espíritus*. Es _____.
6. Oprah Winfrey es una presentadora de televisión de Estados Unidos.
   Es _____.
7. Gabriel García Márquez es un escritor de Colombia, autor de *Cien años de soledad*, Premio Nobel, 1982. Es _____.
8. Ricky Martin es un cantante de Puerto Rico. Es _____.

**SEGUNDA FASE.** Which of the personalities in the *Primera fase* is interesting to you? Why?

**MODELO:**　*Para mí, ...es interesante. Es un actor famoso/una actriz famosa.*

 **2-9 Adivinanzas (*Guesses*).** Think of a well-known person. A classmate will try to guess the identity by asking you questions.

**MODELO:**　E1:　*¿De dónde es?*
　　　　　　E2:　*Es estadounidense./Es de Estados Unidos.*
　　　　　　E1:　*¿Cómo es?*
　　　　　　E2:　*Es de estatura mediana, rubio y muy rico.*
　　　　　　E1:　*¿Qué es?/¿En qué trabaja?*
　　　　　　E2:　*Es actor.*
　　　　　　E1:　*¿Es Brad Pitt?*
　　　　　　E2:　*¡Sí!*

 **2-10 Entrevista.** **PRIMERA FASE.** Interview a classmate to find out the following information:

1. his/her name
2. his/her age
3. what he/she is like
4. the things he/she likes to do
5. where he/she is from
6. ...

**SEGUNDA FASE.** Write an introduction to the interview and a description of this person, including physical traits. Then share it with the class.

**2-11 ¡Hola!** **PRIMERA FASE.** You will hear a student describe himself. Before you listen, mark (✔) in the *Antes de escuchar* column the information you think he may provide.

CD 1
Track 41

|  | ANTES DE ESCUCHAR | DESPUÉS DE ESCUCHAR |
|---|---|---|
| 1. name |  |  |
| 2. age |  |  |
| 3. parents' names |  |  |
| 4. physical description |  |  |
| 5. country where he was born |  |  |
| 6. place where he intends to work |  |  |

**SEGUNDA FASE.** Now, listen and pay attention to the general idea of what is said. Then, in the *Después de escuchar* column, indicate which information the speaker provided.

# EN ACCIÓN

## Diarios de bicicleta: ¿Una cantante divina?

### Antes de ver

**2-12** **PRIMERA FASE.** How well do you remember? Indicate whether the following statements refer to Javier (**J**) or to Daniel (**D**).

1. ___ Es mexicano.     2. ___ Es muy puntual.     3. ___ Es colombiano.

**SEGUNDA FASE.** In this segment a singer is scheduled to audition for a role in an up-coming musical. Guess what she looks like by underlining one sentence in each pair.

1. Es bonita. Es fea.
2. Es joven. Es vieja.
3. Tiene el pelo corto. Tiene el pelo largo.
4. Tiene los ojos verdes. Tiene los ojos negros.

### Mientras ve

**2-13** Indicate whether each statement is **cierto** (**C**) or **falso** (**F**) according to the video segment. Correct the statements that are false.

1. ___ Los amigos están en la cafetería.
2. ___ Luciana y Gabi necesitan escuchar audiciones para un nuevo musical.
3. ___ Beatriz Condes canta una canción tradicional mexicana.
4. ___ Beatriz Condes canta mal.

### Después de ver

**2-14** At the end of the video segment, a new character appears. Write five sentences in Spanish describing her.

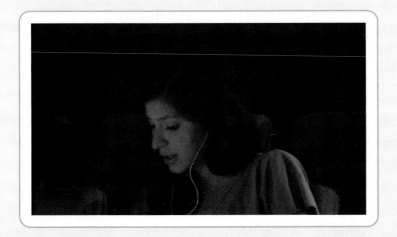

# FUNCIONES Y FORMAS

## 1. Describing people, places, and things: Adjectives

Ana, Patricia y Teresa estudian mucho. Son inteligent**es** y trabajador**as**.

Eduardo es alt**o** y atlétic**o**.

Adriana es baj**a** y es muy elegant**e**.

Carlos, Luis y Carmen son sociabl**es** y activ**os**. Conversan y bailan mucho en los clubes.

**Piénselo.** Complete the descriptions of the people in the drawings by supplying their names.

1. _____ es joven y delgad**a**.
2. _____ , _____ y _____ son interesant**es** y estudios**as**.
3. _____ **es** moren**o** y guap**o**.
4. _____ , _____ y _____ son popular**es** y activ**os**.
5. _____ es colombian**o**.
6. _____ , _____ y _____ son español**as**.

- Adjectives are words that describe people, places, and things. Like articles (**el, la, los, las**) and nouns (**chica, chicas; libro, libros**), they generally have more than one form. In Spanish an adjective must agree in gender (masculine or feminine) and number (singular or plural) with the noun or pronoun it describes. Adjectives that describe characteristics usually follow the noun.
- Most masculine adjectives end in **-o**, and most feminine adjectives end in **-a**. To form the plural, these adjectives add **-s**.

|  | MASCULINE | FEMININE |
|---|---|---|
| SINGULAR | el chic**o** alt**o** | la chic**a** alt**a** |
| PLURAL | los chic**os** alt**os** | las chic**as** alt**as** |

■ Adjectives that end in **-e** and some adjectives that end in a consonant have the same form for both masculine and feminine. To form the plural, adjectives that end in **-e** add **-s**; those that end in a consonant add **-es**.

|  | MASCULINE | FEMININE |
|---|---|---|
| SINGULAR | un libro interesante | una revista (*magazine*) interesante |
|  | un cuaderno azul | una mochila azul |
| PLURAL | unos libros interesantes | unas revistas interesantes |
|  | unos cuadernos azules | unas mochilas azules |

■ Other adjectives that end in a consonant add **-a** to form the feminine and **-es** or **-as** to form the plurals.

|  | MASCULINE | FEMININE |
|---|---|---|
| SINGULAR | el alumno español | la alumna española |
|  | el alumno hablador | la alumna habladora |
| PLURAL | los alumnos españoles | las alumnas españolas |
|  | los alumnos habladores | las alumnas habladoras |

■ Adjectives that end in **-ista** are both masculine and feminine. To form the plurals, add **-s**.

Pedro es muy optim**ista**,        *Pedro is very optimistic,*
   pero Alicia es pesim**ista**.        *but Alicia is pessimistic.*
Ellos no son material**istas**.        *They are not materialistic.*

**2-15 ¿Cómo son estas personas?** Choose the correct completion to describe the following people. More than one answer may be possible.

1. Muchos alumnos de mi universidad son…
   **a.** latinoamericano.      **b.** hispanos.          **c.** norteamericanas.    **d.** mexicanos.

2. Mi profesora favorita es muy…
   **a.** joven.            **b.** activo.             **c.** inteligente.       **d.** delgado.

3. Mi amigo Nicolás es muy…
   **a.** tonta.           **b.** fuerte.             **c.** callado.          **d.** antipática.

4. Las dos chicas más inteligentes de la clase son…
   **a.** activos y sociables.    **b.** trabajadoras y estudiosas.    **c.** altos y morenos.    **d.** interesante y optimista.

**2-16 Cualidades necesarias.** Your school is hiring recent graduates to help recruit students interested in studying other languages and cultures. Mark (✓) the qualities you think these new employees should have and then describe them to a partner, making sure that adjectives agree with nouns. Your partner will mention additional qualities.

**MODELO:**      dos empleados bilingües en inglés y español
       E1: *Los empleados bilingües hablan bien inglés y español. Son activos y extrovertidos.*
       E2: *Sí. Son simpáticos, no son antipáticos. Hablan con los estudiantes y los padres de los estudiantes.*

1. dos especialistas en computadoras para el laboratorio de lenguas

   ____ activo      ____ bilingüe      ____ competente      ____ pasivo
   ____ agradable      ____ callado      ____ extrovertido      ____ trabajador

2. una recepcionista para la Oficina de Admisiones

   ____ eficiente      ____ imparcial      ____ perezoso      ____ simpático
   ____ hablador      ____ interesante      ____ perfeccionista      ____ tímido

**2-17 Personas importantes.** PRIMERA FASE. With your partner, take turns describing the people in the photos. Use at least three of the following descriptions: *atlético, cómico, extrovertido, guapo, inteligente, liberal, serio, simpático, tiene el pelo..., tiene los ojos..., trabajador,* ...

Jimmy Smits es un actor famoso de cine (*movies*) y televisión.

Tish Hinojosa es una cantante mexicano-americana. Canta y escribe canciones también.

Julia Álvarez es una novelista y poeta dominicana. También es profesora.

Alex Rodríguez es un jugador de béisbol muy bueno.

 SEGUNDA FASE. Now, take turns describing someone important in your life. Your partner will ask questions to get more information about that person.

## En directo

To address someone on the phone about an ad:

**Hola, buenos días, llamo por el anuncio...**

To respond:

**¡Ah, sí, hola! Buenos días...**

To greet someone you know on the phone:

**Hola, ¿qué tal?**

**Soy María... /Habla María...**

To respond:

**Ah, ¡hola!**

**¿Qué tal, María?/¿Cómo estás?**

## SITUACIONES

1. **Role A.** You have just rented an apartment near campus and are looking for a roommate (**compañero/a de apartamento**). You receive a call from an interested student. Verify the student's name and ask a) where he/she is from; b) what his/her personality traits are; c) if he/she works and, if so, where; and d) what he/she likes to do in his/her free time (**tiempo libre**).

   **Role B.** Through an ad (**anuncio**) on a campus bulletin board, you see that someone is looking for a roommate (**compañero/a de apartamento**). You call that person. Answer his/her questions in detail and ask any questions you may have.

2. **Role A.** Your friend calls to tell you that he/she has been dating someone new. Ask a) where your friend's new boyfriend/girlfriend (**novio/a**) is from; b) what he/she is like; c) what he/she studies; d) if he/she has a car and, if so, what it looks like (color, size); and e) at least one other question of your own invention.

   **Role B.** You call your friend to talk about your new boyfriend/girlfriend. Your friend asks a lot of questions. Answer in as much detail as possible.

## 2. Identifying and describing; expressing origin, possession, location of events, and time: Present tense of *ser*

Marc Anthony **es** un artista neoyorquino muy talentoso y versátil. **Es** cantante y actor. Sus padres **son** de Puerto Rico. También **es** compositor. Canta y escribe canciones de salsa, de pop y de pop latino, y **es** un actor muy bueno de cine y de teatro. Sus (*His*) conciertos **son** en Estados Unidos y en muchos países latinoamericanos.

**Piénselo.** Read the sentences about Marc Anthony on the left. Select the meaning expressed by **es** or **son** in each sentence from the list on the right.

1. ____ Marc Anthony **es** de ascendencia puertorriqueña.

2. ____ El próximo (*next*) concierto de Marc Anthony **es** en California.

3. ____ La esposa de Marc Anthony **es** Jennifer López.

4. ____ Las películas de Marc Antony **son** muy populares.

5. ____ Este álbum de Marc Antony **es** de Daniel. Es su álbum favorito.

6. ____ Marc Anthony **es** muy famoso como artista de salsa y de pop.

a. identificación
b. descripción
c. nacionalidad/origen
d. posesión
e. eventos (localización, hora)

■ You have practiced some forms of **ser** and have used them for identification (**Esta señora es la profesora de historia**) and to tell time (**Son las cuatro**). Here are other uses of this verb.

| SER (*to be*) | | | |
|---|---|---|---|
| yo | **soy** | nosotros/as | **somos** |
| tú | **eres** | vosotros/as | **sois** |
| Ud., él, ella | **es** | Uds., ellos/as | **son** |

■ As you have seen, **ser** is used with adjectives to describe an intrinsic feature of a person, place, or thing.

| | |
|---|---|
| ¿Cómo **es** ella? | *What is she like?* |
| **Es** atlética y extrovertida. | *She is athletic and outgoing.* |
| ¿Cómo **es** el apartamento? | *What is the apartment like?* |
| El apartamento **es** pequeño pero **es** muy cómodo. | *The house is small, but it is very comfortable.* |

### Lengua

Adjectives of nationality that end in a consonant form the feminine by adding **-a.**

**español → español*a***

Note that the feminine and plural forms do not have a written accent.

**portugués → portugues*a***
**portugues*es* → portugues*as***

**alemán → aleman*a***
**aleman*es* → aleman*as***

Adjectives of nationality are not capitalized.

### Lengua

**De + el** contracts to **del,** but **de + la** and **de + los/las** do not contract.

El diccionario **es del** profesor, no **es de la** estudiante.
*The dictionary is the professor's, not the student's.*

◼ **Ser** is used to express nationality; **ser + de** is used to express origin.

**NATIONALITY**

| | |
|---|---|
| Gonzalo **es** chileno. | *Gonzalo is Chilean.* |
| Adriana **es** venezolana. | *Adriana is Venezuelan.* |

**ORIGIN**

| | |
|---|---|
| ¿De dónde **son** Gonzalo y Adriana? | *Where are Gonzalo and Adriana from?* |
| Gonzalo **es** de Chile. | *Gonzalo is from Chile.* |
| Adriana **es** de Venezuela. | *Adriana is from Venezuela.* |

◼ **Ser + de** is used to express possession. The equivalent of the English word *whose?* is **¿de quién?**

| | |
|---|---|
| **¿De quién es** el apartamento? | *Whose apartment is it?* |
| El apartamento **es de** Marta. | *The apartment is Marta's.* |

◼ **Ser + de** is also used to express the material of which something is made.

| | |
|---|---|
| El reloj **es de** oro. | *The watch is (made of) gold.* |
| Las sillas **son de** madera. | *The chairs are made of wood/wooden.* |

◼ **Ser** is also used to express where an event takes place or time of an event.

| | |
|---|---|
| El concierto **es** en el estadio. | *The concert is (takes place) in the stadium.* |
| La clase **es** a las nueve. | *The class is (takes place) at nine.* |

**2-18 ¿Cómo somos?** **PRIMERA FASE.** Look at the following descriptions and write an X under the appropriate heading.

| | SÍ | NO |
|---|---|---|
| 1. Yo soy muy estudioso/a y trabajador/a. | _____ | _____ |
| 2. A veces soy callado/a. | _____ | _____ |
| 3. Soy norteamericano/a. | _____ | _____ |
| 4. Mis abuelos son de otro (*another*) país. | _____ | _____ |
| 5. Mi familia es muy religiosa y tradicional. | _____ | _____ |
| 6. Mi mejor amigo/a es extrovertido/a y conversador/a. | _____ | _____ |
| 7. Mis amigos y yo somos sociables y activos. | _____ | _____ |
| 8. Mis clases este semestre son interesantes. | _____ | _____ |

 **SEGUNDA FASE.** Now compare your answers with your partner's. Ask questions to get additional information.

**2-19 ¿Cómo y dónde?** Ask what the following people, places, and objects are like. For your Spanish class, ask when and where it takes place, and for the computer lab, ask where it is located, as well as what the computers are like.

MODELO: tu profesor/a de inglés

E1: *¿Cómo es tu profesor de inglés?*

E2: *Es alto, moreno y muy simpático.*

1. tus amigos
2. tu cuarto (*bedroom*)
3. tu compañero/a de cuarto (*roommate*)
4. el auto de tu mejor amigo/a
5. la clase de español
6. el laboratorio de computadoras

**2-20 ¿Qué es esto?** Take turns to describe an object and its location in the classroom. Your partner will ask you questions and guess what it is.

MODELO: E1: *Es grande, es de plástico, está al lado de la ventana.*

E2: *¿De qué color es?*

E1: *Es roja.*

E2: *¿Es la mochila de Juan?*

> ### Lengua
>
> **Madera** (*wood*), **plástico**, **tela** (*fabric*), **metal**, **oro** (*gold*), **vidrio** (*glass*) are some words used to describe what something is made of.

**2-21 Eventos y lugares.** You are working at the university's information booth, and a visitor (your classmate) stops by. Answer his/her questions. Then switch roles.

MODELO: la exposición del club de fotografía

VISITANTE: *Perdón/Disculpe, ¿dónde es la exposición del club de fotografía?*

EMPLEADO/A: *Es en la biblioteca.*

VISITANTE: *¿Dónde está la biblioteca?*

EMPLEADO/A: *Está en la calle Madison, enfrente del edificio (building) de biología.*

1. el concierto de música salsa
2. la conferencia (*lecture*) sobre el arte mexicano
3. el banquete para los estudiantes internacionales
4. la reunión de profesores
5. la fiesta del club de español
6. la ceremonia de graduación

## SITUACIONES

1. **Role A.** You meet a student from a Spanish-speaking country in one of your classes. Introduce yourself and find out a) the student's name; b) his/her city and country of origin; c) characteristics of his/her city; and d) what his/her friends are like.

   **Role B.** You are an international student from a Spanish-speaking country. Answer your classmate's questions and then ask questions to get the same information he/she obtained from you.

2. **Role A.** A friend has invited you to a party at his/her house on Saturday. Ask a) where the house is located; b) what it looks like (so you can find it easily); and c) what time the party is.

   **Role B.** You have invited a friend to a party at your house on Saturday. Answer your friend's questions. Then explain that the house belongs to your parents (**padres**), and tell your friend why your parents are not at home that weekend.

## 3. Expressing inherent qualities and changeable conditions: *Ser* and *estar* with adjectives

Todos los estudiantes **están** aburridos porque la profesora **es** aburrida.

**Piénselo.** Read the statements below and classify them as to whether they describe either a) a personality trait/physical characteristic or b) a feeling or perception that may change.

1. \_\_\_\_ La profesora **es** aburrida. Sus clases no son interesantes.
2. \_\_\_\_ Sofía **está** delgada en ese vestido (*dress*) negro.
3. \_\_\_\_ Los estudiantes **están** nerviosos. Tienen un examen difícil hoy.
4. \_\_\_\_ Normalmente, las modelos **son** altas y muy delgadas.
5. \_\_\_\_ Hoy los niños **están** contentos. Van (*They are going*) al parque.
6. \_\_\_\_ Roberto **es** estudioso y trabajador. Estudia mucho todos los días.

■ **Ser** and **estar** are often used with the same adjectives. However, the choice of verb determines the meaning of the sentence.

■ **Ser** + *adjective* states the norm—what someone or something is like.

| | |
|---|---|
| Jorge **es** delgado. | *Jorge is thin.* (He is a thin man.) |
| Sara **es** muy nerviosa. | *Sara is very nervous.* (She is a nervous person.) |
| El libro **es** nuevo. | *The book is new.* (It is a new book.) |

■ **Estar** + *adjective* expresses a change from the norm, a condition, or how one feels about the person or object being discussed.

| | |
|---|---|
| Jorge **está** delgado. | *Jorge is/looks thin.* (He lost weight recently, or he looks thin in a picture or because of the clothes he is wearing.) |
| Sara **está** muy nerviosa. | *Sara is very nervous.* (She is feeling nervous.) |
| El libro **está** nuevo. | *The book is/looks new.* (It is used, but it seems like a brand new book.) |

■ The adjectives **contento/a**, **cansado/a**, **enojado/a** are always used with **estar**.

| | |
|---|---|
| Ella **está contenta** ahora. | *She is happy now.* |
| Los niños **están cansados**. | *The children are tired.* |
| Carlos **está enojado**. | *Carlos is angry.* |

■ Some adjectives have one meaning with **ser** and another with **estar**.

| | |
|---|---|
| Ese señor **es** malo. | *That man is bad/evil.* |
| Ese señor **está** malo. | *That man is ill.* |
| La chica **es** lista. | *The girl is clever/smart.* |
| La chica **está** lista. | *The girl is ready.* |
| La manzana **es** verde. | *The apple is green.* |
| La manzana **está** verde. | *The apple is not ripe.* |
| La profesora **es** aburrida. | *The professor is boring.* |
| La profesora **está** aburrida. | *The professor is bored.* |

**2-22 ¿Qué pasa aquí?** Look at the drawings and then complete the descriptions about each one with the appropriate form of **ser** or **estar**.

1. Esteban _____ (1) un joven listo y estudioso. Este semestre saca buenas notas, excepto en la clase de economía. _____ (2) una clase muy difícil. Esteban _____ (3) nervioso porque mañana hay un examen sobre la Comunidad Económica Europea, pero él no _____ (4) listo. Debe estudiar toda la noche.

2. ¡Pobres niños! (*Poor children!*) La fruta _____ (5) buena y saludable (*healthful*), pero estas manzanas _____ (6) verdes, no _____ (7) buenas. Ahora los niños no _____ (8) contentos. Una niña _____ (9) mala porque le duele el estómago (*her stomach hurts*).

**2-23 Cambios (*Changes*).** Imagine that you and your partner know the people mentioned below. One of you will describe a person, using an adjective in the list. The other explains how the person has changed and why. Then switch roles.

**MODELO:** Arturo/fuerte
    E1: *Arturo es fuerte.*
    E2: *Pero por su enfermedad (illness), ahora está muy débil.*

| PERSONAS | CARACTERÍSTICAS | RAZONES |
|---|---|---|
| 1. Ramón | alegre | por sus problemas |
| 2. Laura y Gustavo | callado/a | por la dieta |
| 3. Cristina | conversador/a | por el ejercicio |
| 4. Andrés | débil | por el exceso de estudio |
| 5. Ana y Sofía | extrovertido/a | por la falta (*lack*) de motivación |
| 6. Teresa | feliz | por su depresión |
| | fuerte | por sus buenas notas |
| | introvertido/a | |
| | optimista | |
| | perezoso/a | |
| | pesimista | |
| | trabajador/a | |
| | triste | |

**2-24 Termómetro emocional.** PRIMERA FASE. Indicate (✓) how you feel in each situation. Then write two adjectives to further describe how you feel and how you think your classmate feels in these situations.

| LUGARES | ABURRIDO/A | CONTENTO/A | TRANQUILO/A | NERVIOSO/A | YO | MI COMPAÑERO/A |
|---|---|---|---|---|---|---|
| en la cafetería con mis compañeros | | | | | | |
| en los exámenes finales | | | | | | |
| en la oficina de un profesor/una profesora | | | | | | |
| en un concierto con mis amigos | | | | | | |
| en una fiesta formal | | | | | | |
| en mi casa por la noche | | | | | | |

SEGUNDA FASE. Now compare your responses with those of your partner and write down one similarity and one difference between the two of you. Report to the class.

MODELO:  en la clase de español

E1: *En la clase de español, yo estoy contento/a. Tú también estás contento/a en la clase de español, ¿verdad?*

E2: *Tienes razón. Yo estoy contento/a. O Estás equivocado/a. Yo estoy aburrido/a.*

E1: *[a la clase] Yo estoy contento/a en la clase de español, pero Amanda está aburrida.*

## SITUACIONES

1. **Role A.** You have traveled to another city for a job interview. A friend of a friend who lives in that city has offered to show you around. Make arrangements over the phone to meet this person, whom you do not know. Find out what the person looks like, so you will be able to spot him/her at your meeting place.

   **Role B.** You have offered to get together with a friend of a friend who has a job interview in your city. You do not know this person, so when you arrange over the phone to meet, you have to find out what the person looks like and something about his/her personality, so you can decide what to show him/her.

2. **Role A.** Show your classmate a photo. Identify the people and explain what they are like. Then respond to your friend's questions and comments about them.

   **Role B.** After your classmate tells you about the people in the photo, ask and comment about a) how they seem to be feeling, based on their facial expressions or what they are doing and b) where they appear to be.

## 4. Expressing ownership: Possessive adjectives

### Mis amigos y yo

Condorito—the main character of the comic strip magazine of the same name—introduces some of his closest friends. Look at the group portrait to follow what he says.

Condorito y sus amigos

**Mi** nombre es Condorito. Soy un cóndor simpático, listo y sincero.

Yayita y **su** pequeña hija (*daughter*) Yuyito son **mis** dos grandes amores (*sweethearts*). **La** hija **de** Yayita es muy atractiva, pero es muy dependiente de **su** mamá y de **su** abuelo Don Tremendón. **Nuestra** relación es especial. Nosotros pasamos mucho tiempo juntos.

**Mi** sobrino (*nephew*) Coné es amoroso, pero un poco llorón (*whiner*). **Su** mejor amiga es Yuyito. La actividad favorita **de ellos** es comer chocolate y jugar en el parque. Finalmente, Doña Tremebunda es la madre de **mi** novia Yayita. Honestamente no me gusta mucho hablar con ella porque es muy materialista. También es dominante y ambiciosa. Y **tu** familia y amigos, ¿cómo son?

### Cultura

*Condorito*, a comic strip created by the Chilean cartoonist René Ríos (Pepo), is popular throughout Latin America. The main character, Condorito, is an anthropomorphic condor who uses his wit, rather than his work or talents, to solve the problems of everyday life. The multifaceted Condorito, usually in black pants and red shirt, adopts new identities to tell the latest gossip in town. With his ability to transcend social class, nationality, and ideology, he can be a peasant, a scientist, or a beggar, an Egyptian or an Argentinian. The comic strip in which he appears portrays with humor the personality and struggles of the Chilean people. For more information go to the *Mosaicos* web page.

**Piénselo.** Complete the following statements, using the information in Condorito's description.

1. Condorito tiene una novia. ____ nombre es _____ .
   **a.** Tu... Yayita    **b.** Mi... Doña Tremebunda    **c.** Su... Yayita

2. Condorito dice (*says*): *Nuestra relación es especial.* ¿A qué relación se refiere Condorito en esta afirmación?
   **a.** La relación de Condorito con Yayita y su familia.
   **b.** La relación de Yayita con la familia de ella.
   **c.** La relación entre Coné, Yayita, la familia de Yayita y él (Condorito).

3. Coné es ____ Condorito.
   **a.** la hija de    **b.** el sobrino de    **c.** el hijo (*son*) de

4. Condorito prefiere no pasar tiempo con Doña Tremebunda. ¿Por qué?
   **a.** por la apariencia física de ella    **b.** por la personalidad de ella
   **c.** por el hijo de ella

■ Possessive adjectives modify nouns to express possession. They always precede the noun they modify.

   **mi** amigo          **tu** familia

| POSSESSIVE ADJECTIVES | |
|---|---|
| **mi(s)** | *my* |
| **tu(s)** | *your (familiar)* |
| **su(s)** | *your (formal)*, *his, her, its, their* |
| **nuestro(s), nuestra(s)** | *our* |
| **vuestro(s), vuestra(s)** | *your (familiar plural)* |

■ Possessive adjectives change number to agree with the thing possessed, not with the possessor.

  mi *clase*, mis *clases*

■ The **nosotros/as** and **vosotros/as** forms must agree also in gender.

  **nuestro** *profesor*, **nuestros** *amigos*; **nuestra** *profesora*, **nuestras** *amigas*

■ **Su** and **sus** have multiple meanings. To ensure clarity, you may use **de** + *the name of the possessor* or *the appropriate pronoun* instead of *su/sus*. For example, the multiple meanings of *su compañera* can be expressed as follows:

la compañera +
- **de ella** (la compañera de Elena)
- **de él** (la compañera de Jorge)
- **de usted**
- **de ustedes**
- **de ellos** (la compañera de Elena y Jorge)
- **de ellas** (la compañera de Elena y Olga)

**2-25 Mi mundo (*world*). PRIMERA FASE.** Write down two things that you own (**pertenencias**) and two people whom you value very much. You may use the words in the box or choose others.

| Pertenencias: | un carro | una computadora portátil | un iPod |
|---|---|---|---|
| Personas: | un amigo/ una amiga | un profesor ideal/ una profesora ideal | un actor/ una actriz |

PERTENENCIAS
1. _____
2. _____

PERSONAS
1. _____
2. _____

**SEGUNDA FASE.** Take turns describing your selections. Take notes so that you can share with the class the similarities and differences between you and your classmate.

**Pertenencias**

E1: *Yo tengo un auto. Es rápido y moderno. Y tú, tienes un auto?*
E2: *Sí.*
E1: *¿Y cómo es tu auto?*
E2: *Mi auto es rojo y muy viejo.*

**Personas**

E1: *Mi madre es importante en mi vida (life). Es muy alegre y activa. Y tu mamá, ¿cómo es?*
E2: *Mi madre es tranquila y muy inteligente.*

**2-26 Mi familia.** Which of these statements apply to your family and friends? Mark (✓) your answers in the spaces under **Yo**. Then interview a classmate.

|  | YO | MI COMPAÑERO/A |
|---|---|---|
| 1. Mi familia es grande. | _____ | _____ |
| 2. Otros miembros de mi familia viven en nuestro barrio (*neighborhood*). | _____ | _____ |
| 3. A veces pasamos las vacaciones con mis abuelos (*grandparents*). | _____ | _____ |
| 4. Siempre conversamos sobre temas políticos. | _____ | _____ |
| 5. A veces no estamos de acuerdo y discutimos. | _____ | _____ |
| 6. Nuestros amigos visitan la casa frecuentemente. | _____ | _____ |

**2-27 Nuestra universidad. PRIMERA FASE.** In preparation for the *Segunda fase*, write some words that generally describe the following aspects of your university.

1. los profesores: _____

2. las clases: _____

3. los estudiantes: _____

4. los equipos (*teams*) de fútbol, baloncesto, béisbol, etc.: _____

5. el campus: _____

**SEGUNDA FASE.** Now write 1 or 2 sentences about each topic in the *Primera fase*. Be prepared to present your sentences to the class. The class will decide which sentences a) describe the school most accurately and b) present an appealing view of the school for prospective students.

## SITUACIONES

1. **Role A.** You are a Spanish professor. You inform a student about a lecture by another professor. Explain that a) the professor is visiting the university; b) there is a lecture by the professor (**una conferencia del profesor**) on Thursday; c) it will take place in the library.

   **Role B.** Your professor invites you to a lecture. Find out a) the time of the lecture; b) the speaker's name; and c) the topic (**tema**).

2. **Role A.** You are a student from Peru studying in the United States. You phone your parents and ask how they are. Tell about your host parents (**madre americana/padre americano**), brother (**hermano**), and sister (**hermana**). Describe their ages, appearance, personalities, and occupations.

   **Role B.** You live in Peru, and your child is studying in the United States. When he/she calls, ask about a) the host family schedule (**horario**) and b) activities of the host family.

### En directo

To initiate the conversation:

**Oye** (*Hey*)**, mi hermano americano es...**

**¿Sabes?** (*You know?*) **Mi hermano americano es...**

To acknowledge information by showing surprise:

**Ah, ¿sí?**

**¡No me digas!**
*Oh, really?, No way!, Wow!*

## 5. Expressing likes and dislikes: *Gustar*

The following is a transcript of a chat over the Internet between Marisa, a Mexican student living in Mexico City, and Carla, a Mexican American living in El Paso, Texas.

**Marisa:** Hola. ¿Quién eres? ¿Cómo te llamas?

**Carla:** Carla Chandía. Mucho gusto, Marisa.

**Marisa:** Y tú, ¿de dónde eres? ¿Dónde vives?

**Carla:** Mi familia y yo somos de Guanajuato, pero vivimos en El Paso, Texas.

**Marisa:** ¿**Te gusta** vivir en Estados Unidos?

**Carla: Me gusta** este país y en particular El Paso. Hay muchas actividades interesantes para los jóvenes. **A mí me gusta** hablar español e inglés con mis amigos. **Me gustan** las oportunidades para estudiar y trabajar. Y tú, ¿dónde vives?

**Marisa:** Vivo en la Ciudad de México y **me gusta** mucho vivir aquí. El D.F. es una ciudad enorme y muy bonita. **Me gusta** caminar por el parque Chapultepec y jugar con mi perro, Lassie.

**Carla:** ¿Qué **te gusta hacer** en tu tiempo libre?

**Marisa: Me gustan** muchas cosas, como escuchar música, ir a los museos, mirar tele, y más…

**Piénselo.** Indicate whether each paraphrase best refers to Marisa (**M**) or Carla (**C**).

1. ____ **Me gustan** las posibilidades académicas que ofrece Estados Unidos.
2. ____ **Me gusta** vivir en la capital de México.
3. ____ **Me gusta** ser bilingüe.
4. ____ **Me gustan** las actividades al aire libre (*open air*).
5. ____ **Me gusta** el arte.

■ To express what you like to do, use **me gusta** + *infinitive*. To express what you don't like to do, use **no me gusta** + *infinitive*.

| | |
|---|---|
| **Me gusta** hablar español. | *I like to speak Spanish.* |
| **No me gusta** mirar televisión. | *I don't like to watch television.* |
| **Me gusta** practicar deportes y salir con mis amigos. | *I like to play sports and go out with my friends.* |

■ To express that you like something or someone, use **me gusta** + *singular noun* or **me gustan** + *plural noun*.

| | |
|---|---|
| **Me gusta** la música clásica. | *I like classical music.* |
| **Me gustan** las personas alegres. | *I like happy people.* |

■ To ask a classmate what he/she likes, use **¿Te gusta(n)… ?** To ask your instructor, use **¿Le gusta(n)… ?**

| | |
|---|---|
| **¿Te gusta/Le gusta** tomar café? | *Do you like to drink coffee?* |
| **¿Te gustan/Le gustan** los chocolates? | *Do you like chocolates?* |

■ To state what another person likes, use **a** + *name of person* + **le gusta(n)…** When you are talking about the preferences of more than one person, use **a** + *name of person* + **les gusta(n)…**

| | |
|---|---|
| **A Diego le gustan** las fiestas. | *Diego likes parties.* |
| **A Carlos le gusta** el fútbol. | *Carlos likes soccer.* |
| **A Diego y a Carlos les gusta** ir de vacaciones con sus padres. | *Diego and Carlos like to go on vacation with their parents.* |

**2-28 Mis preferencias.** PRIMERA FASE. Mark (✓) your preferences in the following chart.

| ACTIVIDAD | ME GUSTA MUCHO | ME GUSTA UN POCO | NO ME GUSTA |
|---|---|---|---|
| escribir correos electrónicos en español | | | |
| comer en restaurantes de comida mexicana | | | |
| bailar salsa | | | |
| escuchar música rock en español | | | |
| aprender sobre la cultura de otros países | | | |
| visitar lugares históricos | | | |

SEGUNDA FASE. Now, compare your answers with those of a classmate. Share with the class one similarity and one difference between you and your partner in terms of your preferences.

**2-29 ¿Te gusta… ?** PRIMERA FASE. Ask if a classmate likes the following. Be sure to ask follow-up questions as appropriate.

1. el gimnasio de la universidad
2. los teléfonos celulares con conexión a Internet
3. la informática
4. los autos de este año
5. los animales
6. los conciertos de música clásica

SEGUNDA FASE. Write a brief note to another classmate in which you share two pieces of information about yourself and two pieces of information you discovered about your partner.

**2-30 ¿Qué te gusta hacer?** PRIMERA FASE. Write down some questions that you would ask a classmate to find out the following:

1. what he/she likes to do in his/her free time
2. in what restaurant he/she likes to eat with his/her family

SEGUNDA FASE. Interview two classmates and ask each of them the questions you prepared in the *Primera fase*. Compare their responses and be prepared to share with others your conclusions regarding how your classmates spend their time.

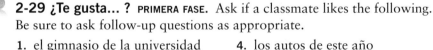

## SITUACIONES

1. **Role A:** You are at a park where you hear someone giving Spanish commands to a dog. Break the ice and introduce yourself. Ask a) the person's name; b) the dog's name and age; and c) if the dog is friendly (**manso**). Compliment the dog (smart, strong, very pretty, etc.). Tell the person that you like dogs very much and that you also like cats. Answer the questions this person asks.

   **Role B:** You are in the park training your dog and someone approaches. Answer this person's questions and ask if he/she has a dog, and if so, what it looks like. Say that you don't like cats because they are not active or fun. Finally, ask where this person is from and where he/she is studying Spanish.

2. **Role A:** You are at Panchero's, a Mexican restaurant. While you are waiting to be seated, you hear someone speaking Spanish to a child. Introduce yourself and ask the child's name and age. Compliment the parent on his/her beautiful child. Also ask the parent if he/she likes Panchero's and likes to eat at American restaurants like McDonald's.

   **Role B:** You and your two-year-old daughter are waiting to be seated at Panchero's, a Mexican restaurant. Someone asks you about your child. React to the person's comments and answer his/her questions.

# MOSAICOS

## A escuchar

**Listen for specific information**

When you ask a person specific questions, he/she may provide not only the answers you need, but also additional information. To listen efficiently, focus on the answers you requested. This will help you obtain the information you need.

### Antes de escuchar

**2-31 Preparación.** You will listen to a student telling her mother about how different her roommates are. Before listening to their conversation, write the name(s) of your own roommate(s) and a sentence that describes each of them.

### Escuchar

CD 1
Track 42

**2-32 ¿Comprende usted?** Listen to the conversation between a student and her mother. Mark (✓) the appropriate column(s) to indicate whether the following statements describe Rita, Marcela, or both.

|  | RITA | MARCELA |
|---|---|---|
| 1. Estudia economía. |  |  |
| 2. Le gusta bailar. |  |  |
| 3. Es alta, morena y tiene los ojos negros. |  |  |
| 4. Es muy seria, baja y delgada. |  |  |
| 5. Estudia arte moderno. |  |  |

### Después de escuchar

**2-33 Ahora usted.** Complete the following sentences to say how you feel about your roommate(s).

1. Me gusta(n) mi(s) compañero/a(s) de cuarto porque...
2. A veces no me gusta(n) mi(s) compañero/a(s) de cuarto porque...
3. Mi(s) compañero/a(s) de cuarto y yo somos semejantes/diferentes porque...

# A conversar

**Describe a person**

Descriptions are most effective when they are well organized. When describing a person, you may want to include demographic information (e.g., age, nationality/origin), physical characteristics, and personality traits. A well-organized description presents information by category, beginning with an introductory phrase to prepare your listener.

**ESTRATEGIAS**

## Antes de conversar

 **2-34 Preparación.** *Mafalda*, like *Condorito*, featured earlier in this chapter, is a popular comic strip in the Spanish-speaking world. Go to the *Mosaicos* web page, choose one of the characters shown there, and read the description about him/her.

## Conversar

 **2-35 Entre nosotros.** Describe the physical characteristics and personality traits of the *Mafalda* character you read about in **2-34**. Your partner will ask questions or comment as appropriate. Then switch roles.

## Después de conversar

**2-36 Un poco más.** Find out about another popular comic character, like those mentioned in the *Cultura* box below, and tell the class about him/her.

### Cultura

Mafalda is the name of a character in a comic strip of the same name created by the Argentinian cartoonist Quino. Extremely popular in the Spanish-speaking world, she is a six-year-old girl deeply concerned with political issues and world peace. Her naive yet sharp criticism of society has made her an icon for the defense of human rights. For more information go to the *Mosaicos* web page.

### En directo

To introduce information about physical characteristics:

**En cuanto a lo físico,...
/ Físicamente, es...**

To introduce information about personality:

**Es una persona... /Tiene un carácter...**

### Cultura

Many Hispanics who emigrate to other countries maintain connections to their culture by reading and listening to music in Spanish. In areas with large Hispanic populations, Spanish-language newspapers and magazines are available.

These carry some of the many comic strips popular in the Hispanic world, including *Mafalda* (Argentina), *Condorito* (Chile), and *Mortadelo y Filemón* (Spain). You will find information about these comic strips on the Internet.

# A leer

ESTRATEGIAS

### Scan a text for specific information

When you read in Spanish, your goal should be to read for ideas, not for the meaning of every word. One way to read for ideas is to search for particular pieces of information that you think will be in the text. Often the comprehension questions after the text will help you decide what information to search for as you read. This approach to reading, called *scanning*, works best if you a) focus on the information you are seeking and b) read the text through quickly at least twice, looking for specific information each time.

## Antes de leer

**2-37 Preparación.** PRIMERA FASE. Read the title of the text and examine its format. (This is the reading strategy you learned in *Capítulo 1*.) What type of text is it?

1. a series of e-mail messages
2. personal ads
3. ads for items for sale

SEGUNDA FASE. Scan the text and use your highlighter to mark the following information in each paragraph.

1. el nombre de la persona
2. la edad (*age*) de la persona
3. la dirección electrónica de la persona

## Leer

**2-38 Primera mirada.** Read the personal ads that follow and scan them for the information needed in the form. In some cases, it may not be possible to provide all the information requested.

| | PERSONA 1 | PERSONA 2 | PERSONA 3 | PERSONA 4 |
|---|---|---|---|---|
| nombre | | | | |
| edad | | | | |
| nacionalidad | | | | |
| estado civil | | | | |
| personalidad (1 ó 2 adjetivos) | | | | |
| le gusta... | | | | |

### Amigos sin fronteras

Soltera, sin hijos y sin compromiso. Me llamo Susana y tengo 24 años. Soy guatemalteca. Busco amigos extranjeros, solteros, separados o divorciados, jóvenes o mayores. Soy amable, cariñosa y muy trabajadora. Por mi trabajo, viajo mucho, pero me gusta la compañía de otras personas. Soy bilingüe. Hablo español e inglés. Escriban a sincompromiso@comcast.net.

Soy Ricardo Brown. 21 años, sincero, dedicado. Me gustan las fiestas. Soy soltero. Deseo conocer a una chica de unos 23 años, preferiblemente venezolana como yo. Prefiero una mujer activa e independiente. Me gusta practicar deportes y explorar lugares nuevos. Escríbanme a amigosincero@msn.com.

Me llamo Pablo Sosa, tengo 31 años, y soy chileno. Soy agradable y muy trabajador. Me gusta hacer mi trabajo a la perfección, pero soy tolerante. Los autos convertibles son mi pasión. Deseo mantener correspondencia por correo electrónico con jóvenes del extranjero para intercambiar información sobre los convertibles europeos o americanos. Mi dirección electrónica es locoporlosautos@yahoo.com.

Soy Xiomara Stravinsky, decoradora y fotógrafa argentina. Me gusta el arte, especialmente el impresionismo. Tengo 27 años y soy divorciada. Soy dinámica, agradable y generosa, pero tengo pocos amigos porque tengo dos trabajos y paso muchas horas con mis clientes. Necesito un cambio en mi vida. ¿Deseas ser mi amigo/a? Por favor, escríbeme a xiomarastravinsky@hotmail.com.

---

#### Lengua

The letter **y** changes to **e** when it precedes a word beginning with **i** or **h**.

**inglés y español**, but **español e inglés**

**inteligente y agradable**, but **agradable e inteligente**

---

## Después de leer

**2-39 Ampliación.** PRIMERA FASE. What qualities do you associate with Susana (**S**), Ricardo (**R**), Pablo (**P**), and Xiomara (**X**)? Why? With a classmate, write the person's initial next to each quality, and support your opinions.

a. ____ sociable
b. ____ simpático/a
c. ____ divertido/a
d. ____ perfeccionista
e. ____ mayor
f. ____ flexible
g. ____ trabajador/a
h. ____ ocupado/a

SEGUNDA FASE. Find the best match for Susana, Ricardo, Pablo and Xiomara from the following responses received.

1. Tengo 22 años y me gustan todos los deportes. Mis padres viven en Caracas pero yo vivo en Miami.
2. Enseño arte en la escuela secundaria. Tengo tiempo para mis amigos los fines de semana.
3. Soy de Nicaragua. Soy muy sociable y deseo perfeccionar mi inglés.
4. Trabajo para *Autos de hoy*, una revista de Internet.

# A escribir

**Consider audience and purpose**

Writing is an act of communication between writer and reader. Writers usually have a purpose in mind, such as compiling information, informing the reader, describing something or someone, or expressing a point of view. Readers rely on their prior knowledge and on the quantity and quality of information presented to derive meaning from the text.

As you write, keep in mind your purpose and make the necessary adjustments to form and content to facilitate your audience's comprehension of the message.

## Antes de escribir

**2-40 Preparación.** PRIMERA FASE. Read the following ad written by a movie fan in your local Spanish-language newspaper.

Fanático del cine necesita amigos para discutir películas los fines de semana. Tengo 24 años y estudio cinematografía. Me fascinan las películas de acción y también las románticas. Soy fuerte, activo, atlético y aventurero. Me gusta practicar deportes, especialmente el tenis y el esquí. Siempre estoy muy ocupado, pero tengo unas horas todas las semanas para conversar sobre películas y hacer deportes. Interesados, favor de enviar correo electrónico a fanaticodelcine@yahoo.com.

SEGUNDA FASE. You decide to respond to the ad. First, think about the following questions and mark (✓) your responses accordingly.

1. What is the purpose that *fanaticodelcine* has in mind when he writes the e-mail?
   a. ____ to find a girlfriend
   b. ____ to find someone (male or female) to talk with about movies

2. What would your purpose be if you responded to his personal ad?
   a. ____ to share your interest in movies with someone who is knowledgeable about the topic.
   b. ____ to date *fanaticodelcine*

TERCERA FASE. Now jot down information that will help you meet the goal of becoming the conversation partner of *fanaticodelcine*.

1. your age
2. your place of origin
3. words (adjectives) that describe you physically
4. expressions (adjectives) that describe your personality
5. activities (verbs) that you like to do that may match the needs of the person in the ad

## Escribir

**2-41 Manos a la obra.** Write an e-mail to *fanaticodelcine* using the information you prepared in the *Tercera fase* of **2-40**.

**Para:**

**Asunto:** Anuncio

Hola,_____

Respondo a tu anuncio del periódico.(*Provide your name.*)
_____

Primero, aquí tienes alguna información personal.(*Provide personal information.*)_____
_____
_____
_____

En segundo lugar, estas son algunas de las actividades que, al igual que tú, yo hago en mi tiempo libre.(*Provide activities that you, like fanaticodelcine, like to do in your free time.*)_____
_____
_____
_____

En tercer lugar, los fines de semana… (*Tell what you like to do.*)_____
_____
_____
_____

Finalmente, deseo ser tu amigo/a. Por favor, escríbeme un correo electrónico a mi dirección:_____
_____

Hasta pronto.

_____

## Después de escribir

**2-42 Revisión.** After writing your e-mail, read it again and check the following:

1. Did you include all the information *fanaticodelcine* needs? Do you think your information will be interesting to him?
2. Did you use punctuation correctly? Did you verify that there are no spelling or grammatical mistakes that may hinder comunication?
3. Make any necessary changes that will make your e-mail clear and comprehensible to *fanaticodelcine*.

# ENFOQUE CULTURAL

## Los hispanos y la expansión de Estados Unidos

Inicialmente, Estados Unidos está formado por trece colonias de Inglaterra. Estas trece colonias ocupan principalmente el noreste y la región del Atlántico. Las trece colonias se independizan de Inglaterra en la larga y violenta Guerra de Independencia. George Washington es un líder muy importante de esta guerra. El 4 de julio de 1776, el Congreso Continental firma la Declaración de Independencia en Filadelfia y George Washington es el primer presidente de la nueva república.

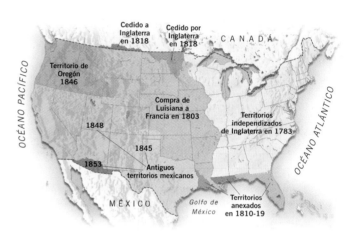

La expansión de Estados Unidos

Moneda de 25 centavos en honor de Luisiana, 2002

La primera expansión de las trece colonias hacia el oeste ocurre en 1803 durante la presidencia de Thomas Jefferson. En este año, el gobierno de Estados Unidos compra a Francia el inmenso territorio de Luisiana por 23 millones de dólares. Esta región ocupa unos 2.100.000 km². La compra de Luisiana incorpora todo el valle del Río Misisipi al territorio de Estados Unidos.

En 1810, el presidente James Madison anexa al territorio de Estados Unidos la región de Florida Occidental. Esta región está en la costa norte del Golfo de México y hoy pertenece a los estados de Luisiana, Misisipi, Alabama y Florida. Pero anteriormente, pertenece a España, Francia y también a Inglaterra. Durante un tiempo se llama la República Independiente de Florida Occidental. España disputa esta anexión, pero en 1819 acepta ceder todo el territorio de Florida, incluyendo la península de Florida.

*Bonnieblue,* la bandera de la República Independiente de Florida Occidental

Dinero de República Independiente de Texas

Entre 1845 y 1853, Estados Unidos anexa extensos territorios mexicanos. La anexión de Texas en 1845 causa la guerra entre México y Estados Unidos. En 1848, México cede otra parte muy grande de su territorio, incluyendo partes de Texas, Colorado, Arizona, Nuevo México y Wyoming, además de toda la extensión de California, Nevada y Utah. En 1853 Estados Unidos compra un área adicional en la frontera de México y el presidente Franklin Pierce paga diez millones de dólares. Los habitantes mexicanos de estas regiones son los ancestros de muchos latinos de Estados Unidos.

En 1898 Puerto Rico se convierte en un protectorado de Estados Unidos a causa de la guerra de Estados Unidos contra España. Los habitantes de Puerto Rico son ciudadanos de Estados Unidos desde 1917.

El escudo de Puerto Rico tiene el símbolo de San Juan y la inscripción en latín: "Su nombre es Juan".

---

### En otras palabras

Expresiones puertorriqueñas:

No le des **cabuya**.
*Don't give him/her ammunition to bother you.*

Yo no compro la lotería porque tengo una **macacoa** terrible.
*I don't buy lottery tickets because I have terrible luck.*

Dejó su cuarto hecho un **majarete**.
*He/She left his/her room a complete mess.*

---

### En otras palabras

Expresiones chicanas (*Mexican-American*):

**Ando brujo.**
*I am broke.*

**¡Ándale, güero!**
*Let's go, blondie!*

**2-43 Comprensión.** PRIMERA FASE. **Reconocimiento de palabras clave.** Find in the text the Spanish word or phrase that best expresses the meaning of the following concepts:

1. war          _____
2. valley       _____
3. ancestors    _____
4. border      _____
5. coat of arms   _____
6. citizen      _____

SEGUNDA FASE. **Oraciones importantes.** Underline the statements that contain ideas found in the text. Then indicate where in the text those words appear.

1. The colonies became independent after a long and violent war.
2. The Continental Congress signed the Declaration of Independence in Philadelphia.
3. George Washington was a good soldier, but a poor politician.
4. The purchase of the Mississippi Valley turned out to be a poor decision by President Jefferson.
5. Spain gave up its claim to Florida and West Florida without any resistance.
6. The United States and Mexico went to war over the annexation of Texas.
7. Puerto Ricans are citizens of the United States.

TERCERA FASE. **Ideas principales.** Write a brief paragraph in English summarizing the main ideas expressed in the text.

**2-44 Use la información.** Prepare an oral presentation describing the current flag or a historic flag of one of the states that has a Hispanic heritage. Consult the *Mosaicos* web page where you will find a worksheet and relevant links to collect information about the flag.

# VOCABULARIO

| Las descripciones | Descriptions |
|---|---|
| agradable | nice |
| alegre | happy, glad |
| alto/a | tall |
| antipático/a | unpleasant |
| bajo/a | short (in stature) |
| bilingüe | bilingual |
| bonito/a | pretty |
| callado/a | quiet |
| cansado/a | tired |
| casado/a | married |
| contento/a | happy, glad |
| conversador/a | talkative |
| corto/a | short (in length) |
| débil | weak |
| delgado/a | thin |
| divertido/a | funny, amusing |
| enojado/a | angry |
| estatura mediana | average, medium (height) |
| feo/a | ugly |
| fuerte | strong |
| gordo/a | fat |
| guapo/a | good-looking, handsome |
| joven | young |
| largo/a | long |
| listo/a | smart; ready |
| mayor | old |
| moreno/a | brunette |
| nervioso/a | nervous |
| nuevo/a | new |
| oscuro/a | dark |
| pelirrojo/a | redhead |
| perezoso/a | lazy |
| pobre | poor |
| rico/a | rich, wealthy |
| rubio/a | blond |
| simpático/a | nice, charming |
| soltero/a | single |
| tonto/a | silly, foolish |
| trabajador/a | hardworking |
| triste | sad |
| viejo/a | old |

| Las nacionalidades | Nationalities |
|---|---|
| alemán/alemana | German |
| argentino/a | Argentinian |
| boliviano/a | Bolivian |
| canadiense | Canadian |
| chileno/a | Chilean |
| colombiano/a | Colombian |
| costarricense | Costa Rican |
| cubano/a | Cuban |
| dominicano/a | Dominican |
| ecuatoriano/a | Ecuadorian |
| español/a | Spanish |
| estadounidense | U.S. citizen |
| francés/francesa | French |
| guatemalteco/a | Guatemalan |

| | |
|---|---|
| hispano/a | Hispanic |
| hondureño/a | Honduran |
| japonés/japonesa | Japanese |
| marroquí | Moroccan |
| mexicano/a | Mexican |
| nicaragüense | Nicaraguan |
| nigeriano/a | Nigerian |
| panameño/a | Panamanian |
| paraguayo/a | Paraguayan |
| peruano/a | Peruvian |
| polaco/a | Polish |
| portugués/portuguesa | Portuguese |
| puertorriqueño/a | Puerto Rican |
| salvadoreño/a | Salvadorian |
| uruguayo/a | Uruguayan |
| venezolano/a | Venezuelan |

| Los colores | Colors |
|---|---|
| amarillo/a | yellow |
| anaranjado/a | orange |
| azul | blue |
| blanco/a | white |
| marrón | brown |
| gris | gray |
| morado/a | purple |
| negro/a | black |
| rojo/a | red |
| rosado/a, rosa | pink |
| verde | green; not ripe |

| Verbos | Verbs |
|---|---|
| desear | to wish, to want |
| ser | to be |
| usar | to use |

| Palabras y expresiones útiles | Useful words and expressions |
|---|---|
| el auto, el coche, el carro | car |
| de | of, from |
| ¿de quién? | whose? |
| del | of the (contraction of de + el) |
| la flor | flower |
| le gusta(n) | you (formal) like; he/she likes |
| los lentes de contacto | contact lenses |
| me gusta(n) | I like |
| mucho (adv.) | much, a lot |
| mucho/a (adj.) | many |
| el ojo | eye |
| el pelo | hair |
| te gusta(n) | you (familiar) like |
| Tengo... años. | I am . . . years old. |
| tiene | he/she has; you (formal) have |
| todos/as | everybody |

See the English-Spanish and Spanish-English glossaries for other adjectives of nationality.

See page 74 for possessive adjectives.

87

# El tiempo libre

En este cuadro anónimo del siglo XVIII, vemos la boda de un hombre y una mujer.
Ella es la princesa inca Nusta Beatriz y él es un noble español, D. Martín de Loyola.

# In this chapter you will learn how to:

- discuss daily activities and leisure
- talk about food
- express where you are going
- make plans

Cultural Focus: **Perú**

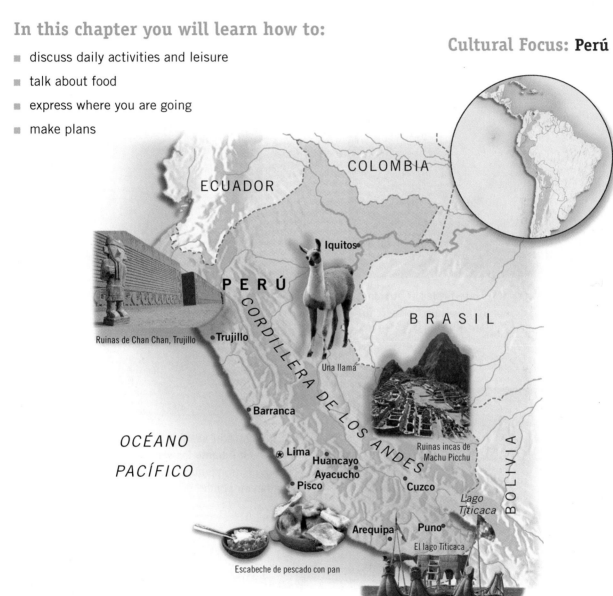

COLOMBIA

ECUADOR

Iquitos

P E R Ú

Ruinas de Chan Chan, Trujillo • Trujillo

CORDILLERA DE LOS ANDES

Una llama

B R A S I L

OCÉANO PACÍFICO

Barranca

⊛ Lima
Huancayo
Ayacucho
• Pisco

Cuzco

Ruinas incas de Machu Picchu

BOLIVIA

Lago Titicaca

Arequipa Puno•

El lago Titicaca

Escabeche de pescado con pan

**A vista de pájaro.** Based on what you know about Peru, indicate if the statement is true (**Cierto**) or false (**Falso**).

1. _____ Perú está al sur de Colombia.
2. _____ La capital de Perú está en la costa del Atlántico.
3. _____ La comida de Perú es muy variada.
4. _____ Algunos peruanos son de origen inca y español.
5. _____ El Amazonas está entre Perú y Ecuador.
6. _____ La llama es un animal débil.

## ◀)) Las diversiones

CD 2
Track 1

En muchos **países** hispanos hay **fiestas** y **reuniones**.
Los **jóvenes** bailan, escuchan **música** o conversan.
A veces **tocan la guitarra** y **cantan canciones**
populares.

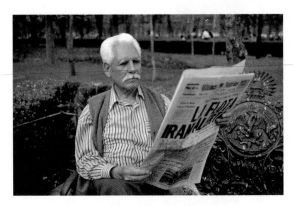

Estas **mujeres van** a la playa en su **tiempo libre** y
también **durante** las **vacaciones**. Allí, caminan y
conversan **mientras** otras personas **toman el sol**,
**nadan** en **el mar**, corren o **descansan**.

Este **hombre** lee el **periódico al aire libre** en un
parque de su **ciudad**. Y usted, ¿lee el
periódico? ¿Qué periódicos o **revistas** lee?

Muchos jóvenes van al **cine**,
especialmente los fines de
semana. También es común
**alquilar películas** para ver en
casa.

**3-1 Asociaciones.** Which leisure activities do you associate with the following places?

1. _____ la playa
2. _____ la fiesta
3. _____ el cine
4. _____ la biblioteca
5. _____ la casa

a. ver una película
b. leer el periódico
c. tomar el sol
d. mirar televisión
e. bailar y conversar

**3-2 Nuestro tiempo libre.** PRIMERA FASE. What do all of you do in the following places? Take turns asking one another, and take notes on the responses.

MODELO: las fiestas
E1: *¿Qué haces en las fiestas?*
E2: *En las fiestas bailo mucho. ¿Y tú?*
E1: *Bailo y hablo con mis amigos.*
E2: *Y tú (E3), ¿qué haces en… ?*

| | COMPAÑERO/A 1 | COMPAÑERO/A 2 | COMPAÑERO/A 3 | YO |
|---|---|---|---|---|
| 1. en la universidad después de clase | | | | |
| 2. en la biblioteca pública de tu ciudad | | | | |
| 3. en casa el fin de semana | | | | |
| 4. en un parque de tu ciudad | | | | |
| 5. en la playa durante las vacaciones | | | | |
| 6. en la discoteca con tus amigos | | | | |

SEGUNDA FASE. With the other members of your group, prepare a report to share with the class about the activities most popular among group members.

MODELO: *En nuestro grupo, dos personas practican fútbol después de clases.*

**3-3 ¿Qué hacen Pedro y Carmen?** PRIMERA FASE. Look at the drawings and explain what Pedro and Carmen do on weekends.

SEGUNDA FASE. Write an e-mail to Rafael, your new friend in Peru, explaining what you and your friends do on weekends.

Hola Rafael,

¿Cómo estás? Nosotros estamos muy bien. Los fines de semana mis amigos y yo _____

_____

_____

_____ .

¡Hasta pronto!

_____

### En otras palabras

Telephone greetings vary from country to country. **¿Diga?** and **¿Dígame?** are used to answer the phone in Spain; **¡Bueno!** in Mexico; **¿Aló?** in Argentina, Peru, and Chile; **¡Oigo!** and **¿Qué hay?** in Cuba. Terms of endearment such as **mi amor, corazón, mi vida, querido/a,** and **mi cielo** also reflect regional preferences.

# ꓬ)) Los planes

**CD 2 Track 2** **Una conversación por teléfono entre Manuel y Lola**

LOLA: ¿Aló?

MANUEL: Hola, mi amor, **¡felicidades** por tu cumpleaños!

LOLA: Ay, gracias, Manuel.

MANUEL: **¿Qué te parece** si **vamos** al cine esta tarde y **después** a un restaurante para **cenar?**

LOLA: Me parece **fabuloso.** ¿Qué película vamos a ver?

MANUEL: Hay una nueva de Alfonso Cuarón.

LOLA: Muy bien. Me gustan mucho sus películas. ¿Dónde **ponen** la película?

MANUEL: **Cerca de** El Jardín Limeño, tu restaurante peruano favorito.

LOLA: **Estupendo,** ¿entonces **luego** vamos a cenar allí?

MANUEL: **¡Claro!** ¿Nos vemos en tu casa a las cinco?

LOLA: Sí, sí, perfecto. ¡Hasta luego!

**3-4 Una invitación.** PRIMERA FASE. Using the preceding dialogue as a model, role-play a phone call to invite a classmate to join you in a weekend activity. He/She should accept or decline the invitation.

SEGUNDA FASE. Repeat the activity with two other classmates. Then explain to the class your weekend plans and how many people are joining you.

MODELO: *El sábado por la tarde Juan, Verónica y yo vamos al gimnasio para ver un partido de básquetbol.*

### En directo

To extend an invitation:

**Te llamo para ver si quieres** (*if you want*) **+ infinitive…**

**Tengo una idea. ¿Por qué no +** *nosotros/as form…of the verb…?*

To accept an invitation:

**¡Estupendo! ¿Dónde quedamos?** *Where do we meet?*

**Sí, gracias/¡Ah, qué bien!/ ¡Qué buena idea!**

**¡Qué bueno!**

**¡Fabuloso!**

To decline an invitation:

**Lo siento, pero no tengo tiempo/tengo mucho trabajo/tengo mucha tarea…**

**Ese día no puedo** (*I can't*), **tengo un examen.**

## Cultura

Traditionally, Mexico, Spain, and Argentina have had important film industries, but films are made in other Spanish-speaking countries as well. Outstanding Spanish-language film directors like Pedro Almodóvar and Icíar Bollaín in Spain, Alfonso Cuarón and Alejandro González in Mexico, Sergio Cabrera in Colombia, and Juan Carlos Tabío in Cuba, among others, are internationally known.

**3-5 ¿Adónde vamos?** PRIMERA FASE. You and your partner are in a study abroad program in Lima and are looking for something to do together over the weekend. Underline three activities in the cultural section of the newspaper that you find interesting. Then fill in the chart, including the day and time for each activity.

## AGENDA CULTURAL
## La guía de Lima

### Cine

El amor en los tiempos del cólera. Dir. Mike Newell. C.C. Británico. Calle Bellavista 531. Miraflores. 7:30 pm. Libre.

### Teatro

La casa de Bernarda Alba. Grupo de Teatro Lorca. C.C. Británico. Av. La Marina 2554. San Miguel. 7:30 pm. Libre.
Entre visillos. Basada en "La cantante calva", de Eugenio Ionesco. Auditorio Municipalidad de San Isidro. La República 455. El Olivar. 8 pm. Boletería.

### Música

Los andinos en concierto. Huainos, yaravíes, mulizas. ICPNA. Jr. Cuzco 446. Lima. 7 pm. S/. 10.00.
Noche flamenca. Ballet La flor de Sevilla. ICPNA. Av. Angamos Oeste 120. Miraflores. 7:30 p.m. S/. 25.00.
Amalia Sánchez en concierto. A beneficio del C.C. de Rehabilitación de Ciegos. C.C. Ricardo Palma. Larco 770. Miraflores. 8 pm. S/. 10.00.

### Exposición

Maestros en acción. Asociación de Docentes de la ENSABAP. Bellas Artes de La Molina. Av. Rinconada del Lago 1515. 7 pm.

### Libro

Lectura de poemas de Óscar Liria. Av. La Paz 646. 7:30 pm. Libre.

### Conferencia

La mujer en el arte. Con Lola Reyes. C. C. San Marcos. Parque Universitario. Lima. 6:30 pm. Libre.

### Literatura

Perú en la literatura francesa. Con Pierre Brillat. Alianza Francesa. Av. Arequipa 4595. Miraflores. 8 pm. S/.15.00, S/.10.00.

### Cultura

*Huainos*, *yaravíes*, and *mulizas* are Peruvian songs of pre-Columbian origin that are popular in the Andean region of the country. They are often performed and danced in the *peñas*, music clubs that promote traditional (Afro-Andean and Creole) music. In the *peñas* people dance all night long and enjoy excellent regional food.

| ¿ADÓNDE VAMOS? | ¿QUÉ VAMOS A VER/HACER/ESCUCHAR? | ¿CUÁNDO? |
|---|---|---|
|  |  |  |
|  |  |  |
|  |  |  |

SEGUNDA FASE. Explain your plans to another pair. Decide if you can do some of the activities together.

# ·)) La comida

CD 2
Track 3 **En el restaurante.** Ahora Lola y Manuel están en el restaurante El Jardín Limeño para **celebrar el cumpleaños** de Lola. Hablan con el **camarero**.

CAMARERO: Buenas noches. ¿Qué desean los señores?

MANUEL: Lola, ¿qué vas a comer?

LOLA: Para mí, una **ensalada** primero y después **pollo** con **verduras**.

MANUEL: Yo, para empezar, **ceviche** de **pescado**. Y luego un **bistec** con **papas**.

CAMARERO: ¿Y para beber?

LOLA: Vamos a beber **vino** blanco. Y también **agua** con gas, por favor.

CAMARERO: ¿Algo más?

MANUEL: Nada más, gracias.

### ESPECIALIDADES DE LA CASA

ENTRADAS

| | |
|---|---|
| Ensalada de la casa | S/.10 |
| Ceviche de pescado | S/.15 |
| Papa a la huancaína | S/.10 |
| Causa a la limeña | S/.12 |

PLATOS PRINCIPALES

| | |
|---|---|
| Chupe de camarones | S/.22 |
| Ají de gallina | S/.18 |
| Lomo saltado | S/.17 |
| Bistec con papas | S/.17 |
| Pollo con verduras | S/.16 |

POSTRES

| | |
|---|---|
| Suspiro de limeña | S/.8 |
| Alfajor | S/.8 |
| Mazamorra morada | S/.6 |

BEBIDAS

| | |
|---|---|
| Chicha morada | S/.4 |
| Jugo de maracuyá | S/.4 |
| Inca Kola | S/.3 |

## Cultura

Peruvian cooking mostly uses regional ingredients and follows preparation methods inherited from indigenous cultures. Ceviche is a typical dish of Peru and other countries in Latin America. It is generally made with seafood that is not cooked but rather marinated in lime juice and spices.

yuca frita
adobo de chancho
papas cocidas
aceitunas
frijoles
ceviche de pescado
tamales
rocotos rellenos

La comida peruana es muy variada. Sobre esta mesa hay ceviche de pescado, tamales, papas cocidas, rocotos (pimientos) rellenos, adobo de chancho (cerdo), yuca frita, frijoles y aceitunas.

## En directo

Expressions to take an order:

**¿Qué desean los señores?**

**¿Qué van a tomar/beber?**

Expressions to order food:

**Para mí, una ensalada, arroz con…**

**Me gustaría/Quisiera comer/tomar…**
*I would like to eat/ drink…*

**Yo quiero/deseo…**

## Cultura

The *Cultura* box above mentions one of the most typical dishes in Perú, *el ceviche*. Some other typical Peruvian dishes include *papa a la huancaína* (sliced boiled potatoes covered with a spicy creamy cheese sauce); *causa a la limeña* (seasoned mashed potato stuffed with tuna, egg, shrimp, or avocado); *chupe de camarones* (shrimp chowder); *ají de gallina* (shredded chicken casserole with walnuts, parmesan cheese, and Peruvian hot peppers); *suspiro de limeña* (a dessert made with milk and eggs); *alfajor* (two-layer cookies with *dulce de leche* between the layers; *mazamorra morada* (purple corn pudding).

## Más comidas y bebidas

CD 2
Track 4

el desayuno

el cereal
la leche
el té
el jugo de naranja
el café caliente
el pan tostado/las tostadas
los huevos fritos

el almuerzo

la ensalada de lechuga y tomate
el sándwich de jamón y queso
una cerveza fría
las papas fritas
la fruta
el refresco
la hamburguesa

la comida/la cena

el pescado
el arroz
el helado
el pollo
el agua
los vegetales/las verduras
la sopa
los espaguetis

**3-6 Calorías. PRIMERA FASE.** Which item in each group contains the most calories?

1. la sopa de tomate, una hamburguesa, la sopa de pollo
2. el pollo frito, el pescado, la ensalada
3. los vegetales, las frutas, las papas fritas
4. la cerveza, la leche desnatada (*skim*), el café
5. el helado de chocolate, el cereal, el arroz

**SEGUNDA FASE.** Mention items in the *Primera fase* that you eat or drink frequently. Do you both have the same preferences?

**MODELO:** E1: *Frecuentemente como ensaladas y bebo cerveza. ¿Y tú?*
E2: *Yo frecuentemente como hamburguesas con papas fritas y bebo refrescos.*

**3-7 Las comidas.** Tell a classmate what you usually have for breakfast, lunch, and dinner. Then find out what he/she usually eats for those meals.

**MODELO:** *En el desayuno, como tostadas y bebo café. ¿Y tú?*

**3-8 Dietas especiales.** Which is the best option from this menu for the following people?

1. Su amiga Luisa está un poco delgada y desea subir de peso (*gain weight*). ¿Qué va a comer de este menú?
2. Su mamá es alérgica a los mariscos (*seafood*). ¿Cuál de las ensaladas va a comer?
3. Su amigo José está un poco gordo y quiere bajar de peso (*lose weight*). ¿Cuál de los platos principales no debe comer?
4. El profesor/La profesora de español está enfermo/a (*sick*) del estómago hoy. ¿Qué debe comer?

### Cultura

Fast food is popular among young Hispanics, and American-style hamburger places may be found in Hispanic countries. They often adapt to local tastes, and it is not unusual to have hamburgers served with rice and black beans instead of fries. Beer and wine may also be sold in addition to soft drinks.

### MENÚ

**SOPAS**

| | |
|---|---|
| Sopa de pollo | S/. 9 |
| Sopa de tomate | S/. 7 |
| Sopa de vegetales | S/. 7 |
| Sopa de pescado | S/. 12 |

**ENSALADAS**

| | |
|---|---|
| Ensalada de lechuga y tomate | S/. 8 |
| Ensalada de pollo | S/. 14 |
| Ensalada de atún | S/. 12 |

**PLATOS PRINCIPALES**

| | |
|---|---|
| Bistec con papas y vegetales | S/. 20 |
| Hamburguesa con papas fritas | S/. 16 |
| Pescado con papas fritas | S/. 18 |
| Arroz con vegetales | S/. 15 |

**3-9 ¿Qué te gusta más?** Using the words below, ask what your partner prefers to drink **por las mañanas, para el almuerzo, por las noches.** Alternate asking questions and taking notes. Then explain your partner's preferences to the class.

MODELO: E1: *¿Qué te gusta beber por las mañanas, té o café?*
E2: *Me gusta más el café.*

| | | |
|---|---|---|
| el agua mineral con gas | una copa de vino | un refresco |
| el agua mineral sin gas | una cerveza | el té (helado) |
| un batido (*shake*) | un chocolate caliente | un vaso (*glass*) |
|    de yogur y fruta | el jugo de naranja |    de leche |

**3-10 En el café.** It is 9:00 on Saturday morning, and you and a friend are in a café in Lima. Ask what your friend wants to order. Then say what you are going to order.

MODELO: E1: *El desayuno es muy bueno aquí.*
        *¿Qué deseas comer?*
E2: _____ *¿Y tú?*
E1: _____ *¿Y qué vas a tomar?*
E2: _____

| DESAYUNOS | |
|---|---|
| café | S/.3 |
| té | S/.3 |
| café con leche | S/.5 |
| jugo de naranja | S/.5 |
| chocolate | S/.6 |
| tostadas | S/.5 |
| pan con mantequilla | S/.5 |
| pan dulce | S/.6 |
| cereal | S/.8 |
| huevos fritos | S/.10 |

**3-11 Un viaje (*trip*).** You are in Peru and are planning a day trip to Machu Picchu. Arrange to take some food and beverages with you.

1. Make a list of the food and beverages that you need to take.
2. Talk about the things that you are going to do.

**3-12 Nuestro menú.** You and your roommate want to have guests over for dinner tonight. Decide whom each of you is going to invite and what you are going to serve. Finally, compare your menu with that of another pair of classmates.

■ Vamos a invitar a _____ .

■ Vamos a servir _____ .

**3-13 ¿Qué hacen estos estudiantes?** PRIMERA FASE. You will listen to two students, Rafael and Miguel, talk about their activities and weekend plans. Before you listen, write down three activities you normally do during the week, and three that you plan for this weekend.

CD 2
Track 5

actividades de la semana: _____

planes para el fin de semana: _____

SEGUNDA FASE. Now, listen to Rafael and Miguel and pay attention to the general idea of what they say. Then check (✓) the activities they mention they will do during the weekend.

1. —— estudiar para los exámenes
2. ___ comer en un restaurante
3. ___ descansar y tomar el sol
4. ___ trabajar en la librería
5. ___ celebrar el cumpleaños de Rafael

# EN ACCIÓN

## Diarios de bicicleta: La invitación

### Antes de ver

**3-14** In this video segment, Javier is at a restaurant. Based on your knowledge of Mexican restaurants in the United States, mark (✓) the sentences that you think describe restaurants in Mexico.

1. ___ Hay muchos colores.
2. ___ Hay música de mariachis.
3. ___ La comida cuesta mucho dinero.
4. ___ Muchos platos tienen chile.

### Mientras ve

**3-15** Mark (✓) the correct answer according to the information provided.

1. Javier va al restaurante para…
   a. ___ desayunar        b. ___ almorzar        c. ___ cenar
2. Para comer, Javier pide…
   a. ___ pollo con papas fritas    b. ___ pollo con papas    c. ___ sopa azteca.
      y chile habanero.               fritas y chile verde.
3. Para beber, Javier pide…
   a. ___ agua mineral bien fría.   b. ___ un té frío con limón.   c. ___ una limonada bien fría.

### Después de ver

**3-16 PRIMERA FASE.** Mark (✓) the statement that describes the problem that Javier has in this segment.

1. ___ Javier no tiene dinero para pagar la cuenta (*bill*).
2. ___ Gabi no puede almorzar con Javier.
3. ___ A Javier no le gusta la comida del restaurante.

**SEGUNDA FASE.** Write a sentence indicating how Javier's problem is solved.

# FUNCIONES Y FORMAS

## 1. Talking about daily activities: Present tense of *hacer*, *poner*, *salir*, *traer*, and *oír*

### Unos amigos nuevos conversan sobre sus actividades

CAROLINA: Bueno, para conocernos mejor, ¿por qué no jugamos a *Decir la verdad*? José Manuel, la primera pregunta es para ti. ¿Qué **haces** cuando estás aburrido?

JOSÉ MANUEL: **Pongo** la tele para ver películas. Ahora, Tomás, ¿adónde **sales** cuando tienes tiempo? ¿Y con quién?

TOMÁS: Bueno, **salgo a comer** con mi novia Pilar. Pero cuando tengo exámenes, debo **salir para** la biblioteca. Carolina, cuando **oyes** música salsa, ¿qué **haces**?

José Manuel    Carolina    Tomás

CAROLINA: Eso es muy fácil. Siempre bailo cuando **oigo** música salsa. Mi pregunta es para los dos. ¿Qué **hacen** ustedes en casa que no les gusta **hacer**?

TOMÁS: Yo **hago** mi cama porque me gusta el orden.

JOSÉ MANUEL: Mis hermanitos me **traen** su ropa y lavo ropa sucia (*dirty*) todo el fin de semana. La ropa sucia de ellos es repugnante. ¡Qué asco! ¿Y tú, Carolina?

CAROLINA: ¿Yo? Pues, **pongo la mesa** todos los días. ¡Qué lata!

**Piénselo.** Match each idea on the left with a logical ending on the right. More than one answer may be possible.

1. \_\_\_\_ **Pongo** la tele…
2. \_\_\_\_ **Pongo la mesa**…
3. \_\_\_\_ **Oigo** música…
4. \_\_\_\_ Debo **salir para** la biblioteca…
5. \_\_\_\_ **Hago** mi cama…
6. \_\_\_\_ Lavo la ropa que **traen** mis hermanos…

a. porque me gusta el orden.
b. cuando **salgo** con mis amigos.
c. para pasarlo bien (*have a good time*).
d. para ayudar (*help*) con el trabajo de casa.
e. porque me gusta ver películas.
f. porque deseo aprender mucho.

■ In the present tense, the verbs **hacer**, **poner**, **salir**, **traer**, and **oír** have irregular **yo** forms, but are regular in all other forms.

| HACER (*to make, to do*) | | | |
|---|---|---|---|
| yo | **hago** | nosotros/as | **hacemos** |
| tú | **haces** | vosotros/as | **hacéis** |
| Ud., él, ella | **hace** | Uds., ellos/as | **hacen** |

■ **Hacer** means *to do* or *to make*. It is used frequently in questions to ask in a general sense what someone does, is doing, or likes to do.

| | |
|---|---|
| ¿Qué **haces** para sacar buenas notas? | *What do you do to get good grades?* |
| **Hago** la tarea para mis clases todos los días. | *I do the homework for my classes every day.* |

| PONER (*to put*) | | | |
|---|---|---|---|
| yo | **pongo** | nosotros/as | **ponemos** |
| tú | **pones** | vosotros/as | **ponéis** |
| Ud., él, ella | **pone** | Uds., ellos/as | **ponen** |

■ **Poner** means *to put*. When used with some electrical appliances, **poner** means *to turn on*; **poner la mesa** means *to set the table*.

| | |
|---|---|
| Por la mañana **pongo** mis libros en mi mochila. | *In the morning I put my books in my backpack.* |
| Mi abuelo **pone** la televisión después de la cena. | *My grandfather turns on the TV after dinner.* |
| Yo **pongo** la mesa a la hora de la cena. | *I set the table at dinner time.* |

| SALIR (*to leave*) | | | |
|---|---|---|---|
| yo | **salgo** | nosotros/as | **salimos** |
| tú | **sales** | vosotros/as | **salís** |
| Ud., él, ella | **sale** | Uds., ellos/as | **salen** |

■ **Salir** can be used with several different prepositions. To express that you are leaving a place, use **salir de**; to express your destination, use **salir para**; to express with whom you go out or the person you date, use **salir con**; to express what you are going to do, use **salir a**.

| | |
|---|---|
| Yo **salgo de** mi cuarto a las 7:15 de la mañana. | *I leave my room at 7:15 in the morning.* |
| **Salgo para** la cafetería. | *I am leaving for the cafeteria.* |
| Mi mejor amiga **sale con** Mauricio. | *My best friend is dating Mauricio.* |
| Ellos **salen** a bailar los sábados. | *They go out dancing on Saturdays.* |

| TRAER (*to bring*) | | | |
|---|---|---|---|
| yo | **traigo** | nosotros/as | **traemos** |
| tú | **traes** | vosotros/as | **traéis** |
| Ud., él, ella | **trae** | Uds., ellos/as | **traen** |

| | |
|---|---|
| Yo siempre **traigo** un postre a estas fiestas. | *I always bring a dessert to these parties.* |

| OÍR *(to hear)* | | | |
|---|---|---|---|
| yo | **oigo** | nosotros/as | **oímos** |
| tú | **oyes** | vosotros/as | **oís** |
| Ud., él, ella | **oye** | Uds., ellos/as | **oyen** |

■ **Oír** means *to hear* in the sense of *to perceive sounds*. Note the spelling and the accent marks in the infinitive, **nosotros/as**, and **vosotros/as** forms.

Yo **oigo** música.              *I hear music.*

— ¿**Oyes** la alarma?           — *Do you hear the alarm?*

— No, no **oigo** nada.          — *No, I don't hear anything.*

**3-17 La perfección andante (*Perfection in motion*). PRIMERA FASE.** Are you organized, considerate, studious, and/or punctual? Check (✔) the statements that refer to things you do or don't do regularly.

1. _____ Yo **hago** mi cama temprano por la mañana.
2. _____ Cuando **oigo** que un amigo está triste, lo invito a salir.
3. _____ Siempre **pongo** música rock cuando estudio.
4. _____ Generalmente, **traigo** el periódico a la mesa para leer las noticias mientras desayuno.
5. _____ En general, no **traigo** el periódico a la mesa mientras desayuno porque prefiero conversar con mi familia.
6. _____ Por las mañanas, **hago** ejercicio y luego **salgo** para la universidad.

 **SEGUNDA FASE.** Take turns talking about the activities you both do that show off your best qualities.

**MODELO:**  E1: *Yo soy organizado. Siempre hago mi cama temprano. ¿Y tú?*
      E2: *Pues, yo también... /No, yo no...*

**3-18 ¿Usa usted bien su tiempo libre? PRIMERA FASE.** Check (✔) the version of each activity that best describes your habits.

1. _____ Pongo la mesa para cenar.       _____ Como en cualquier lugar de la casa.
2. _____ Hago el desayuno.             _____ Salgo a desayunar fuera de casa.
3. _____ Hago la cama cada día.         _____ Hago la cama una vez por semana.
4. _____ Oigo las noticias en la radio.   _____ Veo las noticias en la televisión.
5. _____ Traigo el periódico a la casa.    _____ Leo el periódico en el cibercafé.
6. _____ Pongo la televisión para ver películas.   _____ Salgo al cine para ver películas.

**SEGUNDA FASE.** Working with a partner, compare your answers and determine which of you has more fun doing these things. Explain why.

**3-19 Mi rutina. PRIMERA FASE.** Talk about the activities that you routinely do. Then ask your classmate about his/her activities.

**MODELO:**        tener clases por la mañana/por la tarde
        E1:  *Yo tengo clases por la mañana. ¿Y tú?*
        E2:  *Yo tengo clases por la mañana y por la tarde./Yo también tengo clases por la mañana.*

1. normalmente salir de su casa temprano/tarde por la mañana
2. generalmente poner la radio/tele para escuchar su música favorita por la mañana
3. hacer la tarea en casa/en la biblioteca
4. frecuentemente salir a comer/ver películas con su familia por la noche
5. con frecuencia traer muchos libros a casa después de las clases

**SEGUNDA FASE.** Write a brief paragraph comparing your routine with that of your classmate. In your opinion, who has a more interesting routine, and why? Provide a few reasons.

**3-20 Para pasarlo bien. PRIMERA FASE.** Write a check (✓) next to the activities that, in your opinion, your classmates probably do to have fun.

1. _____ Ponen películas los fines de semana.
2. _____ Oyen música y bailan mientras estudian para los exámenes.
3. _____ Frecuentemente hacen fiestas con sus amigos.
4. _____ Asisten a conciertos y exposiciones de arte.
5. _____ Hacen ejercicio en el gimnasio o en el parque.
6. _____ Escuchan programas en la radio pública.
7. _____ Salen a comer en grupo.
8. _____ ...

**SEGUNDA FASE.** Using the activities you marked in the *Primera fase* as a starting point, ask if your instructor does the same activities to have fun. Refer to *En directo* to help you express your reactions to your instructor's responses.

**MODELO:**    PAREJA:  *Para pasarlo bien, nosotros asistimos a conciertos de música rock. ¿Asiste a conciertos de música rock para pasarlo bien?*
    PROFESOR/A:  *No asisto a conciertos de música rock. Para pasarlo bien escucho conciertos de música clásica en la radio pública.*
    PAREJA:  *¡Qué aburrido!*

---

### En directo

To react to what someone has said:

**¡Qué interesante!**

**¡Qué divertido!**
*How funny!*

**¡Qué aburrido!**

---

### SITUACIONES

1. **Role A.** You are interviewing a potential roommate for your two-bedroom apartment. Find out a) if he/she likes things to be neat (**si le gusta el orden**); b) what household chores he/she likes to do and does not like to do; and c) what he/she likes to do at home in his/her free time. Your interviewee will have questions for you also. At the end of the conversation, decide whether to accept this person as a roommate.

   **Role B.** You are new in town and are being interviewed by someone who has a room to rent in his/her apartment. Answer the questions in as much detail as possible and ask some questions of your own. At the end of the conversation, decide whether you are interested in the room.

2. **Role A.** You have just been hired to take care of a five-year-old boy for the summer. Ask what time the parent leaves the house in the morning and find out a) what the child eats and drinks for breakfast and lunch; b) whether he has to make his bed or set the table; and c) what his favorite activities are.

   **Role B.** You have just hired a college student to take care of your five-year-old son for the summer. Answer his/her questions. To get to know him/her better, ask a) what he/she studies at school and b) what he/she likes to do in his/her free time.

## 2. Expressing movement and plans: Present tense of *ir* and *ir a + infinitive*

### Elena, la chica en el centro, habla de sus amigos

Mis amigos y yo somos diferentes, pero somos muy unidos. Para mi cumpleaños, nosotros **vamos a** un restaurante todos los años. Los sábados, yo **voy a** la casa de mi amiga Estela, y luego ella **va** conmigo al gimnasio para hacer ejercicio. A veces Rafael, Humberto y Rodrigo también **van al** gimnasio con nosotras. Mi amiga Teresa, no sale mucho porque prefiere estudiar. Yo siempre bromeo (*joke*) con ella: "Tere, ¿**vas a** la biblioteca a pasarlo bien?" Fernando, es muy tranquilo y artístico y le fascina el silencio. Con frecuencia él y Estela **van a** la librería a comprar libros.

**Piénselo.**  Read the following statements about Elena and her friends. Then indicate (✓) if the statement is **probable** or **improbable**, based on the information Elena provides.

|  | PROBABLE | IMPROBABLE |
|---|---|---|
| 1. Elena y sus amigos **van a** lugares juntos para celebrar su cumpleaños. | —— | —— |
| 2. Fernando **va a** los conciertos de música rock. | —— | —— |
| 3. Estela afirma: "Frecuentemente, yo **voy a** la librería a comprar libros". | —— | —— |
| 4. Teresa comenta: "Fernando y yo **vamos al** museo de arte esta tarde". | —— | —— |
| 5. Elena no **va a** las fiestas de cumpleaños de sus amigos. | —— | —— |

■ After the verb **ir**, use **a** to introduce a noun that refers to a place. When **a** is followed by the article **el**, the two words contract to form **al**.

| | |
|---|---|
| Voy **a la** fiesta de María. | *I am going to María's party.* |
| Vamos **al** gimnasio. | *We are going to the gym.* |

■ Use **¿adónde?** when asking *where (to)?* with the verb **ir**.

| | |
|---|---|
| **¿Adónde** vas ahora? | *Where are you going now?* |

| IR (*to go*) | | | |
|---|---|---|---|
| yo | **voy** | nosotros/as | **vamos** |
| tú | **vas** | vosotros/as | **vais** |
| Ud., él, ella | **va** | Uds., ellos/as | **van** |

■ To express a future action or condition, use the present tense of **ir a** + the infinitive form of the verb.

| | |
|---|---|
| Mis amigos **van a nadar** después. | *My friends are going to swim later.* |
| ¿**Vas a ir** a la fiesta? | *Are you going to go to the party?* |

■ The expression **vamos a** + *infinitive* can mean *let's*.

| | |
|---|---|
| **Vamos a cenar** en mi casa. | *Let's have dinner at my house.* |
| **Vamos a bailar** después. | *Let's go dancing afterward.* |

### Lengua

The following expressions denote future time:

**después, más tarde, esta noche, mañana, pasado mañana, la próxima semana, el próximo mes/año.**

**3-21 ¿Adónde van?** PRIMERA FASE. Josh and Steve are North American students visiting Peru for their summer vacation. Match the descriptions on the left with the places they plan to see on the right.

1. ____ Steve estudia historia. Por eso, desea ver la universidad prestigiosa y más antigua de América de Sur. Está en Lima. Él va a...

2. ____ Los dos amigos van a visitar uno de los lugares más misteriosos del planeta. Allí hay enormes figuras geométricas trazadas (*drawn*) en la tierra que son visibles solamente desde el aire. Ellos van a...

3. ____ Josh conoce (*meets*) a Susana en Perú. Ella lo invita a un evento folclórico donde las personas oyen poesía, música tradicional y comen y bailan también. Josh y Susana van a...

4. ____ Steve y Josh van a un lugar histórico imposible de ignorar. Es considerado el símbolo del imperio inca. Está cerca de Cuzco. Steve y Josh van a...

**a.** Machu Picchu

**b.** las líneas de Nazca

**SEGUNDA FASE.** Now indicate where you will go to do the following in Peru.

1. Para hacer amigos, conversar y bailar ritmos peruanos, yo voy a

   _____ .

2. Voy a _____ para tomar fotos de los alumnos y el edificio de una universidad muy antigua.

3. Para escalar unas montañas altas de mucha importancia histórica, voy a

   _____ .

**c.** la Universidad de San Marcos

**3-22 Intercambio.** PRIMERA FASE. Your classmate's friends are busy today. Find out when each friend is leaving the place listed and where he/she is going afterward.

MODELO: E1: *¿A qué hora sale del trabajo tu amigo Armando?*
E2: *(Sale) a las seis de la tarde.*
E1: *¿Adónde va después?*
E2: *Va al cine.*

**d.** una peña

| NOMBRE | HORA | LUGAR |
|--------|------|-------|
| Juan | 8:00 a.m. | gimnasio |
| Alicia | 9:30 a.m. | laboratorio de computadoras |
| Sofía | 8:30 p.m. | oficina |
| Tú | ... | ... |

**SEGUNDA FASE.** Exchange information with your partner about what each of you does at the times listed in the *Primera fase*.

MODELO: E1: *¿Qué haces a las 8:00 de la mañana?*
E2: *Salgo de mi casa para la universidad.*
E1: *¿Adónde vas cuando llegas a la universidad?*
E2: *Voy a mi clase de español. ¿Qué haces tú a las 8:00 de la mañana?*

**3-23 ¡Qué lío! (*What a mess!*)** PRIMERA FASE. Cristina had a party at her house while her parents were out of town, and now her friends are helping her clean up. Match each situation on the left with its probable solution.

1. ____ Hay muchos platos sucios.
2. ____ Cristina ve mucha comida en la mesa.
3. ____ La casa está desordenada.
4. ____ Cristina y sus amigos necesitan energía para limpiar la casa.
5. ____ Los amigos de Cristina están cansados después de la fiesta.

a. Dos chicos van a ordenar todo.
b. Algunos amigos van a recoger (*pick up*) los platos.
c. Una amiga va a refrigerar la comida.
d. Una amiga va a preparar café.
e. Van a descansar.

 SEGUNDA FASE. Brainstorm how Cristina's parents are going to react when they find out about her party. Some suggestions may include: *cancelar las tarjetas de crédito, prohibir fiestas/amigos, conversar seriamente, ...*

## SITUACIONES

1. **Role A.** Your friend has invited you to a concert. Call him/her to find out a) where and when the concert is going to be; b) who is going to sing; c) who is going to introduce (**presentar**) the group; and d) how much the ticket (**el boleto/el billete/la entrada**) costs.

   **Role B.** Your friend calls to find out about a concert you invited him/her to. Answer all the questions with as much information as possible.

2. **Role A.** You call to invite a friend to a café tonight where a mutual friend is going to sing. After your friend responds, ask about his/her plans for later in the evening: a) where he/she is going; b) with whom; and c) what time, etc.

   **Role B.** A friend calls to invite you to a café tonight where a mutual friend is going to sing. Inquire about the event to find out a) what time and where it will be and b) if other friends are going to go. Accept the invitation and mention your plans for later in the evening.

**3-24 Mi agenda para la semana.** Invite six classmates individually to do the following activities with you. Each will accept or reject your invitation according to his/her schedule for the week. Indicate the day, the activity and the name of the classmate who accepted your invitation.

MODELO:      estudiar en la biblioteca el lunes
   E1:   *¿Vamos a estudiar en la biblioteca el lunes?*
   E2:   *Lo siento, Miguel, el lunes voy a ir al cine con David. Pero, ¿por qué no salimos a comer el martes?*
   E3:   *Buena idea. Vamos a salir el martes.*

1. ir a un concierto
2. mirar televisión en casa
3. tomar algo en un café
4. estudiar para un examen difícil
5. bailar en la discoteca
6. hacer ejercicio

| DÍA | ¿QUÉ VA A HACER? | ¿CON QUIÉN? |
|---|---|---|
| martes | comer en un restaurante peruano | Miguel |
|  |  |  |
|  |  |  |

**3-25 Los planes de Maribel.** PRIMERA FASE. Take turns saying what Maribel is going to do at the times indicated.

SEGUNDA FASE. Tell your classmate what you are going to do at those times on Friday.

# 3. Talking about quantity: Numbers 100 to 2.000.000

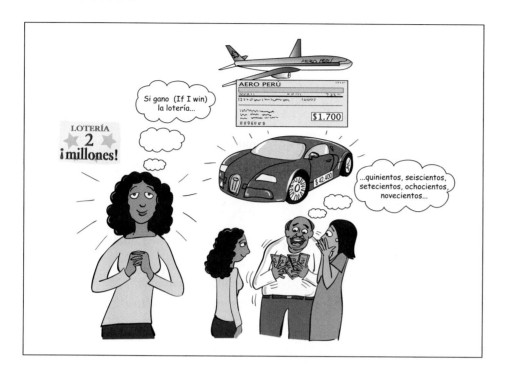

**Lengua**

In Spanish, numbers higher than one thousand, such as dates or street addresses, are not stated in pairs as they often are in English. For example, 1942 is expressed as **mil novecientos cuarenta y dos**, whereas in English it is almost always given as *nineteen forty-two*.

**Piénselo.** Your instructor will say a number from each of the following series. Identify each number you hear. The numbers in the last row are dates.

| | | | |
|---|---|---|---|
| **1.** 114 | 360 | 850 | 524 |
| **2.** 213 | 330 | 490 | 919 |
| **3.** 818 | 625 | 723 | 513 |
| **4.** 667 | 777 | 984 | 534 |
| **5.** 1.310 | 1.420 | 3.640 | 6.860 |
| **6.** 10.467 | 50.312 | 100.000 | 2.000.000 |
| **7.** 1492 | 1776 | 1890 | 2001 |

■ You have already learned the numbers up to 99. In this section you will learn numbers to use to talk about larger quantities.

| | | | |
|---|---|---|---|
| 100 | cien/ciento | 1.000 | mil |
| 200 | doscientos/as | 1.100 | mil cien |
| 300 | trescientos/as | 2.000 | dos mil |
| 400 | cuatrocientos/as | 10.000 | diez mil |
| 500 | quinientos/as | 100.000 | cien mil |
| 600 | seiscientos/as | 150.000 | ciento cincuenta mil |
| 700 | setecientos/as | 500.000 | quinientos mil |
| 800 | ochocientos/as | 1.000.000 | un millón (de) |
| 900 | novecientos/as | 2.000.000 | dos millones (de) |

■ Use **cien** to say 100 when used alone or when followed by a noun. Use **ciento** for numbers from 101 to 199.

| 100 | **cien** |
| 100 chicos | **cien** chicos |
| 120 profesoras | **ciento** veinte profesoras |
| 177 libros | **ciento** setenta y siete libros |

■ Multiples of 100 agree in gender with the noun they modify.

| 200 periódicos | **doscientos** periódicos |
| 1.400 revistas | **mil cuatrocientas** revistas |

■ Use **mil** for *one thousand*. Multiples of 1,000 are also **mil**.

| 1.000 | **mil** alumnos, **mil** alumnas |
| 12.000 | **doce mil** residentes |

■ Use **un millón** to say *one million*. Use **un millón de** when a noun follows.

| 1.000.000 | **un millón** |
| 1.000.000 de personas | **un millón de personas** |
| 12.000.000 de dólares | **doce millones de dólares** |

■ In many Spanish-speaking countries, a period is used to separate thousands, and a comma is used to separate decimals.

| $1.000 | $19,50 |

 **3-26 ¿Cuándo va a ocurrir?** Exchange opinions with a classmate about when each of the following events will occur.

MODELO: Todos los libros van a ser electrónicos.
E1: *En el año 2020.*
E2: *Estoy de acuerdo.* Or
*No estoy de acuerdo. Todos los libros van a ser electrónicos en 2050.*

1. Los adultos van a trabajar sólo 20 horas por semana.
2. Los estudiantes no van a ir a clases. Van a estudiar en universidades virtuales.
3. Todos los autos van a ser eléctricos y van a ser muy rápidos.
4. Los turistas van a ir de un país a otro sin pasaporte.
5. La contaminación va a ser muy grande, y las personas van a usar máscaras (*masks*) en los parques y en las calles.
6. Los robots, y no las personas, van a servir la comida en los restaurantes.
7. Las personas van a comunicarse por telepatía.
8. Muchas personas van a comer solamente la comida artificial.
9. Muchos turistas van a viajar (*travel*) al espacio interplanetario.
10. Los viajes en avión van a ser más rápidos y van a costar poco.

**3-27 Unas vacaciones. PRIMERA FASE.** Your classmate has chosen one of the destinations in the ad for an upcoming vacation. To find out where he/she is going, ask the following questions. Then switch roles.

1. ¿Adónde vas?
2. ¿Qué lugares vas a ver?
3. ¿Cuántos días vas a estar allí?
4. ¿Cuánto cuesta la excursión?

**SEGUNDA FASE.** Based on your classmate's answers, fill in the information and share it with the class.

1. planes que su compañero/a necesita hacer (sacar un pasaporte, obtener una visa, hacer reservaciones, etc.):

   _____

2. lugar(es) que va a visitar: _____

3. tiempo que va a estar allí: _____

4. costo de la excursión: _____

5. dinero extra que usted cree que su compañero/a va a necesitar: _____

**AGENCIA MUNDIAL**

**A SU SERVICIO SIEMPRE** *20 años de experiencia, responsabilidad y profesionalidad.*

TODOS LOS PRECIOS INCLUYEN PASAJES AÉREOS Y SERVICIOS TERRESTRES POR PERSONA

**PERÚ Y BOLIVIA**

**LIMA, AREQUIPA, CUZCO, MACHU PICCHU, PUNO, LA PAZ,** 15 días. La Ruta del Inca. Hoteles de 3 y 4 estrellas. Desayuno incluido. **$2.760**

**PERÚ**

**LIMA, CUZCO, MACHU PICCHU, NAZCA,** 12 días. Visite fortalezas incas. Vea las misteriosas líneas de Nazca desde el aire. Hoteles de primera. Desayuno y cena incluidos. **$3.150**

**LIMA, NAZCA, AREQUIPA, LAGO TITICACA,** 10 días. Admire la arquitectura colonial de Lima y Arequipa. Vea las líneas de Nazca desde el aire. Navegue en el lago más alto del mundo. Hoteles de primera. **$2.620**

**ARGENTINA**

**BUENOS AIRES, BARILOCHE, MENDOZA,** 12 días. Disfrute de una gran metrópoli. Esquíe en uno de los lugares más bellos del mundo. Hoteles de 4 y 5 estrellas. Desayuno y cena. **$3.590**

**CHILE Y ARGENTINA**

**SANTIAGO, PUERTO MONTT, BARILOCHE, BUENOS AIRES,** 12 días. Excursión a Viña del Mar y Valparaíso. Cruce de los Andes en minibús y barco. Hoteles de 3 y 4 estrellas. **$4.075**

**CARIBE**

**JAMAICA,** 7 días. Happy Inn, todo incluido. Exclusivo para parejas. **$2.480**

**PUERTO RICO**

**SAN JUAN,** 5 días. Hotel de 5 estrellas. Excursión a Ponce. Visita con guía al Viejo San Juan. Desayuno incluido. **$1.995**

**MÉXICO**

**MÉXICO, TAXCO, ACAPULCO,** 7 días. Hoteles de 3 y 4 estrellas. Excursión a Teotihuacán. Desayuno bufet incluido. **$1.800**

**CANCÚN,** 5 días. Hotel de 4 estrellas. Excursión a Cozumel. Visita a ruinas mayas. Las mejores playas. **$1.510**

*Solicite los programas detallados con variantes de hoteles e itinerarios a su agente de viajes.*

Tel. 312-785-4455   Fax: 312-785-4456

# SITUACIONES

1. **Role A.** You have been saving up for a special trip (**viaje**) during the next school vacation, and you are now making plans. Call a friend to explain a) where you plan to go; b) who will travel with you; and c) what you plan to do.

   **Role B.** Your friend calls to tell you about his/her travel plans for the next school break. Ask a) with whom he/she is planning to go; and b) what places he/she is going to visit. You are curious about the cost of the trip (**viaje**), so you inquire about the cost of the flight (**el vuelo**), the hotel, and the activities your friend plans to do.

2. **Role A.** You have been working hard, and you would like to splurge on a weekend trip to do some special (but expensive) activities, like rent a car, go to a professional sports event or rock concert, eat in good restaurants, and shop (**ir de compras**). Call and invite your friend to go. Explain your plan and be prepared to answer questions about the cost of this weekend adventure.

   **Role B.** Your friend calls to invite you on an exciting (but expensive) weekend trip. After your friend explains the plan, ask questions to get an idea of the cost. Decide whether you can afford it, and either accept or decline the invitation.

## En directo

To call attention to an unusual fact:

**¡Fíjate qué noticia!** *How about that!*

**¡Imagínate!**

To react to good news:

**¡Qué suerte!**

**¡Qué maravilla!**

**¡Qué bien!**

To convince someone:

**¡Ven/Anda, anímate!** *Come on, cheer up!*

**Lo vamos a pasar muy bien.** *We are going to have a good time.*

# 4. Stating what you know: *Saber* and *conocer*

ALFREDO: Me gustan mucho los músicos y ella **sabe** cantar muy bien.

ELENA: Sí, es una cantante fabulosa.

MARIO: Luisa, **conoces** a Liliana, ¿no?

LUISA: Sí, las dos estamos en la clase de arte de la profesora Ruiz.

**Piénselo.** Indicate (✓) in the appropriate box whether each sentence refers to knowing a fact, knowing how to do something, knowing a person, or being familiar with a place, an event, or a thing.

| | KNOWING A FACT | KNOWING HOW TO DO SOMETHING | KNOWING A PERSON | BEING FAMILIAR WITH A PLACE, EVENT, ETC. |
|---|---|---|---|---|
| 1. ¿**Conoces** la música afro-peruana? | ___ | ___ | ___ | ___ |
| 2. Me gusta mucho la música, pero no **sé** bailar. | ___ | ___ | ___ | ___ |
| 3. ¿**Sabes** los nombres de esos grupos musicales? | ___ | ___ | ___ | ___ |
| 4. ¿**Conoces** a Alfredo Roncal? Toca la guitarra. | ___ | ___ | ___ | ___ |
| 5. ¿**Sabes** si hay un club de música hispana en la ciudad? | ___ | ___ | ___ | ___ |
| 6. Alfredo **conoce** todos los clubes de música en la ciudad. | ___ | ___ | ___ | ___ |

■ Both *saber* and *conocer* mean *to know*, but they are not used interchangeably.

| | SABER | CONOCER |
|---|---|---|
| yo | **sé** | conozco |
| tú | sabes | conoces |
| Ud., él, ella | sabe | conoce |
| nosotros/as | sabemos | conocemos |
| vosotros/as | sabéis | conocéis |
| Uds., ellos/as | saben | conocen |

■ Use **saber** to express knowledge of facts or pieces of information.
  Él **sabe** dónde está el club.     *He knows where the club is.*

■ Use **saber +** *infinitive* to express knowing how to do something.

Yo **sé** tocar la guitarra.          *I know how to play the guitar.*

■ Use **conocer** to express familiarity with someone or something. **Conocer** also means *to meet.* Remember to use the *personal* **a** when referring to people.

| **Conozco a** los músicos. | *I know the musicians.* |
| **Conozco** bien ese club. | *I am very familiar with that club.* |
| Ella va a **conocer a** Luis. | *She is going to meet Luis.* |

**3-28 Un encuentro entre dos estudiantes.** Raúl just arrived on campus, and he asks Sergio some questions. Select the correct words to complete their conversation.

| | | |
|---|---|---|
| RAÚL: | Soy un estudiante nuevo y no (1) _____ dónde está la biblioteca. | **a.** sé   **b.** conozco |
| SERGIO: | Es muy fácil. Tú (2) _____ dónde está la cafetería, ¿no? Pues, está al lado. | **a.** sabes   **b.** conoces |
| RAÚL: | Gracias. ¿Y (3) _____ si hay un club de español? | **a.** sabes   **b.** conoces |
| SERGIO: | Sí, claro, y (4) _____ que esta noche tiene una reunión. | **a.** sé   **b.** conozco |
| RAÚL: | Magnífico. Sólo (5) _____ a dos o tres personas en la universidad. | **a.** sé   **b.** conozco |
| SERGIO: | Pues allí vas a (6) _____ a muchos estudiantes. | **a.** saber   **b.** conocer |

**3-29 ¿Sabes quién es...?** Ask your partner if he/she knows who is being referred to and if he/she knows that person. Take turns asking questions.

**MODELO:**      el actor principal de *El ultimátum de Bourne*

E1:  *¿Sabes quién es el actor principal de* El ultimátum de Bourne?

E2:  *Sí, sé quién es. Es Matt Damon.*

E1:  *¿Conoces a Matt Damon en persona?*

E2:  *No, no conozco a Matt Damon./Sí, conozco a Matt Damon, pero solamente en fotografías.*

**1.** el/la representante de la Cámara de Representantes (*Congress*) de su distrito

**2.** el decano/la decana de la facultad

**3.** su profesor/a de español

**4.** el rey de España

**5.** el gobernador de su estado

**6.** el vicepresidente de Estados Unidos

**3-30 Adivina, adivinador.** In small groups, take turns reading the descriptions and guessing who is being described.

**MODELO:**  E1:  *Es una chica muy pobre que va a un baile. Allí conoce a un príncipe, pero a las 12:00 de la noche ella debe volver a su casa.*

E2:  *Sé quién es. Es Cenicienta* (Cinderella).

**1.** Es un gorila gigante con sentimientos (*feelings*) humanos. En una película aparece en el edificio Empire State de Nueva York.

**2.** Fue (*She was*) una mujer muy importante en Argentina. Su esposo gobernó (*governed*) ese país por varios años. Hay un musical con su nombre y también una película donde Madonna la representa.

**3.** Es una diseñadora de ropa y joyas, hija de un famoso pintor cubista español. Su perfume más famoso lleva su nombre.

**4.** Es un hombre de otro planeta con doble personalidad. Trabaja en un periódico, pero cuando se pone una ropa azul especial, puede volar (*fly*).

## SITUACIONES

1. **Role A.** If you have not already done so, make a list of five people, at least some of whom you think your partner knows personally. Choose three of them and ask a) if your partner knows them and b) what your partner knows about them. Be ready to answer similar questions.

   **Role B.** If you have not already done so, make a list of five people, at least some of whom you think your partner knows personally. Your partner will tell you the names of three people on his/her list and will ask a) if you know them and b) what you know about them. Answer and then ask your partner the same questions about three of the people on your list.

2. **Role A.** You are looking for a third roommate for your apartment. Your partner knows a student from Peru who is looking for a place to live. Ask your partner a) the Peruvian student's name; b) where in Peru he/she is from; and c) if your partner knows the Peruvian student well. Also find out if the Peruvian student knows how to cook Peruvian dishes and how to play soccer (**fútbol**).

   **Role B.** Your partner is looking for a third roommate for his/her apartment. Mention that you know a student from Peru who is looking for a place to live. Answer your partner's questions about that person.

**3-31 ¿Qué sabes hacer?** Ask your partner if he/she knows how to do the following things. If your partner says yes, ask more questions to get additional information.

**MODELO:** bailar salsa y merengue
E1: *¿Sabes bailar salsa y merengue?*
E2: *Sí, sé bailar salsa y merengue./No, no sé bailar salsa y merengue. ¿Y tú?*

1. tocar un instrumento musical
2. cantar bien
3. preparar ceviche
4. manejar (*drive*) un autobús
5. cocinar platos muy elaborados
6. sacar (*take*) fotos con una cámara digital
7. hablar muchas lenguas
8. …

**3-32 Bingo.** To win this game of bingo, you have to fill in three boxes (horizontal, vertical, or diagonal) with the names of classmates who answer the answers correctly.

| ¿Quién sabe dónde está la ciudad de Cuzco? | ¿Quién sabe cuál es la capital de Perú? | ¿Quién sabe qué es Machu Picchu? |
|---|---|---|
| ¿Quién conoce al presidente de Perú? | ¿Quién sabe cuál es la unidad monetaria de Perú? | ¿Quién sabe el nombre de un lago importante que está entre Perú y Bolivia? |
| ¿Quién conoce unos platos típicos de la cocina (*cuisine*) peruana? | ¿Quién conoce algún país hispanoamericano? | ¿Quién sabe cómo se llaman las montañas de Perú? |

**3-33 Saber y conocer.** Complete the conversation with the correct forms of **saber** and **conocer**. Review your answers with a partner.

PACO: ¿ _____ (1) a esa chica?
AUGUSTO: Sí, yo _____ (2) a todas las chicas aquí.
PACO: Entonces, ¿ _____ (3) dónde vive?
AUGUSTO: No, no _____ (4) dónde vive.
PACO: ¿ _____ (5) cómo se llama?
AUGUSTO: Lo siento, pero no _____ (6).
PACO: Pero ¿cómo dices que _____ (7) a la chica? Tú no _____ (8) dónde vive y tú no _____ (9) su nombre.

# 5. Expressing intention, means, movement, and duration: Some uses of *por* and *para*

CARLOS: Papá, necesito tu auto **por** una semana. ¿Está bien?

PADRE: ¿**Por** una semana? ¿**Por** qué?

CARLOS: **Porque** mis amigos y yo vamos a ir la playa **para** las vacaciones de primavera.

PADRE: ¡%$#@!

**Piénselo.** Indicate whether the following statements are true (**Cierto**) or false (**Falso**) according to the conversation.

1. ____ Carlos necesita el auto de su padre **por** una semana.
2. ____ El padre pregunta **por qué** Carlos desea el auto.
3. ____ Carlos desea ir a la playa **para** las vacaciones de primavera.
4. ____ Los amigos de Carlos necesitan el auto **para** trabajar.
5. ____ El padre está alegre **porque** Carlos necesita su auto.

■ **Por** and **para** have different meanings in Spanish, though sometimes they are both translated into English as *for*. The uses presented here include some you have already seen, as well as some new ones.

■ **Para** expresses *for* when you mean *intended for* or *to be used for*. It can refer to a person, an event, or a purpose.

| | |
|---|---|
| Necesito un diccionario **para** la clase. | *I need a dictionary for the class.* |
| Este diccionario es **para** David. | *This dictionary is for David.* |

■ **Para +** *infinitive* means *in order to*.

| | |
|---|---|
| Uso el autobús **para** ir a la universidad. | *I use the bus (in order) to go to the university.* |
| El restaurante hace publicidad **para** traer clientes. | *The restaurant does advertising (in order) to bring in customers.* |

■ **Por** appears in expressions such as **por favor**, **por teléfono**, and **por la mañana/tarde/noche**. Other expressions with **por** that you will find useful include the following:

| | | | |
|---|---|---|---|
| **por ciento** | *percent* | **por fin** | *finally, at last* |
| **por ejemplo** | *for example* | **por lo menos** | *at least* |
| **por eso** | *that is why* | **por supuesto** | *of course* |

■ **Por** and **para** can also be used to express movement in space and time.

**Para** indicates movement toward a destination.

| | |
|---|---|
| Caminan **para** la playa. | *They walk toward the beach.* |
| Vamos **para** el túnel. | *We are going toward the tunnel.* |

**Por** indicates movement through or by a place.

| | |
|---|---|
| Caminan **por** la playa. | *They walk along the beach.* |
| Vamos **por** el túnel. | *We are going through the tunnel.* |

You may also use **por** to indicate length of time or duration of an action.

Many Spanish speakers omit **por** in this case, or they use **durante**.

| | |
|---|---|
| Necesito el auto (**por**) tres días. | *I need the car for three days.* |

**3-34 ¿Por o para?** Match each use of **por** and **para** in the following text with the letter of its appropriate meaning from the list on the right.

Mis amigos y yo siempre estamos ocupados los fines de semana. Los viernes **por**[1] la noche, siempre vamos a un cine cerca de nuestro barrio. Cuando vamos **para**[2] el cine, caminamos **por**[3] el parque. Después del cine, a veces hacemos fiestas en casa. Yo compro una pizza y papas fritas **para**[4] comer con ellos. Si es una fiesta de cumpleaños, compro un regalo especial **para**[5] mi amigo. **Para**[6] celebrar, también invito a todos los miembros del grupo. A veces lo pasamos bien **por**[7] largas horas.

| | |
|---|---|
| 1. ____ | **a.** intended for (person) |
| 2. ____ | **b.** used for (purpose) |
| 3. ____ | **c.** in order to |
| 4. ____ | **d.** length of time |
| 5. ____ | **e.** movement toward a destination |
| 6. ____ | **f.** movement through or by a place |
| 7. ____ | |

 **3-35 ¿Para dónde van?** Guess where these people are going, and compare your guesses with your classmate's. Then find out where your classmate is going after class, and why.

**MODELO:** Jorge busca su uniforme de fútbol.
*Va para el estadio.*

1. Es la una de la tarde y Pedro desea comer.
2. Sebastián lleva una mochila con sus libros de química y una calculadora.
3. Magdalena y Roberto van a consultar unos libros porque tienen un examen.
4. Gregorio va a comprar un libro para su clase de español.
5. Ana María va a ver una película de su actor favorito.
6. Amanda y Clara están muy elegantes y contentas. En este momento llegan Arturo y Felipe en su auto.

**3-36 Caminante.** Your classmate likes to walk. Ask him/her the following questions. Then switch roles.

1. ¿Te gusta caminar con amigos o solo/a? ¿Por qué?
2. ¿Por dónde caminas cuando quieres estar solo/a?
3. ¿Te gusta caminar por la playa o por un parque?
4. ¿Caminas por la mañana o por la tarde?
5. Cuando sales a caminar, ¿caminas por media hora o por más tiempo?

**3-37 ¿Para quiénes son los regalos (*gifts*)?** You are very generous and have bought the following gifts. Your partner asks whom they are for.

MODELO:        un disco compacto
    E1: *¿Para quién es el disco compacto?*
    E2: *Es para mi hermana.*

1. tres libros de español
2. dos billetes de avión
3. una revista de deportes
4. cuatro refrescos dietéticos
5. una guitarra española
6. un kilo de helado
7. una computadora portátil
8. un teléfono celular
9. un buen vino chileno
10. una colección de DVDs

## SITUACIONES

1. **Role A.** You run into a friend on the street who is carrying a large, gift-wrapped box. You are curious about the box, so you ask what it is and whom it is for.

   **Role B.** You are walking home from the store carrying a large, gift-wrapped package. You run into a friend on the way. Answer your friend's questions and explain why you are giving the gift.

2. **Role A.** You see your neighbor leaving his/her apartment, dragging a big suitcase. You are curious, so you ask a) where he/she is going; b) if the plane leaves in the afternoon or evening; c) how long he/she will be there; and d) why he/she is going.

   **Role B.** You are about to go on a long international trip, and as you are leaving your apartment with your suitcase you see your nosy neighbor. He/She asks a lot of questions. Answer in as much detail as possible.

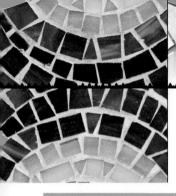

# MOSAICOS

## A escuchar

CD 2
Track 6

### ESTRATEGIA

**Use background knowledge**

When you listen to a conversation, you can use your knowledge of the situation to understand what is being said. Relying on the experience and knowledge you bring to the listening experience will enhance your comprehension.

### Antes de escuchar

**3-38 Preparación.** You will listen to an ad for *ViajaMás*, a travel agency, which mentions several destinations in Latin America, the days of the flights, the flight numbers, and the price of a round-trip ticket from Miami. Before you listen, use your knowledge of Latin America and ticket prices to write down the name of one large city in each of the countries below that you think the ad may mention and the likely cost of each ticket.

| CIUDADES LATINOAMERICANAS | PRECIO DEL BOLETO DE IDA Y VUELTA DESDE MIAMI |
|---|---|
| Perú: | |
| Argentina: | |
| Venezuela: | |

### Escuchar

**3-39 ¿Comprende usted?** Now listen to the ad and complete the chart with the information you hear.

| CIUDAD | VUELO # | DÍAS | PRECIO DEL BOLETO |
|---|---|---|---|
| | | sábados y domingos | |
| Buenos Aires | 479 | | |
| | | | $250 |
| Bogotá | | | |

### Después de escuchar

**3-40 Ahora usted.** A friend who is studying Spanish wants to visit a capital city in Latin America but is unsure where to go. After listening to the ad, write an e-mail to your friend to suggest a city to visit.

**De:** _____

**Para:** _____

**Asunto:** Una ciudad interesante en América Latina

**Hola** _____

¡Tengo una información excelente para ti! Hay tarifas (*fares*) fantásticas para visitar _____! ¡Es una ciudad _____! Los vuelos salen los _____. Los boletos cuestan _____.

¿Por qué no hablamos por teléfono este fin de semana? _____

114

# A conversar

**ESTRATEGIA**

**Organize information for a presentation**

When preparing for an oral presentation, it is helpful to decide on a plan and then organize your information accordingly. In this section, you will make a presentation on students' food preferences. Organizing your information by meal (i.e., foods students would like to have available for breakfast, for lunch, etc.) is one approach; another is to start with categories of food that students like (e.g., **carnes**, **cereales**) and then list specific items in each category that students would like to see on the cafeteria menus. Both organizational plans will result in effective presentations.

## Antes de conversar

**3-41 Preparación.** A new cafeteria is going to open on campus. You have been hired to survey students' food preferences so that the cafeteria menu will feature the most popular foods. Find out what your classmates like to eat and drink. Write down the names of students who answer **Sí** or **No** in the appropriate column.

**MODELO:** E1: *Susana, ¿comes cereal en el desayuno?*
E2: *Sí, como cereal en el desayuno./No, no como cereal.*

|  | DESAYUNO | | ALMUERZO | | CENA | |
|---|---|---|---|---|---|---|
|  | SÍ | NO | SÍ | NO | SÍ | NO |
| cereal con leche |  |  |  |  |  |  |
| café/chocolate caliente |  |  |  |  |  |  |
| jugo de naranja/tomate/manzana |  |  |  |  |  |  |
| hamburguesas |  |  |  |  |  |  |
| ensalada de frutas |  |  |  |  |  |  |
| vino |  |  |  |  |  |  |
| pan |  |  |  |  |  |  |
| ... |  |  |  |  |  |  |
| ... |  |  |  |  |  |  |

## Conversar

**3-42 Entre nosotros.** Analyze the information you collected and write down a proposed menu. Present it to the new cafeteria supervisor (your classmate). Explain what most students (**la mayor parte de los estudiantes**) eat and drink. Be prepared to answer the supervisor's questions.

## Después de conversar

**3-43 Un poco más.** Compare your menu with those of other classmates. Then vote on which menu is the most healthful and the most complete, and explain why.

*Cultura*

Despite differences from country to country, mealtimes in Hispanic countries generally differ from those in the United States. People typically eat breakfast at 7:00 or 8:00 a.m. It normally consists of **café**, **café con leche** (hot milk with strong coffee), **té**, or **chocolate caliente** with bread, a sweet roll, and sometimes juice or fruit. As this is a light breakfast, people sometimes have a snack in the late morning. Cereals are becoming more popular, especially among children and young adults.

In some countries, the main meal of the day is lunch (**el almuerzo** or **la comida**), eaten between 12:30 and 3:00 p.m. Supper (**la cena** or **la comida**) is served after 7:00 or 8:00 p.m., and sometimes as late as 10:00 p.m.

# A leer

**1.**

**NIÑOS**

CORPORACIÓN CULTURAL DE LIMA. Santa María y Gálvez. 2209451. A las 12 y 16 horas. Bagdhadas. S/. 12.

TEATRO INFANTIL A DOMICILIO. 2390176. El patito feo. Adaptación del cuento de Andersen. Compañía Arcoiris.

CENTRO LIMA. Av. Grau y Velásquez. A las 12, show especial de Navidad.

FANTASÍA DISNEY. Desde las 15. Niños, S/. 8; adultos, S/. 14. Parque de entretenimientos.

EL MUNDO FANTÁSTICO DE MAFALDA. Desde las 10. Entrada general a todos los juegos. Niños, S/. 12. Calle Domingo Sarmiento 358.

PLANETARIO DEL MORRO SOLAR. A las 12, 17 y 19. Gratis para niños; adultos, S/. 15. Circunvalación, Nuevo Perú. Tel. 5620841.

PARQUE DE LAS LEYENDAS (ZOO). De 9 a 19 hrs. Niños y 3ʳᵃ edad, S/. 5; S/. 10, otro público. Cerro Tongoy, 3701725.

**2.**

**osta Verde**

**Sabrosa comida tradicional peruana**
**Menú especial los fines de semana**

■ Aperitivo
■ Entrada
■ Segundo
■ Postre
■ Café y plus café (crema de café, crema de menta, anisado)

Valor: S/. 75

Carnes, pescados y mariscos preparados por los mejores cocineros del país

Avenida Arequipa 357
Reservas: 428 9654
Fax: 428 9655

**3.**

**El Chifa Lungfung**

La más exquisita, variada y exótica carta de comida cantonesa-peruana: finas carnes, pescados y todo tipo de mariscos.

**SÁBADOS Y DOMINGOS:**

**Almuerzos y cenas familiares**

...los esperamos

AIRE ACONDICIONADO
MÚSICA AMBIENTAL
CAMAREROS PROFESIONALES
AV. REPÚBLICA DE PANAMÁ 8720
RESERVAS 3817543, 3816532, 3814241

## Antes de leer

**3-44 Preparación.** PRIMERA FASE. The three ads in activity **3-45** come from a newspaper in Lima, Peru. Look them over quickly without reading them. Then mark which ad goes with each of the following descriptions.

1. ____ un restaurante de comida china
2. ____ actividades para niños
3. ____ un restaurante de comida tradicional peruana

SEGUNDA FASE. What word(s) in each ad helped you answer the questions in the *Primera fase*?

## Leer

**3-45 Primera mirada.** Read the ads and offer a solution for the following choices that have to be made. Be prepared to explain your solutions to the class.

1. El señor y la señora Molina tienen cuatro hijos entre tres y ocho años. A los niños les fascinan los animales. ¿Adónde van a ir probablemente? ¿Por qué?
2. Carlos está triste porque se fracturó una pierna y no puede (*he can't*) salir de la casa. Su mamá tiene una sorpresa para él. ¿Qué es?
3. Cuatro médicos franceses visitan el Hospital Central. El Dr. Moreira, director del hospital, desea invitar a sus colegas a cenar en un restaurante cómodo, con comida tradicional peruana. ¿A qué restaurante va a invitarlos? ¿Por qué?

**3-46 Segunda mirada.** Reread the ads **(3-45)** to answer the following questions.

**Anuncio 1:** ¿Qué palabras indican que las actividades son para los niños? ¿Qué significa *3ʳᵃ edad*? ¿Qué significa *otro público*?

**Anuncio 2:** Identifique qué expresión indica que este restaurante prepara comida nacional. ¿Cuánto cuesta el menú especial de los fines de semana?

**Anuncio 3:** ¿Qué expresiones se refieren a la buena calidad del restaurante? ¿Qué palabra significa *reservation*?

## Después de leer

**3-47 Ampliación.** With a classmate, answer the following questions about the four ads from Peru.

1. ¿Cuál de las siguientes actividades desean hacer ustedes en Lima: ir a un parque de entretenimiento (*amusement park*), comer comida tradicional peruana, ver teatro o comer comida china? ¿Por qué?
2. ¿Cuál de los dos restaurantes sirve comida que a ustedes les gusta más, Costa Verde o Chifa Lungfung?

# A escribir

**Use appropriate conventions in letter-writing**

Writing a casual or formal letter requires observing certain basic conventions, such as including the date, a salutation, an introduction, a body, and a closing, as well as carefully selecting information that will interest your reader. Formalities of writing also require developing one idea per paragraph. Remember to follow these conventions even when writing to a friend.

## Antes de escribir

**3-48 Preparación.** You are visiting a great vacation spot and want to write your friend a letter about it. To prepare to write the letter, do the following:

1. Write a tentative date for the letter: _____ (date) de _____ (month), 20____
2. Choose a salutation and a closing from the *En directo* box.
3. Prepare some information for the introduction. Mention the place where you are: Is it a beach, a park, a city, a historical landmark (**lugar histórico**)?
4. Decide on the information for the body of the letter:

   a. Make a list of words (adjectives) that describe the place: Is it small, big, beautiful, fun, interesting, historical?
   b. Write down some enjoyable activities (verbs) that people do there. Are they outdoor activities, sports (**deportes**), culturally oriented activities such as going to museums (**museos**), excursions (**excursiones**), fairs (**ferias**)?
   c. Indicate some of the activities that others do that you also like.

**En directo**

Salutations for casual correspondence:

   **Querido/a...**

   **Estimado/a...**

   **Hola...**

Closings for casual correspondence:

   **Tu amigo/a,**

   **Hasta pronto,**

   **Cariños,**
   *Love*

## Escribir

**3-49 Manos a la obra.** Now write the letter to your friend, telling about your vacation. Use the information you prepared in activity **3-48** and any other that you think may be of interest to your friend.

## Después de escribir

**3-50 Revisión.** After completing your letter, read it at least twice with your friend in mind. Check the following:

1. Did you include the date in your letter?
2. Are your salutation and closing appropriate?
3. Did you include a brief introduction and enough information in the body of the letter to achieve your purpose?
4. Did you check for spelling or grammatical errors?
5. Finally, discuss your letter with one of your peers.

# ENFOQUE CULTURAL

## Breve perfil de Perú

Perú es un país extraordinario por su diversidad y riqueza histórica, geográfica y cultural. En efecto, Perú y México son las dos regiones más importantes durante la época colonial de América Latina. Pero antes de los españoles, en Perú ya existe uno de los imperios indígenas más interesantes del continente. Y, finalmente, en Perú encontramos ruinas espectaculares de las culturas indígenas y de la época colonial, y también ciudades modernas con una mezcla de razas y una diversidad étnica muy grande.

Antes de la llegada de los conquistadores españoles, el imperio de los incas es una de las principales civilizaciones nativas de América. Esta civilización es famosa por su compleja organización social, su avanzada arquitectura y sus sistemas de comunicación. Muchas ciudades conservan restos de esta cultura. Por ejemplo, en Cuzco, la capital del imperio inca, hay espectaculares construcciones, como la gran fortaleza de Sacsayhuamán. Y, naturalmente, una de las ciudades incas más prestigiosas es Machu Picchu.

El Conde de Nieva, virrey de Perú entre 1561 y 1584, depende del rey Felipe II.

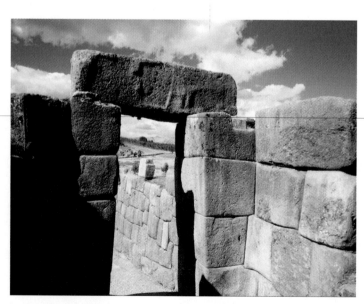

La fortaleza de Sacsayhuamán cerca de Cuzco

Cuando los españoles conquistan América, dividen el territorio en tres tipos diferentes de administración. El tipo más importante de administración en el imperio español es el *virreinato*. Esta palabra "vir**rei**nato" se relaciona con "rey", porque la autoridad más importante es el virrey. El segundo tipo más importante de administración es la *gobernación*, bajo la autoridad del gobernador. Y el tercer tipo es la *capitanía general*, bajo la autoridad principal del capitán general. México, Perú y la Nueva Granada (la actual Colombia) son los tres virreinatos españoles en el continente americano durante la colonia.

La geografía de Perú es variada y compleja. Tiene una multitud de sistemas ecológicos que forman el hábitat de una infinidad de plantas y animales. Hay tres regiones

La geografía de Perú presenta tres regiones diferentes.

**La selva**
**La sierra**
**La costa**

geográficas principales en Perú. La costa del Pacífico es muy rica en una gran variedad de peces y productos agrícolas. Una de las atracciones más famosas de esta región son las misteriosas líneas de Nazca. La segunda región es la sierra, que está formada por los Andes y que tiene algunas montañas muy altas, tales como el Nevado de Huascarán, el pico más alto de Perú, de aproximadamente 6.700 metros. La tercera región es la selva del Amazonas, al oriente de los Andes. Las grandes selvas tropicales de esta región son una de las fuentes principales de oxígeno en el planeta.

Finalmente, la cultura peruana es el resultado de la mezcla de la cultura indígena de los incas con la cultura española. Muchos peruanos, especialmente entre los habitantes de la sierra, hablan quechua, la lengua original de los incas. Pero Perú también tiene una gran influencia de culturas de origen africano y asiático. En resumen, la comida, el arte, la literatura, y todas las manifestaciones culturales peruanas son realmente únicas.

### En otras palabras

**Expresiones peruanas**

Me conseguí una **chamba**.
*I found a job.*

José y yo somos **patas**.
*José and I are buddies.*

¡Juanita es una **chancona**!
*Juanita is a nerd!*

**3-51 Comprensión.** PRIMERA FASE. **Reconocimiento de palabras clave.** Find in the text the Spanish word or phrase that best expresses the meaning of the following concepts:

1. profile _____
2. empire _____
3. rain forest _____
4. fort, fortress _____
5. fish, fishes _____
6. snow-capped peak _____
7. east _____

SEGUNDA FASE. **Oraciones importantes.** Underline the statements that contain ideas found in the text. Then indicate where in the text those ideas appear.

1. Before the arrival of the Spaniards, Cuzco was the capital of the Inca Empire.
2. The viceroyalties of Mexico and Peru were the most important colonies of Spain in the New World.
3. Colombia was one of the three viceroyalties in the Spanish Empire.
4. Peru has some beautiful modern cities, but they are all somewhat run down.
5. The mysterious Nazca drawings are located in the coastal region of Peru.
6. Some mountains, like Peru's highest peak, for example, are capped with snow.
7. A few mountains in the Peruvian Andes are very close to 8,000 meters high.
8. Spanish is not just the main language of Peru; it is the only language spoken there.

TERCERA FASE. **Ideas principales.** Write a brief paragraph in English summarizing the main ideas expressed in the text.

**3-52 Use la información.** You are visiting Peru, and you will spend tomorrow visiting Cuzco and its surroundings. Although it is late and you are tired, you take a few minutes to write a postcard to someone you really care about. Explain your plans for tomorrow: a) mention at least one place you plan to visit; b) if the place is in Cuzco or near/far (**cerca/lejos**); c) how you are going to get there; and d) what you are going to see. For help with this activity, go to the web page of *Mosaicos* and use the links provided there to write your postcard.

*De*..............................
..............................
..............................
..............................
..............................

*Para*..........................
..............................
..............................
..............................
..............................

# �))) ¿Qué hacen los parientes?

CD 2
Track 18

Mis abuelos viven en una casa al lado del parque. Normalmente, ellos **pasean** por las mañanas y **almuerzan** muy temprano. Después, **duermen la siesta** y por la tarde **visitan** a sus **parientes**.

**Lengua**

In Spanish, the direct object of a verb is normally introduced without a preposition. However, the preposition **a** is required when the direct object is a person or a specific animal: **los abuelos visitan a los parientes; la hija pasea al perro.**

Jorgito es mi primo favorito. Es un poco menor que yo. Nosotros corremos y jugamos mucho **juntos**. También nos gusta ver el fútbol en la televisión y montar en bicicleta los domingos.

**Hace dos años que** mi prima Ana tiene **novio**, y **frecuentemente dice** que **quiere casarse** muy pronto. Elenita, su hermana gemela, **piensa** que Ana no debe casarse porque es muy joven.

Mi tío Jorge es un hombre muy **ocupado**. Sale de casa muy **temprano** y **vuelve tarde** todos los días. Mi tía María, su esposa, dice que él **prefiere** el trabajo a su familia. Pienso que en todas las familias hay problemas. En la mía también, pero me gusta mi familia.

**4-7 ¿Cierto o falso?** Conteste (*Answer*) de acuerdo con la información adicional sobre la familia de Pablo.

|   |   | CIERTO | FALSO |
|---|---|---|---|
| 1. | Normalmente los abuelos están muy ocupados. | —— | —— |
| 2. | Jorgito y Pablo montan en bicicleta frecuentemente. | —— | —— |
| 3. | Elenita piensa que su hermana es muy joven para casarse. | —— | —— |
| 4. | El tío Jorge cree que Elenita tiene problemas. | —— | —— |
| 5. | El tío Jorge trabaja mucho. | —— | —— |
| 6. | El tío Jorge llega temprano a su casa. | —— | —— |

**4-8 ¿Y qué hace su familia?** Hágale preguntas a su compañero/a para obtener más información sobre su familia. Use la siguiente guía (*guide*).

1. número de personas en la casa, edad (*age*) y relación de parentesco (*kinship*)
2. ocupación y descripción (física y de personalidad) de algunos (*some*) miembros de la familia
3. actividades de estas personas en su tiempo libre
4. nombre del pariente favorito, relación familiar y razón (*reason*) de su preferencia

## ◄)) Las rutinas familiares

CD 2
Track 19

En casa de Pablo hay mucha actividad por la mañana. Los niños **se despiertan** a las siete. **Se levantan, se lavan** y luego **desayunan** en la cocina con sus padres. Después salen para la escuela.

Poco después, la madre **se ducha, se seca, se viste** y **se maquilla**.

Más tarde, el padre **se afeita**, **se baña** y **se pone la ropa**, pero no sale de casa hasta las nueve.

**4-9 Cada cosa a su tiempo.** Ponga (*Put*) en orden cronológico las siguientes oraciones según (*according to*) las escenas.

_____ La madre se maquilla.
_____ Los niños se despiertan a las siete.
_____ El padre se baña y luego se pone la ropa.
_____ La madre se ducha.
_____ El padre sale de casa a las nueve.
_____ Los niños desayunan y después salen para la escuela.

**4-10 Las rutinas diarias.** Conteste las siguientes preguntas sobre la rutina diaria de la familia de Pablo:

1. ¿Con quién desayunan los niños?
2. ¿Quién se maquilla por las mañanas?
3. ¿A qué hora se despiertan los niños?
4. ¿Quién sale de casa a las nueve?
5. ¿Quién se afeita por las mañanas?
6. ¿Qué hace la madre después de ducharse?

**4-11 Mañanas ocupadas (*busy*).** Marque (✓) las acciones diarias de los miembros de su familia.

> **Lengua**
>
> The following are expressions to organize time sequentially: **Primero, luego, poco después, más tarde,** and **por último.**

| | SE DESPIERTA TEMPRANO | SE DUCHA POR LA MAÑANA | SE PONE ROPA ELEGANTE | DESAYUNA CON LA FAMILIA |
|---|---|---|---|---|
| Mi padre (padrastro) | | | | |
| Mi madre (madrastra) | | | | |
| Mi hermano/a | | | | |
| Mi abuelo/a | | | | |
| Mi tío/a | | | | |

**4-12 ¿Y usted?** Complete el siguiente párrafo indicando el orden de las acciones en la rutina diaria de usted. Use las expresiones siguientes:

me ducho
me despierto
me levanto
salgo para la universidad
desayuno

Primero _____, luego _____ . Poco después _____,
más tarde _____. Por último _____.

 **4-13 ¿A qué hora?** Túrnense para hacerse las siguientes preguntas sobre la rutina diaria.

1. ¿A qué hora se levanta tu madre/padre/hermano?
2. ¿Te duchas por la mañana o por la noche?
3. ¿Quién se levanta temprano en tu familia?
4. ¿Te vistes antes o después de desayunar?
5. ¿Te pones ropa elegante o informal para ir a clase?
6. ¿A qué hora te acuestas durante la semana?
7. ¿A qué hora te acuestas durante los fines de semana?
8. ¿A qué hora te levantas durante los fines de semana?
9. ¿A qué hora tienes la clase de español?
10. ¿Quién se despierta antes los domingos en tu familia?

**4-14 Algunas familias hispanas.** You will listen to descriptions of four Hispanic families. Before you listen, answer these questions: Is your family large or small? How many brothers and sisters, cousins, aunts, and uncles do you have?

CD 2
Track 20

Now pay attention to the general idea of what is said. As you hear each description, write a check mark (✔) in the corresponding column.

|  | TIENE UNA FAMILIA GRANDE | TIENE HERMANOS | TIENE MUCHOS TÍOS | TIENE PRIMOS |
|---|---|---|---|---|
| Pedro |  |  |  |  |
| Alicia |  |  |  |  |
| Magdalena |  |  |  |  |
| Alberto |  |  |  |  |

# EN ACCIÓN

## Diarios de bicicleta: Nada de bromas

### Antes de ver

**4-15** En este segmento, Javier se encuentra con Luciana y su familia en el parque. Marque (✔) las actividades que las personas hacen normalmente cuando están en un parque.

1. ___ Juegan con una pelota (*ball*).
2. ___ Comen sándwiches y beben refrescos.
3. ___ Leen el periódico.
4. ___ Buscan trabajo.
5. ___ Escuchan música.

### Mientras ve

**4-16** Ponga en orden cronológico las acciones de Javier cuando la familia de Luciana le hace una broma (*plays a joke*).

___ Cierra los ojos.          ___ Se levanta y se va enojado.
___ Se pone el sombrero.      ___ Levanta los brazos y los mueve.
___ Se sienta.                ___ Abre los ojos.

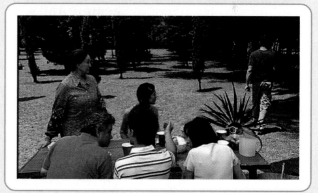

### Después de ver

**4-17** ¿Qué ocurre después de esta escena? Marque (✔) todas las actividades que usted cree que son posibles.

1. ___ Javier come con la familia de Luciana.
2. ___ Javier sale del parque sin despedirse de (*without saying good-bye*) Luciana.
3. ___ La abuela habla con Javier.
4. ___ El padre de Luciana duerme una siesta después del almuerzo.
5. ___ Marcos está enojado y sale del parque.

## 1. Expressing opinions, plans, preferences, and feelings: Present tense of stem-changing verbs: *e → ie*, *o → ue*, and *e → i*

### Carmen habla

**Quiero** conversar seriamente con ustedes y les **pido** su ayuda. **Pienso** que mamá y papá **quieren** algunos cambios en casa. Ellos no **pueden** hacer todo. El día **empieza** muy temprano para ellos y **duermen** muy poco. Con frecuencia, **almuerzan** en la oficina, aunque **prefieren** comer en casa. Nosotros necesitamos ayudar. Luis y Ximena, ustedes **vuelven** a casa a las 2:00. Si ustedes le **sirven** el almuerzo a Juanito y **juegan** con él, nuestros padres van a estar muy contentos. **Cuesta** mucho dinero pagar los servicios de una niñera (*babysitter*). ¿**Piensan** ustedes que mis ideas son buenas o **tienen** otras?

**Piénselo.** Identifique a la(s) persona(s) que probablemente hace(n) estas actividades en la familia del texto anterior: Los padres (**P**), Luis y Ximena (**LX**), Juanito (**J**) o Carmen (**C**). A veces hay más de una respuesta correcta.

1. _____ **Almuerzan** fuera de casa.
2. _____ **Necesita** ayuda para almorzar.
3. _____ **Prefieren** almorzar en casa.
4. _____ **Vuelven** a casa a las 2:00.
5. _____ **Sirven** el almuerzo a su hermanito.
6. _____ **Pide** la colaboración de sus hermanos.

■ Some common verbs in Spanish undergo a vowel change in all forms of the present tense except **nosotros/as** and **vosotros/as**.

| PENSAR (e → ie) (*to think*) | | | |
|---|---|---|---|
| yo | pienso | nosotros/as | pensamos |
| tú | piensas | vosotros/as | pensáis |
| Ud., él, ella | piensa | Uds., ellos/as | piensan |

| VOLVER (o → ue) (*to return*) | | | |
|---|---|---|---|
| yo | vuelvo | nosotros/as | volvemos |
| tú | vuelves | vosotros/as | volvéis |
| Ud., él, ella | vuelve | Uds., ellos/as | vuelven |

| PEDIR (e → i) (*to ask for*) | | | |
|---|---|---|---|
| yo | pido | nosotros/as | pedimos |
| tú | pides | vosotros/as | pedís |
| Ud., él, ella | pide | Uds., ellos/as | piden |

■ Other common verbs that have vowel changes in the stem are:

| e → ie | o → ue | e → i |
|---|---|---|
| **cerrar** (*to close*) | **almorzar** (*to have lunch*) | **repetir** (*to repeat*) |
| **empezar** (*to begin*) | **costar** (*to cost*) | **servir** (*to serve*) |
| **entender** (*to understand*) | **dormir** (*to sleep*) | |
| **preferir** (*to prefer*) | **encontrar** *(to meet)* | |
| **querer** (*to want; to love*) | **poder** (*to be able to, can*) | |

■ Use **pensar +** *infinitive* to express what you or someone else is planning to do.

| **Pienso estudiar** esta noche. | *I plan to study tonight.* |
|---|---|
| **Pensamos comer** a las ocho. | *We are planning to eat at 8:00.* |

■ Note the irregular **yo** form in the following **e → ie** and **e → i** stem-changing verbs.

| **tener** (*to have*) | **tengo**, tienes, tiene, tenemos, tenéis, tienen |
|---|---|
| **venir** (*to come*) | **vengo**, vienes, viene, venimos, venís, vienen |
| **decir** (*to say, to tell*) | **digo**, dices, dice, decimos, decís, dicen |
| **seguir** (*to follow*) | **sigo**, sigues, sigue, seguimos, seguís, siguen |

■ In the verb *jugar* (*to play a game or sport*) **u** changes to **ue**.

| Mario **juega** muy bien al tenis, pero nosotros jugamos regular. | *Mario plays tennis very well, but we play so-so.* |
|---|---|

**4-18 Planes para la boda.** Beatriz y Miguel se casan en un mes. Complete la descripción de los planes para la boda con la forma correcta de un verbo apropiado.

| empezar | poder | querer | servir |
|---------|-------|--------|--------|
| entender | preferir | seguir | volver |

Beatriz y Miguel (1) _____ tener una boda pequeña, pero elegante. La ceremonia (2) _____ a las 7:00. Los sobrinos y primos jóvenes de los novios no asisten a la ceremonia. Ellos no (3) _____ la ceremonia, y (4) _____ jugar con una niñera en otra parte de la iglesia. Después de la ceremonia, todos van a un restaurante, donde los invitados (5) _____ bailar y cenar. Los camareros (6) _____ una cena italiana, porque los padres de Miguel son de Italia. Después de la cena, la familia (7) _____ a la casa de los padres de la novia. Los invitados (8) _____ en la celebración, pero Beatriz y Miguel salen para su luna de miel (*honeymoon*) a Colombia.

**4-19 ¿Qué piensan hacer?** Túrnense para decir qué piensa hacer cada (*each*) miembro de la familia en las situaciones siguientes.

MODELO:     Mi hermano quiere estar delgado.
E1:   *Tu hermano probablemente piensa correr mucho.*
E2:   *Él probablemente piensa empezar una dieta.*
E3:   *Y probablemente piensa ir al gimnasio todos los días.*

1. Mi hermana tiene un examen de matemáticas mañana.
2. Mi hermana estudia bastante, pero no entiende muchos de los problemas.
3. Mi tía está enferma, por eso se siente muy débil y cansada.
4. Mis abuelos están de vacaciones en Colombia.
5. Mis primos quieren ir a Cartagena para visitar a los abuelos.
6. Mi tío lee y escucha comentarios contradictorios sobre Colombia, por eso, quiere aprender más sobre el país.

**4-20 ¿Qué pasa en las reuniones familiares?** PRIMERA FASE. Muchas familias se reúnen (*get together*) para las fiestas, los eventos especiales o sólo para reunirse. Describan las reuniones de su familia a su compañero/a. Tomen nota de las semejanzas (*similarities*) y las diferencias.

MODELO:     preparar la comida
E1:   *En las reuniones de mi familia, mi abuela prepara mucha comida.*
E2:   *En las reuniones de mi familia, tenemos mucha comida también. Pero mi madre y mi tía preparan la comida.*

1. venir
2. jugar con los niños
3. servir la comida
4. dormir en el sofá
5. preferir hablar de temas políticos
6. volver a casa

SEGUNDA FASE. Hablen de una semejanza y una diferencia entre las reuniones de su familia. Estén listos (*Be ready*) para compartir la información con la clase.

---

## Lengua

■ **Pensar en** is the Spanish equivalent of *to think of/about someone or something.*

**¿Piensas en** tu familia cuando estás fuera de casa?
*Do you think of/about your family when you are away from home?*

Sí, **pienso** mucho **en** ellos.
*Yes, I think of/about them a lot.*

■ **Pensar de** is used to ask for an opinion. **Pensar que** is normally used in the answer.

¿Qué **piensas de** los planes de ayuda familiar?
*What do you think of the plans to help families?*

**Pienso que** son excelentes.
*I think they are excellent.*

**4-21 Entrevista.** Túrnense para entrevistarse (*interview each other*). Hablen sobre los siguientes temas (*topics*) y después compartan la información con otro compañero/otra compañera.

1. la hora del almuerzo, qué prefiere comer y dónde
2. los deportes que prefiere practicar o mirar en la televisión
3. a qué hora empieza a hacer la tarea generalmente
4. si duerme una siesta durante el día
5. si vuelve a la casa de sus padres para las vacaciones
6. qué piensa hacer después de la universidad

**4-22 ¿Cuándo y con quién?** PRIMERA FASE. Háganse preguntas para obtener la siguiente información.

1. quiénes son sus amigos y qué actividades hacen juntos durante el año académico, durante la semana y los fines de semana
2. actividades de diversión (o deportivas) que hacen juntos, cuándo y dónde
3. actividades preferidas del fin de semana

SEGUNDA FASE. Preparen una lista de sus actividades semejantes o diferentes. Comparen su lista con la de otra pareja (*pair*).

MODELO: *Durante la semana, nosotros almorzamos en la cafetería de la universidad. ¿Y ustedes?*

**4-23 Una reunión.** En su universidad hay un fin de semana cuando los padres visitan a sus hijos en el campus. Ustedes quieren organizar una reunión para las familias de los miembros de su grupo. Decidan lo siguiente:

1. lugar y hora de la reunión
2. número de niños y adultos que van a participar (especifiquen la relación familiar)
3. comida y bebida que piensan servir
4. actividades y diversiones para los niños y para los adultos

---

### En directo

These expressions help maintain the flow of conversation:

**¡Cuánto me alegro!**
*I am so happy for you!*

**Claro, claro...**
*Of course . . .*

**¡Qué bien/bueno!**
*That's great!*

---

## SITUACIONES

1. **Role A.** You and a member of your family are planning to visit Latin America. Your friend has heard about your plans and calls with some questions. Answer your friend's questions in as much detail as possible.

   **Role B.** Your friend is planning to go to Latin America with a relative. Call to find out a) when he/she is planning to go; b) with whom; c) what country and cities he/she wants to visit and why; d) if his/her relative prefers to go to other places; and e) when they are returning.

2. **Role A.** The entire family has gathered for a party for the holidays. An elderly aunt/uncle is very curious about your life in college. After commenting on the party and several family members, answer her/his questions politely.

   **Role B.** You are at a family holiday gathering and you are very happy to see your young nephew/niece who is in college. After commenting on the party and several family members, ask about these aspects of college life: a) his/her classes; b) which class(es) he/she prefers; c) if the food is good; d) when vacation (**vacaciones**) starts; and e) what he/she plans to do after college.

## 2. Expressing obligation: *Tener que + infinitive*

La señora Rojas no está de buen humor hoy. Se siente muy frustrada con su familia. Acaba de escribir este mensaje.

Planes para nuestra familia

De hoy en adelante, todos **tenemos que ser** más organizados. Verónica **tiene que ver** menos televisión y **hacer** más ejercicio. Luis **tiene que practicar** el piano todos los días. Papá **tiene que escribir** los cheques todos los viernes. Agustín y Toño **tienen que hacer** su tarea por la tarde. Finalmente, todos **tenemos que pasar** más tiempo juntos los fines de semana.

**Mamá**

**Piénselo.** Según el texto anterior, asocie la situación de la columna izquierda con la obligación de cada persona en la columna derecha.

1. ＿＿ Verónica mira mucha televisión.
2. ＿＿ La madre tiene planes para todos.
3. ＿＿ El padre no se preocupa de los cheques.
4. ＿＿ Luis no es muy constante con la música.
5. ＿＿ Agustín y Toño probablemente prefieren practicar deportes y no estudian.
6. ＿＿ Cada miembro de la familia hace sus actividades independientemente.

a. Todos **tienen que pensar** en la importancia de hacer actividades en familia.
b. **Tienen que dedicar** suficiente tiempo a sus estudios.
c. **Tiene que hacer** más actividades físicas.
d. **Tiene que colaborar** con su esposa.
e. **Tiene que practicar** regularmente.
f. La familia **tiene que organizar** sus actividades.

■ **Tener que +** *infinitive.* Use **tener que** to express what someone *has to, needs to,* or *must* do.

Eliana, **tienes que estudiar** más.　　　　　*Eliana, you have to study more.*

**Tengo que visitar** a mis abuelos este fin de semana.　　*I have to visit my grandparents this weekend.*

**4-24 Mis obligaciones. PRIMERA FASE.** Marque (✓) las tareas que usted tiene que hacer regularmente. Luego compare sus obligaciones con las de otro compañero/otra compañera.

＿＿ sacar a caminar al perro
＿＿ hacer ejercicio
＿＿ comprar comida
＿＿ hacer la tarea para sus clases
＿＿ revisar el aceite (*oil*) del carro

＿＿ poner los platos sucios en el lavaplatos (*dishwasher*)
＿＿ escuchar los mensajes (*messages*) telefónicos
＿＿ ir a la universidad
＿＿ trabajar por las tardes
＿＿ visitar a mis parientes

**SEGUNDA FASE.** Ahora dígale (*tell*) a su compañero/a cuándo usted tiene que hacer cada tarea. Luego compare sus obligaciones con las de él/ella.

**MODELO:**　E1: *Tengo que poner la mesa todos los días. ¿Y tú?*
　　　　　E2: *Yo no tengo que poner la mesa, pero tengo que preparar la comida los domingos.*

**4-25 Un viaje (*trip*) a Colombia.** PRIMERA FASE. Su familia va a viajar a Colombia. Escoja la mejor recomendación para cada persona.

1. ___ Mariela quiere visitar un lugar interesante para una persona religiosa.
2. ___ A mis padres les gustaría ver el trabajo que se hace con metales preciosos en Colombia.
3. ___ Mi prima Mónica quiere escuchar música colombiana.
4. ___ Mis abuelitos prefieren las actividades al aire libre.

a. Tiene que asistir a un concierto de Los Príncipes del Vallenato.
b. Tiene que ir a la Catedral de Sal.
c. Tienen que ir al Museo del Oro.
d. Tienen que conocer el Parque Ecológico El Portal.

 SEGUNDA FASE. Preparen una breve descripción de uno de los lugares o eventos mencionados en la *Primera fase*. Incluyan la localización y las actividades que las personas hacen allí. Luego, compartan la información con la clase.

1. los Príncipes de Vallenato
2. la Catedral de Sal
3. el Museo del Oro
4. el Parque Ecológico El Portal

**4-26 Sugerencias.** PRIMERA FASE. ¿Qué tienen que hacer (o no) las personas en estas circunstancias?

MODELO:    Luis no tiene dinero (*money*).
    E1: *¿Qué tiene que hacer Luis?*
    E2: *Tiene que leer el periódico para encontrar trabajo.*

1. Mi amigo Juan tiene un examen el lunes.
2. Francisco siempre está cansado.
3. Manuel y Victoria no tienen una buena relación de pareja (*couple*).
4. Mi hermana Marta ve televisión todos los días y saca malas notas en sus clases.
5. Luis y Emilia quieren aprender español.
6. Isabel y Lucía desean visitar un país hispano, pero no hablan español.

SEGUNDA FASE. Escriban individualmente tres circunstancias. Cada persona explica sus circunstancias y su compañero/a dice qué tiene que hacer.

### SITUACIONES

1. **Role A.** You run into your cousin downtown. Exchange greetings and explain that today is your father's birthday and that you have to buy a gift (**regalo**). You don't have much time because you have to return home at 5:00. Say that you are thinking of buying a DVD and ask what he/she thinks of the idea. Thank your cousin for the advice (**gracias por los consejos**).

   **Role B.** You run into your cousin downtown. Exchange greetings. Your cousin needs some advice. Listen to his/her concerns and ask pertinent questions. Offer your opinion about whether a DVD is a good idea and, if so, what kind of DVD and where your cousin can find it.

2. **Role A.** You are worried about your bad relationship with your parents. They are angry because a) when you go out, you come home late; b) you do not study much; c) you prefer to spend a lot of time with your friends, but not with your family; d) you never play with your little sister; and e) when you are home you watch a lot of TV. Call a friend for advice. Answer your friend's questions in as much detail as possible.

   **Role B.** A friend calls you to discuss family problems. Listen and ask appropriate questions. Say that he/she a) must return home early in the evenings; b) has to spend more time with family and play with his/her little sister; c) has to study every day to get good grades; and d) must not watch TV before studying.

## 3. Expressing when, where, or how an action occurs: Adverbs

Los senderistas (*hikers*) siguen una ruta difícil y tienen que caminar **lentamente**. Si van **rápidamente** van a estar cansados. Cruzan el riachuelo (*creek*) **cuidadosamente**. Hay animales peligrosos en la sierra, pero **afortunadamente** es otoño y **seguramente** no encuentran serpientes.

Sierra de Santa Marta, Colombia

**Piénselo.** Asocie la expresión en negrita (*bold*) en la columna izquierda con su significado (*meaning*) en la columna derecha.

1. \_\_\_\_ Los senderistas piensan escalar **poco a poco.**
2. \_\_\_\_ Si los senderistas suben la montaña **con rapidez,** ellos van a estar cansados.
3. \_\_\_\_ **Por suerte,** ahora es otoño.
4. \_\_\_\_ Los senderistas **saben que** no van a encontrar serpientes.
5. \_\_\_\_ Cruzan el riachuelo **con mucha atención.**

    **a.** rápidamente
    **b.** afortunadamente
    **c.** seguramente
    **d.** cuidadosamente
    **e.** lentamente

■ Adverbs are used to describe when, where, and how an action/event takes place. You may already be familiar with adverbs referring to time (**mañana, siempre, después**) and place (**allí, abajo, afuera**), and you have used adverbs to express how you feel (**bien, muy mal, regular**). These adverbs can also be used to express how things are done.

Diego nada **bien,** pero yo nado muy **mal.**    *Diego swims well, but I swim badly.*

■ Many Spanish adverbs end in **-mente,** an ending that corresponds to the English *-ly*. To form these adverbs, add **-mente** to the feminine singular form of the adjective. With adjectives that do not have a separate feminine form, simply add **-mente** to the singular form.

Abuelita camina **lentamente.**    *Grandma walks slowly.*
Mis tíos cantan **alegremente** en las fiestas.    *My aunts and uncles sing happily at parties.*

■ When two or more adverbs are used in a series, only the last one has the **-mente** ending. The other adverbs in the series have the same form as the feminine singular form of the adjective.

La profesora habla **clara** y **lentamente.**    *The professor speaks clearly and slowly.*
Siempre ganan **rápida** y **fácilmente** el partido.    *They always win the game quickly and easily.*

■ Some commonly used adverbs ending in **-mente** are:

| | | | |
|---|---|---|---|
| **básicamente** | **lógicamente** | **realmente** | **simplemente** |
| **frecuentemente** | **normalmente** | **regularmente** | **tradicionalmente** |
| **generalmente** | **perfectamente** | **relativamente** | **tranquilamente** |

### Lengua

Adjectives with a written accent retain it when forming adverbs ending in **-mente:**
**difícil → difícilmente**

**4-27 ¿Está de acuerdo o no? PRIMERA FASE.** Las características de la familia pueden variar entre una comunidad y otra. Indique si usted está de acuerdo (**Sí** o **No**) con las siguientes afirmaciones.

En mi comunidad...

1. _____ los padres frecuentemente hablan con los hijos adolescentes sobre temas importantes.
2. _____ los nietos regularmente visitan a sus abuelos.
3. _____ generalmente los hijos solteros viven con sus padres.
4. _____ los padres siempre hablan lentamente cuando están enojados con sus hijos.
5. _____ idealmente el padre trabaja fuera de casa y la madre trabaja en casa.
6. _____ los hijos adolescentes siempre tratan a sus padres cortésmente.

**SEGUNDA FASE.** Comparen sus respuestas y digan por qué están de acuerdo.

**MODELO:** E1: *Estoy de acuerdo con el número uno. Generalmente los padres hablan sobre temas importantes con sus hijos.*

E2: *No estoy de acuerdo. Los padres generalmente hablan sobre educación o dinero, pero no hablan de drogas.*

**4-28 ¿Lenta o rápidamente?** Escriba tres actividades de la siguiente lista que usted hace rápidamente y tres que hace lentamente. Indique el lugar y/o las circunstancias.

| | | | |
|---|---|---|---|
| almorzar | escribir composiciones | hablar español | pasear |
| beber | estudiar | leer el periódico | tomar apuntes |

**MODELO:** *Como rápidamente cuando tengo poco tiempo.*

**4-29 ¿Cómo lo hace usted?** Primero, individualmente escriba cómo o cuándo usted hace las siguientes actividades. Usando las palabras en la lista u otras, forme adverbios para escribir sus frases. Luego, comparen sus respuestas.

| | | | |
|---|---|---|---|
| difícil | frecuente | lógico | perfecto |
| fácil | lento | ocasional | rápido |

1. caminar cuando usted está muy cansado/a
2. pensar en la clase de matemáticas
3. respirar (*breathe*) después de una hora de ejercicio en el gimnasio
4. responder en un examen fácil

**4-30 Actividades frecuentes. PRIMERA FASE.** Hágale estas preguntas a su compañero/a. Después él/ella tiene que hacerle las mismas (*same*) preguntas a usted. Tome apuntes sobre las respuestas de su compañero/a.

1. ¿Qué haces normalmente con tu familia?
2. ¿A qué lugares vas regularmente con tu familia? ¿Y con tus amigos?
3. Generalmente, ¿sales por las noches? ¿Adónde vas y con quién?
4. ¿A quiénes llamas por teléfono más frecuentemente, a tus amigos o a tu familia?

**SEGUNDA FASE.** Ahora escriba una breve comparación entre usted y su compañero/a con respecto a cada pregunta en la *Primera fase.* ¿Hacen ustedes actividades semejantes o diferentes?

---

**En directo**

To express surprise at what you hear:

**¡Qué increíble!**
*Incredible!*

**¡No me diga(s)!**
*Really!*

---

**SITUACIONES**

1. **Role A.** Your class is conducting a survey regarding students' movie habits. Ask a classmate a) when and with whom he/she generally goes to the movies; b) the type of movies he/she normally prefers (**románticas, dramáticas, de ciencia ficción**, etc.); c) what he/she often eats or drinks at the movies; and d) the name of his/her favorite movie.

   **Role B.** Answer the questions a classmate will ask about your movie preferences.

2. **Role A.** In your Sociology and the Family course, you are helping to conduct a survey about family traditions and activities. Ask a classmate a) if the members of his/her immediate family generally eat together; b) if they visit other family members frequently; and c) which family member normally organizes family gatherings.

   **Role B.** First answer your classmate's questions about your family. Then ask him/her these questions for the survey: a) Who is generally more organized (**organizado/a**) at home, men or women?; b) Do family members frequently do activities together?; c) Who prepares dinner well in the family?; d) Who talks calmly when angry, your father or your mother?

## 4. Expressing how long something has been going on: *Hace* with expressions of time

PATRICIA: Señora, ¿**cuánto tiempo hace que** practico esta sonata? ¡Estoy muy cansada!

SRA. ESCOBEDO: **Hace dos horas que** trabajas en ella. Pero una vez más, por favor, Patricia. El recital es en dos días.

Sra. Escobedo    Patricia

SRA. ESCOBEDO: Les presento a Patricia Suárez. Estudia el violín conmigo **hace cinco años**. Ahora va a tocar la Sonata N° 4 de Mozart.

**Piénselo.** Diga si las siguientes afirmaciones son lógicas (**L**) o ilógicas (**I**).

1. ____ **Hace mucho tiempo que** Patricia toca el violín perfectamente.
2. ____ **Hace cinco años que** Patricia no pasa mucho tiempo con sus amigos porque tiene que practicar la sonata.
3. ____ Patricia conoce a la profesora de violín **hace cinco años**.
4. ____ **Hace sólo un día que** Patricia trabaja en la sonata de Mozart.
5. ____ **Hace poco tiempo que** la señora Escobedo toca el violín.
6. ____ Los padres de Patricia no le pagan a la profesora por las clases de violín **hace un año**.

■ To say that an action/state began in the past and continues into the present, use **hace** + *length of time* + **que** + *present tense*.

**Hace dos horas que** juegan.          *They have been playing for two hours.*

■ If you begin the sentence with the present tense of the verb, do not use **que**.

Juegan **hace dos horas**.          *They've been playing for two hours.*

■ To find out how long an action/state has been taking place, use **cuánto tiempo** + **hace que** + *present tense*.

¿**Cuánto tiempo hace que** juegan?          *How long have they been playing?*

¿**Cuántas horas hace que** los niños juegan al fútbol?          *How many hours have the children been playing soccer?*

**4-31 Este soy yo. PRIMERA FASE.** Lea esta descripción y conteste las preguntas.

Me llamo Jaime Caicedo y soy de Cali, Colombia. Quiero aprender inglés para poder trabajar en una compañía internacional. Estudio inglés **hace dos años,** pero tengo que estudiar más para hablar correctamente. Siempre miro programas de televisión en inglés. Mis favoritos son *American Idol* y *Grey's Anatomy.* **Hace dos años que** miro estos programas y me gustan mucho. Tengo un auto **hace un año,** y salgo en él con mis amigos y también con mi novia. **Hace seis meses que** somos novios. Somos muy felices.

1. Jaime Caicedo es de...
   **a.** Estados Unidos.    **b.** Cali.    **c.** *Grey's Anatomy.*
2. Hace dos años que Jaime...
   **a.** tiene novia.   **b.** va al cine.    **c.** mira televisión en inglés.
3. Hace seis meses que Jaime...
   **a.** va a fiestas.    **b.** estudia inglés.    **c.** tiene novia.

**SEGUNDA FASE.** Ahora escriba su propia descripción, siguiendo el modelo en la *Primera fase.* Luego, comparta su descripción con un compañero/una compañera.

Me llamo (1) _____ . Soy de (2) _____ , (3) _____ (ciudad y país). Quiero aprender (4) _____ (lengua extranjera) porque (5) _____ . Estudio (6) _____ (lengua extranjera) hace (7) _____ (período de tiempo), pero tengo que estudiar más para hablar correctamente. Miro (8) _____ películas como _____ (películas en español) y escucho la música de (9) _____ (cantante o grupo español) para aprender más. Mi programa favorito es (10) _____ . Hace (11) _____ (período de tiempo) que (12) _____ el programa y me gusta mucho. En mi tiempo libre, (13) _____ . Tengo (14) _____ (vehículo/objeto o animal) hace (15) _____ . Hace (16) _____ (período de tiempo) que estudio en (17) _____ (nombre de la universidad). Espero ser (18) _____ (profesión) (19) _____ en el futuro.

**4-32 ¿Cuánto tiempo hace que...?** Túrnense para hacerse las siguientes preguntas. Después compartan la información con otra pareja.

1. ¿Dónde vive tu familia? ¿Cuánto tiempo hace que viven allí?
2. ¿Dónde trabajas? ¿Cuánto tiempo hace que trabajas allí?
3. ¿Cuánto tiempo hace que estudias en esta universidad? ¿Y por qué estudias español?
4. ¿Practicas algún deporte? ¿Cuánto tiempo hace que juegas al...? ¿Juegas bien?

## SITUACIONES

1. **Role A.** You live in Queens, New York, and a friend has come to visit. Explain that there are many Hispanic restaurants in this neighborhood (**barrio**). You suggest your favorite Colombian restaurant for dinner. When your friend asks about the Colombian food that they serve, you may want to mention **ajiaco de pollo** (a chicken stew made with potatoes, corn, and cream), **papas chorreadas** (potatoes covered with a sauce made with onions, tomatoes and milk), and **arroz con coco** (rice cooked in coconut milk).

   **Role B.** You are visiting a friend in Queens, New York. He/She suggests a Colombian restaurant for dinner. Ask a) how long he/she has been living in Queens; b) if he/she knows the restaurant well; c) what Colombian dishes they serve, and what they are like; and d) how much they cost.

2. **Role A.** You go to see your counselor (**consejero/a**) to talk about a personal problem (**un problema**). Greet the counselor and explain your problem. Answer the counselor's questions in as much detail as possible. When the session is over, thank the counselor.

   **Role B.** You are a student counselor (**consejero/a**). A student comes to you with a problem (**un problema**). Exchange greetings and ask a) how long the student has been at the university; b) how long he/she has been having the problem; and c) what he/she is doing to solve (**resolver**) the problem and for how long. Finally, suggest several things he/she has to do to improve (**mejorar**) the situation.

## 5. Talking about daily routine: Reflexive verbs and pronouns

Yo **me llamo** Óscar Torres. Mi esposa Rosa y yo tenemos una vida muy ocupada. Nosotros **nos levantamos** a las seis todos los días. Yo **me ducho** mientras Rosa se viste rápidamente. Después, Rosa **despierta** a Carlitos y a Roberto, nuestros hijos. Roberto **se viste**, y Rosa **viste** a Carlitos. Desayunamos y luego todos **nos lavamos** los dientes y a las siete salimos de la casa.

**Piénselo.** Para cada acción, indique si cada persona hace la acción a sí misma(s) (*him/her/themselves*) o a otra persona.

| ACCIÓN | A SÍ MISMO/A | A OTRA PERSONA |
|---|---|---|
| 1. Óscar **se ducha** por la mañana. | —— | —— |
| 2. Rosa **despierta** a Carlitos. | —— | —— |
| 3. La madre **viste** al niño porque es muy pequeño. | —— | —— |
| 4. Roberto **se viste** rápidamente. | —— | —— |
| 5. Nosotros **nos lavamos** los dientes después de desayunar. | —— | —— |
| 6. Rosa probablemente **se baña** por la noche, porque no tiene tiempo por la mañana. | —— | —— |

■ Reflexive verbs express what people do to or for themselves.

REFLEXIVE: Mi hermana **se lava.** *My sister washes (herself).*

NONREFLEXIVE: Mi hermana **lava** el auto. *My sister washes the car.*

| LAVARSE (to wash oneself) | | | |
|---|---|---|---|
| yo | **me lavo** | nosotros/as | **nos lavamos** |
| tú | **te lavas** | vosotros/as | **os laváis** |
| Ud., él, ella | **se lava** | Uds., ellos/as | **se lavan** |

■ A reflexive pronoun refers back to the subject of the sentence. English sometimes uses the pronouns ending in *-self/-selves* to express reflexive meaning. In many cases, Spanish uses reflexives where English does not.

Yo **me levanto, me ducho, me seco** y **me visto** rápidamente.

*I get up, take a shower, dry myself, and get dressed quickly.*

■ Place reflexive pronouns after the word **no** in negative constructions.

Rosa **no se ducha** por la mañana. *Rosa does not take a shower in the morning.*

- The pronoun **se** attached to the end of an infinitive indicates the verb is reflexive.

  | | |
  |---|---|
  | **vestir** | *to dress (someone else)* |
  | **vestirse** | *to get dressed (oneself)* |

- With a conjugated verb followed by an infinitive, place the reflexive pronoun before the conjugated verb or attach it to the infinitive.

  Yo **me** voy a levantar a las siete. ⎤
  Yo voy a levantar**me** a las siete. ⎦ *I am going to get up at seven.*

- When referring to parts of the body and articles of clothing, use definite articles rather than possessives with reflexive verbs.

  | | |
  |---|---|
  | Me lavo **los** dientes. | *I brush my teeth.* |
  | Roberto se pone **la** chaqueta. | *Roberto puts on his jacket.* |

- Some verbs change meaning when used reflexively.

  | | | | |
  |---|---|---|---|
  | **acostar** | *to put to bed* | **acostarse** | *to go to bed, to lie down* |
  | **dormir** | *to sleep* | **dormirse** | *to fall asleep* |
  | **levantar** | *to raise, to lift* | **levantarse** | *to get up* |
  | **llamar** | *to call* | **llamarse** | *to be called* |
  | **poner** | *to put, to place* | **ponerse** | *to put on* |
  | **quitar** | *to take away* | **quitarse** | *to take off* |

**4-33 ¿Qué hacemos todos los días?** Ponga estas actividades en el orden más lógico.

____ Me duermo.  ____ Salgo para mis clases.  ____ Me lavo la cara (*face*).
____ Me levanto.  ____ Me acuesto.  ____ Desayuno.

**4-34 ¿Tenemos las mismas rutinas?** Hablen sobre sus actividades diarias.

MODELO:    despertarse
E1: *Yo me despierto a las siete. ¿Y tú?*
E2: *Generalmente, me despierto a las ocho.*

1. levantarse      3. vestirse      5. acostarse
2. ducharse        4. desayunar     6. dormirse

**4-35 Los horarios. PRIMERA FASE.** Usen la información en la tabla para escribir un párrafo sobre el horario de las hermanas gemelas (*twins*) Alicia y Blanca y su hermanito Carlitos.

| | CARLITOS | ALICIA Y BLANCA | YO |
|---|---|---|---|
| despertarse | 8:00 | 7:00 | |
| levantarse | 8:15 | 7:05 | |
| bañarse | 8:20 | 7:10 | |
| vestirse | 8:30 | 7:20 | |

**SEGUNDA FASE.** Ahora escriba individualmente sus actividades en la tabla. Luego, hablen de su horario y hagan comparaciones entre su horario y el de las personas de la *Primera fase*.

---

**SITUACIONES**

1. **Role A.** A young person in your family has to do a report for school based on an interview of a family member. That person is going to interview you. Exchange greetings and answer his/her questions as completely as possible.

   **Role B.** You are a middle school student who has to write a report about a family member (your classmate). Greet him/her and explain the purpose of the interview. Then find out a) where he/she lives and for how long he/she has lived there; b) what his/her daily routine is; and c) some differences between the routine of a college student and that of a middle school student.

2. **Role A.** You live in Bogota, and you would like your niece to attend a summer camp (**campamento de verano**) in the United States so she will learn English. Ask the camp director questions to find out a) how many children there are per counselor (**por consejero/a**); b) what time the children get up; c) what sports they play; d) what they eat; e) what they do in the evenings; and f) what time they go to bed.

   **Role B.** You are the director of the summer camp (**campamento de verano**). Answer the questions of the aunt/uncle of a prospective camper. Add as much information as possible.

# MOSAICOS

## A escuchar

### ESTRATEGIA

**Listen for a purpose**

Listening with a purpose in mind will help you focus your attention on what is important and relevant to meet your goal. As you focus your attention, you screen what you hear and select only the information you need, letting go of what seems irrelevant to your purpose.

### Antes de escuchar

**4-36 Preparación.** Usted va a escuchar el mensaje de Pedro para Julio sobre una fiesta sorpresa (*surprise*) que está organizando Pedro. Antes de escuchar, escriba el propósito (*purpose*) posible de un mensaje como este. ¿A qué información específica es importante poner atención?

propósito posible: _____

información específica: _____

### Escuchar

**4-37 ¿Comprende usted?** First read the information you will need to have in order to attend the party Pedro is organizing. Then, as you listen, complete the sentences with the rest of the information. Don't worry if you do not understand every word.

CD 2
Track 21

1. La fiesta es para…
2. La fiesta va a ser en la casa de…
3. El día de la fiesta es…
4. Julio debe llevar (*take*)…
5. Julio tiene que llegar a la casa a las…
6. La dirección es…

### Después de escuchar

**4-38 Ahora usted.** Usted va a dar una fiesta sorpresa para un amigo/una amiga en la clase de español y desea invitar a su profesor/a de español. Complete la nota que usted va a poner en el buzón (*mailbox*) de su profesor/a.

> Estimado/a profesor/a _____:
>
> Este fin de semana, pienso dar una fiesta sorpresa para _____.
>
> ¿Le gustaría venir? Vamos a comer _____ y _____. Vamos a tener refrescos para todos.
>
> La fiesta va a ser el _____ en mi casa a las _____ de la noche.
> Mi dirección es _____.
>
> Lo/La espero el _____.
>
> Hasta pronto.
>
> _____

# A conversar

## Antes de conversar

**4-39 Preparación.** Complete las siguientes afirmaciones con los nombres de sus parientes, la relación de parentesco y sus actividades.

**MODELO:** <u>*Mi primo David come*</u> en restaurantes los fines de semana.

1. ... cerveza frecuentemente cuando mira(n) fútbol en la televisión.
2. ... mucho y con frecuencia está(n) cansado/a(s).
3. ... a conciertos de música popular.
4. ... en casa los fines de semana. Descansan, leen, escuchan música, etc.
5. ... ejercicio físico tres o cuatro veces por semana.
6. ... con amigos o con la familia en casa el día de su cumpleaños.
7. ... música romántica a todas horas.
8. ... por el teléfono celular. Llama(n) a sus amigos día y noche.

## Conversar

**4-40 Entre nosotros.** Conteste las preguntas de sus compañeros/as con los nombres de los miembros de su familia para comparar las dos categorías.

**MODELO:** E1: *¿Quiénes son las personas artísticas en tu familia, las mujeres o los hombres?*
E2: *En mi familia, las mujeres son muy artísticas. Por ejemplo, mi hermana Carlota pinta y escribe poemas. En contraste con las mujeres, los hombres son deportistas. Mi primo Alberto, por ejemplo, practica tenis y fútbol.*

1. ¿Quiénes son las personas activas en tu familia, las mujeres o los hombres?
2. ¿Qué miembros de la familia pasan mucho tiempo en casa, los jóvenes o los mayores?
3. ¿Quiénes son muy sociables, las mujeres o los hombres, los jóvenes o los mayores? ¿Por qué?

## Después de conversar

**4-41 Un poco más.** Completen un pequeño informe (*report*) con la información de su grupo de la actividad **4-40**. Luego compartan la información con el resto de la clase.

1. En nuestras familias (los hombres/las mujeres) _____ son muy activos/as. Por ejemplo, _____. Por otro lado, _____ no son muy activos. Por ejemplo, _____.
2. (Los jóvenes/Los mayores) _____ pasan mucho tiempo en casa porque _____. Por ejemplo, _____ . En cambio, _____ no pasan mucho tiempo en casa porque _____. Por ejemplo, _____ .
3. (Las mujeres/Los hombres/Los jóvenes/Los mayores) _____ son muy sociables. Por ejemplo, _____ . En contraste, _____ no son muy sociables. Por ejemplo, _____ .

# A leer

## Antes de leer

**4-42 Preparación.** Lea el título y los subtítulos del artículo a continuación y observe las fotos. Luego, use la información del título, los subtítulos y las fotos para contestar las siguientes preguntas.

1. Basándose en el título del artículo, los subtítulos, las fotos y sus leyendas (*captions*), adivine el tema del artículo.
   a. la comunicación entre amigos
   b. la comunicación entre los miembros de una familia
   c. la comunicación con los colegas en el trabajo

2. En su opinión, ¿cuáles de las siguientes ideas va a incluir el artículo? (Hay más de una respuesta correcta.)
   a. Hoy en día la comunicación entre padres e hijos es mejor que (*better than*) en el pasado.
   b. Los jóvenes no hablan con sus padres sobre sus problemas porque los padres siempre están ocupados.
   c. La vida moderna afecta la comunicación entre padres e hijos.
   d. La tecnología tiende a reducir la comunicación sobre temas importantes.

3. Marque (✓) las actividades de la siguiente lista que usted asocia usted con una buena relación entre padres e hijos.

   a. ___ conversar
   b. ___ pasar tiempo juntos
   c. ___ hablar por teléfono
   d. ___ pelear (*argue*)
   e. ___ escribir correos electrónicos a un miembro de la familia que vive lejos (*far*)
   f. ___ comprar regalos con frecuencia
   g. ___ expresar cariño (*affection*) verbalmente
   h. ___ no hablar de sus problemas con los padres

## Leer

**4-43 Primera mirada.** Lea los dos primeros párrafos del texto y siga las instrucciones.

Subraye (*Underline*)...

1. las palabras en el título que probablemente indican el tema del artículo.
2. una palabra que describe la condición de la familia de hoy.
3. una palabra que indica la importancia de la comunicación dentro de la familia.

Escriba...

4. una causa de los problemas de comunicación en la familia.
5. dos necesidades de los hijos que tienen padres que trabajan fuera de casa.
6. dos efectos de la ausencia de los padres de la casa.

# La importancia de la comunicación familiar

## La familia en crisis

Los expertos afirman que la familia de hoy está en crisis por la falta[1] de comunicación entre sus miembros o por la mala comunicación que existe entre ellos. También dicen que la comunicación es vital en todas las relaciones, especialmente en las relaciones familiares.

La comunicación entre padres e hijos sobre temas importantes forma relaciones familiares fuertes y cariñosas.

## Ausencia de los padres

¿Por qué hay problemas de comunicación en las familias? Hay varias razones. Una razón es que la madre y el padre trabajan largas horas fuera de casa y los hijos están solos mucho tiempo, sin la compañía y la supervisión de sus mayores. La ausencia casi todos los días de los padres puede crear cierta independencia en los hijos y una distancia emocional que causa dificultades en la comunicación entre padres e hijos.

## La tecnología

Un segundo factor es la tecnología. Nuestro mundo está controlado por la tecnología en casa, en el trabajo, etc. Evidentemente la tecnología facilita muchas cosas, pero su uso excesivo puede complicar la vida. Un gran número de hogares[2] están conectados a Internet, así que muchos jóvenes tienen acceso ilimitado al correo electrónico y a la Red, sobre todo a los sitios web de comunicación social y entretenimiento, como MySpace y YouTube. Idealmente, el bajo costo de la conexión debería afectar positivamente la comunicación en la familia, pero la realidad indica que la comunicación moderna (e.g., correo electrónico, mensajes de texto) tiende a ser más breve y más superficial. Los hijos prefieren no discutir sus problemas por correo electrónico o mensajes de texto. Prefieren hablar directamente con sus padres, si es que sus padres tienen el tiempo. Lo mismo ocurre con el teléfono celular. Es cierto que muchos jóvenes usan celulares para llamar a sus padres, pero no muchos usan el celular para conversar largamente con sus padres sobre temas personales importantes. ¡Muy pocos!

La tecnología puede facilitar la comunicación familiar.

## Conclusión

En conclusión, el tiempo limitado que los padres pueden dar a sus hijos y la tendencia a usar la tecnología para comunicaciones muy breves pueden afectar negativamente las relaciones familiares. Por eso es importante crear oportunidades para una comunicación real y profunda dentro de la familia. Si usted usa la tecnología de manera positiva para pasar tiempo con sus familiares y para expresar el amor y el cariño que siente por ellos, su familia va a ser más fuerte y unida.

[1] lack    [2] homes

**4-44 Segunda mirada.** Ahora lea el resto del artículo y siga las indicaciones.

En el párrafo sobre la tecnología, el artículo presenta otra razón de la mala comunicación entre padres e hijos.

Indique...

1. una palabra asociada con los problemas de comunicación familiares.
2. por qué la tecnología probablemente afecta las relaciones de la familia.
3. dos ejemplos de cómo la tecnología puede causar problemas en la familia.
4. dos palabras que indican la calidad de la comunicación cuando usamos el correo electrónico o los mensajes de texto.
5. dos formas de usar la tecnología positivamente en la comunicación con la familia.

# Después de leer

**4-45 Ampliación.** Se pueden aplicar las ideas del artículo a la situación de los estudiantes que viven en la universidad y ya no viven en casa con su familia. Hable con su compañero/a sobre el impacto en la comunicación familiar entre los estudiantes universitarios y sus padres. Enfóquese (*Focus*) en los dos temas principales del artículo:

■ la separación física entre los padres y los hijos
■ el uso de la tecnología como medio de comunicación

# A escribir

## ESTRATEGIA

**Choose between informal and formal language to express the desired tone**

Choosing the appropriate level of formality when you write to someone depends on your relationship to that person. When writing to elders in your family, such as parents or grandparents, a more formal tone may be needed than when writing to friends. The abbreviated format and casual language of computer-based communication may not be the best choice to show your elders love and respect. When you write to them, either in letters or on the computer, choose your language more carefully and write about issues more seriously than you would when corresponding with friends.

The salutation, closing, and forms of address used in letter writing also reflect your degree of closeness and formality. The expressions in *En directo* include some common salutations and forms of address that are appropriate to use when you write to elders in your family.

## Antes de escribir

**4-46 Preparación.** **PRIMERA FASE.** La madre de Julián, un alumno universitario colombiano, está triste y preocupada porque su hijo estudia en la Universidad de los Andes y vive lejos de casa. Ella le escribe la siguiente carta a su hijo. Lea la carta.

---

Querido Julián:

¿Qué tal estás? ¿Cómo van tus clases? Hace un mes que no tenemos información sobre ti. ¡No escribes correos electrónicos, no llamas por teléfono! ¿Qué ocurre?

Bueno, es el fin del semestre y debes tener mucho trabajo. ¿Estás muy estresado? ¿Duermes suficiente? ¿Comes bien en la universidad? En tu próxima visita, pienso preparar tus platos favoritos. Tu hermana Mariela, tus abuelos y tíos van a estar con nosotros y vamos a conversar largas horas.

Tengo una sorpresa para ti. Gustavo tiene novia. Se llama Alicia. Pasan mucho tiempo juntos; van al cine, salen a comer por las noches, etc. La semana próxima ambos tienen vacaciones y, para conocerla un poco más, Gustavo piensa ir a Cartagena con ella. Las temperaturas allí están perfectas para nadar y descansar un poco.

Tengo que confesarte que tu padre y yo pensamos mucho en ti. ¿Por qué no escribes? ¿Tienes problemas en tus clases? ¿Trabajas mucho? ¿Estás desconectado de Internet? Por favor, escribe o llama pronto.

Un beso de papá, Mariela y toda la familia.

Abrazos,

Tu madre

**SEGUNDA FASE.** Usted es Julián. Prepárese para responder a la carta de su madre. Haga lo siguiente:

1. Identifique las preguntas de su madre que usted quiere contestar y escriba algunas ideas que piensa incluir. Seleccione las palabras adecuadas para lograr (*achieve*) el tono adecuado.
2. Escriba algunas preguntas que usted quiere hacerle a su madre: sobre su padre, sus hermanos, sus abuelos, su perro o gato, etc.

## Escribir

**4-47 Manos a la obra.** Ahora responda a la carta de su madre. Use la información de la *Segunda fase* de la actividad **4-46**. Seleccione cuidadosamente las palabras para mostrar respeto a su madre. Recuerde incluir la fecha, un saludo y una despedida (*closing*) apropiados.

Querida madre:

## Después de escribir

**4-48 Revisión.** Revise los siguientes aspectos de su carta.

1. Primero, el grado de intimidad (*intimacy*) y formalidad para comunicarse con su madre. ¿Incluye usted un saludo y una despedida apropiados en la carta? ¿Usa usted el vocabulario adecuado para dirigirse (*address*) a su madre?
2. La coherencia de sus ideas y la cantidad de información que su madre probablemente desea
3. Luego, la precisión gramatical: la estructura de las oraciones, la concordancia, etc.
4. Finalmente, la ortografía, la acentuación

# ENFOQUE CULTURAL

## La riqueza de Colombia

Normalmente asociamos a Colombia con el café de Juan Valdez, un personaje inventado por las agencias de publicidad, como el representante de Colombia ante el mundo. En realidad, Colombia se conoce en todas partes por la calidad suave de su café y el símbolo de Juan Valdez es una de las imágenes corporativas más famosas del mundo. Sin embargo, Colombia es mucho más que su café. Su diversidad geográfica y climática, y la variedad natural, étnica y cultural de sus regiones hacen de Colombia un país con un inmenso potencial.

Para empezar, Colombia es el único país de América del Sur que tiene costas en los dos mares. La costa Atlántica, que es la región caribeña, tiene playas espectaculares, montañas impresionantes en la Sierra Nevada de Santa Marta, selvas tropicales en el Urabá y un desierto en La Guajira. Los habitantes de la costa Atlántica tienen fama de tener un carácter alegre y festivo. La costa Pacífica es la región con mayor biodiversidad del mundo y es la región más lluviosa del planeta. Una gran parte de la población afro-colombiana habita en las dos costas.

Las cinco regiones de Colombia continental

En contraste, la Amazonía colombiana forma parte de la zona de selvas tropicales que se extienden a Perú, Brasil y Venezuela para formar el "pulmón del mundo". Se llama así porque es la zona donde se produce la mayor cantidad del oxígeno que respiramos. En esta región se hablan más de cien idiomas indígenas, y hay una gran variedad de animales y plantas. Los indígenas de la región usan muchas de estas plantas como medicinas y muchos científicos investigan los beneficios de estas plantas para la medicina. En la Amazonía, por ejemplo, hay una estación científica para el estudio de la malaria, donde el Dr. Manuel Patarroyo hace investigación para encontrar una vacuna contra esta enfermedad.

La región de los Llanos Orientales está formada por grandes praderas que se extienden a Venezuela. Colombia y Venezuela son dos países hermanos que están unidos por su historia y geografía. La ganadería y la agricultura son las actividades más importantes de esta región. En efecto, los llaneros o habitantes de esta región, son muy aficionados a los caballos y en las fiestas populares practican un deporte similar al rodeo para demostrar sus destrezas. Además, los Llanos Orientales son el hábitat de una gran variedad de aves, reptiles, mamíferos y peces. Esta es la única región de Colombia donde habita el oso hormiguero, un bello animal que come hormigas.

El oso hormiguero habita en los Llanos Orientales de Colombia.

Medellín, conocida como "la capital de la montaña"

La región andina de Colombia es la zona central del país. Precisamente en esta región, cerca de la ciudad de Armenia, se produce el mejor café de Colombia. Está formada por la Cordillera de los Andes y es el lugar donde vive la gran mayoría de los colombianos. Aquí están las ciudades más grandes del país: Bogotá, la capital; Medellín, la ciudad más industrial; Cali, la tercera ciudad más grande de Colombia. La mayoría de la clase media de Colombia vive en las ciudades de la zona central y aquí se encuentran también las universidades más importantes del país, que atraen a jóvenes de todas las regiones colombianas.

Además de las cinco regiones continentales, Colombia tiene una región insular. Las Islas de San Andrés y Providencia están en el Caribe y son un verdadero paraíso tropical. Sus playas blancas, las aguas cristalinas y tranquilas del mar, sus bellas palmeras y sus excelentes restaurantes hacen de estas islas un lugar ideal para el turismo. Las otras islas colombianas están en el Océano Pacífico y son una reserva natural y ecológica. Cerca de la Isla Gorgona se pueden ver ballenas durante gran parte del año.

**4-49 Comprensión.** PRIMERA FASE. **Reconocimiento de palabras clave.** Encuentre en el texto la palabra o expresión que mejor expresa el significado de las siguientes ideas.

1. mild, soft          _____
2. to begin with        _____
3. rainy               _____
4. lung                _____
5. research            _____
6. vaccine             _____
7. ant                 _____

SEGUNDA FASE. **Oraciones importantes.** Subraye las afirmaciones que contienen ideas que se encuentran en el texto. Luego indique en qué parte del texto están.

1. Juan Valdez was created by a marketing agency.
2. The Pacific coast of Colombia is the rainiest region in the world.
3. Most of the oxygen in the Earth's atmosphere is produced in the Amazon region.
4. Manuel Patarroyo is a Colombian who is searching for a cure for HIV.
5. Spanish is the only language spoken in the Amazonian region of Colombia.
6. The Eastern Prairies (*Llanos Orientales*) of Colombia extend into Venezuela, giving these sister countries a common geography.
7. Different varieties of anteaters can be found all over Colombia.
8. Most Colombians live in the Andean region.

TERCERA FASE. **Ideas principales.** Escriba un párrafo breve en inglés resumiendo (*summarizing*) las ideas principales expresadas en el texto.

 **4-50 Use la información.** Prepare un afiche (*poster*) para hacer una presentación sobre dos colombianos famosos. Elija personas que representen áreas diferentes de la vida colombiana, como la política, las artes, la música, los deportes, etc. Incluya fotos y la siguiente información: lugar donde viven, el trabajo que hacen y otra información de interés. Para preparar esta actividad visite la página web de *Mosaicos* y siga los enlaces útiles.

# VOCABULARIO

| La familia | The family |
|---|---|
| la abuela | grandmother |
| el abuelo | grandfather |
| el ahijado/la ahijada | godchild |
| la esposa | wife |
| el esposo | husband |
| la hermana | sister |
| el hermano | brother |
| el hermanastro | stepbrother |
| la hermanastra | stepsister |
| la hija | daughter |
| el hijo | son |
| el hijo único/la hija única | only child |
| la madrastra | stepmother |
| la madre | mother |
| la madrina | godmother |
| la mamá | mom |
| la media hermana | half-sister |
| el medio hermano | half-brother |
| la nieta | granddaughter |
| el nieto | grandson |
| el niño/la niña | child |
| la novia | fiancée, girlfriend |
| el novio | fiancé, boyfriend |
| el padrastro | stepfather |
| el padre | father |
| los padres | parents |
| el padrino | godfather |
| el papá | dad |
| el pariente | relative |
| el primo/la prima | cousin |
| la sobrina | niece |
| el sobrino | nephew |
| la tía | aunt |
| el tío | uncle |

| Verbos | Verbs |
|---|---|
| acostar(se) (ue) | to put to bed; to go to bed |
| afeitar(se) | to shave; to shave (oneself) |
| almorzar (ue) | to have lunch |
| bañar(se) | to bathe; to take a bath |
| casar(se) | to get married |
| cerrar(ie) | to close |
| costar (ue) | to cost |
| decir (g, i) | to say, to tell |
| desayunar | to have breakfast |
| despertar(se) (ie) | to wake (someone up); to wake up |
| dormir(se) (ue) | to sleep; to fall asleep |
| dormir (ue) la siesta | to take a nap |
| duchar(se) | to give a shower to; to take a shower |
| empezar (ie) | to begin, to start |

| | |
|---|---|
| entender (ie) | to understand |
| jugar (ue) | to play (a game, sport) |
| lavar(se) | to wash (oneself) |
| levantar(se) | to raise; to get up |
| maquillar(se) | to put makeup on (someone); to put makeup on (oneself) |
| pasar | to spend (time) |
| pasear | to take a walk, to stroll |
| pedir (i) | to ask for; to order |
| peinar(se) | to comb (someone's hair); to comb (one's hair) |
| pensar (ie) | to think |
| pensar (ie) + infinitive | to plan to + verb |
| poder (ue) | to be able to, can |
| poner(se) (g) la ropa | to put one's clothes on |
| preferir (ie) | to prefer |
| querer (ie) | to want |
| quitar(se) | to take away; to take off |
| secar(se) | to dry (oneself) |
| seguir (i) | to follow, to go on |
| sentarse (ie) | to sit down |
| sentir(se) (ie) | to feel |
| servir (i) | to serve |
| tener (g, ie) | to have |
| venir (g, ie) | to come |
| vestir(se) (i) | to dress; to get dressed |
| visitar | to visit |
| volver (ue) | to return |

| Las descripciones | Descriptions |
|---|---|
| divorciado/a | divorced |
| gemelo/a | twin |
| ocupado/a | busy |

| Palabras y expresiones útiles | Useful words and expressions |
|---|---|
| el bautizo | baptism, christening |
| la derecha | right |
| la foto(grafía) | photo(graph) |
| la izquierda | left |
| juntos/as | together |
| el/la mayor | the oldest |
| el/la menor | the youngest |
| la noticia | news |
| tarde | late |
| temprano | early |
| un poco | a little |

> See *Lengua* box on page 129 for time expressions.
> See *Lengua* box on page 134 for other expressions with *pensar*.
> See page 138 for a list of adverbs.
> See page 140 for time expressions with *hacer*.

153

CAPÍTULO

5

# Mi casa es su casa

*Cuadro de un pueblo hondureño*, Jorge Fermán, pintor de Honduras

# In this chapter you will learn how to:

- discuss housing, furnishings, and architecture
- talk about daily chores and household activities
- talk about activities in progress
- describe physical and emotional states

**Cultural focus: Nicaragua, El Salvador, Honduras**

*Mar Caribe*

BELICE

MÉXICO

Ruinas mayas

HONDURAS

GUATEMALA

Copán    Tegucigalpa ⊛

El café

EL SALVADOR
San Salvador ⊛

NICARAGUA

Mango verde
con limón y sal

León •

Un edificio de arquitectura colonial

Managua ⊛

El Volcán de Izalco

Granada

COSTA
RICA

OCÉANO PACÍFICO

PANAMÁ

**A vista de pájaro.** Mire el mapa y después asocie la información de las dos columnas.

1. ___ Tegucigalpa...
2. ___ El mango verde con limón y sal...
3. ___ Al oeste de El Salvador...
4. ___ Las ruinas de Copán...
5. ___ El café...
6. ___ Granada y otras ciudades de Nicaragua...

a. es un plato típico de El Salvador.
b. es un producto de exportación de los tres países.
c. es la capital de Honduras.
d. tienen arquitectura colonial.
e. son de la civilización maya.
f. está el volcán de Izalco.

## ·)) En casa

CD 2
Track 26
or CD 3
Track 1

En las ciudades de Nicaragua, El Salvador, Honduras, y hay **viviendas** de diferentes **estilos**. La ciudad de Granada, en Nicaragua, tiene **calles** y plazas como esta, con casas coloniales de colores alegres. En Tegucigalpa, la capital de Honduras, hay **edificios** de **apartamentos**. Algunas personas prefieren vivir **cerca** del **centro**. **Creen** que los **barrios** de las **afueras** están muy **lejos** del **trabajo** y de los centros de diversión.

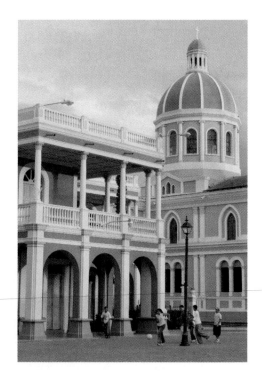

| Alquileres | |
|---|---|
| **Categoría:** | Alquiler Apartamentos |
| **Ciudad:** | Tegucigalpa |
| **Ubicación:** | Palmira |
| **Descripción:** | PALMIRA ALQUILER DE APARTAMENTO MUY AMPLIO, CÉNTRICO Y ACCESIBLE, 2 HABITACIONES, SALA–COMEDOR, COCINA, 1 BAÑO, ÁREA DE LAVANDERÍA, ESTACIONAMIENTO, TELÉFONO. |
| **Precio:** | $ 450,00 |

### En otras palabras

Some words for the parts of a house vary from one region to another in the Spanish-speaking world. Here are some examples:

**habitación, dormitorio, cuarto, alcoba, recámara**

**sala, salón, living**

**planta, piso**

**piscina, pileta, alberca**

# El apartamento del anuncio

CD 2
Track 27
and
CD 3
Track 2

MARTA DÍAZ: Hola, buenos días. Me llamo Marta Díaz. ¿Es posible visitar el apartamento del anuncio?

DIEGO LÓPEZ: Sí, claro. Mucho gusto, señorita Díaz. Yo soy Diego López. Pase, pase. Como usted puede ver, el apartamento es muy alegre.

MARTA DÍAZ: ¡Ah, sí! Tiene muchas ventanas.

DIEGO LÓPEZ: Esta es la **sala**. Es muy grande. Junto a la sala hay un **comedor** pequeño y al lado está la **cocina**.

MARTA DÍAZ: ¡La cocina es lindísima!

DIEGO LÓPEZ: Sí, todos los **electrodomésticos** son nuevos. A la izquierda del **pasillo** hay dos **habitaciones** y un **baño**.

MARTA DÍAZ: Esta habitación tiene muy buena **vista** al **jardín**. Además, los **muebles** son de buena calidad. Me gusta el apartamento. ¿Cuánto es el **alquiler**?

DIEGO LÓPEZ: 8.000 lempiras al mes.

MARTA DÍAZ: Pues, señor López, me encantan el apartamento y esta **zona** céntrica. Y el precio es muy bueno. Voy a decidir esta noche y lo llamo mañana.

DIEGO LÓPEZ: Perfecto, señorita Díaz. Hasta mañana.

---

**En otras palabras**

The Spanish word for *apartment* varies according to the country. **El apartamento** is used in Central America, Colombia, and Venezuela, while **el departamento** is common in Mexico, Argentina, Peru and Chile. The word used in Spain is **el piso**.

---

**En otras palabras**

The expressions **Pase(n)** and **Adelante** invite people to enter a room or a house in many Spanish-speaking countries. In others, like Colombia, the expression **Siga(n)** is preferred.

---

**5-1 Asociación.** Indique si las siguientes afirmaciones son ciertas (**C**) o falsas (**F**), según el diálogo anterior.

1. ___ Marta Díaz quiere comprar el apartamento.
2. ___ La sala es pequeña.
3. ___ El apartamento tiene dos baños.
4. ___ Los electrodomésticos son nuevos.
5. ___ Los muebles son de buena calidad.
6. ___ A Marta no le gusta la zona céntrica.

**5-2 ¿En qué piso viven?** Pregúntele a su compañero/a dónde viven las diferentes personas. Su compañero/a debe contestarle de acuerdo con el dibujo (*drawing*).

MODELO: E1: *¿Dónde viven los Girondo?*
E2: *Viven en el cuarto piso, en el apartamento 4-A.*

---

**Lengua**

Ordinal numbers are adjectives and agree in gender and number with the noun they modify (e.g., **la segunda casa, el cuarto edificio**). **Primero** and **tercero** drop the final **-o** when used before a masculine singular noun.

el **primer** apartamento
el **tercer** piso

---

*Cultura*

Notice that the first floor is normally called **la planta baja** in most Hispanic countries. The second floor is called **el primer piso**.

---

décimo: Rodríguez
noveno: Peralta
octavo: Elizondo
séptimo: Díaz
sexto: Gómez
quinto: Lizaur
cuarto: Sánchez
tercero: Carreras
segundo: Iglesias
primer piso: Olmos
planta baja

| | |
|---|---|
| 5-A López | 5-B Alemán |
| 4-A Girondo | 4-B Mujica |
| 3-A Ozollo | 3-B Ponce |
| 2-A Cárdenas | 2-B García-Gil |
| 1-A Jiménez | 1-B Valbuena |
| PB-A Martínez | PB-B Casal |

**5-3 Un hotel de lujo.** Ustedes van a gastar los millones que ganaron (*won*) en la lotería para construir un hotel de lujo en la Bahía de Jiquilisco, cerca de San Salvador. Decidan cómo distribuir los siguientes espacios del hotel.

MODELO:      el restaurante
  E1: *¿En qué piso vamos a poner el restaurante?*
  E2: *Debe estar en la planta baja.*

1. la discoteca
2. la recepción
3. el gimnasio
4. la oficina de seguridad

5. las habitaciones
6. la piscina
7. la cafetería con vista a la playa
8. el salón de computadoras

 **5-4 Agentes de bienes raíces (*real estate*). PRIMERA FASE.** Los fines de semana ustedes trabajan en una agencia de bienes raíces. Para vender o alquilar la casa del dibujo escriban un anuncio similar al anuncio de la página 156.

Incluyan la siguiente información en su anuncio:

1. número de habitaciones
2. número de baños
3. distribución (*layout*) de los cuartos
4. color de la sala
5. otras características (garaje, jardín, sótano [*basement*], ático, etc.)

6. localización de la casa en relación al centro de la ciudad
7. localización de la casa en relación a la universidad
8. precio de la casa

**SEGUNDA FASE.** Presenten su anuncio al resto de la clase y contesten las preguntas de sus compañeros sobre la casa que quieren vender o alquilar.

 **5-5 Ventajas y desventajas.** Discutan los aspectos positivos y negativos de los siguientes temas relacionados con la vivienda. Escriban una ventaja y una desventaja para cada uno de los siguientes puntos. Después compartan sus opiniones con el resto de la clase.

| | VENTAJAS | DESVENTAJAS |
|---|---|---|
| 1. vivir en un apartamento | | |
| 2. vivir en una casa | | |
| 3. tener una piscina | | |
| 4. vivir con un compañero/una compañera de cuarto/casa | | |

# La casa, los muebles y los electrodomésticos

CD 2
Track 28
or CD 3
Track 3

## 5-6 ¿Aparatos eléctricos, muebles o accesorios? PRIMERA FASE. Escriba cada una de las siguientes palabras en la columna apropiada.

| la alfombra | el cuadro | el/la radio |
| el armario | la butaca | el refrigerador |
| la cómoda | el horno | las sábanas |
| las cortinas | el lavaplatos | la silla |

| APARATOS ELÉCTRICOS | MUEBLES | ACCESORIOS |
|---|---|---|
|  |  |  |
|  |  |  |
|  |  |  |
|  |  |  |

**SEGUNDA FASE.** Respondan a las siguientes preguntas relacionadas con la *Primera fase*.

1. Según ustedes, ¿qué aparato eléctrico cuesta más dinero?
2. ¿Qué muebles necesita todos los días un/a estudiante? ¿Necesita un aparato electrónico también? ¿Cuál?
3. ¿Qué accesorios tienen ustedes en su cuarto?
4. ¿En qué parte de la casa generalmente están estos objetos?

**5-7 El curioso.** Intercambien preguntas para describir los cuartos de la casa/el apartamento de cada uno/a. Traten (*Try*) de obtener la mayor información posible.

MODELO:   E1:   *¿Cómo es la sala de tu casa?*
          E2:   *Es pequeña. Hay una alfombra verde y un sofá grande. También hay dos sillas modernas y una mesa con una lámpara. ¿Y cómo es tu dormitorio?*

**5-8 Preparativos. PRIMERA FASE.** Usted va a mudarse (*move*) a una casa muy grande y tiene que comprar muchas cosas. Organice su lista de compras según las siguientes categorías.

|  | MUEBLES | ACCESORIOS | ELECTRODOMÉSTICOS/ APARATOS ELECTRÓNICOS |
|---|---|---|---|
| para el dormitorio |  |  |  |
| para la sala |  |  |  |
| para el comedor |  |  |  |
| para la cocina |  |  |  |

**SEGUNDA FASE.** Comparta la lista con su compañero/a. Él/Ella le va recordar (*remind you about*) otras cosas que probablemente va a necesitar.

MODELO:   E1:   *Voy a comprar una cama nueva para el dormitorio.*
          E2:   *¿No vas a comprar sábanas y mantas?/¿Y no necesitas un sofá?*

**5-9  Por catálogo.** Miren las fotos del catálogo y elijan (*choose*) un producto de cada categoría. Intercambien sus preferencias y expliquen en qué lugar de la casa van a poner estos accesorios. Las palabras de la lista los/las pueden ayudar.

barato/a       caro/a          de buena calidad      grande        pequeño/a
bonito/a       confortable     de color...           lindo/a

MODELO:   E1:   *Me gusta la primera toalla porque no es cara y es muy linda. Es para el cuarto de baño.*
          E2:   *Yo prefiero la tercera porque es más grande.*

# •)) Las tareas domésticas

CD 2
Track 29
or CD 3
Track 4

Gustavo **lava** los **platos**.

Beatriz **seca** los platos.

Beatriz **cocina**. Ella usa mucho los electrodomésticos.

Gustavo **limpia** el baño y **pasa** la **aspiradora**.

Gustavo **saca** la **basura**.

Gustavo **barre** la terraza.

la lavadora    la secadora

Beatriz **tiende** la **ropa**.

Después la **dobla** cuando está **seca**.

Beatriz **plancha** la ropa.

**5-10 Por la mañana.** ¿En qué orden hace usted estas actividades por la mañana? Use las siguientes expresiones para indicar el orden: **primero, luego, más tarde, después, finalmente.** Compare sus respuestas con las de su compañero/a.

___ lavar los platos        ___ desayunar
___ preparar el café        ___ secar los platos
___ salir para la universidad     ___ hacer la cama

**5-11 Actividades en la casa.** Pregúntele a su compañero/a dónde hace estas cosas normalmente cuando está en casa.

MODELO:    E1:   *¿Dónde ves televisión?*
           E2:   *Veo televisión en mi cuarto. ¿Y tú?* O
               *No veo televisión. ¿Y tú?*

1. dormir la siesta             5. pasar la aspiradora
2. escuchar música            6. estudiar para un examen
3. planchar                    7. tender la ropa
4. lavar la ropa               8. hablar por teléfono con amigos/as

**5-12 ¡A compartir las tareas!** PRIMERA FASE. Ustedes van a compartir una casa el próximo año académico. Preparen una lista de todas las tareas domésticas que van a hacer.

SEGUNDA FASE. Discutan qué tareas va a hacer cada uno/a de ustedes según sus gustos. Finalmente, hagan un calendario de tareas y compártanlo con el resto de la clase.

MODELO: *A mí me gusta planchar la ropa pero a mi compañero/a no le gusta. Por eso, yo voy a planchar la ropa los lunes por la tarde.*

CD 2
Track 30
or CD 3
Track 5

**5-13 El agente de bienes raíces.** PRIMERA FASE. Mr. and Mrs. Mena and their two children live in San Salvador. They have decided to move to a larger place and they are talking to a real estate agent. Before you listen, write down the kind of dwelling and the characteristics of the neighborhood they may be looking for.

SEGUNDA FASE. Now, as you listen, circle the letter next to the correct information.

1. Los señores Mena quieren comprar…
   a. una casa.
   b. un apartamento.

2. El señor y la señora Mena prefieren vivir…
   a. en una buena zona.
   b. lejos de un parque.

3. El agente de bienes raíces…
   a. no sabe cómo ayudarlos.
   b. tiene una casa buena para ellos.

4. El agente dice que la casa del barrio La Mascota…
   a. cuesta mucho.
   b. tiene un buen precio.

5. El señor Mena dice que…
   a. los niños necesitan estar al aire libre para jugar.
   b. los niños no necesitan jugar al aire libre.

# EN ACCIÓN

## Diarios de bicicleta: El apartamento

### Antes de ver

**5-14** **PRIMERA FASE.** En este segmento, Javier está buscando un lugar para vivir. Escriba cuatro muebles o accesorios que probablemente va a necesitar para su habitación o apartamento.

**SEGUNDA FASE.** ¿Qué características le parecen a usted más importantes cuando busca un apartamento o una habitación? Marque (✓) sus respuestas.

1. ___ Está cerca de la universidad o del trabajo.
2. ___ Es barato/a.
3. ___ Tiene mucha luz natural.
4. ___ Es grande.
5. ___ Está amueblado/a.

### Mientras ve

**5-15** Marque (✓) lo que Javier menciona cuando le describe un apartamento a Daniel.

En la sala:
___ la mesa
___ el sofá
___ la silla
___ el televisor
___ la lámpara

En la cocina:
___ el microondas
___ la estufa
___ el lavaplatos
___ el fregadero
___ el refrigerador

En el baño:
___ el inodoro
___ la ducha
___ la bañera
___ el lavabo
___ el jacuzzi

En el cuarto:
___ el clóset
___ la mesa de noche
___ la lámpara
___ la cama
___ la alfombra

### Después de ver

**5-16** Al final de este segmento, Javier decide compartir casa con Daniel. Imagine cómo es esta casa y escriba cinco oraciones para describirla.

# FUNCIONES Y FORMAS

## 1. Expressing ongoing actions: Present progressive

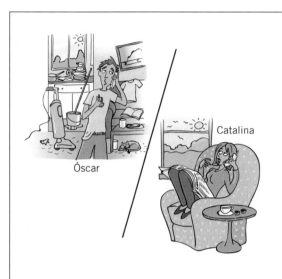

Óscar

Catalina

| | |
|---|---|
| ÓSCAR: | ¿Aló? |
| CATALINA: | Hola, Óscar. Te habla Catalina. ¿Qué **estás haciendo**? |
| ÓSCAR: | Hola, Catalina. **¡Estoy trabajando** mucho! |
| CATALINA: | ¿Por qué? |
| ÓSCAR: | Mis padres **están pasando** sus vacaciones en la playa y vuelven mañana. ¡La casa es un desastre total! |
| CATALINA: | ¿Así que **estás limpiando**? |
| ÓSCAR: | ¡Claro! **Estoy barriendo** el piso, **ordenando** la sala, **recogiendo** la ropa… de mi cuarto. Y tú, ¿qué **estás haciendo**? |
| CATALINA: | ¿Yo?… Nada. **Estoy leyendo** el periódico y **tomando** un café. |

**Piénselo.** Indique las oraciones que son **ciertas** (**C**) o **falsas** (**F**), de acuerdo con la conversación entre Catalina y Óscar.

1. ___ Catalina y Óscar **están trabajando** juntos.
2. ___ Óscar **está descansando**.
3. ___ Óscar **está pasando** sus vacaciones con sus padres en la playa.
4. ___ Óscar **está limpiando** la casa de sus padres.
5. ___ Óscar no está contento porque él **está trabajando** mucho en casa.

■ Use the present progressive to emphasize that an action or event is in progress at the moment of speaking, rather than a habitual action.

| | |
|---|---|
| Óscar **está limpiando** la casa. | *Oscar is cleaning the house.* (at this moment) |
| Óscar **limpia** la casa. | *Oscar cleans the house.* (habitually) |

■ Form the present progressive with the present tense of **estar** + *present participle*. To form the present participle, add **-ando** to the stem of **-ar** verbs and **-iendo** to the stem of **-er** and **-ir** verbs.

| ESTAR | | PRESENT PARTICIPLE |
|---|---|---|
| yo | **estoy** | |
| tú | **estás** | hablando |
| Ud., él, ella | **está** | comiendo |
| nosotros/as | **estamos** | escribiendo |
| vosotros/as | **estáis** | |
| Uds., ellos/as | **están** | |

■ When the verb stem of an **-er** or an **-ir** verb ends in a vowel, add **-yendo**.

leer → le**yendo**

oír → o**yendo**

■ Stem-changing **-ir** verbs (**o → ue**, **e → ie**, **e → i**) change **o → u** and **e → i** in the present participle.

dormir (ue)  (**o → u**)  d**u**rmiendo

sentir (ie)  (**e → i**)  s**i**ntiendo

pedir (ie)  (**e → i**)  p**i**diendo

■ Spanish does not use the present progressive to express future time, as English does; Spanish uses the present tense instead.

**Salgo** mañana.  *I am leaving tomorrow.*

¿**Te levantas** temprano mañana?  *Are you getting up early tomorrow?*

**5-17 Un día ocupado.** Hoy es un día muy ocupado para la familia Villa. Asocie las acciones de la columna de la izquierda con las explicaciones de la columna de la derecha para averiguar (*find out*) por qué.

1. ___ La Sra. Villa está preparando una cena deliciosa y un pastel (*cake*) especial.
2. ___ Su hijo Marcelo está barriendo la terraza.
3. ___ Su hija Ana está lavando los platos en el fregadero.
4. ___ Alicia está decorando la mesa.
5. ___ Pedro está hablando por teléfono.

a. Está llamando a su mejor amigo para invitarlo a la fiesta.
b. El lavaplatos no está funcionando.
c. Es una ocasión especial.
d. Es el cumpleaños de su esposo.
e. Está muy sucia (*dirty*) y unos amigos vienen a celebrar el cumpleaños.

Rodrigo   Soledad

**5-18 La vida activa.** Túrnense para describir lo que está haciendo cada persona en estas escenas. Indiquen en qué lugar de la casa está cada uno de ellos. Luego, imaginen lo que, según ustedes, cada persona va a hacer más tarde.

**MODELO:** E1: *Rodrigo y Soledad están cantando en una fiesta. Están en la terraza.*
E2: *Después van a bailar y conversar con sus amigos.*

Pepe   Catalina   Arturo   Gonzalo   Carlos

**5-19 Lugares y actividades.** PRIMERA FASE. Miren las siguientes fotografías de celebraciones y hagan lo siguiente:

## SITUACIONES

1. **Role A.** Your best friend calls to invite you to go out. Respond that you and your housemates are busy cleaning the apartment. Explain the chores that each of you is doing.

   **Role B.** Call your best friend to invite her/him to go out with you. Ask what your friend and her/his roommates are doing. Ask if your friend can go out later (**más tarde**).

2. **Role A.** There is a big family gathering at your aunt's house today, but you are away at school. Call and greet the family member who answers the phone. Explain that you will not be attending, and excuse yourself for not being there. Ask how everyone is and what each family member is doing at the moment.

   **Role B.** You are at a big family gathering today. A family member calls to say he/she can't attend. Answer the phone. Greet the caller and answer his/her questions. Finally, mention that everyone says hello (**todos te mandan saludos**) and say good-bye.

1.

3.

2.

Asocien las fotos con el país/los países en que probablemente se realiza cada una: Foto **1.** ____, **2.** ____, **3.** ____
a. España          c. México          e. Uruguay
b. Estados Unidos  d. Ecuador         f. en muchos países

SEGUNDA FASE. Descríbanle a otra pareja dos o tres actividades que las personas están haciendo en la escena de una de las fotos. La otra pareja debe adivinar el nombre del lugar. Luego, entre todos, escriban una descripción completa de una de las fotos. Incluyan el nombre de la fiesta o celebración, su significado cultural y las actividades de las personas en la foto.

# 2. Describing physical and emotional states: Expressions with *tener*

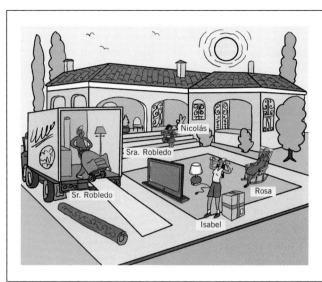

Hoy es un día de verano y los Robledo se mudan. **Tienen prisa** porque ya son las tres de la tarde. El señor Robledo y su hija Isabel **tienen calor** porque hace cuatro horas que trabajan bajo (*under*) el sol. Ella **tiene mucha sed** y está bebiendo agua. El bebé, Nicolás, llora porque **tiene hambre**. La señora Robledo le da de comer mientras la abuelita Rosa duerme la siesta. Después de empacar su ropa y todas sus fotografías, libros y plantas, Rosa **tiene mucho sueño**. ¡Qué día para los Robledo!

**Piénselo.**  Asocie la descripción del estado físico con la(s) persona(s) del dibujo. Escriba el nombre de la(s) persona(s) al lado de la descripción.

_____ 1. Va a comer porque **tiene hambre**.
_____ 2. Está tomando agua porque **tiene sed**.
_____ 3. No **tienen frío** porque es verano y hace calor.
_____ 4. Está cansada y **tiene sueño**.
_____ 5. **Tienen calor** porque están trabajando bajo el sol.
_____ 6. **Tienen prisa** porque quieren salir pronto.

■ Spanish uses **tener** + *noun* for many conditions and states where English uses *to be* + *adjective*. You have already seen the expression **tener... años: Eduardo tiene veinte años.** Here are some other useful expressions.

| TENER + *NOUN* | | |
|---|---|---|
| | hambre | *hungry* |
| | sed | *thirsty* |
| | sueño | *sleepy* |
| | miedo | *afraid* |
| tener { | calor | *hot* |
| | cuidado | to be { *careful* |
| | frío | *cold* |
| | suerte | *lucky* |
| | prisa | *in a hurry/rush* |
| | razón | *right, correct* |

■ With these expressions, use **mucho/a** to indicate *very*.

Tengo **mucho** calor (frío, miedo, sueño, cuidado).      *I am very hot (cold, afraid, sleepy, careful).*

Tienen **mucha** hambre (sed, suerte).      *They are very hungry (thirsty, lucky).*

**5-20 Asociaciones.** Lea las situaciones en que están usted y algunos miembros de su familia. Luego asocie las situaciones con las expresiones de la derecha.

1. Mi hermano siempre tiene _____ y, por eso, está comiendo ahora.
2. Mi hermana duerme a todas horas porque siempre tiene _____ .
3. En este momento mis primos están visitando la Antártida; probablemente tienen _____ .
4. Mis abuelos están bebiendo agua en la cocina porque tienen _____ .
5. Mi mamá tiene _____ ; siempre gana (*wins*) cuando juega a la lotería.
6. ¡Uf! Todavía estoy planchando mi blusa y mis amigos van a llegar en cinco minutos. Yo tengo _____ .

     **a.** sed
     **b.** prisa
     **c.** suerte
     **d.** sueño
     **e.** mucho frío
     **f.** hambre

**5-21 ¿Qué están haciendo, dónde están y cómo se sienten?** PRIMERA FASE. Observen a las personas en los dibujos y hagan lo siguiente.

1. Digan qué está(n) haciendo la(s) persona(s) y dónde está(n).
2. Describan su estado físico.

MODELO: *El padre y su hijo están durmiendo en el sofá. Tienen sueño.*

1.

2.

3.

4.

**SEGUNDA FASE.** Respondan a las siguientes preguntas sobre las escenas de la *Primera fase*. Expliquen.

1. ¿Cuál de los dibujos describe mejor cómo se sienten ustedes en este momento?
2. ¿Qué dibujo refleja (*reflects*) el clima de su región en diciembre?
3. ¿A qué hora se sienten ustedes como las personas del dibujo del modelo?

## 5-22 ¿Estados de ánimo (*moods*) semejantes o diferentes? PRIMERA FASE. Primero, termine las siguientes ideas y, luego, compare sus respuestas con las de su compañero/a. Tome apuntes de las respuestas de su compañero/a. Use expresiones con **tener**.

1. En las mañanas de invierno, yo siempre _____ .
2. Cuando mi madre pasa mucho tiempo limpiando nuestra casa, ella

   _____ .
3. Generalmente, cuando mis hermanos y yo hacemos barbacoa, nosotros

   _____ .
4. Cuando yo leo un libro aburrido, siempre _____ .
5. Inmediatamente yo _____ cuando llego a casa y mi esposo está preparando mi plato favorito.

**SEGUNDA FASE.** Usando sus apuntes de la *Primera fase*, escriba una semejanza y una diferencia entre usted y su compañero/a.

## SITUACIONES

1. **Role A.** You share an apartment with a messy friend. Complain to him/her that a) his/her books, backpack, etc., are always all over the living room; b) he/she uses a lot of dishes, but never washes them; c) his/her bottles of soft drinks (**botellas de refrescos**) are always on the table; and d) he/she makes a lot of noise (**ruido**) during the night and you can't sleep.

   **Role B.** The friend with whom you share an apartment has some complaints about you. Apologize and explain that you a) don't pick up your books or wash the dishes because you are always in a rush to do homework; b) drink a lot of soft drinks because you are always thirsty; and c) go to bed late because you're not sleepy before midnight or later and also because you're scared at night. Say as convincingly as you can that you are going to be more careful in the future.

2. **Role A.** You are a young child. It is a busy Saturday morning at your house, and nobody is paying any attention to you. Go to your parent and say the following: a) You are hungry and want to eat; b) you are thirsty and want some juice; and c) you are bored and want to play outside. What you really want is your parent's attention, so you react negatively to suggestions that you entertain yourself.

   **Role B.** You are the parent of a young child. You are really busy, and you think your child is old enough to take care himself/herself for awhile. When your child makes demands, say that if he/she a) is hungry, there is fruit in the kitchen; b) is thirsty, there is orange juice in the refrigerator; c) is bored, he/she has a lot of toys (**juguetes**) in his/her room. Explain that you are in a hurry and cannot play outside. Suggest things your child can do while you are busy with your household tasks.

## 3. Avoiding repetition in speaking and writing: Direct object nouns and pronouns

### A.

## ¿Qué hacen estas personas?

### B.

### C.

La abuela cuida (*takes care of*) a la niña.
**La** cuida todos los días.

El padre lava los platos y los niños **los** secan.

Las señoras preparan la comida en la cocina del restaurante y después **la** sirven.

**Piénselo.** Ponga la letra de la foto correcta al lado de la descripción.

1. ___ La niña está contenta porque su abuela **la** cuida.
2. ___ El padre trabaja y los niños **lo** ayudan.
3. ___ Las señoras tienen una parrilla (*grill*) enorme. Ellas **la** usan todos los días.
4. ___ Las cocineras (*cooks*) están preparando mucha carne en la parrilla. Después, los clientes van a comer**la**.
5. ___ La abuela está cuidando a la niña. La abuela **la** quiere mucho.
6. ___ El padre está en la cocina con sus hijos. Él **los** mira con cariño y habla con ellos mientras trabajan.

■ Direct objects answer the question *what?* or *whom?* in relation to the verb.

| | |
|---|---|
| ¿Qué dobla Pedro? | *What does Pedro fold?* |
| (Pedro dobla) **las toallas.** | *(Pedro folds) the towels.* |

■ Direct objects may be nouns or pronouns. When direct object nouns refer to a specific person, a group of persons, or a pet, the word **a** precedes the direct object. This **a** is called the *personal a* and has no equivalent in English. The personal **a** followed by **el** contracts to **al.**

| | |
|---|---|
| Amanda seca **los platos.** | *Amanda dries the dishes.* |
| Amanda seca **al perro.** | *Amanda dries off the dog.* |
| ¿Ves la piscina? | *Do you see the swimming pool?* |
| ¿Ves **al** niño en la piscina? | *Do you see the child in the swimming pool?* |

■ With the verb *tener* the personal **a** is not needed.

María tiene un hijo.    *María has a child.*

■ Direct object pronouns replace direct object nouns and are used to avoid repeating the noun while speaking or writing. These pronouns may refer to people, animals, or things already mentioned.

| DIRECT OBJECT PRONOUNS | | | |
|---|---|---|---|
| **me** | *me* | **nos** | *us* |
| **te** | *you* (familiar, singular) | **os** | *you* (familiar plural, Spain) |
| **lo** | *you* (formal, singular), *him, it* (masculine) | **los** | *you* (formal and familiar, plural), *them* (masculine) |
| **la** | *you* (formal, singular), *her, it* (feminine) | **las** | *you* (formal and familiar plural), *them* (feminine) |

■ Place the direct object pronoun before the conjugated verb form.

| ¿Barre **la cocina** Mirta? | *Does Mirta sweep the kitchen?* |
|---|---|
| No, no **la** barre. | *No, she does not sweep it.* |
| ¿Cuidas **a tu hermanito**? | *Do you take care of your little brother?* |
| Sí, **lo** cuido. | *Yes, I take care of him.* |

■ With compound verb forms (a conjugated verb and an infinitive or present participle), a direct object pronoun may be placed before the conjugated verb, or may be attached to the accompanying infinitive or present participle.

| ¿Vas a ver **a Rafael**? | *Are you going to see Rafael?* |
|---|---|
| Sí, **lo** voy a ver mañana. ⎤<br>Sí, voy a ver**lo** mañana. ⎦ | *Yes, I am going to see him tomorrow.* |
| ¿Están limpiando **la casa**? | *Are they cleaning the house?* |
| Sí, **la** están limpiando. ⎤<br>Sí, están limpiándo**la**. ⎦ | *Yes, they are cleaning it.* |

■ Since the question word **quién(es)** refers to people, use the *personal a* when **quién(es)** is used as a direct object.

| ¿**A quién** vas a ayudar? | *Whom are you going to help?* |
|---|---|
| Voy a ayudar **a** Pedro. | *I am going to help Pedro.* |

> ### Lengua
>
> You have seen that words that stress the next-to-the-last syllable do not have a written accent if they end in a vowel: **lav<u>a</u>ndo**. If we attach a direct object pronoun, we are adding a syllable, so the stress now falls on the third syllable from the end and a written accent is needed: **lav<u>á</u>ndo<u>lo</u>**.

**5-23 La división del trabajo.** Sus compañeros Martín, Pedro y Julio comparten un apartamento y usted le hace las siguientes preguntas a Julio para saber cómo dividen las tareas domésticas entre ellos. Escriba la letra de la respuesta más apropiada de Julio.

1. ¿Quién limpia la nevera?
   **a.** Yo lo limpio.       **b.** Pedro la limpia.   **c.** Nosotros las limpiamos.
2. ¿Quién hace las camas?
   **a.** Pedro la hace.      **b.** Yo los hago.       **c.** Martín las hace.
3. ¿Quién tiende la ropa?
   **a.** Los tres lo tendemos.   **b.** Pedro los tiende.   **c.** Martín la tiende.
4. ¿Quién saca la basura?
   **a.** Martín lo saca.     **b.** Pedro las saca.    **c.** Yo la saco.
5. ¿Quién pasa la aspiradora?
   **a.** Martín y yo las pasamos.   **b.** Pedro la pasa.   **c.** Ellos lo pasan.

**5-24 ¿Qué es lógico hacer?** PRIMERA FASE. Las afirmaciones de la columna de la izquierda describen la situación doméstica de esta familia. Léalas y, luego, asocie cada afirmación con una acción lógica.

1. ___ Las camas están sin hacer.
2. ___ La ropa está seca.
3. ___ Los dormitorios están desordenados.
4. ___ El aire acondicionado no funciona.
5. ___ Las ventanas están sucias.
6. ___ No pueden poner el auto en el garaje porque hay muchos muebles viejos y cajas con libros.

a. Los hijos los van a ordenar.
b. La madre las hace después de leer el periódico.
c. El padre las va a limpiar.
d. La hija va a plancharla.
e. Los hijos lo van a organizar y limpiar.
f. El hijo mayor lo va a reparar (*fix*).

 SEGUNDA FASE. Dígale a su compañero/a cuál(es) de las afirmaciones de la *Primera fase* describe(n) mejor su apartamento o casa en este momento. Luego, explíquele qué va a hacer usted y cuándo.

**5-25 Mis responsabilidades en casa.** PRIMERA FASE. Averigüe (*Find out*) si su compañero/a es responsable de las siguientes tareas domésticas en su casa.

MODELO:     sacar la basura
            E1:  *¿Sacas la basura?*
            E2:  *Sí, la saco. O No, no la saco. ¿Y tú?*

1. lavar los platos
2. ordenar el garaje
3. tender las cortinas después de lavarlas
4. limpiar la ducha y la bañera
5. lavar las sábanas
6. cortar el césped

SEGUNDA FASE. Ahora, comparen sus respuestas. Después díganle a otra pareja cuáles son las tareas domésticas que ustedes dos hacen y averigüen si ellos las hacen también.

MODELO:     E1:  *Nosotros no lavamos los platos en casa porque tenemos lavaplatos. ¿Y ustedes los lavan?*
            E2:  *Sí, nosotros los lavamos y hacemos las camas también.*

**5-26 El apartamento de mi compañero/a.** Usted va a cuidar el apartamento de su compañero/a por una semana, y quiere saber lo que debe hacer y lo que puede hacer allí.

MODELO:  E1:  *¿Debo sacar la basura?*
         E2:  *Sí, la debes sacar/debes sacarla todos los días.*

| ¿DEBO O NO DEBO? | SÍ | NO | ¿PUEDO O NO PUEDO? | SÍ | NO |
|---|---|---|---|---|---|
| regar (*water*) las plantas | _____ | _____ | leer los libros | _____ | _____ |
| pasear al perro | _____ | _____ | usar los electrodomésticos | _____ | _____ |
| limpiar el apartamento | _____ | _____ | invitar a un amigo/una amiga | _____ | _____ |
| poner la alarma | _____ | _____ | hacer la tarea en la computadora | _____ | _____ |
| ... | _____ | _____ | ... | _____ | _____ |

**5-27 Los preparativos para la visita.** La familia Granados está muy ocupada porque espera la visita de unos parientes. Conteste las preguntas de su compañero/a sobre lo que está haciendo cada miembro de la familia.

MODELO:  E1:  *¿Quién está preparando la comida?*
         E2:  *La abuela la está preparando/está preparándola.*

**5-28 Una mano amiga. PRIMERA FASE.** Su compañero/a le va a hacer preguntas sobre sus relaciones con otras personas. Conteste, escogiendo a una de las personas de la lista.

| | | |
|---|---|---|
| mi madre | mi novio/a | ¿...? |
| mi mejor amigo/a | mi padre | |

**MODELO:**   ayudar económicamente
E1:   *¿Quién te ayuda económicamente?*
E2:   *Mis padres me ayudan económicamente.*

1. querer mucho
2. escuchar en todo momento
3. llamar por teléfono con frecuencia
4. ayudar con los problemas
5. aconsejar (*advise*) cuando estás indeciso/a
6. entender siempre

**SEGUNDA FASE.** Dígale a su compañero/a lo que usted hace por las siguientes personas. Indique en qué circunstancias lo hace.

**MODELO:**   su esposo/a
E1:   *Lo/La ayudo cuando está cansado/a.*
E2:   *Y yo lo/la escucho cuando tiene problemas en el trabajo.*

1. su papá
2. su mamá
3. su mejor amigo/a
4. su novio/a
5. sus vecinos (*neighbors*)
6. su compañero/a de cuarto

## SITUACIONES

1. **Role A.** You are at a furniture store buying a sofa. Tell the salesperson which sofa you want and ask when they can deliver (**entregar**) it. Explain that you are not going to be home at that time, but that you can be home in the afternoon. Agree to the time and thank the salesperson.

   **Role B.** You are a salesperson at a furniture store. Tell the customer that the sofa he/she wants is a very good one and that you can deliver (**entregar**) it next Monday morning. Mention that you can deliver it between three and five o'clock in the afternoon if the customer prefers.

2. **Role A.** You and your little brother/sister have to do some chores at home. Since you are older, you tell your sibling three or four things that he/she has to do. Be prepared to respond to complaints and questions.

   **Role B.** You and your older brother/sister have to do some chores at home. Because you are younger, you get some orders from your sibling about what you have to do. You do not feel like working, and you especially do not like being bossed around, so respond to everything you hear with a complaint or a question.

### En directo

To assist a customer in a store:

**¿Qué desea?**
*What would you like?*
(lit., *What do you desire?*)

**¿En qué puedo ayudarlo/a?**
*How can I help you?*

To request a product:

**Quisiera...**
*I would like . . .*

**¿Podría ver...?**
*Could I see . . .?*

**¿Podría mostrarme...?**
*Could you show me . . .?*

## 4. Pointing out and identifying people and things: Demonstrative adjectives and pronouns

AGENTE: **Esta** casa blanca es muy moderna y el precio es bueno.

CLIENTE: Pero **esa** tiene jardín y **esta** no tiene, ¿verdad?

AGENTE: No, **esta** casa y **aquella** no tienen jardín. Por eso, la casa amarilla es más cara.

**Piénselo.** En su presentación, el señor Mendoza describe algunos tipos de vivienda para un grupo de salvadoreños que desean comprar una casa. Indique si cada una de las siguientes descripciones se refiere a la vivienda que está cerca (**C**), un poco lejos (**P**) o lejos (**L**) del señor Mendoza.

1. ___ **Esta** casa de dos pisos está en una ciudad. Tiene muchas ventanas en cada piso, pero no tiene jardín.
2. ___ **Aquella** casa donde están la madre y su hija es de material sólido y de un color alegre.
3. ___ **Esa** casa es de construcción sólida y tiene dos pisos y un garaje. Tiene una pequeña área verde enfrente.

## Demonstrative Adjectives

■ Demonstrative adjectives agree in gender and number with the noun they modify. English has two sets of demonstratives (*this*, *these* and *that*, *those*), but Spanish has three sets.

| *this* | **este** cuadro<br>**esta** butaca | *these* | **estos** cuadros<br>**estas** butacas |
|---|---|---|---|
| *that* | **ese** horno<br>**esa** casa | *those* | **esos** hornos<br>**esas** casas |
| *that (over there)* | **aquel** camión<br>**aquella** casa | *those (over there)* | **aquellos** camiones<br>**aquellas** casas |

■ Use **este, esta, estos,** and **estas** when referring to people or things that are close to you in space or time.

**Este** escritorio es nuevo.          *This desk is new.*

Traen el sofá **esta** tarde.          *They will bring the sofa this afternoon.*

■ Use **ese, esa, esos,** and **esas** when referring to events, people, or things that are not relatively close to you. Sometimes they are close to the person you are addressing.

| | |
|---|---|
| **Esa** lámpara es muy bonita. | *That lamp is very pretty.* |
| **Ese** amigo de Lola vende su auto, ¿verdad? | *That friend of Lola's is selling his car, isn't he?* |

■ Use **aquel, aquella, aquellos,** and **aquellas** when referring to people or things that are more distant, or to events that are distant in time.

| | |
|---|---|
| **Aquel** edificio es muy alto. | *That building (over there) is very tall.* |
| En **aquella** visita los niños jugaron en el parque. | *During that (long ago) visit, the children played in the park.* |

## Demonstrative pronouns

■ Demonstratives can be used as pronouns to mean *this one/these* or *that one/those*, thus avoiding repetition when speaking or writing.

| | |
|---|---|
| Compran este espejo y **ese**. | *They are buying this mirror and that one.* |
| Estas lámparas y **aquellas** son mis favoritas. | *These lamps and those over there are my favorites.* |

■ To refer to a general idea or concept, or to ask for the identification of an object, use **esto, eso,** or **aquello**. These forms are invariable.

| | |
|---|---|
| Trabajan mucho y **eso** es muy bueno. | *They work a lot, and that is very good.* |
| ¿Qué es **esto**? | *What is this?* |
| Es un espejo. | *It is a mirror.* |
| **Aquello** es un edificio de la universidad. | *That (over there) is a university building.* |

### 5-29 Cerca, relativamente cerca o lejos. Decida qué adjetivo demostrativo debe usar de acuerdo con el lugar donde se encuentran los siguientes objetos.

**Cerca de usted**

1. ___ mesa es de Honduras.  a. Esta  b. Esa  c. Aquella
2. ___ cuadros también son de Honduras.  a. Estos  b. Esos  c. Aquellos

**Relativamente cerca de usted**

3. ___ sofá es muy grande.  a. Este  b. Ese  c. Aquel
4. ___ alfombra tiene unos colores muy alegres.  a. Esta  b. Esa  c. Aquella

**Lejos de usted**

5. ___ espejo es nuevo.  a. Este  b. Ese  c. Aquel
6. ___ lámparas son antiguas.  a. Estas  b. Esas  c. Aquellas

**5-30 ¿Quién es?** Coloque (*Place*) sus fotos en la clase de acuerdo con las instrucciones del profesor/de la profesora. Luego pregunte a un compañero/una compañera quién es el sujeto de cada foto.

**MODELO:** E1: *¿Quién es este/ese/aquel hombre?* (según la distancia de la foto de E1)

E2: *Este/Ese/Aquel hombre es Antonio Banderas.* (según la distancia de la foto de E2)

**5-31 En una mueblería en Managua.** Usted y su compañero/a van a hacer los papeles de dos amigos/as nicaragüenses que deciden vivir juntos/as. Van a una mueblería para comprar muebles y accesorios. Usen las palabras y frases para hablar sobre lo que ven. Sigan el modelo.

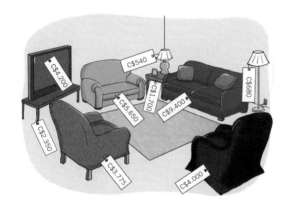

| | | |
|---|---|---|
| bonito/a | feo/a | (no) me gusta(n) |
| caro/a | me encanta(n) | |

**MODELO:** E1: *¿Te gusta el sofá?*
E2: *¿Cuál? ¿Aquel sofá verde?*
E1: *No, ese sofá azul.*
E2: *Sí, me encanta.* O *No, es muy feo.*

**5-32 Descripciones.** Cada uno de ustedes va a pensar en tres objetos o muebles y va a decir en qué parte de la casa están. Su compañero/a va a hacerle preguntas para adivinar qué mueble u objeto es.

**MODELO:** E1: *Este mueble está generalmente en el comedor.*
E2: *¿Es grande?*
E1: *Puede ser grande o pequeño.*
E2: *¿Lo usamos para comer?*
E1: *Sí.*
E2: *Es la mesa.*

## SITUACIONES

1. **Role A.** You have a good job and want to move to a nicer apartment. The property manager of several apartment complexes has already shown you pictures of one apartment (**ese apartamento**) and is now showing you pictures of a second one (**este apartamento**). Discuss with the property manager a) the rent (**el alquiler**); b) the number of rooms; and c) the facilities, such as laundry room (**lavandería**), garage, and pool, of both apartments. Say which of the two apartments you want to see and explain why.

   **Role B.** You are the property manager of several apartment complexes. You have already shown your client pictures of one apartment (**ese apartamento**) and now are showing pictures of a second one (**este apartamento**). Answer his/her questions by saying that a) the rent of the first apartment is $900 dollars per month and the second one is $1,100; b) both apartments have two bedrooms; and c) the first apartment comes with a one-car garage, while this one has a two-car garage. Also tell him/her the advantages of each of the two apartments.

2. **Role A.** You are in a car with a real estate agent, who is showing you some houses for sale in the neighborhood where you hope to live. You are interested in knowing more about one house on the side of the street closer to you (**esta casa**), another house on other side of the street (**esa casa**), and a third house (**aquella casa**) a couple of blocks away.

   **Role B.** You are a real estate agent driving with a client who is interested in three houses. Answer the client's questions about the three houses.

# MOSAICOS

## A escuchar

### Antes de escuchar

**ESTRATEGIA**

**Create mental images**
You have already learned that visual cues can increase your listening comprehension. For example, seeing the pictures or objects that a speaker refers to can help you understand what is being said. Even when visuals are not present, you can form images in your mind by using your imagination or by making associations with experiences you have had. As you listen, practice creating mental images to help you develop your listening skills in Spanish.

**5-33 Preparación.** Usted va a escuchar la descripción de una casa. Antes de escuchar, piense en las casas que conoce y haga una lista de cuatro cuartos y de tres objetos (muebles, aparatos eléctricos o accesorios) que usted espera encontrar en cada uno de los cuartos.

### Escuchar

**5-34 ¿Comprende usted?** Now, look at the following drawing, and as you hear the different statements about the location of pieces of furniture and objects, mark (✔) the appropriate column to indicate whether each of the statements is true (**Cierto**) or false (**Falso**).

CD 2
Track 31
or CD 3
Track 6

| | CIERTO | FALSO |
|---|---|---|
| 1. | —— | —— |
| 2. | —— | —— |
| 3. | —— | —— |
| 4. | —— | —— |
| 5. | —— | —— |
| 6. | —— | —— |
| 7. | —— | —— |
| 8. | —— | —— |

### Después de escuchar

**5-35 Ahora usted.** Describa su vivienda (número de cuartos, colores, muebles, etc.) a un compañero/una compañera. Él/Ella va a tomar notas para describirle su casa a otra persona de la clase. Verifique si la información es correcta. Luego, intercambien roles.

# A conversar

## Antes de conversar

**5-36 Preparación.** Usted necesita alquilar un apartamento. Escriba algunas características esenciales y algunas secundarias del apartamento que usted necesita.

## Conversar

**5-37 Entre nosotros.** Usted y su mejor amigo/a estudian en San Salvador este año y quieren alquilar un apartamento. Van a conversar por teléfono sobre unos apartamentos que se anuncian en el periódico.

**PRIMERA FASE.** Trabajando individualmente, piense en las características esenciales y secundarias de un buen apartamento. Lea los anuncios y decida qué apartamento prefiere. Organice mentalmente lo que va a decir. Luego, piense en el lenguaje que va a usar para expresarse y para negociar con su amigo/a, por ejemplo, *en mi opinión…, entiendo tu punto de vista pero…, (no) estoy de acuerdo porque…*

---

### *ALQUILERES*

1. Se alquila condominio residencial privado, 3er nivel, 2 dormitorios, 1 baño, cuarto y baño, empleada, cocina con despensa, sala y comedor separados, garaje 2 carros, área recreación niños. SVC 4.500 vigilancia incluida. 22 24 46 30.

2. Alquilo apartamento cerca de centro comercial. Transporte público a la puerta. Ideal para profesionales. 1 dormitorio, 1 baño con jacuzzi, con muebles y electrodomésticos, terraza, sistema de seguridad, garaje doble. SVC 7.500. Tfno. 22 65 16 92.

3. Alquilo apartamento, cerca zona universitaria. 3 dormitorios. 1ra planta. Ideal para estudiantes. (SVC 1.800) Contactar al 22 35 37 83.

4. Alquilo preciosa habitación en casa particular. Semi-amueblada. Amplia, enorme clóset, cable gratis. Alimentación opcional. Información al teléfono 22 63 28 07.

---

**SEGUNDA FASE.** Hable con su amigo/a por teléfono para llegar a un acuerdo sobre el apartamento que los/las dos quieren alquilar. En su conversación, pueden referirse a algunos de los siguientes temas: el alquiler, la localización, el número de habitaciones y baños, si tiene muebles o no, si tiene aire acondicionado/calefacción.

## Después de conversar

**5-38 Un poco más.** Ya que usted y su compañero/a saben qué apartamento les gusta más, tienen que dar el próximo paso (*next step*). Conversen para decidir lo siguiente:

1. ¿Por qué es este apartamento el favorito de ustedes?
2. ¿Qué preguntas quieren hacerle al dueño del apartamento para obtener más información?

Tomen apuntes, porque van a presentar sus ideas a la clase.

# A leer

## Antes de leer

**5-39 Preparación.** Muchas casas modernas tienen los aparatos que aparecen en la siguiente lista. Para cada función, escriba el/los aparato(s) correspondiente(s).

| | |
|---|---|
| aire acondicionado central | red (*network*) inalámbrica |
| música ambiental en todos los cuartos | reproductor de DVD |
| computadora | sensor de temperatura |
| fotocopiadora | teléfono |
| lámpara | televisor |
| microondas | ventilador |

**FUNCIÓN**  **APARATOS**

1. para trabajar desde (*from*) casa  _____
2. para hacer trabajos domésticos  _____
3. para controlar la temperatura de la casa  _____
4. para comunicarse con otras personas  _____
5. para entretenerse (*have fun*) en casa  _____

## Leer

**5-40 Primera mirada.** El siguiente artículo describe la casa del futuro. Léalo y pase un marcador (*highlighter*) por las palabras en cada párrafo que se asocian con tecnología.

**Segunda mirada.** Lea el artículo otra vez y haga lo siguiente.

1. En el primer párrafo, el autor del artículo da una definición de una casa inteligente. Escriba la definición.
2. El segundo párrafo contrasta la casa inteligente con la casa tradicional. ¿Cuál es la diferencia? Escríbala.
3. El segundo párrafo también indica algunas formas en que la casa inteligente ayuda a las personas que viven en ella. Indique una función útil para una persona de su familia. ¿Por qué es útil?
4. En el tercer párrafo, se mencionan algunas de las funciones múltiples de los aparatos eléctricos y electrónicos. ¿Cuál de estas funciones múltiples es más beneficiosa para un/a estudiante? ¿Por qué?
5. En el cuarto párrafo se explica cómo la tecnología ayuda a los miembros de la familia a mantenerse en contacto (to *stay in touch*). ¿A su familia le gustaría (*would like*) usar esta tecnología?
6. En el quinto párrafo se mencionan algunos beneficios de la tecnología para divertirse en casa. ¿Cuál de las opciones le gusta más?
7. En el último párrafo, el autor introduce una duda sobre los beneficios de la casa del futuro. Subraye la frase donde se introduce la duda.

## La casa inteligente del futuro

Las casas inteligentes o automatizadas ya existen en el presente. Tienen un gran número de aparatos eléctricos y electrónicos, controlados por una computadora, que se comunican entre ellos. Pero, ¿cuáles son las diferencias entre una casa tradicional y una inteligente?

Básicamente, la casa inteligente incorpora los últimos avances tecnológicos en beneficio de las personas que viven en ella. A través de complejos dispositivos[1] y sensores, estas casas facilitan el trabajo doméstico de sus dueños: abren y cierran cortinas y puertas, hacen funcionar electrodomésticos (microondas, ventiladores, etc.), el aire acondicionado y la calefacción central, por ejemplo. Los sensores también controlan el movimiento de unos robots móviles que limpian las alfombras y los pisos y, en el patio, limpian la piscina y cortan el césped.

Además, la casa inteligente ofrece un uso más eficiente y múltiple de los aparatos eléctricos y electrónicos en su interior. Un microondas se puede usar para calentar comida y también para ver televisión. De la misma manera, un refrigerador puede conectarse a Internet y permitir a una persona navegar por la red o enviar mensajes electrónicos.

La casa inteligente del futuro facilita también las relaciones entre los miembros de la familia. Por ejemplo, cuando los miembros de la familia no están juntos, pueden reunirse para cenar o para pasar tiempo juntos, gracias a las tecnologías de videoconferencia en Internet. Con el video y la voz sobre IP, los miembros de la familia en todo el mundo pueden conversar, interactuar y cenar juntos de forma virtual.

La sala en la casa inteligente es el centro de entretenimiento, donde todos los dispositivos están conectados a la red inalámbrica central. Los juegos bajo demanda están disponibles[2] a través de la televisión de banda ancha[3] y satélite. Las películas de alta definición, la televisión sin anuncios y el contenido digital a petición[4] son normales. También es normal distribuir música y películas a cada habitación de la casa desde el servidor central.

En resumen, la casa del futuro es una versión técnicamente más sofisticada de la casa del presente. Es difícil predecir con exactitud cómo vamos a vivir dentro de 50 años. Sin embargo, muchos se preguntan si esta abundancia de tecnología va a afectar nuestra vida positiva o negativamente.

[1]*devices*  [2]*available*  [3]*broadband*  [4]*on demand*

## Después de leer

**5-41 Ampliación.** PRIMERA FASE. Lea la siguiente nota que el arquitecto de una casa inteligente le escribe a uno de sus colegas. Complete los espacios en blanco con la palabra adecuada.

| | | |
|---|---|---|
| funcionar | juegos bajo demanda | tecnológicos |
| funciones | películas de alta definición | urgentemente |
| inteligente | sensores | ventanas |

Manolo,

¡Te tengo una gran sorpresa! El diseñador (*designer*) Óscar de la Renta necesita (1) _____ construir una casa (2) _____ en Managua. Como sabes, de la Renta es muy rico y quiere los últimos avances (3) _____ en ella. Desea una casa con dispositivos para abrir y cerrar puertas y (4) _____ . También quiere incorporar electrodomésticos con (5) _____ múltiples. Quiere calefacción controlada por (6) _____ . Desde luego (*Of course*) quiere un centro de entretenimiento que le permita mirar (7) _____ y recibir programación digital y (8) _____ . Tú sabes mucho de sistemas automatizados y yo de construcción, y pienso que eres la persona ideal para ayudarme en este proyecto. Vamos a darle una casa espectacular. Todo va a (9) _____ perfectamente.

Debemos responder pronto. Llámame.

Ricardo

 **SEGUNDA FASE.** Ahora comparen sus propias viviendas con la casa inteligente de la lectura. Hablen de la tecnología, los electrodomésticos y los aparatos electrónicos.

# A escribir

## Antes de escribir

**5-42 Preparación. PRIMERA FASE.** El periódico *La Prensa* de Tegucigalpa, Honduras, invita al público a participar en el concurso (*contest*) *La casa automatizada del futuro*. Uno de los requisitos del concurso es escribir un panfleto, según se explica en el anuncio del periódico.

---

El diario *La Prensa* invita al público a participar en el concurso *La casa automatizada del futuro*.

**Bases del concurso:**

Los participantes deben enviar la siguiente información por correo electrónico al Comité de Selección de *La casa automatizada del futuro*:

1. información personal: nombre completo, dirección, teléfono y dirección de correo electrónico
2. un panfleto descriptivo de la casa automatizada con la siguiente información:
   a. tamaño de la casa en pies (*feet*) o metros cuadrados (*square meters*)
   b. número y nombre de las habitaciones
   c. aparatos eléctricos y electrónicos de la casa y sus funciones
   d. dispositivos y sensores y su(s) función(es)
3. si es posible, un dibujo o foto digital de la casa automatizada

Fecha límite: el 30 de marzo
Premio: Una computadora portátil de último modelo y alta resolución, con programas de alta capacidad y funcionalidad.

---

**SEGUNDA FASE.** Usted decide participar en el concurso con un proyecto excepcional. Para preparar su proyecto para el comité que selecciona a los ganadores (*winners*), tenga en cuenta las bases del concurso y tome notas de los puntos 1, 2 y 3 que aparecen en el anuncio.

## Escribir

**5-43 Manos a la obra.** Ahora prepare su panfleto. Para hacer la descripción de *La casa automatizada del futuro*, use sus ideas de la *Segunda fase* de la actividad **5-42**. Recuerde incluir toda la información que pide el concurso. Considere la cantidad de información necesaria y el tono apropiado para sus lectores, los miembros del Comité de Selección. ¡Buena suerte!

## Después de escribir

**5-44 Revisión.** Antes de presentar su panfleto, revise:

1. primero, la claridad de sus ideas
2. la cantidad y la sofisticación de la información dada
3. lo apropiado del tono (impersonal, serio) para un comité de periodistas
4. la precisión gramatical (el vocabulario común y corriente y el vocabulario más técnico, las estructuras que utiliza para describir, la concordancia, etc.)
5. finalmente, la ortografía y la acentuación

# ENFOQUE CULTURAL

## La geografía espectacular de Nicaragua, El Salvador y Honduras

**U**na característica de la geografía de Nicaragua, El Salvador y Honduras es la gran cantidad de volcanes que hay en estos países. En realidad, toda la región centroamericana del Pacífico es rica en volcanes. Algunos son grandes montañas de una belleza impresionante; algunos están activos y producen explosiones de lava o ceniza; otros, en cambio, no tienen actividad volcánica notable. Algunos son muy viejos, otros, en cambio, como el Volcán de Cerro Negro, que nació en 1850, son relativamente jóvenes.

Muchos volcanes tienen una actividad constante que consiste en pequeñas explosiones internas, expulsión de gases y temblores de tierra que los humanos no perciben, pero que se pueden medir usando instrumentos científicos. Algunas veces, esa actividad normal aumenta sin presentar un peligro inmediato. Sin embargo, los científicos y el gobierno se preocupan cuando esto ocurre. El volcán de San Cristóbal, por ejemplo, tuvo un aumento importante (pero no peligroso) de su actividad normal en mayo de 2006.

El volcán Cerro Negro de Nicaragua durante una explosión en 1995

Otra característica importante de toda la región centroamericana es la propensión a producir terremotos. Managua, la capital de Nicaragua, constantemente se ve afectada por grandes terremotos. En 1931, por ejemplo, un terremoto destruyó muchos edificios y causó la muerte de más de mil personas. También en 1972, un terremoto destruyó una gran parte del centro de esta ciudad, como muestra la foto. El 13 de enero de 2001, un violento terremoto mató a más de 700 personas y dejó a más de medio millón de personas sin casa en El Salvador. Y el 13 de febrero de 2001, un terremoto de 6, 6 de intensidad destruyó en El Salvador más de 30,000 casas y dejó más de 300 muertos.

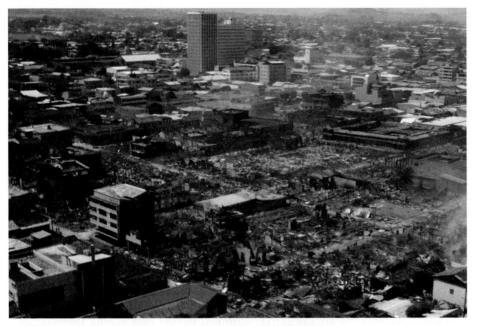

El terremoto de 1972 destruyó muchas casas del centro de Managua.

En otras palabras

Expresiones nicaragüenses

Él es **ñeque**.
*He is strong/vigorous.*

Ella **está jalando** con Luis.
*She is Luis's girlfriend.*

Ese **chavalo** es terrible.
*That kid is terrible.*

En otras palabras

Expresiones salvadoreñas

María **chinea** a su hijo.
*María holds her child in her arms continuously.*

Sólo es un **cipote**.
*He is only a child.*

—¿Vas a la playa mañana?
*—Are you going to the beach tomorrow?*

—**Primero** Dios.
*—God willing.*

Finalmente, esta región también se caracteriza por ser muy montañosa y por tener selvas y playas espectaculares. El Salvador, por ejemplo, aunque es el país más densamente poblado de las Américas, tiene montañas, selvas y playas naturales de gran belleza. Las playas salvadoreñas del Pacífico son bellísimas y son un paraíso para los aficionados al surfing. Más del 80% del terreno de Honduras consiste de montañas, pero tiene también selvas. Honduras es uno de los países con mayor biodiversidad, porque tiene muchas especies diferentes de plantas y animales.

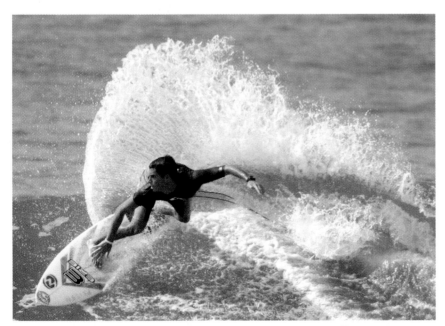

En otras palabras

Expresiones hondureñas

Parece que José **me agarró de ojo de gallo**.
*It looks like José has ill will towards me.*

¿Qué está haciendo ese **güirro**?
*What is that child doing?*

Gustavo Estrasser en una competencia en La Libertad, El Salvador

185

**5-45 Comprensión.** PRIMERA FASE. **Reconocimiento de palabras clave.** Encuentre en el texto la palabra o expresión que mejor expresa el significado de las siguientes ideas.

1. ash _____
2. increases _____
3. danger _____
4. earthquakes _____
5. mountainous _____
6. jungles _____
7. paradise _____

SEGUNDA FASE. **Oraciones importantes.** Subraye las afirmaciones que contienen ideas que se encuentran en el texto. Luego indique en qué parte del texto están.

1. Many volcanoes in this region are located near the Pacific Ocean.
2. Some volcanoes are amazingly beautiful.
3. One can find some young volcanoes in this region.
4. Volcanoes are dangerous, and people are afraid of them.
5. Most volcanoes are always active, although people may not be able to feel it.
6. Although small increments in volcano activity are not dangerous, scientists usually worry about them.
7. Central America is prone to earthquakes.
8. Earthquakes and volcanoes have destroyed the biodiversity of the surrounding area.

TERCERA FASE. **Ideas principales.** Escriba un párrafo breve en inglés resumiendo las ideas principales expresadas en el texto.

 **5-46 Use la información.** Usted tiene $300.000 dólares y quiere comprar una casa en Nicaragua, Honduras o El Salvador. Siguiendo los enlaces, busque la mejor casa, apartamento o propiedad rural que puede comprar con ese dinero. Prepare un afiche (*poster*) para mostrar en la clase. Debe incluir: localización, tipo de propiedad, características más importantes de la propiedad y su precio. Incluya también información adicional de interés para usted. Para preparar esta actividad, visite la página web de *Mosaicos* y siga los enlaces útiles.

# VOCABULARIO

| | |
|---|---|
| **La arquitectura** | *Architecture* |
| el alquiler | *rent* |
| el apartamento | *apartment* |
| el edificio | *building* |
| el estilo | *style* |
| las ruinas | *ruins* |
| la vivienda | *housing* |
| **En una casa** | *In a home* |
| el aire acondicionado | *air conditioning* |
| el armario | *closet, armoire* |
| el baño | *bathroom* |
| la basura | *garbage, trash* |
| la calefacción | *heating* |
| la chimenea | *fireplace* |
| la cocina | *kitchen* |
| el comedor | *dining room* |
| el cuarto | *room; bedroom* |
| la escalera | *stairs* |
| el garaje | *garage* |
| la habitación | *bedroom* |
| la lavandería | *laundry room* |
| el pasillo | *corridor, hall* |
| la piscina | *swimming pool* |
| el piso | *floor; apartment* |
| la planta baja | *first floor, ground floor* |
| la sala | *living room* |
| la terraza | *terrace* |
| **Los muebles y accesorios** | *Furniture and accessories* |
| la alfombra | *carpet, rug* |
| la butaca | *armchair* |
| la cama | *bed* |
| la cómoda | *dresser* |
| la cortina | *curtain* |
| el cuadro | *picture, painting* |
| el espejo | *mirror* |
| la lámpara | *lamp* |
| el sofá | *sofa* |
| **Los electrodomésticos** | *Appliances* |
| la aspiradora | *vacuum cleaner* |
| la lavadora | *washer* |
| el lavaplatos | *dishwasher* |
| el (horno) microondas | *microwave (oven)* |
| el/la radio | *radio* |
| el refrigerador | *refrigerator* |
| la secadora | *dryer* |
| el ventilador | *fan* |
| **Para la cama** | *For the bed* |
| la almohada | *pillow* |
| la manta | *blanket* |
| la sábana | *sheet* |
| **En el baño** | *In the bathroom* |
| la bañera | *bathtub* |
| la ducha | *shower* |
| el inodoro | *toilet* |
| el jabón | *soap* |

| | |
|---|---|
| el lavabo | *bathroom sink* |
| la toalla | *towel* |
| **En la cocina** | *In the kitchen* |
| la estufa | *stove* |
| el fregadero | *kitchen sink* |
| el plato | *dish, plate* |
| **En el jardín** | *In the garden* |
| la barbacoa | *barbecue pit; barbecue (event)* |
| el césped | *lawn* |
| la hoja | *leaf* |
| **Los lugares** | *Places* |
| las afueras | *outskirts* |
| el barrio | *neighborhood* |
| la calle | *street* |
| el centro | *downtown, center* |
| cerca (de) | *near, close (to)* |
| lejos (de) | *far (from)* |
| el pueblo | *village* |
| la zona | *area* |
| **Las descripciones** | *Descriptions* |
| limpio/a | *clean* |
| ordenado/a | *tidy* |
| seco/a | *dry* |
| sucio/a | *dirty* |
| **Verbos** | *Verbs* |
| ayudar | *to help* |
| barrer | *to sweep* |
| cocinar | *to cook* |
| cortar | *to cut; to mow (lawn)* |
| creer | *to believe* |
| doblar | *to fold* |
| limpiar | *to clean* |
| ordenar | *to tidy up* |
| pasar la aspiradora | *to vacuum* |
| planchar | *to iron* |
| preparar | *to prepare* |
| recoger (j) | *to pick up* |
| regar (ie) | *to water* |
| sacar | *to take out* |
| tender (ie) | *to hang (clothes)* |
| **Palabras útiles** | *Useful words* |
| la desventaja | *disadvantage* |
| el trabajo | *work* |
| la ventaja | *advantage* |
| la vista | *view* |

See page 157 for ordinal numbers.
See *Lengua* box on page 160 for more electronic items.
See page 167 for expressions with **tener**.
See page 171 for direct object pronouns.
See pages 175–176 for demonstrative adjectives and pronouns.

# 6

# De compras

Simón Bolívar (1783-1830), nacido en Caracas, Venezuela, es un héroe de la independencia latinoamericana.

# In this chapter you will learn how to:

- talk about clothing, prices, and shopping
- talk about past events
- express likes and dislikes

## Cultural focus: **Venezuela**

*Mar Caribe*

La industria del petróleo

islas
Los Roques

Isla Margarita

OCÉANO ATLÁNTICO

Maracaibo
Barquisimeto

Valencia

Caracas ✸

Barcelona

Maturín

Lago Maracaibo

Mérida

CORDILLERA DE MÉRIDA

La moderna ciudad de Caracas

*Río Orinoco*

Ciudad Bolívar

Ciudad Guayana

**VENEZUELA**

Salto Ángel

GUYANA

Las hayacas, un plato típico venezolano

Puerto Ayachucho

COLOMBIA

El pájaro turpial, símbolo de Venezuela

Salto Ángel

B R A S I L

**A vista de pájaro.** Piense en lo que sabe de Venezuela e indique si la afirmación es cierta (**C**) o falsa (**F**).

1. ___ Venezuela es una república independiente.
2. ___ La fauna de Venezuela es muy variada.
3. ___ El río Amazonas pasa por Venezuela.
4. ___ El petróleo es la industria más importante de Venezuela.
5. ___ Caracas está cerca del océano Pacífico.
6. ___ Panamá está al sur de Venezuela.

189

# A PRIMERA VISTA

## ◀)) Las compras

CD 3
Track 19

En este **centro comercial venden** de todo. Hay tiendas de **ropa** y de **zapatos**. También hay **tiendas** de muebles y accesorios para la casa, hay librerías, tiendas de **juguetes** para los niños e incluso hay un **supermercado**.

Muchas personas **van de compras** a los **mercados** al aire libre. Este es un mercado de la calle en Sabana Grande, Venezuela. En los mercados tradicionales venden **telas**, objetos de **artesanía**, **joyas**, **bolsos**, etc., pero a veces también hay discos, aparatos electrónicos y otras **cosas** para la casa.

En los mercados tradicionales los turistas a veces compran **regalos** para su familia y sus amigos. A esta señora le gustan las joyas artesanales. Ella compra un **collar** de **plata** para su mejor amiga, una **pulsera** para su hermana, unos **aretes** para su hija y un **anillo** de **oro** para sí misma (*herself*).

190

## De compras

**CD 3
Track 20**

José Manuel va a un **almacén** a comprar un regalo para su novia. Él necesita la ayuda de la dependienta.

DEPENDIENTA: **¿En qué puedo servirle?**

JOSÉ MANUEL: **Quisiera** comprar un regalo para mi novia. Un bolso o una **billetera**, por ejemplo.

DEPENDIENTA: Hay unos bolsos de **cuero** preciosos y no son muy **caros**. **Enseguida** le **muestro** los que tenemos.

[La dependienta trae unos bolsos.]

JOSÉ MANUEL: No sé. M**e gustaría** comprar este bolso, pero no puedo **gastar** mucho. ¿Cuánto cuesta?

DEPENDIENTA: Sólo **vale** 80 bolívares. Es bastante **barato**.

JOSÉ MANUEL: Sí, no es mucho **dinero**. Es un buen **precio**.

DEPENDIENTA: Y **están** muy **de moda**. Las chicas jóvenes los **llevan** mucho.

JOSÉ MANUEL: Bueno, lo voy a comprar.

DEPENDIENTA: Muy bien, señor. ¿Va a **pagar** con **tarjeta de crédito** o **en efectivo**?

JOSÉ MANUEL: En efectivo.

**6-1 ¿Adónde van?** Las siguientes personas necesitan comprar algunas cosas. Indique a qué tienda deben ir.

1. ___ María necesita unos libros para su clase de literatura.
2. ___ Juan quisiera cocinar comida venezolana para sus amigos.
3. ___ Rosa piensa comprar unos regalos para sus sobrinos.
4. ___ Felipe necesita una cómoda para su cuarto.
5. ___ Olga necesita unos zapatos nuevos para una entrevista de trabajo.
6. ___ Catalina va a comprar un collar elegante para ir a una fiesta.

a. mueblería
b. juguetería
c. zapatería
d. supermercado
e. joyería
f. librería

> ### Lengua
>
> To soften requests, Spanish uses the forms **me gustaría** (instead of **me gusta**) and **quisiera** (instead of **quiero**). English does this with the phrase *would like*.
>
> **Me gustaría/Quisiera ir a ese almacén.**
> *I would like to go to that department store.*

**6-2 ¿Qué tienen que hacer?** Ustedes tienen que hacer muchas cosas esta semana. Hablen de lo que necesitan comprar y decidan a qué tiendas van a ir.

MODELO: planear nuestro viaje a Venezuela
*Necesitamos comprar un billete de avión para Caracas. Vamos a ir a una agencia de viajes.*

1. preparar un postre para la fiesta de Jaime
2. hacer un regalo para mi novio/a por su cumpleaños
3. entretener a mi sobrino de cinco años
4. comprar zapatos para mi viaje
5. amueblar el comedor de mi apartamento
6. leer una novela divertida

**6-3 En el mercado tradicional. PRIMERA FASE.** Túrnense para comprar unos recuerdos (*souvenirs*) en un mercado tradicional en Caracas. Pregunten el precio de los siguientes productos. Regateen (*haggle*) para obtener un precio más barato.

cuadros de Venezuela · bolsas de cuero · platos de artesanía · aretes · collares · anillos · casas en miniatura · joyas · pulseras

**MODELO:**
E1: *Quisiera comprar este cuadro ¿Cuánto cuesta?*
E2: *Cuesta 50 bolívares.*
E1: *¡Uy, es muy caro! Lo compro por 38.*
E2: *Pero, es muy bonito. Tiene colores muy alegres.*
E1: *Sí, es muy bonito, pero no tengo suficiente dinero.*
E2: *Bueno, está bien. Lo vendo por 40.*

**SEGUNDA FASE.** Ahora está con su mejor amigo/a (otro compañero/otra compañera). Muéstrele sus compras y explique:

1. qué es
2. para quién lo compra
3. cuánto cuesta

**MODELO:** *Esto es un collar de plata para mi prima Isabel. Cuesta 35 bolívares.*

# La ropa

CD 3
Track 21

**La ropa formal**
- el traje de chaqueta
- la camisa
- la corbata
- el saco
- el pañuelo
- el cinturón
- los pantalones
- el impermeable
- los zapatos
- **Roberto**

- la blusa
- la falda
- el paraguas
- los zapatos de tacón
- **Marisa**

**La ropa informal**
- la sudadera
- la camiseta
- **Miguel**
- las zapatillas de deporte
- **Sonia**
- los vaqueros/los jeans
- las sandalias

**La ropa interior y de estar en casa**
- la bata
- las pantimedias
- el camisón
- el/la piyama
- el sostén
- los calzoncillos
- las medias/los calcetines
- las zapatillas

**6-4 ¿Cuándo se usa?** Indique qué prenda(s) (*article[s]*) de vestir se usa(n) en cada situación.

1. Para ir a correr o al gimnasio nos ponemos (*put on*) _____.
2. Para ir a dormir llevamos (*wear*) _____.
3. Para ir a una fiesta nos ponemos _____.
4. Después de bañarnos y antes de vestirnos nos ponemos _____.

# Telas y diseño

CD 3
Track 22

- Vestidos en todas las telas
- algodón
- lana
- de color entero
- de cuadros
- seda
- poliéster
- de rayas
- de lunares

**6-5 ¿Qué ropa llevan? PRIMERA FASE.** Túrnense para describir la ropa que llevan algunas personas de la clase y adivinen (*guess*) quiénes son.

**SEGUNDA FASE.** Cuenten (*Count*) cuántas personas de la clase llevan los siguientes accesorios y prendas de vestir. Después comparen sus números.

1. aretes en las orejas _____
2. anillos en las manos _____
3. zapatillas de deporte _____
4. camisas de cuadros _____
5. camisas de color entero _____
6. vestidos o faldas _____

---

### En otras palabras

Some words referring to clothing differ from one region to another. For example, in Spain **el/la piyama** is **el pijama**, **medias** means *stockings*, but in some countries of Latin America it also means *socks*. Depending on the country, the words **aros**, **aretes**, **pendientes**, **pantallas**, or **zarcillos** are used for *earrings*. In Argentina and Uruguay **pollera** is used instead of **falda**.

### Lengua

Here is some useful vocabulary for the body (**el cuerpo**): **la cabeza** (*head*), **las orejas** (*ears*), **la nariz** (*nose*), **los brazos** (*arms*), **las manos** (*hands*), **las piernas** (*legs*), **los pies** (*feet*). You will learn more words related to parts of the body in *Capítulo 11*.

**Las rebajas**

CD 3
Track 23

MARTA: Las **rebajas** son **magníficas**. Mira esa falda de rayas. Está **rebajada** de 60 bolívares a 50. ¿Por qué no vemos si tienen tu **talla**?

ANA: Sí, y **me pruebo** la falda para ver si **me queda** bien. Uso la talla 38 y a veces es difícil **encontrarla**. Esta falda es de algodón y es **preciosa**.

MARTA: O te pruebas la falda en casa y si te queda mal, la **cambias**.

[**Entran en** la tienda.]

ANA: Buenos días, señorita, **quisiera** probarme la falda que está en **el escaparate** en la talla 38.

DEPENDIENTA: Lo siento, pero las únicas tallas que **nos quedan** son más grandes, la 42 y la 44.

ANA: ¡Qué lástima! Gracias.

Le queda **estrecha**. Le queda **ancha**.

La chaqueta y la falda están **rebajadas**.

**Lengua**

The word **talla** is normally used when talking about clothing size; **número** refers to shoe size. **Tamaño** means size in all other contexts: ¿**Cuál es su número de zapatos?**

The word **calzado** is used to express footwear in general. The verb **calzar** is also used to ask about someone's shoe size; ¿**Qué número calzas? ¿Cuánto calzas?**

**6-6 La falda de rayas.** Describa la experiencia de Ana, buscando la afirmación de la derecha que lógicamente se asocia con la afirmación de la izquierda.

1. ___ Ana necesita una falda en la talla 38.
2. ___ La falda no es de color entero.
3. ___ Ana prefiere las telas naturales.
4. ___ Ana entra en la tienda, pero no se prueba la falda.
5. ___ La falda no es muy cara.
6. ___ Marta dice que Ana debe cambiar la falda.

a. La dependienta dice que no tienen su talla.
b. Está rebajada.
c. Sabe que la talla 42 le va a quedar ancha.
d. Como no la va a comprar, no la va a cambiar.
e. Es de rayas.
f. Le gusta la falda porque es de algodón.

 **6-7 El cumpleaños de Nuria.** Ustedes van a una tienda para comprarle un regalo a una buena amiga, pero cada artículo que ven presenta un problema. Piensen en la solución.

| ARTÍCULO | PROBLEMA | SOLUCIÓN |
|---|---|---|
| collar | Es muy caro. | *Debemos buscar uno más barato.* |
| impermeable | Le queda ancho. | |
| vaqueros | Son de poliéster. | |
| sudadera | Es pequeña. | |
| blusa | Las rayas son muy anchas. | |
| bolso | No es de cuero. | |

# ◄)) ¿Qué debo llevar?

CD 3
Track 24 En el **invierno** hace frío. ¿Qué ropa llevamos?

el suéter    los guantes    la chaqueta

las botas    el abrigo

la bufanda

Cuando hace calor en el **verano,** ¿qué nos ponemos para ir a la playa?

las gafas de sol    la gorra    el sombrero

el traje de baño    los pantalones cortos    las sandalias

la camisa de manga corta    el vestido de verano

Y cuando llueve en la **primavera** y en el **otoño,** usamos impermeable y paraguas.

**6-8 ¿Frío o calor?** Indique cuándo se usa la siguiente ropa, asociando las palabras de la izquierda con la oración más lógica de la derecha.

1. ___ los guantes
2. ___ el traje de baño
3. ___ las botas
4. ___ el suéter
5. ___ los pantalones cortos
6. ___ el sombrero

a. Sirve para protegernos del sol.
b. Los llevamos en las manos cuando hace frío.
c. Son más cómodos cuando hace buen tiempo.
d. Nos lo ponemos para ir a la playa.
e. Es de lana, para llevar cuando hace frío.
f. Las llevamos en los pies en invierno.

**6-9 Vacaciones en Venezuela.** PRIMERA FASE. Usted y su amigo/a van a pasar sus vacaciones en Venezuela. Primero escojan el plan que más les interesa de las siguientes opciones.

1. Quince días en Isla Margarita. Por el día: ir a la playa; por la noche: ir a las discotecas.
2. Tomar un curso de verano en la Universidad Central de Venezuela en Caracas. Por la mañana: clases de español; por las tardes: lugares de interés turístico.
3. Explorar la fauna y flora de la región de Canaima. Por el día: caminar mucho; por las noches: estar en un campamento.

**SEGUNDA FASE.** Ahora, preparen una lista de la ropa y accesorios que van a necesitar para su plan de vacaciones.

| PLAN #____ | YO | MI COMPAÑERO/A |
|---|---|---|
| por la mañana | | |
| por la tarde | | |
| por la noche | | |

**TERCERA FASE.** Informen a la clase sobre sus planes y la ropa y accesorios que van a necesitar.

**MODELO:** *Vamos a ir a la ciudad venezolana de Mérida. Yo necesito unos zapatos de tenis para caminar por la ciudad. Mi compañero/a necesita unos pantalones cortos. También necesitamos suéteres porque Mérida está en las montañas.*

**6-10 Comprando ropa para todos.** Cada uno/a de ustedes debe comprar ropa para hacer unos regalos a tres personas diferentes de la lista. Expliquen para quiénes son los regalos. Su compañero/a le va a dar algunas ideas de qué comprar y el lugar donde puede comprar, según la información de los anuncios.

1. su sobrinita de 6 años
2. su mamá para el Día de la Madre
3. un amigo/una amiga que necesita ropa informal
4. un hermano que va a pasar unos días en el Caribe
5. su padre para su cumpleaños
6. su novio/a para el Día de los Enamorados

**CD 3 Track 25**

**6-11 Ropa para cada ocasión.** You will listen to a brief conversation regarding the clothes people will wear for an event. Before you listen, list what you would wear on the following occasions.

fiesta elegante _____

fiesta informal _____

Now as you listen, indicate [✓] the clothes and event mentioned.

**ROPA**

___ ropa elegante

___ falda y chaqueta

___ traje pantalón y blusa

___ pantalones cortos y camiseta

**EVENTO**

___ entrevista de trabajo

___ reunión de jóvenes

___ excursión de fin de semana

___ fiesta formal

# EN ACCIÓN

## Diarios de bicicleta: Una camisa de moda

### Antes de ver

**6-12** En este segmento, Luciana y Gabi están preparándose para su musical. Marque (✓) los accesorios o ropa que probablemente van a llevar.

Accesorios:

___ un anillo
___ aretes
___ una bufanda
___ un collar
___ gafas de sol
___ una gorra

Ropa:

___ una falda y una blusa
___ pantalones cortos
___ una bata
___ un vestido
___ zapatos de tacón
___ una sudadera

### Mientras ve

**6-13** Indique si las siguientes afirmaciones son ciertas (**C**) o falsas (**F**) según este segmento. Si son falsas (**F**), corrija la información.

1. ___ Luciana y Gabi se están probando ropa para ir a una fiesta de graduación.
2. ___ Javier va a tener una cita (*date*) con Carmen.
3. ___ Luciana y Gabi creen que Javier debe probarse ropa distinta.
4. ___ Javier necesita comprar una nueva camisa.
5. ___ Marcos cree que está muy guapo con la camisa que le da Luciana.
6. ___ Gabi dice que es muy torpe (*clumsy*).

### Después de ver

**6-14** ¿Qué puede recomendar usted para resolver los siguientes problemas?

1. La falda que le gusta a Gabi es muy formal.
2. La camisa que compró Javier no está de moda.
3. Los pantalones que se prueba Javier le quedan muy anchos.

# FUNCIONES Y FORMAS

### 1. Talking about the past: Preterit tense of regular verbs

Querido diario,

Esta mañana Álvaro y yo **gastamos** mucho dinero en ropa para vernos bien en la fiesta de boda de mi cuñada Gabriela esta tarde. Yo **compré** un hermoso vestido de fiesta y un chal de encaje (*lace shawl*). Álvaro **compró** un traje, una camisa y una corbata.

A las 7:00 de la tarde, **empezó** la ceremonia religiosa. La fiesta con familia y amigos **comenzó** a las 9:00 y **terminó** a las 4:00 de la mañana. Todos **comimos**, **bailamos** y **cantamos** mucho. Vamos a recordar este día especial por mucho tiempo. Gabriela y Gonzalo son una pareja perfecta.

Ahora voy a dormir. Estoy muy cansada.
Camila

**Piénselo.** ¿Qué pasó el día de la boda? Ordene cronológicamente la siguiente información (1 = primer evento, etc.), según lo que Camila escribe en su diario.

___ La fiesta con familia y amigos **comenzó** a las 9:00.

___ Camila **compró** un hermoso vestido de fiesta y un chal de encaje.

___ La fiesta **terminó** a las 4:00 de la mañana.

___ Todos **comieron**, **bailaron** y **cantaron** mucho.

- Spanish has two simple tenses to express the past: the preterit and the imperfect (**el pretérito** y **el imperfecto**). Use the preterit to talk about past events, actions, and conditions that are viewed as completed or ended.

|  | HABLAR | COMER | VIVIR |
|---|---|---|---|
| yo | hablé | comí | viví |
| tú | hablaste | comiste | viviste |
| Ud., él, ella | habló | comió | vivió |
| nosotros/as | hablamos | comimos | vivimos |
| vosotros/as | hablasteis | comisteis | vivisteis |
| Uds., ellos/as | hablaron | comieron | vivieron |

198

■ Note that the **nosotros/as** forms of the preterit of **-ar** and **-ir** verbs are the same as their present tense forms. Context will help you determine if a **nosotros/as** verb form is present or past.

**Llegamos** a la tienda a las tres. $\left\{\begin{array}{l}\text{\textit{We arrive at the store at three.}}\\ \text{\textit{We arrived at the store at three.}}\end{array}\right.$

Salí de la universidad a las dos y **llegamos** a casa a las tres.

*I left the university at two and we arrived home at three.*

■ Stem-changing verbs ending in **-ar** and **-er** do not have a stem change in the preterit.

| | |
|---|---|
| **pensar:** | pensé, pensaste, pensó, pensamos, pensasteis, pensaron |
| **volver:** | volví, volviste, volvió, volvimos, volvisteis, volvieron |

■ Verbs ending in **-car** and **-gar** have a spelling change in the **yo** form of the preterit that reflects how the word is pronounced. Verbs ending in **-zar** have a spelling change in the **yo** form because Spanish rarely uses a **z** before **e** or **i**.

| | |
|---|---|
| **sacar:** | sa**qué**, sacaste, sacó… |
| **llegar:** | lle**gué**, llegaste, llegó… |
| **empezar:** | empe**cé**, empezaste, empezó… |

> ### Lengua
> The **yo** and the **usted/él/ella** preterit verb forms are stressed on the last syllable and end in a vowel. Therefore, they carry a written accent: **hablé, comí, viví; habló, comió, vivió.**

■ There are some expressions you can use with the preterit to denote past time.

| | | | |
|---|---|---|---|
| **anoche** | *last night* | **la semana pasada** | *last week* |
| **anteayer** | *day before yesterday* | **una semana atrás** | *a week ago* |
| **ante(a)noche** | *night before last* | **hace un día/mes/año (que)** | *it has been a day/month/year since* |
| **ayer** | *yesterday* | | |
| **el año/mes pasado** | *last year/month* | | |

**6-15 Ayer yo...** **PRIMERA FASE.** Marque (✓) sus actividades de ayer y añada una actividad en cada grupo.

| POR LA MAÑANA | POR LA TARDE | POR LA NOCHE |
|---|---|---|
| ____ Desayuné. | ____ Almorcé en la cafetería. | ____ Preparé la cena. |
| ____ Llegué a tiempo a mis clases. | ____ Saqué libros de la biblioteca. | ____ Miré televisión. |
| ____ Estudié varias horas. | ____ Lavé la ropa. | ____ Planché mi ropa. |
| ____ Llamé por teléfono a un amigo/una amiga. | ____ Compré comida para toda la semana. | ____ Salí con mis amigos. |

**SEGUNDA FASE.** Comparen sus respuestas. ¿Tienen actividades semejantes o diferentes? Expliquen.

**6-16 El sábado pasado. PRIMERA FASE.** Miren las siguientes escenas y expliquen cómo pasaron el sábado Carmen y Rafael.

El sábado por la mañana          El sábado por la tarde

El sábado por la noche

**SEGUNDA FASE.** Escriban un párrafo para compartir oralmente con la clase sobre el sábado pasado de Carmen y Rafael.

**6-17 ¿Cómo pasaron el fin de semana? PRIMERA FASE.** Conversen sobre el fin de semana de ustedes.

1. ¿Cuáles fueron (*were*) las actividades de cada uno/a de ustedes?
2. ¿Dónde y con quién?
3. ¿A qué hora?
4. ¿Gastó mucho dinero? ¿Cómo lo gastó?

**SEGUNDA FASE.** Decidan qué persona de su grupo pasó el mejor fin de semana. Describan las actividades de esta persona en una presentación oral a la clase.

## SITUACIONES

1. **Role A.** You run into a classmate whose parents visited campus the previous weekend. Ask a) what day and time his/her parents arrived; b) where they ate breakfast and lunch; c) what places on campus they visited; and d) what time his/her parents left. Express your reactions to the information.

   **Role B.** Your classmate wants to know about your parents' visit to campus last weekend. Answer his/her questions in as much detail as possible. Ask if your classmate's parents are going to visit soon.

2. **Role A.** Your classmate and his/her significant other (**pareja**) went on a shopping spree last weekend. Ask a) what store(s) they shopped in; b) what each of them bought; c) what time they returned home; and d) what his/her plans are for wearing or using the items he/she bought.

   **Role B.** Answer your classmate's questions about your shopping spree with your significant other (**pareja**) over the weekend. Then find out if your classmate went shopping over the weekend, played a sport, or watched a lot of TV.

## 2. Talking about the past: Preterit of *ir* and *ser*

Una semana después...

CLIENTA: Compré este vestido aquí el sábado pasado. Pero ahora me queda estrecho.

SUPERVISORA: ¿Quién **fue** el vendedor que le vendió el vestido, señorita?

CLIENTA: No sé su nombre, pero **fue** su compañero, un señor alto y delgado.

SUPERVISORA: ¿Qué pasó? ¿Lavó el vestido en casa?

CLIENTA: Claro que no. Hay que lavar este vestido en seco (*dry clean*). **Fui** a una lavandería (*dry cleaner*).

SUPERVISORA: Los irresponsables **fueron** los empleados de la lavandería. No limpiaron en seco su vestido. Lo lavaron.

**Piénselo.** Indique si las siguientes afirmaciones son ciertas (**C**) o falsas (**F**), según la conversación entre la clienta y la supervisora.

1. ___ El vendedor **fue** el compañero de la supervisora.
2. ___ La clienta **fue** a una tienda especializada para limpiar el vestido.
3. ___ Lavar el vestido **fue** un error por parte de los empleados de la lavandería.
4. ___ La supervisora **fue** amable con la clienta porque trató de comprender el problema.
5. ___ Los vendedores de la tienda de ropa **fueron** las personas responsables del problema con el vestido.

■ The verbs **ir** and **ser** have identical forms in the preterit. They are used often in speaking and writing, and the context will help you to determine the meaning.

| IR and SER | | | |
|---|---|---|---|
| yo | **fui** | nosotros/as | **fuimos** |
| tú | **fuiste** | vosotros/as | **fuisteis** |
| Ud., él, ella | **fue** | Uds., ellos/as | **fueron** |

■ You will also be able to differentiate between **ir** and **ser** in the preterit because **ir** is often followed by the preposition **a**.

| | |
|---|---|
| Ernesto **fue** a la tienda. | *Ernesto went to the store.* |
| **Fue** vendedor en esa tienda por dos años. | *He was a salesman at that store for two years.* |

**6-18 ¿Quién fue a este lugar?** Las siguientes personas fueron a Venezuela para conocer algunos lugares, según sus intereses personales. Primero, lea cada situación y luego, relacione las fotos con cada una de ellas.

**A.** Salto Ángel

**B.** Isla Margarita

**C.** Maracaibo

**D.** El puente Angostura
sobre el río Orinoco

1. ___ Andrés visitó un lugar con agua para navegar. Le fascinan los deportes acuáticos, pero no le gusta el mar.
2. ___ Alguien habló sobre este lugar espectacular y único en el mundo. Dice que es semejante a las cataratas de Niágara. Usted decidió ir para ver el lugar.
3. ___ Los estudiantes del primer año de español de su universidad fueron de viaje a una playa exótica. Allí conocieron a otros turistas de muchas partes del mundo. Hablaron mucho español y un poco de inglés.
4. ___ Los ingenieros Roberto y Angélica decidieron ir a un lugar para investigar las últimas tecnologías en el procesamiento del petróleo. Por eso, fueron a este lugar con una población de más de dos millones y medio de personas.

 **6-19 ¿Quiénes fueron estas personas?** Investiguen la siguiente información sobre uno de estos famosos y hagan una breve presentación en clase.

| | | | |
|---|---|---|---|
| Alfonso X | Atahualpa | Roberto Clemente | Frida Kahlo |
| Doroteo Arango | Simón Bolívar | Ernesto Guevara | Mario Molina |
| Arámbula | Pablo Casals | Nicolás Guillén | Pablo Luis Picasso |

1. ¿Quién fue él/ella?
2. ¿Dónde nació, vivió y murió (*died*) esta persona?
3. ¿Por qué fue famoso/a? Indiquen como mínimo dos o tres hechos (*facts*) sobre su vida.

## SITUACIONES

1. **Role A.** A classmate tells you that he/she went to a concert last weekend. Ask a) where the concert was; b) what time it started; c) with whom he/she went; d) what time the concert ended; and e) where he/she went afterward. Express your reactions to the information.

   **Role B.** Your classmate wants to know about the concert you went to last weekend. Answer your classmates questions to find out if he/she went to a party or concert over the weekend, if he/she went out with friends, and so on. Ask for details about where, when, and with whom he/she went.

2. **Role A.** As part of your coursework in Spanish, you have been asked to interview a classmate to find out about the role some people may have had in his/her life. Ask a) who was an important authority figure (*figura de autoridad*) in his/her childhood (**infancia**); b) who was his/her best childhood friend; and c) who was his/her favorite teacher in elementary school (**escuela primera**). Express your reactions and ask additional questions.

   **Role B.** Your classmate will interview you to find out about some important people in your childhood (**infancia**). Answer the questions in as much detail as possible.

## 3. Indicating to whom or for whom an action takes place: Indirect object nouns and pronouns

LUCY: Oye, Panchito, ¿qué **te** compran tus padres para tu cumpleaños, ropa, chocolates o qué?

PANCHITO: No **me** dan ni ropa ni chocolates. Siempre **me** compran libros súper interesantes. Y tus padres, ¿qué **te** compran a ti, Lucy?

LUCY: Mi mamá siempre **nos** compra ropa a mi hermano y a mí. A mí **me** gusta mucho la ropa nueva.

PANCHITO: ¿Y qué **les** das tú a tus padres para su cumpleaños?

LUCY: ¡A mi mamá **le** doy muchos besitos y a mi papá **le** doy muchos problemas porque no hago mi tarea!

Lucy

Panchito

**Piénselo.** Primero, identifique **quién hace** la acción: Lucy, Panchito, Lucy y su hermano, los padres de Panchito, la mamá o el papá de Lucy. Luego, en la línea de la derecha, indique **quién recibe** el beneficio de la acción.

1. ———————————— **le** compran libros a ———————————— .
2. ———————————— **les** compra ropa a ———————————— .
3. ———————————— **le** da muchos besos a ———————————— .
4. ———————————— **le** causa problemas a —————— porque no hace la tarea.

■ Indirect object nouns and pronouns tell *to whom* or *for whom* an action is done, in other words, who is affected by an action.

| INDIRECT OBJECT PRONOUNS | | | |
|---|---|---|---|
| **me** | *to/for me* | **nos** | *to/for us* |
| **te** | *to/for you* (familiar) | **os** | *to/for you* (familiar) |
| **le** | *to/for you* (formal), *him, her, it* | **les** | *to/for you* (formal), *them* |

■ Indirect object pronouns have the same form as direct object pronouns except in the third person: **le** and **les**.

| | |
|---|---|
| Mi madre **me** compró ropa la semana pasada. | *My mother bought me clothes last week. [My mother bought clothes for me last week.]* |
| Yo **te** presto mis zapatos para la fiesta. | *I will lend you my shoes for the party. [I will lend my shoes to you for the party.]* |
| ¿El dependiente? Ella **lo** ve todas las mañanas. (*direct object*) | *The salesperson? She sees him every morning.* |
| ¿El dependiente? Ella **le** da los recibos por la mañana. (*indirect object*) | *She gives him the receipts in the morning.* |

■ Place the indirect object pronoun before a conjugated verb form. It may be attached to a present participle, in which case an accent mark is added, or to an infinitive.

**Les** voy a vender mi carro. ⎫
Voy a vender**les** mi carro. ⎬ *I am going to sell them my car.*

Juan **nos** está preparando la cena. ⎫
Juan está preparándo**nos** la cena. ⎬ *Juan is preparing dinner for us.*

■ Use indirect object pronouns even when the indirect object noun is stated explicitly.

Yo **le** presté mi libro a **Victoria**.  *I lent my notes to Victoria.*

■ To eliminate ambiguity, **le** and **les** are often used with the preposition **a +** *pronoun.*

**Le** hablo **a usted**.  *I am talking to you.* (not to *him/her*)

Siempre **les** cuento mis secretos **a ellos**.  *I always tell my secrets to them.* (not to *you/ustedes*)

■ For emphasis, use **a mí, a ti, a nosotros/as**, and **a vosotros/as** with indirect object pronouns.

Pedro **te** habla **a ti**.  *Pedro is talking to you.* (not to someone else)

■ **Dar** is almost always used with indirect object pronouns. Notice the difference in meaning between <u>dar</u> (*to give*) and **regalar** (*to give as a gift*). Other verbs of transmission (of things, ideas, words) that are generally used with indirect object pronouns include **decir, describir, escribir, explicar, mostrar, prestar**, and **vender**.

Ella le **da** el cinturón a Pedro.  *She gives (hands) Pedro the belt.*
Ella le **regala** el cinturón a Pedro.  *She gives Pedro the belt (as a gift).*

**6-20 La Academia de la Moda.** Ustedes están tomando una clase (Elegancia con Poco Dinero) en La Academia de la Moda. Marquen (✓) las sugerencias que su profesor les da a ustedes.

1. _____ Nos da nombres de tiendas de ropa buena y barata.
2. _____ A mí me recomienda artículos sobre la moda actual.
3. _____ Nos muestra telas que son elegantes y que no son muy caras.
4. _____ A mí me da ejemplos de cómo combinar ropa y accesorios.

**6-21 Para estar a la última moda.** Cada uno/a de ustedes desea o necesita lo que se indica en la lista a continuación. Explíquense (*to each other*) la situación. Después pidan y den una recomendación.

MODELO:  E1: *Quiero llevar zapatos muy cómodos. ¿Qué me recomiendas?*
     E2: *Te recomiendo unas sandalias de la marca Teva.*

1. Quiero llevar pantalones de moda (*in style*).
2. Deseo protegerme del sol.
3. Quiero ropa buena y barata.
4. Quiero verme (*look*) más delgado/a.
5. Me gustaría llevar ropa elegante y fina a la entrevista de trabajo.

---

## Lengua

**Dar** uses the same endings as **-er** and **-ir** verbs in the preterit:
**di, diste, dio, dimos, disteis, dieron**
Jorge le **dio** a Elena una copia de sus apuntes.
*Jorge gave Elena a copy of his notes.*

Mis padres me **dieron** dinero para la matrícula.
*My parents gave me money for tuition.*

**6-22 Afortunados.** Ustedes ganaron la lotería ayer y quieren compartir su fortuna con su familia y sus compañeros de clase.

1. Hagan una lista de dos o tres miembros de su familia a quienes desean regalarles algo.
2. Indiquen el regalo que piensan hacerle a cada uno/a.

**MODELO:** E1: *A nuestros padres les vamos a regalar un crucero por el Caribe.*
E2: *A Sara vamos a comprarle una mochila.*

**6-23 Entrevista.** **PRIMERA FASE.** Basándose en la siguiente lista, pregúntense sobre sus hábitos de compras y los regalos que ustedes hacen y reciben de otras personas.

1. ir de compras: ¿Qué? ¿Tienda(s) favoritas?
2. comprar regalos caros: ¿A quién(es)? ¿Cuándo?
3. le compran regalos a usted: ¿Quién(es)?

**SEGUNDA FASE.** Escriba una comparación entre sus hábitos y los de su compañero/a en la *Primera fase*. Use las siguientes preguntas como guía (*as a guide*). Prepárese para compatir su texto con otro compañero/otra compañera.

1. ¿Tienen ustedes hábitos de compras semejantes o diferentes?
2. ¿Compran en las mismas tiendas? ¿Compran regalos semejantes o diferentes?
3. ¿A quién(es) le(s) dan regalos? ¿Quiénes les dan regalos a ustedes? ¿Qué tipos de regalos reciben?

## SITUACIONES

1. **Role A.** You are a customer at a department store. Tell the salesperson a) you are looking for a present for a friend (specify male or female); b) you are not sure what you should buy for him/her; and c) the amount that you can spend.

   **Role B.** You are a salesperson. A customer asks for your advice. Inquire about the friend's age, taste, size, favorite color, and any other pertinent information. Make suggestions and offer information about the quality of the products, prices, sales, and so forth.

2. **Role A.** You are shopping for clothes for your new job. Tell the salesperson that you like a garment (specify) in the window and inquire if they have your size. Answer the salesperson's questions and decide what you want to try on.

   **Role B.** You are a salesperson. First ask the customer for more details to identify the garment the customer is referring to. Then explain that: a) you have it in brown, blue, gray, and black; b) you also have some new items that you can show him/her (describe the styles); and c) ask if he/she would like to see them.

## 4. Expressing likes and dislikes: *Gustar* and similar verbs

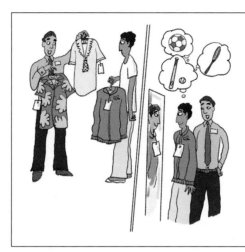

| | |
|---|---|
| DEPENDIENTE: | ¿**Le gustan** estas camisas? |
| JORGE: | No, no **me gustan**, pero **me gusta** esta chaqueta. |
| DEPENDIENTE: | Es una buena chaqueta para el otoño. ¿**Le interesan** los deportes, señor? |
| JORGE: | **Me encanta** practicar deportes, pero no **me gusta** mirar los partidos en televisión. **Me fascinan** el tenis, el béisbol y el fútbol. |

**Piénselo.** Indique si las siguientes afirmaciones son ciertas (**C**) o falsas (**F**), según la información en esta escena. Si no hay información suficiente para contestar, indique que usted no sabe (**NS**).

1. ___ A Jorge **le gusta** una de las camisas que le muestra el dependiente.
2. ___ A Jorge **le interesa** comprar una chaqueta.
3. ___ A Jorge **le queda** poco dinero, porque la chaqueta es muy cara.
4. ___ A Jorge **le encantan** varios deportes.
5. ___ A Jorge **le gusta** mirar los partidos de fútbol en la televisión.
6. ___ A los amigos de Jorge **les interesa** jugar al fútbol con él.

- In previous chapters you have used the verb **gustar** to express likes and dislikes. As you have seen, **gustar** is not used the same way as the English verb *to like*. **Gustar** is similar to the expression *to be pleasing (to someone)*.

| | |
|---|---|
| **Me gusta** esta chaqueta. | *I like this jacket.* |
| | (lit. *This jacket is pleasing to me.*) |

- The subject of **gustar** is the person or thing that is liked. The indirect object pronoun shows to whom the person or thing is pleasing.

| | | | |
|---|---|---|---|
| me | | *I* | |
| te | | *you* (familiar) | |
| le | gusta el traje. | *you* (formal), *he/she* | *like(s) the suit.* |
| nos | | *we* | |
| os | | *you* (familiar) | |
| les | | *they*, *you* (formal and familiar) | |

- The most frequently used forms of **gustar** in the present tense are **gusta** and **gustan** and for the preterit **gustó** and **gustaron**. If one thing is liked, use **gusta/gustó**. If two or more things are liked, use **gustan/gustaron**.

  | | |
  |---|---|
  | Me **gusta** ese **collar**. | *I like that necklace.* |
  | No me **gustaron** los anillos. | *I did not like the rings.* |

- To express what people like or do not like to do, use **gusta** followed by one or more infinitives.

  | | |
  |---|---|
  | Nos **gusta caminar** por la mañana. | *We like to walk in the morning.* |
  | ¿No te **gusta correr** y **nadar**? | *Don't you like to run and swim?* |

- Some other Spanish verbs that follow the pattern of **gustar** are **encantar** and **fascinar** (*to like a lot, to love*), **interesar** (*to interest; to matter*), **parecer** (*to seem*), and **quedar** (*to fit; to have something left*).

  | | |
  |---|---|
  | No te **interesan** las humanidades. | *You are not interested in the humanities.* |
  | Leí la novela y me **encantó**. | *I read the novel and I loved it.* |
  | El curso me **parece** muy difícil. | *The course seems very difficult to me.* |
  | No me **queda** mucho dinero. | *I don't have much money left.* |
  | No le **quedan** bien los pantalones. | *His/her pants don't fit well.* |
  | Nos **fascina** la moda europea. | *We love European fashion.* |

- To express that you like or dislike a person, use **caer bien** or **caer mal**, which follow the pattern of **gustar**.

  | | |
  |---|---|
  | **Les cae bien** Miriam. | *They like Miriam.* |
  | Esa dependienta **me cae mal**. | *I do not like that salesclerk.* |

- To emphasize or clarify to whom something is pleasing, use **a + mí, a + ti, a + él/ella, a usted(es)**, etc. or **a + *noun***.

  | | |
  |---|---|
  | **A mí** me gustaron los zapatos, pero **a Pedro** no le gustaron. | *I liked the shoes, but Pedro did not like them.* |

### 6-24 Mis preferencias en la ropa. PRIMERA FASE. Indique si le encanta(n), le gusta(n) o no le gusta(n) la ropa que sigue.

| | | |
|---|---|---|
| la ropa deportiva | los suéteres de lana | los vaqueros |
| las chaquetas de cuero | las gorras | los pantalones cortos |

**SEGUNDA FASE.** Comparen sus preferencias, y luego, explíquenle al resto de la clase si ustedes coinciden en sus gustos.

**MODELO:** E1: *A dos de nosotros nos gusta la ropa deportiva.*
E2: *Y a todos nos encantan los vaqueros.*

### 6-25 ¿Cuánto dinero les queda? Lean estas situaciones y calculen cuánto dinero queda.

**MODELO:** Pilar tiene 50 bolívares. Paga 25 bolívares por un vestido y 10 por unos aretes. ¿Cuánto dinero le queda?
*Le quedan 15 bolívares.*

1. Ernesto tiene 75 bolívares. Le da 15 a su hermano. ¿Cuánto dinero le queda?
2. Érica tiene 25 bolívares. Va al cine y a cenar con una amiga. El cine cuesta 5 y la cena 12. ¿Cuántos bolívares le quedan?
3. Gilberto tiene 40 bolívares. Compra un suéter por 39. ¿Cuánto dinero le queda?
4. Mis amigos tienen 30 bolívares. Van a la playa y almuerzan en un restaurante por 25 bolívares. ¿Cuántos les quedan?

En directo

To state that doing something is appropriate or not:

**(No) Es apropiado +** *infinitivo…*

**Es inapropiado +** *infinitivo…*

To explain why some clothes are inappropriate:

**… no es apropiado/a porque la ocasión es formal/informal.**

**En un/a…** (*evento*) **no es elegante/apropiado llevar…**

(*Ropa*)**… no va bien con…** (*accesorio*)

**6-26 ¿Qué les parece a ustedes?** Los famosos en las siguientes fotos asisten a eventos públicos. Den su opinión sobre su ropa y accesorios.

**MODELO:** E1: *No me gusta el traje de… No es apropiado llevar un traje blanco en el invierno.*

E2: *Me gusta la combinación de colores del hombre, pero la corbata no va bien con la camisa.*

La jugadora de tenis Serena Williams llega a una recepción formal.

La Reina Isabel II de Inglaterra con Ricky Martin, Paul McCartney y otros cantantes

El Dalai Lama de Tibet y la actriz Penélope Cruz en una exposición de arte en Barcelona

## SITUACIONES

1. **Role A.** You are shopping at an outdoor market where haggling is the norm. You select an item that you plan to give as a gift. In your interaction with the vendor a) say how much you like what the vendor is selling; b) ask the price of the item you are interested in; c) react to what you hear and offer a lower price; d) comment on the item, saying whom you plan to give it to; and e) come to an agreement on the price.

   **Role B.** You are a vendor at an outdoor market. A customer is interested in an item of yours. In your interaction with the customer a) respond to his/her compliments; b) give the price of the item; c) explain why you cannot accept the customer's offer of a lower price; d) respond to his/her comments on the item; and e) come to an agreement on the price.

2. **Role A.** You are at the store where you bought a pair of shorts last week. Tell the clerk that a) you tried them on at home and they didn't fit well; b) you don't like the color; and c) you want to return (**devolver**) them.

   **Role B.** You are the clerk at a clothing store. A customer wants to return (**devolver**) a pair of shorts. Listen to his/her case, and a) ask why the customer bought them if they didn't fit well and he/she didn't like the color; b) explain that the he/she can exchange the shorts for something else (**otra cosa**), but cannot return them; and c) show the person some other shorts and ask if he/she likes them.

# 5. Describing people, objects, and events: More about *ser* and *estar*

ABUELA: Cuidado, Susana, el café **está** muy caliente. [*A la madre*] ¡La niña **está** muy grande!

MADRE: Claro, tiene cinco años. **Es** muy alta para su edad.

SUSANA: Abuelita, ¿qué **es** ese cuadro?

ABUELA: **Son** montañas de la cordillera de los Andes en Chile.

**Piénselo.** Clasifique las frases a continuación de acuerdo con la función de **ser** o **estar**.

|  | CONDICIÓN | CARACTERÍSTICA |
|---|---|---|
| 1. El café **está** caliente. | ____ | ____ |
| 2. ¡La niña **está** muy grande! | ____ | ____ |
| 3. **Es** muy alta para su edad. | ____ | ____ |
| 4. **Son** montañas de los Andes. | ____ | ____ |
| 5. La nieve (*snow*) en las montañas **es** fría. | ____ | ____ |

■ In *Capítulo 2*, you learned to use **ser** to identify, describe, and express nationality, ownership, and origin. You also learned to use **ser** to talk about dates and time and to tell where an event takes place.

| | |
|---|---|
| Víctor **es** de Venezuela. | *Victor is from Venezuela.* (nationality) |
| **Es** un bailarín profesional. | *He is a professional dancer.* (profession) |
| **Es** alto y delgado y **es** muy fuerte. | *He is tall and thin, and he is very strong.* (distinguishing characteristics) |
| Estas figuras pintadas **son** de Víctor, tiene una colección grande. | *These painted figures belong to Victor; he has a big collection.* (possession) |
| El próximo espectáculo de su compañía de baile **es** mañana a las ocho. **Va a ser** en el Centro de Bellas Artes. | *The next performance of his dance company is tomorrow at eight o'clock. It is going to take place in the Fine Arts Center.* (time/location of event) |

■ **Ser** is also used to talk about what something is made of.

| | |
|---|---|
| El reloj **es** de oro. | *The watch is (made of) gold.* |

■ You also learned in *Capítulo 2* that **estar** is used to indicate location, to talk about health and similar conditions, and to describe changes in feelings or perceptions. It is also used to express ongoing actions, presented in *Capítulo 4*.

| | |
|---|---|
| El Centro de Bellas Artes **está** en el centro. | *The Fine Arts Center is downtown.* (location) |
| Víctor **estaba** (*was*) enfermo la semana pasada, pero ahora **está** bien. | *Victor was sick last week, but now he is fine.* (health) |
| Víctor **está** nervioso antes del espectáculo, pero siempre **está** contento después. | *Victor is nervous before the performance, but he is always happy afterward.* (feelings, condition) |
| Algunos bailarines **están** ensayando ahora. | *Some dancers are rehearsing now.* (ongoing action) |

■ When describing people or objects, use **ser** to convey an intrinsic characteristic. Use **estar** to convey a feeling or perception. The difference in meaning is sometimes so pronounced that the adjectives have different English translations.

| ADJECTIVE | WITH SER | WITH ESTAR |
|---|---|---|
| **aburrido/a** | *boring* | *bored* |
| **bueno/a** | *good* (character) | *well* (health); *physically attractive* |
| **grave** | *serious* (situation) | *seriously ill* |
| **listo/a** | *clever* | *ready* |
| **malo/a** | *bad* (character) | *ill* |
| **muerto/a** | *dead* (atmosphere) | *deceased* |
| **rico/a** | *rich, wealthy* | *delicious* (food) |
| **verde** | *green* | *unripe* |
| **vivo/a** | *lively* (personality) | *alive* |

| | |
|---|---|
| Javier **es** malo, les roba dinero a sus compañeros y dice mentiras. | *Javier is bad; he steals money from his classmates and tells lies.* |
| Roberto Tovares **es** rico. Tiene una casa en California, un rancho en México y un apartamento en París. | *Roberto Tovares is wealthy. He has a house in California, a ranch in Mexico, and an apartment in Paris.* |
| ¡Esta sopa **está** riquísima! ¿Usaste una receta diferente? | *This soup is delicious! Did you use a different recipe?* |

**6-27 Una familia va de compras.** Observen la foto de una familia venezolana que sale de un centro comercial en Caracas. Describan a las personas que ven, e incluyan la información de las preguntas. Si es necesario, usen su imaginación.

1. ¿Quiénes son las personas?
2. ¿Cómo son?
3. ¿Dónde están?
4. ¿Cómo están?
5. ¿Qué están haciendo?

**6-28 La mañana horrible de Javier.** Lea el cuento sobre la mañana de Javier y complételo con la forma apropiada de **ser** o **estar**.

Javier se despierta temprano. (1) _____ las seis de la mañana. La casa (2) _____ muy fría, y el agua en la ducha (3) _____ fría también. ¡Javier no (4) _____ nada contento! Su reunión con la profesora de historia (5) _____ a las 10:00 y él no (6) _____ listo. Necesita leer un artículo antes de la reunión, pero no sabe dónde (7) _____. Tiene hambre, pero no hay pan, los plátanos (8) _____ verdes y (9) _____ demasiado tarde para hacer café. La situación (10) _____ grave, piensa Javier.

Javier entra en la oficina de la profesora Guzmán a las 10:00. Ella (11) _____ normalmente relajada, pero hoy (12) _____ tensa. Le dice a Javier que su borrador (*draft*) no (13) _____ bueno y que tiene que trabajar mucho más. Cuando sale de la reunión, Javier (14) _____ muy preocupado.

**6-29 ¿Quiénes son y cómo están?** Mire las siguientes fotos y explique quiénes son estas personas, cómo son y cómo están en estas situaciones.

## SITUACIONES

1. **Role A.** Your classmate asks about the photo of your family (or friends). Explain a) who the people are; b) where they are; c) what they are like; and d) how they are feeling in the photo.

   **Role B.** Ask your classmate to see the photo he/she is holding. Ask as many questions as you can about the people in the photo, their activities, and the setting.

2. **Role A.** You have lost your favorite sweater. You think you may have left it in your Spanish class, so you go to the department office, where they have a lost-and-found box (**una caja de objetos perdidos**). Explain to the secretary a) what you lost (**perder**); b) where your Spanish class is held; and c) what your sweater is made of and what it looks like. Answer the secretary's questions.

   **Role B.** You are the department secretary, and the lost-and-found box (**la caja de objetos perdidos**) is in your office. A student comes to ask about a lost sweater. Ask the student a) to identify himself/herself; b) what the sweater looks like; and c) where and when the student lost (**perder**) it.

# MOSAICOS

## A escuchar

**Take notes to recall information**

When you want to remember something that you are listening to, like an academic lecture, you benefit from taking notes. Taking notes in other situations is helpful also. For example, when you ask for directions, you will remember them better if you take notes.

### Antes de escuchar

**6-30 Preparación.** Usted va a escuchar una conversación entre Andrea, una adolescente, y sus padres. Andrea habla con ellos sobre la ropa que va a necesitar durante el año escolar. Antes de escuchar, prepare una lista de las cosas que usted tuvo que comprar para el invierno antes del comienzo de las clases este año.

accesorios de invierno: _____

ropa de invierno: _____

### Escuchar

🔊 **6-31 ¿Comprende usted?** Now listen to the conversation between Andrea
CD 3 and her parents. As you listen, take notes on what she needs. Write at least
Track 26 three items per category that Andrea mentions.

1. Para ir a clases Andrea necesita. . .
2. Para practicar deportes Andrea tiene que comprar. . .
3. Para salir con sus amigos Andrea quiere. . .

### Después de escuchar

 **6-32 Ahora usted.** Responda oralmente a las siguientes preguntas. Su compañero/a debe tomar apuntes. Luego, intercambien papeles. Finalmente, cada uno debe verificar si su compañero/a tiene la información correcta.

1. ¿Qué ropa, muebles para su cuarto y/o aparatos electrónicos compró cada uno/a de ustedes antes de comenzar sus clases en la universidad este semestre?
2. ¿Qué accesorios compró cada uno/a de ustedes? ¿Dónde los compró?
3. ¿Fueron ustedes a las rebajas? ¿Gastó cada uno/a mucho dinero?

# A conversar

**Negotiate a price**

In Hispanic cultures, negotiating the price of an item in an open-air market or other location in which the price is not fixed is an activity that has both linguistic and cultural rules. You should haggle over a price only if you intend to buy the item. Your initial offer, while lower than the selling price given by the vendor, should be reasonable, because an excessively low price may be insulting. In your negotiation, which may last several turns, you may include a brief comment about the desirability of the item and a reaction to the price suggested by the vendor.

**ESTRATEGIA**

*En directo*

To haggle:
**CLIENTE/A**
  Me gusta este/a _____, pero no tengo tanto dinero.

  Sólo puedo pagar...

  ¡Es muy caro/a!

  ¿Qué le parece(n)... bolívares/dólares (etc.)?

  Le doy... bolívares/dólares (etc.).

**VENDEDOR/A**
  ¡Imposible!

  Me cuesta(n) más...

  El material es importado/de primera calidad.

  Lo siento, pero no puedo darle... por ese precio.

## Antes de conversar

**6-33 Preparación.** Usted quiere comprar unos regalos o algunas cosas para su cuarto/apartamento en un mercado al aire libre. Complete la tabla con la información.

| ¿QUÉ QUIERE COMPRAR? | ¿PARA QUIÉN(ES)? | DESCRIPCIÓN DEL PRODUCTO |
|---|---|---|
|  |  |  |
|  |  |  |
|  |  |  |
|  |  |  |

## Conversar

**6-34 Entre nosotros.** Usted está en un mercado al aire libre. Pregúntele al vendedor/a la vendedora (su compañero/a) el precio de los productos que usted desea comprar. Regatee (*Haggle*) para obtener el mejor precio posible. Use las expresiones más apropiadas. Luego, cambien de papel.

## Después de conversar

**6-35 Un poco más.** Conversen sobre su experiencia de regateo en el mercado al aire libre de la actividad **6-34**. Cuéntense lo siguiente:

1. qué productos compró y para quién los compró
2. qué precio le dio el vendedor/la vendedora por cada producto
3. cuánto dinero le ofreció usted
4. cuánto pagó finalmente

# A leer

**Use context to figure out the meaning of unfamiliar words**

All readers encounter unknown words and phrases, even in their native language. In our native language we automatically use the surrounding context and our overall comprehension of the text to figure out the meaning of these unknown words and phrases, and we can learn to use the same strategy in the second language. As you read, think about what each sentence or paragraph means. When you come to a word you don't know, reread the last line or two, focusing on the overall meaning. In many cases, this strategy will enable you to understand the unknown word without using a dictionary.

## Antes de leer

**6-36 Preparación.** PRIMERA FASE. Mire rápidamente el texto en la actividad **6-37** y use su conocimiento del tema para responder a las preguntas. Hay más de una respuesta correcta.

1. ¿Qué tipo de texto es?
   a. sugerencias para comprar en Internet
   b. publicidad (*advertising*) para una tienda virtual
   c. una lista de tiendas que venden sus productos por Internet
2. ¿Qué información lo/la ayudó a responder a la pregunta 1?
   a. el título
   b. los gráficos
   c. unas palabras clave (*key*) en el texto
3. Según su experiencia, ¿qué información sobre las compras espera encontrar en el texto?
   a. productos que están a la venta (*for sale*) y los precios
   b. formas de pago
   c. precios especiales para algunos productos

 **SEGUNDA FASE.** Converse con su compañero/a sobre lo siguiente:

1. ¿Les gusta comprar en Internet, o prefieren ir a las tiendas? ¿Por qué?
2. ¿Conocen algunas megatiendas en Internet? ¿Cuál(es)?
3. ¿Qué cosas compran en las megatiendas en Internet?
4. ¿Qué cosas no compran en Internet? ¿Por qué?

# Leer

**6-37 Primera mirada.** Lea la página web de CompreenInternet.net que aparece a continuación.

Bienvenido a CompreenInternet.net

| Menú | Nuestro Proceso | Beneficios |
|---|---|---|

**Menú**
- Nuestra compañía
- Nuestros servicios
- Cómo puede comprar
- Recomendaciones prácticas
- Preguntas frecuentes
- Nuestras filiales

- Póngase en contacto con nosotros
- Recomiéndenos y gane puntos
- Búsqueda

**Dirección en EE.UU.**
1438 Flagler Street
Miami, Florida (Fl)
Código Zip:  33166
Tel : 305-328-6289
Utilice esta
dirección para
su envío (shipping)

- Asistencia para afiliados
- Actualizar datos personales
- Modificación de clave
- Salida

**Nuestro Proceso**
1. Hágase miembro
2. Busque su producto
3. Calcule los gastos de su envío
4. Pague con tarjeta de crédito
5. Espere su envío y disfrútelo

3. Calcule los gastos de su envío
2. Busque su producto
4. Pague con tarjeta de crédito
1. Hágase miembro
5. Espere su envío y disfrútelo

**Beneficios**
- Excelentes precios
- Pagos en bolívares
- Entrega en todo el país
- Nuestras filiales de Nueva York o Miami hacen los envíos

**Servicios**

Compra de una gran variedad de productos en Internet:

- Aparatos eléctricos/electrónicos
- Muebles accesorios, ropa, juguetes, software, etc.
- Asistencia de expertos durante y después de su compra
- Envío gratis en Venezuela
- Descuentos por recomendarnos a otras personas
- Lista de las mejores tiendas en Internet
- Ofertas y gangas de la semana

Ahora, indique si las siguientes afirmaciones son correctas (**C**) o incorrectas (**I**). Si son incorrectas (**I**), corrija la información.

1. ___ Los productos y servicios que CompreenInternet.com ofrece son principalmente para personas que viven fuera de Venezuela.
2. ___ La sección **Nuestro proceso** de la página web les indica a los clientes las fases de una compra en Internet.
3. ___ Las tiendas que promociona (*advertises*) CompreenInternet.com incluyen sólo tiendas que están en Venezuela.
4. ___ CompreenInternet.com tiene su oficina central en Venezuela.
5. ___ Los clientes pueden comprar ropa solamente.
6. ___ Los clientes pueden ahorrar (*save*) dinero si compran en Internet.

**6-38 Segunda mirada.** Lea otra vez la página web de CompreenInternet.net y seleccione la alternativa correcta.

1. En el **Menú** de CompreenInternet.net, la frase **Nuestras filiales** significa...
   a. los clientes de CompreenInternet.net.
   b. las tiendas asociadas con CompreenInternet.net.
   c. un producto que vende CompreenInternet.net.

2. Los clientes que compran en CompreenInternet.net pagan en...
   a. dólares
   b. bolívares
   c. dólares y bolívares

3. La expresión **Hágase miembro** en la sección **Nuestro proceso** probablemente significa que para comprar, las personas deben...
   a. subscribirse a una lista de clientes de la tienda en Internet.
   b. trabajar para la compañía para comprar a precios especiales.
   c. comprar un mínimo al año.

4. La expresión **envío gratis** significa que los clientes...
   a. van a un almacén (*warehouse*) para recoger sus compras.
   b. no pagan por recibir los productos en su casa.
   c. pagan un precio reducido por algunos productos.

## Después de leer

 **6-39 Ampliación.** Lean una vez más la página web de CompreenInternet.net y completen la tabla con los productos que, según ustedes, las chicas, los chicos o ambos visitan con más frecuencia. Compartan sus respuestas con las de otra pareja.

| LAS CHICAS | LOS CHICOS | AMBOS |
| --- | --- | --- |
|  |  |  |
|  |  |  |
|  |  |  |
|  |  |  |

# A escribir

**ESTRATEGIA**

**Sequence events**

In our interactions with others, we all talk about or write about experiences and events that occur over time in a sequence. That sequence can serve as the basis of the step-by-step chronological organization of the piece we are writing. Using the correct connectors to indicate the succession of events or transitions will help you make your writing clearer and easier for readers to follow.

## Antes de escribir

**6-40 Preparación.** Usted compró un producto en Internet (ropa, un mueble, un accesorio, etc.), pero el producto resultó ser diferente de sus expectativas. Usted está muy decepcionado/a (*disapppointed*) y decide escribirle una carta a alguien de su familia para contarle su experiencia. Haga lo siguiente:

1. Escriba el nombre de la tienda donde usted compró el producto.
2. Indique qué producto compró en Internet y si compró más de uno.
3. Prepare una lista de nombres y adjetivos para describir lo que usted compró, por ejemplo, un vestido negro largo, una camisa blanca ancha, un plato decorativo de cerámica.
4. Narre lo que ocurrió en orden cronológico. ¿Cuándo hizo (*did you make*) la compra en Internet? ¿Qué ocurrió después de hacer la compra? ¿Qué hizo usted primero, después, más tarde, etc.? ¿Cuánto costó y cómo pagó usted, con una tarjeta de crédito?
5. Escriba la razón de su insatisfacción con el producto.

## Escribir

**6-41 Manos a la obra.** Ahora escríbale la carta a alguien de su familia para contarle qué le ocurrió. Use la información que preparó en la actividad **6-40**. Incluya la fecha, el saludo, el cierre de la carta y la despedida.

## Después de escribir

**6-42 Revisión.** Ahora lea su carta por lo menos dos veces. Piense en la persona que la va a leer. Verifique lo siguiente:

1. ¿Incluyó usted toda la información necesaria?
2. ¿Escribió en su carta la fecha, el saludo, el cierre de la carta y la despedida?
3. ¿Organizó los eventos cronológicamente para contar paso a paso lo que ocurrió? ¿Usó algunas expresiones que indican transición temporal para hacer más comprensible su narración?
4. ¿Revisó la gramática de su texto: el vocabulario correcto, la concordancia (*agreement*), el tiempo (presente, pasado)?
5. ¿Usó la puntuación y ortografía correctas?

---

### En directo

To indicate the succession of events or temporal transitions, you may use the following connectors: **primero, luego, más tarde, antes de eso, después (de eso), finalmente**

---

### Cultura

Although big department stores are increasingly popular in Spanish-speaking countries, people still enjoy shopping at local neighborhood stores. For example, instead of buying bread from a large supermarket, some prefer to go to the neighborhood bakery (**panadería**), where they probably have a long-standing relationship with the bakery owner and employees.

# ENFOQUE CULTURAL

## El mundo fascinante de Simón Bolívar

El nombre completo de Bolívar es Simón José Antonio de la Santísima Trinidad Bolívar y Ponte Palacios y Blanco. Nace en Caracas en 1783 en una familia aristocrática y muy rica. Cuando Bolívar tiene siete años de edad, su padre muere y dos años después también muere su madre. El joven Simón vive entonces con un tío y es educado por dos de los más importantes intelectuales de la época, Simón Rodríguez y Andrés Bello. A los catorce años es un oficial en el ejército español y a los quince, viaja por primera vez a Europa. Allí se casa con una mujer española y regresa a Venezuela. Ocho meses después, su joven esposa muere, posiblemente de una enfermedad tropical, y a los 20 años, Bolívar regresa a Europa, se une a los movimientos revolucionarios de esa época y promete ganar la independencia de los países americanos.

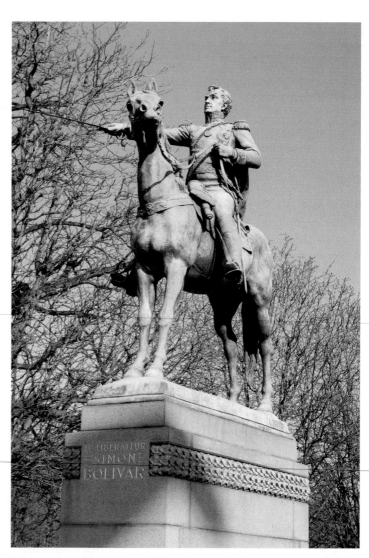

Estatua de Simón Bolívar, el Libertador, en París

Manuela Sáenz

Su vida es muy apasionada y romántica, llena de aventuras, amor y heroísmo. Las guerras de la independencia son muy violentas y demandan mucho esfuerzo e inteligencia política. Bolívar viaja a caballo por Venezuela, Colombia, Ecuador, Perú y Bolivia en condiciones muy difíciles. Varias veces casi lo asesinan sus adversarios y sólo milagrosamente salva su vida. Durante muchos años mantiene una relación amorosa con Manuela Sáenz, una mujer de carácter fuerte y muy valiente, reconocida como una de las primeras feministas de la América hispana.

Durante más de veinte años, hasta su muerte en 1830, Bolívar es el líder político y militar más importante de la América española. Consigue la independencia de Venezuela en 1813; la de Colombia y Panamá en 1820; la de Ecuador en 1823; y la de Perú y Bolivia en 1825. Durante once años, Bolívar unifica estos cinco países, bajo el nombre de la Gran Colombia, pero después de su muerte, la Gran Colombia se divide nuevamente.

Estos países tienen mucho en común. En primer lugar, frecuentemente se llaman *países bolivarianos* porque Bolívar los liberó. Para ellos Bolívar es tan importante como George Washington para los estadounidenses. Muchos latinoamericanos recuerdan el ideal de Bolívar de hacer un país grande y fuerte de las antiguas colonias españolas. Y este ideal está presente en los Juegos Bolivarianos que se celebran cada cuatro años en distintas ciudades de estos países (en Armenia y Pereira, Colombia, en 2005 y en Sucre, Bolivia, en 2009).

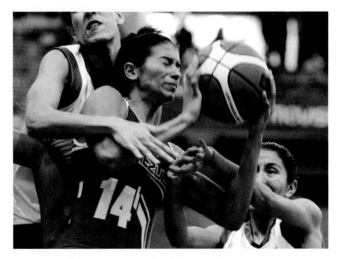
Jugadoras de baloncesto en los juegos bolivarianos

**6-43 Comprensión.** PRIMERA FASE. **Reconocimiento de palabras clave.** Encuentre en el texto la palabra o expresión que mejor expresa el significado de las siguientes ideas.

1. at age fourteen      _____
2. officer      _____
3. disease      _____
4. wars      _____
5. travels by horse      _____
6. several times      _____
7. feminists      _____
8. unifies      _____

SEGUNDA FASE. **Oraciones importantes.** Subraye las afirmaciones que contienen ideas que se encuentran en el texto. Luego indique en qué parte del texto están.

1. There was a difference of fifteen years in the ages of Bolivar's parents.
2. After both of his parents died, Bolivar lived with an uncle.
3. Bolívar had a long and happy marriage to a Spanish woman.
4. Many times Bolívar came close to being assassinated, but managed to escape with his life.
5. He had a long love affair with a woman known as an early Latin American feminist.
6. Bolivar's ideal was to create one large, strong country out of all of the old Spanish colonies.
7. The games in honor of Bolívar are played regularly in Caracas.
8. Venezuela won the most gold medals in the most recent games.

TERCERA FASE. **Ideas principales.** Escriba un párrafo breve en inglés resumiendo las ideas principales expresadas en el texto.

 **6-44 Use la información.** Prepare una presentación oral sobre algo relacionado con el nombre de Bolívar. Puede ser un país, una región de un país, una ciudad, dinero, una universidad, etc. Explique cuál es el objeto de su presentación, en qué país está y otras características interesantes. Para preparar esta actividad, visite la página web de *Mosaicos* y siga los enlaces útiles.

**7-1 Deportes: ¿Quién es?** PRIMERA FASE. Asocie los deportes de la columna de la izquierda con los jugadores hispanos a la derecha.

1. ____ ciclismo
2. ____ tenis
3. ____ béisbol
4. ____ golf

a. Sergio García
b. Alex Rodríguez
c. Rafael Nadal
d. Alberto Contador
e. David Nalbandian

SEGUNDA FASE. Ahora hablen entre ustedes de dos de sus jugadores favoritos/jugadoras favoritas. Expliquen quiénes son y a qué deporte juegan, dónde juegan, qué campeonatos ganaron y por qué son sus jugadores favoritos/jugadoras favoritas.

## Deportes y equipos deportivos

CD 3
Track 34

el béisbol — el bate — los jugadores — el guante

el golf — los palos de golf

la raqueta — la cancha — el tenis

el cesto / la cesta — el básquetbol / el baloncesto

la pelota — la red — el vóleibol

**7-2 ¿Qué necesitamos para jugar?** PRIMERA FASE. Escriba el equipo que se necesita para practicar cada deporte.

| DEPORTE | EQUIPO |
| --- | --- |
| béisbol | |
| golf | |
| vóleibol | |
| baloncesto | |
| tenis | |

**SEGUNDA FASE.** Entreviste a su compañero/a para conversar sobre el equipo que necesita para practicar deportes.

1. ¿Qué deporte(s) practicas? ¿Por qué?
2. ¿Qué equipo necesitas para practicarlo(s)?
3. ¿Dónde compras el equipo y la ropa que necesitas?

 **7-3 ¿Qué deporte es?** Túrnense para identificar los siguientes deportes.

1. Hay nueve jugadores en cada equipo y usan un bate y una pelota.
2. Es un juego para dos o cuatro jugadores; necesitan raquetas y una pelota.
3. En este deporte los jugadores no deben usar las manos.
4. Para practicar este deporte necesitamos tener una bicicleta.
5. En cada equipo hay cinco jugadores que lanzan (*throw*) el balón a un cesto.
6. Para este deporte necesitamos una red y una pelota. Mucha gente lo juega en la playa.

### En otras palabras

Different words are used in Spanish for *ball*, depending on the context. The ball in basketball and volleyball is usually called a **balón**. Both **pelota** and **balón** are used for the soccer ball. **Pelota** is also used in golf and tennis. **Bola** or **bolo** is used in bowling.

 **7-4 Su deporte favorito.** Háganse las preguntas necesarias para averiguar lo siguiente.

1. el deporte favorito para practicar
2. el lugar donde lo practica, con quién y cuándo
3. el deporte favorito para ver
4. el lugar y las personas con quienes ve su deporte favorito
5. los nombres de sus equipos favoritos/as
6. la marca (*brand*) de ropa deportiva que más le gusta

 **7-5 Concurso.** Ustedes van a organizar un concurso sobre deportes. En grupos de tres o cuatro, elijan a uno/a de los/las deportistas en las fotos y hagan lo siguiente en tres minutos:

1. Identifiquen al/a la atleta y su deporte. (5 pts)
2. Digan algún campeonato/torneo (*tournament*) que este/a atleta ganó. (5 pts)
3. Digan el equipo que necesita para practicar su deporte. (5 pts)
4. Cuenten algún dato personal o profesional de esta persona. (5 pts)

**SEGUNDA FASE.** Compartan con la clase la información sobre este/a atleta. El grupo con la información más completa es campeón.

# ■)) El tiempo y las estaciones

CD 3
Track 35

## Verano

¿Qué tiempo hace? Hace buen tiempo y hace calor. Es un día perfecto para jugar al vóleibol en la playa. El cielo **está despejado** y **hace mucho sol.**

## Otoño

**Hace fresco** y mucho **viento.** No es fácil jugar al golf cuando hace viento. Pero el otoño es muy bonito porque muchos **árboles** cambian de color antes de **perder** las hojas.

## Invierno

Hoy hace mal tiempo. Anoche **nevó** y hoy hace frío. Hay mucha **nieve** y **hielo** en las calles. Los **lagos** también **se congelaron** y algunas personas **aprovechan** para **patinar sobre el hielo.**

## Primavera

Hoy **está nublado** y **está lloviendo.** Por eso, estos chicos no pueden jugar al fútbol y están **jugando a los bolos.** Pero **la lluvia** es muy buena para las plantas y las flores, y además limpia la **atmósfera contaminada.**

> ### En otras palabras
> In some Spanish-speaking countries the expressions **jugar (al) boliche** or **ir de bowling** are preferred to **jugar a los bolos.**

**7-6 Condiciones meteorológicas.** Asocie la situación de la columna de la izquierda con la oración más lógica de la derecha.

1. ___ Las calles están blancas.
2. ___ Las personas llevan impermeable y paraguas.
3. ___ La casa es un horno y vamos a ir a la playa.
4. ___ Los árboles se mueven (*move*) mucho.
5. ___ Vamos a celebrar mi cumpleaños en el parque porque el clima está perfecto.
6. ___ El cielo (*sky*) está cubierto (*overcast*) y parece que va a llover.

a. Hace muy buen tiempo.
b. Hace mucho viento.
c. Está lloviendo.
d. Hace mucho calor.
e. Está nevando.
f. Está nublado.

> ### En directo
> To thank a friend for calling:
>
> **Mil gracias por llamar. ¡Fue un gusto escucharte!**
> *Many thanks for calling. It was a pleasure to hear your voice!*
>
> **Gracias por llamar. ¡Qué placer escucharte!**
> *Thanks for calling. What a pleasure to hear from you!*

**7-7 ¿Qué tiempo hace?** Un amigo/Una amiga lo/la llama por teléfono desde otra ciudad. Pregúntele qué tiempo hace allí y averigüe cuáles son sus planes. Su amigo/a debe hacerle preguntas a usted también.

MODELO: E1: *¡Qué sorpresa! ¿Dónde estás?*
E2: _____
E1: *¿Qué tiempo hace allí?*
E2: _____

**7-8 El tiempo y las actividades.** PRIMERA FASE. Túrnense para explicar qué les gusta hacer a usted y a sus amigos en las siguientes condiciones.

1. Cuando llueve yo…
2. Cuando hace mucho calor me gusta…
3. A veces cuando nieva…
4. Mis amigos y yo… cuando hace mal tiempo.
5. En invierno…
6. Los estudiantes… cuando hace buen tiempo.
7. Cuando está nublado…
8. Hoy hace viento pero…

 SEGUNDA FASE. Preparen un breve diálogo que incluya al menos (*at least*) los siguientes elementos:

1. una pregunta
2. tres expresiones de tiempo
3. un deporte

MODELO:  E1:  *Hola, Carmen. ¿Vamos a la playa esta tarde? Hace mucho calor.*
E2:  *Sí, pero en la televisión dicen que esta tarde va a llover.*
E1:  *Está nublado pero pienso que no va a llover.*
E2:  *Bueno, pues vamos. Es mejor jugar al vóleibol cuando está nublado.*

**7-9 Las temperaturas.** PRIMERA FASE. Escojan una ciudad de este mapa de Uruguay y túrnense para completar la siguiente conversación.

E1:  *¿Qué temperatura hace en _____?*
E2:  *_____ grados. Su equivalente en Fahrenheit es _____.*
E1:  *¿Y qué tiempo hace allí?*
E2:  *_____. ¿Y qué temperatura hace en _____?*

SEGUNDA FASE. Siguiendo el modelo de la *Primera fase*, preparen un pronóstico del tiempo (*weather report*) de su región para presentar por televisión. Indiquen:

1. la temperatura de tres ciudades
2. el tiempo que hace hoy
3. el tiempo que va a hacer mañana

> ### Cultura
>
> In Hispanic countries the Celsius system is used. To convert degrees Fahrenheit to the Celsius system, subtract 32, multiply by 5, and divide by 9.
>
> $86°F - 32 = 54$
>
> $54 \times 5 = 270$
>
> $270/9 = 30°C$

**Sol y Luna de Hoy**

**Sol**
sale .........06:30 hs
se pone...17:29 hs
**Luna**
sale .........23:42 hs
se pone...11:03 hs

**Fases de la luna**

🌘 menguante
Jul. 24

🌑 nueva
Jul. 30

🌒 creciente
Ago. 6

🌕 llena
Ago. 15

ARTIGAS 17°c
RIVERA 18°c
SALTO 14°c
TACUAREMBÓ 15°c
PAYSANDÚ 16°c
FRAY BENTOS 12°c
DURAZNO 9°c
MONTEVIDEO 14°c

cielo claro | algo nuboso | nuboso | inestable | lluvioso | tormenta eléctrica

# ◀)) ¿Qué pasó ayer?

CD 3
Track 36 ## Un partido importante

Ayer fue el juego decisivo del campeonato de fútbol.

Rigoberto **se despertó** temprano.

**Se levantó**.

**Se vistió.**

> ### Cultura
>
> Hispanic sports fans generally do not boo opposing teams or particular players. Instead they whistle to show their displeasure. This behavior may occur at a soccer game, boxing match, or other popular sports events.

**Se sentó** a comer un buen desayuno. Después **se fue** para el **campo** de fútbol.

Durante el partido el árbitro **pitó** un **penalti.**

Un jugador del equipo **contrario se enfadó** y **discutió** con el **árbitro,** pero el equipo de Rigoberto **metió un gol** y **ganó.**

Después del partido Rigoberto **se quitó** el uniforme, **se bañó** y **se puso la ropa.**

Luego fue a una fiesta para celebrar el triunfo.

**Volvió** a casa muy tarde, **se acostó** y **se durmió** enseguida.

**7-10 ¿Qué significa?** Busque la definición de estas palabras relacionadas con los deportes.

| | | | |
|---|---|---|---|
| 1. ___ ganar | | a. | jugador/a número 1 en un deporte |
| 2. ___ equipo | | b. | persona que mantiene el orden en un partido |
| 3. ___ gol | | c. | tener más puntos al terminar un juego |
| 4. ___ partido | | d. | juego entre dos equipos o individuos |
| 5. ___ árbitro | | e. | punto en un partido de fútbol |
| 6. ___ campeón/campeona | | f. | un grupo de jugadores |

**7-11 El partido de Rigoberto.** Contesten las preguntas sobre las actividades de Rigoberto el día del partido.

1. ¿Qué hizo (*did*) Rigoberto primero?
2. ¿Qué hizo después de levantarse?
3. ¿Qué desayunó Rigoberto?
4. ¿Por qué se enfadó un jugador del equipo contrario?
5. ¿Quién ganó el partido?
6. ¿Adónde fue Rigoberto después del partido?

**7-12 ¿Las actividades de ayer?** PRIMERA FASE. Háganse preguntas para obtener la siguiente información sobre las actividades de cada uno/a de ustedes ayer.

1. hora de despertarse y de levantarse ayer
2. desayuno que tomó
3. número de horas de estudio
4. deporte(s) que practicó y por cuánto tiempo
5. hora de acostarse

SEGUNDA FASE. Después, comparen sus actividades, contestando las siguientes preguntas:

1. ¿Quién de ustedes se levantó más temprano ayer?
2. ¿Quién tomó un desayuno más nutritivo?
3. ¿Quién estudió más?
4. ¿Quién practicó deportes por más tiempo?
5. ¿Quién se acostó más tarde?

**7-13 El clima en Hispanoamérica.** You will listen to the weather forecast for four cities in Latin America. Before you listen, write down the information that you might hear in a weather forecast in each season.

CD 3
Track 37

primavera  _____
verano      _____
otoño       _____
invierno    _____

Now, focus on the general idea of what is said. As you listen, indicate (✓) whether each forecast predicts good or bad weather.

| | BUEN TIEMPO | MAL TIEMPO |
|---|---|---|
| Montevideo | _____ | _____ |
| Buenos Aires | _____ | _____ |
| Caracas | _____ | _____ |
| Ciudad de México | _____ | _____ |

# EN ACCIÓN

## Diarios de bicicleta: Aficionados al fútbol

### Antes de ver

**7-14** Los deportes juegan un papel importante en el mundo hispano. Escriba los nombres de algunos atletas españoles y latinoamericanos que usted asocia con los siguientes deportes: tenis, béisbol, fútbol y boxeo.

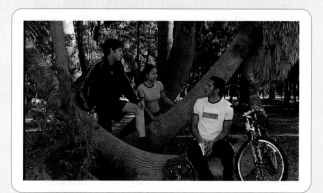

### Mientras ve

**7-15** Ponga en orden cronológico las siguientes acciones de Javier, según lo que le dice a Daniel.

___ Me desperté.
___ Fui al parque.
___ Me invitaron a jugar al fútbol.
___ Me senté junto a un árbol.
___ Me encontré con un señor y me dijo cómo llegar al parque.
___ Me dormí por unos minutos.
___ Me encontré con Martín y Claudia.
___ Dejé la bicicleta junto al árbol.
___ Ahora necesito encontrar mi bicicleta.
___ No usé el candado de mi bicicleta.

### Después de ver

**7-16** Cuéntele a su compañero/a una experiencia en la que usted perdió algo. Incluya el mayor número de detalles posible.

# FUNCIONES Y FORMAS

## 1. Talking about the past: Preterit of reflexive verbs and pronouns

Rodolfo

REPORTERO: ¡Felicitaciones por el triunfo! ¡Jugaron como campeones!

RODOLFO: Gracias. El triunfo es de todo el equipo. Fue un partido difícil, pero **nos preparamos** bien.

REPORTERO: ¿Y cómo empezó este día de victoria para ti, Rodolfo?

RODOLFO: Bueno, anoche **me acosté** temprano. Hoy, yo **me levanté** a las 5:30, **me duché** muy rápido para el entrenamiento, **me vestí** y **me fui** a la cancha.

REPORTERO: ¿Y cómo **se prepararon** ustedes para enfrentar al equipo rival?

RODOLFO: Eh… Primero, es fundamental **sentirse** ganador y también es importante tener un buen entrenador como el nuestro.

**Piénselo.** Indique si las siguientes afirmaciones son probables (**P**) o improbables (**I**), según la conversación entre Rodolfo y el reportero.

1. ___ Todos los jugadores del equipo **se acostaron** tarde la noche antes del partido.
2. ___ Rodolfo **se levantó** temprano el día del partido.
3. ___ Rodolfo **se duchó** rápidamente para llegar a tiempo a la cancha.
4. ___ El equipo no **se preparó** bien para el partido, por eso, ganó.
5. ___ Según Rodolfo, lo más importante para ganar es **sentirse** nervioso.

■ In *Capítulo 4* you learned about reflexive verbs. Now you will use these verbs in the preterit. The rules that apply to reflexive verbs are the same in the past tense as in the present.

■ As you have seen, reflexive verbs express what people do *to* or *for themselves*.

| | |
|---|---|
| Los jugadores **se levantaron** a las cinco. | *The players got up at five o'clock.* |
| Yo **me preparé** rápidamente. | *I got ready quickly.* |

| LEVANTARSE | | | |
|---|---|---|---|
| yo | **me levanté** | nosotros/as | **nos levantamos** |
| tú | **te levantaste** | vosotros/as | **os levantasteis** |
| Ud., él, ella | **se levantó** | Uds., ellos/as | **se levantaron** |

■ With a conjugated verb followed by an infinitive, place the reflexive pronoun before the conjugated verb or attach it to the infinitive.

Yo **me** empecé a preparar a las cinco.
Yo empecé a preparar**me** a las cinco.
} *I started to get ready at five.*

■ With the present progressive (**estar + -ndo**), place the reflexive pronoun before the conjugated form of **estar** or attach it to the present participle. When attaching a pronoun to the present participle, add a written accent mark to the stressed vowel (the vowel preceding **-ndo**).

Amelia **se** está duchando ahora.
Amelia está duch**á**nd**ose** ahora.
} *Amelia is taking a shower now.*

Nosotros **nos** estamos lavando los dientes.
Nosotros estamos lav**á**nd**onos** los dientes.
} *We are brushing our teeth.*

■ Remember that when referring to parts of the body and clothing, the definite articles are used with reflexive verbs.

Me lavé **el** pelo.　　　　　*I washed my hair.*

Alicia se quitó **la** sudadera.　*Alicia took off her sweatshirt.*

■ Some verbs that use reflexive pronouns do not necessarily convey the idea of doing something to or for oneself. These verbs normally convey the idea of mental or physical states.

María **se enfermó** gravemente la semana pasada.
*María got seriously sick last week.*

**Nos preocupamos** mucho cuando fue al hospital.
*We got very worried when she went to the hospital.*

■ Reflexive verbs that convey the idea of mental or physical states do not take an object. The following verbs are in that category.

| | | | |
|---|---|---|---|
| **arrepentirse (ie)** | *to regret* | **enfadarse** | *to get upset, angry* |
| **atreverse** | *to dare* | **quejarse** | *to complain* |
| **divertirse (ie)** | *to have fun* | **sentirse (ie)** | *to feel* |
| **disculparse** | *to apologize* | | |

La entrenadora **se disculpó** de no asistir a la práctica del viernes pasado.
*The coach apologized for not attending last Friday's practice.*

El público **se quejó** del pobre desempeño de los jugadores.
*The public complained about the poor performance of the players.*

> **Lengua**
>
> Do you know why the verb forms **duchándose** and **lavándonos** have an accent mark?

**7-17 ¿Cómo fue su día ayer?** Ponga estas actividades en el orden más lógico.

___ Me preparé para un examen.
___ Me dormí.
___ Me levanté.
___ Me fui a la universidad.
___ Me acosté.

___ Me desperté temprano.
___ Me senté a desayunar.
___ Me bañé.
___ Al final del día, me sentí cansado/a.

**7-18 ¿Cómo reaccionan?** PRIMERA FASE. Cuando ustedes tienen un partido importante, ¿hacen actividades semejantes o diferentes? ¿Reaccionan bien o mal?

MODELO:  E1:  *Yo me acuesto temprano la noche anterior.*
         E2:  *Yo no. Yo me acuesto a la hora de siempre.*

1. Yo me despierto…
2. A veces yo me enfado si…
3. Nuestro entrenador se queja cuando nosotros…
4. Cuando el entrenador está enfadado, yo no me atrevo a…
5. Cuando los jugadores cometen un error en la cancha, ellos…
6. Cuando esperamos el comienzo de un partido importante, nosotros siempre…
7. Cuando jugamos muy bien, nosotros…
8. Después de un partido difícil, siempre…

SEGUNDA FASE. Comparen la información de la *Primera fase* con la de otra pareja. ¿Son semejantes o diferentes sus actividades? ¿Reaccionan igual o de una manera diferente?

MODELO:  E1:  *Juan y yo nos despertamos muy temprano el día de un partido importante. ¿Y ustedes?*
         E2:  *Yo me despierto temprano también, pero Susana se levanta tarde. Dice que no está nerviosa antes de los partidos.*

**7-19 Mis actividades de ayer.** Haga una lista de por lo menos tres actividades físicas que usted hizo ayer para cuidar de su salud.

**7-20 ¿Qué les ocurrió a estas personas?** Lean las siguientes situaciones y hablen de lo que hicieron (*did*) estas personas después. Usen los verbos de la lista u otros propios. Después, comparen sus opiniones con las de otros compañeros/otras compañeras.

| afeitarse | despertarse | lavarse | mirarse | perfumarse | quitarse |
| bañarse | enfadarse | maquillarse | peinarse | probarse | secarse |

MODELO:      Bernardo se despertó cuando sonó el despertador.
         E1:  *Luego se levantó lentamente. En tu opinión, ¿qué pasó después?*
         E2:  *Probablemente se afeitó.*

1. Teresa se miró en el espejo.
2. Juan y Tomás entraron en el vestuario (*locker room*) del gimnasio después del partido.
3. Marisa y Erica salieron de una tienda deportiva.
4. Ramón salió de la ducha.
5. Marta no está contenta. Habló con la capitana del equipo de unos temas personales y luego la capitana les contó todo a otras jugadoras.
6. Pablo llegó tarde a la cancha.

**7-21 Nuestra preparación para el campeonato.** El mes pasado ustedes representaron a su universidad en un campeonato de tenis en Montevideo. Digan lo que hicieron (*you did*)...

1. para prepararse físicamente.
2. para prepararse mentalmente.
3. para cumplir (*to fulfill*) con las responsabilidades académicas.

**7-22 Loreta se levantó con el pie izquierdo (*got up on the wrong side of the bed*).** **PRIMERA FASE.** Observen las siguientes escenas y cuenten lo que ocurrió. Usen su imaginación y los verbos de la lista u otros, si es necesario.

| | | | |
|---|---|---|---|
| acostarse | ducharse | explicar | practicar |
| despertarse | enfadarse | golpear (*to knock*) | sentarse |
| disculparse | enojarse | levantarse | sonar |

**SEGUNDA FASE.** Cuenten lo que ocurrió entre las 8:00 y las 9:00 de la mañana.

## SITUACIONES

1. **Role A.** You are a well-known athlete who is greatly admired by young people in your country. A television reporter will interview you to prepare a special feature about your life. Answer the reporter's questions as fully as possible. Remember that you are considered a role model by young people.

   **Role B.** You are a television reporter. Today you are interviewing a highly respected and admired sports figure. After introducing yourself and greeting the athlete, find out a) what school he/she went to; b) when he/she started to play; c) what his/her daily routine is to keep in shape (**estar en forma**); and d) what sports he/she practiced yesterday.

2. **Role A.** You are visiting a friend who is preparing for the Olympics (**Olimpiadas**) at a training resort (**centro de entrenamiento**). Ask a) how many athletes are there; b) what time the athletes went to bed last night; c) what time they got up today; d) when they started practice today; e) what they ate for breakfast and where they ate; and d) if these activities are similar to his/her usual routine.

   **Role B.** A friend is visiting you today at the training resort (**centro de entrenamiento**) where you are preparing for the Olympics. Answer your friend's questions and add any information of interest.

## 2. Talking about the past: Preterit of *-er* and *-ir* verbs whose stem ends in a vowel

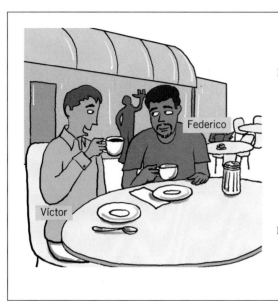

VICTOR: Federico, ¿miraste el partido entre la selección de Argentina y la de Colombia?

FEDERICO: No, Víctor. Pero **oí** las noticias por la radio, y mi hermano **leyó** la crónica del partido en el periódico. La selección colombiana ganó dos a uno. Los argentinos no jugaron bien ¿Y tú? ¿Viste el partido?

VICTOR: Desafortunadamente no, pero **leí** en Internet que los jugadores argentinos no **oyeron** las instrucciones de su entrenador y cometieron muchos errores. Por eso, el árbitro les marcó un penalti.

FEDERICO: Tienes razón, yo **oí** que el plan estratégico de defensa que **construyeron** no fue bueno. Ellos **creyeron** que ganarles a los colombianos es fácil, pero es un equipo muy bueno.

**Piénselo.** ¿Quién lo hizo (*Who did it*): Federico (**F**), Víctor (**V**), el hermano de Federico (**HF**), los jugadores argentinos (**JA**)?

1. ___ **Oyó** las noticias del partido por la radio.
2. ___ **Leyó** la crónica en el periódico.
3. ___ **Leyó** en Internet comentarios sobre el partido.
4. ___ No **oyeron** las instrucciones.
5. ___ **Creyeron** que ganar es fácil.
6. ___ **Construyeron** (*They built*) una mala estrategia de defensa.

■ You have already learned the preterit forms of regular **-er** and **-ir** verbs. For verbs whose stem ends in a vowel, the preterit ending for the **usted/él/ella** form is **-yó** and for the **ustedes/ellos/ellas** form, the ending is **-yeron**.

| LEER | | | |
|---|---|---|---|
| yo | leí | nosotros/as | leímos |
| tú | leíste | vosotros/as | leísteis |
| Ud., él, ella | leyó | Uds., ellos/as | leyeron |

| OÍR | | | |
|---|---|---|---|
| yo | oí | nosotros/as | oímos |
| tú | oíste | vosotros/as | oísteis |
| Ud., él, ella | **oyó** | Uds., ellos/as | **oyeron** |

| | |
|---|---|
| Los jugadores **oyeron** los comentarios negativos de los reporteros deportivos. | *The players heard the negative comments of the sports commentators.* |
| Cuando el entrenador **oyó** el pitazo final, abrazó a los jugadores. | *When the coach heard the final whistle, he hugged the players.* |
| Los miembros del equipo **construyeron** una casa con la organización Hábitat para la Humanidad. | *The members of the team built a house with Habitat for Humanity.* |

**Lengua**

Note that **-er** and **-ir** verbs whose stems end in a vowel (**creer**, **leer**, **oír**) have an accent mark on the **i** in the infinitive and in the preterit endings that begin with **i**.

No la **oí** llegar anoche.
*I didn't hear her arrive last night.*

**7-23 ¿Cómo se enteraron (*found out*) de los resultados?** El fin de semana pasado se jugó la Copa Davis. Las siguientes personas son fanáticas del tenis. Indique cómo se enteró cada uno de ellos de los resultados de los partidos. Use los verbos creer, leer, mirar y oír.

1. Paula y su novio pasaron el fin de semana en las montañas y _____ los resultados en la radio durante su viaje de regreso a la ciudad.
2. Mercedes trabajó en la biblioteca todo el fin de semana. Cuando su hermano le contó los resultados, ella no lo _____.
3. Ricardo participó en un partido de fútbol entre su universidad y una universidad rival. Él _____ los resultados en el periódico.
4. Los Belmar salieron a hacer ejercicio a la hora del partido. Prefieren el aire libre a mirar televisión y _____ los resultados en el periódico al día siguiente.

 **7-24 La semana pasada.** Miren la lista de actividades e indiquen en cuáles participaron todos ustedes la semana pasada.

| | |
|---|---|
| concluir un proyecto importante | ir a la biblioteca |
| construir algo | leer el periódico de la universidad |
| contribuir con su tiempo a una organización sin fines de lucro (*non-profit*) | mirar una película para una clase |
| | oír música en español |

## SITUACIONES

1. **Role A.** You have just written a book on Hispanics in professional sports in the United States. A reporter for your local newspaper is interviewing you. Respond to the reporter's questions about your work.

   **Role B.** You are a newspaper reporter interviewing the author of a new book on professional Hispanic athletes in the United States. After introducing yourself, ask a) what sports he/she wrote about; b) whether he/she read newspapers from Latin America to write the book; c) what contributions the first Hispanic players made to professional sports in the United States; and d) what he/she concluded from the research (**investigación**).

2. **Role A.** Call a friend to invite him/her to go to a sports event with you. Mention a) what the event is; b) that you read about it in the newspaper; and c) that you want to see the city's new stadium (**estadio**).

   **Role B.** Your friend calls to invite you to a sports event. Respond to the invitation with questions and comments. Then decide if you want to go and either accept or decline the invitation.

## 3. Talking about the past: Preterit of stem-changing *-ir* verbs

Querido Sr. López,

°Nos encanta Argentina! Anoche salimos a bailar, excepto Raquel y Estela, que no **durmieron** en el avión. Ellas no **se divirtieron** anoche, ¡pero nosotras sí!

Esta mañana desayunamos en un café cerca del hotel. Todas nosotras **pedimos** desayunos enormes excepto Laura, que **pidió** sólo café. Rafael, el camarero que nos **sirvió**, se **rió** de lo mucho que comimos. Pero como somos atletas, tenemos que comer bastante.

Esta mañana comenzamos su plan de entrenamiento bajo la dirección del Sr. Lucero. Marcela tiene problemas en su pierna derecha, por eso **prefirió** no caminar mucho. María Jesús y Paulina **se sintieron** cansadas después de bailar toda la noche, pero **siguieron** las instrucciones y se quejaron solamente un poco.

Mañana se celebra el Carnaval de Primavera en Buenos Aires. Le vamos a escribir en un par de días.

Muchos saludos de su equipo

**Piénselo.** Después de cada oración, escriba a qué persona(s) se refiere, según la breve nota anterior.

1. No **durmieron** en el avión. _____ y _____
2. No desayunó esta mañana; **pidió** un café solamente. _____
3. Se **rió** de lo mucho que comieron las jugadoras. _____
4. **Prefirió** no caminar mucho. _____
5. No **se divirtieron** anoche porque no salieron con sus amigas. _____ y _____
6. **Se sintieron** cansadas, pero **siguieron** el plan de entrenamiento. _____ y _____

■ In the preterit, stem-changing **-ir** verbs change **e → i** and **o → u** in the **usted, él, ella** and **ustedes, ellos/as** forms. The endings are the same as those of regular **-ir** verbs.

Marta **prefirió** salir temprano.    *Marta preferred to leave early.*

Las jugadoras **durmieron** tranquilamente.    *The players slept calmly.*

| PREFERIR (e → i) | | | |
|---|---|---|---|
| yo | preferí | nosotros/as | preferimos |
| tú | preferiste | vosotros/as | preferisteis |
| Ud., él, ella | prefirió | Uds., ellos/as | prefirieron |

| DORMIR (o → u) | | | |
|---|---|---|---|
| yo | dormí | nosotros/as | dormimos |
| tú | dormiste | vosotros/as | dormisteis |
| Ud., él, ella | durmió | Uds., ellos/as | durmieron |

■ The following are other stem-changing **-ir** verbs:

| despedirse | to say goodbye | Los hinchas se despidieron de su equipo. *The fans said goodbye to their team.* |
|---|---|---|
| divertirse | to have fun | Todos se divirtieron con la presentación de las barras paralelas. *Everyone had fun with the performance of the parallel bars.* |
| morir | to die | Un hincha murió de un ataque al corazón cuando su equipo perdió. *A fan died of a heart attack when his team lost.* |
| pedir | to ask for/order | El entrenador pidió agua para los jugadores. *The coach asked for water for the players.* |
| reír | to laugh | El árbitro se rió cuando un perro cruzó la cancha. *The referee laughed when a dog crossed the field.* |
| repetir | to repeat | El reportero repitió el nombre del jugador que marcó el gol. *The reporter repeated the name of the player who scored the goal.* |
| seguir | to follow | Los jugadores siguieron las instrucciones de su entrenador. *The players followed the instructions of their coach.* |
| sentirse | to feel | Todos se sintieron felices con el triunfo. *Everyone felt happy about the victory.* |
| servir | to serve | Los hinchas le sirvieron perros calientes gratis al público. *Fans served free hot dogs to the public.* |
| vestirse | to get dressed | Los jugadores se vistieron para ir a celebrar. *The players got dressed to go out and celebrate.* |

**7-25 Carrera de un campeón.** Un famoso deportista recibió muchas medallas durante su carrera. ¿Cómo lo logró (*accomplished*)? Marque (✔) la alternativa más apropiada, según usted.

1. ___ **a.** Durmió poco antes de cada partido.
   ___ **b.** Siempre durmió por lo menos ocho horas.
2. ___ **a.** Prefirió evitar el alcohol.
   ___ **b.** Prefirió beber alcohol moderadamente.
3. ___ **a.** Se preparó solo.
   ___ **b.** Prefirió prepararse con un entrenador.
4. ___ **a.** Prefirió comer poco, pero bien.
   ___ **b.** Comió mucho durante toda su vida, pero hizo mucho ejercicio físico.
5. ___ **a.** Practicó sólo antes de los partidos importantes.
   ___ **b.** Practicó constantemente.
6. ___ **a.** Repitió sus victorias con frecuencia.
   ___ **b.** Raras veces repitió sus victorias.
7. ___ **a.** Cuando no ganó un partido, se sintió deprimido y no continuó tratando.
   ___ **b.** Se sintió triste cuando no ganó un partido, pero pidió ayuda para mejorar.

**7-26 Momentos cruciales.** Indique lo que hicieron las siguientes jugadoras del equipo femenino de básquetbol unos minutos antes del partido.

1. Marta (vestirse) _____ con la camiseta número 3.
2. Ana y Luisa Fernanda (seguir) _____ con atención los pasos del calentamiento (*warm-up*).
3. Carmen (preferir) _____ no beber agua antes del partido.
4. Las jugadoras del equipo contrario (reírse) _____ cuando su entrenador les hizo una broma (*joke*).
5. La entrenadora les (repetir) _____ las instrucciones a todas las jugadoras.
6. El equipo (sentirse) _____ animado (*encouraged*) con los aplausos del público.

**7-27 Celebrando la victoria.** Uno de los equipos de su universidad ganó un campeonato importante y ustedes organizaron una fiesta en su honor. Explíquenle a otra pareja los siguientes detalles de la fiesta. Usen los verbos de la lista.

| | | | |
|---|---|---|---|
| despedirse | pedir | repetir | servir |
| divertirse | reír | sentirse | vestirse |

1. hora y lugar de la fiesta
2. número de personas que asistieron y cómo se vistieron para la fiesta
3. tipo de cooperación que ustedes pidieron para los gastos de la fiesta
4. cómo se divirtieron en la fiesta
5. comida y bebida que sirvieron en la fiesta y tipo de música que escucharon
6. reconocimiento (*recognition*) que les dieron a los jugadores
7. sentimientos de los jugadores durante la fiesta
8. a qué hora los invitados se despidieron y se fueron de la fiesta

## SITUACIONES

1. **Role A.** You had to work late last night and missed an important basketball game at your school. Call a friend who went to the game. After greeting your friend, a) explain why you did not go; b) ask questions about the game; c) answer your friend's questions; and d) accept your friend's invitation to go to another game next Saturday.

   **Role B.** A friend calls to find out about last night's basketball game. Answer your friend's questions and then a) say that there is another game on Saturday; b) find out if your friend is free that evening; and c) if free, invite him/her to go with you.

2. **Role A.** You read in today's newspaper that your favorite football (**fútbol americano**) player was interviewed on TV last night. Call your friend, who watched the interview, to find out a) on which channel (**canal**) he/she watched the interview; b) the time of the interview; c) who interviewed (**entrevistar**) the football player; and d) what they talked about.

   **Role B.** Your friend calls to get the details of a TV interview of his/her favorite football (**fútbol americano**) player. Answer all of your friend's questions in as much detail as possible.

# 4. Emphasizing or clarifying information: Pronouns after prepositions

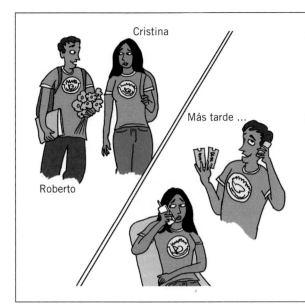

ROBERTO: Estas flores son **para ti**, Cristina.

CRISTINA: **¿Para mí?** Gracias, Roberto.

* * *

ROBERTO: Oye, Cristina. El partido es mañana. ¿Quieres ir **conmigo**?

CRISTINA: No puedo ir **contigo**, Roberto. Mis primos están aquí, y voy al partido **con ellos**.

**Piénselo.** Indique quién dice cada oración, Roberto (**R**) o Cristina (**C**).

1. ___ ¿Quieres ir **conmigo**?
2. ___ Estas flores son **para ti**.
3. ___ No puedo ir **contigo**.
4. ___ **¿Para mí?**
5. ___ Voy **con ellos**.

■ In *Capítulo* 6 you used **a + mí**, **a + ti**, and so on, to clarify or emphasize the indirect object pronoun: **Le di el suéter a él.** These same pronouns are used after other prepositions, such as **de**, **para**, and **sin**.

| a | | mí |
|---|---|---|
| de | | ti |
| para | | usted, él, ella |
| por | + | nosotros/as |
| sin | | vosotros/as |
| sobre | | ustedes, ellos/as |

| | |
|---|---|
| Siempre habla **de ti**. | *He is always talking about you.* |
| Las raquetas son **para mí**. | *The racquet are for me.* |
| No quieren ir **sin nosotros**. | *They do not want to go without us.* |

■ In a few cases, Spanish does not use **mí** and **ti** after prepositions. After **con**, use **conmigo** and **contigo**. After **entre**, use **tú y yo**.

| | |
|---|---|
| ¿Vas al partido **conmigo**? | *Are you going to the game with me?* |
| Sí, voy **contigo**. | *Yes, I am going with you.* |
| **Entre tú** y **yo**, ella tiene unos problemas serios. | *Between you and me, she has some serious problems.* |

**7-28 Un amigo preguntón.** Un amigo de Rosario le hace muchas preguntas. Conecte sus preguntas en la columna de la izquierda con un comentario lógico de Rosario en la columna de la derecha.

1. ¿Con quién vas a ir al partido de tenis, Rosario?
2. ¿Por qué no vemos las finales del campeonato con Sofía?
3. Rosario, ¿para quién es esta raqueta de tenis?
4. ¿Pueden mis amigos ir a la cancha con nosotros?
5. Después del partido de ayer encontramos una sudadera. ¿Es de Carlos?
6. ¿De quién van a recibir el trofeo los ganadores?

a. La compré para ti. ¿Te gusta?
b. Imposible. No podemos ir con ellos. Tengo sólo dos billetes.
c. Contigo, ¡por supuesto!
d. Sí, es de él.
e. De nosotros. De ti y de mí. ¡Qué emocionante!
f. Prefiero verlas sin ella. Habla mucho y no puedo concentrarme.

**7-29 Haciendo planes.** ¿Cuándo van a hacer las siguientes actividades? Escojan individualmente una opción en cada número y, luego pregúntense entre ustedes.

**MODELO:** E1: *¿Cuándo puedes ir al cine conmigo?*
E2: *Puedo ir contigo el sábado.*

1. estudiar español/historia/biología
2. ir al parque/al partido de béisbol/al concierto
3. jugar al golf/al tenis/al vóleibol

**7-30 ¿Con quién va?** Completen el siguiente diálogo, usando pronombres.

JULIA: Yo salgo ahora. ¿Vienes conmigo?
CELIA: No, no puedo ir _____. Tengo que trabajar media hora más en la tienda.
JULIA: ¡Cuánto lo siento! Entonces, ¿vas a ir con Roberto?
CELIA: Sí, voy a ir con _____ más tarde.
JULIA: Seguro que él no quiere ir sin _____ . Tú eres su mejor amigo/a.
CELIA: Sí, somos muy buenos amigos. ¿Y sabes dónde te vas a sentar?
JULIA: Sí, voy a sentarme entre _____ y _____ .

## SITUACIONES

1. **Role A.** One of your friends is a basketball player. He gave you two tickets for today's game, but you have no transportation. Call a friend who has a car. After greeting him/her a) explain how you got the tickets for the game; b) invite your friend to go with you; and c) explain that you have no transportation.

   **Role B.** A friend calls you to invite you to today's basketball game. After exchanging greetings, a) thank your friend for the invitation; b) respond that you would be delighted to go with him/her; c) say that you can pick him/her up in your car; and d) agree on a time and place.

2. **Role A.** Your friend calls to chat and tells you that he/she went to a surprise party (*una fiesta sorpresa*) last weekend. Ask a) who gave the party; b) who it was for; c) who your friend went with; and d) what happened at the party.

   **Role B.** You call a friend to chat. Talk about the surprise party (*fiesta sorpresa*) you went to last weekend. Answer your friend's questions about the party in as much detail as possible.

# 5. Talking about the past: Some irregular preterits

ABUELA: ¡Bienvenidos! Pasen, por favor. ¿No **vino** Carmencita? ¿Está enferma?

MADRE: Está trabajando. **Estuvo** en la biblioteca hasta muy tarde anoche, pero no **pudo** terminar su proyecto. Nos **dijo** que es largo y difícil.

\* \* \*

CARMENCITA: ¿Mis padres? **Tuvieron** que ir a la casa de mi abuela, pero no **quise** ir a otra cena aburrida. Les **dije** una pequeña mentira sobre un proyecto...

**Piénselo.** Marque (✓) si las afirmaciones en la columna de la izquierda probablemente expresan la **verdad**, una **mentira** (*lie*) o si **no se sabe**, según la información en las conversaciones.

|  | VERDAD | MENTIRA | NO SE SABE |
|---|---|---|---|
| 1. Carmencita **tuvo** que terminar un proyecto. | —— | —— | —— |
| 2. Los padres de Carmencita **tuvieron** que ir a la casa de la abuela. | —— | —— | —— |
| 3. Carmencita no **quiso** ir a la casa de su abuela. | —— | —— | —— |
| 4. Carmencita **estuvo** en la biblioteca por muchas horas. | —— | —— | —— |
| 5. Carmencita **hizo** un proyecto para una clase. | —— | —— | —— |
| 6. Carmencita les **dijo** la verdad a sus padres. | —— | —— | —— |

▪ Some verbs have irregular forms in the preterit because they use different stems than in the present tense. The preterit endings are added to those stems. Note that the **yo, usted, él,** and **ella** preterit endings of these verbs are unstressed and therefore do not have written accents.

▪ The verbs **hacer, querer,** and **venir** have an **i** in the preterit stem.

| INFINITIVE | NEW STEM | PRETERIT FORMS |
|---|---|---|
| **hacer** | hic- | hice, hiciste, hizo, hicimos, hicisteis, hicieron |
| **querer**[1] | quis- | quise, quisiste, quiso, quisimos, quisisteis, quisieron |
| **venir** | vin- | vine, viniste, vino, vinimos, vinisteis, vinieron |

---

[1]The verb **querer** in the preterit followed by an infinitive normally means to *try (but fail) to do something.*
  **Quise hacerlo** ayer.               *I tried to do it yesterday.*

■ The verbs **estar**, **tener**, **poder**, **poner**, and **saber** have a **u** in the preterit stem.

| INFINITIVE | NEW STEM | PRETERIT FORMS |
|---|---|---|
| estar | estuv- | estuve, estuviste, estuvo, estuvimos, estuvisteis, estuvieron |
| tener | tuv- | tuve, tuviste, tuvo, tuvimos, tuvisteis, tuvieron |
| poder[2] | pud- | pude, pudiste, pudo, pudimos, pudisteis, pudieron |
| poner | pus- | puse, pusiste, puso, pusimos, pusisteis, pusieron |
| saber[3] | sup- | supe, supiste, supo, supimos, supisteis, supieron |

■ The verbs **decir**, **traer**, and all verbs ending in **-ducir** (e.g., **traducir**, *to translate*) have a **j** in the stem and use the ending **-eron** instead of **-ieron**. **Decir** also has an **i** in the stem.

| INFINITIVE | NEW STEM | PRETERIT FORMS |
|---|---|---|
| decir | dij- | dije, dijiste, dijo, dijimos, dijisteis, dijeron |
| traer | traj- | traje, trajiste, trajo, trajimos, trajisteis, trajeron |
| traducir | traduj- | traduje, tradujiste, tradujo, tradujimos, tradujisteis, tradujeron |

 **7-31 ¿Qué hizo usted ayer? PRIMERA FASE.** De la siguiente lista de quehaceres (*chores*), usted sólo pudo hacer dos o tres. Marque (✓) lo que hizo y lo que no pudo hacer.

|  | SÍ | NO |
|---|---|---|
| 1. lavar la ropa | _____ | _____ |
| 2. comprar los zapatos de tenis | _____ | _____ |
| 3. probarse el uniforme nuevo | _____ | _____ |
| 4. conocer al nuevo entrenador | _____ | _____ |
| 5. mirar el video del último partido | _____ | _____ |
| 6. comentar las estrategias del próximo partido | _____ | _____ |

 **SEGUNDA FASE.** Hágale preguntas a su compañero/a para averiguar qué pudo hacer ayer.

MODELO:    comprar el trofeo para el campeonato
    E1:  *¿Compraste el trofeo para el campeonato?*
    E2:  *Quise comprarlo, pero no pude.*
    E1:  *¿Por qué no pudiste comprarlo?*
    E2:  *Porque tuve que regresar al laboratorio.*

---

[2]**Poder** used in the preterit usually means *to manage to do something.*
    **Pude hacerlo** esta mañana.        *I managed to do it this morning.*
[3]**Saber** in the preterit normally means *to learn* in the sense of *to find out.*
    **Supe** que llegó anoche.        *I learned that he arrived last night.*

**7-32 ¿Qué ocurrió?** Expliquen qué le ocurrió a Javier el día de su cumpleaños. Den la mayor cantidad de información posible.

1.
2.
3.
4.
5.
6.

**7-33 Unos días de descanso.** Su compañero/a estuvo unos días en Argentina. Hágale preguntas sobre los siguientes puntos para saber más de su viaje.

1. lugares adonde fue
2. tiempo que estuvo en Argentina
3. cosas interesantes que hizo
4. los lugares que le gustaron más
5. si pudo hablar español y con quién(es)

## SITUACIONES

1. **Role A.** Congratulations! You won a contest (**concurso**) to attend the World Cup. Tell your classmate that you won the contest and that you went to the World Cup. Answer all of his/her questions in detail.

   **Role B.** Your classmate won a contest and tells you about it. Ask a) how he/she found out about the contest; b) how long he/she was away; c) how many games he/she attended; d) with whom he/she went; and e) details about the last game.

2. **Role A.** Imagine that yesterday you went to a sports event and had the opportunity to meet your favorite sports star. Explain to a friend a) where you went; b) what happened and where; c) what you did when you saw this person; d) what he/she said to you; and d) what happened finally.

   **Role B.** Your friend tells you that he/she met a very famous sports star yesterday. Ask about what happened and what they talked about.

---

### En directo

To express interest and to ask for details:

**¡No me digas! ¿Qué pasó?**
*You don't say! What happened?*

**¿Y qué más pasó?**
*And what else happened?*

**¡Cuenta, cuenta!**
*Tell me more!*

---

### Lengua

**Hace**, meaning *ago*
▪ To indicate the time that has passed since an action was completed, use **hace +** *length of time* **+ que +** *preterit verb*.

**Hace** dos meses **que** fui a la Copa Mundial.
*I went to the World Cup two months **ago**.*

**Hace** una hora **que** empezó el partido.
*The game started an hour **ago**.*

▪ When **hace +** *length of time* ends the sentence, omit **que**.

Fui a la Copa Mundial **hace** dos meses.

El partido empezó **hace** una hora.

# MOSAICOS

## A escuchar

**ESTRATEGIA**

**Differentiate fact from opinion**

When you listen to a report or a newscast on the radio, television, or the Internet, you need to differentiate facts from opinions. Unlike opinions, which express personal attitudes, beliefs, or points of view, facts are provable. You may distinguish facts from opinions by identifying fact indicators, which include information that refers to data, statistics, numbers, and other verifiable evidence.

### Antes de escuchar

**7-34 Preparación.** Usted va a escuchar una conversación entre un reportero y Nicolás, un esquiador argentino que habla sobre su viaje al centro de esquí en Bariloche, Argentina. Antes de escuchar la conversación, escriba una oración con información concreta sobre el tiempo o sobre las pendientes (*slopes*) en las canchas de esquí. Después escriba una opinión sobre la gente del lugar que, según usted, Nicolás probablemente va a conocer.

### Escuchar

**7-35 ¿Comprende usted?** Now listen to the conversation and write down in Spanish three pieces of factual information and three opinions Nicolás offered about the place and/or the people.

CD 3
Track 38

información concreta:

1. _____
2. _____
3. _____

opinión personal:

1. _____
2. _____
3. _____

### Después de escuchar

**7-36 Ahora usted.** Hágale preguntas a su compañero/a para averigüar la siguiente información.

1. un deporte que practica y dónde lo practica
2. el tiempo que hace cuando lo practica
3. su atleta favorito/a en ese deporte y por qué

# A conversar

## Antes de conversar

**7-37 Preparación.** PRIMERA FASE. Hagan una lista de los deportes que se practican en Argentina y/o Uruguay, según su conocimiento de la región.

SEGUNDA FASE. En la página web de *Mosaicos*, busquen los deportes que escribieron en la *Primera fase*. Elijan uno que se practica en Argentina o Uruguay, busquen la siguiente información sobre ese deporte y tomen apuntes.

1. el nombre del deporte
2. dos o tres datos históricos básicos sobre el deporte: a) cuándo empezó a practicarse; b) dónde empezó; c) algo interesante sobre los comienzos (*beginnings*) del deporte
3. una persona argentina o uruguaya famosa en la historia de este deporte: a) nombre, fecha y lugar de nacimiento y b) datos sobre su carrera deportiva

## Conversar

**7-38 Entre nosotros.** Hagan una presentación de no más de un minuto sobre el deporte que investigaron, usando la información que aprendieron. Divídanse el trabajo de preparar y hacer su presentación entre ustedes. Pueden usar *PowerPoint* e imágenes de Internet para crear una presentación interesante.

## Después de conversar

**7-39 Un poco más.** Elija un deporte y un/a atleta de las presentaciones que hicieron sus compañeros/as de clase. Usando sus apuntes, prepare dos informes breves (de no más de un minuto). Incluya la información indicada en las fichas (*note cards*) a continuación.

| Deporte | Atleta |
|---|---|
| Nombre: | Nombre y nacionalidad: |
| Dónde y cuándo empezó a practicarse: | Fecha de nacimiento: |
| Dónde se practica ahora: | Campeonatos que ganó: |
| Su popularidad: | Su reputación nacional e internacional: |

# A leer

**Predict and guess content**

You may enhance your comprehension of a text by predicting and guessing its content before you start to read. Begin by brainstorming the information you are likely to find in the text and identifying the text format. Try this with a magazine article in English and think consciously about how you rely on your own knowledge and reading experiences, as well as textual information, to anticipate what you will read. When you read in Spanish, try to use the strategies that you deploy automatically when you read in your native language.

## Antes de leer

**7-40 Preparación.** PRIMERA FASE. Mire el texto "Los deportes: Una pasión uruguaya". Lea el título y examine las fotos. Tome un minuto máximo para escanear el texto, buscando nombres de lugares y deportes conocidos. Luego responda a las preguntas.

1. Después de examinar el texto, seleccione su tema entre las posibilidades a continuación.
   **a.** los lugares en Uruguay dónde se practican los deportes
   **b.** los atletas más famosos de Uruguay
   **c.** el amor de los uruguayos por los deportes

2. Marque (✓) las ideas que usted anticipa encontrar en el texto.
   **a.** ___ los deportes más populares de Uruguay
   **b.** ___ el origen de los deportes de Uruguay
   **c.** ___ los lugares donde se practican algunos deportes en Uruguay
   **d.** ___ los campeonatos que ganaron los equipos de fútbol uruguayo
   **e.** ___ los deportes favoritos de los uruguayos en comparación con los de otros países latinoamericanos

SEGUNDA FASE. Ahora, respondan a estas preguntas.

1. ¿Les gustan los deportes individuales o prefieren los de equipo? ¿Por qué?
2. ¿Saben esquiar? ¿Esquían en la nieve o en el agua? ¿Esquían bien o regular?
3. ¿Qué tipos de surf conocen? ¿Han oído hablar (*Have you heard about*) del surf en la arena? ¿Qué saben acerca del deporte?
4. ¿Conocen el fútbol de salón? ¿Se practica en su país? ¿Dónde?

# Leer

## Los deportes: Una pasión uruguaya

Uruguay es un país pequeño donde los deportes forman una parte integral de la vida de la mayor parte de sus habitantes.

Entre las grandes pasiones nacionales, desde luego, está el fútbol. Desde su infancia, muchos uruguayos acompañan fielmente a sus equipos predilectos. En varias ocasiones, la selección nacional uruguaya ganó títulos y campeonatos importantes.

Pero los uruguayos son un pueblo inquieto, de una personalidad versátil que no limita su interés a un solo deporte. El básquetbol, el ciclismo, el fútbol de salón, el rugby, el boxeo y la pelota de mano son otros deportes que tienen muchos aficionados.

Las hermosas y privilegiadas playas del Uruguay también favorecen los deportes acuáticos, como el surf, que, según los expertos, cuenta hoy con un gran número de aficionados. En 1993 en Uruguay se formó la Unión de Surf del Uruguay (USU). Ese mismo año, el país envió a sus representantes a competir internacionalmente en el Primer Campeonato Panamericano de Surf en Isla Margarita, Venezuela. Hoy en día la USU promueve el surf, arbitra las competencias clasificatorias a nivel nacional, apoya a los competidores nacionales, representa a Uruguay en competencias internacionales y compite en los Juegos Olímpicos con la Selección Uruguaya de Surf.

Sin duda, uno de los lugares predilectos de los uruguayos y turistas extranjeros para practicar el surf es Punta del Este. Ubicada al sureste del Uruguay, a 140 kilometros de Montevideo, Punta Este es una hermosa península de enormes playas, con arenas finas y gruesas, rocas y un entorno de bosques y médanos[1].

Precisamente en estos médanos nació, en el siglo pasado, una variante del surf que está despertando grandes polémicas en el país: el surf en la arena o sandsurf. Los brasileños inventaron este deporte en los años ochenta para no aburrirse cuando no había olas. La agradable temperatura de las playas uruguayas, la escasez de olas que a veces impide practicar el surf en el agua y la formación arenosa de algunas playas aumentaron considerablemente el número de personas que practican el surf en la arena. Por ejemplo, los médanos de Valizas son los más grandes de Sudamérica y los terceros más grandes del mundo, algunos con 30 metros de altura y una longitud de bajada[2] de aproximadamente 125 metros. Sin embargo, las autoridades uruguayas están controlando e incluso prohibiendo la práctica de este deporte por el posible deterioro ecológico que ocasiona. No hay duda de que la prohibición del surf en la arena no va a detener el espíritu activo de los uruguayos. Su creatividad los incentivará a buscar o inventar otras opciones para entretenerse.

[1]*dunes*  [2]*slope*

**7-41 Primera mirada.** Diga si las siguientes citas textuales (*quotations*) representan información concreta (**C**) o una opinión (**O**) del autor.

1. ___ Desde su infancia, muchos uruguayos acompañan fielmente a sus equipos predilectos.
2. ___ Pero los uruguayos son un pueblo inquieto, de una personalidad versátil que no limita su interés a un solo deporte.
3. ___ En 1993 en Uruguay se formó la Unión de Surf del Uruguay (USU).
4. ___ Punta del Este es una hermosa península de enormes playas, con arenas finas y gruesas, rocas y un entorno de bosques y médanos.
5. ___ La agradable temperatura de las playas uruguayas, la escasez de olas que a veces impide practicar el surf en el agua y la formación arenosa de algunas playas aumentaron considerablemente el número de personas que practican el surf en la arena.
6. ___ No hay duda de que la prohibición del surf en la arena no va a detener el espíritu activo de los uruguayos.

Ahora, marque (✓) la estrategia que lo/la ayudó a predecir el contenido del texto.

a. ___ Hice una lluvia de ideas (*brainstorming*) antes de leer el texto.
b. ___ Usé mi experiencia personal con los deportes.
c. ___ Analicé el formato del texto.
d. ___ Observé los elementos visuales del texto como las fotos.

**7-42 Segunda mirada.** Lea el artículo otra vez y, según la información que aparece en él, haga lo siguiente:

1. Indique dos razones que explican la popularidad del fútbol en Uruguay.
2. Diga por qué los uruguayos tienen un carácter inquieto.
3. Nombre tres deportes que se juegan en equipo, dos que son principalmente deportes individuales y uno que no requiere una pelota.
4. Dé dos razones para explicar por qué Punta del Este es un lugar ideal para practicar el surf acuático.
5. Explique dos hechos que provocaron el nacimiento del surf en la arena.
6. En su opinión, ¿deben prohibir el surf en la arena? ¿Por qué?

## Después de leer

**7-43 Ampliación.** Determinen cuál es el deporte favorito del grupo. Luego preparen una hoja descriptiva sobre ese deporte sin mencionar el nombre. Incluyan la siguiente información e intercambien su hoja con otro grupo que debe adivinar cuál es el deporte.

1. lugar donde se practica
2. deporte individual o en grupo (número de personas en el equipo)
3. clima ideal para practicarlo: Se practica en invierno… /cuando hace…
4. un jugador famoso/una jugadora famosa de este deporte
5. su opinión sobre ese jugador/esa jugadora

# A escribir

## Antes de escribir

**7-44 Preparación. PRIMERA FASE.** Los expertos afirman que el ejercicio físico beneficia a las personas. Respondan a las siguientes preguntas:

1. ¿Qué tipos de actividad física puede hacer una persona? Hagan una lista de posibles actividades físicas (ejercicio o deportes).
2. ¿Es la edad de la persona un factor importante en el tipo de actividad física que hace? ¿Por qué? Escriban una o dos razones, según los expertos.
3. ¿Son la frecuencia y la cantidad de actividad factores importantes en el ejercicio físico? ¿Por qué? Indiquen la frecuencia y la cantidad de actividad física que puede beneficiar a una persona joven y a una persona mayor, según los expertos.
4. ¿Cuáles son dos o tres beneficios del ejercicio físico, según los expertos? Escriban por lo menos una palabra (detalle) que apoye (*supports*) cada uno de los beneficios. ¿Conocen ustedes a alguna persona que se benefició con la actividad física? ¿Qué comenzó a hacer esta persona? ¿Cómo se benefició con el ejercicio?

## Escribir

**7-45 Manos a la obra.** Como proyecto final en su clase *Ejercicio y longevidad*, usted debe escribir un artículo electrónico para los jóvenes hispanos de la escuela secundaria que no hacen actividad física. Usando la información que recogió en **7-44**, escriba su artículo. Incluya lo siguiente:

1. Los beneficios del ejercicio físico, según los expertos. Escriba detalles lógicos que apoyen cada uno de los beneficios.
2. Tipos de actividad física que pueden beneficiar a una persona joven. Escriba una o dos razones, según los expertos.
3. Indique cómo la frecuencia y la cantidad de actividad física benefician a una persona, según los expertos. Dé detalles.

## Después de escribir

**7-46 Revisión.** Antes de presentar su proyecto, revise:

1. la organización y la cantidad de información: ¿Es lógica y clara la organización? ¿Hay suficientes detalles que apoyan la idea central de cada párrafo?
2. el vocabulario general y vocabulario especializado, las estructuras que utilizó para presentar la información, la concordancia, etc.
3. las expresiones para presentar la información factual o la opinión de los expertos
4. la división de los párrafos, la ortografía y la acentuación, etc.

**ESTRATEGIA**

**Add supporting details**

Supporting details are sentences, facts, examples, and ideas that follow the topic sentence or main idea and make up the body of a paragraph. Details should be sequenced logically and support the main idea of the paragraph. Paragraph structure may be visualized as follows:

Main idea
  Supporting detail #1
  Supporting detail #2
  Supporting detail #3
Closing sentence

As you write, think of how you will organize the supporting details to develop the main idea of each paragraph. Anticipate and use details that your reader can expect to see after reading the topic sentence.

**En directo**

To express facts:

**Los expertos afirman/dicen/aseguran que…**

**La investigación indica que…**

**Los estudios muestran que…**

To express an opinión:

**A mí me parece que…**

# ENFOQUE CULTURAL

## El arte del asado y la tradición ganadera en Argentina y Uruguay

Si le preguntamos a una persona de Argentina o de Uruguay cuál es su comida favorita, probablemente va a responder que es la carne. En efecto, en estos dos países la carne es más que un producto para la exportación. Es, también, el núcleo de muchas tradiciones y está unida a celebraciones, fiestas familiares y, en general, a la cultura de la región. En otras palabras, la ganadería y todo lo relacionado con el ganado contribuyen no solamente a la economía de los dos países, sino también al modo de vida y a las costumbres de sus habitantes.

Un asado argentino con carne de vaca

Indiscutiblemente, en Argentina y Uruguay el asado es un verdadero arte. Algunas personas comparan el asado de Argentina y Uruguay con la parrillada o *cook-out* de Estados Unidos, pero en realidad, son muy diferentes. Aunque la parrillada tradicional en Estados Unidos se compone principalmente de hamburguesas hechas de carne molida, también incluye pollo, costillas (*ribs*) y otros cortes de carne. Inclusive, en los últimos tiempos se han empezado a usar verduras y frutas, por consideraciones de salud. Por parte, el asado de Argentina y Uruguay incluye diferentes tipos de carne, además de algunos órganos internos de la vaca. La salsa típica que acompaña el asado argentino es el *chimichurri*, una salsa de aceite y una variedad de hierbas, mientras que en Estados Unidos frecuentemente se prepara una mezcla de salsa de tomate con salsa *Worcestershire* y azúcar.

La contribución de la ganadería a la economía es impresionante. En Uruguay, por ejemplo, la ganadería constituye cerca del 20% de la economía. Este porcentaje tan alto no lo produce solamente la carne, sino también el cuero y la lana que se usan para fabricar ropa, zapatos y otros artículos de vestir. El valor de las exportaciones de carne uruguaya supera los 500 millones de dólares, pero es necesario sumar unos 150 millones que valen las exportaciones de lana de ovejas y aproximadamente 300 millones por la venta de cueros. Estos resultados son todavía más impresionantes en el caso de Argentina, donde hay unos 40 millones de vacas y aproximadamente 25 millones de ovejas, en un país que tiene unos 40 millones de personas.

Los vaqueros que trabajan en la ganadería se llaman *gauchos*. Es cierto que el modo de vida de los gauchos está unido al arte, la literatura y la cultura de estos países. En la foto se puede ver a un gaucho en su traje típico. Las imágenes de estos vaqueros y su vida romántica y aventurera pertenecen a la literatura y el arte desde el siglo XIX. Por ejemplo, *Facundo* es uno de los más famosos libros latinoamericanos del siglo XIX. En él, Domingo Sarmiento describió con detalle la vida y las costumbres de los gauchos. José Hernández inventó otro de los grandes estereotipos gauchos en un largo poema en el que cuenta la vida, las aventuras y los sufrimientos de *Martín Fierro*, un gaucho argentino. De otra parte, Ricardo Güiraldes publicó *Don Segundo Sombra*, otro ejemplo de la representación literaria del gaucho, a principios del siglo XX.

sombrero
pañuelo
poncho
camisa
boleadora
cinturón
bombachas
botas de cuero

El traje típico del gaucho argentino

Domingo Faustino Sarmiento (1811-1888), escritor, fue el primer presidente civil de República Argentina, desde 1868 a 1874.

## En otras palabras

Expresiones argentinas

**Che**, **vos**, ¿dónde está la pelota?
*Hey, you, where is the ball?*

**¡No te mandes la parte!**
*Don't brag!*

## En otras palabras

Expresiones uruguayas

Tengo un **gurí** y dos **gurisas**.
*I have a boy and two girls.*

**¡Qué bárbaro!**
*Great!*

**7-47 Comprensión.** PRIMERA FASE. **Reconocimiento de palabras clave.** Encuentre en el texto la palabra o expresión que mejor expresa el significado de las siguientes ideas.

1. meat or beef        _____
2. cattle ranching      _____
3. barbecue           _____
4. on the other hand    _____
5. leather            _____
6. sheep             _____
7. baggy trousers     _____

SEGUNDA FASE. **Oraciones importantes.** Subraye las afirmaciones que contienen ideas que se encuentran en el texto. Luego indique en qué parte del texto están.

1. Argentinians value meat only as a commodity for export.
2. Cattle and cattle ranching are deeply embedded in the culture of Argentina and Uruguay.
3. Besides meat, some internal organs of the cow are used in a typical Argentinian *asado*.
4. There are more cows and sheep in Uruguay than there are in Argentina.
5. About one-fifth of the economy of Uruguay depends on cattle farming.
6. The combined exports of meat, wool and leather from Uruguay are worth close to one billion dollars.
7. Argentinian cowboys love to dance the tango.
8. Many authors have portrayed the life of Argentinian cowboys in their literature since the nineteenth century.

TERCERA FASE. **Ideas principales.** Escriba un párrafo breve en inglés resumiendo las ideas principales expresadas en el texto.

 **7-48 Use la información.** Haga un afiche para comparar tres de las más importantes regiones ganaderas del continente americano: Texas, los Llanos de Colombia y Venezuela, y la pampa argentina. Para preparar esta actividad, visite la página web de *Mosaicos* y siga los enlaces útiles. Incluya lo siguiente:

1. una foto de cada una de las regiones y una explicación breve para cada una de ellas
2. una descripción de tres características de cada una de las regiones, por ejemplo, el clima, la naturaleza, las personas, las costumbres, la ropa, la comida, etc.

El Día de San Fermín, el 7 de julio, se inicia la **celebración** de los sanfermines en Pamplona, España. Esta celebración, que dura del 7 al 14 de julio, es famosa mundialmente por los encierros. Los jóvenes corren por las calles seguidos de los **toros**, hasta llegar a la plaza donde **encierran** a los toros y más tarde tienen lugar las **corridas**.

**8-1 Definiciones.** Asocie el nombre de la festividad en la columna de la izquierda con su descripción en la columna de la derecha.

1. ____ San Fermín
2. ____ La Diablada
3. ____ El Rocío
4. ____ Carnaval
5. ____ El Día de los Muertos
6. ____ Semana Santa

a. Se celebra durante el carnaval de Oruro en Bolivia. personas bailan en las calles disfrazadas de demonios.

b. Muchas personas se disfrazan y bailan en comparsas por las calles.

c. Todos van al cementerio a hacer ofrendas a los seres queridos que están muertos.

d. Hay procesiones por las calles y en Antigua, Guatemala, se hacen unas alfombras de aserrín, flores y semillas.

e. Los jóvenes corren por las calles delante de los toros.

f. Es una fiesta en el sur de España. La gente va en carretas hasta una ermita.

**8-2 Describir las imágenes.** PRIMERA FASE. Describan las fotos anteriores detalladamente contestando las siguientes preguntas.

1. ¿Qué están haciendo las personas en las fotos?
2. ¿Qué ropa llevan las personas? ¿Qué colores hay en las fotos?
3. ¿Qué objetos hay en las fotos? ¿Para qué sirven?
4. ¿Hay animales? ¿Qué hacen estos animales?
5. ¿Piensan que la festividad de la foto es religiosa? ¿Por qué?
6. Según ustedes, ¿es la festividad divertida? ¿Por qué?

SEGUNDA FASE. Elijan una de las fotos y descríbanla en un párrafo. Incluyan las ideas sobre las que conversaron en la *Primera fase*.

**8-3 Contextos.** PRIMERA FASE. Hablen sobre las ideas, sentimientos o costumbres que evocan las siguientes palabras.

MODELO: el carnaval
*La palabra carnaval me hace pensar en música, baile, alegría, carrozas, desfiles, calles.*

1. los cementerios
2. los toros
3. las flores
4. los disfraces
5. las alfombras de aserrín
6. el baile

SEGUNDA FASE. Elijan una de las palabras de la *Primera fase* y escriban una oración en la que la palabra aparezca en un contexto familiar para ustedes. Compartan esta oración con la clase.

MODELO: *Cuando visitamos a los amigos llevamos flores.*

*Cultura*

El Día de Acción de Gracias (*Thanksgiving*) no se celebra en los países hispanos y tampoco es tradicional el Día de las Brujas (*Halloween*), aunque empieza a celebrarse en algunas ciudades de Hispanoamérica y de España. Por otro lado, debido a la importancia e influencia de la religión católica en los países hispanos, algunas fiestas católicas se consideran también fiestas oficiales y son días feriados. Pero lo más importante es la gran diversidad de fiestas locales. Muchas personas trabajan todo el año para garantizar el éxito de estas celebraciones en las que la gente baila y se divierte durante días enteros.

## Cultura

En muchos países hispanos, los niños reciben regalos de Papá Noel o del Niño Dios el día de Navidad. Sin embargo, la Nochebuena se considera el día más importante. Muchas personas van a la **iglesia** a la medianoche para asistir a la Misa del Gallo (*Midnight Mass*). El 6 de enero, día de la Epifanía, se celebra la llegada de los Reyes Magos con sus regalos para el Niño Jesús. La noche del 5 de enero, muchos niños se acuestan esperando la visita de los tres reyes que llegan montados en sus camellos con regalos para ellos.

# ꙮ) Otras celebraciones

CD 4
Track 2

la Nochebuena     la Navidad     la Nochevieja     el Año Nuevo

el Día de la Independencia de México

la Pascua

el Día de la Madre

el Día del Padre

el Día de Acción de Gracias

el Día de las Brujas

el Día de los Enamorados/del Amor y la Amistad

**8-4 Asociaciones. PRIMERA FASE.** Asocie las fechas de la izquierda con los días festivos de la derecha.

1. ___ el 25 de diciembre
2. ___ el 2 de noviembre
3. ___ el 6 de enero
4. ___ el 4 de julio
5. ___ el 24 de diciembre
6. ___ el 31 de diciembre
7. ___ el 14 de febrero
8. ___ el 31 de octubre

a. el Día de la Independencia de Estados Unidos
b. el Día de las Brujas
c. la Nochebuena
d. la Nochevieja/el Fin de Año
e. el Día de los Enamorados/del Amor y la Amistad
f. el Día de los Reyes Magos
g. el Día de los Muertos
h. la Navidad

**SEGUNDA FASE.** Comenten entre ustedes las respuestas a las siguientes preguntas.

1. ¿Cuál(es) de estas fiestas celebra cada uno/a de ustedes?
2. ¿Cuál es la fiesta favorita de la mayoría de las personas del grupo, y por qué?
3. ¿En cuál de estas fiestas reciben regalos? ¿Qué tipo de regalos?
4. ¿En cuál de estas fiestas hay una comida especial?

**8-5 Festivales o desfiles.** Piense en algunos festivales o desfiles importantes y complete el cuadro. Su compañero/a va a hacerle preguntas sobre ellos.

**MODELO:**   E1: *¿En qué fiesta o desfile importante estás pensando?*
        E2: *En el Cinco de Mayo.*
        E1: *¿Dónde lo celebran?*
        E2: *En México y en algunas ciudades de Estados Unidos, como Austin, Texas.*

| FESTIVAL O DESFILE | FECHA | LUGAR | DESCRIPCIÓN | OPINIÓN |
|---|---|---|---|---|
|  |  |  |  |  |
|  |  |  |  |  |
|  |  |  |  |  |
|  |  |  |  |  |

El Cinco de Mayo es una fiesta que celebra la victoria de México contra Francia en la Batalla de Puebla en 1862. Ese día hay desfiles y los mexicanos visten sus trajes típicos.

**8-6 Unos días festivos.** Hablen sobre cómo celebran ustedes estas fechas.

**MODELO:**   E1: *¿Cómo celebras tu cumpleaños?*
        E2: *Lo celebro con mi familia y mis amigos. Recibo regalos, y mi madre prepara mi comida favorita con pastel de chocolate de postre. Después escuchamos música, conversamos y a veces bailamos.*

1. la Nochevieja/el Fin de Año
2. el Día de las Brujas
3. el Día de Acción de Gracias
4. el Día de la Independencia
5. el Año Nuevo
6. el Día de la Madre

 **8-7 Una celebración importante. PRIMERA FASE.** Escojan una celebración importante del mundo hispano (Carnaval, Semana Santa, Año Nuevo, Las Posadas, La Diablada, Día de la Independencia, etc.) y busquen información en Internet sobre:

1. el lugar donde se celebra
2. la época del año
3. las actividades
4. los vestidos o disfraces
5. la comida

**SEGUNDA FASE.** Imagínese que usted y su compañero/a estuvieron en un país hispano durante la celebración que investigaron en la *Primera fase.* Explíquenles a otros/as dos compañeros/as cómo celebraron y qué pasó. Ellos les van a hacer preguntas para obtener más información.

**Lengua**

The words **fiesta**, **festividad**, and **festival** are often used interchangeably. **Fiesta** may mean a holiday or a party or celebration. **Festividad** normally refers to a public festivity or a holiday. **Festival** often involves a series of events or celebrations of a public nature. Another term for holiday is **día festivo**. **Día feriado** is a legal holiday.

## ♦)) **Las invitaciones**

CD 4
Track 3 **¿Quieres salir conmigo?**

LUISA: Hola, Arturo, ¿cómo estás?

ARTURO: Bien, Luisa, ¿y tú?

LUISA: Estupendamente. Mira, me gustaría **invitarte** a cenar conmigo el sábado. Es la ocasión perfecta para hablar de tu viaje a México.

ARTURO: La verdad es que me gustaría mucho, pero mañana no puedo porque tengo un partido de fútbol.

LUISA: ¡Qué lástima! ¿Y el domingo, día 15?

ARTURO: El domingo está bien. Si quieres, podemos **quedar** antes para **dar un paseo** por la ciudad. Las calles están adornadas para las fiestas, y la ciudad está muy **animada**.

LUISA: ¡Qué buena idea! Nos vemos en la plaza a las seis.

ARTURO: Bueno, pues nos vemos allí y luego decidimos adónde vamos a cenar.

LUISA: Gracias, Arturo, hasta el domingo.

ARTURO: Hasta el domingo.

### En directo

To accept an invitation:

**Gracias. Me encanta la idea.**

**Con mucho gusto.**

**Encantado/a.**

**Será un placer.**
*It will be a pleasure.*

To apologize:

**Me gustaría ir, pero...**

**¡Qué lástima/pena! Ese día tengo que...**

**No puedo, tengo un compromiso.**
*I can't, I have a prior engagement.*

**8-8 Una invitación. PRIMERA FASE.** Completen el siguiente cuadro según la conversación de Luisa y Arturo.

| FECHAS DE LAS INVITACIONES | EXPRESIONES QUE USA ARTURO |
|---|---|
| primera invitación: | para disculparse por no aceptar: |
| segunda invitación: | para aceptar la invitación: |

**SEGUNDA FASE.** Ahora invite a su compañero/a a cenar, o a ir al teatro o a un partido importante. Después, su compañero/a va a invitarlo/la a usted. Pueden usar las expresiones del diálogo y de *En directo*.

# Celebraciones personales

CD 4
Track 4

La boda del príncipe Felipe en mayo de 2004 fue un gran acontecimiento histórico y social en España y millones de hispanos pudieron ver por televisión. En los países hispanos, el padrino de la boda es la persona que acompaña a la novia al altar y generalmente es su padre. La madrina está en el altar con el novio y normalmente es su madre.

**8-9 Una invitación de boda.** Lean la invitación de boda y la de la recepción, y contesten las preguntas. Luego preparen una lista con las diferencias que encuentran ustedes entre estas invitaciones y las de su país.

Agradecemos su presencia
después de la ceremonia religiosa
en el Club de Golf Chapultepec
Av. Conscripto N° 425, Lomas
Hipódromo

R.S.V.P.
529-99-43
520-16-85

Personal

Pedro Martín Salda
Juana Montoya de Martín

Eduardo Calderón Solís
Elisa Noriega de Calderón

participan el matrimonio de sus hijos

Estelita
y
Alberto

y tienen el honor de invitarle a la ceremonia
religiosa que se celebrará el viernes 9 de febrero,
a las diecinueve treinta horas en el Convento de
San Joaquín, Santa Cruz Cocalco N° 15,
Legaria, dignándose impartir la
bendición nupcial
el R.P. José Ortuno S.J.
Ciudad de México

1. ¿Cómo se llaman los padres de la novia? ¿Y los del novio?
2. ¿Cómo se llaman los novios?
3. ¿Qué día es la boda?
4. ¿A qué hora es?
5. ¿En qué país se celebra esta boda?
6. ¿Adónde van a ir los invitados después de la ceremonia?

**8-10 Una ocasión memorable.** Lean la invitación y contesten las preguntas.

Nuestro querido hijo

*Davi∂*

será llamado a la lectura de la Tora
con motivo de su Bar Mitzvah
el jueves 18 de noviembre
a las ocho de la mañana en la Sinagoga
Centro Hebreo, Avenida 13-15 Zona 9.

Nos sentiremos muy honrados en compartir
con ustedes tan memorable ocasión
y será un placer recibirles en el desayuno
que seguidamente ofreceremos en el
salón de fiestas de la sinagoga.

**David y Ruth Bauman**
Fax: (502) 238-2042
Ciudad de Guatemala, Guatemala

1. ¿Cuál es el motivo de la celebración?
2. ¿Qué día es la celebración? ¿A qué hora?
3. ¿Hay otra actividad, además de la celebración religiosa?
4. ¿Quiénes son David y Ruth Bauman?
5. ¿En qué país tiene lugar esta celebración?

**8-11 Una fiesta especial.** PRIMERA FASE. Piense en una celebración o fiesta en la que usted participó recientemente. Escriba algunas notas sobre lo siguiente:

1. ¿Cuál es el nombre de la fiesta?
2. ¿Dónde se celebró? ¿Cuántos invitados asistieron?
3. Describa la comida que sirvieron.
4. ¿Cómo se divirtió la gente? ¿Tocaron música?
5. ¿Gastaron mucho los anfitriones (*hosts*)?

SEGUNDA FASE. Ahora explíquense los detalles de esta fiesta. Incluyan detalles de la *Primera fase*.

**8-12 Identificar la fiesta.** You will listen to four short dialogues about different holidays celebrated in the Hispanic world. Before you listen, write down the names of two holidays that you have studied or read about in this chapter.

CD 4
Track 5

Pay attention to the general idea of what is said. As you listen, identify the holiday each conversation refers to by writing the appropriate conversation number next to it.

____ el Día del Amor y la Amistad/Día de los Enamorados
____ el Día de los Muertos
____ el Día de los Reyes Magos
____ el Día de las Brujas

# EN ACCIÓN

## Diarios de bicicleta: La ponchera

### Antes de ver

**8-13** En este segmento, Marcos, Luciana y Javier están organizando una fiesta de cumpleaños para Gabi. Escriba cinco preguntas para averiguar si todo está listo para la fiesta.

**MODELO:** *¿Hicieron el pastel de cumpleaños?*

### Mientras ve

**8-14** Indique si las siguientes afirmaciones se refieren a Marcos (**M**), a Luciana (**L**) o a Javier (**J**).

1. ____ Quería hacer un pastel de cumpleaños.
2. ____ Invitó a toda la gente.
3. ____ Pusieron la mesa.
4. ____ Dejó caer (*dropped*) la ponchera.

### Después de ver

**8-15** Responda a las siguientes preguntas.

1. ¿Cuándo recibió la ponchera la mamá de Luciana y Marcos?
2. Según Marcos, ¿quién rompió la ponchera?
3. Según su hermana, ¿de quién fue la culpa?
4. ¿Quién le dijo la verdad a la mamá?

# FUNCIONES Y FORMAS

### 1. Expressing ongoing actions and descriptions in the past: The imperfect

ABUELA: **Antes** la música **era** suave y romántica. **Tenía** más melodía y las orquestas **eran** magníficas. **Hoy en día** no **hay** música, sólo ruido, y a la gente **no le interesa** bailar.

NANCY: **Antes** las familias **cenaban** juntas. **Conversaban** mientras **comían**, y los hijos **se aburrían** (*got bored*) mucho. **¡Era** una tortura! **Ahora** es mucho mejor. Cuando **tengo** hambre, **preparo** algo para comer. Además, los padres no **controlan** tanto la vida de sus hijos.

**Piénselo.** Indique (✓) a qué función se refiere cada afirmación.

| ACTIVIDAD | DESCRIPCIÓN EN EL PASADO | ACCIÓN O DESCRIPCIÓN HABITUAL EN EL PASADO | ACCIÓN EN EL PRESENTE |
|---|---|---|---|
| **1.** La música del pasado **tenía** más melodía. | ———— | ———— | ———— |
| **2.** Hoy en día no **hay** música. | ———— | ———— | ———— |
| **3.** Antes las familias **cenaban** juntas. | ———— | ———— | ———— |
| **4.** Los hijos **se aburrían** mucho. | ———— | ———— | ———— |
| **5.** Cuando **tengo** hambre, **preparo** algo para comer. | ———— | ———— | ———— |
| **6.** Los padres no **controlan** tanto la vida de sus hijos. | ———— | ———— | ———— |

■ You have already learned to use the preterit to talk about actions in the past. In these scenes, the grandmother and granddaughter use a different past tense, the **imperfect**, because they are focusing on how things used to be and what usually took place 50 or 60 years ago. If they were talking about a specific completed action, like something they did yesterday, they would use the preterit. Generally, the imperfect is used to:

■ express habitual or repeated actions in the past (without focus on the completion of the action).

Nosotros **íbamos** a casa para cenar todos los días a las seis.

*We used to go home to eat dinner every day at six o'clock.*

■ express an action or state that was in progress in the past (not whether the action or state was completed).

| | |
|---|---|
| Todos los invitados **hablaban** y **bailaban**. **Estaban** muy contentos. | *All the guests were talking and dancing. They were very happy.* |

■ describe characteristics and conditions in the past.

| | |
|---|---|
| El desfile **era** muy largo y **había** muchos espectadores. | *The parade was very long and there were many spectators.* |

■ tell time in the past.

| | |
|---|---|
| **Era** la una de la tarde; no **eran** las dos. | *It was one in the afternoon; it was not two.* |

■ express a person's age in the past.

| | |
|---|---|
| Ella **tenía** quince años entonces. | *She was fifteen years old then.* |

■ Some expressions of time and frequency that often accompany the imperfect to express ongoing or repeated actions or states in the past are **mientras, a veces, siempre, generalmente,** and **frecuentemente.**

| IMPERFECT | | | |
|---|---|---|---|
| | **HABLAR** | **COMER** | **VIVIR** |
| yo | hablaba | comía | vivía |
| tú | hablabas | comías | vivías |
| Ud., él, ella | hablaba | comía | vivía |
| nosotros/as | hablábamos | comíamos | vivíamos |
| vosotros/as | hablabais | comíais | vivíais |
| Uds., ellos/as | hablaban | comían | vivían |

■ Note that the endings for **-er** and **-ir** verbs are the same and have a written accent over the **í** of the ending.

■ The Spanish imperfect has several English equivalents.

| | |
|---|---|
| Mis amigos **bailaban** mucho. | *My friends danced a lot.* *My friends were dancing a lot.* *My friends used to dance a lot.* *My friends would dance a lot.* (implying a repeated action) |

■ There are no stem changes in the imperfect.

| | |
|---|---|
| Ella no d**ue**rme bien ahora, pero antes d**o**rmía muy bien. | *She does not sleep well now, but she used to sleep very well before.* |

■ Only three verbs are irregular in the imperfect.

**ir**  iba, ibas, iba, íbamos, ibais, iban

**ser**  era, eras, era, éramos, erais, eran

**ver**  veía, veías, veía, veíamos, veíais, veían

■ The imperfect form of **hay** is **había** (*there was, there were, there used to be*). It is invariable.

| | |
|---|---|
| **Había** una invitación en el correo. | *There was an invitation in the mail.* |
| **Había** muchas personas en la fiesta. | *There were many people at the party.* |

**8-16 Cuando tenía cinco años.** Marque (✓) cuáles eran sus actividades cuando usted tenía cinco años.

1. _____ Jugaba en el parque con mi perro.
2. _____ Ayudaba a mi mamá en la casa, especialmente cuando teníamos invitados.
3. _____ Salía con mis padres los fines de semana.
4. _____ Iba a la playa en el verano.
5. _____ Veía televisión hasta muy tarde.
6. _____ Celebraba el Año Nuevo con mis amigos.
7. _____ Asistía a las fiestas de la familia.
8. …

 **8-17 En mi escuela secundaria.** PRIMERA FASE. Marque (✓) la frecuencia con que usted y sus amigos/as hacían estas cosas. Luego compare sus respuestas con las de su compañero/a.

MODELO: decorar los salones de clase
*Frecuentemente decorábamos los salones de clase.*

| ACTIVIDADES | SIEMPRE | FRECUENTEMENTE | A VECES | NUNCA |
|---|---|---|---|---|
| hablar sobre las competencias deportivas en las clases | | | | |
| organizar reuniones para aumentar el espíritu de la escuela (*pep rallies*) | | | | |
| ir a los partidos de fútbol y otros deportes | | | | |
| asistir a conciertos y obras de teatro | | | | |
| participar en un equipo, en la banda, etc. | | | | |
| otra actividad | | | | |

 SEGUNDA FASE. Hablen de los siguientes temas.

1. ¿Cuáles eran las tradiciones en su escuela para celebrar y aumentar el espíritu de equipo (*team spirit*) que realizaban con más frecuencia?
2. ¿Cuáles eran sus actividades favoritas?

**8-18 El apagón (*blackout*).** El sábado pasado los señores Herrera organizaron una fiesta en su casa. Desafortunadamente durante la fiesta hubo un apagón en su barrio. Basándose en el dibujo escriba un párrafo para explicar lo que hacían las personas cuando se fue la luz.

**8-19 Mi casa.** Descríbale a su compañero/a cómo era la casa o apartamento donde usted vivía cuando era niño/a. Después, su compañero/a debe hacer lo mismo.

**8-20 Las fiestas infantiles.** Comenten cómo eran las fiestas de cumpleaños cuando ustedes eran pequeños/as. Incluyan los siguientes puntos:

1. lugar de la celebración
2. horas (comienzo y final)
3. dos o tres actividades que hacían
4. personas que participaban
5. comida y bebida que servían
6. ropa que llevaban

**8-21 Antes y ahora.** Expliquen cómo era la vida antes y cómo es ahora con respecto a los siguientes temas:

1. la familia (tamaño, grado de movilidad, porcentaje de divorcios)
2. la mujer en la sociedad (participación en el mundo del trabajo/de la política, su independencia económica)
3. las ciudades (tamaño, los problemas ambientales (*environmental*) como la contaminación, la delincuencia, el crimen)

## SITUACIONES

1. **Role A.** You are a famous public figure (a singer, professor, scientist, athlete, etc.) being interviewed by a television reporter. Offer as many details about your background as possible.

   **Role B.** You are interviewing a famous person for a television program. Ask a) what his/her family life and hometown were like when he/she was young; b) the type of music he/she used to listen to; c) the books he/she used to read; d) the holidays he/she celebrated most.

2. **Role A.** You are an exchange student and would like to find out about your host's weekend and summer activities when he/she was in high school. Ask a) what activites there were for high school students in his/her community, b) what he/she generally did on Saturday evenings and with whom; and c) what he/she usually did in the summer.

   **Role B.** You are the host of an exchange student. Answer his/her questions about your weekend and summer activities when you were in high school. Describe a summer trip to a friend's house in Guadalajara, Mexico, and say that you a) spoke Spanish every day; b) went to the outdoor markets often; c) listened to the mariachis very often; and d) used to eat excellent Mexican food every day.

## 2. Narrating in the past: The preterit and the imperfect

**Había** una vez una chica que **vivía** con su padre, porque su madre **estaba** muerta. La chica **se llamaba** Cenicienta. **Era** muy bella y muy buena, y todos los vecinos la **querían** mucho. Pero un día, su vida **cambió**. Su padre **se casó** con una mujer muy mala que **tenía** dos hijas. La mujer y sus hijas **vinieron** a vivir a la casa de Cenicienta. Las hijas **eran** muy crueles y **odiaban** (*hated*) a Cenicienta, su hermanastra...

**Piénselo.** Lea las afirmaciones y marque (✓) su función en el cuento: contar los eventos, o dar información de fondo (*background information*) sobre el contexto o los personajes.

|  | CONTAR LOS EVENTOS | DAR INFORMACIÓN DE FONDO |
|---|---|---|
| 1. La chica **se llamaba** Cenicienta. | _____ | _____ |
| 2. **Era** muy bella y muy buena. | _____ | _____ |
| 3. Todos los vecinos la **querían** mucho. | _____ | _____ |
| 4. Pero un día, su vida **cambió**. | _____ | _____ |
| 5. Su padre **se casó** con una mujer muy mala. | _____ | _____ |
| 6. La mujer y sus hijas **vinieron** a vivir a la casa de Cenicienta. | _____ | _____ |

■ The preterit and the imperfect are not interchangeable. They fulfill different functions when telling a story or talking about an event in the past.

■ Use the preterit:

1. to express a sequence of actions completed in the past (note that there is a forward movement of narrative time).

**Oyeron** un ruido, se **levantaron**, y **bajaron** las escaleras.   *They heard a noise, got up, and went downstairs.*

2. to talk about the beginning or end of an event, action, or condition.

Pepito **leyó** a los cinco años.   *Pepito read (began to read) at age five.*

El niño **se enfermó** el sábado.   *The child got sick (became sick) on Saturday.*

Pepito **leyó** el cuento.   *Pepito read (finished) the story.*

El niño **estuvo** enfermo ayer.   *The child was sick yesterday (and is no longer sick).*

3. to talk about an event, action, or condition that occurred over a specified period of time.

**Vivieron** en México por diez años.   *They lived in Mexico for ten years.*

■ Use the imperfect:

**1.** to talk about customary or habitual actions, events, or conditions in the past.

| | |
|---|---|
| Todos los días **llovía** y por eso **leíamos** mucho. | *It used to rain every day, and that's why we read a lot.* |

**2.** to express an ongoing part of an event, action, or condition.

| | |
|---|---|
| En ese momento **llovía** mucho y los niños **estaban** muy tristes. | *At that moment it was raining a lot, and the children were very sad.* |

■ In a story, the imperfect provides the background information, whereas the preterit tells what happened. Frequently an action or situation (expressed with the imperfect) is ongoing when something else (expressed with the preterit) suddenly happens.

| | |
|---|---|
| **Era** Navidad. Todos **dormíamos** cuando los niños **oyeron** un ruido en el techo. | *It was Christmas. All of us were sleeping when the children heard a noise on the roof.* |

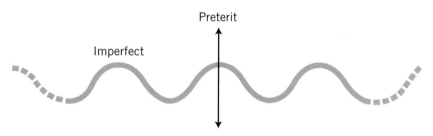

**8-22 ¡Qué día más malo!** Ayer iba a ser un día especial para Pedro, pero sus planes terminaron mal. Marque (✔) las tres cosas más graves que le ocurrieron a Pedro mientras trataba de realizar sus planes.

**1.** _____ Mientras se bañaba temprano por la mañana, se cayó en el baño.
**2.** _____ Mientras desayunaba tranquilamente, el teléfono sonó y no pudo terminar de comer.
**3.** _____ Iba a la tienda para comprarle un anillo a su novia cuando alguien le robó el dinero.
**4.** _____ Mientras llamaba por teléfono a un restaurante para reservar una mesa, el restaurante se incendió.
**5.** _____ Iba a proponerle matrimonio a su novia cuando su ex-novia lo llamó por teléfono.
**6.** _____ Mientras preparaba una cena deliciosa para celebrar el cumpleaños de su novia, el perro se comió el pastel.

**8-23 La última vez.** Túrnense para preguntarse cuándo fue la última vez que cada uno de ustedes hizo estas cosas y cómo se sentía mientras las hacía.

MODELO:      ver un partido de béisbol
    E1: *¿Cuándo fue la última vez que viste un partido de béisbol?*
    E2: *Vi un partido de béisbol la semana pasada.*
    E1: *¿Y cómo te sentías mientras veías el partido?*
    E2: *Estaba aburrido/a, porque no me gusta mucho el béisbol.*

**1.** participar en un campeonato
**2.** ganar un premio
**3.** estar en un desfile
**4.** disfrazarse
**5.** bailar en un carnaval
**6.** …

Compradores en un mercado
de Mérida.

**8-24 Una visita al mercado.** Imagínese que usted fue de compras a un mercado al aire libre de Mérida y ahora le cuenta a un amigo/una amiga lo que pasó. Complete las oraciones usando el imperfecto del verbo en la primera columna y el pretérito del verbo en la segunda columna.

**MODELO:** Ser las once cuando…
*Eran las once cuando llegué al mercado.*

1. Caminar al mercado cuando…   ver unas botellas bonitas
2. Mirar las botellas cuando…   hablarme la vendedora
3. Probarse un cinturón de cuero cuando…   empezar a llover
4. Ser las dos de la tarde cuando…   ver a mi amigo José
5. Tomar un café para escapar de la lluvia cuando…   (nosotros) volver al mercado para hacer nuestras compras

 **8-25 Un cuento.** Completen esta narración usando el pretérito o el imperfecto.

En el mes de abril del año pasado mi familia y yo (1) _____ (ir) a México de vacaciones. Primero nosotros (2) _____ (estar) en Ciudad de México por dos días. Allí (3) _____ (ver) a unos parientes y (4) _____ (visitar) lugares muy interesantes, como el Museo Nacional de Antropología, donde (5) _____ (poder) admirar una excelente colección de objetos de la cultura azteca, y a las tiendas de la Zona Rosa, donde mi mamá (6) _____ (comprar) unas blusas preciosas.

En la mañana del tercer día, nosotros (7) _____ (irse) a Iztapalapa, que está bastante cerca de la capital. (8) _____ (Hacer) un tiempo fabuloso. Como (9) _____ (ser) primavera, muchos árboles y plantas (10) _____ (tener) flores, y todo (11) _____ (estar) muy verde. Nosotros (12) _____ (salir) del hotel cerca de las cinco de la tarde y poco después (13) _____ (llegar) a una plaza donde (14) _____ (haber) mucha gente. Allí (15) _____ (ver) las procesiones de la Semana Santa. El ambiente (16) _____ (ser) impresionante; las personas (17) _____ (llevar) túnicas largas y (18) _____ (caminar) lentamente por la calle. ¡Nunca vamos a olvidar esa experiencia!

 **8-26 Un evento inolvidable.** Cuéntele a su compañero/a algo inesperado que le ocurrió el año pasado. Indique qué pasó, dónde y cuándo. Describa la escena y los personajes.

**SITUACIONES**

1. **Role A.** Tell your friend about your nephew's first birthday party, which you attended recently.

   **Role B.** Your friend is going to tell you about his/her nephew's first birthday party. Ask a) where the party took place; b) who went to the party; c) what people did; and d) how the little boy reacted to all the attention.

2. **Role A.** You have just come back from a vacation in Mexico. Tell your classmate about a particular place you visited. Explain what it was like and what you did there.

   **Role B.** Your classmate has just returned from a vacation to Mexico. Ask about a particular place he/she visited while there. Find out a) what the place looked liked; b) what he/she did there; c) what special event he/she can tell you about.

## 3. Comparing people and things: Comparisons of inequality

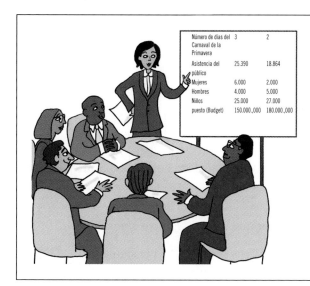

| Número de días del Carnaval de la Primavera | 3 | 2 |
|---|---|---|
| Asistencia del público | | |
| Mujeres | 25.390 | 18.864 |
| Hombres | 6.000 | 2.000 |
| Niños | 4.000 | 5.000 |
| puesto (Budget) | 25.000 | 27.000 |
| | 150.000.,000 | 180.000.,000 |

Para planificar el Carnaval de la Primavera debemos mirar las estadísticas de los años recientes. ¿Vamos a celebrar el carnaval **más de** dos días? En el año 2008, la asistencia fue **mayor que** la del 2009. En el 2008, había **más** mujeres **que** hombres, pero en el 2009 participaron **menos** mujeres **que** en el año anterior. Para tener un **mejor** carnaval **que** en años anteriores, vamos a necesitar **más** dinero **que** en los años pasados.

**Piénselo.** Indique si las siguientes afirmaciones son ciertas (**C**), falsas (**F**) o posibles (**P**), según las estadísticas.

1. ____ En el año 2009 había **menos** participación del público **que** en el 2008.
2. ____ En el año 2009 participaron **menos** niños **que** adultos en el carnaval.
3. ____ Los organizadores probablemente gastaron **más** dinero en el año 2009 **que** en el 2008.
4. ____ En el futuro el carnaval va a durar **más de** dos días.
5. ____ En el futuro, los carnavales van a ser **mejores que** los del pasado.

■ Use **más... que** or **menos... que** to express comparisons of inequality with nouns, adjectives, and adverbs.

| COMPARISONS OF INEQUALITY | | |
|---|---|---|
| Cuando Alina era joven tenía { más / menos } amigos que Pepe. | | When Alina was young she had { more / fewer } friends than Pepe. |
| Ella era { más / menos } activa que él. | | She was { more / less } active than he. |
| Salía { más / menos } frecuentemente que él. | | She went out { more / less } frequently than he. |

■ Use **de** instead of **que** before numbers.

En el año 2008, había **más de** diez carrozas en el desfile.

*In 2008, there were **more than** ten floats in the parade.*

El año pasado había **menos de** diez carrozas.

*Last year there were **fewer than** ten floats.*

■ The following adjectives have both regular and irregular comparative forms.

| | | |
|---|---|---|
| bueno/a | más bueno/a o mejor | *better* |
| malo/a | más malo/a o peor[1] | *worse* |
| pequeño/a | más pequeño/a o menor | *smaller* |
| joven | más joven o menor | *younger* |
| grande | más grande o mayor | *bigger* |
| viejo/a | más viejo/a o mayor[2] | *older* |

Esta banda es { mejor / peor } que aquella. *This band is { better / worse } than that one.*

■ **Bien** and **mal** are adverbs. They have the same irregular comparative forms as the adjectives **bueno** and **malo**.

bien → mejor   Yo canto **mejor** que Héctor.   *I sing better than Héctor.*
mal → peor   Héctor canta **peor** que yo.   *Héctor sings worse than I.*

**8-27 Comparación de dos desfiles. PRIMERA FASE.** Lea la siguiente información sobre dos desfiles mexicanos, uno de Veracruz y el otro de Mérida. Complete las frases con **más que, menos que, más de** o **menos de**, según la información en la tabla.

| | VERACRUZ | MÉRIDA |
|---|---|---|
| habitantes | 444.438 | 649.770 |
| promedio (*average*) de público que participa | 14.000 personas | 12.000 personas |
| número de bandas | 8 | 6 |
| número de policías | 200 | 175 |

1. Mérida tiene _____ habitantes _____ Veracruz.
2. _____ personas asisten al desfile de Veracruz _____ al desfile de Mérida.
3. Los dos desfiles tienen _____ _____ cinco bandas.
4. Mérida gasta _____ dinero en seguridad (*security*) _____ Veracruz.
5. _____ _____ medio millón de personas viven en Veracruz.
6. Probablemente el público de Mérida es _____ entusiasta _____ el de Veracruz.

**SEGUNDA FASE.** La banda de su universidad piensa participar en uno de estos desfiles, pero no puede gastar mucho dinero. Con la información de la *Primera fase* y la que aparece a continuación, decidan a qué desfile debe asistir. Expliquen por qué.

| COSTO POR PERSONA | DESFILE DE VERACRUZ | DESFILE DE MERIDA |
|---|---|---|
| transporte | 5.824,50 pesos | 6.552,60 pesos |
| hotel por día | 880,50 pesos | 915,25 pesos |
| comidas por día | 450,00 pesos | 348,00 pesos |

---
[1]**Más bueno/a** and **más malo/a** are not used interchangeably with **mejor** and **peor**. **Más bueno/a** and **más malo/a** refer to a person's moral qualities. **Mejor** and **peor** refer to skills and abilities.

[2]Use **mayor** to refer to a person's age. **Más viejo/a** is generally used with nouns other than people.

**8-28 Las alfombras de aserrín.** Los artesanos de Guatemala hacen alfombras de aserrín para celebrar la Semana Santa. Comparen las dos alfombras según los siguientes criterios. Pueden usar estas expresiones u otras.

| | | | |
|---|---|---|---|
| colores fuertes | corto | figuras | rectangular |
| colores suaves | diseño | imágenes | simple |
| colorido | elaborado | largo | sofisticado |

1. el tamaño
2. los colores
3. el estilo
4. su preferencia por una de las alfombras

**A.**

**B.**

**8-29 Personas famosas.** Compare a las siguientes personas. Considere lo siguiente.

1. su aspecto físico
2. su edad
3. el tipo de trabajo que hacen
4. el dinero o popularidad que tienen

Brad Pitt

Salma Hayek en el papel de Frida Kahlo en la película *Frida*

**SITUACIONES**

1. **Role A.** You and your fiancé/fiancée disagree about wedding plans. You prefer small weddings. Try to persuade your groom/bride by comparing small and large weddings with regard to: a) expenses (**gastos**); b) stress (**estrés**); c) work involved; and d) possible problems.

   **Role B.** You and your fiancé/fiancée are planning your wedding. You prefer big weddings. Listen to the opinions of your fiancé/fiancée and try to come to an agreement.

2. **Role A.** You are a student government representative presenting a proposal to the dean to change the graduation ceremony. Compare the ceremony at your school with one at a rival institution. Say that the other ceremony is better because it is smaller, better organized, less expensive, and usually has better music and speeches (**discursos**).

   **Role B.** You are the dean. A student government representative is proposing changes in the graduation ceremony. Listen to the presentation and ask questions to compare the advantages of both types of ceremonies.

## 4. Comparing people and things: Comparisons of equality

**PRESIDENTA DEL COMITÉ ORGANIZADOR:** Este año tuvimos un Carnaval de Primavera **tan** espectacular **como** el de 2008, que hasta este año era nuestro carnaval más grande. En los tres días del carnaval asistió **tanto** público **como** en el año 2008, un total de 25.400 personas. Además, los grupos musicales tocaron música **tan** buena **como** la música del carnaval de 2008. También el número de bailarines se mantuvo igual. Hubo **tantos** bailarines **como** en el 2008. Estoy muy agradecida de ustedes porque colaboraron **tanto como** en otros años. Vamos a planificar el carnaval del próximo año **tan bien como** el de este año.

**Piénselo.** Indique si las siguientes afirmaciones interpretan correcta (**C**) o incorrectamente (**I**) la información que dio la Presidenta del Comité Organizador.

1. ____ En 2008 asistieron unas 25.400 personas al carnaval y este año asistió el mismo número de personas.
2. ____ Este año los grupos musicales tocaron música que al público le gustó **menos que** en otros años.
3. ____ Este año el Comité Organizador hizo un trabajo **tan bueno como** el trabajo de otros años.
4. ____ La planificación del carnaval fue buena este año y la del próximo año va ser buena también.

■ In the previous section you learned to express comparisons of inequality. In this section you will learn how to indicate that two people, things, or activities are equal in some way.

| COMPARISONS OF EQUALITY | |
|---|---|
| tan... como | *as ... as* |
| tanto/a... como | *as much ... as* |
| tantos/as... como | *as many ... as* |
| tanto como | *as much as* |

■ Use **tan... como** to express comparisons of equality with adjectives and adverbs.

La boda fue **tan** elegante **como** la fiesta.
*The wedding was as elegant as the party.*

El padre bailó **tan** bien **como** su hija.
*The father danced as well as his daughter.*

■ Use **tanto/a... como** and **tantos/as... como** to express comparisons of equality with nouns.

| | |
|---|---|
| Había **tanta** alegría **como** en el Carnaval. | *There was as much joy as at Mardi Gras.* |
| Había **tantos** invitados **como** en mi fiesta de graduación. | *There were as many guests as at my graduation party.* |

■ Use **tanto como** to express comparisons of equality with verbs.

| | |
|---|---|
| Los invitados bailaron **tanto como** nosotros. | *The guests danced as much as we did.* |

## 8-30 Cuatro estudiantes afortunados.

Lean algunos datos personales sobre cuatro estudiantes. Luego, indiquen si las afirmaciones a continuación son ciertas (**C**) o falsas (**F**). Si son falsas (**F**), corrijan la información.

| | PEDRO | VILMA | MARTA | RICARDO |
|---|---|---|---|---|
| hermanos | 2 | 3 | 3 | 2 |
| clases | 5 | 5 | 4 | 6 |
| dinero para gastos personales cada mes | 5.000 pesos | 8.500 pesos | 5.000 pesos | 8.500 pesos |
| películas en DVD | 200 | 180 | 180 | 215 |
| viajes a otros países | 3 | 8 | 3 | 8 |

1. \_\_\_\_ Pedro tiene **tantos** hermanos **como** Vilma.
2. \_\_\_\_ Vilma tomó **tantas** clases este semestre **como** Ricardo.
3. \_\_\_\_ La familia de Marta es **tan** grande **como** la familia de Vilma.
4. \_\_\_\_ Cada mes, Ricardo recibe **tanto** dinero de sus padres **como** Vilma.
5. \_\_\_\_ Marta probablemente gasta **más** dinero en películas **que** Vilma.
6. \_\_\_\_ La familia de Pedro viaja **tanto como** la familia de Ricardo.

## 8-31 Sus opiniones. PRIMERA FASE. Haga lo siguiente.

1. Escriba los nombres de dos celebridades en su cultura.
2. Escriba los nombres de dos festividades o desfiles que se realizan en su ciudad, región o país.
3. Escriba dos programas cómicos de la televisión.

**SEGUNDA FASE.** Ahora, expresen su opinión y comparen los nombres que escribieron en la *Primera fase.* Usen la información dada y modifiquen los adjetivos cuando sea necesario.

| MODELO: | *Tom Cruise y Johnny Depp*: calidad de su trabajo (bueno/a, mediocre, malo/a) |
|---|---|
| | E1: *Tom Cruise es tan buen actor como Johnny Depp.* |
| | E2: *Sí, estoy de acuerdo. O: No, Johnny Depp es mejor actor que Tom Cruise.* |

1. Dos celebridades: apariencia física, calidad de su trabajo (atractivo, alto, famoso, bueno...)
2. Dos desfiles o celebraciones locales o nacionales: número de personas, carrozas (divertido, colorido, numeroso, alegre)
3. Dos programas cómicos de la televisión: calidad, grado de interés para el público (bueno, malo, mediocre, cómico, loco, divertido)

## SITUACIONES

1. **Role A.** You are reminiscing about Independence Day celebrations when you were a child. Tell your son/daughter (your classmate) that you think that a) in the past Americans were more patriotic (**patrióticos**); b) the celebrations were less expensive; and c) the celebrations were more family oriented (**se celebraban en familia**) than today.

   **Role B.** Your dad/mom (your classmate) argues that today's Independence Day celebrations are less family oriented than in the past. You disagree. State that a) today Americans are as patriotic as they were in the past; b) people used to spend less money because they made less money; and c) today families celebrate Independence Day together as much as in the past.

2. **Role A.** Your next-door neighbors are three students, two of whom are identical twins (**gemelos/as**). Even though you have lived there for a year, you cannot tell them apart. When you run into the third roommate on campus, you mention all the ways in which the twins seem absolutely alike to you. Ask your neighbor's help in telling them apart.

   **Role B.** You and your long-time friends, who are identical twins (**gemelos/as**), share an apartment. When your neighbor asks you for help in telling them apart, describe a) two ways in which they are exactly alike in appearance, abilities, and preferences and b) two ways in which they are different that allow you to tell them apart.

# 5. Comparing people and things: The superlative

PERLA: Lupita, ¿tienes algún plan especial para el Día de los Muertos?

LUPITA: Claro que sí. En mi comunidad, visitamos a familiares y amigos muertos en el cementerio. Les llevamos **la mejor** música mexicana y su comida preferida. Es el día **más importante del** año para recordarlos. Creemos que ellos vuelven a su tumba el 1 y 2 de noviembre para disfrutar de **la mejor** compañía, la de su familia y amigos.

PERLA: ¡Qué interesante! Para mi familia **el** acto **más** importante es recordarlos con **las** flores **más** hermosas **de** la estación.

**Piénselo.** Complete las siguientes oraciones con el nombre de la persona que expresa la información.

1. _____ lleva al cementerio **la mejor** música mexicana.
2. Según _____, el Día de los Muertos es **el** día **más importante del** año para recordar a los familiares y amigos muertos.
3. _____ dice que **la** compañía **más** agradable para los muertos es la de sus familiares y amigos.
4. _____ dice que su familia lleva la comida que les gustaba **más** a sus familiares muertos.
5. _____ dice que para su familia, **la** manera **más** apropiada **de** recordar a los muertos es llevarles flores.

▪ Use superlatives to express *most* and *least* as degrees of comparison among three or more entities. To form the superlative, use *definite article* + *noun* + **más/menos** + *adjective*. To express *in* or *at* with the superlative, use **de**.

| | |
|---|---|
| Es **el** disfraz **menos** creativo (**de** la fiesta). | *It is the least creative costume (at the party).* |
| México es **el** país con **más** fiestas **de** América del Norte. | *Mexico is the country with the most holidays in North America.* |

▪ Do not use **más** or **menos** with **mejor**, **peor**, **mayor**, or **menor**.

| | |
|---|---|
| ¿Esos desfiles? Son **los mejores** desfiles **del** país. | *Those parades? They are the best parades in the country.* |
| Ivonne es **la mejor** bailarina **del** grupo. | *Ivonne is the best dancer of the group.* |

▪ You may delete the noun when it is clear to whom or to what you refer.

| | |
|---|---|
| Son **los mejores del** país. | *They are the best (ones) in the country.* |

---

### Lengua

Spanish and English often use adjectives as nouns. Whereas English frequently uses *one* or *ones* after the adjective, Spanish simply drops the noun.

*El traje rojo* es más bonito.

*El rojo* es más bonito.
*The red one is prettier.*

El rojo es el más bonito.
*The red one is the prettiest.*

■ To express the idea of *extremely*, add the ending **-ísimo** (**-a, -os, -as**) to the adjective. If the adjective ends in a consonant, add **-ísimo** directly to the singular form of the adjective. If it ends in a vowel, drop the vowel before adding **-ísimo**.

| | | |
|---|---|---|
| **fácil** | Este baile es **facilísimo**. | *This dance is extremely easy.* |
| **grande** | La carroza es **grandísima**. | *The float is extremely big.* |
| **bueno** | Las orquestas son **buenísimas**. | *The orchestras are extremely good.* |

> ### Lengua
> A Spanish word can have only one written accent. Therefore, an adjective with a written accent loses the accent when **-ísimo/a** is added.
>
> **fácil > facilísimo/a**
> **rápido > rapidísimo/a**

**8-32 Estadísticas demográficas.** Lea la información de la tabla. Luego indique a qué país de la columna B se refiere cada oración de la columna A.

| | **MÉXICO** | **GUATEMALA** | **ESTADOS UNIDOS** |
|---|---|---|---|
| **población (aprox.) del país** | 104.700.000 habitantes | 12.728.000 habitantes | 302.688.000 habitantes |
| **población de la capital** | México, DF: 19.232.000 | Ciudad de Guatemala: 3.942.000 | Washington, DC: 588.292 |
| **número de lenguas indígenas** | 62 | 24 | aprox. 150 familias de lenguas |
| **religión predominante** | 89% son católicos (aprox. 93.180.000) | 49% son católicos (aprox. 6.237.000) | 52% son protestantes (aprox. 157.398.000) |
| **número de estados o departamentos** | 32 estados | 22 departamentos | 50 estados |

**A**

1. ____ Este país tiene **el mayor número** de habitantes.
2. ____ Esta ciudad capital es **la más** grande.
3. ____ Es el país donde existe **el mayor** número de lenguas indígenas.
4. ____ Este es el país con **menos** lenguas indígenas.
5. ____ Este país tiene **el menor** porcentaje de personas que profesan el catolicismo.
6. ____ Este país tiene **el mayor** número de gobiernos estatales o departmentales.

**B**

a. Guatemala
b. México
c. Estados Unidos

**8-33 ¿En qué pueblo o ciudad?** Respondan a las siguientes preguntas y, luego, comparen sus respuestas con las de otra pareja. ¿Están de acuerdo o tienen opiniones diferentes?

¿En qué pueblo o ciudad de su país...

1. sirven la mejor comida étnica?
2. se come la comida más picante (*spicy*)?
3. se vende el café cubano más fuerte?
4. celebran las mejores fiestas de Año Nuevo?
5. hay el mayor número de desfiles hermosos?
6. tocan la mejor música folclórica estadounidense?

## SITUACIONES

1. **Role A.** You are interviewing a well-known film critic about American movies. Ask a) which is the best American film and why; b) who is the best actor/actress; c) which is the worst film of the year; and d) what he/she thinks of Hispanic films.

   **Role B.** You are a well-known film critic. Answer the questions according to your own opinions regarding the best/worst American films and actors. Mention that a) there are some excellent Mexican, Argentinian, and Spanish films and b) several of them won Oscars in the last ten years.

2. **Role A.** You travelled to Mexico for Spring Break and liked the country very much. Tell your classmate the five things you liked best about Mexico and if there was something you found extremely interesting. Provide examples.

   **Role B.** Ask questions about your classmate's trip. Then tell where you went during Spring Break. Share five of the best things you liked about the place you visited.

# MOSAICOS

## A escuchar

**Draw conclusions based on what you know**

Understanding what someone says involves comprehending the literal meaning of the words you hear. It also may involve using the context and the information the speaker provides in order to draw conclusions that go beyond literal comprehension. This process is called inferencing, or making inferences.

When you talk to someone or overhear a conversation, you can understand what is said even when the speaker does not express the meaning explicitly. For example, if you are driving with a friend and get lost, you may say, "There is a gas station up there on the right." Your friend will probably infer that you want to stop to ask for directions.

### Antes de escuchar

**8-34 Preparación.** Es el fin de año y dos amigos conversan sobre el feriado que se aproxima. Antes de escuchar la conversación, escriba el nombre de una festividad de la cual probablemente ellos van a hablar. Luego, escriba dos preguntas que en su opinión alguien va a hacer sobre este feriado.

### Escuchar

CD 4
Track 6

**8-35 ¿Comprende usted?** First, read the statements below, and then listen as two friends talk about a Mexican holiday. After listening, mark (✓) the statements that provide information you can infer from what you heard.

1. ___ Daniel es mexicano.
2. ___ Sandra es una persona muy tímida.
3. ___ Sandra no es estadounidense.
4. ___ Daniel está triste porque no va a celebrar la Navidad con su familia.
5. ___ Pedir posada es una costumbre en que participa solamente la familia.
6. ___ Daniel no conoce algunas costumbres mexicanas.

### Después de escuchar

**8-36 Ahora usted.** Comparta sus respuestas a estas preguntas con su compañero/a.

1. ¿Qué fiesta o tradición religiosa le gustaría celebrar en un país hispano? ¿Por qué?
2. ¿Celebran esa fiesta en su ciudad o país? ¿Cómo la celebran?
3. ¿Qué fiesta o tradición celebra usted solamente con sus amigos?

# A conversar

**Conduct an interview**

To conduct an interview, you need to ask two types of questions: (a) questions to open up a topic and (b) follow-up questions to get additional information. Open-ended questions that function as invitations to speak—such as **¿Podría hablar de los deportes que practicaba de niño/a?**—will elicit longer and more detailed responses than direct, closed-ended questions like **¿Qué deportes practicaba cuando era niño/a?** Questions that can be answered with **Sí** or **No** are not likely to elicit much information, unless you follow up with **¿Por qué?** Listen carefully to what your interviewee says so that you can ask relevant follow-up questions.

## Antes de conversar

**8-37 Preparación.** ¿Tuvieron usted y uno/a de sus compañeros/as una infancia y adolescencia semejantes? Escriban preguntas que los/las ayuden a obtener información en las siguientes áreas, u otras áreas de interés para ustedes.

1. deportes que su compañero/a practicaba y miraba en la televisión entre los siete y los doce años de edad
2. la(s) fiesta(s) más importantes para la familia de su compañero/a y cómo la(s) celebraba
3. una o dos costumbres de la familia que a él/ella le gustaba(n) y otras que no le gustaban y por qué
4. ...

## Conversar

**8-38 Entre nosotros.** Entreviste a su compañero/a usando las preguntas de la actividad **8-37** y tome notas de sus respuestas.

## Después de conversar

**8-39 Un poco más.** Anónimamente, escriban un breve informe comparativo de la infancia y adolescencia de ustedes. Sus compañeros van a leer su informe y van a tratar de averiguar quiénes son ustedes. Sigan los modelos y frases a continuación o combínenlos, de acuerdo con sus experiencias. Mantengan su identidad en secreto.

**MODELO:**

**ALMAS GEMELAS**

*Somos dos almas gemelas. Tanto mi compañero/a como yo nacimos en...*

**MUNDOS APARTES**

*Somos dos mundos apartes. Mi compañero/a nació en.... Yo nací en...*

1. Durante la infancia/adolescencia...
2. Con respecto a los deportes/las fiestas...
3. La persona A y la persona B tuvieron una niñez/adolescencia semejante/diferente porque...

---

### En directo

To ask someone to talk about a topic:

**¿Me podría(s) hablar sobre... ?**
*Can you talk to me more about . . . ?*

**¿Qué me puede(s) decir usted sobre/de... ?**
*What can you tell me about . . . ?*

**Me gustaría saber...**
*I would like to know . . .*

To ask someone to expand on a topic:

**¿Podría(s) hablar más sobre... ?**

**¿Qué más me puede(s) decir sobre... ?**

---

### En directo

To show empathy:

**¡Oh! ¡Qué lástima!**
**¡Cuánto lo siento!**
*How sad! I'm so sorry.*

To share someone's happiness:

**¡Qué fabuloso/bueno!**
*How fabulous/great!*

**¡Cuánto me alegro!**
*I'm so happy to hear that!*

To express interest in what someone said:

**¡Qué interesante!**
*How interesting!*

# A leer

## Antes de leer

**8-40 Preparación.** Las creencias sobre la muerte varían de una cultura a otra. Indiquen si creen que las siguientes prácticas se asocian con la cultura egipcia (**E**), con alguna cultura indígena americana (**I**) o con ambas (**A**).

1. ____ Creían que había vida después de la muerte.
2. ____ Construían pirámides para honrar a los muertos.
3. ____ Vestían a los muertos con ropa funeraria especial.
4. ____ Ponían una máscara sobre la cara del muerto.
5. ____ Enterraban (*They buried*) al muerto en las pirámides, en tumbas o sepulcros, de acuerdo al estatus social de la persona muerta.
6. ____ La familia de la persona muerta depositaba joyas y objetos de valor en la tumba o pirámide.
7. ____ Rociaban (*They sprayed*) el cadáver con un polvo de color rojo para simbolizar el renacimiento (*rebirth*).

## Leer

### Creencias y costumbres mayas sobre la muerte

El origen de los mayas es incierto. Sin embargo, se sabe que esta civilización ocupó y se desarrolló[1] en los actuales territorios de Guatemala, México, Belice, Honduras y El Salvador. Durante su período de mayor esplendor, los mayas construyeron ciudades y pirámides, donde enterraban a sus gobernantes y los veneraban después de muertos.

Los mayas compartían con otras culturas mesoamericanas algunas creencias y costumbres. Entre otras cosas, creían en la vida después de la muerte y en la interacción entre el mundo humano y el mundo espiritual. Creían que el destino de una persona después de la muerte dependía de la forma en que moría y no de su conducta mientras vivía. Las tumbas y los vestuarios funerarios confirman que los mayas creían que el espíritu se prolongaba más allá de la muerte. La mayoría de los muertos iba a Xibalbá, un lugar en el mundo de abajo.

Para llegar a Xibalbá había que superar numerosos peligros. El espíritu debía comer bien y cuidarse. Por eso, los mayas dejaban en la tumba una vestimenta funeraria. También colocaban comida, agua y amuletos protectores, de acuerdo con el estatus social del muerto.

Los mayas rociaban el cadáver con un polvo rojo que simbolizaba el renacimiento. También lo adornaban con joyas, collares, pulseras y anillos de jade, hueso[2] o concha[3] y un cinturón ceremonial. En muchas tumbas ponían una máscara sobre la cara del muerto para ocultar su identidad. En la boca le ponían una cuenta[4] de jade, símbolo de lo precioso y lo perenne, para preservar su espíritu inmortal.

Algunas de estas creencias y costumbres todavía se conservan, con ciertas variaciones, en algunas comunidades de Guatemala, México y El Salvador.

[1]*developed*   [2]*bone*   [3]*shell*   [4]*bead*

**8-41 Primera mirada.** Determine si las siguientes afirmaciones representan información explícita (**E**) en el texto o si son inferencias (**I**) basadas en el contenido. Si es una inferencia, indique la oración o las oraciones en el texto en que se basa(n).

1. \_\_\_\_ Los expertos no saben de dónde vinieron los mayas.
2. \_\_\_\_ Los mayas crearon una gran civilización.
3. \_\_\_\_ Las comunidades mayas tenían autoridades que los gobernaban.
4. \_\_\_\_ Como los egipcios, los mayas construyeron edificios magníficos para honrar la memoria de personas de alto estatus en su comunidad.
5. \_\_\_\_ Los mayas, como otros grupos indígenas, pensaban que la vida continuaba después de la muerte.
6. \_\_\_\_ Para los mayas, el tipo de muerte determinaba el destino de una persona.
7. \_\_\_\_ No todos los mayas iban al mismo destino después de la muerte.
8. \_\_\_\_ La comida, el agua y los amuletos ayudaban al espíritu del muerto a llegar a su destino final.

**8-42 Segunda mirada.** Complete las siguientes ideas con información explícita en el texto.

1. Los mayas, como otras culturas indígenas de Mesoamérica, creían en…
2. Dos costumbres que demuestran que los mayas tenían estas creencias son…
3. Para llegar a su destino final, el espíritu de los muertos tenía que…
4. Para indicar que el espíritu del muerto nacía otra vez, los mayas…
5. Para simbolizar la importancia y la inmortalidad del espíritu, los mayas…

## Después de leer

**8-43 Ampliación.** Mencionen qué objetos probablemente ponían los mayas en la tumba o pirámide de un gobernante con las siguientes características:

1. Era físicamente activo.
2. Le gustaba mucho el arte.
3. Estudiaba astronomía.
4. Le fascinaba la guerra.
5. Tenía ocho hijas, todas muy bellas.

# A escribir

**Select and sequence details to write effective narratives**

A successful narrative is characterized by a logical, clear, and believable sequence of events, and a good description of setting and characters.

Use organizational strategies such as a graphic organizer or a story map to visualize the order of events in and the time frame (present, past). Use dialogue to make your story more believable.

To describe the main characters, select feelings and traits that will make them stand out. Place the characters in the appropriate setting (rural, mysterious, etc.).

Structure your narration:

■ Introduce the character(s), describe the setting, and begin the action.

■ Present the unfolding of the action. Describe the characters and the tensions caused by their actions or by the events around them.

■ Present a closure to the actions/tensions, or leave it open for your reader to imagine the ending.

## Antes de escribir

**8-44 Preparación.** PRIMERA FASE. Lea la siguiente narración y siga las instrucciones.

Eran alrededor de las siete de la tarde del 24 de mayo cuando ocurrió algo totalmente inesperado. Era una noche de otoño y hacía viento. Empezaba a oscurecer.

Era el cumpleaños de nuestra gran amiga Guadalupe Martínez. Aunque tenía sólo veinte años, Guadalupe era una chica excepcional. Estudiaba en la UNAM[1] y también trabajaba para ayudar a su familia de ocho hermanos. Todos sus amigos la admirábamos por su generosidad, optimismo y alegría. Guadalupe era la hermana y amiga que todos soñábamos[2] tener.

El día de su cumpleaños por la mañana, Francisco y yo rompimos nuestra rutina. Pensábamos darle una sorpresa para su cumpleaños. Después de todo, ¡sólo se cumplen veintiún años una vez en la vida! Primero, fuimos a un centro comercial y le buscamos un regalo especial. Encontramos un plato decorativo guatemalteco y un CD. Francisco también le compró un perfume, y yo agregué un libro al cesto de regalos. Más tarde, volvimos a casa y envolvimos los regalos.

A las seis de la tarde Francisco y yo caminábamos a casa de Guadalupe. Estábamos a unos 80 metros de su casa cuando la ambulancia pasó a gran velocidad. Francisco y yo intuitivamente nos miramos y empezamos a caminar con más rapidez, pero en silencio. A sólo unos metros de su casa, supimos que algo pasaba en casa de Guadalupe. Corrimos. Cuando llegamos a la puerta, un enfermero nos dijo: "La señorita Martínez tuvo un accidente. Se quebró una pierna y dos costillas. La llevamos al hospital".

Inmediatamente, Francisco y yo llamamos al resto de nuestros amigos. Esa noche, todos los amigos de Guadalupe fuimos a saludarla al hospital. Fue un cumpleaños diferente a todos los anteriores, porque lo celebramos en el hospital, al lado de la cama de nuestra gran amiga Guadalupe.

[1]Universidad Nacional Autónoma de México
[2]*dreamed*

**SEGUNDA FASE.** Conteste las siguientes preguntas basadas en la historia que acaba de leer.

1. ¿Cuál es el propósito de la historia? Márquelo (✓).
   a. ___ describir un evento emocional e inesperado
   b. ___ entretener a los lectores
   c. ___ informar a los lectores sobre una experiencia triste
   d. ___ enseñar algo
2. ¿Son efectivos la selección de los personajes y los detalles de ellos, el entorno (*setting*) y la trama (*plot*)? ___ Sí ___No
3. ¿Cuáles son las razones posibles para su respuesta a la pregunta 2? Márquelas (✓).
   a. ___ La protagonista se describe de una manera interesante.
   b. ___ La historia es ágil: la acción ocurre rápidamente y hay suficiente descripción.
   c. ___ Hay demasiada descripción y la historia es lenta.
   d. ___ Hay suficiente información sobre el entorno.
   e. ___ La historia sigue un orden cronológico.
   f. ___ La narración tiene una organización clara: una introducción, un desarrollo y un fin.
   g. ___ La historia es realista para el lector.

## Escribir

**8-45 Manos a la obra. PRIMERA FASE.** Usted va a narrar una historia personal, real o imaginaria. Primero, determine lo siguiente:

1. ¿Cuál es el objetivo de su narración, informar, relatar, entretener o enseñar?
2. ¿Cuántos protagonistas hay? ¿Qué características físicas y de personalidad tienen?
3. ¿Va a relatar usted en el pasado o en el presente? ¿Va a organizar los hechos en orden cronológico?
4. Escriba una lista de verbos que lo/la ayuden a describir el ambiente (*setting*), y otros que cuenten la acción.
5. ¿Qué información va a presentar en la introducción? ¿Cuál va a ser el conflicto? ¿Usted va a resolverlo o el lector va a imaginar el final de la historia?

> ### En directo
> To indicate chronological order:
> **Primero,...**
> **Después,.../Después de (un tiempo),...**
> **Luego,...**
> **Más tarde,...**
> **Finalmente,.../Por fin,...**

**SEGUNDA FASE.** Ahora, use la información de la *Primera fase* para escribir su narración, empezando del presente al pasado. Las siguientes expresiones en *En directo* pueden ser muy útiles.

## Después de escribir

**8-46 Revisión.** Lea su narración, pensando en su lector. Verifique lo siguiente:

1. ¿Incluyó la información que su lector necesita? ¿Es la trama creíble? ¿Describió suficientemente a los personajes y el ambiente?
2. ¿Tiene su narración una introducción, un conflicto y una conclusión?
3. ¿Usó expresiones apropiadas para indicar el orden cronológico, concordancia de tiempos (presente, pasado), etc.?
4. ¿Revisó la gramática, vocabulario, puntuación y ortografía?

Ahora, comparta su narración con un/a compañero/a. Converse con él/ella sobre los áreas débiles de su narración, si los hay.

# ENFOQUE CULTURAL

## Cultura y tradiciones mexicanas

La cultura popular de México es una de las más ricas y variadas de toda América Latina. En México se conservan muchas tradiciones y celebraciones nacionales, regionales, religiosas, políticas y familiares. Además, existe una gran riqueza en otros aspectos de la cultura, tales como la comida, la música e inclusive el idioma. En gran parte, esta riqueza cultural se debe a la mezcla de las antiguas culturas indígenas que existían en México y la europea, en particular la española. Esta mezcla resultó en una cultura popular tradicional y original a la vez.

Aunque en México existe una separación de la iglesia y el estado, la religión es, ciertamente, uno de los aspectos más

Aunque México es hoy un país industrializado y moderno, su cultura popular es rica en tradiciones.

sobresalientes de la cultura popular. Son muchas las tradiciones y celebraciones que tienen relación con aspectos de la cultura religiosa en México. Indudablemente una de las tradiciones religiosas más importantes es la veneración a la Virgen de Guadalupe. Según la tradición, la virgen María se le apareció a un indígena pobre llamado Juan Diego y le habló en náhuatl, el idioma de los aztecas. La virgen le pidió construir una iglesia en el Tepeyac, al norte de la actual Ciudad de México. Más tarde, una imagen de la virgen apareció milagrosamente en la camisa de Juan Diego. Esta imagen se convirtió en un símbolo de la identidad de México. Así la iglesia del Tepeyac es uno de los lugares religiosos más visitados en todo el continente americano.

La Virgen de Guadalupe es uno de los íconos más representativos de la identidad mexicana.

La celebración del Día de los Muertos también tiene sus orígenes en la cultura azteca. Los aztecas daban mucha importancia a la muerte y muchos de sus ritos se centraban en la muerte. La unión de esa tradición azteca con las tradiciones cristianas españolas produjo en México un culto muy especial de la muerte. Un aspecto interesante de este culto es el tratamiento a veces humorístico de la muerte, muy diferente del tratamiento solemne de la muerte en Estados Unidos o en otros países. En efecto, símbolos de la muerte como los esqueletos y las calaveras se representan en galletas, dulces y todo tipo de juguetes para niños. Las familias construyen altares en

Los Voladores de Papantla descienden girando alrededor de un poste de 30 metros de alto en una ceremonia relacionada con el calendario maya.

sus casas para ofrecer a los muertos las comidas y bebidas que disfrutaban en vida. Resulta interesante comparar la fiesta de *Halloween* en Estados Unidos y el Día de los Muertos, porque existen muchas diferencias entre ellas, a pesar de algunas semejanzas superficiales. En primer lugar, el origen celta de *Halloween* contrasta con el origen cristiano-azteca de la fiesta mexicana. En segundo lugar, mientras en Estados Unidos se trata de una fiesta principalmente para los niños que recorren las calles con disfraces macabros pidiendo dulces, la fiesta mexicana es principalmente una fiesta familiar dedicada a honrar a los muertos de cada familia.

Otra tradición muy espectacular de origen indígena es la de los Voladores de Papantla. Cuatro hombres de origen totonaca, uno de los muchos pueblos indígenas de México, se suben a un poste de 30 metros de altura que representa el árbol de la vida. Atados por la cintura, se lanzan dando círculos alrededor del poste, mientras otro hombre toca instrumentos prehispánicos y baila en lo alto del poste. Esta ceremonia se realiza en honor del Sol y tiene sus raíces en el calendario maya. Los voladores representan los cuatro elementos y los cuatro puntos cardinales.

Finalmente, la comida mexicana popular incluye muchos productos autóctonos, poco utilizados en la cocina europea, o en otras regiones americanas, tales como diferentes especies de hongos, cactus y flores. Por otra parte, la música y danza mexicanas también se unen a las tradiciones indígenas, como en el caso de la Mazoyiwua o Danza del Venado, que es una de las formas de más pura tradición prehispánica. La artesanía mexicana, con raíces en la cultura tradicional, es una de las más interesantes, coloridas y variadas de todo el mundo hispano. Y desde luego, la riqueza lingüística de México incluye más de 60 lenguas indígenas, además de innumerables variaciones del castellano.

### En otras palabras

Expresiones mexicanas

¿Cómo estás, mi **cuate?**
*How are you, my friend?*

Pablo es **chaparro**, pero su abuelo era alto.
*Pablo is short, but his grandfather was tall.*

Mi amiga Stephanie es **güera** y tiene los ojos azules.
*My friend Stephanie is blonde and has blue eyes.*

Mi **recámara** tiene una ventana grande.
*My bedroom has a large window.*

**8-47 Comprensión.** PRIMERA FASE. **Reconocimiento de palabras clave.** Encuentre en el texto la palabra o expresión que mejor expresa el significado de las siguientes ideas.

1. at the same time   _____
2. outstanding   _____
3. undoubtedly   _____
4. skulls   _____
5. cookies   _____
6. pole   _____
7. roots   _____
8. mushrooms   _____

SEGUNDA FASE. **Oraciones importantes.** Subraye las afirmaciones que contienen ideas que se encuentran en el texto. Luego indique en qué parte del texto están.

1. Native cultures of Mexico mixed with Spanish traditions to produce an original culture.
2. Religion is probably not a major component of Mexican popular culture.
3. Decorations for the All Souls' Day celebration sometimes include humorous images of Death.
4. The Tree of Life is represented by a 30–meter pole in the **Flyers of Papantla** ceremony.
5. The **Flyers of Papantla** ceremony is rooted in the Mayan calendar.
6. Flowers are used as ingredients in some Mexican dishes.
7. Traditional Mexican dances are very similar to (or are modeled on) traditional Spanish dances.
8. Many native languages, as well as variations of Spanish, are regularly spoken in Mexico.

TERCERA FASE. **Ideas principales.** Escriba un párrafo breve en inglés resumiendo las ideas principales expresadas en el texto.

 **8-48 Use la información.** Usted fue a México y asistió a una de las siguientes celebraciones. Escríbale un correo electrónico a su profesor/a y cuéntele cuál de las siguientes celebraciones vio y dónde las vio. Incluya al menos cuatro datos sobre ella. Para preparar esta actividad, visite la página web de *Mosaicos* y siga los enlaces útiles.

a. el Cinco de Mayo
b. el Día de los Muertos
c. el Baile de los Viejitos
d. la Danza del Venado
e. el Día de la Virgen de Guadalupe

# VOCABULARIO

**Las fiestas y las
celebraciones** / *Holidays and
celebrations*

| | |
|---|---|
| la alegría | *joy* |
| el aserrín | *sawdust* |
| el carnaval | *carnival* |
| la carreta | *cart, wagon* |
| la carroza | *float (in a parade)* |
| la celebración | *celebration* |
| la comparsa | *group dressed in similar costumes* |
| la corrida (de toros) | *bullfight* |
| la costumbre | *custom* |
| el desfile | *parade* |
| el día feriado | *legal holiday* |
| el día festivo | *holiday* |
| el festival | *festival* |
| la festividad, la fiesta | *festivity; holiday; celebration* |
| la invitación | *invitation* |
| el preparativo | *preparation* |
| la procesión | *procession* |
| la semilla | *seed* |
| el toro | *bull* |
| la tradición | *tradition* |

**Las personas** / *People*

| | |
|---|---|
| el antepasado | *ancestor* |
| la gente | *people* |
| el rey/la reina | *king/queen* |

**La música** / *Music*

| | |
|---|---|
| la melodía | *melody* |
| la orquesta | *orchestra* |
| el ruido | *noise* |

**Los lugares** / *Places*

| | |
|---|---|
| el camino | *road; way* |
| el cementerio | *cemetery* |
| la iglesia | *church* |
| el teatro | *theater* |

**El tiempo** / *Time*

| | |
|---|---|
| antes | *before* |
| el comienzo | *beginning* |
| entonces | *then* |
| hoy en día | *nowadays* |
| mientras | *while* |

**Las descripciones** / *Descriptions*

| | |
|---|---|
| adornado/a | *decorated* |
| animado/a | *lively* |
| difunto/a, muerto/a | *dead* |
| maravilloso/a | *marvelous* |
| suave | *soft* |
| último/a | *last* |

**Verbos** / *Verbs*

| | |
|---|---|
| acompañar | *to accompany* |
| comenzar (ie) | *to begin* |
| dar un paseo | *to take a walk* |
| disfrazarse (c) | *to wear a costume* |
| divertirse (ie, i) | *to have a good time* |
| encerrar (ie) | *to lock up, shut in* |
| invitar | *to invite* |
| mantener (g, ie) | *to maintain* |
| quedar | *to arrange to meet* |
| recordar (ue) | *to remember* |
| reunirse | *to get together* |

See page 260 for the names of popular celebrations.
See page 267 for expressions of time and frequency.
See pages 273, 274, and 276 for expressions to use to make comparisons.

# Hay que trabajar

Tapices de lana en un mercado de Antigua, Guatemala. Se elaboran a mano en la región de Momostenango, que está al oeste de la capital.

# In this chapter you will learn how to:

- talk about the workplace and professions
- talk about the past
- give instructions

## Cultural focus: **Guatemala**

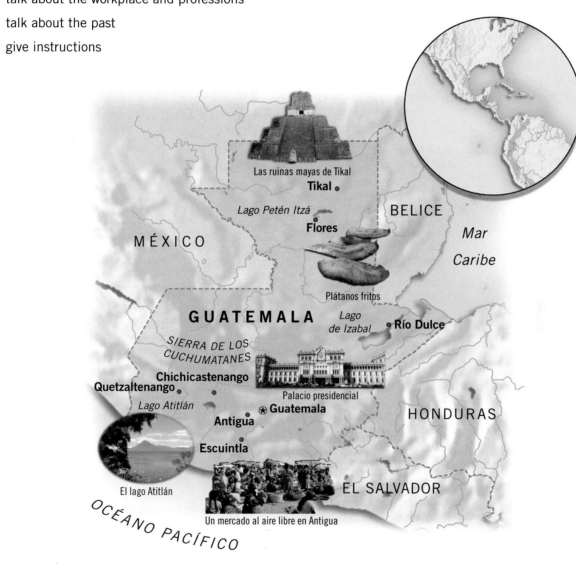

Las ruinas mayas de Tikal

**Tikal**

*Lago Petén Itzá*

**Flores**

**BELICE**

**MÉXICO**

*Mar Caribe*

Plátanos fritos

**GUATEMALA**

*Lago de Izabal* **Río Dulce**

*SIERRA DE LOS CUCHUMATANES*

**Chichicastenango**

**Quetzaltenango**

*Lago Atitlán*

Palacio presidencial

⊛ **Guatemala**

**Antigua**

**HONDURAS**

**Escuintla**

El lago Atitlán

Un mercado al aire libre en Antigua

**EL SALVADOR**

*OCÉANO PACÍFICO*

**A vista de pájaro.** Piense en lo que sabe de Guatemala y conteste las siguientes preguntas.

1. ¿Cómo se llaman los habitantes de Guatemala?
2. ¿Cuál era la antigua capital de Guatemala?
3. ¿Qué país está al este de Guatemala?
4. ¿Qué civilización fue muy importante en Guatemala?
5. ¿Qué idiomas habla la gente (*people*)?
6. ¿Cuáles son probablemente algunos recursos económicos importantes?

291

## �»)) El trabajo

CD 4
Track 14

En muchos lugares de Latinoamérica la **agricultura** es un sector significativo de la economía nacional. En estos cuadros del pintor guatemalteco Pedro Rafael González Chavajay vemos a algunos **agricultores cosechando** el café y los plátanos.

Los productos del **campo** se venden después en los mercados locales junto con las telas y las joyas que **elaboran** los **artesanos**.

Este **carpintero** está trabajando la **madera** en su **taller** para hacer una silla. Otras personas que trabajan con materias primas son los **herreros**, los **peleteros**, los **ceramistas** y los **joyeros**. Desafortunadamente, para muchas personas es difícil encontrar un buen trabajo para **sobrevivir** y tienen que **emigrar** a las grandes ciudades o a otros países.

**9-1 ¿A qué se dedican?** Diga si las siguientes afirmaciones son ciertas (**C**) o falsas (**F**). Si la respuesta es falsa (**F**), corrija la información.

1. ___ Los peleteros hacen zapatos, bolsas y chaquetas.
2. ___ Los ceramistas trabajan con el hierro.
3. ___ Los herreros trabajan los metales.
4. ___ Los carpinteros hacen los trabajos del campo.
5. ___ Los joyeros trabajan la plata y el oro para hacer pulseras y collares, por ejemplo.
6. ___ Los agricultores plantan y cosechan productos naturales.

**9-2 Las preparaciones.** Varios estudiantes planeaban una fiesta para celebrar su graduación. Indique adónde fueron y con quiénes hablaron para conseguir lo que necesitaban para la fiesta.

MODELO: María quería comprar un kilo de carne para hacer una parrillada en el jardín.
*Fue a la carnicería y habló con el carnicero/la carnicera.*

1. Juan necesitaba pescado para preparar un ceviche.
2. Paula tenía que comprar unos zapatos.
3. Carlos y Laura querían regalarle un collar elegante a Felicia.
4. Elisa quería encargar (*order*) una mesa de madera pequeña para poner los aperitivos.
5. Sofía pensaba regalarle un libro a Diego.
6. Martín y Luis necesitaban unos pantalones formales nuevos para ir a la fiesta.
7. Lorenzo quería comprar algo de fruta para hacer el postre.
8. Pilar quería adornar la casa con flores.

**9-3 Descripciones.** Miren los cuadros en la p. 292 y descríbanse las escenas con el mayor detalle posible. Tengan en cuenta las siguientes ideas:

1. lugar donde están estas personas
2. rasgos físicos
3. edad aproximada
4. ropa que llevan
5. lo que están haciendo
6. lo que están pensando algunas de las personas en la escena
7. cómo se sienten

---

## Lengua

The suffix **-ero/-era** is often used in Spanish to designate trades and professions, e.g., **camarero/a** (*server*), **plomero/a** (*plumber*), **peluquero/a** (*hairdresser*). Another common suffix is **-ista**, e.g., **electricista** (*electrician*); **contratista** (*contractor*).

# •)) Los oficios y las profesiones

CD 4
Track 15

Una **chef** muestra algunas de sus **especialidades**.

Dra. Alicia Gonica de Pérez

CARDIÓLOGA

Consultorio
La Concepción 81
Calle 18, 402, Ciudad de Guatemala
Teléfono: (502) 23622001
Fax: (502) 23670721

Una **médica** le inyecta antibióticos a una paciente en su **consultorio**.

Unos **bomberos apagan** un **incendio** en Ciudad de Guatemala.

Una **ejecutiva** llama por teléfono a un **cliente**.

Una **locutora espera** la **señal** para comenzar un programa de noticias en una estación de radio.

Un **técnico** revisa los controles de una **compañía** petrolera.

## Cultura

Un importante cambio social en los países hispanos en las últimas décadas es el ingreso masivo de las mujeres al mercado laboral. Sin embargo, aún existen desigualdades: el desempleo entre las mujeres es mayor; su representación en las empresas de alta productividad es mucho menor; y los salarios de las mujeres son más bajos de los que reciben los hombres por el mismo tipo de trabajo.

Además, el trabajo doméstico no remunerado todavía se considera una obligación asociada con las mujeres y las niñas. No obstante, en muchos países hispanos ya se ofrecen programas educativos para combatir la discriminación. Algunos países, como Perú y Chile, tienen Ministerios de la Mujer para proteger y atender las necesidades de las mujeres.

Un **peluquero** le corta el pelo a una clienta.

# Otras ocupaciones

CD 4
ack 16

la juez

el abogado

el actor

el ama de casa

el policía

la bibliotecaria

la cajera

el chofer

la científica

el contador

la electricista

la enfermera

la mujer de
negocios

el ingeniero

el intérprete

el obrero

el psicólogo

el plomero

la arquitecta

la periodista

**9-4 ¿Qué profesión debe tener?** Lean las siguientes descripciones y digan qué profesión u oficio de la lista deben tener las personas con estas características. **OJO:** A veces, más de una respuesta es posible.

| | | |
|---|---|---|
| abogado/a | científico/a | médico/a |
| actor/actriz | ingeniero/a | plomero/a |
| artista | mecánico/a | psicólogo/a |

1. A Pablo le gusta observar y analizar el comportamiento (*behavior*) de las personas.
2. Los hermanos Pedraza siempre resuelven los problemas del auto de su padre. Lo examinan y lo reparan a la perfección.
3. Eva y Ana tienen facilidad para resolver los problemas de otras personas. También tienen la habilidad de exponer oralmente.
4. A Jaime le fascina desarmar (*disassemble*) aparatos electrónicos para estudiar cómo funcionan.
5. Daniela es una chica muy sensible y una gran observadora. Le fascina expresar sus sentimientos y experiencias de manera artística.
6. Adela siempre lee libros sobre anatomía. Ella sabe el nombre de cada parte del cuerpo humano.

**9-5 Las profesiones y la personalidad. PRIMERA FASE.** Digan cómo deben ser estos/as profesionales. Seleccionen las palabras de la lista para describir las características deseadas.

**MODELO:** un bombero
*Debe ser valiente, serio y responsable. No debe ser descuidado* (careless).

| | | | | | |
|---|---|---|---|---|---|
| autoritario | dedicado | detallista | inteligente | perezoso | serio |
| calculador | delgado | estudioso | irónico | responsable | simpático |
| cuidadoso | descuidado | guapo | paciente | romántico | valiente |

1. un médico/una médica
2. un actor/una actriz
3. un hombre/una mujer de negocios
4. un peluquero/una peluquera
5. un locutor/una locutora
6. un ama de casa
7. un ejecutivo/una ejecutiva
8. un mecánico/una mecánica
9. un cocinero/una cocinera
10. un abogado/una abogada

**SEGUNDA FASE.** Intercambien ideas sobre lo siguiente.

1. ¿Conoce a algún/a... (*nombre de la profesión*)? ¿Cómo se llama? ¿Dónde trabaja?
2. ¿Qué características personales o especiales, en su opinión, lo/la ayudan en su profesión?

**9-6 Asociaciones.** Asocien una o más profesiones con los siguientes lugares de trabajo, y digan lo que hacen estas personas.

| LUGAR | PROFESIÓN | ¿QUÉ HACE? |
|---|---|---|
| **1.** el hospital | enfermero/a, médico/a | Atiende a los pacientes. |
| **2.** el restaurante | | |
| **3.** la clase | | |
| **4.** la estación de radio | | |
| **5.** la tienda de ropa | | |
| **6.** el consultorio médico | | |
| **7.** la peluquería | | |

**9-7 ¿Cuál es la profesión?** Primero identifiquen la ocupación o profesión, según la descripción. Luego, digan dos ventajas y una desventaja de esta ocupación o profesión.

MODELO:     Trabaja en una biblioteca haciendo catálogos de libros.
E1: *Es un bibliotecario/una bibliotecaria.*
E2: *Dos ventajas de ser bibliotecario/a son estar en contacto con muchos libros y trabajar en un lugar tranquilo.*
E3: *Una desventaja es la falta de ejercicio físico.*

| | PROFESIÓN | 2 VENTAJAS | 1 DESVENTAJA |
|---|---|---|---|
| **1.** Escribe artículos para el periódico. | | | |
| **2.** Presenta programas de televisión. | | | |
| **3.** Traduce simultáneamente. | | | |
| **4.** Mantiene el orden público. | | | |
| **5.** Apaga incendios. | | | |
| **6.** Defiende o acusa a personas delante de un/a juez. | | | |

**9-8 Mi ocupación ideal para el futuro. PRIMERA FASE.** Piense en su ocupación o profesión ideal. Su compañero/a le va a hacer preguntas para adivinar la ocupación o profesión en que piensa.

MODELO:  E1: *En tu profesión ideal, ¿las personas deben viajar mucho?*
E2: *Sí.*
E1: *¿Y deben hablar con clientes para hacer negocios?*
E2: *Sí.*
E1: *¡Ah! ¡Tú quieres ser hombre/mujer de negocios!*

SEGUNDA FASE. Haga una lista de tres requisitos de su trabajo ideal y compruebe si usted los tiene. Intercambie esta información con su compañero/a.

MODELO: *Me gustaría ser actor/actriz. Un actor/una actriz debe leer mucho; debe saber representar emociones y sentimientos y debe ser flexible para trabajar muchas horas. A mí me gusta leer y soy flexible, pero no puedo representar muy bien las emociones.*

# ·))) **Buscando trabajo**

CD 4
Track 17 **La entrevista de trabajo**

SRA. ARCE: Buenos días, Sr. Solano. Soy Marcela Arce, presidenta de la compañía.

SR. SOLANO: Mucho gusto, señora.

SRA. ARCE: Siéntese, por favor. Usted **solicitó** el **puesto** de **gerente de ventas**, ¿verdad?

SR. SOLANO: Sí, señora. Leí en *El Diario de Centro América* que había una **vacante**. Después pedí y **llené** una **solicitud**.

SRA. ARCE: Sí, aquí la tengo, y también su **currículum**. **Por cierto**, es excelente.

SR. SOLANO: Muchas gracias.

SRA. ARCE: **Actualmente** usted trabaja en la empresa Badosa. ¿Por qué quiere **dejar** su puesto?

SR. SOLANO: Bueno, **en realidad** yo estoy muy contento allí, pero a mí me gustaría trabajar en una compañía internacional y poder usar otras lenguas. Como usted ve en mi currículum, yo hablo español, inglés y francés.

SRA. ARCE: En su solicitud, usted indica que desea un **sueldo** de 30.000 quetzales al mes. **Sin embargo**, para el puesto que tenemos, el sueldo que **se ofrece** es de 25.500 quetzales.

SR. SOLANO: Sí, lo sé, pero la diferencia no es tan importante. **Lo importante** es que aquí puedo tener la oportunidad de comunicarme con los clientes en su **propia** lengua. Yo creo que esto puede mejorar las ventas de Computel notablemente.

SRA. ARCE: Pues si le parece bien el sueldo, ¿por qué no pasamos a la oficina del director general para seguir hablando?

SR. SOLANO: ¡Cómo no!

## *Cultura*

The **quetzal** (GQT) is the national currency of Guatemala. The exchange rate is about 7,56 GQT to $1 U.S. The word **quetzal** comes from the Náhuatl language and it refers to the strikingly colored bird that is the symbol of Guatemala.

## Lengua

In Spanish, **actualmente** refers only to the present time.

**Actualmente** yo trabajo en Antigua.
*At the present time/Now I work in Antigua.*

Therefore, *actualmente* is a false cognate of *actually*. The equivalents of *actually* in Spanish are **realmente** or **en realidad**.

**Realmente/En realidad** yo sólo trabajé en Ciudad de Guatemala un mes.
*Actually I only worked in Ciudad de Guatemala for a month.*

👥👥 **9-9 Los datos de la entrevista.** Busquen los siguientes datos en el diálogo anterior.

1. nombre de la presidenta de la compañía
2. puesto que solicita el Sr. Solano
3. nombre de la compañía donde el Sr. Solano trabaja actualmente
4. nombre de la compañía donde desea trabajar
5. lenguas que habla
6. sueldo que desea el Sr. Solano
7. sueldo que se ofrece en el nuevo puesto
8. motivo para cambiar de puesto

**9-10 ¿En qué orden?** Cuando alguien busca un trabajo, normalmente ¿en qué orden ocurren las siguientes actividades? Ordénelas de 1 a 8.

____ Me llaman de la Compañía Rosell para una entrevista.
____ Les contesto que no, que se cerró el almacén.
____ Leo los anuncios del periódico.
____ Envío la solicitud a la Compañía Rosell.
____ Voy a la compañía para la entrevista.
____ Me preguntan si me despidieron (*fired*) del trabajo anterior.
____ Preparo mi currículum y lleno la solicitud para la Compañía Rosell.
____ Me ofrecen el puesto de vendedor/a.

**9-11 El arte de entrevistarse. PRIMERA FASE.** Escoja el anuncio más interesante del periódico *La Hora* e imagínese que solicita ese puesto. Su compañero/a, en el papel de jefe/a de personal, lo/la entrevista a usted y toma notas para obtener la siguiente información. Luego cambien de papel.

1. nombre de la persona que solicita el puesto
2. estudios que tiene
3. lenguas que habla
4. lugar donde trabaja y responsabilidades
5. experiencia anterior
6. razones para querer trabajar en esta compañía

**INSTITUTO DE CIRUGÍA PLÁSTICA: CLÍNICA CÁRDENAS**
**Necesita enfermera**

**Prótesis:**
implantes faciales (Botox, silicona)
liposucción papada, abdomen, muslos

**Informes:**
Clínica Centro, Zona 10
**Tel: (502) 2534147**

*Llamar a secretaria: Marta*

**Hotel VILLA ANTIGUA**
Necesita
**RECEPCIONISTA**
• Experiencia
• Bilingüe español-inglés
**CAMARERA**
• Mín. 2 años de experiencia
• Disponible trabajar por las mañanas y tardes
Dirigirse al Hotel VILLA ANTIGUA
Jefe de Personal
9a. Calle Poniente, Carretera a Ciudad Vieja, Antigua, Guatemala
**Teléfono:** +(502) 78323956 ó +(502) 78323955

**EMPRESA EXPORTADORA DE ARTESANÍAS**
Requiere
**CONTADOR**
**Requisitos:**
• Experiencia mínima de 5 años
• Graduado del Colegio de Contadores Públicos
• Para cita llamar al Sr. López al (502) 2764532

**EMPRESA MINERA**
*Requiere*
**3 Ingenieros de sistemas**
REQUISITOS:
1. Mayor de 25 años
2. Experiencia en minas de cobre
3. Flexibilidad horaria (incluidos fines de semana)
OFRECEMOS:
1. Ingreso superior a 20.000 quetzales
2. Capacitación profesional
3. Bonos de participación
*Interesados enviar currículum a: Minas de Guatemala S.A.*
**Oficina de Personal**
Diagonal 19, 29-78, Zona 11
Ciudad de Guatemala, Guatemala
Teléfono: (502) 2762147
Fax: (502) 2763482

**SEGUNDA FASE.** Ahora informe al presidente de la empresa (otro compañero/otra compañera) sobre las calificaciones del candidato/de la candidata.

**9-12 ¿Comportamiento apropiado?** Preparen una lista de cinco acciones que se deben hacer antes de una entrevista y cinco que no se deben hacer durante una entrevista. Después comparen su lista con la de otros compañeros/otras compañeras.

| LO QUE SE DEBE HACER ANTES DE UNA ENTREVISTA | LO QUE NO SE DEBE HACER DURANTE UNA ENTREVISTA |
|---|---|
| | |
| | |
| | |
| | |
| | |

**9-13 Mi profesión.** You will listen to Julieta Odriozola talk about her profession. Before you listen, write down the names of four professions that have traditionally been associated with women.

CD 4
Track 18

Now, pay attention to the general idea of what is said. As you listen mark (✔) the appropriate ending to each statement.

1. Julieta Odriozola es...
   ____ artista.
   ____ política.
   ____ periodista.

2. Julieta tiene un horario...
   ____ de 9 a 5.
   ____ variable.
   ____ de lunes a sábado.

3. Julieta hace casi todo su trabajo en...
   ____ su auto.
   ____ su casa.
   ____ diferentes lugares.

4. Julieta trabaja básicamente con...
   ____ artistas jóvenes.
   ____ personas importantes.
   ____ empleados de la comunidad.

## Diarios de bicicleta: ¿Qué quieres ser?

### Antes de ver

**9-14** Asocie cada una de las profesiones de la izquierda con una palabra relacionada en la columna derecha.

1. ____ ingeniero/a          **a.** salud
2. ____ bombero/a            **b.** cine
3. ____ médico/a             **c.** comida
4. ____ chef                 **d.** documentos legales
5. ____ abogado/a            **e.** máquinas y computadoras
6. ____ actor/actriz         **f.** incendios

### Mientras ve

**9-15** Escriba todas las profesiones que se mencionan en este segmento.

### Después de ver

**9-16** Exprese su opinión sobre los siguientes temas:

- la profesión en que es posible ayudar a más gente
- la profesión más difícil
- la profesión más lucrativa
- la profesión más peligrosa (*dangerous*)

# FUNCIONES Y FORMAS

## 1. Avoiding repetition: Review of direct and indirect object pronouns

Bárbara

Carlota

BÁRBARA: Carlota, ¿por qué llevas chanclas (*flip-flops*)?

CARLOTA: **Le** di mis zapatos al zapatero porque se rompieron.

BÁRBARA: ¿Y no tienes frío?

CARLOTA: Sí, pero no tengo otra opción. El zapatero va a arreglarlos en una hora. Y tú, Bárbara, ¿por qué no tienes chaqueta? Hace frío.

BÁRBARA: **La** dejé en casa.

CARLOTA: Bueno, yo **te** presto mi suéter.

**Piénselo.** Para cada oración, escriba las palabras en negrita (*boldface*) en la columna apropiada. **OJO:** En algunas oraciones hay más de un objeto directo u objeto indirecto.

| | OBJETO DIRECTO | OBJETO INDIRECTO |
|---|---|---|
| 1. **Le** di mis **zapatos** al **zapatero**. | ——— | ——— |
| 2. El zapatero va a arreglar los **zapatos** de Carlota. | ——— | ——— |
| 3. El zapatero va a arreglar**los**. | ——— | ——— |
| 4. ¿Por qué no tienes **chaqueta**? | ——— | ——— |
| 5. **La** dejé en casa. | ——— | ——— |
| 6. **Te** presto mi **suéter**. | ——— | ——— |

■ In *Capítulo 5* you learned that direct objects answer the question *what?* or *whom?* in relation to the verb. They can refer to people, animals, or objects. When a direct object noun refers to a specific person, a group of people, or a pet, the *personal* **a** precedes the direct object. To avoid repetition in speaking or writing, direct object pronouns can replace direct object nouns if the noun has already been mentioned.

| | |
|---|---|
| ¿Ves **al chef**? | *Do you see the **chef**?* |
| Sí, **lo** veo. Está al lado de la cocina. | *Yes, I see **him**. He is next to the kitchen.* |
| La Dra. Martín recibe **a sus pacientes** en la clínica. | *Dr. Martín sees **her patients** in the clinic.* |
| **Los** recibe todos los días. | *She sees **them** every day.* |

302

■ In *Capítulo 6* you learned that indirect object nouns and pronouns tell *to whom* or *for whom* an action is done. They most often occur in the context of transferring information or objects, such as giving someone a gift, telling someone a story, or asking someone for something.

| | |
|---|---|
| La maestra siempre **les** dice la verdad a los niños. | *The teacher always tells the children the truth.* |
| El camarero no **nos** trajo la sopa. | *The waiter did not bring us the soup.* |

■ Direct and indirect object pronouns are placed before conjugated verbs. When a conjugated verb is followed by an infinitive or present participle, the pronouns can either precede the conjugated verb or be attached to the infinitive or present participle.

| | |
|---|---|
| ¿Las fotos de la casa? La arquitecta está compilándo**las**. | *The photos of the house?* |
| ¿Las fotos de la casa? La arquitecta **las** está compilando. | *The architect is compiling them.* |
| Su asistente va a mandar**nos** todos los documentos. | *Her assistent is going to send us all the documents.* |
| Su asistente **nos** va a mandar todos los documentos. | |

■ Direct and indirect object pronouns have the same form, except in the third person. Note that **le/les** refer to either males or females.

| DIRECT OBJECT PRONOUNS | | INDIRECT OBJECT PRONOUNS | |
|---|---|---|---|
| me | nos | me | nos |
| te | os | te | os |
| lo | los | le | les |
| la | las | | |

**9-17 Los preparativos para la evaluación. PRIMERA FASE.** Usted trabaja en la oficina de una arquitecta y mañana empieza la evaluación anual. Indique qué empleado/a está haciendo cada uno de los preparativos para la visita de los evaluadores: la arquitecta (**A**) o el asistente administrativo (**AA**).

1. ____ Está terminando el último informe.
2. ____ Está examinando los materiales para ver si hay errores.
3. ____ Está sacando las fotocopias.
4. ____ Está organizando el horario.

 **SEGUNDA FASE.** Compare sus respuestas con las de su compañero/a, siguiendo el modelo.

**MODELO:** E1: *¿Quién está examinando el presupuesto (budget)?*
E2: *El asistente administrativo está examinándolo.*

**9-18 Comunicaciones y transacciones.** Mire los dibujos y explique dónde ocurre la escena y lo que pasa en cada una.

dependienta

Pancho

**MODELO:** enviar/flores

*Pancho está en la floristería. Le va a enviar flores a su esposa porque es el Día de los Enamorados.*

**1. Role A.** You meet with a career counselor (**consejero/a vocacional**) for tips on how to look for a job. Explain the type of job you are looking for, and answer the counselor's questions about your past experience. Ask the counselor questions of your own.

**Role B.** You are a career counselor (**consejero/a vocacional**) who is meeting with a new client. After listening to the client, ask whether he/she a) prepared a résumé; b) looked for job ads (and where); c) applied for a job (which one); and d) prepared questions to ask in an interview. Be ready to answer the client's questions.

**2. Role A.** You are at an outdoor market in Antigua, Guatemala. You are at a stand that has blouses, tapestries, and jewelry. Tell the vendor that a) you want to give your sister a blouse for her birthday; b) you would like to take your parents a tapestry; and c) you want to buy a necklace for a good friend. Respond to the vendor's questions and ask an additional question about each item.

**Role B.** You are a Guatemalan artisan selling your goods at a market in Antigua. An American student is interested in buying some gifts. Ask questions to help the customer make appropriate choices, and answer his/her questions about the items.

Juan

María

jefa

asistente

artesana     turistas

**1.** mandar/mensaje de texto     **2.** dar/documentos     **3.** vender/telas tradicionales

**9-19 Gerentes y empleados. PRIMERA FASE.** La compañía Hipertermo fabrica casas modulares que utilizan la energía solar y es famosa por la buena relación entre sus empleados. Escriban los factores que, según ustedes, contribuyen a la buena comunicación entre los gerentes y los empleados.

1. sugerir formas más eficientes de hacer el trabajo
2. dar las gracias por la alta calidad de su trabajo
3. explicar los beneficios de usar la energía solar
4. ofrecer ayuda para resolver conflictos
5. comunicar inmediatamente problemas con las máquinas
6. pedir ayuda cuando tienen dudas

| LOS GERENTES... | LOS EMPLEADOS... |
| --- | --- |
| les explican a los empleados claramente sus responsabilidades. | les dan buenas ideas a los gerentes. |
|  |  |
|  |  |
|  |  |

**SEGUNDA FASE.** Los gerentes quieren premiar (*reward*) a los empleados al final del año. ¿Qué van a hacer los gerentes para los empleados?

**MODELO:** escribir una carta de agradecimiento
*Los gerentes van a escribirles una carta de agradecimiento.*

1. subir el salario
2. dar una fiesta
3. escribir evaluaciones negativas de su trabajo
4. comprar regalos
5. decir que están muy contentos con su trabajo
6. pedir más horas de trabajo por semana

## 2. Avoiding repetition: Use of direct and indirect object pronouns together

CONSEJERA: ¿Ya **le** mandó su currículum al director?

CLIENTE: Sí, **se lo** mandé la semana pasada.

CONSEJERA: ¿Recibió alguna confirmación?

CLIENTE: Sí, ellos **me la** mandaron rápidamente. **La** recibí hoy.

**Piénselo.** Lea las oraciones y escriba en la columna apropiada los objetos directos y los indirectos, tanto los pronombres como los sustantivos (*nouns*).

|  | OBJETO INDIRECTO | OBJETO DIRECTO |
|---|---|---|
| MODELO: La secretaria **me** dio una cita para el lunes. | me | cita |
| 1. ¿Ya **le** mandó su currículum al director? | | |
| 2. **Se lo** mandé la semana pasada. | | |
| 3. Ellos **me la** mandaron rápidamente. | | |
| 4. **La** recibí hoy. | | |

■ You have already learned how to use indirect object pronouns or direct object pronouns in sentences. In this section you will learn how to use both types of pronouns in the same sentence.

| INDIRECT OBJECT PRONOUNS | | DIRECT OBJECT PRONOUNS | |
|---|---|---|---|
| me | nos | me | nos |
| te | os | te | os |
| le (se) | les (se) | lo | los |
| | | la | las |

■ When direct and indirect object pronouns are used in the same sentence, the indirect object pronoun precedes the direct object pronoun. Place double object pronouns before conjugated verbs.

Ella **me** dio **la solicitud**.
   i.o.     d.o.

*She gave me the application.*

Ella **me la** dio.
   i.o. d.o.

*She gave it to me.*

■ In compound verb constructions, you may place double object pronouns before the conjugated verb or attach them to the accompanying infinitive or present participle.

Él quiere dar**me el contrato**. *He wants to give me the contract.*
         i.o.    d.o.

Él quiere dár**me lo**.
         i.o.d.o.           } *He wants to give it to me.*

Él **me lo** quiere dar.
   i.o. d.o.

Ella **te** está diciendo **la verdad**. *She is telling you the truth.*
     i.o.                    d.o.

Ella **te la** está diciendo.
     i.o. d.o.              } *She is telling it to you.*

Ella está diciéndo**te la**.
                   i.o.d.o.

■ The indirect object pronouns **le** and **les** change to **se** before **lo, los, la,** or **las.**

**Le** dio **el puesto** a Verónica. *He gave the job to Veronica.*
i.o.      d.o.

**Se lo** dio. *He gave it to her.*
i.o. d.o.

**Les** va a mostrar **el anuncio**. *She is going to show them/you*
i.o.                    d.o.         *(ustedes) the ad.*

**Se lo** va a mostrar. *She is going to show it to*
i.o. d.o.                *them/you (ustedes).*

■ When a direct object pronoun and a reflexive pronoun are used together, the reflexive pronoun precedes the direct object pronoun.

Siempre **me** envío **correos electrónicos** *I always send myself e-mails to*
        i.o.        d.o.                       *remember what I have to do.*
para recordar lo que debo hacer.

Siempre **me los** envío. *I always send them to myself.*
        i.o. d.o.

 **9-20 ¿Qué hizo el supervisor?** Usted es el dueño/la dueña de una compañía. Habla con un empleado nuevo/una empleada nueva para saber si el supervisor hizo todo lo que tenía que hacer para explicarle cómo funciona su departamento.

**MODELO:**     darle el manual de la compañía
        E1:  *¿Le dio el manual de la compañía?*
        E2:  *Sí, me lo dio.*

1. explicarle la campaña de publicidad
2. mostrarle los anuncios
3. traerle las revistas
4. pedirle un documento que faltaba
5. dejarle las fotos
6. describirle los modelos que se necesitan.

**9-21 ¿Qué hace usted? PRIMERA FASE.** La imparcialidad, la amabilidad y la confidencialidad son fundamentales en el trabajo. Lea las siguientes situaciones y seleccione lo que usted haría (*would do*) en cada una.

1. Un cliente le pide a usted el teléfono de la oficina del presidente de la compañía.
   **a.** ____ Usted se lo da.        **b.** ____ Usted no se lo da.
2. Alguien quiere leer un documento confidencial.
   **a.** ____ Usted se lo muestra.        **b.** ____ Usted no se lo muestra.

**3.** La nueva jefa de personal viene a una reunión de su departamento. Alguien tiene que presentarla a los empleados.

**a.** ___ Usted se la presenta.          **b.** ___ Usted no se la presenta.

**4.** Una empleada nueva le dice a usted que quiere dos semanas de vacaciones después de trabajar sólo tres meses.

**a.** ___ Usted se las da.          **b.** ___ Usted decide no dárselas.

**SEGUNDA FASE.** ¿Están de acuerdo usted y su compañero/a? Justifiquen su respuesta entre ustedes.

MODELO:    Un cliente le pide a usted información personal sobre las finanzas de otro cliente. Los dos clientes son hermanos.

E1: *No se la doy porque no le gustaría al segundo cliente.*
E2: *Yo se la doy porque los dos clientes son hermanos.*

**9-22 ¡El cliente siempre tiene razón! PRIMERA FASE.** Ustedes se entrevistan sobre el servicio en un restaurante donde cada uno de ustedes comió recientemente. Tomen notas sobre las respuestas de su compañero/a para compartir con la clase.

**1.** ¿Cuándo les sirvieron el agua?
**2.** ¿Les trajeron pan a la mesa?
**3.** ¿Les dijo el camarero cuáles eran los platos especiales del día?
**4.** ¿Se los describió?
**5.** ¿Les ofreció postres y café?
**6.** ¿Cómo fue el servicio en general?

**SEGUNDA FASE.** Presenten a la clase un breve resumen del servicio en sus respectivos restaurantes.

## SITUACIONES

**1. Role A.** You are a reporter for *El Quetzalteco*, a regional newspaper en Quetzaltenango, and you have just arrived in Guatemala City to cover a story. You were in such a rush to leave Quetzaltenango that you left your laptop and camera (**cámara**) in the taxi. Call a fellow reporter in the capital city and a) explain what happened; b) ask if he/she can lend you a laptop and camera; and c) say that you need them right away.

**Role B.** You are a reporter for *El Súper Canal 3* in Guatemala City. A reporter from Quetzaltenango calls to tell you about an urgent problem. Ask a) when he/she left the laptop and computer in the taxi and b) if he/she called the taxi company. When the reporter asks you for a favor, say that he/she can come to your office to pick them up right away.

**2. Role A.** As manager of a large bank, you asked an employee to deliver (**entregar**) an important package (**un paquete**) to another bank. When he/she returns, ask a) if he/she delivered it; b) at what time he/she delivered it; c) to whom he/she gave it.

**Role B.** You work at a large bank. You have just returned from delivering (**entregar**) an important package (**un paquete**) to another bank. The manager is anxious about whether the package reached its destination. Answer the manager's questions to ease his/her concerns.

### 3. Talking about the past: More on the imperfect and preterit

PERIODISTA: Sr. Mario Parada, usted estaba en el Bancafé cuando entraron los ladrones (*robbers*), ¿verdad? ¿Qué **estaba haciendo**?

SR. PARADA: Yo **estaba hablando** con la cajera. **Iba a** hacer un depósito, pero claro, no **pude** realizar la transacción.

PERIODISTA: ¿Qué hicieron los empleados cuando **supieron** que había ladrones en el banco?

SR. PARADA: Todo pasó muy rápido. En el momento del robo, los cajeros **estaban respondiendo** a las preguntas de los clientes. Los oficiales de seguridad vieron a los ladrones y **quisieron** detenerlos (*stop them*) pero no **pudieron**.

**Piénselo.** Indique quién(es) estaba(n) haciendo las siguientes actividades cuando ocurrió el asalto: Mario Parada (**M**), los cajeros de Bancafé (**CA**), los clientes (**CL**) o los oficiales de seguridad (**O**).

1. _____ **Estaban trabajando** en Bancafé.
2. _____ **Estaba poniendo** dinero en su cuenta de Bancafé.
3. _____ **Estaban haciendo** alguna transacción en Bancafé.
4. _____ **Estaban ayudando** a los clientes que tenían preguntas.

■ You have used the imperfect to express an action or event that was in progress in the past. You may also use the imperfect progressive to emphasize the ongoing nature of the activity in the past. Form the imperfect progressive with the imperfect of **estar** and the present participle (**-ndo**).

| | |
|---|---|
| Mario **estaba hablando** con la cajera cuando entraron los ladrones. | *Mario was talking to the teller when the robbers came in.* |
| Los vicepresidentes del banco **estaban trabajando** en el segundo piso cuando oyeron los gritos. | *The vice presidents of the bank were working on the second floor when they heard the shouts.* |

■ To express intentions in the past, use the imperfect of **ir + a +** *infinitive*.

| | |
|---|---|
| **Iba a salir**, pero era muy tarde. | *I was going to go out, but it was very late.* |

■ In *Capítulo 7* you practiced the preterit of **saber** with the meaning of finding out about something. You also practiced the preterit of **querer** with the meaning of wanting or trying to do something, but failing to accomplish it.

**Supe** que Jorge consiguió trabajo.    *I found out that Jorge got a job.*

**Quise** entrevistarme con el gerente, pero fue imposible.    *I wanted (and tried) to get an interview with the manager, but it was impossible.*

In the negative, the preterit of **querer** conveys the meaning of refusing to do something.

**No quise** ir.    *I refused to go.*

■ Other verbs that convey a different meaning in English when the preterit is used are **conocer** and **poder**.

| IMPERFECT | | PRETERIT | |
|---|---|---|---|
| Yo **conocía** a Ana. | *I knew Ana.* | **Conocí** a Ana. | *I met Ana.* |
| **Podía** hacerlo. | *I could (was able to) do it.* | **Pude** hacerlo. | *I accomplished (managed to do) it.* |
| **No podía** hacerlo. | *I couldn't (wasn't able to) do it.* | **No pude** hacerlo. | *I couldn't do it. (I tried and failed.)* |

**9-23 Una oficina muy ocupada.** Ustedes visitaron la oficina que aparece en la siguiente escena. Túrnense para preguntar qué estaban haciendo las personas cuando cada uno/a de ustedes llegó.

MODELO:    E1:  *¿Qué estaba haciendo Alicia cuando tú llegaste a la oficina?*
E2:  *Estaba conversando con un cliente.*

**9-24 Una explicación lógica.** Ayer ustedes tuvieron una reunión en su compañía para mostrarles unos productos nuevos a unas empresas extranjeras. Den una explicación lógica de todo lo que salió mal.

> MODELO: La secretaria no contestaba el teléfono.
> E1: *Estaba buscando un intérprete para la reunión.*
> E2: *No, estaba buscando un salón más grande.*

1. Varios empleados llegaron tarde.
2. El técnico no pudo arreglar una computadora que se necesitaba para la presentación.
3. Los periodistas no podían comprender lo que decía un director extranjero.
4. No les sirvieron café ni refrescos a los invitados.
5. Uno de los vendedores no quiso mostrar los productos nuevos.
6. No se pusieron anuncios en los periódicos.

**9-25 ¡A usar la imaginación!** Estas descripciones indican lo que estaban haciendo varias personas ayer. Identifiquen cuál era el oficio o profesión de ellos y qué iban a hacer después.

> MODELO: Esta persona llevaba un traje espacial, guantes, botas muy grandes y un plástico transparente frente a los ojos para poder ver.
> E1: *Era un astronauta.*
> E2: *Iba a caminar en la Luna.*

1. Un señor tenía un secador en la mano y le arreglaba el pelo a una señora que estaba sentada enfrente de él.
2. Unos señores iban en un camión rojo con una sirena. El camión iba muy rápido y los autos paraban al lado derecho de la calle.
3. Una joven que llevaba un vestido similar a los que se llevaban en la época de Cleopatra hablaba frente a una cámara. Estaba muy maquillada y tenía una línea negra alrededor de los ojos.
4. Un señor estudiaba los planos de un edificio y decía que ciertas cosas no estaban bien.

**9-26 El diario de vida de Arturo.** Lea una página del diario de Arturo, un estudiante de antropología enamorado de Guatemala. Escriba en el espacio la forma apropiada del verbo entre paréntesis, según el contexto.

En el ano 2007, yo (1) _____ (conocí/conocía) a mi novia Elizabeth en mi segundo viaje a Guatemala. En ese momento, yo ya (2) _____ (conocí/conocía) Antigua y un par de lugares de interés para los turistas. Después de nuestro encuentro, yo inmediatamente (3) _____ (supe/sabía) que mis visitas a Guatemala (4) _____ (fueron/iban) a ser más frecuentes. Ese año nosotros no (5) _____ (pudimos/podíamos) viajar juntos por el país, pero el año siguiente lo hicimos. Su familia, ella y yo (6) _____ (pudimos/podíamos) explorar juntos la reserva ecológica Calahuar. Caminamos todo el día por el bosque (*forest*). Después de caminar tantas horas, yo no (7) _____ (pude/podía) dar un paso más, pero al día siguiente (8) _____ (pudimos/podíamos) continuar el viaje a San Pedro La Laguna en Atlitán.

**9-27 ¡Malas sorpresas!** Lean las siguientes situaciones y digan cuáles eran los planes probables de estas personas.

**MODELO:**    Martín está enfadado porque su bicicleta se descompuso (*broke*).
E1:  *Martín no pudo ir al parque con sus amigos.*
E2:  *Él quiso arreglar la bicicleta, pero fue imposible.*

1. Lorena está molesta porque la fotocopiadora de la oficina no funciona.
2. Usted y su pareja caminaron a su restaurante favorito, pero el restaurante estaba cerrado.
3. El jefe de producción llamó a una reunión urgente ayer. Anoche comenzó a nevar y muchos empleados no llegaron a su trabajo porque los caminos estaban en malas condiciones.
4. Al carro de Marta y Francisco se le acabó (*ran out of*) la gasolina cerca de la playa. Tuvieron que dejarlo en la carretera.
5. Esteba tenía una entrevista con el jefe de personal a las 9 pero no llegó a tiempo.

## SITUACIONES

1. **Role A.** One of your employees did not come to an important meeting, so you call him/her to your office. Greet your employee and ask why he/she was not present. After listening to the explanation, say that a) this is the second time this happened and b) he/she has to attend all meetings in the future.

   **Role B.** You were expected to attend an important meeting at work, but you could not make it. After greeting your boss, apologize and explain the circumstances. As you were driving to work, your spouse called to say that a) there was a fire in the kitchen; b) the firefighters were there; and c) the children were fine but scared. Explain that you had to go home.

2. **Role A.** You are the caterer (**proveedor/a de comida**) hired for a large wedding party. While the party was taking place, the deck (**terraza**) of the house collapsed (**colapsar**), resulting in several injured people (**heridos**). An investigator (your classmate) interviews you about the accident.

   **Role B.** You are a police officer investigating the accident. Ask the caterer a) approximately how many guests and servers were on the deck (**terraza**) when it collapsed (**colapsar**); b) what the guests were doing there; and c) what the caterer was doing when the deck collapsed. Then thank the caterer for the information.

# 4. Giving instructions or suggestions: Formal commands

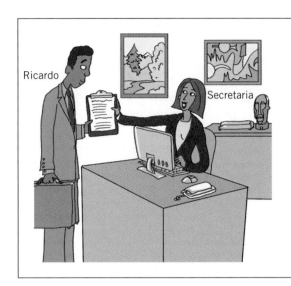

Ricardo

Secretaria

RICARDO: Buenos días, señorita. Me llamo Ricardo Roldán Díaz. ¿Podría darme una solicitud para el puesto de asistente de contador?

SECRETARIA: Claro que sí, Sr. Roldán. Por favor, **llene** la solicitud y **mándenosla** pronto.

RICARDO: ¿Puedo mandársela por correo electrónico?

SECRETARIA: Sí, **envíela** por correo electrónico, pero también por correo postal.

**Piénselo.** Ricardo llega a casa con la solicitud que le dio la secretaria. Lea las sugerencias que Ricardo leyó en un manual sobre cómo buscar puestos profesionales y marque (✓) las que le parecen apropiadas en la cultura de usted.

1. \_\_\_\_ Llene la solicitud inmediatamente.
2. \_\_\_\_ Escriba con letra clara.
3. \_\_\_\_ Mándele flores a la secretaria.
4. \_\_\_\_ No se olvide de incluir su currículum.
5. \_\_\_\_ Firme la solicitud.
6. \_\_\_\_ No deje ningún espacio en blanco.

■ Commands (**los mandatos**) are the verb forms used to tell others to do something. Use formal commands with people you address as **usted** or **ustedes**. To form these commands, drop the final **-o** of the **yo** form of the present tense and add **-e(n)** for **-ar** verbs and **-a(n)** for **-er** and **-ir** verbs.

■ Verbs that are irregular in the **yo** form of the present tense maintain the same irregularity in the command form.

### Cultura

En Guatemala, los niños se dirigen normalmente a sus padres y a otras personas mayores con la forma **usted**. El uso del **tú** y del **usted** varía mucho en el mundo hispano, pero en general la forma **tú** es más común para comunicarse con los padres.

|  |  | | USTED | USTEDES |  |
|---|---|---|---|---|---|
| pensar | → | piens~~o~~ | piense | piensen | *think* |
| dormir | → | duerm~~o~~ | duerma | duerman | *sleep* |
| repetir | → | repit~~o~~ | repita | repitan | *repeat* |
| poner | → | pong~~o~~ | ponga | pongan | *put* |

■ The use of **usted** and **ustedes** with command forms is optional. When used, they normally follow the command.

Pase/Pase **usted**.          *Come in.*

■ To make a formal command negative, place **no** before the affirmative command.

**No salga** ahora.          *Do not leave now.*

■ Object pronouns and reflexive pronouns are attached to the end of affirmative commands. (Note the written accent over the stressed vowel). Object pronouns and reflexive pronouns precede negative commands and are not attached.

| | |
|---|---|
| **Cómpre**la. | *Buy it.* |
| **No** la **compre**. | *Do not buy it.* |
| **Háblen**le. | *Talk to him/her.* |
| **No** le **hablen**. | *Do not talk to him/her.* |
| **Siénte**se. | *Sit down.* |
| **No** se **siente**. | *Do not sit down.* |

■ The verbs **dar, ir, ser,** and **saber** have irregular command forms.

dar: **dé, den** ir: **vaya, vayan** ser: **sea, sean** saber: **sepa, sepan**

■ Verbs ending in **-car, -gar, -zar, -ger,** and **-guir** have spelling changes in command forms.

| | | | |
|---|---|---|---|
| sacar | sac**o** | → | sa**que**, sa**quen** |
| jugar | jueg**o** | → | jue**gue**, jue**guen** |
| almorzar | almuerz**o** | → | almuer**ce**, almuer**cen** |
| recoger | recoj**o** | → | reco**ja**, reco**jan** |
| seguir | sig**o** | → | si**ga**, si**gan** |

**9-28 Preguntas de un/a estudiante.** Usted no asistió a clase durante la semana dedicada a Guatemala y quiere saber qué tiene que hacer para ponerse al día. Su compañero/a, en el papel de profesor/a, va a contestar afirmativamente a sus preguntas. Después, cambien de papel.

MODELO:      estudiar el Capítulo 9
       E1: *¿Estudio el Capítulo 9?*
       E2: *Sí, estúdielo.*

1. contestar las preguntas sobre los lugares turísticos en Guatemala
2. mirar los DVDs de bailes folklóricos de Guatemala
3. escribir algunas expresiones populares entre los jóvenes guatemaltecos
4. leer el *Enfoque cultural* sobre Guatemala
5. hacer la tarea sobre las culturas indígenas de Guatemala

**9-29 En el hospital.** Un enfermero/Una enfermera entra en la habitación y le hace las siguientes preguntas al/a la paciente. Túrnense para hacer los papeles de enfermero/a y paciente.

**MODELO:** E1: *¿Le abro las cortinas?*
E2: *Sí, ábramelas, por favor. Quisiera leer.*

1. ¿Le pongo la televisión?
2. ¿Le traigo un jugo?
3. ¿Le pongo otra almohada?
4. ¿Me llevo estas flores?
5. ¿Le traigo el teléfono?
6. …

 **9-30 Mandatos del entrenador de un equipo.** Preparen una lista de sugerencias que el entrenador/la entrenadora puede darles a los miembros de su equipo para lograr los objetivos siguientes. Comparen su lista con la de otra pareja.

**MODELO:** para mantenerse en buen estado físico
*Practiquen todos los días. No se acuesten tarde.*

1. para tener mejor rendimiento (*performance*)
2. para prepararse mentalmente para un partido difícil
3. para evitar problemas con el árbitro
4. para dormir bien cuando tienen mucho estrés
5. para ser buenos alumnos y buenos deportistas también

## Cultura

En la ciudad de Cobán, en el centro de Guatemala, se celebra anualmente un festival de personas nativas de Guatemala, La Fiesta Nacional Indígena de Guatemala (Festival Folclórico). Incluye un certamen (*contest*) de belleza para mujeres indígenas de Guatemala. Participan aproximadamente 100 señoritas que expresan sus ideales en su idioma materno y en español. La ganadora es coronada con el título de *Rabin Ajau*, que significa Hija del Rey en Q'eqchi', un idioma maya.

**9-31 ¿Qué deben hacer estas personas?** Busquen una solución a los siguientes problemas y díganle a cada persona lo que debe hacer.

**MODELO:** El Sr. Álvarez dice: "No estoy contento en mi trabajo".
E1: *Sr. Álvarez, busque otro trabajo inmediatamente.*
E2: *Hable con su jefe y explíquele la situación.*

1. La Sra. Jiménez dice: "Necesito más vendedores en mi compañía".
2. El Sr. Jiménez se queja (*complains*): "Tengo que terminar un informe económico mensual pero mi computadora no funciona".
3. Unos hombres de negocios van a ir a Ciudad de Guatemala, pero no saben hablar español.
4. La Sra. Peña tuvo un accidente serio con su auto; el chofer que provocó el accidente no quiere darle la información que ella necesita para informar a su seguro.
5. La Sra. Hurtado entra en su apartamento y ve que hay agua en el piso de la cocina.
6. Su esposa quiere ir al Festival Folclórico Nacional de Cobán, pero el Sr. Fernández no se siente bien.

## SITUACIONES

1. **Role A.** Tell your neighbor that you are leaving for three days for job interviews. Ask if your neighbor can do a few things for you. After he/she agrees, tell him/her to a) feed (**dar de comer a**) the cat and play with her every day; b) water the plants; c) pick up the mail (**correspondencia**); and d) any other things that you may need. Thank him/her for helping out.

   **Role B.** Your neighbor tells you that he/she is going to be away. Agree to help him/her out. After you find out what you will have to do, ask: a) whom should you call if there is an emergency (**emergencia**) and b) get the telephone number of the vet (**veterinario/a**).

2. **Role A.** You have moved to Quetzaltenango, Guatemala, and want to open a checking account (**cuenta corriente**) at Bancafé. Since you are not familiar with their system, ask an employee for help. After the employee gives you all the details, thank him/her, and say that you are very happy with the service the bank provides the customers.

   **Role B.** You are an employee at Bancafé in Quetzaltenango, Guatemala. Explain to a new customer a) how to write a check in Spanish (see example below); b) how to write the date in Spanish; c) where to put the name of the person to whom he/she is writing the check; d) how to write the amount (**cantidad**) in numbers; e) how to write the amount in words; and f) where to sign the check (**firmar el cheque**).

Serie AD 6703690 $ _____

12 Av. 5-50 Zona 1   012-0587 / 446

_____ - _____ DE _____ AÑO _ _ _ _ _

PÁGUESE A LA ORDEN DE _____   O AL PORTADOR

LA CANTIDAD DE _____

_____ PESOS M/L

**BANCO DE CAFÉ, S.A.** _____

06703690   0190587446004 2102   01

# MOSAICOS

## A escuchar

**ESTRATEGIA**

**Use contextual guessing**

When you have a conversation in a second language, it is very possible that you may not understand everything the other person says. You can figure out the overall message by using contextual cues; that is, by paying attention to the topic or to the words that precede or follow what you did not understand.

### Antes de escuchar

**9-32 Preparación.** En la siguiente conversación, dos amigas hablan sobre las ventajas y desventajas de su trabajo. Antes de escuchar, escriba el nombre de una profesión relacionada con los negocios y otra con la salud. Luego, escriba una ventaja y una desventaja para cada una de las profesiones.

| PROFESIÓN | VENTAJA | DESVENTAJA |
|-----------|---------|------------|
| _____ | _____ | _____ |
| _____ | _____ | _____ |

### Escuchar

CD 4
Track 19

**9-33 ¿Comprende usted?** First, read the words in the left column and listen to the conversation between Estela and Susana. Then state the probable meaning of each word in English based on the contextual cues you heard in the conversation. Finally, write down the cue words that helped you understand.

| ESCUCHÉ... | POSIBLE SIGNIFICADO | ADIVINÉ EL SIGNIFICADO PORQUE... |
|------------|---------------------|----------------------------------|
| 1. neuróloga | | |
| 2. primordial | | |
| 3. guardias | | |

### Después de escuchar

 **9-34 Ahora usted.** Compartan las respuestas a las siguientes preguntas.

1. ¿Cuáles son las ventajas y desventajas de la profesión que le gusta a usted?
2. En general, ¿qué profesión u ocupación le parece a usted que es menos estresante?
3. ¿Qué profesión u ocupación, según usted, da más satisfacciones personales? ¿Por qué?

# A conversar

## Antes de conversar

**9-35 Preparación.** Lea los siguientes anuncios con ofertas de trabajo, escoja un anuncio para un puesto que a usted le interese y prepare una lista de requisitos que, en su opinión, usted cumple (*meet*). Comparta su lista con su compañero/a.

INSTITUTO PRIVADO

*necesita*

**DIRECTOR/A**

**Lugar de residencia, Región de los Lagos**

Empresa de Hotelería necesita
Director/a

Requisitos: Estudios universitarios avanzados. Experiencia mínima de 1 a 2 años en ventas directas, preferiblemente en el área de servicios. Edad 26 a 32 años. Excelente presentación. Poseer vehículo propio. Buenas relaciones interpersonales.

Ofrecemos: Salario a convenir según experiencia, gasolina, comisiones sobre ventas. Excelente ambiente de trabajo. Oportunidades de crecimiento.

*Sueldo compatible con calificaciones*

**Interesados,** enviar currículum a
gruporecursoshumanos@hotmail.com

---

**EMPRESA DE EXPORTACIONES**
**necesita para Chile y el extranjero**

**VENDEDORES/AS REPRESENTANTES**

**Sueldo inicial 1,000.000**
**Comisión de ventas**

Casa Tadeo necesita
Asistente de Ventas y Mercadeo
Requisitos: Estudios universitarios de administración de empresas o mercadeo. De preferencia con experiencia en puesto similar de 1 año, no indispensable. Proactivo, extrovertido, dinámico, con autoridad, con iniciativa, organizado, colaborador. Habilidad para trabajar independientemente. Excelente manejo de equipos de cómputo. Buen dominio del inglés. Filosofía de servicio al cliente.
Ofrecemos: Salario competitivo. Oportunidades de capacitación. Excelente oportunidad de desarrollo en una empresa de alto crecimiento. Ambiente agradable de trabajo.

**Interesados,** llamar al teléfono
2533-2459
Lunes a viernes de 8:30 a 15:00 hrs.

---

**JEFE DE SERVICIO**
necesita importante empresa
**MANUFACTURERA DE PLÁSTICOS**

Nos urge un buen diseñador gráfico
Requisitos: Conocer al 100% PhotoShop y Freehand. Manejar ambiente Mac y PC. De preferencia estudiante de diseño en la U, con ideas frescas. Dispuesto a trabajar bajo presión.
Ofrecemos: Salario a convenir. Capacitación constante. Desarrollo dentro de la organización. Horario flexible. Seguro de vida y médico.

**Interesados,** enviar currículum y fotografía reciente, especificando pretensiones de sueldo, a Casilla 2568, Correo Guatemala, zona 1, Guatemala

---

**BANCO AZTECA**
*necesita*
**10 CONTADORES AUDITORES**
**Lugar de trabajo ideal: Viña del Mar**

- Título universitario
- Mínimo dos años de experiencia
- Flexibilidad horaria
- Deseo de viajar a otras regiones del país
- Capacidad de organización y trabajo

*Sueldo atractivo*

**Interesados,** enviar currículum, con fotografía a:
Bco. Azteca, 7 Av. 19-28, zona 5

## Conversar

**9-36 Entre nosotros.** Ahora escojan un papel. Uno/a de ustedes es el jefe/la jefa de personal de una compañía representada en los anuncios y dos son personas que solicitan el mismo trabajo en esa compañía. Sigan las siguientes instrucciones para cada papel.

**Jefe/a de personal:** Entreviste separadamente a dos personas que están interesadas en el mismo puesto. Pregúnteles sobre su experiencia, sus estudios, sus preferencias de sueldo, etc. y decida cuál es la persona indicada para el puesto.

**Personas que buscan trabajo:** Escojan el anuncio con el trabajo que los dos necesitan. Respondan a las preguntas del jefe/de la jefa de personal y háganle preguntas para saber más acerca del puesto.

## Después de conversar

**9-37 Un poco más. PRIMERA FASE.** Los jefes de personal y las personas que buscaban trabajo deben informar a la clase sobre lo siguiente:

**Informe de las personas que buscaban trabajo:**

1. ¿Qué puesto buscaba usted? ¿Qué requisitos para el puesto cumple usted?
2. ¿Qué aspecto de la oferta de trabajo le pareció más atractivo?
3. ¿Cree usted que va a recibir la oferta de trabajo? ¿Por qué?

**Informe de los jefes de personal:**

1. ¿Qué puesto ofrecía su compañía en el anuncio?
2. ¿Qué requisitos debía tener el candidato/la candidata que buscaba su compañía?
3. ¿A qué candidato/a(s) va a contratar usted? ¿Por qué?

**SEGUNDA FASE.** Presenten la entrevista ideal entre el jefe de personal y el candidato más apropiado para cada anuncio de trabajo.

# A leer

**Organize textual information into categories**

To understand what you are reading, you need to focus on what is being conveyed by the text. By *focus* we mean organizing the information into meaningful categories, which helps you connect the information to what you already know. As you read, focus on the main points in each of the three sections. Use the subtitles to help you anticipate the content.

## Antes de leer

**9-38 Preparación.** Lea el título y los subtítulos del texto y mire la foto. Basándose en esta información y en lo que usted sabe sobre la inmigración, marque (✓) las ideas que piensa encontrar en el texto.

1. ____ Muchas mujeres guatemaltecas en Estados Unidos se casan con hombres mexicanos.
2. ____ El término "guatemexicoestadounidense" se refiere a familias cuyos (*whose*) miembros pertenecen a estas tres culturas.
3. ____ La concentración más grande de guatemaltecos en Estados Unidos está en Los Ángeles.
4. ____ La inmigración de guatemaltecos a Estados Unidos tiene un impacto económico positivo en Guatemala.

## Leer

### Los guatemaltecos en Estados Unidos

**Matrimonios entre guatemaltecos y mexicanos**

Gustavo Rivera conoció a Marta Rodríguez en un club hispano de Los Ángeles y la invitó a bailar.

"¿De dónde eres?", preguntó Marta. "De México", respondió Gustavo.

Después de esa noche, los dos empezaron a conversar por teléfono y a salir juntos. Marta, que era de Ciudad de México, se dio cuenta que Gustavo hablaba español con un acento diferente y usaba unas palabras diferentes también. Después de un tiempo, ella le preguntó: "¿De dónde eres realmente, Gustavo?" Esta vez, Gustavo le dijo la verdad: "Soy de Guatemala". Pasaron dos años y Gustavo y Marta se casaron. Ahora tienen tres hijos: Martita, de tres años, Gustavo, de dos y la bebé Rosita, de seis meses. Esta familia representa una tendencia demográfica que está aumentando en Los Ángeles y en otras ciudades del suroeste: más inmigrantes guatemaltecos y mexicanos se casan entre sí y tienen hijos, creando familias hispanas mixtas que tienen conexiones con tres países al mismo tiempo. Esa mezcla es ahora tan común que dio lugar al nombre de "guatemexicoestadounidense" para describir a esas familias.

**Nuevas tendencias demográficas**

Hay varias razones que explican esta nueva tendencia demográfica. Primero, el número de personas de ascendencia guatemalteca en Estados Unidos está creciendo. Según la Organización Internacional para las Migraciones (OIM), en 2006 había 1.178.000 guatemaltecos en Estados Unidos. La mayoría de ellos son jóvenes, entre 15 y 44 años, y hay muchos más hombres que mujeres. Se estima que el 72% son hombres y el 28% mujeres. Es evidente que, por esta razón, cuando los guatemaltecos en Estados Unidos se casan, muchos se casan con mujeres no guatemaltecas.

Segundo, cuando llegan a Estados Unidos, los inmigrantes guatemaltecos buscan vivienda en comunidades hispanas establecidas, donde viven principalmente inmigrantes mexicanos, el grupo hispano más grande del país. La constante interacción de hombres guatemaltecos y mujeres mexicanas inevitablemente resulta en más matrimonios entre los dos grupos.

Esta mezcla de culturas hispanas no se limita a guatemaltecos y mexicanos. Los hispanos son, como los estadounidenses, de diversas nacionalidades. Una persona puede decir, por ejemplo, "la madre de mi madre es de Irlanda, y los padres de mi padre eran alemanes". Lo mismo está ocurriendo con los hispanos.

**Impacto económico en Guatemala**

En muchos sentidos, Gustavo Rivera es un inmigrante guatemalteco típico. Como el 88% de los guatemaltecos que viven en Estados Unidos, Gustavo se mantiene activo económicamente, trabaja en una fábrica que manufactura materiales para tejados (*roofs*). Como el 33% de los guatemaltecos en Estados Unidos, vive en Los Ángeles. Y como el 93% de los emigrantes guatemaltecos, mantiene contacto con su familia en Guatemala. Llama a sus padres todas las semanas y les envía remesas todos los meses. Según la OIM, más de 600.000 familias en Guatemala reciben remesas de familiares que viven en el extranjero.

El impacto económico de las remesas en Guatemala es considerable. Se estima que las remesas estimulan la economía de Guatemala, igual que la de otros países centroamericanos. También ayudan a estos países a evitar la recesión.

**9-39 Primera mirada.** Indique a qué categoría pertenecen las siguientes afirmaciones, según el contenido del artículo: información personal sobre una familia (**P**), información general sobre los inmigrantes guatemaltecos en Estados Unidos (**EU**) o información sobre Guatemala (**G**).

1. ____ Viven en comunidades donde el grupo predominante son los mexicanos.
2. ____ Se conocieron en un club de baile.
3. ____ Reciben dinero de sus familiares que viven en el extranjero.
4. ____ Se casan con personas de otras culturas.
5. ____ El dinero que viene del exterior estimula la economía.
6. ____ No dijo la verdad sobre su país de origen.
7. ____ Hay más hombres que mujeres.
8. ____ Muchas veces sus hijos nacen en un país diferente de donde nacieron los padres.

**9-40 Segunda mirada.** El artículo explica algunos fenómenos de causa y efecto. Conecte cada fenómeno en la columna de la izquierda con su resultado lógico en la columna de la derecha.

1. ____ La mayoría de los inmigrantes son jóvenes.
2. ____ Hay más hombres que mujeres entre los inmigrantes guatemaltecos.
3. ____ Los mexicanos son el grupo hispano más numeroso en Estados Unidos.
4. ____ La gran mayoría de los inmigrantes guatemaltecos tienen trabajo.
5. ____ Hay una tendencia en Estados Unidos a casarse con personas de diferentes ascendencias culturales.

a. Hay muchas parejas en las que una persona es mexicana y la otra es de otra cultura hispana.
b. Mandan remesas a sus familiares en Guatemala.
c. Se casan en su nuevo país.
d. Se casan con mujeres no guatemaltecas.
e. Hay cada vez más familias hispanas compuestas de (*composed of*) personas de diferentes países.

## Después de leer

**9-41 Ampliación.** Con su compañero/a, escriban una lista de la información nueva que aprendieron del artículo. Luego, indiquen qué información les parece más interesante.

# A escribir

ESTRATEGIA

**Focus on purpose, content, and audience**

Getting the job you want may be a challenge in today's competitive labor market. Responding effectively to an employment ad is an important first step. Answering an ad takes as much skill as being interviewed.

To get the job that is right for you, whether during college or after graduation, consider the following when responding to an ad in any language:

■ Your purpose: What kind of job do you want (management or entry level; full- or part-time; permanent or temporary, etc.)?
■ Your response: What academic degree do you need for the job (high school, college, other)? What general abilities and job-specific skills should you possess?
■ Your audience: What experience does the employer require? What personality characteristics will you need to be considered a serious candidate?

## Antes de escribir

**9-42 Preparación.** Usted ve un anuncio de trabajo en Internet de la señora Álvarez de Colón de Guatemala. La familia va a mudarse a Estados Unidos y quiere contratar a dos estudiantes en Estados Unidos para el verano, uno/a para cuidar a sus dos hijos (de 4 y 6 años) y enseñarles inglés y el otro/la otra para preparar comidas típicamente americanas. Planee un correo electrónico para solicitar uno de los trabajos. Haga una lista de las categorías de información sobre su experiencia y sus talentos que piensa mencionar.

## Escribir

**9-43 Manos a la obra.** Ahora escríbale un correo electrónico a la señora Álvarez de Colón. En un mensaje breve, organizado y convincente, preséntese y explique cómo su experiencia, su conocimiento y sus talentos lo/la preparan para el puesto.

## Después de escribir

**9-44 Revisión.** Lea lo que escribió, pensando en su lectora. Verifique lo siguiente:

1. ¿Qué categorías de información incluyó? ¿Falta alguna categoría importante?
2. Como usted no conoce a esta persona, ¿se dirigió a ella usando la forma *usted*?
3. ¿Tiene su correo electrónico una organización clara, es decir, una introducción, un cuerpo y un cierre?
4. ¿Revisó el vocabulario, expresiones de cortesía y de despedida, la concordancia, el tiempo (presente, pasado), el uso de los mandatos, etc.?

Comparta su mensaje electrónico con un compañero/una compañera. Esto puede darle la perspectiva de un lector/una lectora sobre la claridad de su texto y sobre la cantidad de información que usted incluyó.

# ENFOQUE CULTURAL

## Historia y trabajo en Guatemala

Los restos de la gran civilización maya sobreviven hoy día en sitios como Tikal, Yaxha y Naachtun en Guatemala. Las ruinas que se conservan nos permiten imaginar cómo fueron esas ciudades en sus momentos de esplendor. Cuando las visitamos, frecuentemente pensamos en la complejidad y el simbolismo religioso de muchas de esas construcciones, o en el lujo de los palacios, o en la avanzada técnica de construcción. Y sin embargo, un aspecto muy importante que con

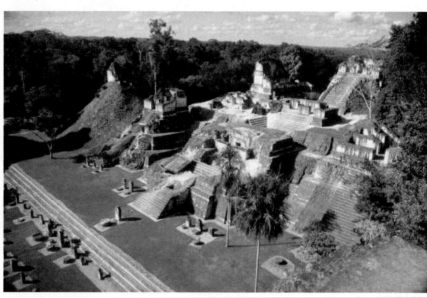

Gran Plaza de Tikal

frecuencia olvidamos es la diversidad de profesiones, trabajos y artes que tuvieron que desarrollar los mayas para construir dichas ciudades. En efecto, fue necesario especializar a los trabajadores, de manera que surgieron profesiones independientes para realizar actividades específicas. Pintores, escultores, cortadores de piedra, carpinteros, ceramistas, astrónomos, todos contribuyeron con su trabajo especializado.

Xaman-ek, considerado el dios de los comerciantes, según está representado en el Códice Dresden

Mientras estas personas trabajaban en la construcción de las ciudades, los agricultores tenían que cultivar la comida para alimentar a todos estos trabajadores urbanos que no tenían tiempo para producir su propia alimentación. Y como es lógico, cuando el centro de producción es diferente del centro de consumo, los comerciantes se ocupan de llevar los productos del campo y venderlos en los mercados de la ciudad. Pero los comerciantes mayas hicieron más que eso, pues desarrollaron unas rutas comerciales que los llevaron más allá de las fronteras locales. Efectivamente, la red de caminos de los comerciantes mayas cubría una inmensa parte de México y Centroamérica.

El mercado indígena de Antigua, un ejemplo del llamado "capitalismo del centavo"

## Cultura

**La economía guatemalteca**
El 50% de la fuerza laboral de Guatemala trabaja en la agricultura. Los productos principales son el café, la caña de azúcar y los plátanos, que constituyen dos tercios (*thirds*) de las exportaciones del país. Guatemala exporta también madera y níquel. El turismo también es un motor importante de la economía guatemalteca. Guatemala recibe aproximadamente 1.800.000 turistas cada año.

Cuando vemos la sofisticación y la complejidad de la antigua civilización maya, nos preguntamos por qué es hoy Guatemala uno de los países más pobres del continente. Aunque la respuesta a esta pregunta es demasiado compleja para contestarla en pocas palabras, sí podemos decir que la sociedad creada a partir de la colonia española marginó a la población indígena y limitó su posibilidad de participar en la economía. Y, puesto que más del 60% de la población guatemalteca hoy día se considera indígena, un porcentaje muy elevado de la población tiene que encontrar su subsistencia en una economía limitada, a la que Sol Tax, un famoso antropólogo de la Universidad de Chicago, llamó "capitalismo del centavo". Lo más interesante, sin embargo, es que a pesar de tantos años de marginalización, el espíritu comerciante de los indígenas no ha desaparecido y continúa muy visible hoy día en los mercados indígenas.

Desafortunadamente, en la actualidad, los más emprendedores entre los marginados de Guatemala buscan en la emigración mejores condiciones de trabajo y formas para participar en la economía. Esta necesidad de buscar oportunidades económicas fuera de Guatemala se ve reforzada por las periódicas catástrofes naturales que ocurren en la región, tales como terremotos y huracanes. Otro factor que afecta a la ola migratoria son los acontecimientos de carácter político, tales como las guerras civiles o las dictaduras militares que persiguen a los indígenas. En la actualidad, más de una cuarta parte de los inmigrantes centroamericanos en Estados Unidos son de Guatemala, y se calculan en cerca del millón.

## En otras palabras

**Expresiones guatemaltecas**

Me gusta Luis, pero es muy **codo**.
*I like Luis, but he is very stingy.*

¡Me muero de hambre! Necesito **una refacción**.
*I am starving! I need a snack.*

¡Anda rápido que ya viene **la camioneta**!
*Hurry up! The bus is coming!*

**9-45 Comprensión.** PRIMERA FASE. **Reconocimiento de palabras clave.** Encuentre en el texto la palabra o expresión que mejor expresa el significado de las siguientes ideas.

1. remnants _____
2. stonecutters _____
3. to feed _____
4. merchants _____
5. trade routes _____
6. complexity _____
7. civil wars _____

SEGUNDA FASE. **Oraciones importantes.** Subraye las afirmaciones que contienen ideas que se encuentran en el texto. Luego indique en qué parte del texto están.

1. For all their complexity, Mayan cities lacked religious symbolism.
2. We often fail to see the variety of trades that were required to build a Mayan city.
3. Mayan farmers were forced to stop growing food crops to work on the construction of the great Mayan cities.
4. Mayan merchants traded their products well beyond the borders of the Maya Empire.
5. Guatemala is one of the poorest countries in the continent today.
6. Well over half of the population of Guatemala is considered to be indigenous.
7. Military dictatorships have been successful in curbing emigration.
8. Natural disasters are one of the factors that motivate Guatemalans to emigrate.

TERCERA FASE. **Ideas principales.** Escriba un párrafo breve en inglés resumiendo las ideas principales expresadas en el texto.

 **9-46 Use la información.** Escriba una carta contestando a un anuncio de trabajo en Guatemala. Su carta debe incluir lo siguiente:

1. qué trabajo solicita usted
2. dónde trabaja actualmente y por cuánto tiempo
3. qué experiencia tiene usted en ese tipo de trabajo
4. cuándo puede empezar a trabajar

Para preparar esta actividad, visite la página web de *Mosaicos* y siga los enlaces útiles.

# VOCABULARIO

CD 4
s 20–24

| Las profesiones, oficios y ocupaciones | Professions, trades, and occupations |
|---|---|
| el/la abogado/a | lawyer |
| el actor/la actriz | actor/actress |
| el/la agricultor/a | farmer |
| el ama/o de casa | housewife, homemaker |
| el/la arquitecto/a | architect |
| el/la artesano/a | craftsman/woman, craftsperson |
| el/la bibliotecario/a | librarian |
| el/la bombero/a | firefighter |
| el/la cajero/a | cashier |
| el/la carpintero/a | carpenter |
| el/la ceramista | potter |
| el/la chef | chef |
| el/la chofer | driver |
| el/la científico/a | scientist |
| el/la contador/a | accountant |
| el/la contratista | contractor |
| el/la ejecutivo/a | executive |
| el/la electricista | electrician |
| el/la empleado/a | employee |
| el/la enfermero/a | nurse |
| el/la gerente (de ventas) | (sales) manager |
| el herrero | blacksmith; ironworker |
| el hombre/la mujer de negocios | businessman/woman |
| el/la ingeniero/a | engineer |
| el/la intérprete | interpreter |
| el jefe/la jefa | boss |
| el/la joyero/a | jeweller |
| el/la juez | judge |
| el/la locutor/a | radio announcer |
| el/la médico/a | medical doctor |
| el/la obrero/a | worker |
| el/la peletero/a | furrier |
| el/la peluquero/a | hairdresser |
| el/la periodista | journalist |
| el/la plomero/a | plumber |
| el/la policía | policeman/woman |
| el/la (p)sicólogo/a | psychologist |
| el/la técnico/a | technician |
| el/la vendedor/a | salesman, saleswoman |

| Los lugares | Places |
|---|---|
| el banco | bank |
| el campo | countryside |

| la compañía/la empresa | company |
|---|---|
| el consultorio | office (of doctor, dentist, etc.) |
| la peluquería | beauty salon, barbershop |
| el taller | workshop |

| El trabajo | Work |
|---|---|
| la agricultura | farming |
| el anuncio | ad, advertisement |
| el cliente/la clienta | client |
| el currículum | résumé |
| la entrevista | interview |
| la especialidad | specialty |
| la experiencia | experience |
| el incendio | fire |
| la madera | wood |
| el puesto | position |
| la solicitud | application |
| el sueldo | salary |
| la vacante | opening |
| las ventas | sales |

| Verbos | Verbs |
|---|---|
| apagar | to extinguish, to turn off |
| cosechar | to harvest |
| dejar | to leave |
| elaborar | to produce |
| emigrar | to emigrate |
| enviar | to send |
| esperar | to wait for |
| llenar | to fill (out) |
| mandar | to send |
| ofrecer (zc) | to offer |
| sobrevivir | to survive |
| solicitar | to apply (for) |

| Palabras y expresiones útiles | Useful words and expressions |
|---|---|
| actualmente | at the present time |
| ¡Cómo no! | Of course! |
| en realidad/realmente | in fact, really |
| lo importante | the important thing |
| por cierto | by the way |
| propio/a | own |
| la señal | signal |
| sin embargo | nevertheless |

325

# ¡A comer!

Este cuadro del siglo XVIII presenta a un indígena yumbo cerca de Quito, Ecuador. Junto a él hay árboles y frutas típicas de su país.

# In this chapter you will learn how to:

- discuss food, menus, diets, and shopping for food
- state impersonal information
- give instructions
- talk about the recent past and the future

## Cultural focus: **Ecuador**

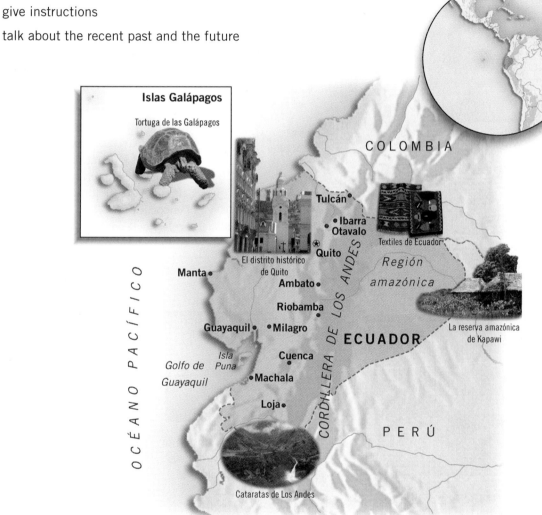

Islas Galápagos

Tortuga de las Galápagos

COLOMBIA

Tulcán

Ibarra
Otavalo

Textiles de Ecuador

Quito

El distrito histórico
de Quito

Región
amazónica

Manta

Ambato

Riobamba

CORDILLERA DE LOS ANDES

ECUADOR

La reserva amazónica
de Kapawi

Guayaquil    Milagro

OCÉANO PACÍFICO

Golfo de
Guayaquil

Isla
Puna

Cuenca

Machala

Loja

PERÚ

Cataratas de Los Andes

**A vista de pájaro.**  Mire los siguientes grupos de palabras y ponga un círculo alrededor de la palabra que no corresponde.

1. pescado, comida, lima, tomate, papaya, volcán
2. tela, diseño, artesanía, bombero, mercado, joyas
3. catedral, toro, casa, calle, iglesia, ciudad
4. selva, río, plato, planta, árbol, calor
5. montaña, tortilla, catarata, agua, nube, verde
6. tortuga, isla, naturaleza, textil, animal, roca

327

# A PRIMERA VISTA

## ◀)) Los productos y las recetas

CD 4
Track 25
or CD 5
Track 1

En Ecuador se cultiva mucha fruta, sobre todo **piña**, **limón**, **melón**, **papaya**, **maracuyá** y **plátano**. Mucha de esta fruta se exporta a Estados Unidos y otros países. Aquí vemos a unas personas trabajando en una compañía de exportación de plátanos cerca de Guayaquil.

En los mercados ecuatorianos, como en los de otros países hispanoamericanos, hay buenos puestos de **pasteles** donde se venden los **dulces** típicos de la región.

El pescado y los **mariscos** son muy importantes en la dieta de algunos países hispanoamericanos como Chile, Perú y Ecuador. En la provincia de Esmeraldas, en Ecuador, uno de los platos típicos es el encocado, pescado que se cocina con **leche de coco**.

Esta mujer ecuatoriana vende frutos secos mientras cuida las **ovejas**. De las ovejas se aprovechan la carne en comida y la lana en suéteres, mantas, etc. Además, los **campesinos** usan la leche para hacer queso y yogur. Junto a la carne de **cordero**, la de **res** y la de cerdo son las que más se usan en la comida de Ecuador y se venden en los mercados y en las carnicerías.

En el mercado de Zumbahua se encuentran los productos que se usan en las muchas **recetas** de la comida de Ecuador. La forma de combinar estos productos con el cilantro y otras **hierbas** y **especias** dan fama a la gastronomía ecuatoriana.

### En otras palabras

The words for some vegetables and spices vary from region to region. **Aguacate** is known as **palta** in some South American countries; **maíz** is known as **elote** in Mexico and in some Central American countries and as **choclo** in parts of South America. Other examples are **cilantro/culantro**, **achiote/pimentón** (paprika), and **frijoles/porotos**. Names of fruits also vary: **plátano** in Spain becomes **cambur** in Venezuela; in other places, like Colombia, **banano** is used, and elsewhere (in Uruguay, for example) it is **banana**. Other examples include **melocotón** (Spain)/**durazno** (Latin America); **fruto de la pasión** (Spain)/**maracuyá** (Colombia)/**parchita** (Venezuela, Mexico).

**10-1 Definiciones.** Asocie las definiciones a continuación con las palabras que aparecen en los textos y fotos anteriores.

1. una lista de ingredientes y de instrucciones para elaborar una comida
2. un animal del que se aprovecha la lana, la leche y la carne
3. una fruta alargada que se pela y que les gusta mucho a los monos
4. un plato ecuatoriano que se cocina con pescado y leche de coco
5. una tienda donde se vende pescado
6. las personas que cultivan productos del campo
7. dulces que se venden en las pastelerías y en los mercados
8. la carne de una oveja pequeña

**10-2 Una receta ecuatoriana.** Lea la siguiente receta y clasifique sus ingredientes según las siguientes categorías.

a. carnes o pescados:
b. vegetales:
c. condimentos:
d. frutas:

### Lengua

These are some useful words that appear in the recipe: **almejas** (*clams*), **perejil** (*parsley*), **paiteña** (*a type of onion*), **diente de ajo** (*clove of garlic*), **picado** (*chopped*), and **comino** (*cumin*). Other cooking expressions include **picar** (*chop*), **pelar** (*peel*), **machacar** (*crush*), **tapar** (*cover*), **agregar/añadir** (*add*), **taza** (*cup*), and **cucharada** (*spoonful*).

## Pescado encocado

**Ingredientes:**
1 coco
1 libra de camarones
2 libras de pescado crudo

**Refrito:**
1 cebolla paiteña finamente picada
¼ taza de cebolla blanca finamente picada
1 pimiento picado
4 cucharadas de cilantro picado
4 cucharadas de perejil picado
2 dientes de ajo machacados
4 cucharadas de aceite

1 un tomate grande rojo, pelado y picado
un poquito de achiote
sal, pimienta, comino al gusto

**Elaboración:**
Haga un refrito con los ingredientes. Agréguele una libra de camarones crudos, pelados y limpios y dos libras de pescado crudo, cortado en trozos. Refríalos durante un rato y luego agregue la mitad de la leche del coco. Tape la olla y deje cocinar durante 20 ó 30 minutos. Después, añada la otra mitad de la leche del coco. Sirva inmediatamente, acompañado de arroz blanco y plátano verde asado.

### Lengua

To give instructions on how to prepare a recipe, the following grammatical constructions may be used: 1. commands (**cocine el arroz, añada la sal**); 2. **se** + verb (**se cocina el arroz, se añade la sal**); 3. the infinitive (**cocinar el arroz, añadir la sal**).

**10-3 Mi receta favorita.** Escojan una receta simple. Escriban los ingredientes y después explíquenle a otra pareja cómo se prepara el plato. Las siguientes palabras pueden facilitarles la explicación:

**batir** (*to beat*)     **cortar** (*to cut*)     **freír** (**i**) (*to fry*)     **hervir** (**ie**) (*to boil*)

# ·)) En el supermercado

CD 4
Tracks 26–30
or CD 5
Tracks 2–6

## Las frutas y las verduras

| el ajo | los pimientos verdes | las zanahorias |

| los pepinos | las espinacas | el maíz, el elote el choclo |

| las cebollas | los plátanos/ las bananas | las peras |

| las manzanas | las toronjas/ los pomelos | las uvas |

| los aguacates | las cerezas | las fresas |

## Los productos lácteos

la leche   el queso   la crema

el queso crema                    la mantequilla

los huevos   la margarina   el yogur   la crema agria

# El pescado y la carne

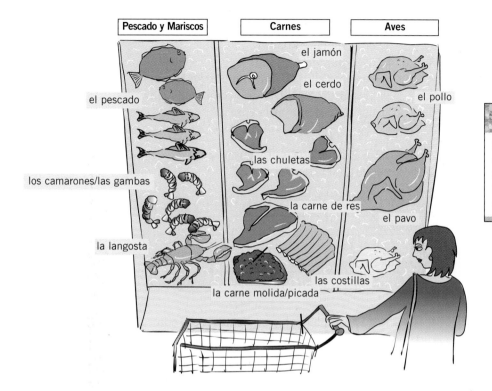

| Pescado y Mariscos | Carnes | Aves |
| --- | --- | --- |

el pescado

los camarones/las gambas

la langosta

el jamón

el cerdo

las chuletas

la carne de res

la carne molida/picada

las costillas

el pollo

el pavo

### En otras palabras

Other names of foods that vary by country are **pavo**, which is **guajolote** in Mexico, and **camarones**, which are **gambas** in Spain.

# Los condimentos y las legumbres

la sal

la pimienta

la mostaza

la vainilla

la harina

el/la azúcar

el aderezo

el vinagre   el aceite

la manteca   la salsa de tomate   la mayonesa

los frijoles   las lentejas   los garbanzos

# El pan y las bebidas

el pan

los churros

las galletas

el pan dulce

los refrescos   el vino tinto   el vino blanco

**10-4 Asociaciones.** Después de asociar cada explicación con la palabra adecuada, comenten si les gustan o no estos alimentos.

1. ____ Se toma mucho en el verano, cuando hace calor.
2. ____ Se pone en la ensalada.
3. ____ Se usan para hacer vino.
4. ____ Se come en el desayuno con huevos fritos.
5. ____ Se prepara para el Día de Acción de Gracias.
6. ____ Se usa para preparar la ensalada de atún o de pollo.

a. el jamón
b. las uvas
c. la mayonesa
d. el helado
e. el aderezo
f. el pavo

**10-5 Dietas diferentes.** PRIMERA FASE. Completen la tabla con comidas adecuadas para estas dietas.

| DIETA | SE DEBE COMER | NO SE DEBE COMER |
|---|---|---|
| vegetariana | | |
| para diabéticos | | |
| para desarrollar músculos | | |
| para bajar de peso (*lose weight*) | | |

SEGUNDA FASE. Completen las siguientes ideas con sus recomendaciones para cada una de estas personas. Digan por qué.

1. Laura, que es vegetariana, debe comer...
2. Mi padre, que es diabético,...
3. Luis, que levanta pesas (*weights*),...
4. Joaquín y Amalia quieren bajar de peso. Por lo tanto...

**10-6 ¿Qué necesitamos?** PRIMERA FASE. Ustedes son estudiantes de intercambio en Ecuador. Le quieren preparar una cena a su familia ecuatoriana. Hagan lo siguiente.

1. Describan el menú: ¿Qué plato principal van a servir? ¿Van a hacer ensaladas? ¿Van a servir bebidas? ¿Qué bebidas?
2. Hagan una lista de los ingredientes que necesitarán. ¿Van a necesitar verduras, vegetales, legumbres, especias, frutas?

SEGUNDA FASE. Ahora compartan sus planes con otra pareja.

**10-7 Los estudiantes y la comida.** PRIMERA FASE. Hablen de las comidas típicas de los estudiantes de su universidad. Respondan a las siguientes preguntas.

1. ¿Qué comieron hoy?
2. ¿Cuándo y dónde comieron?
3. ¿Cuánto gastaron en comida?

SEGUNDA FASE. Hagan una lista de recomendaciones para una dieta estudiantil más saludable (*healthy*) y compártanla con el resto de la clase. Piensen en el desayuno, el almuerzo, la cena y las meriendas (*snacks*).

# 🔊 La mesa

CD 4
ck 31
CD 5
ack 7

**10-8 Entrenamiento de un camarero/una camarera.** Ustedes son camareros en un restaurante pero uno/a de ustedes es nuevo/a en el puesto. Dígale a al camarero nuevo/a la camarera nueva dónde debe poner cada cosa de acuerdo con el dibujo. Después cambien de papel.

**MODELO:**   E1: *Ponga el cuchillo a la derecha del plato.*
E2: *Muy bien. ¿Y dónde pongo la copa?*
E1: _____

**10-9 Los preparativos de un banquete.** Ustedes trabajan en el servicio de comidas de la universidad y tienen que organizar un banquete para sus profesores. Primero preparen un menú, una lista de lo que tienen que comprar para el banquete y un presupuesto (*budget*). Luego deben dividirse el trabajo. Cada uno/a de ustedes es responsable de dar instrucciones a los otros/las otras sobre lo siguiente:

1. cómo elaborar el menú
2. cómo preparar la mesa
3. cómo decorar la sala

**En directo**

To express that you had a good time:

**Lo pasé muy bien./Lo pasamos muy bien.**

**Fue estupendo.**

**Estuvo muy divertido.**

**10-10 Una cena.** Usted estuvo muy ocupado/a ayer porque tuvo invitados a cenar. Dígale a su compañero/a todas las cosas que hizo. Él/Ella le va a preguntar dónde hizo las compras, a quién invitó, qué sirvió, y si lo pasaron bien. Después cambien de papel.

CD 4
Track 32
or CD 5
Track 8

**10-11 Una cena perfecta.** You will listen to a married couple talk about their plans for their dinner party tonight. Before you listen, make a list of four ingredients you would need to prepare a salad and an entrée.

ensalada _____

plato principal _____

Now, pay attention to the general idea of what is said. As you listen, mark (✓) the appropriate ending to each statement.

1. Rodolfo es...
   ___ un buen cocinero.
   ___ muy perezoso.
   ___ vegetariano.

2. Manuela va a...
   ___ cocinar ceviche.
   ___ poner la mesa.
   ___ llamar a los invitados.

3. Rodolfo va a comprar...
   ___ pescado y maíz.
   ___ limón y camarones.
   ___ espinacas y aguacates.

4. Manuela tiene...
   ___ todos los ingredientes.
   ___ muchos vegetales y frutas.
   ___ casi todos los ingredientes.

## Cultura

La comida de los países hispanoamericanos es muy variada. En Ecuador, al igual que en Perú, el ceviche de pescado o de camarón es muy popular. Otro plato muy popular es la fritada, un combinado de diversas carnes con plátano (*plantain*) maduro, plátano tostado y maíz. Y entre los postres, además de la pastelería, es muy sabroso el dulce de higos (*candied figs*).

# EN ACCIÓN

## Diarios de bicicleta: Lección de cocina

### Antes de ver

**10-12** Prepare una lista de algunos problemas inesperados que pueden ocurrir antes de una fiesta o de una cena importante.

### Mientras ve

**10-13** Muchas recetas para pozole incluyen los siguientes ingredientes. Marque (✓) los que menciona Luciana.

1. ___ carne de cerdo
2. ___ chiles
3. ___ ajos
4. ___ cebollas
5. ___ tomates
6. ___ cilantro
7. ___ maíz
8. ___ aceite

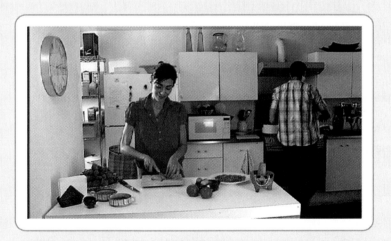

### Después de ver

**10-14** Ponga en el orden apropiado los siguientes pasos para hacer pozole.

___ Se quitan las semillas de los chiles y se cocinan con el tomate.

___ Se licuan los chiles, los tomates y el cilantro.

___ Se pone a cocinar la carne con las cebollas y ajos.

___ Se unen la carne, los chiles y tomates y el maíz.

___ Se corta la carne ya cocinada en trocitos muy pequeños.

___ Se sirve en platos hondos y se adorna con tostadas.

___ Se agrega sal y se deja sazonar unos minutos.

# FUNCIONES Y FORMAS

## 1. Stating impersonal information: *Se* + verb constructions

PROFESOR: **Se consumen** muchos carbohidratos y mucha grasa. ¿Sabían ustedes que en Estados Unidos **se comen** 23 libras de pizza por persona al año?

RICARDO: [piensa] ¿Cuánta cerveza **se bebe** con 23 pizzas?

PROFESOR: **Se comen** sólo 16 libras de manzanas, bla bla bla…

RICARDO: [piensa] En esta clase **se duerme** mucho.

**Piénselo.** ¿Cuánto más sabe usted sobre la dieta estadounidense? Indique si las siguientes afirmaciones son ciertas (**C**) o falsas (**F**), según la información del profesor y lo que usted sabe.

1. ____ **Se consumen** muchas grasas (*fats*).
2. ____ **Se compra** más fruta en el supermercado ahora que en el pasado.
3. ____ **Se dice** que los niños comen más y hacen menos actividad física.
4. ____ **Se bebe** mucho café, especialmente en las universidades.
5. ____ **Se consume** más pizza que manzanas.
6. ____ **Se recomienda** desayunar todos los días.

---

■ Spanish uses the **se +** *verb* construction to emphasize the occurrence of an action rather than the person(s) responsible for that action. The noun (what is bought, sold, offered, etc.) usually follows the verb. The person(s) who buy(s), sell(s), offer(s), and so on, is not mentioned. This is normally expressed in English with the passive voice (is/are **+** *past participle*).

**Se habla** español en este restaurante.   *Spanish is spoken in this restaurant.*

■ Use a singular verb with singular nouns and a plural verb with plural nouns.

**Se necesita** un horno para hacer galletas.   *An oven is needed to make cookies.*

**Se venden** vegetales allí.   *Vegetables are sold there.*

■ Use a singular verb when the **se +** *verb* construction is followed not by a noun, but rather by an adverb, an infinitive, or a clause. This is expressed in English with indefinite subjects such as *they, you, one,* and *people.*

| | |
|---|---|
| **Se trabaja** mucho en ese manzanal. | *They work a lot in that apple orchard.* |
| **Se puede** encontrar muchos tipos de manzanas allí. | *You can find many different types of apples there.* |
| **Se dice** que venden sidra excelente también. | *People say they sell excellent cider too.* |

**10-15 Asociaciones.** PRIMERA FASE. Asocie las actividades con los lugares donde ocurren.

1. ____ Se cambian cheques en...
2. ____ Se vende ropa en...
3. ____ Se toma el sol y se nada en...
4. ____ Se sirven comidas en...

a. un almacén.
b. un restaurante.
c. un banco.
d. una playa.

SEGUNDA FASE. Piense en un edificio o lugar público que le gusta mucho. Luego dígale a su compañero/a qué se hace allí.

MODELO: *Me gusta mucho la zona peatonal (pedestrian area) de mi ciudad. Allí se camina mucho y en el verano se escucha la música de conjuntos locales.*

**10-16 El supermercado y las tiendas de conveniencia.** Indique (✓) los productos y/o servicios que se encuentran en los supermercados solamente y los que se encuentran comúnmente en las tiendas de conveniencia también. Compare sus respuestas con las de su compañero/a.

| PRODUCTOS/SERVICIOS | SUPERMERCADO SOLAMENTE | SUPERMERCADO Y TIENDA DE CONVENIENCIA |
|---|---|---|
| productos lácteos | | |
| carnes orgánicas | | |
| frutas de América del Sur | | |
| detergente para lavadoras | | |
| alimentos enlatados (*canned*) | | |
| pescado fresco | | |
| DVDs para alquilar | | |

### En otras palabras

The concept of *convenience stores* is expressed differently according to the country. In Mexico they are **tiendas de conveniencia**, translated directly from English. In Costa Rica the term **tiendas de gasolinera** is used because of where such stores are usually located. In Spain they are **tiendas de 24h** to convey the convenience of being always open.

**10-17 Recetas creativas.** PRIMERA FASE. Lean estas recetas originales. Luego, intercambien opiniones sobre cuáles les gustaría probar y cuáles no.

1. Plátano derretido (*melted*): Se corta un plátano en rebanadas (*slices*) no muy finas. Se echa azúcar. Se calienta en el microondas por uno o dos minutos.
2. Batido de tarta de manzana (*apple pie smoothie*): Se ponen en la licuadora (*blender*): media taza de jugo de manzana, tres cucharadas de helado de vainilla y media cucharadita de canela (*cinnamon*). Se bate por un minuto.
3. Hamburguesa y salsa con queso (*nacho cheese sauce*): Se calienta la parrilla. Se pone la hamburguesa en la parrilla. Se pone la salsa con queso en el panecillo y se calienta. Se pone la hamburguesa en el panecillo.
4. Ensalada de pollo: Se abre una bolsa de lechuga prelavada. Se cortan en rebanadas dos pechugas de pollo (*chicken breasts*) cocidas, y se corta media libra de queso en cubos pequeños. Se combinan los ingredientes en una fuente (*bowl*). Se agrega un aliño de vinagre balsámico.

SEGUNDA FASE. Preparen juntos una receta para compartir con la clase.

**10-18 ¿Cómo se prepara este plato? PRIMERA FASE.** Usted y su compañero/a quieren darle una sorpresa a otra persona. Por eso, deciden prepararle su plato favorito. Primero, seleccionen uno de estos platos:

Luego, escriban en la caja una lista de los ingredientes que se necesitan para hacer el plato.

| CARNES | VERDURAS/VEGETALES | ESPECIAS | OTROS |
|--------|--------------------|----------|-------|
|        |                    |          |       |
|        |                    |          |       |
|        |                    |          |       |

**SEGUNDA FASE.** Usted sabe cocinar, pero su amigo/a no. Responda a sus preguntas mientras ustedes preparan el plato. Los siguientes verbos pueden ser útiles.

| | | |
|---|---|---|
| asar | dorar (*brown*) | rallar (*grate*) |
| cocinar | hervir | (so)freír |
| cortar | hornear | tostar |

**MODELO:** E1: *Vamos a preparar pollo asado. ¿Qué se hace con el pollo?*
E2: *Primero se lava bien el pollo. Luego se ponen sal y pimienta.*
E1: *¿Y después?*
E2: *Se asa en el horno por dos horas y se dora.*

## SITUACIONES

1. **Role A.** You are an international student who has just arrived in town. A student has offered to help with your orientation. You are not familiar with shopping in the United States, so you ask a) where one buys personal items like vitamins and toothpaste (**pasta de dientes**); b) where on campus one can find a decent meal; c) where one goes to buy fresh fruit; and d) where one can get good American pizza. Ask follow-up questions to be sure you understand the answers.

   **Role B.** You have offered to show a new international student around campus. Answer his/her questions about where one goes to buy different things. Offer several options, and be prepared to answer your new friend's questions.

2. **Role A.** You have just moved into your own apartment, and you are living away from home for the first time. You have never done your own food shopping and are not sure how to go about it. Ask a friend for help and ask questions so he/she will expand on the explanation.

   **Role B.** A friend has just told you that he/she does not know how to go food shopping. Explain the process step by step, starting with the shopping list (**se hace una lista...**). Provide additional explanation or clarification in response to your friend's questions.

## 2. Talking about the recent past: Present perfect and participles used as adjectives

ALICIA: Hola, César, ¿qué tal?

CÉSAR: Hola, Alicia. **¿Has visto** a Javier? ¡Estoy muy molesto!

ALICIA: ¿Por qué? ¿Qué te pasa?

CÉSAR: Como sabes, el examen de historia es pasado mañana y yo no **he leído** el libro todavía. ¿Lo **has leído** tú? ¿Lo **ha leído** Javier? ¿Javier te **ha dado** sus notas? No sé qué voy a hacer sin sus notas. ¡Las necesito para estudiar!

ALICIA: Cálmate, César. Yo **he leído** el libro y **he escrito** unas notas. **He hablado** con Javi. No **ha terminado** el libro todavía, pero va a llamarte esta tarde.

**Piénselo.** Lea las afirmaciones e indique a quién(es) se aplica cada una: a Alicia (**A**), a César (**C**) y/o a Javier (**J**).

1. \_\_\_\_ **Ha hablado** con Javier.
2. \_\_\_\_ **Ha escrito** unas notas.
3. \_\_\_\_ **Ha leído** una parte del libro.
4. \_\_\_\_ No **ha hecho** mucho en su curso de historia.
5. \_\_\_\_ No **han visto** a Javier.
6. \_\_\_\_ No **ha abierto** el libro.

■ Both Spanish and English have perfect tenses that are used to refer to past actions, events, and conditions. Both languages use an auxiliary verb (**haber** in Spanish, *to have* in English) followed by a past participle.

■ Use the present perfect to refer to a past event, action, or condition that has some relation to the present.

Lucho, ¿ya **has leído** la receta de paella?

*Lucho, have you read the recipe for paella yet?*

No, no **he leído** la receta todavía.

*No, I have not read the recipe yet.*

| PRESENT TENSE OF HABER | + | PAST PARTICIPLE |
|---|---|---|
| yo | he | |
| tú | has | |
| Ud., él, ella | ha | hablado |
| nosotros/as | hemos | comido |
| vosotros/as | habéis | vivido |
| Uds., ellos/as | han | |

▪ Form the present perfect by using the present tense of **haber** as an auxiliary verb with the past participle of the main verb. **Tener** is never used as the auxiliary verb to form the perfect tense.

| | |
|---|---|
| Los cocineros **han trabajado** mucho en el banquete. | *The cooks have worked a lot on the banquet.* |
| Unos miembros de la organización ya **han traído** los manteles. | *Some members of the organization have already brought the tablecloths.* |

▪ All past participles of **-ar** verbs end in **-ado**, whereas past participles of **-er** and **-ir** verbs generally end in **-ido**. If the stem of an **-er** verb ends in a vowel, use a written accent on the **i** of **-ido** (leer → le**í**do). In English, past participles are often formed with the endings *-ed* and *-en*, as in *finished* and *eaten*.

▪ Some **-er** and **-ir** verbs have irregular past participles. Here are some of the more common ones:

| IRREGULAR PAST PARTICIPLES | | | |
|---|---|---|---|
| hacer | **hecho** | abrir | **abierto** |
| poner | **puesto** | escribir | **escrito** |
| romper | **roto** | cubrir | **cubierto** |
| ver | **visto** | decir | **dicho** |
| volver | **vuelto** | morir | **muerto** |

▪ Place object and reflexive pronouns before the auxiliary **haber**. Do not place any word between **haber** and the past participle.

| | |
|---|---|
| ¿**Le** has dado las servilletas a César? | *Have you given César the napkins?* |
| No, todavía no **se las** he dado. | *No, I have not given them to him yet.* |

▪ The present perfect of **hay** is **ha habido** with both singular and plural nouns.

| | |
|---|---|
| **Ha habido** más trabajo últimamente. | *There has been more work lately.* |
| **Ha habido** varios banquetes y otros eventos. | *There have been several banquets and other events.* |

▪ **OJO:** To state that something has just happened use the present tense of **acabar + de +** *infinitive*, not the present perfect.

| | |
|---|---|
| **Acabamos de volver** del supermercado. | *We have just returned from the supermarket.* |
| **Acabo de probar** la sopa y está deliciosa. | *I have just tasted the soup, and it is delicious.* |

▪ Spanish uses **estar +** *past participle* to express a state or condition resulting from a prior action.

| ACTION | RESULT |
|---|---|
| Ella preparó la sopa. | La sopa **está preparada**. |
| Luego cerró las ventanas. | Las ventanas **están cerradas**. |

■ When a past participle is used as an adjective, it agrees with the noun it modifies.

| | |
|---|---|
| una puerta **cerrada** | *a closed door* |
| los restaurantes **abiertos** | *the open restaurants* |
| unas botellas **lavadas** | *some washed bottles* |

**10-19 Lo que no he hecho.** Usted y su compañero/a deben decir las cosas de cada lista que no han hecho. Después, comparen sus respuestas con las de otros estudiantes.

1. Yo nunca he estado en…
   **a.** Paraguay.    **b.** Guatemala.    **c.** Ecuador.
2. Yo nunca he visto…
   **a.** las Islas Galápagos.    **b.** un volcán activo.    **c.** un huracán.
3. Yo nunca he comido…
   **a.** aguacate.    **b.** un postre con leche de coco.    **c.** langosta.
4. Yo nunca he escrito…
   **a.** una receta.
   **b.** una lista de compras (*shopping list*) en español.
   **c.** el menú para una cena formal.
5. Yo nunca he roto…
   **a.** una taza.    **b.** un vaso.    **c.** un plato.
6. Yo nunca he dicho…
   **a.** "no" a una invitación a cenar.
   **b.** una broma (*joke*) de mal gusto durante una comida formal.
   **c.** una palabra en español en un resturante hispano en este país.

**10-20 Hispanos famosos/Hispanas famosas. PRIMERA FASE.** Piensen en un hispano famoso/una hispana famosa y preparen una lista de cinco cosas que ustedes creen que ha hecho para tener éxito (*to be successful*). Después compartan su lista con la de otra pareja y háganse preguntas.

**MODELO:**    *Cameron Díaz es una actriz famosa.*
       *Ha actuado en más de treinta películas.*

| HISPANO FAMOSO/HISPANA FAMOSA | LO QUE HA HECHO PARA TENER ÉXITO |
|---|---|
| _____ | _____ |
| | _____ |
| | _____ |
| | _____ |

**SEGUNDA FASE.** Digan tres cosas que ustedes han hecho que los/las ha ayudado a tener éxito en su vida personal, académica o profesional.

**10-21 Para hacer una cena importante.** Usted y su compañero/a van a preparar una cena para la visita de una persona importante a su universidad. Háganse preguntas para ver qué preparativos ha hecho cada uno/a para la cena.

MODELO: comprar la carne
E1: *¿Has comprado la carne?*
E2: *No, no la he comprado todavía.*

1. determinar el número de invitados
2. leer las recetas
3. cortar los vegetales
4. hacer el postre
5. decidir qué música se va a tocar
6. poner la mesa
7. asignar los asientos
8. decorar el lugar de la cena

**10-22 Justo ahora.** Con su compañero/a, digan qué acaban de hacer estas personas. Den la mayor información posible.

MODELO: Juan y Ramiro salen del estadio.
E1: *Acaban de ver un partido de béisbol muy importante.*
E2: *Fueron a ver a los Calcetines Rojos porque es su equipo favorito.*

1. Maricarmen y sus amigos ya no tienen hambre.
2. Pedro y Alina salen de una tienda donde se alquilan películas.
3. Mercedes y Paula traen palomitas de maíz (*popcorn*) para todo el grupo.
4. Un hombre sale corriendo de un banco.
5. Jorge y Rubén salen de un supermercado.
6. Frente a todos sus amigos, Rubén le da una sorpresa a su novia.

**10-23 Robo (*Robbery*) en un restaurante.** El siguiente párrafo cuenta algo que ocurrió en el restaurante del chef Marco Tovares. Para saber lo que pasó, llene los espacios en blanco con la forma correcta del participio pasado de los verbos entre paréntesis.

El chef Marco Tovares salió de la cocina de su restaurante en Nueva York para asegurarse de que todo iba bien en el comedor esa noche. Vio que el locutor de televisión Jorge Ramos y otras tres personas estaban (1) _____ (sentar) en una mesa. De repente Marco vio que la bolsa de una de las mujeres estaba (2) _____ (abrir) y que un hombre en otra mesa la estaba mirando. Como la mujer estaba (3) _____ (distraer), el ladrón aprovechó el momento (4) _____ (esperar). Sacó la billetera de la bolsa de ella. La mujer no se dio cuenta, pero Marco lo vio todo. Se acercó a la mesa y le dijo al hombre: —¿Cómo está la comida esta noche? ¿Todo bien? El hombre parecía muy nervioso, y curiosamente tenía las manos (5) _____ (cerrar). Marco le dijo: —¿Podría acompañarme un momento, por favor? El hombre fue con Marco al fondo del restaurante, le dio la billetera (6) _____ (robar) y salió. Marco se acercó a la mesa de Jorge Ramos y les explicó lo ocurrido. Todos estaban muy (7) _____ (sorprender). La mujer víctima del robo dijo: —Hace diez años que vivo en Nueva York, y ¡nunca he (8) _____ (ser) víctima de un robo hasta esta noche! Muchísimas gracias por su ayuda.

**10-24 ¿Qué ha pasado?** PRIMERA FASE. Su compañero/a y usted han ordenado su apartamento esta mañana. Pero acaban de entrar por la tarde, y ven que todo está muy desordenado. Túrnense para describirle al/a la policía lo que han hecho para ordenar el apartamento y lo que ven ahora, usando las palabras entre paréntesis. Añadan más información donde sea posible.

MODELO:     las ventanas (cerrar, abrir)

POLICÍA: *¿Qué ha pasado con las ventanas?*

E1: *Las he cerrado esta mañana...*

E2: *pero ahora están abiertas.*

1. el espejo del baño (usar, romper)
2. la cama (tender, desordenar)
3. el televisor (apagar, encender)
4. las camisas (colgar, tirar al piso)
5. la puerta del apartamento (cerrar, abrir)
6. la comida en el refrigerador (cubrir, descubrir [*to uncover*])

SEGUNDA FASE. Después de escuchar el relato de ustedes, el/la policía hace lo siguiente:

1. Les hace preguntas para conseguir más información.
2. Les dice tres cosas que hay que hacer ahora.

## SITUACIONES

1. **Role A.** You are a reporter who has been assigned to interview the new chef of a restaurant in your community. Ask about a) other restaurants where he/she has worked; b) prizes (*premios*) he/she has won; c) some examples of dishes he/she has developed; and d) changes he/she has already made in the restaurant.

   **Role B.** You are the new chef of one of the nicest restaurants in town, and a reporter is interviewing you for the local newspaper. Answer the reporter's questions, adding as many details possible.

2. **Role A.** You are in charge of discipline at a strict boarding school. Call one of the students to your office to ask about his/her activities. Explain that the teachers have just told you that a) he/she has not attended classes for four days; b) he/she has not done homework for two weeks; and c) he/she has not eaten in the cafeteria all week. Say that the teachers are worried. You want to track his/her every movement to determine the problem. Start with **¿A qué hora te has levantado hoy?** and continue from there.

   **Role B.** You are a student at a strict boarding school. You have been acting strangely, and you don't want to explain why. The teacher in charge of discipline has asked to speak to you. Answer the teacher's questions with enough detail to fool him/her into thinking you are telling the truth.

## 3. Giving instructions in informal settings: Informal commands

Carnes y sustitutos (2 raciones)

Grasas, dulces sal, etc

Aceites y frutos secos
(3 a 6 raciones)

Lácteos (2 a
4 raciones)

Verduras (2 a
4 raciones)

Marcos

Frutas (2 a 3 raciones)
Féculas (3 a 6 raciones)

Marcos, la buena alimentación es fundamental para la buena salud. **Toma** desayuno siempre. Es la comida más importante del día. Para tener energía, **consume** carbohidratos y proteínas en las tres comidas. **Come** carbohidratos complejos, como pasta y pan, pero siempre integrales (*made from whole grains*). **No olvides** las frutas, las verduras y la leche, son muy buenas para la salud. **Evita** comer grasas y azúcares, excepto en cantidades moderadas.

**Piénselo.** Según las sugerencias del enfermero, escoja los alimentos o bebidas que Marcos debe consumir o evitar para alimentarse bien.

1. _____ Come...
2. _____ Evita...
3. _____ Bebe...

a. helado todos los días.
b. pan blanco.
c. manzanas, peras, plátanos, uvas.

d. suficiente leche.
e. pollo y pescado.
f. refrescos.

■ To ask a friend to do or not to do something, use an informal command. Use that form with anyone else you address as **tú**, such as someone your own age or someone with whom you have a close relationship.

■ To form the affirmative **tú** command, use the present indicative **tú** form without the final **-s**.

|  | PRESENT INDICATIVE | AFFIRMATIVE *TÚ* COMMAND |
|---|---|---|
| cocinar | cocinas | **cocina** |
| beber | bebes | **bebe** |
| consumir | consumes | **consume** |

■ For the negative **tú** command, use the negative **usted** command form and add the final **-s**.

|  | NEGATIVE *USTED* COMMAND | NEGATIVE *TÚ* COMMAND |
|---|---|---|
| preparar | no prepar**e** | no prepar**es** |
| comer | no com**a** | no com**as** |
| subir | no sub**a** | no sub**as** |

■ Placement of object and reflexive pronouns with **tú** commands is the same as with **usted** commands.

| AFFIRMATIVE COMMAND | NEGATIVE COMMAND |
|---|---|
| Prepárelo (usted). | No **lo** prepare (usted). |
| Bébela (tú). | No **la** bebas (tú). |

■ The plural of **tú** commands in Spanish-speaking America is the **ustedes** command.

| | |
|---|---|
| **Cocina (tú).** | **Cocinen (ustedes).** |
| **Bebe (tú).** | **Beban (ustedes).** |
| **Sube (tú).** | **Suban (ustedes).** |

■ Some **-er** and **-ir** verbs have shortened affirmative **tú** commands, but their negative command is regular.

| | AFFIRMATIVE | NEGATIVE |
|---|---|---|
| poner | **pon** | **no pongas** |
| salir | **sal** | **no salgas** |
| tener | **ten** | **no tengas** |
| venir | **ven** | **no vengas** |
| hacer | **haz** | **no hagas** |
| decir | **di** | **no digas** |
| ir | **ve** | **no vayas** |
| ser | **sé** | **no seas** |

| | |
|---|---|
| **Sal** a las tres si quieres llegar a las cuatro. | *Leave at 3:00 if you want to arrive at 4:00.* |
| **No salgas** sin paraguas; va a llover. | *Don't leave without an umbrella; it is going to rain.* |
| **Sé** generoso con tus amigos. | *Be generous with your friends.* |
| No **seas** impaciente. | *Don't be impatient.* |
| **Dime** la verdad. | *Tell me the truth.* |
| **No nos digas** mentiras. | *Don't tell us any lies.* |

**10-25 Consejos.** Escoja los consejos más adecuados, según cada situación.

1. Su compañero/a comió demasiado en una fiesta de cumpleaños y ahora le duele mucho el estómago.
   a. Come más para recuperarte.
   b. Llama al médico.
   c. Ve a la farmacia y compra medicamentos.
   d. Camina una hora esta tarde.
   e. Practica deportes para olvidarte del dolor de estómago.
   f. No te acuestes.

2. Su hermana está enferma. Está congestionada y tiene fiebre.
   a. Toma sopa de pollo.
   b. Come una hamburguesa.
   c. No duermas mucho.
   d. Bebe jugos y agua.
   e. No bebas vino ni cerveza.
   f. No consumas mucha cafeína.

3. A su hijo le fascina la comida chatarra (*junk food*), por eso, subió diez libras en un mes.
   a. Ve a los restaurantes de comida rápida.
   b. Bebe muchas gaseosas.
   c. Come en casa, no en restaurantes.
   d. No tomes alcohol.
   e. Evita los batidos de McDonald's.
   f. No pidas ensaladas.

4. Su mamá quiere alimentarse mejor para tener más energía y bajar de peso.
   a. Evita la grasa.
   b. Toma muchos helados.
   c. Come huevos moderadamente.
   d. Compra papas fritas.
   e. Acuéstate y descansa.
   f. Si no tienes energía, consume mucha cafeína.

5. Su mejor amigo quiere preparar una cena espectacular para su novia.
   a. Compra pizza.
   b. Haz un plato sofisticado.
   c. No olvides de comprar un buen vino.
   d. Prepara la mesa el día anterior.
   e. No le pongas chile picante al plato. Ella detesta la comida picante.
   f. Ponle mucha sal a la comida.

**10-26 Una cura de reposo.** Su amigo/a estuvo muy enfermo/a y su médico le recomendó pasar dos semanas de descanso en las Termas de Papallacta o en la reserva natural Playa de Oro en Ecuador. Como usted ha visitado los dos lugares, dígale a su amigo/a qué debe hacer allí. Después cambien de papel.

**MODELO:** visitar la reserva/no pensar en los negocios
*Visita la reserva Playa de Oro./No pienses en los negocios.*

1. disfrutar del sol
2. respirar aire puro y descansar
3. no hacer tarea
4. tomar fotos y hacer videos
5. probar un plato típico ecuatoriano
6. salir por las noches y conversar con las personas del lugar
7. tomar baños termales a diario
8. asistir a un concierto de música andina

**10-27 Buenos hábitos alimenticios. PRIMERA FASE.** Ustedes están preocupados por los hábitos de comida de uno/a de sus amigos/as. Lean lo que esta persona come y bebe en un día típico e identifiquen los problemas que tiene.

Se levanta al mediodía todos los días. Tan pronto se levanta, toma varias tazas de café. Una hora más tarde, come tres huevos fritos con tocino y tostadas. Toma dos tazas de café cubano con bastante azúcar. Luego lee el periódico en su dormitorio, mira televisión y come chocolate mientras habla por teléfono con sus amigos. Por la tarde, llama por teléfono al restaurante de la esquina y pide una hamburguesa con papas fritas y toma unas cervezas. Después, duerme una siesta larga. Por la noche, tiene problemas para dormir, por eso, toma un batido.

**SEGUNDA FASE.** Hagan una lista con cinco recomendaciones o instrucciones que su amigo/a debe seguir. Comparen su lista con las de otros grupos.

**10-28 Cocina paso a paso (*step by step*). PRIMERA FASE.** Busquen una receta para el sancocho, una sopa que se come en Ecuador. Escriban la lista de los ingredientes y estén listos/as para describirlos.

**SEGUNDA FASE.** En el papel de dos chefs de televisión, presenten la preparación del sancocho. Sigan los siguientes pasos: a) describan el plato; b) presenten sus ingredientes; y c) expliquen cómo se prepara el plato.

## SITUACIONES

1. **Role A.** You are not feeling well, so you call your friend to ask for the recipe to make chicken soup. Take notes as your friend gives you the recipe. Ask questions as necessary.

   **Role B.** Your friend is not feeling well and calls to ask for the recipe for chicken soup. Tell him/her to a) buy skinless chicken (**pollo sin piel**); b) wash and cut garlic, onions, carrots, and celery (**apio**); c) sauté (**saltear**) the chicken and vegetables with a little olive oil; and d) add water, salt, and pepper and cook for 30 minutes.

2. **Role A.** To improve your health, you visit a nutritionist. Explain what you generally eat for breakfast, lunch, and dinner. Ask questions and answer the nutritionist's questions.

   **Role B.** A client comes to you for help with eating habits. Ask what he/she eats for breakfast, lunch, and dinner. Advise your client a) to eat fruits, vegetables, fish, and chicken; b) not to drink soft drinks or alcohol; c) to consume foods with lots of fiber; and d) to do physical activity daily. Answer your client's questions.

## 4. Talking about the future: The future tense

CIENTÍFICA: Según los expertos, para el año 2030 la población geriátrica **se duplicará** en comparación con la del presente. La gente **comerá** mejor y **vivirá** más años porque **tendrá** buena salud.

JULIA: ¿Y nuestra dieta **será** semejante a la de hoy? ¿Qué **comeremos**?

CIENTÍFICA: Se piensa que **consumiremos** más alimentos naturales, porque más gente **comprenderá** sus beneficios. Al mismo tiempo, muchos alimentos **serán** modificados genéticamente. Los individuos **tratarán** de protegerse de ciertas condiciones y enfermedades, como la diabetes y el cáncer.

**Piénselo.** Indique si las siguientes afirmaciones son ciertas (**C**) o falsas (**F**), según la científica. Si la respuesta es falsa (**F**), corrija la información.

1. \_\_\_\_ **Habrá** menos personas mayores en el futuro.
2. \_\_\_\_ Las personas **tendrán** una vida más larga.
3. \_\_\_\_ Más personas **comprenderán** el beneficio de los alimentos naturales.
4. \_\_\_\_ La gente **podrá** comer grasas y dulces porque la ciencia los protegerá contra las enfermedades.

■ You have been using the present tense and *ir a + infinitive* to express future plans. Spanish also has a future tense. Although you have these other ways to express a future action, event, or state, it is important to be able to recognize the future tense in reading and in listening.

■ The future tense is formed by adding the endings **-é, -ás, -á, -emos, -éis**, and **-án** to the infinitive. All verbs, **-ar, -er, -ir**, regular or irregular, use these endings.

| | HABLAR | COMER | VIVIR |
|---|---|---|---|
| FUTURE TENSE | | | |
| yo | hablar**é** | comer**é** | vivir**é** |
| tú | hablar**ás** | comer**ás** | vivir**ás** |
| Ud., él, ella | hablar**á** | comer**á** | vivir**á** |
| nosotros/as | hablar**emos** | comer**emos** | vivir**emos** |
| vosotros/as | hablar**éis** | comer**éis** | vivir**éis** |
| Uds., ellos/as | hablar**án** | comer**án** | vivir**án** |

| | |
|---|---|
| Rafael **visitará** Ecuador el mes próximo. | *Rafael will visit Ecuador next month.* |
| Él y sus colegas **volverán** después de dos semanas. | *He and his colleagues will return after two weeks.* |
| **Se reunirán** con los dueños de unas haciendas de café. | *They will meet with the owners of some coffee plantations.* |

■ Some verbs have irregular stems in the future tense and can be grouped into three categories according to the irregularity. The first group drops the **-e** from the infinitive ending.

| IRREGULAR FUTURE—GROUP 1 | | |
|---|---|---|
| **INFINITIVE** | **NEW STEM** | **FUTURE FORMS** |
| poder | **podr-** | podré, podrás, podrá, podremos, podréis, podrán |
| querer | **querr-** | querré, querrás, querrá, querremos, querréis, querrán |
| saber | **sabr-** | sabré, sabrás, sabrá, sabremos, sabréis, sabrán |

■ The second group replaces the **e** or **i** of the infinitive ending with a **-d.**

| IRREGULAR FUTURE—GROUP 2 | | |
|---|---|---|
| poner | **pondr-** | pondré, pondrás, pondrá, pondremos, pondréis, pondrán |
| salir | **saldr-** | saldré, saldrás, saldrá, saldremos, saldréis, saldrán |
| tener | **tendr-** | tendré, tendrás, tendrá, tendremos, tendréis, tendrán |
| venir | **vendr-** | vendré, vendrás, vendrá, vendremos, vendréis, vendrán |

■ The third group consists of two verbs that have completely different stems in the future tense.

| IRREGULAR FUTURE—GROUP 3 | | |
|---|---|---|
| decir | **dir-** | diré, dirás, dirá, diremos, diréis, dirán |
| hacer | **har-** | haré, harás, hará, haremos, haréis, harán |

| | |
|---|---|
| Los estudiantes **sabrán** más sobre la nutrición después de tomar el curso. | *The students will know more about nutrition after taking the course.* |
| **Tendrán** que leer mucho. | *They will have to read a lot.* |
| También **harán** un proyecto de investigación. | *They will also do a research project.* |
| ¿A qué hora **vendrán** a cenar? | *What time will they be coming for dinner?* |
| **Querrán** probar un poco de todo. | *They will want to try a little of everything.* |

**Cultura**

Ecuador tiene muchos parques nacionales y reservas ecológicas cuyo propósito es conservar la riqueza natural de las cuatro regiones del país: las Islas Galápagos, la costa, la sierra y la selva amazónica. En las reservas se encuentran muchas especies de flora y fauna. Para los visitantes, hay muchas maneras de explorar las reservas y gozar de la naturaleza.

**10-29 ¿Qué lugares de Ecuador visitarán estas personas?** Complete las oraciones de la izquierda con la forma correcta del verbo en la columna de la derecha.

1. A Carlos y Eugenia les gusta comer bien. Ellos ____ al restaurante especializado en la cocina de Guayaquil.
2. A doña Lourdes y a su hija les fascinan la zoología y la botánica. Ellas ____ un viaje a las Islas Galápagos para ver la gran variedad de especies animales.
3. Don Jorge y yo ____ el mercado indígena de Cuenca para comprar artesanía ecuatoriana.
4. A ti te gusta disfrutar del aire libre, ver la arquitectura colonial y las montañas. Tú ____ por la Plaza San Blas en Quito.
5. A mí me interesa la protección de los animales y la flora. Yo ____ a la Reserva Cuyabeno que está a 500 kilómetros de Quito.

a. viajaré
b. caminarás
c. irán
d. visitaremos
e. harán

**10-30 Intercambio: Un viaje a Guayaquil. PRIMERA FASE.** Ramiro va a Guayaquil a visitar a su familia. Háganse preguntas y contesten de acuerdo con la agenda que Ramiro preparó.

MODELO: E1: *¿Qué hará Ramiro el miércoles por la noche?*
E2: *Cenará con unos amigos.*
E1: *¿Cuándo irá al cine con los primos?*
E2: *Irán al cine el martes.*

| LUNES | MARTES | MIÉRCOLES | JUEVES | VIERNES |
|---|---|---|---|---|
| salir para Guayaquil | visitar el Parque de las Iguanas | salir de compras al Mercado Artesanal | viajar al Parque Nacional El Cajas | empacar las maletas |
| cenar con los tíos | conocer a otros familiares | ir a un museo | caminar en la reserva, sacar fotos | almorzar con toda la familia |
| acostarse temprano | ir al cine con los primos | cenar con unos amigos | dormir en el parque | regresar a Estados Unidos |

**SEGUNDA FASE.** Hagan una lista de cinco actividades que Ramiro probablemente hará al regresar a Estados Unidos. Expliquen por qué.

**10-31 Planes para una fiesta para celebrar un matrimonio. PRIMERA FASE.** Sus amigos José y Silvia se casaron durante sus vacaciones en Ecuador. Regresarán a Estados Unidos en dos semanas y ustedes van a organizar una fiesta para celebrar su matrimonio. Planifiquen la fiesta considerando lo siguiente: número de invitados, lugar de la fiesta, menú que ofrecerán (comida y bebida), música, baile y otras actividades en la fiesta.

**SEGUNDA FASE.** Compartan sus planes con otra pareja. Hagan una lista de tres semejanzas y tres diferencias entre las fiestas que las dos parejas organizarán.

**10-32 ¿Qué recomendaciones seguirá?** Maricela sufre de estrés, insomnio y anemia. Por eso les pide sugerencias a su mejor amiga y a su nutricionista. A continuación aparecen sus recomendaciones. Discutan qué recomendaciones probablemente seguirá Maricela y expliquen por qué.

| RECOMENDACIONES DE LA NUTRICIONISTA | RECOMENDACIONES DE SU MEJOR AMIGA |
|---|---|
| 1. Coma en pequeñas cantidades por lo menos cuatro veces al día. | 1. Come cuando quieras. Si subes de peso puedes seguir una dieta. |
| 2. No consuma cafeína para tener energía. Consuma proteínas para obtener energía. | 2. Para tener energía, come mucho chocolate y, luego, haz ejercicio. |
| 3. Consuma calcio. Beba leche y coma frutas. | 3. Toma helado todos los días porque la leche tiene mucho calcio. |
| 4. Para eliminar la tensión y relajarse, haga yoga. | 4. Escucha música suave y no contestes el teléfono de la oficina. |
| 5. Compre verduras y carnes orgánicas en supermercados especializados en productos naturales. | 5. Pide ensalada con pollo en los restaurantes de comida rápida y un refresco de dieta. |

## SITUACIONES

1. **Role A.** You are organizing a picnic and some of the guests are vegetarians. Call your nutritionist friend (your classmate) to discuss what food to serve. Say that a) you will prepare vegetarian and non-vegetarian food; b) for the vegetarians, you will make salads and a Spanish tortilla; c) for the meat eaters, you will serve a chicken salad and want to have hamburgers; and d) you will serve beer, soft drinks, and juice. Ask your friend for advice.

   **Role B.** A friend is calling to ask for advice regarding the menu for a picnic that will include both vegetarian and non-vegetarian guests. Give your friend feedback on the proposed menu and offer additional advice.

2. **Role A.** You and a friend are concerned about people's quality of life and the food they eat. Tell your friend that you think in ten years from now people will eat a) more healthful foods; b) fewer fats and sugars; and c) less junk food (**comida chatarra**). Add that you think food will be more expensive but of better quality and that people will live longer because they will be healthier.

   **Role B.** You don't agree with your friend's opinions about what people will eat ten years from now. In your view, a) people will continue to eat unhealthful food; b) people will continue to eat fats and sugar; c) children will have more opportunities to eat junk food (**comida chatarra**) because parents will be very busy; d) food will cost less, so people will eat more; and e) people will die younger but happier.

# MOSAICOS

## A escuchar

### Antes de escuchar

**10-33 Preparación.** Usted escuchará una lista de productos que compraron Andrea, Carolina, Roberto y Darío. Antes de escuchar, prepare una lista de productos que usted compra regularmente y otra de aquellos que usted compra en ocasiones especiales.

### Escuchar

**10-34 ¿Comprende usted?** Andrea, Carolina, Roberto, and Darío have each offered to contribute a dish for their friend Óscar's birthday party. Each has bought some kind of vegetable and meat or seafood to prepare his/her dish. As you listen, mark (✓) the foods that each of them bought.

CD 4
Track 33
or CD 5
Track 9

| ANDREA | CAROLINA | ROBERTO | DARÍO |
|---|---|---|---|
| ___ sal | ___ ajos | ___ mermelada | ___ huevos |
| ___ pollo | ___ cerdo | ___ pepinos | ___ ajos |
| ___ carne molida | ___ espinacas | ___ pimienta | ___ fruta |
| ___ azúcar | ___ jamón | ___ aceite | ___ jamón |
| ___ zanahorias | ___ langosta | ___ pavo | ___ aderezo |
| ___ aguacates | ___ maíz | ___ aguacates | ___ pimientos verdes |
| ___ camarones | ___ pollo | ___ zanahorias | ___ pasta |

### Después de escuchar

**10-35 Ahora usted.** Compartan las respuestas a las siguientes preguntas.

1. ¿Cuál es su plato favorito?
2. ¿Qué productos o ingredientes compra usted para prepararlo?
3. ¿Con quién comparte generalmente su plato favorito? ¿Por qué?
4. ¿Qué dice esta persona cuando usted prepara este plato?

# A conversar

## Antes de conversar

**10-36 Preparación.** PRIMERA FASE. Marque cuáles de los siguientes alimentos son más saludables (**+**) o menos saludables (**–**).

___ los camarones      ___ las espinacas      ___ el jamón      ___ el pollo
___ la carne de res    ___ la fruta           ___ las legumbres ___ el queso
___ la cerveza         ___ las galletas       ___ el pan blanco ___ los refrescos
___ los dulces         ___ el helado          ___ las papas     ___ el vino

SEGUNDA FASE. Escriban en la tabla los productos o alimentos de la *Primera fase* que en general producen los siguientes efectos. Prepárense para explicar por qué. **OJO:** Algunos se pueden poner en más de una categoría.

| ENGORDAN | ADELGAZAN (*ARE SLIMMING*) | DAN ENERGÍA | AUMENTAN EL COLESTEROL |
|---|---|---|---|
|  |  |  |  |
|  |  |  |  |

## Conversar

**10-37 Entre nosotros.** Averigüen las preferencias de comida de los miembros del grupo en las siguientes categorías. Después, sumen los números en las columnas para saber qué comida les gusta más y cuál les gusta menos.

MODELO:    los mariscos
    E1:  *¿Te gustan los mariscos?*
    E2:  *Me encantan. ¿Y a ti?*
    E1:  *A mí no me gustan.*

| ALIMENTO | ENCANTAR | GUSTAR MUCHO | GUSTAR | NO GUSTAR |
|---|---|---|---|---|
| la fruta |  |  |  |  |
| las verduras |  |  |  |  |
| la carne |  |  |  |  |
| los mariscos |  |  |  |  |
| los productos lácteos |  |  |  |  |
| los dulces |  |  |  |  |

## Después de conversar

**10-38 Un poco más.** Comparen los resultados de **10-37** para determinar las categorías de alimentos que se consumen más en la clase. Luego, respondan a estas preguntas.

1. ¿Qué tipos de comida se comen más en la clase?
2. En general, ¿ustedes se alimentan bien o mal? ¿Por qué?
3. ¿Deben ustedes mejorar su dieta? ¿Qué deben hacer?

ESTRATEGIA

**Give and defend reasons for a decision**

When you make a decision that you wish to communicate effectively to others, it is important to a) state your decision clearly; b) present and explain your reasons logically; and c) urge your listeners to consider your point of view.

En directo

To influence someone's decision:

**Es mejor/menos dañino** (*harmful*) **+** infinitive.

**¿No te/le(s) parece más saludable +** infinitive?

**¿Qué te/le(s) parece si +** indicative... ?

# A leer

## Antes de leer

**10-39 Preparación.** Lea el título y los subtítulos de la lectura en la p. 355, mire las fotos y lea sus leyendas. Luego, conteste las preguntas, usando esos elementos y también su conocimiento general.

1. ¿Qué información espera encontrar en el artículo?
   a. una definición del término *fusión culinaria*
      Sí   No
   b. una dieta para bajar de peso
      Sí   No
   c. recetas para platos de cocina fusión
      Sí   No
   d. información sobre la influencia china en la cocina de un país
      Sí   No
   e. información sobre la cocina Tex-Mex
      Sí   No

2. Marque (✔) los elementos que lo/la ayudaron a responder a la pregunta 1.
   a. ___ el título y los subtítulos
   b. ___ las fotos junto con sus leyendas
   c. ___ mi conocimiento de cocina

3. ¿Qué es la fusión culinaria? Marque (✔) la definición más lógica, según su conocimiento general.
   a. ___ La combinación de la cocina con otras artes, como la decoración de interiores
   b. ___ Una cocina que combina la influencia de dos tradiciones culinarias
   c. ___ Una manera tradicional de preparar la comida que la gente conserva por muchas generaciones

4. Prepare una lista de comidas Tex-Mex que usted conoce. ¿Cuáles le gustan más? Luego, indique si aparecieron en el artículo.

# Leer

## La fusión culinaria: una tendencia nueva con una historia larga

Tortilla española envuelta en una tortilla mexicana

### La fusión en la cocina contemporánea

Todos hemos comido platos que combinan la cocina de dos países o culturas. El llamado *California roll*—el sushi japonés con un relleno[1] de cangrejo[2], queso crema y aguacate—es un ejemplo; la *taco pizza*, que se hace con la masa de una pizza cubierta de los ingredientes típicos del taco—carne molida, frijoles refritos, salsa, queso amarillo y especias picantes—es otro. La fusión culinaria, o cocina fusión, es un concepto que señala la mezcla de ingredientes y estilos culinarios de diferentes culturas en el menú de un restaurante o aun en un mismo plato. El término *cocina fusión* fue inventado en California en la década de los 1960s por unos chefs que combinaban los estilos de las cocinas de Asia (china, japonesa, tailandesa) con las legumbres frescas y naturales de California y las salsas hechas de frutas cítricas y tropicales. Hoy en día es común encontrar restaurantes en Estados Unidos con nombres como *Roy's Hawaiian Fusion Cuisine* o *Fusion Restaurant and Lounge*. Hay muchas posibles combinaciones, limitadas solamente por la creatividad del chef y los gustos de los clientes.

### La fusión en la historia culinaria

A pesar de la creciente popularidad de estas combinaciones gastronómicas, sería un error pensar que la cocina fusión es un fenómeno nuevo. Siempre donde conviven grupos de personas de dos culturas nace una fusión de sus tradiciones culinarias. Dos ejemplos de este antiguo fenómeno en las Américas son la cocina chino-peruana y la cocina mexicano-norteamericana, o Tex-Mex.

### El Chifa: La cocina fusión de Perú

La cocina peruana es una mezcla de muchas influencias: indígena, española, africana, china y japonesa. El Chifa, o cocina chino-peruana, es el resultado de la mezcla de la comida criolla de Lima con la cocina traída por los inmigrantes chinos desde mediados del siglo XIX. El término *el Chifa* se refiere tanto a la comida como a los restaurantes donde se sirve.

Los chinos que fueron a Perú se adaptaron a la sociedad y sus costumbres, pero siempre mantuvieron sus tradiciones culinarias. Con el progreso económico, luego pudieron importar de China unas especias y otros productos esenciales para su comida, pero por lo general tenían que cultivar las verduras que necesitaban o sustituirlas por ingredientes locales.

No es una exageración decir que la cultura chino-peruana de los inmigrantes chinos asimilados a la sociedad peruana revolucionó la gastronomía. Algunos platos considerados típicamente peruanos, como el arroz chaufa (preparado con carne picada, cebollitas, pimentón, huevos y salsa de soja) y el tacu-tacu (una tortilla hecha de un puré de frijoles, arroz, ajo, ají y cebolla) reflejan la influencia de la cocina china.

### La comida Tex-Mex: La cocina mexicana en Estados Unidos

Un ejemplo de la cocina fusión que se conoce en todas partes de Estados Unidos es la cocina Tex-Mex. Se trata de una fusión de dos estilos, el de México y el de Texas. La cocina que conocemos hoy en día como Tex-Mex se originó en una mezcla de la comida del pueblo nativo de Texas y la cocina española. Los indígenas contribuyeron con ingredientes como los frijoles pintos, los nopales (las hojas de un cacto), las cebollas silvestres[3] y el mesquite. La influencia española empezó con la llegada del ganado[4] a la región, traído por los colonizadores al final del siglo XVI. También hay influencias del norte de África en la comida Tex-Mex. Un grupo de colonizadores de las Islas Canarias y de Marruecos inmigraron a lo que es ahora San Antonio, Texas en el siglo XVIII. De ellos vinieron combinaciones nuevas de especias (sobre todo el comino), cilantro y chiles en la comida Tex-Mex. El chili con carne de San Antonio todavía retiene los sabores de la cocina marroquí.

Nachos, un plato popular de la cocina Tex-Mex

En los últimos treinta años ha habido esfuerzos de separar lo que se considera *la cocina mexicana* de lo que conocemos como *la cocina mexicana americanizada*, o Tex-Mex. En comparación con la cocina mexicana, la Tex-Mex utiliza más carne y usa las tortillas para envolver una mayor variedad de rellenos. Los nachos, los tacos fritos, las chalupas, el chile con queso y el chile con carne son invenciones Tex-Mex que no se encuentran en la cocina mexicana tradicional. La costumbre universal en los restaurantes Tex-Mex de servir las *tortilla chips* con salsa picante como aperitivo tampoco existe en la cocina mexicana tradicional.

---

[1]*filling*   [2]*crab*   [3]*wild*   [4]*cattle*

**10-40 Primera mirada.** Según el contenido del artículo, ¿son las siguientes afirmaciones ciertas (**C**) o falsas (**F**)? Si la afirmación es falsa, corrija la información.

1. ___ El término *cocina fusión* fue inventado por unos chefs en Estados Unidos.
2. ___ El artículo afirma que la cocina fusión se limita a la combinación de influencias asiáticas en la cocina del Oeste.
3. ___ La cocina peruana incorpora influencias culinarias de muchos países.
4. ___ Llegaron inmigrantes chinos a Perú en el siglo XVIII.
5. ___ Los chinos en el Perú han mantenido su tradición culinaria sin cambios.
6. ___ El Chifa es un término que se refiere a la cocina chino-peruana.
7. ___ La cocina Tex-Mex es igual a la cocina mexicana.
8. ___ Se usa menos carne y menos queso en la cocina Tex-Mex que en la cocina mexicana tradicional.
9. ___ Los nachos y las fajitas son invenciones de la cocina Tex-Mex.
10. ___ El chile con carne que se come en San Antonio, Texas usa especias similares a las que se usan en Marruecos, en el norte de África.

**10-41 Segunda mirada.** Busque en el artículo palabras que se asocien con lo siguiente.

1. dos sinónimos de *fusión culinaria*: _____

2. carnes: _____

3. Asia: _____

4. platos de la cocina Chifa: _____

5. platos de la cocina Tex-Mex: _____

6. referencias a países: _____

## Después de leer

 **10-42 Ampliación. PRIMERA FASE.** Preparen una lista de platos que ustedes comen o que han visto en restaurantes que, en la opinión del grupo, son ejemplos de la cocina fusión. Luego, seleccionen uno de estos platos.

**SEGUNDA FASE.** Preparen una presentación sobre el plato y sus antecedentes culinarios y preséntenla a la clase. Recuerden de dirigirse a su público cuando hacen la presentación.

# VOCABULARIO

**Las especias y los condimentos** — *Spices and seasonings*

| | |
|---|---|
| el aceite | oil |
| el aderezo | salad dressing |
| el azúcar | sugar |
| las especias | spices |
| las hierbas | herbs |
| la mayonesa | mayonnaise |
| la mostaza | mustard |
| la pimienta | pepper |
| la sal | salt |
| la salsa de tomate | tomato sauce |
| la vainilla | vanilla |
| el vinagre | vinegar |

**Las frutas y las verduras** — *Fruits and vegetables*

| | |
|---|---|
| el aguacate | avocado |
| el ajo | garlic |
| la cebolla | onion |
| la cereza | cherry |
| las espinacas | spinach |
| la fresa | strawberry |
| el limón | lemon |
| el maíz | corn |
| la manzana | apple |
| el maracuyá | passion fruit |
| el melón | melon |
| la papaya | papaya |
| el pepino | cucumber |
| la pera | pear |
| el pimiento verde | green pepper |
| la piña | pineapple |
| el plátano/la banana | banana, plantain |
| la toronja/el pomelo | grapefruit |
| la uva | grape |
| la zanahoria | carrot |

**El pescado y la carne** — *Fish and meat*

| | |
|---|---|
| las aves | poultry, fowl |
| el camarón/la gamba | shrimp |
| la carne | meat |
| molida/picada | ground meat |
| de res | beef/steak |
| el cerdo | pork |
| la chuleta | chop |
| el cordero | lamb |
| la costilla | rib |
| la langosta | lobster |
| los mariscos | shellfish |
| la oveja | sheep |
| el pavo | turkey |

**Otros productos** — *Other products*

| | |
|---|---|
| los churros | fried dough |
| la crema | cream |
| el dulce | candy/sweets |
| la galleta | cookie |
| la harina | flour |
| la leche de coco | coconut milk |
| las legumbres | legumes |
| las lentejas | lentils |
| la manteca/la mantequilla | butter |
| la margarina | margarine |
| el pan dulce | bun, small cake |
| el pastel | pastry |
| el queso crema | cream cheese |
| el yogur | yogurt |

**En la mesa** — *On the table*

| | |
|---|---|
| la bandeja | tray |
| la botella | bottle |
| la copa | (stemmed) glass |
| la cuchara | spoon |
| la cucharita | teaspoon |
| el cuchillo | knife |
| el mantel | tablecloth |
| el plato | plate, dish |
| la servilleta | napkin |
| la taza | cup |
| el tenedor | fork |
| el vaso | glass |

**Verbos** — *Verbs*

| | |
|---|---|
| agregar/añadir | to add |
| batir | to beat |
| disfrutar | to enjoy |
| freír (i) | to fry |
| hervir (ie, i) | to boil |
| probar (ue) | to try, to taste |
| recomendar (ie) | to recommend |

**Las descripciones** — *Descriptions*

| | |
|---|---|
| agrio/a | sour |
| lácteo/a | dairy (product) |

**Palabras y expresiones útiles** — *Useful words and expressions*

| | |
|---|---|
| el campesino/la campesina | peasant |
| la receta | recipe |
| todavía | still, yet |
| ya | already |

See *Lengua* boxes on p. 329 and on p. 352 for additional food vocabulary.

# *La salud es lo primero*

**Sin título, del pintor cubano Wilfredo Lam (1902-1982)**
Source: Super Stock, Inc./ARS

# In this chapter you will learn how to:

- discuss health and medical treatments
- talk about the body
- express emotions, opinions, expectations, and wishes

## Cultural focus: Cuba, República Dominicana

OCÉANO
ATLÁNTICO

La Habana
Pinar del Río
El Malecón de la Habana
Cienfuegos
**CUBA**
Camagüey
Un mojito cubano
Santiago de Cuba   Guantánamo

REPÚBLICA
DOMINICANA
Puerto Plata
Sabana de
HAITI   Santiago   La Mar
San Juan
Santo
Domingo
La playa de Punta Cana
Punta Cana
Isla
Saona

Mar Caribe

JAMAICA

La Catedral de Santo Domingo

Paracaidismo en
el Isla Saona

**A vista de pájaro.** Compruebe lo que sabe sobre Cuba y República Dominicana contestando las siguientes preguntas.

1. ¿Cuál es la capital de Cuba?
2. ¿Qué país limita por tierra (*land*) con República Dominicana?
3. ¿Qué lugar de República Dominicana es muy popular entre los turistas?
4. ¿Con qué tres ingredientes se prepara el mojito cubano?
5. ¿Cuáles son algunas de las industrias más importantes de esta región?
6. ¿Cuál es el deporte favorito en estos países?

363

CD 5
Track 18

## Médicos, farmacias y hospitales

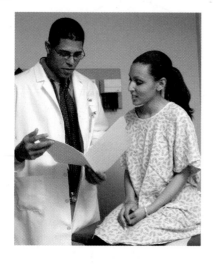

En la mayor parte de los países hispanos existen **hospitales, clínicas** y **centros de salud** financiados por el **gobierno** donde los **enfermos** pueden ir sin tener que pagar nada por los servicios o **medicinas** que reciben.

En las **farmacias** se venden todo tipo de **remedios** y **artículos de belleza**. Al igual que en Estados Unidos, en muchos lugares se necesita tener **receta** médica para comprar **antibióticos**. Muchas veces los clientes de la farmacia le preguntan **al farmacéutico/a la farmacéutica** qué remedio deben comprar para **curar** o **tratar** su **enfermedad**.

Esta enfermera le toma la **tensión/presión arterial** a una **paciente** en un **sanatorio**.

Algunas personas prefieren curarse con hierbas medicinales. Por ejemplo, para el **dolor de estómago** se recomienda tomar un té de manzanilla (*chamomile*) o un té de ruda (*rue*). Otra hierba medicinal muy conocida es la uña de gato (*cat's claw*), que se considera buena para el **tratamiento** del **cáncer**.

### Cultura

Los indígenas del continente americano nos han transmitido muchos conocimientos de medicina natural. Gracias al conocimiento que tenían de hierbas, animales y minerales, los indígenas elaboraban remedios que utilizaban contra las fiebres o como antídotos para otros males. Conocían los efectos positivos de los baños e infusiones de hierbas y tenían fórmulas para cerrar las heridas (*wounds*) y curar las úlceras. También trataban fracturas de huesos, aplicando una pasta de semillas, polvo de ciertas plantas y resina. Acompañaban muchas de estas prácticas con ceremonias en las que invocaban a sus dioses, pidiéndoles protección y ayuda.

**11-1 Definiciones.** Complete las siguientes oraciones con las palabras apropiadas.

1. En las _____ se venden medicinas y productos de belleza.
2. El té de manzanilla se recomienda para el _____ de estómago.
3. Los/Las _____ ayudan a los médicos en los hospitales y cuidan de los enfermos.
4. Según la creencia popular las _____ medicinales pueden curar las enfermedades.
5. Los/Las _____ les venden a sus clientes los remedios que necesitan.
6. El _____ financia muchos hospitales y centros de salud en los países hispanos.
7. Los/Las _____ son las personas que sufren enfermedades.
8. Algunas personas piensan que la uña de gato es un buen tratamiento contra el _____.

**11-2 Conversación.** PRIMERA FASE. Háganse las siguientes preguntas para intercambiar información.

1. Cuando necesitas una operación o tienes un accidente, ¿adónde vas? ¿Tienes que pagar o no?
2. ¿Hay muchos hospitales en tu ciudad? ¿Cómo se llaman?
3. Cuando estás enfermo/a y necesitas medicinas, ¿adónde vas a comprarlas? ¿Qué necesitas del médico/de la médica para poder comprarlas?
4. ¿Qué venden en las farmacias de tu país? ¿En qué farmacia compras normalmente?
5. ¿Usas hierbas medicinales? ¿Para qué las usas? ¿Alguien en tu familia las usa?
6. ¿Te interesa la medicina alternativa? ¿Alguna vez usaste la acupuntura, la homeopatía o alguna otra? ¿Cómo fue tu experiencia?

> **En otras palabras**
>
> In some Spanish-speaking countries, the word **sanatorio** is used instead of **hospital**; in others, **sanatorio** connotes a hospital that specializes in pulmonary and respiratory diseases. In some countries **clínica** refers to a private hospital. **Hospital** may refer to a government- or church-run facility that may provide free medical care.

SEGUNDA FASE. En Cuba y en otros países hispanoamericanos, hay una Academia de Ciencias que protege la investigación y organiza numerosas actividades relacionadas con la salud, la botánica, la física y otras áreas. Busquen en Internet la siguiente información sobre la Academia de Ciencias de Cuba y preparen un breve informe:

1. cuándo se fundó
2. los nombres de tres instituciones que se relacionan con ella
3. alguna de las actividades que organiza

**11-3 Una emergencia.** PRIMERA FASE. Usted y su amigo/a están de viaje en República Dominicana, y su amigo/a tiene un problema de salud. En un cibercafé de Santo Domingo, han encontrado este anuncio con información sobre médicos y farmacias de turno. Decidan cuál es el número más apropiado para llamar, basándose en el problema médico de su amigo/a.

SEGUNDA FASE. Haga la llamada para pedir la dirección del consultorio o de la farmacia. El/La recepcionista le debe explicar cómo llegar allí.

# Las partes del cuerpo

CD 5
Track 19

el pelo/cabello
la cara
la frente
la boca
el hombro
los dedos
la oreja
la espalda
el brazo
el codo
el pecho
la muñeca
la cintura
la cadera
la mano
la rodilla
la pierna
el tobillo
el pie

el cerebro
los nervios
los pulmones
el corazón
los músculos
el estómago
el hueso
las venas
la sangre

la cabeza
la ceja
la mejilla
las pestañas
el ojo
la nariz
los labios
los dientes
el cuello

**11-4 Asociación. PRIMERA FASE.** Indique en qué parte del cuerpo se ponen estos accesorios y esta ropa.

1. ____ los calcetines
2. ____ los guantes
3. ____ el cinturón
4. ____ el collar
5. ____ los aretes
6. ____ el reloj

a. la muñeca
b. la cintura
c. las orejas
d. el cuello
e. los pies
f. las manos

**SEGUNDA FASE.** Digan qué accesorios de la lista en la *Primera fase* no tienen ustedes y mencionen tres que consideren indispensables. Comparen sus respuestas.

**11-5 ¿Para qué sirve(n)?** Lean las siguientes definiciones y asócienlas con la parte del cuerpo correspondiente.

| | |
|---|---|
| los brazos | la nariz |
| el cerebro | los ojos |
| el corazón | las piernas |
| los dientes | los pulmones |
| las manos | la sangre |

1. _____ unen las manos con el cuerpo.
2. _____ permiten que las personas vean.
3. _____ toman el oxígeno del aire y lo pasan a la sangre.
4. _____ es un líquido rojo que circula por el cuerpo.
5. _____ unen el cuerpo con los pies.
6. _____ se deben lavar después de comer.
7. _____ están al final de los brazos.
8. _____ le da órdenes al cuerpo.
9. _____ impulsa la sangre por las venas del cuerpo.
10. _____ está entre la frente y la boca.

**11-6 Partes del cuerpo.** PRIMERA FASE. Indiquen qué parte(s) del cuerpo probablemente se relaciona(n) con cada una de las siguientes situaciones.

| SITUACIÓN | PARTE DEL CUERPO |
|---|---|
| 1. A Felipe le gusta escuchar música muy fuerte. | |
| 2. María se maquilla todos los días. | |
| 3. Necesito ponerme gafas porque veo mal. | |
| 4. Un futbolista le pasa la pelota a un compañero de su equipo. | |
| 5. Se necesita mucha agilidad para tocar el piano. | |
| 6. Esta paciente ha perdido 30 libras. Los pantalones le quedan anchos. | |
| 7. Daniela lleva siempre muchas pulseras. | |
| 8. El té de hierbas es muy bueno para la digestión. | |

SEGUNDA FASE. Ahora inventen ustedes dos adivinanzas cada uno/a para hacer asociaciones con partes del cuerpo.

MODELO:  E1: *sirven para besar (*to kiss)
         E2: *los labios*

# La salud

**CD 5
Track 20**

### Jorgito está enfermo

| | |
|---|---|
| SRA. VILLA: | Jorgito, **tienes muy mala cara. ¿Estás enfermo?** |
| JORGITO: | **Me siento** muy mal y **tengo dolor de garganta.** Anoche tosí mucho. |
| SRA. VILLA: | (Le pone el **termómetro.**) Tienes 39 grados de **fiebre.** Enseguida voy a llamar a la Dra. Bosque. |
| | [En la clínica…] |
| DOCTORA: | Vamos a ver, Jorgito. Cuéntame cómo te sientes. |
| JORGITO: | Ahora **me duele** la cabeza y también me duelen los **oídos.** Además **estornudo** mucho. |
| DOCTORA: | Vamos a **examinarte** los oídos y la garganta. Abre bien la boca y di "Ah". Tienes una **infección.** No es **grave,** pero es necesario que **te cuides.** |
| JORGITO: | Doctora, no quiero que me ponga una **inyección.** |
| DOCTORA: | ¡No, qué va! Te voy a **recetar** unas **pastillas.** Debes tomarlas **cada cuatro horas.** |
| JORGITO: | Está bien, doctora. |
| DOCTORA: | Además, tienes **gripe.** Debes descansar y beber mucho líquido. Aquí está la receta, señora. |
| SRA. VILLA: | Gracias, doctora. |

**11-7 La enfermedad de Jorgito.** Complete la tabla con la información correcta.

| SÍNTOMAS | RECOMENDACIONES | NOMBRE Y ESPECIALIDAD DE LA MÉDICA |
|---|---|---|
| | | |

## ¿Qué les pasa a estas personas?

CD 5
Track 21

Juan **se torció** el tobillo.     Joaquín **se cayó** y **se fracturó** el brazo.

**11-8 Remedios y consejos.** Usted es médico/a y va a aconsejar remedios a sus pacientes. Primero, escoja la mejor recomendación. Luego compare sus respuestas con las de su compañero/a, y piensen en otras dos sugerencias.

1. Su paciente tiene una infección en los ojos. Le recomiendo…
   **a.** nadar en la piscina.     **b.** tomar antibióticos.     **c.** leer mucho.

2. Su paciente tiene fiebre y le duele el cuerpo. Le aconsejo…
   **a.** descansar y tomar aspirinas.     **b.** comer mucho y caminar.     **c.** ir a su trabajo.

3. Su paciente se torció un tobillo. Le sugiero…
   **a.** correr todos los días.     **b.** tomar clases de baile.     **c.** descansar y no caminar.

4. Su paciente se fracturó un brazo. Le recomiendo…
   **a.** jugar al tenis.     **b.** no usar el ordenador por una semana.     **c.** hacer ejercicio.

**11-9 ¿A quién debo llamar?** Lea los anuncios a continuación. Luego, explíquele a su compañero/a sus síntomas o lo que usted necesita. Él/Ella le va a decir a quién debe llamar de acuerdo con la información de los anuncios.

MODELO:     necesitar un examen médico para el trabajo.
   E1:  *Necesito un examen médico para el trabajo.*
   E2:  *Debes llamar a la Dra. Corona López.*

**Dr. Fco. Javier Amador Cumplido**
*Cirugía y enfermedades de los ojos*
**86-43-57**
Consultorio 204

**Dra. Silvia Corona López**
*Medicina Interna*
**86-51-49**

*Clínica de Asma y Alergias*
*Dr. Rubén Shturman*
Amsterdam 219-A
2º piso
294-3866
584-0153

**Dr. Héctor Molina Oviedo**
*Psiquiatra*
**86-51-49**
Consultorio 402

**Dr. Jaime A. Rodríguez Peláez**
*Pediatra*
Niños y Adolescentes
**86-17-15**

**Dra. Gabriela Jacobo de Alcaraz**
Cirujano Dentista
**86-48-44**
Consultorio 314

**Dr. Raúl Elguezábal R.**
**Medicina Familiar y Cirugía**
86-34-73 EU.
428-4846
**Consultorio 309**

1. dolerle la cabeza cuando lee o mira televisión
2. sentirse triste y deprimido/a
3. estar enfermo/a y tener fiebre
4. no poder dormir
5. no poder respirar bien y tener la piel (*skin*) irritada
6. dolerle los dientes cuando come
7. buscar un médico/una médica para un sobrino de cinco años
8. …

**11-10 En el consultorio.** Usted tiene un catarro terrible y va a ver a su médico/a. Dígale cómo se siente y pregúntele qué debe hacer. El médico/La médica debe hacerle alguna recomendación y contestar sus preguntas.

MODELO:  E1: *Me siento… /Tengo…*
E2: *Creo que…*
E1: *¿Es bueno comer muchas frutas y verduras?*
E2: *Es excelente comer frutas y verduras porque tienen muchas vitaminas.*

**11-11 Me duele mucho.** You will listen to a young man talk to his father about how he feels after hurting his toe. Before you listen, list two symptoms you think he probably has.

CD 5
Track 22

Now, pay attention to the general idea of what is said. As you listen, circle the letter that indicates the appropriate ending to each statement.

1. Esteban tiene…
   a. una infección en el dedo.
   b. mucho dolor.
   c. fiebre.

2. El padre de Esteban cree que…
   a. su hijo se ha fracturado el dedo del pie.
   b. Esteban debe acostarse.
   c. es necesario que Esteban ponga hielo en el pie.

3. El padre de Esteban quiere…
   a. que Esteban descanse y se cuide.
   b. llevar a Esteban al hospital.
   c. que Esteban tome una aspirina.

4. El padre de Esteban le dice que…
   a. lo ayuda a caminar para llevarlo al hospital.
   b. decida si prefiere descansar o ir al hospital.
   c. el médico puede verlo esa tarde.

5. Esteban decide…
   a. no escuchar a su padre.
   b. jugar al fútbol al día siguiente.
   c. ir al hospital con su padre.

# EN ACCIÓN

## Diarios de bicicleta: El "accidente"

### Antes de ver

**11-12** Empareje los síntomas de la izquierda con las sugerencias de la derecha.

1. ___ Me duele el estómago.
2. ___ Me torcí el tobillo.
3. ___ Me duele una muela.
4. ___ Tengo fiebre.

a. Tome mucho líquido.
b. Vaya al dentista.
c. Póngase hielo.
d. No coma nada.

### Mientras ve

**11-13** Indique si Javier (**J**) o Gabi (**G**) menciona los siguientes problemas de salud.

1. ___ Tengo catarro.
2. ___ Tengo gripe.
3. ___ Estoy tosiendo.
4. ___ Me torcí el tobillo.

### Después de ver

**11-14** Al final del segmento, Gabi y Javier se dan cuenta de que se han mentido (*they have lied to each other*). Con un compañero/una compañera, haga un diálogo que ilustre qué pasa ahora entre los dos.

page

x

# FUNCIONES Y FORMAS

## 1. Expressing expectations and hopes: Introduction to the present subjunctive

PABLO: ¿Qué me recomienda, doctor?

MÉDICO: Le **recomiendo** que **tome** agua y caldo de pollo. **Quiero** que **duerma** mucho y que no **vaya** a clase.

ALICIA: ¿Qué dice el médico?

PABLO: **Dice** que **me quede** en cama. También **quiere** que tú me **prepares** un caldo de pollo, que **limpies** mi apartamento, que me **traigas** helado...

**Mas tarde...**

**Piénselo.** Para cada oración, marque (✓) quién recomienda (**R**) la acción y quién va a hacer (**H**) la acción.

|  | MÉDICO | PABLO | ALICIA |
|---|---|---|---|
| 1. Le **recomiendo** que **tome** agua y caldo de pollo. | ___ | ___ | ___ |
| 2. **Quiere** que tú me **prepares** un caldo de pollo. | ___ | ___ | ___ |
| 3. **Deseo** que **duerma** mucho. | ___ | ___ | ___ |
| 4. **Dice** que **me quede** en cama. | ___ | ___ | ___ |
| 5. **Quiere** que **limpies** mi apartamento. | ___ | ___ | ___ |
| 6. **Quiere** que me **traigas** helado. | ___ | ___ | ___ |

■ To form the present subjunctive, use the **yo** form of the present indicative, drop the final **-o** and add the subjunctive ending. Notice that as with the endings of the **usted/ustedes** commands, **-ar** verbs change the **-a** to **-e**, while **-er** and **-ir** verbs change the **e** and the **i** to **a**.

|  | HABLAR | COMER | VIVIR |
|---|---|---|---|
| yo | hable | coma | viva |
| tú | hables | comas | vivas |
| Ud., él, ella | hable | coma | viva |
| nosotros/as | hablemos | comamos | vivamos |
| vosotros/as | habléis | comáis | viváis |
| Uds., ellos/as | hablen | coman | vivan |

■ The present subjunctive of the following verbs with irregular indicative **yo** forms is as follows:

conocer: cono**zca**, cono**zcas**...          salir: sal**ga**, sal**gas**...

decir: di**ga**, di**gas**...          tener: ten**ga**, ten**gas**...

hacer: ha**ga**, ha**gas**...          traer: tra**iga**, tra**igas**...

oír: o**iga**, o**igas**...          venir: ven**ga**, ven**gas**...

poner: pon**ga**, pon**gas**...          ver: **vea**, **veas**...

■ The present subjunctive of **hay** is **haya**. The following verbs also have irregular subjunctive forms:

dar: **dé, des**...          saber: **sepa, sepas**...

estar: **esté, estés**...          ser: **sea, seas**...

ir: **vaya, vayas**...

■ Stem-changing **-ar** and **-er** verbs follow the same pattern as the present indicative.

pensar: p**ie**nse, p**ie**nses, p**ie**nse, pensemos, penséis, p**ie**nsen
volver: v**ue**lva, v**ue**lvas, v**ue**lva, volvamos, volváis, v**ue**lvan

■ Stem-changing **-ir** verbs follow the same pattern as the present indicative but have an additional change in the **nosotros/as** and **vosotros/as** forms.

preferir: pref**ie**ra, pref**ie**ras, pref**ie**ra, pref**i**ramos, pref**i**ráis, pref**ie**ran
dormir: d**ue**rma, d**ue**rmas, d**ue**rma, d**u**rmamos, d**u**rmáis, d**ue**rman

■ Verbs ending in **-car, -gar, -ger, -zar**, and **-guir** have spelling changes.

sacar: sa**que**, sa**ques**, sa**que**, sa**que**mos, sa**qué**is, sa**quen**
jugar: jue**gue**, jue**gues**, jue**gue**, ju**gue**mos, ju**gué**is, jue**guen**
recoger: reco**ja**, reco**jas**, reco**ja**, reco**ja**mos, reco**já**is, reco**jan**
almorzar: almuer**ce**, almuer**ces**, almuer**ce**, almor**ce**mos, almor**cé**is, almuer**cen**
seguir: s**iga**, s**igas**, s**iga**, s**iga**mos, s**igá**is, s**igan**

**Lengua**

Remember that you have seen these same orthographic changes in the formal commands:

**Saque los platos.**

**No jueguen ahora.**

■ Notice in the examples below that there are two clauses, each with a different subject. When the verb of the main clause expresses a wish or hope, use a subjunctive verb form in the dependent clause (the clause that begins with **que**).

| MAIN CLAUSE | DEPENDENT CLAUSE |
|---|---|
| La doctora **quiere** | que Alfredo **respire** profundamente. |
| *The doctor wants* | *Alfredo to breathe deeply.* |
| Yo **espero** | que Alfredo no **tenga** asma. |
| *I hope* | *Alfredo doesn't have asthma.* |

■ When there is only one subject, use the infinitive instead of the subjunctive.

| | |
|---|---|
| Lola **necesita llamar** a la farmacia para pedir una medicina. | *Lola has to call the pharmacy to order some medicine.* |
| Ella **quiere recogerla** esta tarde. | *She wants to pick it up this afternoon.* |
| **Desea recogerla** antes de las tres. | *She wants to pick it up before 3:00.* |

■ Some common verbs that express expectations, wants and hopes are **desear, esperar, necesitar, preferir,** and **querer.**

| | |
|---|---|
| Los residentes del barrio prefieren que la clínica no **cierre** antes de las siete. | *The residents of the neighborhood prefer that the clinic not close before seven o'clock.* |
| La niña espera que el enfermero no le **ponga** una inyección. | *The girl hopes that the nurse will not give her a shot.* |

■ The expression **ojalá (que)** (*I/we hope [that]*), which comes from Arabic, originally meaning *May Allah grant that . . .* , is always followed by the subjunctive.

| | |
|---|---|
| Ojalá (que) ellos **vengan** temprano. | *I hope (that) they will come early.* |
| Ojalá (que) **puedas** llevarme a la cita con la médica. | *I hope (that) you can take me to the doctor's appointment.* |

**11-15 Comentarios y deseos.** Los miembros del Club de Estudiantes de Pre-Medicina están hablando de la fiesta que van a dar mañana. ¿Cuáles de las afirmaciones siguientes probablemente son comentarios de ellos? Márquelas (✔).

1. ____ Queremos que la fiesta empiece puntualmente.
2. ____ Ojalá que no sirvan comida.
3. ____ Preferimos que pongan música caribeña, porque queremos bailar salsa y merengue.
4. ____ Esperamos que también asistan estudiantes de odontología (*dentistry*) y de enfermería.
5. ____ Necesitamos que la fiesta termine temprano.
6. ____ Deseamos que nuestros profesores vayan a la fiesta.
7. ____ Queremos que todos recojan la basura después de la fiesta.
8. ____ Ojalá que nos divirtamos.

**11-16 Trabajo voluntario en el hospital.** PRIMERA FASE. Unos estudiantes trabajan de voluntarios en el hospital. ¿Qué espera la directora del programa de voluntarios que hagan estas personas? Túrnense para hablar sobre cada escena.

MODELO:  Elena: llevar flores/conversar con los pacientes
E1:  *La directora espera que Elena les lleve flores a los pacientes.*
E2:  *También espera que Elena converse con los pacientes. Algunos pacientes se sienten muy solos.*

**1.**

José y Camila: jugar con los niños/hablar con los padres de los niños/leerles libros infantiles a los niños

**2.**

Marisa: trabajar en la tienda de regalos/hacerles recomendaciones a los clientes/poner flores frescas en el mostrador de la tienda

**3.**

Sofía y Eduardo: conversar con los familiares de los pacientes/ofrecerles café/darles almohadas si quieren dormir mientras esperan

SEGUNDA FASE. ¿Qué más esperan los pacientes que hagan los voluntarios en el hospital? Escriban una lista de cuatro cosas más como mínimo.

MODELO: *Los pacientes esperan que los voluntarios les traigan su comida.*

**11-17 Se abre la Clínica de la Familia.** Se abre una nueva clínica en una semana y usted está ayudando con los preparativos. Haga una lista de las cosas que usted necesita hacer y otra lista de lo que espera que hagan los empleados indicados en la tabla. Después, compare su lista con la de su compañero/a.

MODELO:  E1:  *Necesito pintar la sala de espera.*
E2:  *Y yo necesito limpiar los pisos.*
E1:  *Espero que los carpinteros terminen su trabajo esta semana.*
E2:  *Y yo espero que los empleados lleguen a tiempo.*

| LO QUE YO NECESITO HACER | LO QUE ESPERO QUE HAGAN |
|---|---|
| _____ | los médicos:_____ |
| _____ | los enfermeros:_____ |
| _____ | el/la recepcionista:_____ |
| _____ | el/la chofer de la ambulancia:_____ |

## More about the present subjunctive

- Verbs that express an intention to influence the actions of others (**aconsejar, pedir, permitir, prohibir, recomendar**) also require the subjunctive in the dependent clause. With these verbs, Spanish speakers often use an indirect object.

El médico **le** recomienda que no **salga** por unos días.

*The doctor recommends that he not go out for a few days.*

La enfermera **me** aconseja que no **coma** por una hora.

*The nurse advises me not to eat for an hour.*

- You may also try to impose your will or express your influence, wishes, and hopes through some impersonal expressions such as **es necesario, es importante, es bueno,** and **es mejor**.

Es necesario que los atletas **duerman** un mínimo de siete horas por noche.

*It is necessary that the athletes sleep a minimum of seven hours a night.*

Es mejor que **coman** pescado y pollo, porque tienen menos grasa que la carne de res.

*It is better that they eat fish or chicken, because they have less fat than beef.*

- If you are not addressing or speaking about someone in particular, use the infinitive.

Es mejor **comer** pescado y pollo.

*It is better to eat fish and chicken.*

- With the verb **decir**, use the subjunctive in the dependent clause when expressing a wish or an order. Use the indicative when reporting information.

Dice que los atletas **consumen** mucha proteína. (*report information*)

*She says (that) the athletes consume a lot of protein.*

Dice que los atletas **consuman** mucha proteína. (*express an order*)

*She tells the athletes to eat a lot of protein.*

 **11-18 Normas de conducta en el trabajo.** PRIMERA FASE. Su amiga Rebeca tiene un trabajo nuevo como recepcionista y le pide a usted consejos sobre las normas de conducta. Indique (✓) sus recomendaciones y luego, compárelas con las recomendaciones de su compañero/a.

| | SE PROHÍBE | SE PERMITE | SE RECOMIENDA |
|---|---|---|---|
| 1. fumar | | | |
| 2. comer chocolates | | | |
| 3. hablar por teléfono con amigos | | | |
| 4. almorzar en la oficina | | | |
| 5. conversar con los pacientes | | | |
| 6. llevar vaqueros | | | |

SEGUNDA FASE. Piensen en un trabajo que tienen ahora o que tiene un miembro de su familia. Hagan una lista de las actividades que se prohíben, las que se permiten y las que se recomiendan. ¿Son semejantes o diferentes las normas en sus respectivos lugares de trabajo?

**11-19 Consejos y sugerencias.** Usted está organizando un nuevo programa en República Dominicana para estudiantes que quieren trabajar en las profesiones de salud. Explíqueles a dos compañeros los aspectos del programa que aún no están resueltos. Ellos le recomendarán qué hacer.

MODELO:  viajar a República Dominicana
E1: *Hay varias opciones: podemos viajar en grupo, o cada estudiante puede hacer su propia reservación.*
E2: *Es mejor que viajen en grupo, así se consigue mejor precio.*
E3: *Y también es importante que todos los estudiantes lleguen juntos.*

1. empezar clases de español
2. establecer conexiones con las clínicas en la capital
3. buscar alojamiento (*lodging*)
4. escoger actividades de ocio (*free time*)

**11-20 Excursión a República Dominicana.** PRIMERA FASE. Su clase está planeando una excursión a la playa Boca Chica en República Dominicana. Primero, busquen en Internet la siguiente información y coméntenla entre ustedes.

1. localización
2. clima
3. lugares de interés
4. tipo de alojamiento
5. tipo de transporte para llegar allí
6. costo del viaje

SEGUNDA FASE. Ahora escriban una lista de todas las cosas que hay que hacer para preparar la excursión.

MODELO:  E1: *Es importante reservar los pasajes.*
E2: *Sí, y necesitamos comprar unas mochilas.*

TERCERA FASE. Por último, decidan qué quieren ustedes que haga cada persona de su grupo. Compartan la información con la clase.

MODELO:  reservar los pasajes
*Queremos que Juan reserve los pasajes.*

## SITUACIONES

1. **Role A.** You are sick today so you will miss the review session for the Spanish midterm. Call a classmate and a) say that you need him/her to take notes for you; b) give him/her advice about what you think is most important to write down; c) say when you want your friend to bring you the notes; and d) thank your friend.

   **Role B.** When a friend from your Spanish class calls to ask a favor, say that you will be happy to take notes for him/her. Ask a) when your friend wants you to bring over the notes; b) how your friend is feeling; and c) what the doctor's recommendations are. Say that it is important that your friend rest and that you hope he/she feels better soon.

2. **Role A.** You are allergic to (**ser alérgico/a a**) cats, and you have just come back from spending the weekend with your friend who has two cats. Now you have a headache, your eyes itch (**me pican los ojos**), your lungs hurt, and it is hard to breathe. Call the clinic to a) explain your situation; b) describe your symptoms; and c) ask what the nurse recommends that you do. Ask questions to be sure you understand the recommendations.

   **Role B.** You work as a nurse at the clinic, and someone calls for advice about an allergic reaction. Ask about the person's symptoms and offer advice about what he/she should do.

## 2. Expressing emotions, opinions, and attitudes: The subjunctive with expressions of emotion

ERNESTO:  **Me molesta** que **fumen.** Y no me gusta que **hablen** tan alto.

SARA:  **Estoy contenta de** que **se vayan** pronto. Ya han terminado de comer.

Ernesto    Sara

**Piénselo.**  Indique (✓) si cada verbo expresa un sentimiento o una acción.

| | VERBO/FRASE DE SENTIMIENTO | VERBO DE ACCIÓN |
|---|---|---|
| 1. **Les molesta** que **fumen.** | _____ | _____ |
| 2. No **les gusta** que **hablen** tan alto. | _____ | _____ |
| 3. **Están contentos de** que **se vayan** pronto. | _____ | _____ |
| 4. **Es triste** que **permitan** fumar en su restaurante. | _____ | _____ |
| 5. **Es una lástima** que **fumen** en la mesa, tan cerca de otra gente. | _____ | _____ |

■  When the verb of the main clause expresses emotion (e.g., fear, happiness, sorrow), use a subjunctive verb form in the dependent clause. Note that the subjects of the two clauses must be different.

| **Sentimos** mucho que el niño **tenga** fiebre. | *We are very sorry (that) the child has a fever.* |
| **Me alegro de** que **estés** con él. | *I am glad (that) you are with him.* |

■  Some common verbs that express emotion are **alegrarse (de), estar contento/a (de), sentir, gustar, encantar, molestar,** and **temer** (*to fear*).

■  Impersonal expressions and other expressions that show emotion are also followed by *que* + subjunctive.

| **Es triste que** el niño **esté** enfermo. | *It is sad that the child is sick.* |
| **¡Qué lástima que** no **pueda** ir a la fiesta! | *What a shame that he cannot go to the party!* |

**11-21 Un amigo enfermo.**  Asocie cada comentario sobre la enfermedad de su amigo con la reacción adecuada.

1. ____ Pedro está muy enfermo.
2. ____ Sus padres llegan hoy para estar con él.
3. ____ Creo que el doctor Pérez lo va a operar.
4. ____ Dicen que es una operación seria.
5. ____ No va a poder participar en el campeonato.

a. Me alegro de que vengan.
b. Siento mucho que esté tan mal.
c. ¡Qué bueno que sea ese el médico!
d. Es una lástima que no pueda jugar.
e. Ojalá que no tenga complicaciones.

**11-22 Una visita.** Usted está en la clínica, visitando a su compañero/a, a quien han operado de la rodilla. Él/Ella le cuenta sobre su experiencia en la clínica y cómo se siente. Escoja entre las expresiones de *En directo* para responderle. Intercambien papeles.

**MODELO:**  E1: *No me gusta la comida del hospital.*
E2: *Siento que la comida no sea buena. ¿Qué te sirven?*
E1: …

1. Me duele bastante la rodilla.
2. Tengo fiebre y dolor de cabeza.
3. Tengo dolor de estómago porque las medicinas son muy fuertes.
4. Tengo náuseas por los efectos de la anestesia.
5. Detesto estar en cama tanto tiempo.
6. La comida del hospital es malísima.
7. Las enfermeras vienen a verme cada media hora.
8. La cirujana que me operó es muy simpática.

**11-23 Reacciones.** Luisa y Rafael llegan temprano a su trabajo en el hospital. Su compañero/a le va a decir lo que ellos piensan hacer la semana próxima. Reaccione usando las expresiones de *En directo*. Después cambien de papel.

**MODELO:**  Luisa / no desayunar
E1: *Luisa no va a desayunar.*
E2: *No me gusta que Luisa no desayune. Temo que no tenga energía.*

| PERSONAS | LUNES | MIÉRCOLES | VIERNES | DOMINGO |
|---|---|---|---|---|
| Luisa | empezar una dieta | ir al gimnasio | hacer ejercicio en su casa | caminar 2 kms |
| Rafael | trabajar en el hospital todo el día | salir del hospital temprano para ir al cine | quedarse en su casa | reunirse con sus amigos |

**11-24 ¿Qué me molesta? PRIMERA FASE.** Haga una lista de los hábitos de otras personas que le molestan. Compare su lista con la de su compañero/a.

**MODELO:** *Me molesta que mis amigos lleguen tarde.*

**SEGUNDA FASE.** En pequeños grupos, comparen sus listas y escojan los seis hábitos que les molestan más a todos en el grupo. Digan por qué. Compartan sus resultados con el resto de la clase.

### En directo

To express empathy:
**Siento que…**
**Me alegro de que…**
**Temo que…**
**Espero que…**
**No me gusta que…**
**¡Qué agradable que…**

### SITUACIONES

1. **Role A.** Recently you decided to join an aerobics class (**clase de ejercicios aeróbicos**). You are also following a healthful diet and you feel great. When you run into a friend whom you have not seen for some time, you try to convince him/her to join you in your exercise class.

   **Role B.** You run into a friend whom you have not seen for some time. Say that he/she looks (**verse**) great, and ask what he/she is doing. Inquire a) how many times a week he/she goes to aerobics class (**clase de ejercicios aeróbicos**); b) how she feels about the class; and c) what he/she likes and doesn't like about his/her new plan for eating better. He/She will try to persuade you to join the program.

2. **Role A.** You have gone to your doctor for a physical examination. Describe your symptoms and your lifestyle (**vida activa**, **vida sedentaria**). Respond to the doctor's reactions and recommendations with questions and comments.

   **Role B.** You are a doctor doing a routine physical examination. As the patient talks, you a) ask pertinent questions; b) express approval or disapproval of the patient's lifestyle; and c) give advice or prescribe medication. Respond to the patient's comments about your recommendations.

### 3. Expressing goals, purposes, and means: Uses of *por* and *para*

**Vive más por unos pasos más por día**

- **Para** vivir más no necesitas más dinero. No pagues miles de pesos **por** aparatos de ejercicio. ¡Muévete!
- Sube a tu clase u oficina **por** las escaleras; no tomes el ascensor.
- Camina **para** tu tienda favorita.
- Si caminas 30 minutos **por** día vivirás más. Pasea **por** el parque con tus amigos o tu familia y guarda tu dinero **para** cosas necesarias.
- Relájate mientras caminas al aire libre y vive con menos estrés **por** ti y **para** ti.

**Piénselo.** Indique si las afirmaciones son ciertas (**C**) o falsas (**F**), según la información en el panfleto. Luego escoja el significado de **por** o **para** que corresponde a cada afirmación y escríbalo en el espacio indicado.

a causa de algo o alguien      en dirección a un lugar

en beneficio de alguien      medio de transporte

duración      objetivo

| | CIERTO/FALSO | SIGNIFICADO DE POR/PARA |
|---|---|---|
| 1. **Para** tener una vida larga es importante mantenernos activos. | _____ | _____ |
| 2. Caminar **por** 30 minutos al día ayuda a vivir más años. | _____ | _____ |
| 3. Es mejor ir en automóvil cuando vamos **para** el supermercado y otras tiendas. | _____ | _____ |
| 4. Debemos relajarnos y vivir con menos estrés **por** nosotros mismos. | _____ | _____ |

- As you learned in *Capítulo 3*, the prepositions **por** and **para** have several meanings and uses. You have used them easily in some contexts in which they are similar to "for" in English, as in **Compré estas vitaminas *para* Anita** (*I bought these vitamins for Anita*).

■ Other uses of **por** and **para** that are not similar to English can be learned by grouping them into functional categories: expressions of movement, time, purpose, and means.

| POR | PARA |
|---|---|
| **MOVEMENT** | |
| ■ through or by a place<br>Caminaron **por** el hospital.<br>*They walked through the hospital.* | ■ toward a destination<br>Caminaron **para** el hospital.<br>*They walked toward the hospital.* |
| **TIME** | |
| ■ duration of an event<br>Estuvo con la médica **por** una hora.<br>*He was with the doctor for an hour.* | ■ deadline<br>Necesita el antibiótico **para** el martes.<br>*He needs the antibiotic by Tuesday.* |
| **PURPOSE** | |
| ■ reason or motive<br>Ana fue al consultorio **por** el dolor de garganta.<br>*Ana went to the doctor's office because of a sore throat.* | ■ for whom something is intended or done<br>Compró el antibiótico **para** Ana.<br>*He bought the antibiotic for Ana.* |

**Por** is also used to express the following:

■ means of transportation

Mandaron los órganos para el trasplante **por** avión.    *They sent the organs for the transplant by plane.*

■ exchange or substitution

Irma pagó $120 **por** las pastillas.    *Irma paid $120 for the pills.*

Cambió esas pastillas rojas **por** las amarillas.    *She exchanged those red pills for the yellow ones.*

■ unit or rate

Yo camino 5 kilómetros **por** hora.    *I walk 5 kilometers per hour.*

El seguro de salud cubre el sesenta **por** ciento de las cuentas.    *The health insurance covers 60 percent of the bills.*

■ object of an errand

Sara fue a la farmacia **por** jarabe para la tos.    *Sara went to the drugstore for the cough syrup.*

Pasamos **por** ti a las 5:00.    *We'll come by for you at 5:00.*

**Para** is also used to express the following:

■ judgment or point of view

**Para** nosotros, es la mejor farmacia.    *For us, this is the best drugstore.*

Es un caso difícil **para** un médico joven.    *It is a difficult case for a young doctor.*

■ intention or purpose, when followed by an infinitive

Fueron a la farmacia **para** comprar jarabe para la tos.    *They went to the drugstore to buy cough syrup.*

Come bien **para** vivir más.    *Eat well to live longer.*

**11-25 ¿Quieren decir *por* o *para*?** Trace un círculo alrededor de la preposición que debe usarse, según el significado entre paréntesis.

1. Salimos **por/para** el consultorio del médico a las nueve de la mañana. (*toward a destination*)
2. Fuimos **por/para** el túnel para llegar más rápido. (*through*)
3. Ana fue a ver al médico **por/para** su dolor de garganta y tos. (*reason or motive*)
4. El médico escribió la receta de un antibiótico **por/para** Ana. (*for whom it is intended*)
5. Yo fui a la farmacia **por/para** el antibiótico. (*object of an errand*)
6. ¿Cuánto pagaste **por/para** el antibiótico? (*exchange or substitution*)

 **11-26 En el laboratorio.** Túrnense para averiguar cuándo estarán listos los resultados del análisis (*test*) de unos pacientes. Consulten la tabla para obtener la información correcta.

MODELO:   Alfredo Benítez 2:00 de la tarde
    E1:   *¿Cuándo va a estar listo el análisis del Sr. Benítez?*
    E2:   *Va a estar listo para las dos de la tarde.*

| PACIENTE | RESULTADOS DEL ANÁLISIS |
|----------|--------------------------|
| Hilda Corvalán | 11:00 de la mañana |
| Alfonso González | esta tarde |
| Jorge Pérez Robles | 3:15 de la tarde |
| Aleida Miranda | mañana por la mañana |
| César Gómez Villegas | martes |
| Irene Santa Cruz | … |

 **11-27 Una cura del estrés.** Para curarse del estrés, el médico le recomienda a su amiga que pase quince días de descanso y relajación. Usted le aconseja que vaya a República Dominicana. Indíquele algunas actividades que ella puede hacer allí y el propósito de cada actividad. Use las actividades de la lista. Después cambien de papel.

comer mariscos y pescado

bailar en las calles

disfrutar del paisaje, la flora y
   la fauna

tomar clases de baile caribeño

ver los espectáculos con delfines y
   leones marinos

ver la puesta del sol

MODELO:   visitar el Museo Bacardí/aprender cómo se hace el ron cubano
    *Visita el Museo Bacardí en Santiago de Cuba para aprender cómo se hace el ron cubano.*

1. participar en el Carnaval de Santiago
2. ir al Acuario Nacional en La Habana
3. ir a la Escuela Danza y Movimiento de la Habana
4. caminar por el Malecón en la Habana
5. visitar el Valle de Viñales en Pinar del Río
6. salir a cenar en El Pescador en la playa de Santa Lucía

**11-28 La graduación de un nuevo médico.** Complete estos párrafos sobre la graduación de Fernando con **por** o **para**, según el contexto. Luego escoja la razón de su elección en la columna de la derecha.

El 14 de junio es la graduación de Fernando en la Facultad de Medicina de la Universidad Católica Madre y Maestra de Santiago de los Caballeros en República Dominicana. Sus padres, los señores Rovira, viven en Puerto Plata, pero van a Santiago (1.__) _____ asistir a la graduación y quieren llevarle un regalo. El lunes pasado fueron a una tienda y pagaron $100 (2.__) _____ un regalo muy bonito (3.__) _____ Fernando. Graciela, su hermana gemela, vive en Miami y no puede ir (4.__) _____ su trabajo. Ella también le compró un regalo y se lo envió (5.__) _____ avión porque quiere que llegue (6.__) _____ el día de la graduación.

El día 14, los padres de Fernando salieron (7.__) _____ la universidad. Estaba lloviendo, y (8.__) _____ eso salieron temprano. Normalmente, ellos pueden estar en la universidad en una hora más o menos, pero (9.__) _____ la lluvia, el viaje duró casi dos horas. (10.__) _____ ellos, que son mayores, el viaje fue un poco largo, pero al final pudieron pasar ese día con su hijo.

To express or indicate...

**a.** intention or purpose (with infinitive).
**b.** judgment or point of view.
**c.** means of transportation.
**d.** exchange or substitution.
**e.** toward a destination.
**f.** deadline.
**g.** for whom something is intended or done.
**h.** reason or motive.

## SITUACIONES

1. **Role A.** You hurt your ankle while playing soccer, so you go to the health center at your college or university. Tell the doctor that a) you fell while running to make a goal (**marcar un gol**); b) your ankle is swollen (**hinchado**); and c) you cannot walk. Ask questions and answer your doctor's questions.

   **Role B.** A patient comes see you with a sports injury. After you hear how the injury happened, ask a) what the coach did for him/her and b) how he/she got to the health center. After determining that the ankle is not broken, recommend that the patient a) rest for three or four days; b) take aspirin for the pain; and c) put ice on his/her ankle to reduce the swelling (**reducir la hinchazón**). Add that because of the injury, he/she should not play soccer for a month.

2. **Role A.** You want to rent a furnished apartment at the beach. You see a promising ad and call the landlord. Explain when you will need the apartment and for how long. Inquire about the rent, furnishings and the number of rooms.

   **Role B.** You are a landlord who is renting an apartment at the beach. A prospective renter calls you. Answer his/her questions and ask how many people will be staying at the apartment. Mention that the rent must be paid by the first of the month. Agree on a date and time to show the property.

## 4. Referring to people and things: Relative pronouns

### El perro, ¿el mejor amigo de los diabéticos?

**Científicos** irlandeses, **quienes** investigan la habilidad del perro para detectar los niveles de azúcar de los diabéticos, esperan probar que los caninos pueden ayudar a los **pacientes que** sufren de esta enfermedad a vigilar (*watch*) sus niveles de azúcar en la sangre.

Según los investigadores, los **perros, que** poseen un agudo sentido de olfato, pueden recibir entrenamiento para anticipar la hipoglucemia por su excelente olfato. Si los expertos prueban su hipótesis, los millones de **diabéticos que** existen alrededor del mundo se beneficiarán con este descubrimiento, especialmente los **diabéticos que** además son ciegos, sordos o **que** sufren de otras discapacidades.

**Piénselo.** Primero, compruebe si las siguientes afirmaciones son ciertas (**C**) o falsas (**F**) según el texto anterior. Luego indique a qué palabra se refiere el pronombre en negrita.

1. _____ Los científicos, **quienes** quieren probar su hipótesis sobre la capacidad de los perros para cuidar diabéticos, son franceses.
2. _____ Una persona diabética **que** no puede oír ni ver no podrá vivir independientemente sin la ayuda de estos perros.
3. _____ Los perros **que** vigilan el azúcar de los diabéticos son entrenados.
4. _____ La habilidad **que** tienen los perros para anticipar la baja de azúcar de los pacientes es maravillosa.
5. _____ La persona a **quien** ayuda el canino puede sufrir de una hipoglucemia, pero el canino la detectará con su olfato.

■ The relative pronouns **que** and **quien(es)** combine two clauses into one sentence.

| Los médicos trabajan en ese hospital. | *The doctors work at that hospital.* |
| Los médicos son excelentes. | *The doctors are excellent.* |
| Los médicos **que** trabajan en ese hospital son excelentes. | *The doctors who work at that hospital are excellent.* |

■ **Que** is the most commonly used relative pronoun. It introduces a dependent clause, and it may refer to persons or things.

| Las pastillas **que** tomo son muy caras. | *The pills that I take are very expensive.* |
| Ese es el médico **que** me receta las pastillas. | *That is the doctor who prescribes the pills for me.* |

■ **Quien(es)** refers only to persons and may replace **que** in a clause set off by commas.

| Los García, quienes/que viven en la ciudad, prefieren el campo | *The Garcías, who live in the city, prefer the country.* |

■ Use **quien(es)** after a preposition (**a, con, de, por, para,** etc.) when referring to people.

| Allí está el enfermero **con quien** hablé esta mañana. | *There is the nurse with whom I spoke this morning.* |
| Esos son los pacientes **a quienes** les debes dar la medicina. | *Those are the patients to whom you should give the medicine.* |

**11-29 Una telenovela dominicana.** Joaquín está enfermo hoy. Por eso, empezó a mirar una telenovela en la televisión. Le mandó un correo electrónico a su amigo Ramiro para contarle detalles de la telenovela. Complete el correo electrónico de Joaquín con **que** o **quien** para averiguar qué opina sobre la telenovela.

---

Hola Ramiro,

¡No me vas a creer! He mirado un episodio de la sensacional telenovela que están pasando en el canal 13. Te cuento lo que pasó por si te interesa.

*Mi corazón* es una telenovela dominicana (1) _____ tiene mucho público. El actor principal es Agustín Montalvo. Él es el actor de (2) _____ todos hablan. La crítica cree que este año va a ganar el premio Talía, (3) _____ es el equivalente del Óscar norteamericano. Muchas chicas dicen que Agustín es el actor con (4) _____ les gustaría salir. Agustín hace el papel del médico (5) _____ quiere salvar la vida de Silvina del Bosque, la actriz principal, (6) _____ tuvo un accidente terrible y está inconsciente. Agustín es el hombre al (7) _____ ella quiere, pero Agustín está enamorado de Esmeralda del Valle, una mujer a (8) _____ sólo le interesa el dinero de Agustín. La telenovela es muy melodramática y siempre hay problemas (9) _____ mantienen el interés del público.

Mírala y mañana y me cuentas qué piensas.

Chao,

Joaquín

---

**11-30 Mi dentista. PRIMERA FASE.** Dígale a su compañero/a cómo es su dentista. Mencione por lo menos tres características.

**MODELO:** *Mi dentista es... Es un dentista/una dentista que...*

**SEGUNDA FASE.** Conversen sobre su experiencia médica más reciente. Usen las preguntas como guía.

1. ¿Cuándo fue la última vez que usted visitó al/a la dentista?
2. ¿Le dio algunas recomendaciones que no le gustaron a usted? ¿Le recetó alguna medicina?
3. ¿Le gusta su dentista? ¿Por qué?

**11-31 El médico lo sabe todo.** Describan las siguientes escenas, pensando en las preguntas a continuación.

1. ¿Qué está haciendo el médico que está en la foto de la izquierda? ¿Y la médica en la foto de la derecha?
2. ¿Qué problema de salud tiene cada una de las niñas que están en las fotos?
3. ¿Qué diferencias hay entre las situaciones en las dos fotos?

# MOSAICOS

## ESTRATEGIA

### Listen for the main idea

Whether you are listening to a conversation, a brief news report, or a lecture, you need to understand the speaker's main points.

When listening for the main ideas, the following tips will prove useful:

1. Anticipate content using your knowledge of the topic and/or the context.
2. Before you start to listen, think about or jot down key words or concepts associated with the topic.
3. Pay attention to places where the main ideas usually occur:
   - before details or supporting examples
   - in the introduction, in repeated information, or in the conclusion
4. Listen for transitional phrases that signal main ideas, such as *Lo importante es...*, *Recuerde(n)...*, *Esto es lo importante...*, *Otro punto importante/central...*, etc.

## A escuchar

### Antes de escuchar

**11-32 Preparación.** Usted escuchará una conversación entre un nutricionista y un grupo de estudiantes universitarios hispanos. Antes de escuchar, escriba dos preguntas que los alumnos probablemente le harán al nutricionista y dos sugerencias que les dará el nutricionista.

posibles preguntas:
posibles consejos:

### Escuchar

**11-33 ¿Comprende usted?** First read the following statements and then listen to the exchange between the nutritionist and a group of college students. Mark (✓) the statements that best identify the main ideas of what you have heard.

CD 5
Track 23

1. _____ Consultar al médico una vez por año es importante para evitar enfermedades.
2. _____ El consumo de tomates, lechugas, uvas, naranjas, cerveza y carne de res es recomendable para tener energía.
3. _____ La buena alimentación y el ejercicio tienen un efecto positivo en la salud.
4. _____ Se recomienda comer bastante y hacer muchísimo ejercicio para mantener una vida saludable.
5. _____ Bajar de peso afecta positivamente a la salud y a la apariencia de las personas.
6. _____ La buena salud requiere de disciplina.

### Después de escuchar

**11-34 Ahora usted.** Compartan sus respuestas a las siguientes preguntas.

1. ¿Qué hábitos de comida y actividad física tiene usted? ¿Son sus hábitos buenos o malos?
2. ¿Cree usted que usted es lo que come?
3. ¿Qué aspecto de su vida piensa usted que puede cambiar para mejorar su estado físico?

# A conversar

**Select appropriate phrases to offer opinions**

When you are talking with someone, it is natural to offer opinions and evaluations of what the other person has said and to express agreement or disagreement. An effective way to do this is to acknowledge the value of what the other person has said and then express your reaction to it.

## Antes de conversar

**11-35 Preparación. PRIMERA FASE.** Marque (✓) los hábitos o condiciones que, según usted, ayudan a prolongar la vida de las personas.

1. \_\_\_ hacer ejercicio físico regularmente
2. \_\_\_ trabajar poco
3. \_\_\_ poner el cuerpo bajo mucho estrés
4. \_\_\_ ser vegetariano/a
5. \_\_\_ beber vino con el almuerzo o la cena
6. \_\_\_ llevar una vida sedentaria
7. \_\_\_ tomar remedios de casa para curar el catarro
8. \_\_\_ evitar fracturarse los huesos

**SEGUNDA FASE.** Comparen sus respuestas a las preguntas de la *Primera fase*. Luego, escriban un cuestionario para determinar si las personas hacen lo necesario para vivir más años. Consideren las siguientes áreas en su cuestionario.

| TEMAS | EJEMPLOS |
|---|---|
| 1. actividades/hábitos | ¿Se mantiene usted activo/a? |
| 2. comida | ¿Come verduras regularmente? |
| 3. bebidas | ¿Bebe alcohol? ¿Con qué frecuencia? |

## Conversar

**11-36 Entre nosotros.** Usen el cuestionario de la actividad **11-35** *Segunda fase*, para entrevistarse entre ustedes. Tomen notas de la información adicional importante que mencione su compañero/a durante la conversación. Esto los/las puede ayudar a determinar si cada uno/a de ustedes realmente se cuida para vivir más.

## Después de conversar

**11-37 Un poco más.** Use la información que le dio su compañero/a en **11-36** y converse con él/ella sobre lo siguiente:

1. Mencione a) las actividades y b) los buenos hábitos de alimentación (comida, bebida) de su compañero/a que, según usted, van a contribuir a una vida más larga. Felicítelo/la. (*Congratulate him/her.*)
2. También indique las áreas en las que usted y su compañero/a tienen opiniones diferentes.
3. Si es necesario, déle consejos o recomendaciones para mejorar sus hábitos.

### En directo

To congratulate or praise someone:

**Felicitaciones por +** *verb, noun.*

**Te felicito. Te cuidas muy bien.**

**¡Qué bien! Vas a vivir muchos años.**

To express happiness at someone's success:

**Me alegro de que +** *subjunctive.*

**¡Qué fabuloso que +** *subjunctive!*

To introduce a differing opinion:

**Lo que dices es interesante, pero mi perspectiva es diferente./ Yo lo veo diferente.**

**Entiendo tu punto de vista, pero no estoy de acuerdo contigo.**

### En directo

To make a general recommendation:

**Es importante/bueno/ conveniente/aconsejable +** *infinitive.*

To make a recommendation to someone specific:

**Es importante que +** *name*(s) + *subjunctive.*

# A leer

## Antes de leer

**11-38 Preparación.** PRIMERA FASE. Lea el título y los subtítulos del texto, mire las fotos y lea la nota debajo de la foto. Use esta información y su conocimiento sobre el tema para escoger la mejor respuesta a la pregunta: ¿Qué ideas e información importantes espera encontrar en el artículo?

1. A causa de la globalización, hay cada vez más enfermedades nuevas.
2. Las enfermedades conocidas en una región del mundo pasan a otras regiones, gracias al movimiento de la gente.
3. Unas enfermedades que se consideraban desaparecidas empiezan a reaparecer en el mundo a causa de cambios en el medio ambiente.

 SEGUNDA FASE. Marque (✓) las enfermedades tropicales de la lista que usted conoce. Busque más información sobre la(s) enfermedad(es) en la página web de *Mosaicos*.

1. ___ la viruela (*smallpox*)
2. ___ la tuberculosis
3. ___ el dengue
4. ___ el virus del Nilo
5. ___ la malaria
6. ___ la enfermedad del sueño

## Leer

### Las enfermedades y la globalización

La malaria aumenta a causa de las inundaciones del río Amazonas.

Enfermedades tropicales como el dengue, la viruela, la malaria, la tuberculosis y el virus del Nilo que, según muchos expertos, ya no existían, ahora reaparecen y se extienden por todo el mundo. Las causas de su reaparición son evidentes: cambios en el medio ambiente[1] y el constante movimiento de personas entre los continentes. Los turistas, los trabajadores migratorios y los inmigrantes transportan estos virus e infecciones. De la misma manera, los cambios climáticos facilitan la adaptación de los virus a nuevos ambientes y los hacen resistentes.

#### Bacterias, parásitos y virus viajeros y resistentes

Un claro ejemplo de la adaptabilidad de estas enfermedades infecciosas es la tuberculosis. Los científicos pensaban que estaba controlada en los países desarrollados. Sin embargo, los hechos nos muestran que esta enfermedad ha evolucionado y ha retornado. En varios países de Europa, hay pacientes con tuberculosis porque las bacterias no reaccionan a los medicamentos tradicionales. Se piensa que alrededor de un 32% de la población del mundo sufre y morirá de esta enfermedad. La Organización Mundial de la Salud (OMS) expresa gran preocupación por la malaria. El mosquito que la provoca puede sobrevivir largos viajes interoceánicos. Por eso, hay personas enfermas de malaria en muchas partes del mundo. La malaria es peligrosa si no se detecta a tiempo. Los médicos sin experiencia en este tipo de enfermedades la pueden confundir con la gripe y tratarla con medicamentos inadecuados.

El virus del Nilo constituye otra enfermedad que afecta a los turistas. Se reportaron 3.500 casos de la enfermedad en Estados Unidos en el 2007, de los que murieron más de cien personas.

#### Las enfermedades migratorias

A fines del siglo XX, gracias a una campaña mundial contra la viruela, casi toda la población mundial fue inmunizada contra esta enfermedad. Sin embargo, en la actualidad, la viruela de los monos, una variedad típica de la selva de algunos países africanos, ya se reproduce en otros lugares, como Estados Unidos. En este país es necesario fabricar vacunas contra la viruela que no se producían desde hacía años.

El dengue es indudablemente la enfermedad más extendida del mundo en los últimos años. Los expertos afirman que es posible que el 40% de la población del mundo contraiga[2] esta mortal fiebre. Geográficamente, el dengue nació en el suroeste de Asia, pero rápidamente pasó al Caribe y Centro y Sudamérica. En los últimos años se han descubierto casos incluso en España.

La lista de enfermedades que surgen de nuevo por la movilidad de la población del mundo actual es larga, pero los fondos mundiales para realizar investigaciones sobre las enfermedades que causan el 90% de las muertes en el mundo son mínimos y limitados. Sin duda, la globalización ha resuelto algunos problemas, pero ha creado otros.

[1]*environment*  [2]*contracts*

**11-39 Primera mirada.** De las siguientes afirmaciones, indique cuáles representan ideas principales (**P**) del artículo y cuáles son ideas secundarias (**S**).

1. \_\_\_ La reaparición de algunas enfermedades es causada por la interconexión de los mercados del mundo.
2. \_\_\_ La gran movilidad de las personas por razones económicas causa la reaparición de enfermedades tropicales que en algún momento desaparecieron.
3. \_\_\_ Los cambios de clima, provocados por los cambios en el medio ambiente, ayudan a que algunos virus sean más resistentes.
4. \_\_\_ Las enfermedades migratorias mataron a norteamericanos y europeos.
5. \_\_\_ Algunas enfermedades que nacieron en un punto específico del mundo se expanden a otros continentes.
6. \_\_\_ Los países desarrollados como Estados Unidos están fabricando vacunas para combatir algunas enfermedades contagiosas.

**11-40 Segunda mirada.** Según el contenido del artículo, subraye las expresiones que se relacionan con estos temas.

1. enfermedades tropicales: las infecciones, la viruela, la tuberculosis, el virus del Nilo
2. desafíos de las enfermedades para los expertos: la infección, la adaptabilidad, el desarrollo, la evolución, la resistencia
3. medidas que los gobiernos toman para enfrentar estas enfermedades: campañas, inmunización, reproducción, vacunas, prevención

## Después de leer

**11-41 Ampliación.** En el artículo usted encontró palabras asociadas con los verbos de la siguiente lista. Primero, seleccione la palabra apropiada, y luego use la forma adecuada (sustantivo o forma verbal) de la palabra para completar el texto a continuación.

| | | | |
|---|---|---|---|
| adaptar | globalizar | migrar | reaparecer |
| enfermarse | investigar | mover | retornar |

### La interconexión del mundo actual

Muchos piensan que los efectos de la (1) _____ siempre son positivos. Sin embargo, hay un gran número de personas en todo el mundo que cree lo contrario. Según ellos, es triste ver que muchas de las (2) _____ que ya se creían eliminadas (3) _____ con mucha fuerza y pueden matar a millones de víctimas inocentes en todos los continentes. Piensan que los científicos de los países desarrollados y más ricos deben hacer (4) _____ para descubrir medidas para eliminarlas o controlarlas. No obstante, la realidad indica que el (5) _____ masivo de inmigrantes entre los continentes inevitablemente facilita el (6) _____ de estas.

# A escribir

**Persuade through suggestions and advice**

Persuasion is a social, communicative task that we pursue to gain something we want or to provoke a behavior change in someone else. One method of persuasion is to offer suggestions or advice. Here are some points to remember when offering advice in Spanish.

■ Pay special attention to your degree of familiarity with the person you are trying to persuade. Is he/she a friend, an acquaintance, or someone you don't know personally? Is the person younger or older than you? Your superior at work or someone under your supervision?

■ Use expressions that signal your degree of familiarity. In Spanish this is indicated, among other ways, with the personal pronouns **tú** or **usted**.

## Antes de escribir

**11-42 Preparación.** PRIMERA FASE. Usted acaba de recibir esta carta de uno de sus buenos amigos, quien ha permanecido en silencio por algún tiempo. Léala.

> *Hola amigo/a,*
>
> *Perdón por no escribirte antes, pero tengo algunas razones válidas. Desde hace un mes, no me siento bien. Aunque estoy trabajando sólo cuatro horas por día, a las 3:00 de la tarde ya quiero irme a casa a descansar. No tengo apetito, así es que generalmente preparo una sopa enlatada o huevos fritos con tocino. De vez en cuando cocino una hamburguesa y, a veces, cuando me canso de la carne, tomo una buena porción de helados con galletas. ¡Ah, claro, mis amigos siempre me encuentran en los cafés de la universidad bebiendo un expreso o un capuchino! Necesito la cafeína para tener energía y hacer mi trabajo. El único problema es que por la cafeína no puedo dormir de noche. Las mañanas son una verdadera tortura. Generalmente me levanto tarde, falto a clases a veces y no me alcanza el tiempo para hacer mi trabajo.*
>
> *Creo que debo buscar ayuda. Quisiera ver un médico, pero no tengo dinero ahora. ¿Qué te parece? Estoy pobre y enfermo.*
>
> *Bueno, escríbeme para saber de ti. Te contestaré tan pronto pueda. Cuídate mucho.*
>
> *Un fuerte abrazo,*
>
> *Tomás*

**SEGUNDA FASE.** En la actividad **11-43**, usted va a responder a la carta de Tomás. Pero antes, escriba tres problemas de Tomás en la primera columna y en la otra, algunas ideas para ayudarlo a resolver cada problema.

| PROBLEMAS DE TOMÁS | ALGUNAS POSIBLES SOLUCIONES |
|---|---|
| 1. | 1. |
| 2. | 2. |
| 3. | 3. |

## Escribir

**11-43 Manos a la obra.** Respóndale a la carta a su amigo. Use la información que preparó en la actividad **11-42**. No se olvide de expresarle sus sentimientos o preocupación por los problemas e indicarle algunas sugerencias para que los resuelva.

## Después de escribir

**11-44 Revisión.** Lea su carta de respuesta y verifique lo siguiente, pensando en Tomás.

1. ¿Le demostró a Tomás interés por su situación? ¿Le indicó los problemas más serios, en su opinión? ¿Le dio algunas posibles soluciones? ¿Usó las formas apropiadas para hacerle recomendaciones?
2. ¿Tiene la carta una introducción, un cuerpo, un párrafo de cierre y una despedida?
3. ¿Corrigió la concordancia, la puntuación y la ortografía? ¿Usó comas, puntos, etc. donde eran necesarios?
4. ¿Usó vocabulario apropiado al tema y expresiones de cohesión? ¿Revisó el tiempo (presente, pasado, futuro) y los modos (indicativo, subjuntivo)?

Finalmente, comparta su carta con su compañero editor/compañera editora.

### En directo

To express concern or sympathy:

**Me preocupa (mucho) que...**

**Siento/Lamento que...**

**Qué lástima que...**

To persuade a friend through suggestions:

**Te recomiendo/sugiero/ aconsejo que...**

**Es importante/necesario/ urgente/mejor que...**

**Ojalá (que)...**

### En directo

To put ideas together cohesively:

**Por un lado...**
*On one hand . . .*

**Por otro (lado)...**
*On the other (hand) . . .*

**En primer/segundo lugar...**
*In the first/second place . . .*

**Además...**
*Besides/Furthermore . . .*

To contrast ideas:

**No obstante**
*However*

**Sin embargo**
*Nevertheless*

# ENFOQUE CULTURAL

## Cuba y República Dominicana: la música y el baile

Usted cree que la única manera de hacer ejercicio es correr muchas millas cada semana? ¿Piensa que el ejercicio es siempre una cosa aburrida que se hace por obligación y no por diversión? Pues en el Caribe hispano, sobre todo en Cuba, República Dominicana y Puerto Rico, han descubierto el mejor método de ejercitar el cuerpo y el espíritu, mientras uno se divierte y socializa con sus amigos y amigas. No se trata de un descubrimiento nuevo, sino de una de las prácticas más antiguas de la humanidad: el baile. Lo especial

Una mujer baila la rumba en las calles de La Habana.

en este caso es que bailan al ritmo de una música que reúne características europeas, africanas e indígenas. Pero si esto es lo que usted quiere hacer, prepárese porque en una sesión de baile caribeño usted tendrá que mover la cabeza, el pecho, la cintura, las caderas, los brazos y las manos y, naturalmente, ¡los pies!

La música caribeña es muy rica y variada, aunque la mayoría de nosotros pensamos principalmente en la salsa, el merengue, la bachata o el reguetón. Sin embargo, bailes muy populares en los años 50, tales como el son y el bolero, la rumba y el mambo, por ejemplo, forman parte de la misma tradición musical. Esos bailes, algunos de ritmo lento y sensual, exigen una coordinación en los movimientos de las diferentes partes del cuerpo, pero especialmente de los hombros, las caderas, las rodillas y los pies. En realidad, un componente muy importante es el movimiento

Tito Puente y Celia Cruz, dos de los grandes mitos de la música caribeña

sincronizado de las extremidades inferiores del cuerpo, algo que le da al baile de esta región características eróticas.

La verdad es que el cuerpo humano está presente en la música no sólo a través del movimiento sino también en la letra de las canciones. En las canciones caribeñas frecuentemente se hace referencia a la boca, los labios, los ojos, los hombros, la cintura y las piernas. Algunas canciones populares explican cómo bailar ciertos ritmos y cómo mover los pies a la derecha, a la izquierda, adelante, atrás. Otras canciones, como es el caso de una famosa canción caribeña de Colombia, nos invitan a "mover la colita". Esos movimientos rítmicos del cuerpo hicieron famosos los bailes cubanos y a muchas estrellas del cine latinoamericano en los años 50 y 60. Las actrices del cine cubano y mexicano de esa época cantaban y bailaban con trajes muy pequeños, ceñidos al cuerpo y adornados con plumas y sombreros locos y espectaculares. Los músicos de las orquestas llevaban camisas de seda con grandes mangas de colores brillantes.

El cine europeo adoptó muchos de los ritmos del Caribe. Por ejemplo, La dolce vita, una película del director italiano Federico Fellini, incluyó la música de "Patricia", un mambo de Pérez Prado, uno de los más famosos compositores de música popular cubana. Igualmente, el cine latinoamericano de los años 50 y 60 está lleno de imágenes de cantantes, bailarines y bailarinas, tales como Resortes y Tin Tan, dos cómicos mexicanos, o divas como María Antonieta Pons, Amalia Aguilar o Yolanda Montes "Tongolele", una hispana de Spokane, Washington.

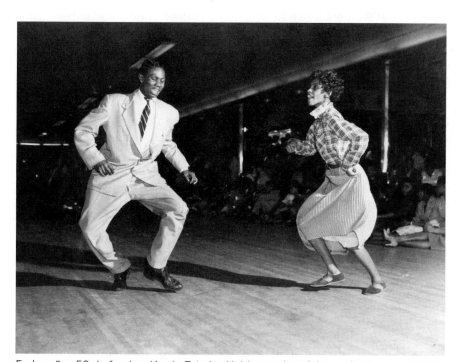

En los años 50, la fascinación de Estados Unidos por la música caribeña era evidente en el concurso semanal de mambo del famosísimo Savoy Ballroom en Harlem.

**11-45 Comprensión.** PRIMERA FASE. **Reconocimiento de palabras clave.** Encuentre en el texto la palabra o expresión que mejor expresa el significado de las siguientes ideas.

1. boring          _____
2. feathers        _____
3. shirts          _____
4. sleeves         _____
5. stars           _____
6. composers       _____
7. singers         _____

SEGUNDA FASE. **Oraciones importantes.** Subraye las afirmaciones que contienen ideas que se encuentran en el texto. Luego indique en qué parte del texto están.

1. Music is important in the culture of Puerto Rico, but not in the cultures of Cuba and the Dominican Republic.
2. People in the Caribbean have invented a way to exercise while also socializing and having a good time.
3. Parts of the body such as shoulders, arms, and legs are seldom mentioned in Caribbean songs.
4. The tradition of Caribbean music includes the bolero, son, rumba, and mambo.
5. The erotic qualities of Caribbean dance are due to the rhythmic movements of the lower body.
6. The most famous Latin American movie stars of the 1950s and 1960s wore crazy hats and revealing clothes adorned with feathers.
7. European films were quick to integrate Caribbean music and dance.
8. The United States only recently became interested in Caribbean rhythms.

TERCERA FASE. **Ideas principales.** Escriba un párrafo breve en español resumiendo las ideas principales expresadas en el texto.

 **11-46 Use la información.** Durante los años 50 y 60 muchas estrellas y orquestas de música caribeña se hicieron muy famosas en todo el mundo. Mire o escuche algunos fragmentos de cine latinoamericano de la época y escoja a una de las estrellas que aparece en un fragmento. Luego, prepare cinco preguntas que usted le haría (*would ask*) si este/a artista estuviera vivo/a (*were alive*). Para preparar esta actividad, visite la página web de Mosaicos y siga los enlaces útiles.

# VOCABULARIO

| El cuerpo humano | The human body |
|---|---|
| la boca | mouth |
| el brazo | arm |
| el cabello | hair |
| la cabeza | head |
| la cadera | hip |
| la cara | face |
| la ceja | eyebrow |
| el cerebro | brain |
| la cintura | waist |
| el codo | elbow |
| el corazón | heart |
| el cuello | neck |
| el dedo | finger |
| el diente | tooth |
| la espalda | back |
| el estómago | stomach |
| la frente | forehead |
| la garganta | throat |
| el hombro | shoulder |
| el hueso | bone |
| el labio | lip |
| la mano | hand |
| la mejilla | cheek |
| la muñeca | wrist |
| el músculo | muscle |
| la nariz | nose |
| el nervio | nerve |
| el oído | (inner) ear |
| la oreja | (outer) ear |
| el pecho | chest |
| la pestaña | eyelash |
| el pie | foot |
| la pierna | leg |
| el pulmón | lung |
| la rodilla | knee |
| la sangre | blood |
| el tobillo | ankle |
| la vena | vein |

| La salud | Health |
|---|---|
| el cáncer | cancer |
| el catarro | cold |
| el dolor | pain |
| la enfermedad | illness |
| el enfermo/la enferma | ill person |
| la fiebre | fever |
| la gripe | flu |
| la infección | infection |
| el/la paciente | patient |
| el síntoma | symptom |
| la tensión/la presión (arterial) | (blood) pressure |
| la tos | cough |

| Los proveedores de salud | Health care providers |
|---|---|
| la clínica/el centro de salud/el sanatorio | clinic |
| el farmacéutico/ la farmacéutica | pharmacist |
| la farmacia | pharmacy |
| el gobierno | government |
| el hospital | hospital |

| Los tratamientos médicos | Medical treatments |
|---|---|
| el antibiótico | antibiotic |
| la inyección | injection |
| la medicina | medicine |
| la pastilla | pill |
| la receta | prescription |
| el remedio | remedy, medicine |
| el termómetro | thermometer |

| Verbos | Verbs |
|---|---|
| alegrarse (de) | to be glad (about) |
| caer(se) | to fall |
| cuidar(se) (de) | to take care of |
| curar | to cure |
| doler (ue) | to hurt, ache |
| enfermarse | to become sick |
| estornudar | to sneeze |
| examinar | to examine |
| fracturar(se) | to fracture, to break |
| fumar | to smoke |
| molestar(le) | to bother, be bothered by |
| recetar | to prescribe |
| respirar | to breathe |
| sentir (ie, i) | to feel |
| temer | to fear |
| torcer(se) (ue) | to twist |
| toser | to cough |
| tratar | to treat |

| Las descripciones | Descriptions |
|---|---|
| deprimido/a | depressed |
| enfermo/a | sick |
| grave | serious |
| serio/a | serious |

| Palabras y expresiones útiles | Useful words and expressions |
|---|---|
| el artículo de belleza | beauty item |
| cada... horas | every . . . hours |
| ¿Qué te/le(s) pasa? | What's wrong (with you/them)? |
| tener dolor de... | to have a(n) . . . ache |
| tener mala cara | to look terrible |

See *Lengua* box on page 368 for words that refer to medical specialists.

# 12

# ¡Buen viaje!

Una mola tradicional de los Kuna, indígenas de Isla San Blas en Panamá

## In this chapter you will learn how to:

- discuss travel arrangements, hotel reservations, and correspondence
- talk about things that may not exist
- express possession
- talk about the past

**Cultural focus:** **Panamá, Costa Rica**

**A vista de pájaro.** Piense en lo que sabe de Panamá y Costa Rica y complete las afirmaciones.

1. ___ El Canal de Panamá se construyó en…
   a. el siglo XVI.
   b. el siglo XXI.
   c. el siglo XX.
2. ___ La capital de Costa Rica es…
   a. San Juan.
   b. San José.
   c. Santo Domingo.

3. ___ Panamá limita al oeste con Costa Rica y al este con…
   a. Colombia.
   b. Nicaragua.
   c. República Dominicana.
4. ___ Una industria muy importante de Costa Rica es…
   a. la carne de res.
   b. el tabaco.
   c. el turismo.

# A PRIMERA VISTA

## ⋆)) Los medios de transporte

**CD 5**
**Track 31**

Mucha gente usa el transporte público. Los **autobuses** son populares en las ciudades y también para **viajar** largas distancias. Son la solución para las personas que no tienen carro, o a quienes simplemente no les gusta **manejar** en las **carreteras** y **autopistas**. El **metro** es otra forma de transporte eficiente en los centros urbanos, como Madrid, Barcelona, Santiago, Buenos Aires, Caracas y Ciudad de México.

El AVE, el **tren** español de alta **velocidad** entre Madrid y otras grandes ciudades españolas, viaja a unos 300 kilómetros por hora. La RENFE (Red Nacional de Ferrocarriles Españoles) es tan importante en España como las **líneas aéreas** en Estados Unidos. Gracias al turismo se ha recuperado en Costa Rica la antigua tradición de **recorrer** el país en tren. Algunas agencias organizan **trayectos** desde San José a la costa este.

El **crucero** es otra forma de viajar. En **barcos** modernos con una capacidad de 400 hasta más de 2.000 **pasajeros**, se puede hacer de todo. En las **escalas** en los diferentes puertos hay excursiones organizadas y oportunidades para ir de compras. De noche, la diversión continúa en la discoteca, el casino y el teatro. El barco es un medio de transporte y también puede servir para pasar las vacaciones.

## En un avión

CD 5
Track 32 El **avión** es la manera, aunque más cara, de viajar rápidamente de un lugar a otro, especialmente en zonas como las selvas y en las montañas, donde es difícil construir carreteras por la geografía o el clima.

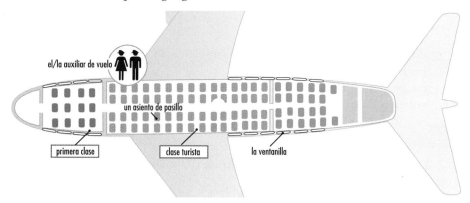

## En el aeropuerto

CD 5
Track 33 Los pasajeros **hacen cola** frente al **mostrador** de la **aerolínea** para **facturar** el **equipaje**, pedir un **asiento** y conseguir la **tarjeta de embarque** para su **vuelo**.

> ### En otras palabras
>
> Other words for **auxiliar de vuelo** are **azafata**, used especially in Spain, and **aeromozo/a**, used mostly in Latin America. Depending on the region, the word **billete** (Spain), **pasaje**, or **boleto** is preferred.

## En el mostrador de la línea aérea

CD 5
Track 34

EMPLEADA: Buenos días. Su **pasaporte** y su **boleto**, por favor.

VIAJERO: Aquí están. Y si es posible, prefiero un asiento cerca de una **salida de emergencia**.

EMPLEADA: Muy bien. ¿Ventanilla o pasillo?

VIAJERO: Pasillo, por favor. Señorita, ¿usted sabe si hay un **cajero automático** aquí en el **aeropuerto**?

EMPLEADA: Sí, hay una oficina del Banco Popular enfrente a la derecha.

VIAJERO: Gracias. ¿Me acreditó los kilómetros a mi programa de viajero frecuente?

EMPLEADA: Sí, y su **pasaje** es **de ida y vuelta**, así que va a tener bastantes kilómetros. Su asiento a San José es el 10F. Aquí tiene su tarjeta de embarque. La puerta de salida es la C20. ¡Que tenga un buen viaje!

**12-1 Asociaciones.** Asocie cada palabra con su descripción. Luego, compare sus respuestas con las de un compañero/una compañera.

1. ___ tren de alta velocidad
2. ___ viaje en un barco grande de pasajeros
3. ___ persona que sirve la comida en un vuelo
4. ___ transporte subterráneo
5. ___ inspección al llegar a otro país
6. ___ documento de identificación necesario para viajar al extranjero
7. ___ pasaje para ir de Panamá a Costa Rica y volver a Panamá
8. ___ se viaja en un asiento cómodo y se come bien

a. el/la auxiliar de vuelo
b. pasaporte
c. primera clase
d. AVE
e. metro
f. aduana
g. boleto de ida y vuelta
h. crucero

 **12-2 Salidas y llegadas.** Miren los horarios y la puerta de salida de los siguientes vuelos y háganse preguntas.

| SALIDA DEPARTURE | ABORDAR BOARDING | PUERTA GATE | DESTINO DESTINATION |
|---|---|---|---|
| 3:30 | 3:00 | 1A | SAN JOSÉ |
| 3:50 | 3:20 | 4 | MANAGUA |
| 4:10 | 3:40 | 6 | GUATEMALA |
| 4:25 | 3:55 | 10 | PANAMÁ |
| 4:45 | 4:15 | 8 | LIMÓN |
| 5:10 | 4:40 | 5 | MÉXICO D.F. |
| 6:00 | 5:30 | 5 | KINGSTON |

**MODELO:**  E1:  *¿A qué hora sale el vuelo para San José?*
E2:  *El avión para San José sale a las tres y media por la puerta 1A.*

 **12-3 Haciendo turismo.** Usted es un/a agente de viajes y su compañero/a es su cliente/a. Hágale preguntas para averiguar la siguiente información. Usen los enlaces a la actividad en la página web de *Mosaicos* para obtener itinerarios posibles. Intercambien roles.

1. destino al que quiere llegar
2. fechas de viaje
3. medio de transporte que desea utilizar
4. tipo de boleto (primera clase, turista,) y asiento (ventanilla, pasillo, etc.)
5. datos del cliente (nombre, tarjeta de crédito, número de viajero frecuente, etc.)

**SEGUNDA FASE.** Hablen entre ustedes de fechas, precios y otras opciones. Después hágale a su compañero/a algunas recomendaciones para el viaje: necesidad de pasaporte, recomendaciones para pasar por la aduana, etc.

# Viajando en coche

CD 5
Track 35

el capó    el espejo retrovisor    el limpiaparabrisas    el maletero/el baúl

el motor

el radiador

la placa

el parachoques    la llanta    el volante

la rueda

la guantera

**12-4 ¿Qué es?**  Busquen en el dibujo la palabra que corresponda a las siguientes descripciones. Después, den una descripción de las otras partes del coche indicadas en el dibujo para ver si otra pareja sabe qué son.

1.  Es para poner el equipaje. _____
2.  Permite ver bien cuando llueve. _____
3.  Son negras y llevan aire por dentro. _____
4.  Controla la dirección del coche. _____
5.  Tiene letras y números y sirve para identificar el coche._____
6.  Hay que ponerle agua si no queremos que se caliente el motor.

_____

**12-5 Mi auto favorito.**  Primero, averigüen qué medio de transporte usa cada uno/a de ustedes con más frecuencia. Después, pregúntense cuál es el auto favorito de cada uno/a y por qué. Cada persona debe dar cuatro razones para explicar por qué le gusta más.

**12-6 Para evitar accidentes.**  Escriban un anuncio con recomendaciones para evitar accidentes de tráfico. El anuncio debe tener la siguiente información:

1.  un título o eslogan (*motto*)
2.  el nombre de la compañía o grupo que patrocina (*sponsors*) el anuncio
3.  tres recomendaciones para evitar accidentes

> ## Cultura
>
> Aunque en los países hispanoamericanos se usa mucho el transporte público, el tráfico y la contaminación son problemas serios en las ciudades grandes. Además, cada vez es más difícil encontrar estacionamiento. Por eso se usan mucho las motos y los carros pequeños.

# El alojamiento y las reservaciones

CD 5
Track 36 **Buscando alojamiento**

EMPLEADA: Buenas tardes. ¿En qué les puedo servir?

SRA. CANO: Buenas tardes. Tenemos dos **habitaciones** reservadas a nuestro nombre, señores Cano.

EMPLEADA: Sí, señora. Tengo una **doble** y una **sencilla**.

SRA. CANO: Muy bien. Una es para nosotros y otra para nuestro hijo. Quisiera dejar los pasaportes en un lugar seguro. ¿Podría usted... ?

EMPLEADA: ¿Por qué no los deja en la **caja fuerte** de su habitación?

SRA. CANO: Muy bien.

EMPLEADA: Bueno, aquí tiene dos **tarjetas magnéticas**. Ya no usamos **llaves**. Sus habitaciones están en el segundo piso.

SR. CANO: Y..., ¿nos puede indicar cómo llegar a la Plaza 5 de Mayo?

EMPLEADA: Sí, cómo no. Mire, **sigan derecho** por esta calle hasta la próxima **esquina**. Allí, **doblen** a la izquierda y caminen una **cuadra** hasta la plaza que está a la derecha. No **se** pueden **perder**.

SR. CANO: Muchísimas gracias.

**12-7 Estoy perdido/a.** Usted está en la Ciudad de Panamá y está perdido. Use el plano siguiente y pregúntele a un ciudadano/una ciudadana (su compañero/a) cómo ir a ciertos lugares. Su compañero/a le debe explicar cómo llegar.

| USTED ESTÁ EN | USTED DESEA IR |
|---|---|
| la Plaza 5 de Mayo | al Palacio Presidencial |
| la Avenida Ancón y la Avenida A | al Casco Viejo |
| el Museo de Historia del Canal de Panamá | al Centro Turístico Mi Pueblito |

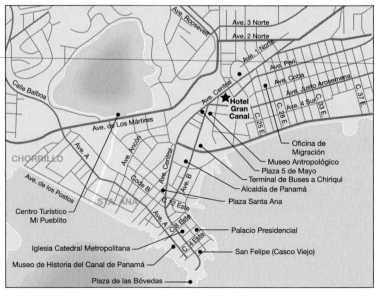

**Ciudad de Panamá**

# El correo y la correspondencia

CD 5
Track 37

una carta

un sello

una postal

un sobre

Sra. Teresa Silva de Granados
504 Edificio Los Pinos
Panamá 3, Rep. de Panamá

el cartero    el paquete

el buzón

**12-8 La correspondencia. PRIMERA FASE.** Complete las oraciones con la palabra adecuada y escriba la letra correspondiente al lado del número.

1. ___ El lugar donde a veces se recoge la correspondencia y se compran sellos es el...
2. ___ La persona que reparte cartas y postales es el/la...
3. ___ El depósito donde ponemos las cartas que queremos enviar es el...
4. ___ Para mandar una carta la ponemos dentro de un...
5. ___ Si queremos mandar un regalo de una ciudad a otra, tenemos que preparar un...
6. ___ No se puede mandar una carta sin escribir la dirección y ponerle un...

a. cartero/a.
b. correo.
c. sello.
d. sobre.
e. paquete.
f. buzón.

**SEGUNDA FASE.** Respondan a las siguientes preguntas.

1. ¿Cuándo fue la última vez que usted fue al correo?
2. ¿Para qué fue? ¿Para comprar sellos o un sobre o para enviar un paquete?
3. ¿Es el correo electrónico un medio de comunicación más eficaz (*efficient*) que el correo postal? ¿Por qué?

### Cultura

Hoy en día las personas prefieren comunicarse mediante los *chats* o el correo electrónico. En todas las ciudades del mundo hay cibercafés desde donde podemos comunicarnos instantáneamente con los familiares y amigos. Sin embargo, en los lugares turísticos venden postales muy lindas para enviar por correo normal. Los sellos para enviar postales y cartas se compran en las tiendas de tabaco y en las oficinas de correos. En algunas épocas del año, estas oficinas están llenas de gente que quieren enviar paquetes a sus conocidos.

**12-9 Un correo electrónico nostálgico.** Envíele un mensaje electrónico o una postal a su compañero favorito/compañera favorita. Cuéntele algunos aspectos especiales de sus últimas vacaciones. Después, su compañero/a le responderá por escrito, reaccionará a sus comentarios y le hará preguntas para obtener más detalles.

1. lugar(es) que visitó
2. personas que conoció
3. experiencias divertidas que vivió
4. otras experiencias que recuerda con nostalgia
5. comida nueva que probó
6. regalos que compró

CD 5
Track 38

**12-10 Antes de viajar.** You will listen to a man who is checking in at the airport. Before you listen, list two questions you think the airline employee will ask him and the answers that you think the man will provide.

Now listen to the exchange, and choose the appropriate ending to each statement.

1. El empleado le pide al viajero...
   a. su boleto de ida y vuelta.
   b. su tarjeta de embarque.
   c. su pasaporte y su pasaje.

2. El viajero va a facturar...
   a. tres maletas.
   b. un maletín de mano.
   c. dos maletas.

3. El viajero prefiere un asiento...
   a. al lado de la ventanilla.
   b. en el pasillo.
   c. en la parte posterior del avión.

4. El empleado le puede conseguir un asiento...
   a. de pasillo, el 28C.
   b. en el centro, entre la ventanilla y el pasillo.
   c. en la ventanilla en primera clase.

5. El empleado le dice al pasajero que...
   a. tiene tiempo para llamar por teléfono.
   b. puede llamar desde el avión.
   c. no tiene que pasar por seguridad.

# EN ACCIÓN

## Diarios de bicicleta: El premio

### Antes de ver

**12-11** Usted está ayudando a un amigo a planear un viaje. ¿Cuáles son, según usted, las cinco cosas que él/ella debería hacer primero?

_____ Es necesario que obtenga un pasaporte.

_____ Recomiendo que haga reservaciones de hotel.

_____ Es importante que compre un boleto de avión.

_____ Sugiero que hable con un agente de viajes.

_____ Es importante que compre una guía turística del país.

_____ Es necesario que haga las maletas.

_____ Recomiendo que compre una cámara de fotos.

_____ Es importante que cargue la batería del iPod.

### Mientras ve

**12-12** Escoja la oración que es equivalente a cada cita (*quote*).

1. Javier: "¿Quién se cree estos engaños?"
   a. No puede ser verdad.
   b. No soy religioso.
2. Gabi: "Me tocó la lotería…"
   a. Voy a cancelar mis planes.
   b. Tengo mucha suerte.
3. Gabi: "…puedo elegir cualquier destino."
   a. Puedo escoger cualquier lugar.
   b. Puedo viajar durante cualquier época del año.
4. Javier: "¿Nos vemos al rato?"
   a. Nos vemos en otro lugar.
   b. Nos vemos más tarde.

### Después de ver

**12-13** En este segmento, tres personajes han recibido un correo electrónico que dice que han ganado un viaje a Centroamérica. Escriba el mensaje que han recibido. Incluya tres instrucciones de cómo reclamar (*reclaim*) este premio.

## 1. Talking about things that may not exist: Subjunctive in adjective clauses

| | |
|---|---|
| MUJER: | Por favor, ¿dónde está el tren que **sale** a las 9:00? |
| AGENTE: | No hay trenes que **salgan** por la noche, señorita. El último tren sale a las 6:00 de la tarde. |
| MUJER: | ¡Ay, Dios mío! ¿Hay un tren que **salga** temprano por la mañana? |
| AGENTE: | Sí, señorita. El primer tren sale a las 7:00. |
| MUJER: | Bueno, tendré que esperar hasta mañana, entonces. ¿Me puede recomendar un hotel que **esté** cerca? Necesito uno que no **sea** caro. |
| AGENTE: | Sí, cómo no. Le recomiendo el Hotel Colonial. Es un buen hotel que **tiene** precios módicos. |

**Piénselo.** Para cada oración, indique si la persona habla de algo que existe (**E**), de algo que no existe (**NE**) o de algo que posiblemente exista (**PE**).

1. ___ ¿Dónde está el tren que **sale** a las 9:00?
2. ___ No hay trenes que **salgan** por la noche.
3. ___ ¿Hay un tren que **salga** temprano por la mañana?
4. ___ ¿Me puede recomendar un hotel que **esté** cerca?
5. ___ Necesito un hotel que no **sea** caro.
6. ___ Es un buen hotel que **tiene** precios módicos (*moderate*).

■ As you have learned, the subjunctive in Spanish is used primarily in sentences that have two clauses. In this section, you will learn about using the subjunctive in adjective clauses.

■ Both adjectives and adjective clauses provide descriptive information about a noun in the independent clause.

ADJECTIVE

Vamos a ir a un hotel muy **moderno.**

ADJECTIVE CLAUSE

Vamos a ir a un hotel **que es muy moderno.**

■ Use the indicative in an adjective clause that refers to a person, place, or thing (antecedent) that exists or is known.

Hay un buen hotel que **queda** cerca de la playa.
*There is a good hotel that is close to the beach.*
(You are familiar with the hotel.)
Quiero visitar el museo que **tiene** la exposición de molas.
*I want to visit the museum that has the exhibit of molas.*
(You know there is such a museum.)

■ Use the subjunctive in an adjective clause that refers to a person, place, or thing that does not exist or whose existence is unknown or in question.

No hay hoteles en esta zona que **tengan** precios módicos.
*There are no hotels in this area that have moderate prices.*

Quiero comer en un restaurante que **sirva** comida vegetariana.
*I want to eat in a restaurant that serves vegetarian food.*
(Any restaurant, as long as it serves vegetarian food.)

■ When the antecedent is a specific person and functions as a direct object, use the indicative and the personal **a**. If the antecedent is not a specific person, use the subjunctive and do not use the personal **a**.

Busco **a** la auxiliar que **trabaja** en ese vuelo.
*I am looking for the flight attendant who is working on that flight.*
(A specific flight attendant, who is among those working on that flight.)

Busco una auxiliar que **trabaje** en ese vuelo.
*I am looking for a flight attendant who is working on that flight.*
(Any flight attendant, as long as she is working on that flight.)

■ In questions, you may use the indicative or the subjunctive according to the degree of certainty you have about the matter.

¿Hay viajeros aquí que **salen** en el vuelo 420?
*Are there any travelers here who are leaving on flight 420?*
(I do not know, but I assume there are.)

¿Hay viajeros aquí que **salgan** en el vuelo 420?
*Are there any travelers here who are leaving on flight 420?*
(I do not know, but I doubt it.)

**12-14 ¿Cuál es la respuesta correcta?** Escriba la letra de la forma verbal (indicativo o subjuntivo) para completar cada grupo de oraciones.

1. No hay ningún vuelo que ___ por la noche.   a. sale
2. Pero hay un vuelo que ___ a las 7:00 de la mañana.   b. salga

3. Me interesa encontrar un hotel (*any hotel*) que ___ cerca del centro.   a. queda
4. Hay un hotel que no es muy caro y que ___ en el centro.   b. quede

5. Busco al empleado que ___ inglés.   a. habla
6. Hay algún empleado (*any employee*) en este departamento que ___ inglés?   b. hable

**12-15 Por curiosidad.** Usted tiene curiosidad por saber algo sobre la familia y los amigos de su compañero/a. Túrnense para hacerse preguntas. Si la respuesta es afirmativa, diga quién es la persona y dé información adicional.

MODELO:   dormir mucho durante los viajes largos por auto/tu familia
E1:  *¿Hay alguien en tu familia que duerma mucho durante los viajes largos por auto?*
E2:  *Sí, mi hermano siempre duerme mucho en el auto. El año pasado fuimos a la casa de mis abuelos y él durmió durante todo el viaje.*

1. viajar mucho/tu famila
2. trabajar en vez de viajar durante las vacaciones de la primavera/tus amigos
3. conocer los parques nacionales de Costa Rica/tus amigos
4. saber pilotear un avión/tu familia
5. ir a esquiar en sus vacaciones/tus amigos
6. viajar a Panamá este año/tu familia

**12-16 Emergencia en el aeropuerto.** Varios empleados de la aerolínea costarricense Travelair están enfermos, y otras personas tienen que hacer su trabajo. Túrnense para hacer los papeles de dos empleados de Travelair que buscan otros empleados que puedan hacer ciertos trabajos. Sigan el modelo.

MODELO:   programar la computadora (alguien)
E1:  *Necesito a alguien que programe la computadora para los itinerarios.*
E2:  *No hay nadie en el aeropuerto que pueda programarla.*
E1:  *Bueno, es necesario buscar a alguien que lo haga.*

1. hablar inglés, japonés y español para el vuelo a Tamarindo (auxiliar)
2. recibir el vuelo que viene de Puerto Jiménez (agente)
3. darles esta información a los pasajeros del vuelo 562 (empleado/a)
4. llevar a los pasajeros a inmigración (empleado/a)
5. poder trabajar este fin de semana (dos auxiliares)
6. ...

**12-17 Un lugar para ir de vacaciones.** PRIMERA FASE. Túrnense para hacerse preguntas sobre un lugar para ir de vacaciones. Contesten según la información de la tabla.

MODELO:   hotel/tener piscina
E1:  *¿Hay un hotel que tenga piscina?*
E2:  *Sí, hay un hotel que tiene piscina. O No, no hay ningún hotel que tenga piscina.*

| HAY | NO HAY |
| --- | --- |
| tiendas/vender ropa para esquiar | autobús/llegar por la mañana |
| cines/dar películas en español | cafetería/servir comida vegetariana |
| restaurantes/tener cajero automático | restaurantes/aceptar cheques personales |

**SEGUNDA FASE.** Ahora ustedes deben describir cómo es su lugar ideal de vacaciones, explicando su localización, ambiente y atracciones. Después, intercambien ideas con otra pareja.

**MODELO:**  E1:  *Quiero ir de vacaciones a una isla que tenga playas blancas y un ambiente tranquilo. ¿Y tú?*

E2:  *Mi lugar de vacaciones ideal es diferente. Quiero ir a una ciudad que tenga muchos conciertos y obras de teatro.*

**12-18 Agencia *Viaje ahora.*** Usted piensa viajar al extranjero, pero no conoce ninguna buena agencia de viajes. Dígale a su compañero/a adónde quiere ir y pídale información sobre una agencia. Su compañero/a le va a dar información basándose en el anuncio de la agencia *Viaje ahora*. Hágale por lo menos tres preguntas adicionales.

**SITUACIONES**

1. **Role A.** You want to visit Panama. Call your travel agent to find out a) the cost of the flight; b) the flight schedule; and c) if you need a visa. Then explain the type of hotel you want in Panama City and where you will spend the first week of your trip.

   **Role B.** You are a travel agent. A customer calls to discuss a possible trip to Panama. Provide all the necessary information.

2. **Role A.** You own a small inn near the college that houses international faculty who visit the campus. You need to hire two people for your staff, so you call an employment agency. Explain that you are looking for a) a receptionist who speaks French, German, or Spanish (preferably two of those languages) and who has experience as a secretary, and b) a chef who is familiar with European cuisines and who is able to work nights and weekends.

   **Role B.** You work at an employment agency, and you receive a call from an innkeeper who is looking for a receptionist and a chef. Listen to the innkeeper's requirements and ask about any other qualifications that may be desired. Tell the innkeeper you will start looking right away.

## 2. Expressing possession: Possessive pronouns

MADRE:   Ramiro, mi maleta casi está lista. ¿Y **la tuya**?

RAMIRO:   **¡La mía** no! Después del programa la empaco. ¿Ya empacaste tus libros, mamá?

MADRE:   **Los míos** ya están en mi maletín. ¿Y los juguetes de Panchito?

RAMIRO:   **Los suyos** están en su mochila, pero **los de** Laurita no sé dónde están.

**Piénselo.** Lea las siguientes afirmaciones tomadas de la conversación anterior e indique si las dijo la madre (**M**) o Ramiro (**R**). Luego, indique (✔) a qué se refiere la palabra en negrita.

1. ___ **¡La mía** no!
   **La mía** se refiere   ___ al programa.   ___ a la maleta.

2. ___ **Los míos** ya están en mi bolso de mano.
   **Los míos** se refiere a   ___ los libros.   ___ los juguetes.

3. ___ **Los suyos** están en su mochila.
   **Los suyos** se refiere a   ___ los maletines de mano.   ___ los juguetes de Panchito.

4. ___ **Los de Laurita** están en su cuarto.
   **Los de Laurita** se refiere a   ___ los libros.   ___ los juguetes.

■ Possessive pronouns express ownership or possession. They are used to avoid repetition of the noun to which they refer.

| SINGULAR | | PLURAL | |
|---|---|---|---|
| **MASCULINE** | **FEMININE** | **MASCULINE** | **FEMININE** |
| mío | mía | míos | mías |
| tuyo | tuya | tuyos | tuyas |
| el { suyo | la { suya | los { suyos | las { suyas |
| nuestro | nuestra | nuestros | nuestras |
| vuestro | vuestra | vuestros | vuestras |

■ The definite article precedes the possessive pronoun, and both article and pronoun agree in gender and number with the noun to which they refer.

¿Tienes la mochila de Mario?            *Do you have Mario's backpack?*

Sí, tengo **la suya** y **la mía** también.    *Yes, I have his and mine too.*

■ After the verb **ser**, the article is usually omitted.

Esa maleta es **mía**.                       *That suitcase is mine.*

■ To be clearer and more specific, the following structures may be used to
replace any corresponding form of **el suyo/la suya**.

la mochila suya → **la suya** *or*

| | |
|---|---|
| la de usted | *yours* (singular) |
| la de él | *his* |
| la de ella | *hers* |
| | |
| la de ustedes | *yours* (plural) |
| la de ellos | *theirs* (masculine, plural) |
| la de ellas | *theirs* (feminine, plural) |

**12-19 ¿De quién(es) son estas cosas?** En su clase de español ustedes
decidieron hacer un viaje de estudios a Costa Rica. En este momento van a
tomar el bus para ir al aeropuerto. Escoja la repuesta correcta para cada una de
las preguntas.

1. Miguel, ¿es tuya esta mochila?      **a.** Sí, es mía.      **b.** Sí, es tuya.
2. ¿Son estas maletas de Pedro?        **a.** Sí, son suyas.   **b.** Sí, son mías.
3. ¿El maletín color café es de Alicia? **a.** No, es tuya.     **b.** No, no es suyo.
4. Este mapa de San José, ¿es tuyo?    **a.** Sí, es mía.      **b.** Sí, es mío.
5. ¿Son nuestros estos boletos?        **a.** Sí, son suyos.   **b.** Sí, son suyas.

> ### En otras palabras
>
> Depending on the region,
> different words for **autobús**
> are used: **camión** (Mexico),
> **ómnibus** (Peru), **bus**,
> **guagua** (Puerto Rico,
> Cuba), **colectivo** (Argentina),
> **micro** (Chile), **chivita**
> (Colombia).

**12-20 ¿Quién tiene carro?** PRIMERA FASE. Entrevístense para saber quién(es)
tiene(n) carro. Hablen de sus carros: marca, modelo, año y color. Tomen
apuntes sobre la información.

MODELO:   E1:  *Mi carro es un Toyota Corolla de 2005. ¿Y los suyos?*
          E2:  *El mío es un Ford Taurus de 2003.*
          E3:  *Yo no tengo carro, pero uso el de mi hermana.*

SEGUNDA FASE. Combinen la información de todos los grupos y preparen un
informe sobre los rasgos (*features*) más comunes de los carros de los miembros
de la clase.

**12-21 Preparándose para un viaje.** Ustedes van a hacer un viaje en auto y
deben tomar varias decisiones antes de salir. Háganse preguntas para decidir lo
que van a hacer, y den una razón. Al conversar, usen un pronombre posesivo
para evitar la repetición.

MODELO:        usar mi coche o tu coche
          E1:  *¿Vamos a usar mi coche o el tuyo?*
          E2:  *Prefiero usar el tuyo porque es más nuevo.*

1. hablar con mi agente o tu agente
2. llevar tus maletas o las de mi hermano
3. usar mis mapas o tus mapas
4. llevar tu cámara o mi cámara
5. llevar tu celular o el de mi madre
6. usar tu GPS o el de mis hermanos

12-22 Recuerdo de vacaciones. **PRIMERA FASE.** Túrnense para hablar de sus vacaciones favoritas. En su conversación, incluyan los siguientes aspectos de sus respectivas vacaciones. Busquen aspectos similares y diferentes entre sus experiencias.

1. adónde fueron y con quiénes
2. cómo viajaron al lugar
3. el alojamiento
4. la comida
5. sus diversiones
6. sus actividades culturales

SEGUNDA FASE. Ahora, comparen sus vacaciones favoritas con las de otra pareja.

MODELO: adónde fueron

E1: *Nuestras vacaciones favoritas fueron en Estados Unidos, las mías en Florida y las de Carlos en Colorado.*

E2: *Las nuestras fueron en otros países, las mías en Costa Rica y las de Isabel en Chile.*

12-23 Objetos perdidos. Durante un viaje por avión usted perdió algunas pertenencias. Converse con el empleado/la empleada (su compañero/a) de la Oficina de Objetos Perdidos de la aerolínea y descríbale detalladamente cada objeto.

MODELO: E1: *Perdón. Anoche perdí mis llaves en el vuelo 1239.*

E2: *Aquí tengo algunas llaves. ¿Puede describirme las suyas?*

E1: *Las mías son negras y están en un llavero (*keyholder*) con otras llaves. El llavero tiene un juguete plástico amarillo.*

E2: *¿Son estas?*

E1: *Sí. Muchas gracias.*

SITUACIONES

1. **Role A.** Yesterday, you lost your wallet (color, size, contents) at a hotel in Panama City. Answer the questions of the employee at the Lost and Found desk. Then show him/her an identification document and thank him/her.

   Role B. You are a hotel employee who is helping a guest who has lost a wallet. Find out a) the person's name; b) a description of the wallet and its contents; and c) when he/she lost it. Ask for identification to verify ownership, and then return the wallet.

2. **Role A.** On the plane home from an ecotourism trip to Costa Rica, you sit next to a student returning from a similar trip. Ask your seatmate a) why he/she went on an ecotourism trip; b) what national park he/she liked best, and why; c) one thing he/she learned from the trip; and d) whether he/she has plans to return to Costa Rica. Answer your seatmate's questions about your trip.

   Role B. On the plane home from an ecotourism trip to Costa Rica, you sit next to a student returning from a similar trip. After answering your seatmate's questions, ask him/her similar questions about his/her trip. Comment on how your experience was similar to that of your seatmate.

## 3. Expressing possession: Stressed possessive adjectives

MANOLO: ¡Ay, Dios mío! Se me perdió la llave. No está en mi bolsillo. Adelita, ¿tienes la tuya?

ADELITA: Por supuesto, mi amor. **La llave mía** está aquí. Dejaste **la llave tuya** en la recepción, ¿no te acuerdas?

MANOLO: Ah, tienes razón. ¿Y los teléfonos celulares?

ADELITA: Sí, tengo **el celular tuyo** y **el celular mío** también. No te preocupes.

**Piénselo.** Mire el dibujo e indique a quién pertenece cada objeto en la lista a continuación.

| | |
|---|---|
| 1. ___ la llave que tiene la mujer | a. a Manolo |
| 2. ___ la llave que está en la recepción | b. a Adelita |
| 3. ___ los teléfonos celulares | c. a los dos |

■ In the previous section, you learned to use possessive pronouns to avoid repetition in speaking and writing. Stressed possessive adjectives, whose forms are the same, emphasize to whom a particular object belongs. Because they are adjectives, they always immediately follow the noun to which they refer.

| SINGULAR | | PLURAL | | |
|---|---|---|---|---|
| **MASCULINE** | **FEMININE** | **MASCULINE** | **FEMININE** | |
| mío | mía | míos | mías | *my, (of) mine* |
| tuyo | tuya | tuyos | tuyas | *your (familiar), (of) yours* |
| suyo | suya | suyos | suyas | *your (formal), his, her, its, their, (of) yours his, hers, theirs* |
| nuestro | nuestra | nuestros | nuestras | *our, (of) ours* |
| vuestro | vuestra | vuestros | vuestras | *your (familiar), (of) yours* |

■ Stressed possessive adjectives agree in gender and number with the noun they modify. An article or demonstrative adjective usually precedes the noun. Use stressed possessives for emphasis.

| | |
|---|---|
| El cuarto **mío** es grandísimo. | *My room is very big.* |
| La maleta **tuya** está en la recepción. | *Your suitcase is at the front desk.* |
| Esos primos **míos** llegan hoy. | *Those cousins of mine arrive today.* |
| Las llaves **nuestras** están encima del escritorio. | *Our keys are on the desk.* |

▪ The third-person possessive adjectives **suyo**, **suya**, **suyos**, and **suyas** have more than one meaning. You can avoid confusion by using **de** + *subject pronoun/name* instead of the possessive adjective.

| la maleta **suya** | la maleta **de él/ella** | *his/her suitcase* |
| | la maleta **de usted/ustedes** | *your (sing./pl.) suitcase* |
| | la maleta **de ellos/ellas** | *their suitcase* |

| los billetes **suyos** | los billetes **de él/ella** | *his/her tickets* |
| | los billetes **de usted/ustedes** | *your (sing./pl.) tickets* |
| | los billetes **de ellos/ellas** | *their tickets* |

**12-24 En la sala de embarque (*departure*). PRIMERA FASE.** La familia Suárez está esperando su vuelo. Complete la conversación entre los padres y sus hijos con la forma apropiada del adjetivo posesivo entre paréntesis.

SR. SUÁREZ: ¡Lalo y Lucy, no se vayan, vengan acá y siéntense! ¿Dónde están sus mochilas?

LALO: La mochila (1) _____ (mío) está aquí.

LUCY: No, Lalo, no es la mochila (2) _____ (tuyo), tú no tienes una mochila rosada. Mamá, Lalo quiere todas las cosas (3) _____ (mío).

SRA. SUÁREZ: Niños, no discutan. ¿Dónde están los bolsos (4) _____ (nuestro)? En uno de ellos están los sándwiches que preparé.

LALO: Sí, tengo hambre. Mamá, ¿cuál es el sándwich (5) _____ (mío)? Quiero un sándwich de jamón.

SRA. SUÁREZ: Tranquilo, Lalo, hay sándwiches para todos. (*Le da un bolso.*) Dale un sándwich a tu hermana. Los almuerzos (6) _____ (suyo) están en este bolso.

**SEGUNDA FASE.** Cada uno de ustedes no encuentra dos objetos personales de la siguiente lista. Usen los adjetivos posesivos y otras formas que sean necesarias para hablar de sus objetos perdidos.

| | |
| --- | --- |
| carnet de estudiante | libro de español |
| gafas de sol | tarjeta magnética para entrar a la residencia |
| iPod | teléfono celular |

**12-25 Identificar los objetos perdidos.** Todas las personas de su grupo han perdido una de sus pertenencias. Un/a agente de la Oficina de Objetos Perdidos les muestra los objetos. Identifique y reclame (*reclaim*) su objeto. Siga el modelo.

**MODELO:** AGENTE: *Aquí tengo un libro de biología.*

E1: *¡Qué bueno! Es el libro mío.*

AGENTE: *X dice que el libro es suyo. ¿Es cierto? ¿Es de él/ella?*

E2: *Sí, es el libro suyo.*

**12-26 Inventos del futuro.** PRIMERA FASE. Lea la descripción de un invento fantástico. Luego diseñe su propio invento. Escriba una lista de sus rasgos, usando adjetivos y pronombres posesivos.

# Este DVD es mucho mejor que el tuyo porque:

- El DVD nuestro es pequeño. Lo puedes llevar en tu bolsillo o cartera.
- El DVD nuestro es desplegable.
- El DVD nuestro te permite ver tus películas favoritas en una pantalla grande.

Para más información, visita nuestro sitio web www.mp3origami.com.

SEGUNDA FASE. Describan sus inventos a su grupo. Decidan entre todos cuál es el más creativo y el más útil. En su opinión, ¿cuáles serán inventados en el futuro?

## SITUACIONES

1. **Role A:** You represent a company that offers a beach-and-sun spring break trip on a Caribbean island. The price includes transportation, hotel, one meal per day, and snorkeling (*buceo*) lessons. Describe your trip to a group of students, contrasting it with the trip being offered by a rival company (your partner's).

   **Role B.** You represent a company that offers a service-oriented spring break trip to a rural area of Panama. Participants will help build a children's community center. The price includes lodging with a local family and all meals. Participants pay $200 toward their airfare. Describe your trip to a group of students, contrasting it with the one being offered by a rival company (your partner's).

2. **Role A.** A friend of yours has been accepted to your college/university and is trying to decide between it and another school. Mention several positive points about your college/university, and respond to your friend's comments about the other school.

   **Role B.** You have been accepted to two colleges/universities and are trying to decide which one to attend. Ask your friend about his/her school. You already know quite a lot about the other school, so explain some of the differences between it and your friend's school.

## 4. Talking about the past: Review of the preterit and imperfect

(José le explica a Alejandra un poco sobre la historia del Canal de Panamá).

JOSÉ: Mira, esta es una foto del Canal de Panamá.

ALEJANDRA: ¡Qué grande! ¿Y cuándo lo **construyeron**?

JOSÉ: **Abrieron** el tránsito por el Canal en 1914, pero sólo en 1999 Panamá **asumió** la responsabilidad total de él. Antes, **estaba** bajo el control de Estados Unidos. Hay datos muy interesantes sobre el Canal.

ALEJANDRA: ¿Cómo cuáles?

JOSÉ: Antes de 1914, los barcos **viajaban** 22.500 km (14.000 millas) para ir de Nueva York a San Francisco. Después de 1914, pasar del Atlántico al Pacífico por el Canal, **resultó** ser un viaje más corto, de 9.5000 km (6.000 millas). **¿Sabías** que en 1928, Richard Halliburton, un aventurero y escritor norteamericano, **transitó** el Canal nadando? **Estuvo** en el agua por diez días y **pagó** el peaje más bajo en la historia del Canal, de sólo treinta y seis centavos.

### Cultura

La construcción del Canal de Panamá, que une el Océano Atlántico con el Océano Pacífico, hizo realidad un sueño de más de tres siglos. Requirió la participación de varios países y es una de las iniciativas internacionales que más positivamente ha influido en la economía mundial. El Canal de Panamá se inauguró en 1914 y tiene 71 kms de largo. Ver *Enfoque cultural* para más información.

**Piénselo.** Identifique los verbos en el diálogo que narran los eventos (**E**) que ocurrieron y los que ofrecen una descripción (**D**) del Canal de Panamá en el pasado.

1. ___ **Abrieron** el tránsito por el Canal en 1914.
2. ___ En 1999 Panamá **asumió** la responsabilidad total de él.
3. ___ Antes, **estaba** bajo el control de Estados Unidos.
4. ___ Antes de 1914, los barcos **viajaban** 22.500 km (14.000 millas) para ir de Nueva York a San Francisco.
5. ___ **Pagó** el peaje (*toll*) más bajo en la historia del Canal.

■ In previous chapters you learned two tenses that Spanish uses to express the past: the preterit (**el pretérito**) and the imperfect (**el imperfecto**). You used the preterit to talk about past events, actions, and conditions that are viewed as completed or ended. You used the imperfect to describe characteristics and conditions in the past, to express habitual or repeated actions, or states in progress at a particular time in the past, and to tell the time and someone's age in the past. In this section you will gain further experience using both tenses to narrate in the past.

Refer to *Capítulos* 6 through 8 for a review of verb endings of regular and irregular verbs.

**12-27 Un viaje accidentado.** Unos turistas hicieron un viaje de turismo al Volcán Arenal en Costa Rica. Mientras viajaban al lugar, el volcán comenzó a erupcionar. Un turista cuenta la historia. Indique si las siguientes afirmaciones narran los eventos (**E**) que ocurrieron o si describen (**D**) el lugar y los personajes.

Una erupción del Volcán Arenal, uno de los volcanes más activos del mundo

Al acercarnos al área del Volcán Arenal, **nos dimos cuenta**[1] ___ de que todos **miraban**[2] ___ desde la distancia el humo y la lava que **salían**[3] ___ del volcán. Algunos **sacaron**[4] ___ sus cámaras de video y **comenzaron**[5] ___ a grabar. El guía turístico nos **indicó**[6] ___ qué hacer. Todos **sabíamos**[7] ___ que acercarnos al volcán no **era**[8] ___ prudente. Después de treinta minutos **llegaron**[9] ___ dos helicópteros y nos **llevaron**[10] ___ a un lugar seguro. Todos **estábamos**[11] ___ aliviados (*relieved*) de estar fuera de peligro. Esa noche, les **contamos**[12] ___ la historia de nuestro escape del volcán a los otros huéspedes del hotel. Nos **hicieron**[13] ___ muchas preguntas y **hablamos**[14] ___ por varias horas. Después, yo no **podía**[15] ___ dormir. **Pensaba**[16] ___ en los eventos del día, y **sentía**[17] ___ la tensión y la incertidumbre otra vez. Finalmente **me dormí**[18] ___ , y **me desperté**[19] ___ al día siguiente con ganas de continuar la excursión.

**12-28 Un viaje inolvidable.** PRIMERA FASE. Ustedes viajaron a Panamá durante sus vacaciones. Tomen apuntes sobre lo siguiente.

1. las fechas del viaje
2. dos o tres actividades relacionadas con estas fotografías que ustedes hicieron en varios lugares
3. el tiempo, las personas que conocieron, la ropa de las personas, la comida
4. algún aspecto de la cultura local que les interesó

Una guacamaya de Panamá

Playa Boca del Toro

Cestos tejidos por los indios emberá de Panamá

Palacio Presidencial Ciudad de Panama

 **SEGUNDA FASE.** Cuéntenles a sus compañeros/as los diversos aspectos de su viaje. Sus compañeros van a hacerles preguntas sobre sus experiencias.

**12-29 La flora y fauna de Costa Rica.** PRIMERA FASE. Ustedes hicieron una excursión a los Canales de Tortuguero en Costa Rica para informarse y luego preparar un panfleto sobre la flora y fauna de esa región para los alumnos de su universidad. Sigan las instrucciones a continuación para preparar su panfleto con estas fotos que tomaron. Visiten la página web de *Mosaicos* y sigan los enlaces para encontrar más fotos e información útil sobre los Canales de Tortuguero.

Tomen apuntes sobre...

1. una descripción del Parque Nacional del Tortuguero: ¿Dónde está? ¿Cómo es?
2. las características de las especies de animales y vegetación que hay allí

Iguana en la jungla costarricense

Flor silvestre en Costa Rica

Madre y crío de monos ardilla (*squirrel monkey*)

SEGUNDA FASE. Ahora escriban el panfleto publicitario para atraer la atención de los alumnos de su universidad. Pueden preparar una presentación visual del panfleto, usando las fotos de la *Primera fase* u otras apropiadas.

---

## SITUACIONES

1. **Role A.** You and a friend just started your trip to the San Blas island in Panama, the home of the Kuna people. Call home to say that a) your plane left your city on time; b) the weather between your city and the city where you will take the connecting flight (**vuelo de conexión**) was very bad, so the airline cancelled your flight; and c) you and your friend are at the airport waiting. Finally, d) promise that you will call again soon.

   **Role B.** Your son/daughter and a friend just left for a trip to Panama. After a few hours, he/she calls you with some bad news. React appropriately and ask pertinent questions. Ask him/her to call you again soon. Wish them a good trip.

2. **Role A.** You just won a trip to the Spanish-speaking country of your choice. Call a friend who has traveled a lot and a) tell him/her the news; b) ask for suggestions about where to go; c) mention how much money you received to spend in the country (**dinero para llevar**); and d) invite her/him to go with you.

   **Role B.** Your friend calls with some good news. React appropriately and: a) answer his/her questions; b) offer ideas about where to go; and c) accept his/her invitation.

# MOSAICOS

## A escuchar

### Antes de escuchar

**12-30 Preparación.** Usted escuchará una conversación telefónica entre una agente de viajes y el señor Hernández, quien busca un hotel para él y su familia en San José. Antes de escuchar, escriba tres características que el Sr. Hernández probablemente desea que tenga el hotel y tres preguntas que él probablemente hará.

### Escuchar

**12-31 ¿Comprende usted?** Read the statements below. Then, as you listen to the conversation between Mr. Hernández and the travel agent, check (✓) the statements that best report what was said.

CD 5
Track 39

1. _____ El Sr. Hernández dice que quiere un hotel económico que esté cerca del centro de la ciudad.
2. _____ La agente tiene varias posibilidades y le describe tres hoteles para que él escoja.
3. _____ El Sr. Hernández afirma que él prefiere que sus hijos y esposa estén cómodos aunque (*even though*) él tenga que tomar un taxi o manejar mucho.
4. _____ La agente le dice al cliente que su elección no es buena porque el hotel es muy caro y está muy lejos del centro de la ciudad.

### Después de escuchar

**12-32 Ahora usted. Compartan sus respuestas a las siguientes preguntas.**

1. Cuando usted busca un hotel, ¿es más importante que sea económico o que sea de lujo (*luxurious*)?
2. ¿Qué servicios o comodidades prefiere usted que ofrezca un hotel?
3. ¿Cuál es el hotel más cómodo en el que usted se ha alojado? Explique.

# A conversar

## Antes de conversar

**12-33 Preparación. PRIMERA FASE.** Cuando alguien vuelve a casa después de un viaje, sus amigos y familiares siempre le dicen: "Cuéntanos de tu viaje. ¿Te pasó algo interesante?" Piense en sus viajes y elija una experiencia durante uno de ellos que podría (*you could*) contarles a sus amigos. Puede usar uno de los temas de la lista.

- perderse en un lugar desconocido
- un artículo perdido
- un error lingüístico o cultural
- un robo
- una situación embarazosa o peligrosa (*dangerous*)

**SEGUNDA FASE.** Ahora, usando la tabla a continuación, organice sus ideas sobre la experiencia que escogió en la *Primera fase*. Después, marque (✓) los elementos que ha escrito que considera más importantes para su cuento.

| EVENTOS | DESCRIPCIÓN<br>(dónde, cuándo, con quiénes y otros detalles) | PARTES<br>IMPORTANTES |
|---|---|---|
| 1. | | |
| 2. | | |
| 3. | | |

## Conversar

**12-34 Entre nosotros.** Usando la tabla que preparó en la actividad **12-33**, cuente su historia. Acuérdese de usar las frases de *En directo* para llamar la atención de sus compañeros/as a las partes más importantes de su historia.

## Después de conversar

**12-35 Un poco más.** Después de cada cuento, los oyentes deben hacer preguntas y sugerencias con los siguientes propósitos:

1. aclarar lo que pasó
2. aclarar información sobre dónde y cuándo pasaron los eventos
3. saber más sobre los sentimientos del narrador/de la narradora durante los eventos
4. sugerir maneras de fortalecer (*strengthen*) el impacto del cuento en los oyentes

# A leer

**Focus on logical relationships**

Magazine articles often address current issues, such as identity theft, sedentary lifestyles, or travel comfort and convenience. When you read an article of this type, you can take advantage of its structure to maximize your comprehension. As you read, look for the issues or problems that the author introduces, and then focus on the logical relationships that the author establishes, such as between problems and their causes, or problems and their solutions. An individual case often appears at the beginning of the article as an example of the problem, and then returns at the end to illustrate a possible solution.

## Antes de leer

**12-36 Preparación.** PRIMERA FASE. Marque (✓) las oraciones que reflejan su opinión y sus experiencias con respecto a los viajes.

1. _____ Prefiero viajar por tierra porque los autobuses y los carros son más seguros que los aviones.
2. _____ Me encantan los viajes por avión porque son más rápidos.
3. _____ Cuando viajo por avión, no facturo mi maleta porque no quiero que la aerolínea la pierda.
4. _____ Me molestan mucho las medidas (*measures*) de seguridad en los aeropuertos, como quitarme los zapatos y limitar la cantidad de líquidos.
5. _____ Prefiero organizar mi propio viaje que comprar un paquete de hotel, comida, excursiones, etc., por medio de una agencia de viajes.
6. _____ Me gusta alquilar un auto cuando viajo para explorar los lugares nuevos.
7. _____ Cuando viajo, siempre llevo el dinero y las tarjetas de crédito en un cinturón especial o en una bolsa debajo de mi ropa, no en la billetera.
8. _____ He tenido problemas alguna vez para cruzar una frontera internacional.

 SEGUNDA FASE. Ahora comparen sus respuestas y respondan a las siguientes preguntas.

1. ¿Qué preferencias de viaje tienen ustedes en común?
2. ¿Qué experiencias de viaje tienen ustedes en común?
3. ¿Qué problema serio ha tenido cada uno/a de ustedes en un viaje?
4. ¿Han tenido problemas semejantes o diferentes?

## Leer

### Vacaciones o pesadilla[1]: Cómo reducir los problemas en los viajes

Isabel y Mario, una pareja de nacionalidad norteamericana y origen uruguayo, decidieron celebrar su aniversario de boda en Costa Rica. Para preparar el viaje se pusieron en contacto por Internet con una agencia de nombre algo pomposo, y desgraciadamente irónico, como comprobarían[2] después: Viajes Reales. La agencia ofrecía paquetes de excursiones que incluían billete de avión, hotel y coche de alquiler por precios bastante módicos. Las fotos prometían una estancia relajada en un hotel de ambiente exótico al noroeste del país. La variedad de piscinas, la cercanía del mar, la apetecible gastronomía local y los cócteles refrescantes que se veían en lujosas mesitas junto a las hamacas de los afortunados clientes confirmaban que se trataba de un verdadero paraíso.

Isabel y Mario pagaron la cantidad requerida y no dudaron ni un momento de lo acertado[3] de su decisión, a pesar de no haber recibido garantías razonables de que sus expectativas se iban a cumplir. Al llegar a su destino comprobaron que las fotos no correspondían a la realidad. El hotel no tenía ni vista al mar ni jardines exóticos. Las habitaciones eran pequeñísimas e incómodas y la comida dejaba mucho que desear.

Lamentablemente, esta no es una anécdota aislada entre los viajeros. ¿Quién no ha sufrido alguna vez la pérdida de su equipaje, las incomodidades de un vuelo cancelado, el robo de su pasaporte o sus tarjetas de crédito, los problemas en la aduana por comprar un producto comestible que no se permite pasar?

Sin embargo, algunos de estos problemas se pueden prevenir. La experiencia de los viajes nos enseña a ser prudentes y prever los riesgos. La facilidad que proporciona Internet es conveniente, pero cuando se viaja por primera vez es preferible dirigirse a una agencia local para que los especialistas de viajes nos ayuden a elegir las mejores opciones. Frecuentemente es más caro hacerlo así, pero se puede ahorrar tiempo y evitar sorpresas desagradables. Por otra parte, a veces resulta más barato comprar un seguro de cancelación que arriesgarse a perder, por una razón u otra, el costo de un billete de avión.

Algunos incidentes ligados a los viajes son naturalmente inevitables, pero otros se pueden prevenir. Por ejemplo, es posible minimizar el riesgo de un robo llevando los pasaportes y papeles importantes en una bolsita colgada del cuello que se oculta debajo de la ropa, o en un bolsillo doble del pantalón. En cuanto a los impedimentos en la aduana, hay que tener en cuenta que las medidas de seguridad son cada vez más estrictas. Ya no se puede subir al avión con productos líquidos de más de tres onzas y sólo se permite viajar con las bebidas y comestibles comprados en las tiendas interiores del aeropuerto. Recuerdo el disgusto de un amigo mío cuando los agentes de aduana le confiscaron el jamón que le habían regalado unos amigos españoles.

Por suerte, las vacaciones de Mario e Isabel no fueron un desastre total. La pareja pudo disfrutar del maravilloso país en sus excursiones a Puntarenas, Puerto Limón y los parques naturales cercanos a Orosí. También pudieron celebrar su aniversario en un magnífico restaurante de primera clase. ¡Qué lástima que la experiencia completa no fuera tan agradable! Como dice el sabio refrán[4]: Más vale prevenir… que curar.

[1]*nightmare*   [2]*would find out*   [3]*the wisdom*   [4]*proverb*

**12-37 Primera mirada.** Marque (✔) los problemas que enfrentan los viajeros, según el artículo.

1. _____ agencias de viajes deshonestas
2. _____ maletas perdidas
3. _____ vuelos cancelados
4. _____ choques de avión
5. _____ robo de las tarjetas de crédito
6. _____ autos aquilados que no funcionan
7. _____ problemas para entrar en otro país
8. _____ enfermedades causadas por la comida

**12-38 Segunda mirada.** Busque en el artículo la siguiente información.

1. Tres problemas que tuvieron Isabel y Mario en sus vacaciones
2. Causa principal de la situación desagradable de Isabel y Mario
3. Recomendaciones para evitar o minimizar los siguientes problemas

## Después de leer

**12-39 Ampliación.** ¿Qué palabras y frases del artículo están asociadas con las siguientes funciones retóricas?

1. Una agencia quiere hacer publicidad para atraer clientes.
2. Los problemas que tienen algunas personas durante un viaje:
   a. la pérdida de su equipaje
   b. un vuelo cancelado
   c. encuentros con los oficiales en los aeropuertos (aduana, seguridad)
3. Presentar el tema del artículo por medio de un refrán.

# A escribir

**Use facts to support a point of view**

In academic life, you are often faced with tasks that require presenting factual information. Facts are considered objective, neutral, or impartial representations of reality. Therefore, to maintain objectivity, you should provide reliable data, such as statistics, opinions, and statements made by experts, and so on.

Facts also serve as the basis to support a personal point of view on an issue. For example, a person may be against drinking and driving (personal point of view) because statistics show that drunk driving causes accidents (facts).

Therefore, to support your point of view on a particular issue in an objective manner...

■ inform yourself by consulting reliable sources.
■ base your statements on the information you gathered.
■ acknowledge your sources of information.

## Antes de escribir

**12-40 Preparación.** En un concurso, su amigo/a ganó diez mil dólares para viajar a San José, Costa Rica. Puesto que él/ella nunca ha hecho un viaje largo, siente mucha ansiedad (*anxiety*). Por eso, le pidió a usted ayuda con la planificación de su viaje. Para escribirle una carta objetiva y ayudarlo/la, haga lo siguiente:

1. En la página web de *Mosaicos*, lea uno o dos artículo(s) sobre el tema o sobre temas relacionados.
2. Subraye las ideas y los datos concretos.
3. Tome nota de los datos objetivos más relevantes que puedan ayudar a su amigo/a.
4. Seleccione la información y las ideas que lo/la ayudarán a sustentar (*support*) su posición personal sobre la planificación de los viajes.
5. Organice la información y las ideas en orden de importancia.
6. Seleccione las palabras adecuadas para lograr (*achieve*) el tono adecuado.

## Escribir

**12-41 Manos a la obra.** Escríbale una carta a su amigo/a. Incluya la información que preparó en la actividad **12-40**. Además, dele buenos consejos para disminuir su ansiedad.

> *Querido/a amigo/a:*

## Después de escribir

**12-42 Revisión.** Ahora lea su carta y verifique lo siguiente, pensando en su lector/a.

1. ¿Es evidente en la carta la posición de usted sobre la planificación de los viajes? ¿Sustenta usted su posición con información objetiva basada en estadísticas, en evidencia o en la opinión de los expertos? ¿Le da algunas sugerencias a su amigo/a?
2. ¿Sigue la carta un orden claro? ¿Hay transiciones claras entre las diferentes ideas?
3. ¿Usó vocabulario relevante al tema? ¿Usó el tiempo (presente, pasado, futuro) y los modos (indicativo, subjuntivo, etc.) apropiados?
4. ¿Utilizó la puntuación necesaria y la ortografía correcta?

San José, Costa Rica

# ENFOQUE CULTURAL

## Centroamérica: un puente entre dos océanos

El poeta nicaragüense Ernesto Cardenal escribió en 1966 un libro de poemas titulado *El estrecho dudoso*[1]. En ese libro, Cardenal reflexiona sobre los viajes de los primeros españoles que llegaron a explorar Centroamérica. Estos conquistadores, entre los que figuran Balboa y Pedrarias Dávila, pronto oyeron hablar de una zona estrecha de tierra que comunicaba el Caribe con otro océano en el sur. Ellos tenían muchas dudas de si verdaderamente existía ese otro océano porque las noticias que tenían eran confusas y contradictorias. Y esta es la razón del título del libro de Cardenal. Sin

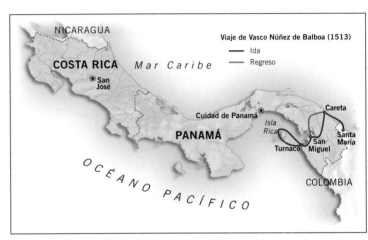

El viaje de Balboa entre los dos océanos

embargo, Balboa hizo amistad con Comogre, un jefe indígena, y este lo guió en un difícil viaje a través de las selvas de la región hasta que el 25 de septiembre de 1513, Balboa pudo ver por primera vez las aguas del mar del sur desde una montaña, de manera que él fue el primer europeo en ver el Océano Pacífico.

El Canal de Nicaragua fue una propuesta alternativa a la del Canal de Panamá, pero nunca se construyó.

Después del "descubrimiento" del Océano Pacífico, la importancia estratégica de Panamá y América Central fue evidente. Esta región se convirtió en un verdadero puente entre los dos océanos, de manera que la distancia entre España y sus colonias en América del Sur se reducía mucho. En los años siguientes, todos los viajes hacia Perú, y más tarde hacia las islas Filipinas en el Pacífico, usaron este puente para el transporte. Es imposible saber con seguridad cuántas personas hicieron el viaje entre los dos océanos siguiendo una ruta semejante a la de Balboa, pero lo que sí podemos asegurar es que una gran cantidad de oro, plata, perlas, seda y otros productos de gran valor hicieron este viaje.

---

[1]*The Doubtful Strait*

Era un viaje muy difícil, lento y costoso. El clima extremo de esta región, con fuertes calores y lluvias intensas, dificultaba el transporte, además de que en esa época los viajes se hacían a pie o a caballo y el terreno era selvático y pantanoso. Por estas razones, desde muy pronto los españoles empezaron a pensar en construir un canal para facilitar el viaje entre los dos océanos.

Los primeros estudios recomendaron la construcción de un canal en un lugar diferente de donde hoy está el Canal de Panamá. Desde muy pronto se hicieron proyectos para construir un canal en territorio que hoy pertenece a Nicaragua, aprovechando ríos

El presidente Theodore Roosevelt maneja una de las modernas máquinas usadas para la construcción del Canal de Panamá.

y lagos que existen en ese país. Durante el siglo XIX, Estados Unidos se interesó muchísimo en este proyecto, pero la oposición de Inglaterra impidió la construcción del canal. Sin embargo, Cornelius Vanderbilt, un empresario de Nueva York, construyó una ruta terrestre, paralela al proyectado canal, que se convirtió en la principal vía de comercio entre Nueva York y San Francisco durante muchos años. Y aunque Vanderbilt tenía planes para construir el canal, ese proyecto nunca se realizó. A pesar de eso, los planes para construir un canal alternativo al de Panamá en Nicaragua vuelven a aparecer periódicamente y esa es una idea que no ha desaparecido completamente.

En la década de 1880, La Compañía del Canal de Panamá, una empresa francesa, inició los trabajos de construcción del actual Canal de Panamá. Ferdinand de Lesseps, el ingeniero que construyó el Canal de Suez, fue nombrado presidente de la compañía, pero el mal diseño del proyecto, la tecnología inadecuada, la corrupción, la mala administración y las malas condiciones de salud de esta región paralizaron la construcción. Muchas personas murieron víctimas de la malaria y otras enfermedades tropicales durante la construcción del canal. Entonces, una compañía de Estados Unidos compró los derechos de construcción y empezó a trabajar en el canal en 1904, cuando Panamá se independizó de Colombia. Esta empresa cambió el diseño del proyecto, introdujo nuevas máquinas y finalmente un viejo barco francés, el "Alexander La Valley", fue el primero en hacer el viaje completo a través del canal el 7 de enero de 1914, casi exactamente 400 años después de que Comogre guiara a Balboa hasta el mar del sur.

**12-43 Comprensión.** PRIMERA FASE. Reconocimiento De Palabras Clave.
Encuentre en el texto la palabra o expresión que mejor expresa el significado de
las siguientes ideas.

1. bridge        _____
2. jungle        _____
3. silk          _____
4. swampy        _____
5. enterprise    _____
6. health        _____
7. machines      _____

SEGUNDA FASE. **Oraciones importantes.** Subraye las afirmaciones que contienen
ideas que se encuentran en el texto. Luego indique en qué parte del texto están.

1. A contemporary poet from Nicaragua wrote a book about the first men
   who explored the region of Panama and Costa Rica.
2. Although the natives gave the Spaniards confusing information, Balboa and
   his friends clearly understood that there was another ocean nearby, and they
   were quick to discover it on their own.
3. Balboa was the first European to see the Pacific Ocean.
4. Many people and products were transported across Panama from Peru and
   other Spanish colonies to Spain.
5. Among the difficulties travelers had to face were extreme weather, travel by
   foot or on horseback, tropical forests, and swampy terrain.
6. The present location of the Panama Canal was favored by the earliest
   studies and recommendations.
7. The American company that finally built the Panama Canal had to make
   major changes to the original design of the project.
8. If Balboa had lived 400 years, he would have been proud to see the
   "Alexander La Valley" sail the canal.

TERCERA FASE. **Ideas principales.** Escriba un párrafo breve en español resumiendo
las ideas principales expresadas en el texto.

**12-44 Use la información.** Usted debe preparar una presentación oral breve
sobre uno de los temas a continuación. Enfóquese sobre el impacto económico
y social de los eventos históricos que trate en su informe.

- Cornelius Vanderbilt
- el Canal de Nicaragua
- el Canal de Panamá
- la ampliación del Canal de Panamá
- la ecología del Canal de Panamá

Para preparar esta actividad, visite la página web de *Mosaicos* y siga los enlaces
útiles.

# VOCABULARIO

| **Los medios de transporte** | **Means of transportation** |
|---|---|
| el autobús/bus | bus |
| el avión | plane |
| el barco | ship/boat |
| el metro | subway |
| el tren | train |

| **En el aeropuerto** | **At the airport** |
|---|---|
| la aduana | customs |
| la aerolínea/línea aérea | airline |
| el asiento | seat |
|   de pasillo/ventanilla | aisle/window seat |
| la clase turista | tourist class |
| el mostrador | counter |
| la primera clase | first class |
| la puerta (de salida) | gate |
| la salida de emergencia | emergency exit |
| el vuelo | flight |

| **Las personas** | **People** |
|---|---|
| el/la agente de viajes | travel agent |
| el/la auxiliar de vuelo | flight attendant |
| el cartero/la cartera | mail carrier |
| el pasajero/la pasajera | passenger |

| **Las partes de un coche** | **Parts of a car** |
|---|---|
| el capó | hood |
| el espejo retrovisor | rearview mirror |
| la guantera | glove compartment |
| el limpiaparabrisas | windshield wiper |
| la llanta | tire |
| el maletero/el baúl | trunk |
| el motor | motor |
| el parachoques | bumper |
| la placa | license plate |
| el radiador | radiator |
| la rueda | wheel |
| el volante | steering wheel |

| **Los viajes** | **Trips** |
|---|---|
| la agencia de viajes | travel agency |
| la autopista | freeway |
| el boleto/el pasaje | ticket |
| la carretera | highway |
| el crucero | cruise |
| el equipaje | luggage |
| la escala | stopover |
| la maleta | suitcase |
| el maletín | briefcase |
| el pasaporte | passport |
| la tarjeta de embarque | boarding pass |
| el trayecto | route |
| la velocidad | speed |

| **En el hotel** | **In the hotel** |
|---|---|
| el alojamiento | lodging |
| la caja fuerte | safe |
| la habitación doble/sencilla | double/single room |
| la llave | key |
| la recepción | front desk |
| la tarjeta magnética | key card |

| **Los lugares** | **Places** |
|---|---|
| la cuadra | city block |
| la esquina | corner |

| **El correo** | **Mail** |
|---|---|
| el buzón | mailbox |
| el correo electrónico | email |
| la carta | letter |
| el paquete | package |
| la postal | postcard |
| el sello | stamp |
| el sobre | envelope |

| **Las descripciones** | **Descriptions** |
|---|---|
| lleno/a | full |
| vacío/a | empty |

| **Verbos** | **Verbs** |
|---|---|
| cancelar | to cancel |
| doblar | to turn |
| facturar | to check in (luggage) |
| manejar | to drive |
| perderse (ie) | to get lost |
| recorrer | to cover, to travel |
| reservar | to make a reservation |
| revisar | to inspect |
| viajar | to travel |
| volar (ue) | to fly |

| **Palabras y expresiones útiles** | **Useful words and expressions** |
|---|---|
| el cajero automático | ATM |
| de ida y vuelta | round trip |
| hacer cola | to stand in line |
| seguir (i) derecho | to go straight |
| una vez | once |

> See pages 410 and 413 for a list of stressed possessive adjectives and pronouns.

# Las artes y las letras

Detalle de tabla de madera pintada, siglo XVI. Museo Casa de Murillo. La Paz, Bolivia

## In this chapter you will learn how to:

- talk about art and culture
- express doubt and uncertainty
- hypothesize about the future
- describe states and conditions

**Cultural focus:** Bolivia, Paraguay

PERÚ

Lago Titicaca

B R A S I L

Las montañas que rodean La Paz

Trinidad

Copacabana

⊛ La Paz

Cochabamba

Mujer indígena en Copacabana

Oruro

**BOLIVIA**

Potosí

Sucre

El festival de Oruro

A L T I P L A N O

Bombilla de yerba mate

Río Paraguay

**PARAGUAY**

Concepción

San Pedro

Salto del Guairá

Río Paraná

Asunción ⊛

Ciudad del Este

Encarnación

El Palacio presidencial en Asunción

ARGENTINA

OCÉANO PACÍFICO

C H I L E

CORDILLERA DE LOS ANDES

**A vista de pájaro.** Piense en lo que sabe de Bolivia y Paraguay e indique si las siguientes afirmaciones son ciertas (**C**) o falsas (**F**).

1. ___ La capital más alta del mundo es Asunción.
2. ___ El río Paraná está en la frontera entre Paraguay y Argentina.
3. ___ Bolivia es más grande que Paraguay.
4. ___ El Altiplano está en la cordillera de los Andes.
5. ___ El lago Titicaca está entre Perú y Bolivia.
6. ___ El guaraní es una de las lenguas oficiales de Paraguay.

# A PRIMERA VISTA

## ◄)) La literatura y el cine

CD 6
Track 1

Uno de los **novelistas** más importantes de Hispanoamérica es el paraguayo Augusto Roa Bastos (1917-2005). Su novela *Yo, el supremo* (1974) **trata** el **tema** de las dictaduras. Su **personaje principal** se basa en la figura de José Rodríguez de Francia, dictador de Paraguay en las primeras décadas del siglo XIX. Este **escritor** fue uno de los iniciadores del movimiento literario conocido como *realismo mágico* que combina elementos mágicos o irracionales con unas situaciones de aparente normalidad.

Gabriel García Márquez (1928- ), colombiano, es otro escritor que se asocia con el realismo mágico. **A través de** sus **novelas** y **cuentos** ha sabido recrear un mundo mítico de gran riqueza humana. En su novela *Cien años de soledad* (1967) narra en tono épico la historia de una familia y la **fundación** y **desarrollo** de Macondo, un pueblo creado en su imaginación. En 1982 este autor recibió el **Premio** Nobel de Literatura. Algunas de sus obras han sido llevadas al cine, por ejemplo, *El amor en los tiempos del cólera* (2007), con el actor español Javier Bardem.

La **poesía** tiene nombres **destacados** en las letras hispanas. Gabriela Mistral (1889-1957), chilena, fue la primera persona de Hispanoamérica en recibir el Premio Nobel de Literatura, en 1945. Algunos de sus temas son el **amor** y la **amistad**. En otros de sus **poemas** habla de la identidad latinoamericana, con su mezcla de sangre mestiza y europea. Otros **poetas** universalmente conocidos son Pablo Neruda, también chileno, y César Vallejo, peruano.

El cine hispano ha dado numerosos ejemplos de **calidad** en películas de todos los países. Entre las que han sido **nominadas** o han ganado algún Óscar se encuentran las españolas *Mar adentro* (2004), de Alejandro Amenábar, y *Volver* (2006), de Pedro Almodóvar. La cubana *Fresa y chocolate* (1994), de Tomás Gutiérrez Alea, ganó el Oso de plata en el festival de Berlín, y la colombiana *La estrategia del caracol* (1993), de Sergio Cabrera, fue premiada en el festival de Valladolid. Entre los directores jóvenes más **prometedores** está la española Iciar Bollaín, autora de *Mataharis* (2007) y de *Te doy mis ojos* (2003), que **denuncia** el tema de la violencia doméstica.

Iciar Bollaín

**Cultura**

Las nominaciones y los premios son muy codiciados (*sought after*) en el mundo del cine. Las películas que compiten en los festivales de cine suelen adquirir más publicidad y tener más éxito económico. Ganar un Óscar a la mejor película extranjera es una de las aspiraciones de muchos directores de todo el mundo, pero hay otros festivales que también tienen mucho prestigio, como el Festival de Venecia en Italia, el Festival de Cannes en Francia, o el de Berlín en Alemania. En el mundo hispano también hay festivales de cine internacionales que tienen gran tradición y repercusión, como los de Valladolid (Seminci) y de San Sebastián en España.

**13-1 Cineastas (*Filmmakers*) y escritores. PRIMERA FASE.** Llenen la tabla con la información que obtuvieron sobre ciertos hispanos prominentes.

| NOMBRE | PROFESIÓN | LUGAR DE ORIGEN | DATOS INTERESANTES | OTRO DATO |
|---|---|---|---|---|
| | director de cine | Colombia | Ganó un premio en el festival de Valladolid. | |
| | poeta | Chile | | |
| Pedro Almodóvar | | | Es el director de la película *Volver*. | |
| | | | Una película suya denuncia el tema de la violencia doméstica. | |
| | escritor | | Ganó el Premio Nobel. | |

**SEGUNDA FASE.** Comparen su tabla con la de otra pareja, y entre todos hagan una lista de otros artistas o escritores hispanos famosos. Pueden incluir a gente del cine, la música, la pintura, el periodismo, la arquitectura, el diseño de ropa, etc. Incluyan el nombre y cubran los siguientes puntos:

**1.** profesión    **2.** lugar de origen    **3.** algunos datos interesantes de su carrera

**13-2 ¿De qué trata? PRIMERA FASE.** Intercambien información sobre un libro que han leído o una película que han visto últimamente. Utilicen las siguientes preguntas como guía.

**1.** ¿Quién es el autor/la autora del libro o el director/la directora de la película?
**2.** ¿Cuál es el tema?
**3.** ¿Quién es su personaje principal? ¿Cómo es?
**4.** ¿Le gustó la película/el libro? ¿Por qué?

**SEGUNDA FASE.** Comparta con la clase la información que ha obtenido de su compañero/a.

**13-3 Un poema.** PRIMERA FASE. Lean el siguiente poema de Gabriela Mistral y digan si las siguientes afirmaciones son ciertas (**C**) o falsas (**F**). Si son falsas, den la respuesta correcta.

### Dame la mano

Dame la mano y danzaremos;
dame la mano y me amarás.
Como una sola flor seremos,
como una flor, y nada más...

5  El mismo verso cantaremos,
al mismo paso bailarás.
Como una espiga ondularemos,
como una espiga, y nada más.

Te llamas Rosa y yo Esperanza;
10  pero tu nombre olvidarás,
porque seremos una danza
en la colina y nada más...

1. ___ Es un poema de amor.
2. ___ El poema habla de tres personas.
3. ___ El tiempo del poema es el pasado.
4. ___ Es un poema alegre.

**SEGUNDA FASE.** Hablen entre ustedes de la importancia de los siguientes temas en el poema y luego escriban un resumen breve del poema.

1. el amor
2. la naturaleza
3. la danza

**TERCERA FASE.** Busquen información en Internet sobre los siguientes poetas hispanos y preparen una breve presentación incluyendo los siguientes datos:

César Vallejo
Alejandra Pizárnik
Pablo Neruda
Federico García Lorca
Blanca Andreu
Adela Zamudio

1. Lugar de origen
2. Época en que viven/vivieron
3. Explicación de uno de sus poemas (tema y características de estilo)

# ■)) La pintura y el arte

CD 6
Track 2

El Museo del Prado tiene una excelente colección de cuadros de **pintores** españoles, como Diego Velázquez, del siglo XVII, y Francisco de Goya, del siglo XVIII. Uno de los cuadros más importantes de Velázquez es *Las Meninas*, donde **retrata** una **escena** en el palacio real. En esta escena vemos a una hija del rey Felipe IV **rodeada** de sus sirvientas. En el cuadro hay un espejo donde **se reflejan** los reyes. También hay un **autorretrato** del pintor.

Algunos de los mejores pintores del siglo XX, como Pablo Picasso y Salvador Dalí, también son españoles. En este cuadro vemos el estilo **surrealista** de Dalí, con sus relojes **blandos** y su obsesión por los insectos. Este **paisaje**, con el mar **al fondo**, es un **recuerdo** del pueblo del Mediterráneo donde él vivió, y se repite en muchos de sus cuadros. Picasso desarrolló el estilo **cubista** y fue muy original en el uso de los colores y las **formas**.

Source: Salvador Dali. "The Persistence of Memory."
© The Museum of Modern Art/Licensed by SCALA/Art Resource, NY. (162.1934). © 2005 Kingdom of spain. © 2005 Salvador Dali, Gala-Salvador Dali Foundation/ Artists Rights Society (ARS), New York.

Los mexicanos Frida Kahlo y Diego Rivera muestran en sus **obras** las costumbres y las condiciones sociales de su país. Este cuadro **se titula** "Danza en Tehuantepec" y en él se ve a una pareja haciendo una danza tradicional. Rivera es muy famoso por sus grandes **murales**. Algunos de ellos se pueden visitar en Ciudad de México.

El **escultor** y pintor colombiano Fernando Botero es conocido por sus voluminosas figuras humanas que **se exponen** en todos los museos del mundo. Botero reconoce la influencia artística de los grandes pintores españoles Velázquez y Goya, así como la de los **muralistas** mexicanos. En su obra, Botero critica con humor una sociedad infantilizada o inmadura en la que **abundan** los **símbolos** de la autoridad y del poder, como clérigos, presidentes y burgueses (*members of the middle class*).

**13-4 Descripciones.**  Relacione las siguientes afirmaciones con los pintores correspondientes que se mencionan en las presentaciones anteriores.

1. Pinta con humor retratos de figuras poderosas.
2. Sus cuadros son de estilo surrealista.
3. Es muy famoso por sus murales.
4. Fue un pintor español del siglo XVIII.
5. Es el pintor de *Las Meninas*.
6. Es una pintora mexicana que retrata las costumbres de su país.
7. Hizo retratos de la familia real.
8. Sus formas de estilo cubista son muy originales.

**13-5 Biografías.**  Escojan uno de los pintores anteriores y busquen información sobre él/ella en la página web de *Mosaicos*. Preparen una presentación visual para la clase que incluya lo siguiente.

1. lugar y fecha de nacimiento
2. título y descripción de una de sus obras más famosas
3. algún acontecimiento (*event*) notable de su vida

**13-6 Comparación.**  Comparen *Las Meninas* de Picasso con *Las Meninas* de Velázquez en la página anterior. Analicen los siguientes aspectos y expliquen cuál les gusta más y por qué.

Source: Pablo Picasso, "Las Meninas, after Velazquez, No. 1." Museu Picasso, Barcelona.
© 2004 Estate of Pablo Picasso/Artists Rights Society (ARS), New York. Bridgeman-Giraudon/
Art Resource, NY.

1. el color
2. la localización de los personajes
3. las formas
4. el estilo

- Negative words may precede or follow the verb. If they follow the verb, use the word **no** before the verb.

**Nadie** va a ese museo.

**No** va **nadie** a ese museo.

*No one/Nobody goes to that museum.*

- **Alguno** and **ninguno** shorten to **algún** and **ningún** before masculine singular nouns.

¿Ves **algún** cuadro interesante?     *Do you see any interesting paintings?*

No veo **ningún** cuadro interesante.     *I do not see any interesting paintings.*

- Use the personal **a** when **alguno/a/os/as** and **ninguno/a** refer to persons and are the direct object of the verb. Use it also with **alguien** and **nadie** since they always refer to people. Note that **ninguno/a** is normally used only in the singular.

¿Conoces a **alguno** de los artistas?     *Do you know any of the artists?*

**No**, no conozco **a ninguno**.     *No, I do not know any (of them).*

¿Conoces **alguna** de sus novelas?     *Do you know any of his/her novels?*

**No**, no conozco **ninguna**.     *No, I do not know any (of them).*

> **Lengua**
>
> **Ningunos/as** is used only with plural nouns that do not have a singular form, like **gafas**, for example. **No tenemos ningunas gafas de seguridad.** (*We don't have any safety glasses.*)

**13-14 Nada de nada.** Asocie cada pregunta con su probable respuesta.

1. ____ ¿Visitó usted Paraguay alguna vez?
2. ____ ¿Conoce a alguien en Bolivia?
3. ____ ¿Baila alguno de los bailes típicos de la región?
4. ____ ¿Alguien sabe quién escribió la novela *Pasiones griegas*?
5. ____ ¿Hay muchos estudiantes que viajaron a Bolivia?
6. ____ ¿Conoce alguna canción de Rubén Blades?

a. No, ninguna.
b. No, ninguno.
c. Nadie lo sabe.
d. No, a nadie.
e. No, nunca.
f. Sólo fueron algunos.

**13-15 ¿Con qué frecuencia?** Indique la frecuencia con que usted participa en cada una de las actividades y diga por qué las hace. Después pregúntele a su compañero/a y anote la información obtenida.

MODELO: ver una película en español
E1: *Veo una película en español todas las semanas porque me gusta escuchar la lengua. ¿Y tú?*
E2: *Yo nunca veo películas en español porque no tengo un DVD en casa.*

| ACTIVIDAD | YO | RAZÓN | MI COMPAÑERO/A | RAZÓN |
|---|---|---|---|---|
| ver obras de teatro | | | | |
| escribir poesía | | | | |
| aprender bailes nuevos | | | | |
| asistir a conciertos | | | | |
| leer novelas como diversión | | | | |
| ir a museos de arte | | | | |
| ver películas extranjeras | | | | |

1. **Role A.** You are a flight attendant on a flight to Asuncion. Ask a passenger if he/she would like to watch the film. Then respond to his/her complaints and requests by saying that a) there are no blankets but you can bring a pillow; b) there are no magazines in Spanish; and c) they do not have iced coffee because nobody ever asks for it.

   **Role B.** You are a passenger on a flight to Asuncion. Tell the flight attendant that you can never sleep on planes. Ask if you can have a magazine in Spanish and some iced coffee. It's a long flight, and you are in a bad mood, so respond negatively to whatever the flight attendant says.

2. **Role A.** You call the box office of a theater to purchase tickets for a children's play. When the clerk answers, ask a) if sometimes they offer free tickets for children under three; b) if they have any tickets for Friday or Saturday; and c) whether there are any family restaurants close to the theater. You may express your annoyance at all the negative answers you receive when you thank the clerk for his/her help.

   **Role B.** You are the clerk in a theater box office. A customer calls to ask about tickets for a children's play. Reply that a) they never give free tickets to young children; b) there aren't any tickets for the first day the customer inquires about, but there are some for the second day (but the seats are not good); and c) there are no suitable restaurants near the theater. You are in a bad mood and you let it show during the conversation.

**13-16 Una exposición de arte mala.** Usted piensa ir a una exposición de arte. Su compañero/a, que vio la exposición y piensa que fue un desastre, va a contestar sus preguntas negativamente.

MODELO:     ofrecer excursiones guiadas
   E1:  *¿Ofrecieron excursiones guiadas de la exposición?*
   E2:  *No, no ofrecieron ninguna excursión guiada.*

1. ver esculturas antiguas
2. gustar algunos cuadros
3. comer un buen plato en el restaurante del museo
4. dejar entrar gratis a los estudiantes universitarios
5. aceptar tarjetas de crédito
6. …

**13-17 ¡La negatividad es contagiosa!** Después de pasar el día con un amigo negativo/una amiga negativa, usted se siente influenciado/a y contesta a todo negativamente.

MODELO:     llamar a un amigo
   E1:  *¿Vas a llamar a un amigo?*
   E2:  *No, no voy a llamar a nadie.*

1. visitar La Paz alguna vez en el futuro
2. ver alguna película argentina esta noche
3. leer una novela o escuchar música
4. salir con algún amigo a un restaurante peruano
5. invitar a alguien a un concierto
6. …

**13-18 Planeando un viaje.** PRIMERA FASE. Ustedes quieren hacer un viaje a Paraguay para conocer su cultura. Comenten qué van a hacer allí.

MODELO:     pasar una semana en la capital
   E1:  *Quiero pasar una semana en la capital.*
   E2:  *Yo también. Es una ciudad bonita.*

1. hacer una excursión al parque nacional en el Chaco
2. visitar el Museo del Barro, un museo de los artes visuales en Asunción
3. conocer las comunidades menonitas (*Mennonite*)
4. comprar unos textiles bordados en ñandutí, el encaje (*lace*) típico de Paraguay
5. asistir a un partido de fútbol
6. probar el tereré, una bebida paraguaya refrescante

SEGUNDA FASE. Conversen sobre dos o tres actividades que quieren hacer en Paraguay. Después, reúnanse con otra pareja, explíquenle sus planes y escuchen los planes de sus compañeros/as. Respondan negativamente a los planes de la otra pareja.

## 2. Expressing doubt and uncertainty: Subjunctive with expressions of doubt

ANA MARÍA: ¡Qué buenos son! Es seguro que **ganan** el premio.

JULIO: No creo que **sean** tan buenos, y dudo que **salgan** bien en el concurso.

ANA MARÍA: Es posible que **tengan** éxito, ¿no?

JULIO: Creo que no. No tienen ni melodía ni ritmo. Es dudoso que **ganen**.

**Piénselo.** Indique (✓) si las siguientes oraciones expresan **certeza** o **duda**.

|  | CERTEZA | DUDA |
|---|---|---|
| 1. Es seguro que **ganan** el premio. | —— | —— |
| 2. No creo que **sean** tan buenos. | —— | —— |
| 3. Dudo que **salgan** bien en el concurso. | —— | —— |
| 4. Es posible que **tengan** éxito. | —— | —— |
| 5. Es dudoso que **ganen**. | —— | —— |

■ You learned in *Capítulo 12* to use the subjunctive in sentences that refer to a person, place, or thing that may not exist, for example, **¿Hay algún cantante en este concurso que sea muy bueno?** In this chapter you will learn to use the subjunctive for a related communicative function: to express doubt and uncertainty.

■ When the verb in the main clause expresses doubt or uncertainty, use a subjunctive verb form in the dependent clause (the clause that begins with **que**).

Dudo que **vendan** libros en español.   *I doubt (that) they sell books in Spanish.*

Es dudoso que el actor **llegue** tarde al teatro.   *It's doubtful (that) the actor will arrive late to the theater.*

- Use the subjunctive with impersonal expressions that denote doubt or uncertainty, such as **es dudoso que**, **es difícil que**, **es probable que**, and **es posible que**.

| | |
|---|---|
| Es dudoso que **encontremos** artesanía paraguaya en ese mercado. | *It is doubtful that we will find Paraguayan handicrafts in that market.* |
| Es posible que **tengan** textiles guatemaltecos. | *It is possible that they have Guatemalan textiles.* |

- Use the indicative with impersonal expressions that denote certainty: **es cierto/verdad que**, **es seguro que**, and **es obvio que**. When these expressions are negative, the following verb is in the subjunctive.

| | |
|---|---|
| Es verdad que el arpa y la guitarra **son** instrumentos muy populares en Paraguay. | *It is true that the harp and the guitar are very popular instruments in Paraguay.* |
| No es cierto que la música paraguaya se **conozca** mucho en Estados Unidos. | *It is not true that Paraguayan music is well known in the United States.* |

- When the verbs **creer** and **pensar** are used in the negative, the subjunctive is used in the dependent clause. In questions with these verbs, the subjunctive may be used to express uncertainty or to anticipate a negative response. If the question simply seeks information, use the indicative.

| SUBJUNCTIVE | |
|---|---|
| Hace sol. No creo que **llueva**. | *It is sunny out. I don't think it will rain.* |
| ¿Crees que **haga** frío en La Paz? | *Do you think it is/ will be cold in La Paz? (I am not sure.)* |

| INDICATIVE | |
|---|---|
| ¿Crees que **hace** frío en La Paz? | *Do you think it is/will be cold in La Paz? (I think so, and I am seeking confirmation.)* |

- Since the expressions **tal vez** and **quizá(s)** convey uncertainty, the subjunctive is normally used.

| | |
|---|---|
| Tal vez el conjunto **toque** una polca paraguaya. | *Perhaps the group will play a Paraguayan polka.* |
| Quizá(s) todos **empiecen** a bailar. | *Perhaps everyone will start to dance.* |

**13-19 Están de acuerdo?** PRIMERA FASE. Lea las siguientes opiniones y marque (✓) si está de acuerdo o no con ellas.

|  | SÍ | NO |
|---|---|---|
| 1. Yo creo que la poesía es fácil de comprender e interpretar. | _____ | _____ |
| 2. Yo dudo que el fútbol sea más popular en Estados Unidos que en América Latina. | _____ | _____ |
| 3. Creo que las películas que se hacen en Hollywood en general son muy buenas. | _____ | _____ |
| 4. Es posible que el cine mexicano sea más artísticamente arriesgado (*risky*) que el cine americano. | _____ | _____ |
| 5. Es obvio que el rock es más popular entre la gente joven que la música clásica. | _____ | _____ |
| 6. No creo que los niños del siglo XXI lean tanto como leían sus padres cuando eran niños. | _____ | _____ |

SEGUNDA FASE. Ahora complete el párrafo sobre los temas de la *Primera fase* con la forma apropiada del verbo.

Algunas personas creen que la poesía es fácil de comprender e interpretar, pero otras personas no creen que la poesía (1) _____ (ser) fácil. No piensan que la música rock (2) _____ (tener) ninguna relación con la poesía. Sin embargo, es posible que las canciones (3) _____ (ser) poemas, ya que muchos profesores las usan en sus clases para enseñar varios aspectos de la poesía, como la rima y las metáforas.

Hay mucho debate sobre el cine hoy en día. Muchas personas dudan que Hollywood (4) _____ (producir) buenas películas, y es cierto que la popularidad del cine de otros países, como México, España e India, (5) _____ (estar) creciendo rápidamente. Es dudoso que las compañías cinematográficas de otros países (6) _____ (poder) gastar tanto dinero en sus películas como las de Estados Unidos. En consecuencia, es verdad que en el cine de Hollywood siempre se (7) _____ (encontrar) más efectos especiales y otros elementos costosos de los que se (8) _____ (ver) en las películas hechas en otros países.

> ### En directo
>
> To report agreement:
>
> **Todos creemos/pensamos que…**
>
> **Nosotros estamos de acuerdo con que…**
>
> To report different opinions:
>
> **No hay consenso entre nosotros/ellos. Unos piensan que… , otros creen que…**

**13-20 Opiniones.** Intercambien opiniones sobre los siguientes temas. Después, comparen sus opiniones con las de otros compañeros/otras compañeras y compartan el resultado con la clase. Usen expresiones de certeza y duda (*creo/no creo*; *dudo/no dudo*; *tal vez/quizás*) en su conversación.

MODELO: el cine de Hollywood
   E1: *Creo que el cine de Hollywood es malo. Prefiero ver películas extranjeras. Y tú, ¿qué opinas?*
   E2: *Dudo que todas las películas de Hollywood sean malas. Hay unas que me gustan mucho.*

1. las películas de acción
2. leer novelas como diversión
3. la música country
4. ver exposiciones de arte

**13-21 Una cena con un/a artista famoso/a.** PRIMERA FASE. Ustedes ganaron un concurso, y su premio es cenar con un/una cantante, pintor/a, autor/a, etc., que ustedes admiran mucho. Escojan a la persona y hagan una lista de tres cosas que esperan que pasen en la cena y tres cosas que dudan que pasen. Expliquen por qué.

Gabriel García Bernal en *Diarios de motocicleta*

MODELO:    *Gael García Bernal*
E1:   *Esperamos que Gael García Bernal nos hable acerca de sus películas, que nos permita sacarle una foto y que se quede por mucho tiempo en la cena.*
E2:   *Dudamos que Gael García Bernal revele información de su vida personal porque él es muy reservado. Dudamos que nos invite a su casa y dudamos que nos cuente los detalles de su próxima película.*

SEGUNDA FASE. Reúnanse con otra pareja y explíquenle a quién escogieron ustedes y por qué. Infórmenle sobre sus esperanzas y dudas con respecto a la situación. Comenten si están de acuerdo con lo que dicen sus compañeros.

## SITUACIONES

1. **Role A.** You are showing a friend how to play the game "Two Truths and a Lie" (**"Dos verdades y una mentira"**). State three pieces of information about yourself, two of which are true and one that is not. Comment on your friend's responses. Then change roles and play the game again.

   **Role B.** A friend is showing you how to play the game "Two Truths and a Lie" (**"Dos verdades y una mentira"**). Your friend will tell you three pieces of personal information, two of which are true and one that is not. Say which statement you think is true, which is possibly true, and which you doubt is true. Then change roles and play the game again.

2. **Role A.** You are the parent of a high school student who went out last night and got home three hours late. Ask your child to explain the late arrival. Express doubt about at least three things your child says. To avoid ongoing conflict with your child, make sure the situation is resolved.

   **Role B.** You are in high school, and you can't wait to be free of your parents and their restrictive rules. Last night you went out with some friends and got home three hours late. Now you have to explain yourself. You know better than to say that you just didn't feel like coming home, so you make up a detailed story about what happened. Your parent is skeptical, so you try to convince him/her to believe you. To avoid ongoing conflict with your parent, make sure the situation is resolved.

# 3. Hypothesizing: The conditional

GLORIA: Aquí veo sólo dos de los instrumentos para el concierto de esta noche. ¿Dónde están los otros?

AMARU: Siempre grabamos digitalmente la música de los otros instrumentos. Yo los **traería** todos, pero **sería** carísimo. **Gastaríamos** demasiado para traer los tambores, las guitarras y las quijadas (*jawbone*), por ejemplo.

GLORIA: ¿Cuánto **costaría** traer los otros instrumentos?

AMARU: Bueno, yo **tendría** que pagar 200 dólares sólo para traer mi guitarra. Para traer todos los instrumentos, **pagaríamos** una fortuna.

**Piénselo.** Indique (✓) en la columna correspondiente si cada una de las siguientes afirmaciones se refiere a la **realidad** o a una **hipótesis**.

| | REALIDAD | HIPÓTESIS |
|---|---|---|
| 1. Aquí **veo** sólo dos de los instrumentos para el concierto. | ___ | ___ |
| 2. Siempre **grabamos** digitalmente la música de los otros instrumentos. | ___ | ___ |
| 3. ¿Cuánto **costaría** traer los otros instrumentos? | ___ | ___ |
| 4. **Sería** carísimo. | ___ | ___ |
| 5. **Tendría** que pagar $200 sólo para traer mi guitarra. | ___ | ___ |
| 6. **Pagaríamos** una fortuna. | ___ | ___ |

■ You have used the expression **me gustaría...** to express what you would like. **Gustaría** is a form of the conditional.

■ The conditional in Spanish is similar to the English construction *would + verb*. It is used to hypothesize about a situation that is not part of the speaker's present reality.

| | |
|---|---|
| Yo **saldría** temprano para el concierto, pero trabajo hasta tarde. | *I would leave early for the concert, but I work late.* |

■ When English *would* implies *used to*, the imperfect is used in Spanish.

| | |
|---|---|
| Cuando era chica, mi papá me **llevaba** a los conciertos al aire libre en el parque. | *When I was little, my father would (used to) take me to open-air concerts in the park.* |

■ The conditional is easy to recognize. It is formed by adding the endings **-ía,
-ías, -ía, -íamos, -íais, -ían** to the infinitive.

| | CONDITIONAL | | |
|---|---|---|---|
| | **HABLAR** | **COMER** | **VIVIR** |
| yo | hablaría | comería | viviría |
| tú | hablarías | comerías | vivirías |
| Ud., él, ella | hablaría | comería | viviría |
| nosotros/as | hablaríamos | comeríamos | viviríamos |
| vosotros/as | hablaríais | comeríais | viviríais |
| Uds., ellos/as | hablarían | comerían | vivirían |

■ Verbs that have an irregular stem in the future have that same stem in the
conditional.

| IRREGULAR CONDITIONAL VERBS | | |
|---|---|---|
| **INFINITIVE** | **NEW STEM** | **CONDITIONAL FORMS** |
| haber | **habr-** | habría, habrías, habría… |
| poder | **podr-** | podría, podrías, podría… |
| querer | **querr-** | querría, querrías, querría… |
| saber | **sabr-** | sabría, sabrías, sabría… |
| poner | **pondr-** | pondría, pondrías, pondría… |
| salir | **saldr-** | saldría, saldrías, saldría… |
| tener | **tendr-** | tendría, tendrías, tendría… |
| venir | **vendr-** | vendría, vendrías, vendría… |
| decir | **dir-** | diría, dirías, diría… |
| hacer | **har-** | haría, harías, haría… |

| | |
|---|---|
| Yo **pondría** la pintura sobre la chimenea. | *I would put the painting over the fireplace.* |
| ¿**Podrías** escribir un poema de amor en español? | *Would you be able to write a love poem in Spanish?* |

**13-22 ¿Qué haría usted?** PRIMERA FASE. Lea las siguientes situaciones y marque con un círculo lo que usted probablemente haría.

1. Es el cumpleaños de su mejor amigo, quien sigue cursos avanzados de español, y usted le quiere regalar algo útil.
   a. Le compraría una novela de Roa Bastos traducida al inglés.
   b. Le regalaría *El Quijote* de Cervantes.
   c. Le daría un buen diccionario.
2. El dúo boliviano Tupay va a dar un concierto en su ciudad este fin de semana.
   a. Invitaría a mi novio/a al concierto.
   b. Llamaría a mis amigos para ir al concierto.
   c. Compraría un charango para tocar con ellos durante el concierto.
3. Van a estrenar (pasar por primera vez) una nueva película de Cecilia Roth.
   a. La iría a ver la noche del estreno.
   b. No vería la película porque no me interesa la actriz.
   c. Leería las reseñas (*reviews*) antes de ir a verla.
4. Usted va a pasar unos días en Madrid. ¿Qué haría de tener tiempo para visitar el Museo del Prado?
   a. Pasaría unos minutos en el museo para conocerlo.
   b. Me informaría sobre lo que se puede ver en el museo.
   c. Visitaría las salas donde están las pinturas de Velázquez.

SEGUNDA FASE. Comparen sus respuestas y después digan qué harían ustedes realmente en esas situaciones.

**13-23 Fantasías de lotería.** PRIMERA FASE. Imagínese que ganó quinientos mil dólares en la lotería. Diga qué haría usted con el dinero y por qué. Considere lo siguiente:

1. lo que haría por un miembro de su familia o un amigo/una amiga
2. lo que haría para alguna organización caritativa (*charitable*)
3. lo que haría para fomentar (*encourage*) las artes en la educación pública

SEGUNDA FASE. Comenten sus planes hipotéticos. Luego, seleccionen el mejor plan, expliquen por qué lo escogieron y compartan esta información con la clase.

**13-24 Buscar soluciones.** Primero digan qué harían ustedes en las siguientes situaciones. Después comparen sus respuestas con las de otros estudiantes.

1. Ustedes entran en un museo donde se muestran obras de pintores famosos y ven que en una de las salas, que está vacía, alguien está tratando de robar un cuadro.
2. Ustedes consiguieron las tres últimas entradas para un concierto de la cantante boliviana Emma Junaro, e invitaron a una persona importante, pero ahora no pueden encontrar las entradas.
3. Ustedes acaban de descubrir que alguien de la Oficina de Estudiantes Extranjeros está vendiendo entradas falsas y muy baratas para un concierto de música folclórica de Paraguay.

**13-25 Mis planes hipotéticos.** PRIMERA FASE. Su nombre aparece en la nómina de posibles Ministros de Cultura de su país. El presidente le ha pedido a cada uno/a de los ministros potenciales un plan hipotético de lo que haría si es elegido/a. Indique por lo menos una medida que usted tomaría con los siguientes propósitos:

1. para educar al ciudadano promedio (*average*) a apreciar las bellas artes (*fine arts*)
2. para identificar y coleccionar algunas formas de arte popular casi extintas
3. para promover la expresión artística entre los niños y los jóvenes
4. para subvencionar (*subsidize*) a artistas jóvenes
5. para exponer obras de arte de manera que lleguen a más personas

 SEGUNDA FASE. Compartan sus planes y escojan uno en cada área para compartir con la clase.

## SITUACIONES

1. **Role A.** You decide to speak to a friend who is majoring in literature because you would like some advice. Explain that a) you have written some short stories and your literature teacher thinks they are of excellent quality and b) you would like to send them to a publishing house (**casa editorial**). Ask whether your friend would be able to read them and would help with any necessary revisions.

   **Role B.** You would like to give your friend good advice, but you need more information. Ask a) what the short stories are about; b) when he/she wrote them; and c) how many he/she has written. Say that you would be glad to read the stories and that it would be a good idea for your friend to ask his/her literature teacher for advice also. Tell your friend that you would have time to help him/her tomorrow.

2. **Role A.** You are considering visiting Paraguay next summer so you call a friend who has been to Paraguay. Include the following in your conversation: a) ask how much money you would need for food and lodging for a month in Paraguay; b) tell your friend that you would like to see a lot of Paraguayan handicrafts; c) ask your friend to recommend some Paraguayan folk music; and d) find out how long it would take to learn Guaraní, the indigenous language of Paraguay.

   **Role B.** Your friend is thinking of visiting Paraguay, a country you love and know a lot about. Tell your friend the following a) he/she would probably need around U.S.$1,500 for food and lodging for a month if he/she stays at youth hostels (**albergues juveniles**); b) he/she can usually find Paraguayan handicrafts in every city square (**plaza**); c) you would recommend the Teatro Nacional in Asuncion for concerts of Paraguayan folk music; and d) he/she would probably be able to learn some basic expressions in Guaraní during the trip, but it's totally different from Spanish.

# 4. Expressing reciprocity: Reciprocal verbs and pronouns

En general, los artesanos hispanos forman comunidades donde abundan las relaciones de solidaridad. **Se conocen** entre ellos y, puesto que generalmente viven modestamente, **se ayudan** mutuamente. Así lo indican las afirmaciones de Camilo, uno de los artesanos de este taller. "Mario y yo somos amigos y compartimos casi todo. Cuando uno de los dos no tiene dinero, **nos prestamos** dinero. Pero aun más importante, **nos respetamos** el uno al otro porque **nos necesitamos**."

**Piénselo.** Busque el significado de las afirmaciones de la columna izquierda en la columna de la derecha.

1. \_\_\_\_ **Se conocen** entre ellos.
2. \_\_\_\_ **Se ayudan** mutuamente.
3. \_\_\_\_ **Nos prestamos** dinero.
4. \_\_\_\_ **Nos respetamos** el uno al otro.
5. \_\_\_\_ **Nos necesitamos**.

a. Yo respeto a Mario y él me respeta a mí.
b. Mario me necesita a mí y yo lo necesito a él.
c. Mario conoce a Camilo y Camilo conoce a Mario.
d. Camilo ayuda a Mario y viceversa.
e. Yo le presto dinero a Mario y él hace lo mismo para mí.

---

■ Use plural reflexive pronouns (**nos, os, se**) to express reciprocal actions. In English, reciprocal actions are usually expressed with *each other* or *one another*.

| | |
|---|---|
| Muchos hispanos **se abrazan** cuando **se saludan**. | *Many Hispanics embrace when they greet each other.* |
| Los artesanos de este taller **se ven** todos los días. | *The artisans in this workshop see each other every day.* |
| En este centro de arte **nos ayudamos** mucho. | *In this art center, we help each other a lot.* |
| **Nos llamamos** cuando hay una nueva exposición de arte para ir juntos. | *We call each other when there is a new art exhibit so that we can go together.* |

*[handwritten annotations:]*
nos + nosotros = we (Brm)
se + ellos = they (Brm)

**13-26 Indicaciones de reciprocidad.** Escoja las ideas de la columna de la derecha que mejor completen las oraciones de la izquierda.

1. Cuando Mario y Camilo no se ven durante el día, ellos \_\_\_\_
2. El perro y el gato de Mario se pelean todo el tiempo. Ellos \_\_\_\_
3. Alberto y yo somos muy buenos amigos, pero vivimos en ciudades diferentes. No hablamos mucho por teléfono, pero \_\_\_\_
4. Mario y Alicia son novios y se quieren mucho. Cuando se despiden por la noche, ellos \_\_\_\_
5. Mario y Camilo dicen que el secreto de su larga amistad es que ellos \_\_\_

a. nos mandamos correos electrónicos.
b. se llaman por teléfono.
c. se aprecian y se respetan.
d. se detestan.
e. se abrazan y se besan.

 **13-27 ¿Qué hacen los buenos colegas?** PRIMERA FASE. Determinen si los buenos colegas deben hacer lo siguiente, y bajo qué circunstancias.

MODELO:  respetarse
   E1: *Yo creo que los buenos colegas se respetan, a pesar de sus diferencias.*
   E2: *Estoy de acuerdo. En las reuniones se escuchan mucho y se tratan con respeto siempre.*

1. \_\_\_ llamarse todos los días
2. \_\_\_ comprenderse
3. \_\_\_ ayudarse cuando tienen jefes problemáticos
4. \_\_\_ insultarse y pelearse
5. \_\_\_ regalarse cosas
6. \_\_\_ darse consejos cuando los necesitan
7. \_\_\_ comunicarse constantemente
8. \_\_\_ criticarse continuamente
9. \_\_\_ pedirse disculpas (*apologize*) después de una discusión
10. \_\_\_ demostrarse empatía

 **SEGUNDA FASE.** Compartan sus ideas con otra pareja. Luego, hagan lo siguiente:

1. Preparen una lista de las actitudes que ustedes consideran importantes para mantener una buena relación con los colegas en el trabajo.
2. Escojan las cuatro actitudes más importantes y justifiquen su selección.
3. Escojan las dos actitudes que consideran las más problemáticas. Den ejemplos de los problemas que podrían causar entre colegas.
4. Compartan su lista con la clase.

**13-28 Consejos.** Identifiquen los problemas de las siguientes personas. Luego, recomiéndenles una solución.

1. Rafael y Magdalena son novios, pero no se ven con mucha frecuencia. Él es un pintor que vive en Monterrey, México, y ella trabaja en Los Ángeles. Mantienen una relación a distancia.
2. Catalina y Raquel trabajan en un taller de arte. Cuando Catalina quiere pintar un cuadro, necesita absoluto silencio para inspirarse. Pero cuando ella llega al taller, siempre encuentra a Raquel hablando por teléfono con su novio.
3. Los empleados de Pablo tienen miedo de expresar sus opiniones sobre las piezas de cerámica que él crea porque Pablo siempre toma los comentarios de sus empleados como un ataque personal o parece no escucharlos. Sus colegas evitan hablar con él de este tema.

**13-29 Mis relaciones con...** Piense en una persona importante en su vida (padre/madre, novio/a, pariente, amigo/a, etc.) y dígale a su compañero/a cómo son las relaciones entre ustedes. Dé ejemplos concretos. Las preguntas siguientes pueden serle útiles.

MODELO: *Mis relaciones con mi hermano son muy buenas. Nosotros nos queremos. A veces...*

1. ¿Se respetan?
2. ¿Se quieren?
3. ¿Se detestan?
4. ¿Se comunican?
5. ¿Se pelean?
6. ...

> **En directo**
>
> To complain about something or someone:
>
> **Tengo una queja.**
> *I have a complaint.*
>
> **Quisiera quejarme de...**
> *I would like to complain about . . .*
>
> **Quisiera hablar con usted sobre un problema que tengo con...**
> *I would like to discuss with you a problem that I have with . . .*

## SITUACIONES

1. **Role A.** You have problems with a colleague at the museum where you work, so you talk to your boss (your classmate). Explain that you and your colleague do not get along (**llevarse bien**) well. Then say that the two of you a) argue with each other a lot at meetings; b) never listen to each other because you are always angry; and c) have to communicate a lot at work, but you never talk in person. Ask your boss for some suggestions to improve your relationship.

    **Role B.** You are the curator of a museum in La Paz. Listen to the complaints of an employee about a colleague. Ask questions to find out a) what they argue about; b) how often they have to see each other at meetings; and c) how they communicate with each other. Suggest that the two meet (**reunirse**) with a mediator (**mediador**) for several sessions of work therapy (**terapia laboral**) to understand and respect each other better.

2. **Role A.** You are talking with the owner of a popular art studio in your community where you are taking a pottery class. You are new in town and think this will be a good place to meet people. You trust this person enough to ask the following personal questions: a) if he/she has many good friends; b) when he/she met his/her best friend (**conocerse**); and c) what the key (**la clave**) to a long friendship (**amistad**) is.

    **Role B.** You own an art studio that is very popular in your community. You are talking with a new student who is eager to make friends with people in the class. Share with him/her some of your own experiences. Explain a) when you and your best friend met (**conocerse**); b) how your friendship (**amistad**) started; c) that you do not see each other every day but you stay in touch (**mantenerse en contacto**); and d) that you respect each other, although you do not always agree on everything.

# MOSAICOS

## A escuchar

### Antes de escuchar

**13-30 Preparación.** Usted va a escuchar a cuatro estudiantes universitarios que hablan sobre actividades culturales. Antes de escuchar, haga una lista de tres actividades culturales que tal vez les interesen.

### Escuchar

CD 6
Track 5 **13-31 ¿Comprende usted?** Now read the following statements, and then listen to the students. As you listen, next to each statement write the number of the passage associated with the student who probably uttered it.

_____ Miguel probablemente quiere escuchar o conversar con los artistas latinoamericanos para decidir sus estudios de posgrado.

_____ Joaquín es el pintor a quien le gusta más la pintura mexicana.

_____ Rosa María piensa ir a ver las obras de teatro este año.

_____ Eugenia es pianista y quiere convencer a otra persona de las ventajas de aprender a tocar el piano.

### Después de escuchar

**13-32 Ahora usted.** Comparta sus respuestas con un compañero/una compañera.

1. ¿Es importante que los jóvenes aprendan a apreciar las diversas expresiones artísticas (la pintura, la música clásica, el teatro, o la escultura)? ¿Por qué?
2. ¿Qué aspecto prefieren ustedes, la música o la pintura?
3. ¿Cuál es su pintor o músico favorito? ¿Por qué le gusta?

# A conversar

## Antes de conversar

**13-33 Preparación.** Escojan a una de las personas de la lista. Luego, busquen la información indicada en la tabla sobre la persona que escogieron. También pueden buscar otra información que les interese a ustedes.

Pablo Casals        Alfonso Gumucio Dagrón
Carlos Colombino      Jaime Laredo
Plácido Domingo       Marina Núñez del Prado
Carlos Gardel         Violeta Parra

| NOMBRE | DATOS PERSONALES | PROFESIÓN | LOGROS |
|---|---|---|---|
| _____ | fecha de nacimiento: <br><br> _____ <br><br> lugar de nacimiento/ muerte: <br><br> _____ | _____ <br><br> contribución a su profesión: <br><br> _____ | premios: <br><br> _____ <br><br> reconocimientos: <br><br> _____ |

## Conversar

**13-34 Entre nosotros.** Hagan una breve presentación sobre la persona escogida en **13-33**. Incluyan la mayor cantidad de información posible.

## Después de conversar

**13-35 ¡Nos quitamos el sombrero (*We take our hats off*)!** Decidan a cuál de las figuras famosas de la actividad **13-34** elegirían ustedes como la persona más admirable. Expliquen por qué, usando las expresiones de *En directo*.

## ESTRATEGIA

**Use your knowledge of narrative structure to support comprehension**

All of us have read short stories and novels in our native language, and we are familiar with their structure: a sequence of events involves a conflict or problem that builds throughout the narrative and is resolved at the end. The skillful author weaves the outcome of the narrative by carefully threading together the conflicts created by characters and circumstance.

When you read a narrative in your second language, you can increase your comprehension by trying to anticipate what the characters will do, and how the story will turn out in the end.

# A leer

## Antes de leer

**13-36 Preparación.** PRIMERA FASE. Lea el título de la narrativa y examine la foto. Luego responda a las preguntas, basándose en su conocimiento general y su conocimiento del tema.

1. ¿Cuál puede ser el tema principal de la narrativa? Indique (✓) los temas posibles.
   ___ a. la vida de un etnógrafo/una etnógrafa mientras estudia una comunidad
   ___ b. una relación romántica que tiene un etnógrafo/una etnógrafa mientras hace su trabajo de campo (*fieldwork*)
   ___ c. una descripción de los miembros de un grupo indígena y de sus viviendas

2. ¿Cómo está organizada la narrativa? Indique (✓) las descripciones probables.
   ___ a. Puede empezar con una escena retrospectiva (*flashback*) en la que el narrador/la narradora presenta el problema.
   ___ b. Se presenta a los personajes principales al comienzo de la narrativa.
   ___ c. Los personajes revelan sus sentimientos y su personalidad por medio de sus acciones.
   ___ d. El conflicto llega a un punto culminante (*climax*).
   ___ e. La narrativa no tiene una conclusión definitiva; los lectores tienen que hacer su propia interpretación.

SEGUNDA FASE. Indique si es probable (**P**) o improbable (**I**) que un etnógrafo/una etnógrafa haga las siguientes afirmaciones sobre las costumbres de una comunidad indígena después de vivir en la comunidad.

| | PROBABLE | IMPROBABLE |
|---|---|---|
| 1. Existen brujos (*sorcerers*) que revelan sus secretos sólo a los iniciados (*apprentices*) que quieren aprender. | ___ | ___ |
| 2. Los indígenas hablan mi lengua mejor que yo. | ___ | ___ |
| 3. Me levantaba al alba, es decir, antes de la salida del sol. | ___ | ___ |
| 4. Me cubría el cuerpo con ropas extrañas. | ___ | ___ |
| 5. Me encantaba comer sus comidas ásperas y desagradables. | ___ | ___ |
| 6. Cuando recién llegué, tomaba notas sigilosamente (*discreetly*) para evitar las sospechas de los indígenas. | ___ | ___ |
| 7. Al clarear el día (*dawn*), siempre tenía sueños extraños. | ___ | ___ |
| 8. Viví tanto tiempo entre los indígenas que comencé a pensar como ellos. | ___ | ___ |

# Leer

## *El etnógrafo* de Jorge Luis Borges

El caso me lo refirieron en Texas, pero había acontecido en otro estado. Cuenta con un solo protagonista, salvo que en toda historia los protagonistas son miles, visibles e invisibles, vivos y muertos. Se llamaba, creo, Fred Murdock. Era alto a la manera americana, ni rubio ni moreno, de perfil de hacha,[1] de muy pocas palabras. Nada singular había en él, ni siquiera esa fingida singularidad que es propia de los jóvenes. Naturalmente respetuoso, no descreía de los libros ni de quienes escriben los libros. Era suya esa edad en que el hombre no sabe aún quién es y está listo para entregarse a lo que le propone el azar,[2] la mística del persa o el desconocido origen del húngaro, las aventuras de la guerra o del álgebra, el puritanismo o la orgía. En la universidad le aconsejaron el estudio de las lenguas indígenas. Hay ritos esotéricos que perduran en ciertas tribus del oeste; su profesor, un hombre entrado en años, le propuso que hiciera su habitación en una toldería,[3] que observara los ritos y que descubriera el secreto que los brujos revelan al iniciado. A su vuelta, redactaría una tesis que las autoridades del instituto darían a la imprenta.[4] Murdock aceptó con alacridad.[5] Uno de sus mayores había muerto en guerras de la frontera; esa antigua discordia de sus estirpes era un vínculo ahora.

Previó,[6] sin duda, las dificultades que lo aguardaban; tenía que lograr que los hombres rojos lo aceptaran como uno de los suyos. Emprendió la larga aventura. Más de dos años habitó en la pradera, bajo toldos de cuero o a la intemperie. Se levantaba antes del alba, se acostaba al anochecer, llegó a soñar en un idioma que no era el de sus padres. Acostumbró su paladar[7] a sabores ásperos, se cubrió con ropas extrañas, olvidó los amigos y la ciudad, llegó a pensar de una manera que su lógica rechazaba. Durante los primeros meses de aprendizaje tomaba notas sigilosas, que rompería después, acaso para no despertar la suspicacia de los otros, acaso porque ya no las precisaba. Al término de un plazo prefijado por ciertos ejercicios, de índole moral y de índole física, el sacerdote le ordenó que fuera recordando sus sueños y que se los confiara al clarear el día. Comprobó que en las noches de luna llena soñaba con bisontes.[8] Confió estos sueños repetidos a su maestro; éste acabó por revelarle su doctrina secreta. Una mañana, sin haberse despedido de nadie, Murdock se fue.

En la ciudad, sintió la nostalgia de aquellas tardes iniciales de la pradera en que había sentido, hace tiempo, la nostalgia de la ciudad. Se encaminó al despacho del profesor y le dijo que sabía el secreto y que había resuelto no publicarlo. —¿Lo ata su juramento?[9]—preguntó el otro. —No es ésa mi razón —dijo Murdock—. En esas lejanías aprendí algo que no puedo decir. —¿Acaso el idioma inglés es insuficiente? —observaría el otro. —Nada de eso, señor. Ahora que poseo el secreto, podría enunciarlo de cien modos distintos y aun contradictorios. No sé muy bien cómo decirle que el secreto es precioso y que ahora la ciencia, nuestra ciencia, me parece una mera frivolidad. Agregó al cabo de una pausa:—El secreto, por lo demás, no vale lo que valen los caminos que me condujeron a él. Esos caminos hay que andarlos. El profesor le dijo con frialdad:—Comunicaré su decisión al Concejo.[10] ¿Usted piensa vivir entre los indios? Murdock le contestó:—No. Tal vez no vuelva a la pradera. Lo que me enseñaron sus hombres vale para cualquier lugar y para cualquier circunstancia. Tal fue, en esencia, el diálogo. Fred se casó, se divorció y es ahora uno de los bibliotecarios de Yale.

[1]*hatchet-faced*  [2]*chance*  [3]*awning-like dwelling consisting of animal hides supported by poles*  [4]*would have it published*  [5]*quickly, gladly*  [6]*foresaw, predicted*  [7]*palate*  [8]*bison*  [9]*bound by your oath*  [10]*council*

## 13-37 Primera mirada. Indique si las siguientes oraciones relacionadas con el cuento son ciertas (**C**) o falsas (**F**).

1. \_\_\_\_ El narrador del cuento es Fred Murdock.
2. \_\_\_\_ No sabemos cómo se llama el narrador.
3. \_\_\_\_ El protagonista es una persona que físicamente llama la atención porque es muy distinto de los demás.
4. \_\_\_\_ Por su edad, el protagonista no había decidido qué quería hacer profesionalmente.
5. \_\_\_\_ Las experiencias que el protagonista vivió no lo afectaron para nada.
6. \_\_\_\_ Al hablar con una persona importante de la comunidad donde vivía, el protagonista experimentó un cambio significativo en su vida.
7. \_\_\_\_ El descubrimiento de un secreto cambió la vida del protagonista.
8. \_\_\_\_ Después de volver a la ciudad, el protagonista publicó un libro sobre sus experiencias.

**13-38 Segunda mirada.** Reconstruya el cuento en el orden cronológico apropiado. La primera situación ya está marcada.

_1_ Alguien en la universidad le sugirió a Murdock que estudiara una lengua indígena.

_____ Entre los indios, se acostumbró a comer su comida, a hablar la lengua de ellos, a vestirse y a pensar como ellos.

_____ Fred aceptó la oferta.

_____ Murdock se casó y ahora trabaja en la biblioteca de la universidad de Yale.

_____ Su profesor le propuso que viviera entre los indígenas para aprender sobre sus ritos y descubrir un secreto.

_____ El joven etnógrafo salió de la comunidad indígena sin decirle adiós a nadie.

_____ Antes de llegar a la comunidad indígena, pensó en los problemas que tendría al vivir en una cultura diferente a la suya.

_____ Al principio, tomaba notas secretamente, las cuales probablemente rompería más tarde.

_____ El gran maestro espiritual le contó el gran secreto.

_____ El profesor le dijo que probablemente, a su regreso, se publicaría su tesis.

_____ Empezó su aventura y se fue a vivir entre los indios por un periodo de dos años.

_____ Después de algunos ejercicios morales y físicos, Murdock tuvo que recordar sus sueños y contárselos a su guía espiritual.

_____ El protagonista fue a la oficina de su profesor y le dijo que había aprendido el secreto, pero que no podía compartirlo con nadie.

## Después de leer

 **13-39 Ampliación.** Comenten las siguientes preguntas y prepárense para compartir las respuestas con la clase.

Sobre la vida de Murdock en la comunidad indígena:

1. ¿Qué cambios en su vida diaria tuvo que hacer Murdock para adaptarse a la comunidad indígena?
2. ¿Qué hacían los indígenas para aceptar a Murdock en su comunidad?
3. ¿Qué decían las notas que tomaba Fred Murdock?

Sobre el secreto que Murdock descubrió:

4. ¿Qué secreto descubrió el etnógrafo? ¿Por qué no podía compartirlo con nadie?
5. ¿Por qué decidió el protagonista trabajar de bibliotecario en la universidad de Yale?

# A escribir

## Antes de escribir

**13-40 Preparación.** PRIMERA FASE. En la página web de *Mosaicos*, busque información biográfica sobre una persona hispana que a usted le interese en uno de estos campos: los deportes, las artes, la ciencia o la política. Obtenga la siguiente información y tome notas.

1. nombre, fecha y lugar de nacimiento: ¿Cuándo y dónde nació?
2. información personal: ¿Es soltero/a, casado/a, divorciado/a? ¿Tiene hijos? ¿Cuántos?
3. estudios y formación profesional: ¿Cuáles son los mayores logros personales y/o profesionales de esta persona? ¿Cómo lo hizo?
4. su comunidad: ¿En qué área se destaca (*stands out*): religiosa, étnica, profesional, científica, artística, etc.? Sus éxitos, ¿han beneficiado a la comunidad? ¿Cómo?

SEGUNDA FASE. Ahora seleccione la información que va a ayudarlo/la a escribir su informe biográfico. Haga lo siguiente:

1. Seleccione los datos personales y/o profesionales más interesantes sobre la vida de la persona escogida en la *Primera fase*.
2. Escriba algunas formas lingüísticas que lo/la ayudarán a expresar información concreta (hechos) y destacar la figura de esta persona.

## Escribir

**13-41 Manos a la obra.** Su comunidad ha decidido empezar una campaña para incentivar a los jóvenes a encauzar (*channel*) mejor sus vidas en un mundo en crisis. Usted es uno/a de los responsables de presentarles a una personalidad del mundo hispano que, en su opinión, representa un excelente ejemplo. Escriba un informe biográfico para una revista electrónica, usando la información obtenida en la actividad **13-40** *Segunda fase*. Su propósito es despertar la curiosidad de los jóvenes por conocer qué sacrificios han hecho los famosos para tener éxito.

## Después de escribir

**13-42 Revisión.** Su compañero editor/compañera editora va a ayudarlo/la a expresar mejor sus ideas para que sus lectores jóvenes se beneficien de las experiencias reales de otros. No se olvide de verificar que…

1. el informe biográfico tenga información interesante para su lector/a, como alguna anécdota o experiencia personal.
2. las ideas estén bien organizadas y el texto se enfoque en la vida y logros de esta persona.
3. su texto tenga un título que capte la atención de su público.
4. haya conexión dentro de los párrafos y entre ellos (use conectores para hacer transiciones).
5. el vocabulario sea variado y dinámico.
6. la ortografía, puntuación, acentuación, etc., sean apropiadas.

# ENFOQUE CULTURAL

## La maravillosa música de los Andes

Normalmente, cuando pensamos en la música andina, nos vienen a la mente las canciones y bailes tradicionales, principalmente de Perú y Bolivia. Sin embargo, la música de los Andes ofrece una gran variedad de otros estilos musicales, muchos de los cuales están relacionados con los ritmos, melodías y cadencias de la música tradicional de esta región. También hay géneros musicales que tienen otras raíces, tanto europeas como propiamente latinoamericanas. En efecto, encontramos en Bolivia documentos que muestran la

Ruinas de la misión jesuita de Trinidad en Paraguay

existencia de una notable corriente de música barroca que empezó en las misiones jesuitas de los siglos XVI y XVII y que todavía perdura. Y en el otro extremo, hay una variedad de géneros de música popular que tiene muchos seguidores entre la gente joven.

Durante la época colonial los jesuitas construyeron misiones en Paraguay, en Bolivia y en otras regiones del imperio español. En varias de estas misiones utilizaron la música como uno de los medios para conseguir la conversión al cristianismo de los indígenas. Esta historia está en el trasfondo de la película *The Mission*, dirigida por Roland Joffé y con música de Ennio Morricone, que trascurre en las misiones de Paraguay. Recientemente se ha descubierto en las misiones de Bolivia, Santa Ana, San Javier y Chiquitos, una gran riqueza de partituras de música barroca en la que se incluyen varios instrumentos típicos de la región andina. Esta tradición de música culta realizada por la población indígena se continúa hoy en Bolivia gracias al trabajo de algunas organizaciones, como por ejemplo la organización no gubernamental SICOR (Sistema de Coros y Orquestas), que se dedican a enseñar y a diseminar este tipo de música entre los jóvenes del Amazonas.

La quena es uno de los instrumentos más distintivos de la música andina.

Además de este importante género culto, la música popular andina se distingue por las peculiares melodías y ritmos de sus instrumentos tradicionales. Esta música se reconoce fácilmente por la interesantísima combinación de varios instrumentos autóctonos de

El charango es un instrumento original de los Andes que une las raíces europeas e indígenas de la región.

viento, instrumentos de cuerda adaptados de la música europea, tales como la guitarra, y otras variaciones locales como el charango, y una percusión basada en grandes tambores de madera y cuero. Entre los instrumentos de viento más característicos de la música andina sobresalen la quena, una flauta dulce hecha de bambú, y la zampoña, o siku, una colección de tubos de caña de diferente tamaño, originaria de la región del Lago Titicaca. El charango, el instrumento de cuerda más característico de la música tradicional popular de los Andes, es un curioso instrumento construido con la concha de un armadillo. Muchas de las canciones populares andinas están compuestas en una clave menor, por lo cual transmiten con frecuencia un sentimiento de tristeza que algunos asocian con la pobreza y la dureza de la vida de los habitantes de esta región después de la caída del imperio inca.

A pesar de la riqueza y popularidad de la música tradicional, los jóvenes de la región han adoptado otras formas musicales más modernas. Mucha de la música que escuchan los jóvenes se basa en la de otros países latinoamericanos, por ejemplo, la cumbia, o en la música rock, de la cual hacen adaptaciones locales. Hay una gran variedad de grupos, cantantes y estrellas de la canción andina que mezclan géneros y utilizan algunas de las marcas de identidad de la música andina para componer piezas de ritmos modernos con influencia de la música internacional. En sus composiciones introducen instrumentos eléctricos y los combinan con otros más tradicionales, lo cual produce un sonido muy característico. Con frecuencia también buscan presentar esta fusión mediante los trajes que usan, ya que los diseños unen lo tradicional y lo moderno. Estos grupos son seguidos con gran pasión por sus admiradores jóvenes.

Un capítulo especial en la música de los Andes se debe a una mujer indígena, nacida en Perú, supuestamente descendiente de Atahualpa, el último rey inca. Desde su infancia, empezó a cantar canciones tradicionales de Perú, y a los trece años ya cantaba en la radio de Argentina. Más tarde viajó a Hollywood, donde se convirtió en una verdadera diva, apareció en muchas películas y finalmente se hizo ciudadana de Estados Unidos. La característica más sorprendente de la voz de Yma Sumac era su amplio espectro, que cubría cerca de cinco escalas. Se dice que sólo algunas pocas mujeres alcanzan las notas más altas que ella producía, pero que no hay otra cantante que tenga un registro tan amplio como ella.

## En otras palabras

Expresiones bolivianas

Es tan desconfiado/a como **gallo tuerto**.
*He/She mistrusts everyone.*

Te voy a dar una **samba canuta**.
*I am going to spank you.*

Expresiones paraguayas

No seas **caigue**.
*Don't be lazy.*

**13-43** PRIMERA FASE. **Reconocimiento de palabras clave.** Encuentre en el texto la palabra o expresión que mejor expresa el significado de las siguientes ideas.

1. roots                    _____
2. followers                _____
3. background               _____
4. musical scores           _____
5. string instruments       _____
6. sound                    _____
7. wide range               _____

SEGUNDA FASE. **Oraciones importantes**. Subraye las afirmaciones que contienen ideas que se encuentran en el texto. Luego indique en qué parte del texto están.

1. The music of the Andean region is richer than its better known traditional forms. It includes other genres that originated elsewhere.
2. Young people from the Andes have developed a more visual culture than their ancestors, and they are less inclined to listen to music.
3. As part of their missionary work in several parts of the Spanish empire, the Jesuits resorted to the musical education of the Indians as a means to convert them to Christianity.
4. The indigenous peoples of the Andes were not interested in adapting the musical forms and instruments brought by the Jesuits.
5. Today, some non-governmental organizations continue to teach indigenous boys and girls how to play classical music.
6. Traditional folk music of the Andes can be easily recognized by its peculiar combination of several kinds of flutes, different string instruments, and large drums made of wood and leather.
7. The most valued trait of Yma Sumac's voice was her wide range, which covered about five scales.
8. Yma Sumac was an American citizen born in Hollywood, but she claimed to be a direct descendant of the last Inca king.

TERCERA FASE. **Ideas principales.** Escriba un párrafo breve en español resumiendo las ideas principales expresadas en el texto.

**13-44 Use la información.** Escuche alguna grabación o vea un video de la actuación de un grupo o cantante boliviano/a o paraguayo/a y escriba un informe breve. Incluya lo siguiente:

1. Mencione y describa algunos de los instrumentos musicales que usted reconozca.
2. Describa el género de la canción (popular tradicional, popular moderno o clásico).
3. Explique si las canciones están cantadas en español, en otro idioma de la región, o en ambos.
4. Describa los vestidos que usan los artistas y otros detalles que le parezcan más notables.

Para preparar su informe, visite la página web de *Mosaicos* en y siga los enlaces útiles.

# VOCABULARIO

**Las personas** | *People*
--- | ---
el bailarín/la bailarina | *dancer*
la compañía (de danza, de teatro) | *(dance, theater) company*
el escritor/la escritora | *writer*
el escultor/la escultora | *sculptor*
la estrella | *star*
el/la guitarrista | *guitar player*
el/la intérprete | *performer, artist*
el/la muralista | *muralist*
el/la novelista | *novelist*
el pintor/la pintora | *painter*
el/la poeta | *poet*

**Las obras de arte** | *Works of art*
--- | ---
el autorretrato | *self-portrait*
el cuento | *story*
la escena | *scene*
la forma | *shape, form*
el mural | *mural*
la novela | *novel*
la obra | *work*
el paisaje | *landscape*
el personaje principal | *main character*
la pintura | *painting*
el poema | *poem*
la poesía | *poetry*
el símbolo | *symbol*
el tema | *theme*
la voz | *voice*

**Verbos** | *Verbs*
--- | ---
abrazar(se) (c) | *to embrace*
abundar | *to abound*
actuar | *to act*
denunciar | *to denounce*
dirigir (j) | *to direct*
distinguir | *to distinguish*
exponer (g) | *to exhibit*

nominar | *to nominate*
--- | ---
popularizar (c) | *to popularize*
reflejar | *to reflect*
retratar | *to portray*
rodear | *to surround*
surgir (j) | *to emerge*
titular(se) | *to be called*
tratar | *to treat, to be about*

**Las descripciones** | *Descriptions*
--- | ---
blando/a | *soft*
destacado/a | *outstanding*
inolvidable | *unforgettable*
prometedor/a | *promising*

*Useful words and expressions* | **Palabras y expresiones útiles**
--- | ---
al fondo | *at the back, in the rear*
la amistad | *friendship*
el amor | *love*
a través de | *through*
la calidad | *quality*
cubista | *cubist*
el desarrollo | *development*
desde | *since*
en la actualidad | *at the present time*
el éxito | *success*
el fracaso | *failure*
la fundación | *founding (noun)*
hasta | *including*
el premio | *award, prize*
el recuerdo | *memory*
la revista de corazón | *gossip magazine*
surrealista | *surrealist*
tener éxito | *to be successful*

See page 440 for a list of affirmative and negative expressions.

# 14 *Los cambios sociales*

Grafiti cultural, Santiago de Chile

# In this chapter you will learn how to:

- discuss demographics and social conditions
- indicate conditions, goals, and purposes
- express conjecture
- talk about the past from a past perspective

Arica
Iquique
El desierto de Atacama
Antofagasta

BOLIVIA

PARAGUAY

ARGENTINA

Isla de Pascua

CHILE

URUGUAY

Viña del Mar
Valparaíso
Santiago
Concepción

Santiago de Chile

Valdivia

Puerto Montt

Viñas en otoño

OCÉANO
ATLÁNTICO

OCÉANO PACÍFICO

CORDILLERA DE LOS ANDES

Desierto de Atacama

Estrecho de
Magallanes

Punta Arenas

Punta Arenas

**A vista de pájaro.** Complete las siguientes oraciones con información que usted conoce de Chile.

1. El desierto de _____, uno de los desiertos más áridos del mundo, está en el norte de Chile.
2. En _____, la capital de Chile, viven más de cinco millones de habitantes.
3. Chile exporta _____ y vino a Estados Unidos.
4. Punta Arenas es la ciudad más al sur del mundo. Está junto al Estrecho de _____.

465

## �))  Cambios en la sociedad

CD 6
Track 11

En las últimas décadas ha habido **cambios** muy importantes en el mundo hispano. Varios países, como Chile, Uruguay, Argentina y España, pasaron de tener **regímenes dictatoriales** a ser **democracias** modernas. Michelle Bachelet ganó la presidencia en las elecciones democráticas de Chile en 2006. Esta mujer **políglota** (habla español, francés, inglés, alemán y portugués), médica de profesión y madre de tres hijos, fue la primera mujer en llegar a la presidencia de su país.

En Argentina, Cristina Fernández de Kirchner fue **elegida** en 2007 por una **amplia mayoría**. Su esposo, Néstor Kirchner, la **precedió** en la presidencia. Aunque es la segunda mujer **presidenta** de su país (en los años 70 **gobernó** Isabel Perón), es la primera en ser elegida en un proceso democrático.

Evo Morales, de origen aymara, ganó las elecciones presidenciales de Bolivia en 2005. Es el primer presidente indígena de su país desde la conquista española hace 470 años. Morales se **destacó** muy pronto por su capacidad de organizar a los campesinos en la **lucha** por sus **derechos**. Es un defensor del cultivo de la coca en la región andina como producto natural de gran tradición que se usa para hacer té y con fines medicinales. Sin embargo, se opone a la comercialización de la coca por las bandas internacionales del **tráfico de drogas**.

Las condiciones de vida aún son difíciles en algunos países de Hispanoamérica donde la **pobreza** y el **analfabetismo** todavía son problemas importantes entre sus **habitantes**. Sin embargo, la economía de Chile y de otros países **ha mejorado** considerablemente en las últimas décadas gracias a la **diversificación** de los cultivos y a la intensificación de las **exportaciones**. Hoy en día Chile exporta vino y fruta a todo el mundo.

| 2002–2008 | CHILE | BOLIVIA | COLOMBIA | GUATEMALA |
|---|---|---|---|---|
| POBLACIÓN | 16.454.143 | 9.247.816 | 45.013.674 | 13.002.206 |
| TASA DE CRECIMIENTO ANUAL | 0,91% | 1,38% | 1,41% | 2,11% |
| ESPERANZA DE VIDA ENTRE LAS MUJERES | 80,59 | 69,33 | 76,5 | 71,86 |
| ESPERANZA DE VIDA ENTRE LOS HOMBRES | 73,88 | 63,86 | 68,71 | 68,22 |
| TASA DE FERTILIDAD | 1,9 HIJOS POR MUJER | 2,7 HIJOS POR MUJER | 2,5 HIJOS POR MUJER | 3,6 HIJOS POR MUJER |
| ANALFABETISMO ENTRE LOS HOMBRES | 4,2% | 6,9% | 7,1% | 24,6% |
| ANALFABETISMO ENTRE LAS MUJERES | 4,4% | 19,3% | 7,3% | 36,7% |
| LA TASA DE DESEMPLEO | 7% | 7,5% | 11,2% | 3,2% |
| MORTALIDAD INFANTIL | 7,9 POR CADA MIL NACIMIENTOS | 49 POR CADA MIL NACIMIENTOS | 19 POR CADA MIL NACIMIENTOS | 29 POR CADA MIL NACIMIENTOS |

Fuente: CIA World Fact Book

Estos **datos** muestran y comparan algunos de los problemas sociales de Hispanoamérica. Por ejemplo, el **desempleo** es muy alto en Colombia. El **porcentaje** de mujeres analfabetas es más alto que el de los hombres en casi todos los países. Las mujeres guatemaltecas tienen el **promedio** más alto de hijos. La **esperanza de vida** es en general más alta para las mujeres que para los hombres, y Bolivia tiene la **tasa** más alta de **mortalidad infantil**.

### 14-1 ¿Cómo es la sociedad en Hispanoamérica?

Determinen si las siguientes afirmaciones son ciertas (**C**) o falsas (**F**) de acuerdo con lo que leyeron. En caso de que sean falsas, corrijan la información.

1. ___ Cristina Kirchner es la primera mujer presidenta de su país.
2. ___ Evo Morales fue elegido presidente de Chile.
3. ___ Michelle Bachelet habla varias lenguas.
4. ___ El presidente de Bolivia defiende el cultivo tradicional de la coca.
5. ___ El analfabetismo en estos países ya no es un problema grande.
6. ___ La economía de Chile es ahora mejor que antes.
7. ___ En Bolivia hay menos analfabetismo entre las mujeres que entre los hombres.
8. ___ Bolivia tiene menos habitantes que Guatemala.
9. ___ Las chilenas tienen más hijos que las guatemaltecas.
10. ___ En Colombia se mueren más niños que en Bolivia por cada mil nacimientos.

## Cultura

El índice de natalidad en los países hispanos ha descendido de manera espectacular en los últimos treinta años. A pesar de las circunstancias particulares de cada país, esta parece ser la tendencia general. En Perú y Bolivia, por ejemplo, los gobiernos han apoyado campañas para mostrar las ventajas de los planes familiares y el control de la natalidad. En Venezuela, sin embargo, el promedio de hijos ha bajado en treinta años de 6,7 a 2,7 sin campañas por parte del gobierno. Esto se debe a varios factores, como la crisis económica, la escasez de vivienda y el mayor acceso de las mujeres al trabajo y a la educación. Pero tal vez el caso más extremo de esta tendencia es el de España, que ha pasado de ser el país de Europa con más hijos por pareja en los años 1960, a ser, junto con Italia, el país con el índice de natalidad más bajo.

**14-2 Los datos demográficos.** PRIMERA FASE. Busquen en los textos y en la tabla en la página anterior la información necesaria para contestar las siguientes preguntas. Después comparen sus respuestas con las de otros compañeros/otras compañeras.

1. ¿Cuál de los países en la tabla está más poblado?
2. ¿Cuál tiene menos habitantes?
3. ¿En qué país viven más años los hombres y las mujeres?
4. ¿En qué país crece con más rapidez la población?
5. ¿De dónde son las mujeres que tienen más hijos?
6. ¿Dónde hay más analfabetos probablemente, en el campo o en las ciudades?
7. ¿En qué país hay menos desempleo?
8. ¿En qué país se mueren más niños cuando son bebés?
9. ¿En qué país mueren antes los hombres?
10. ¿Qué país parece que les ofrece más oportunidades educativas a las mujeres?

SEGUNDA FASE. Compare los siguientes temas con datos sobre su propio país:

1. analfabetismo
2. desempleo
3. promedio de hijos
4. mortalidad infantil
5. esperanza de vida para los hombres
6. esperanza de vida para las mujeres

**14-3 Una encuesta sobre las familias.** PRIMERA FASE. Háganse preguntas para obtener los siguientes datos sobre sus respectivas familias.

1. número de personas que forman la familia nuclear
2. número de hombres y de mujeres
3. edad promedio de los miembros de la familia
4. número de personas que estudian
5. número de personas que trabajan

SEGUNDA FASE. Recopilen (*Compile*) la información obtenida. Con esta información, preparen una tabla que indique el porcentaje de familias que hay en su clase...

1. con menos de tres miembros o más de tres.
2. con mayoría de mujeres o de hombres.
3. con edad promedio de 40 años más o menos.
4. con más o menos de dos personas con estudios universitarios.
5. donde trabajan más o menos de dos miembros.

# ◄)) El papel de la mujer

CD 6
Track 12

■ (FEMPRESS) En un reciente estudio realizado en 553 empresas colombianas, Luz Gabriela Arango encontró que sólo el 23,7% de las directivas están constituidas por mujeres. Con todo, el estudio muestra que en este terreno, así como en otros, ha habido enormes cambios. En los años 1950, por ejemplo, todas las sucursales bancarias tenían un varón como gerente. En los años 1990, una alta proporción era dirigida por mujeres.

La encuesta "clase empresarial", realizada a ejecutivos, señala que la confianza en el desempeño profesional de la mujer es mayor que en el del hombre. De hecho, el 96,8% de los entrevistados le dio la más alta calificación a su honestidad; el 80% a la calidad de su trabajo; el 81,6% en materia de confiabilidad; el 79,2% lo dio a su cumplimiento.

En cuanto al manejo de la autoridad, las ejecutivas entrevistadas por *Dinero* consideran que mientras se valora a un hombre por ser enérgico, cuando una mujer asume posiciones fuertes puede causar rechazo. En cuanto al poder, se sienten menos ambiciosas y le dan menor prioridad que los hombres.

L as gerencias administrativas y de recursos industriales en manos de mujeres están aumentando. En algunas entrevistas de *Dinero,* se destaca y se apoya la participación de las mujeres en la empresa pues las consideran más responsables, más comprometidas, más honestas, se ausentan menos del trabajo que los hombres, demuestran mayor eficiencia en el manejo del tiempo y son más transparentes en el trabajo.

Es interesante ver, dice CIDER (Centro Interdisciplinario de Estudios Regionales), las áreas en las cuales se ha concentrado la presencia femenina. Estas son, en sectores financieros y de servicios en el caso de la empresa privada, y en instituciones de servicio y manejo de relaciones públicas en el sector público, como son los ministerios de salud, educación, trabajo y relaciones exteriores. La mayor concentración de fuerza laboral femenina en un alto nivel se ubica en las labores ejecutivas, mientras que sólo el 8,2% de los funcionarios hombres está en ese nivel no directivo.

Estos fragmentos de información reflejan cómo el papel de la mujer ha cambiado y sigue cambiando desde los años 1950 en Hispanoamérica.

**14-4 La mujer de hoy.** Prepare un informe sobre la situación de la mujer en el mundo hispanohablante, utilizando la información que leyó en las estadísticas (p. 467) y las citas (*quotations*) (p. 469). Compare su informe con el de su compañero/a.

**14-5 Mujeres ejecutivas.** PRIMERA FASE. Cada uno/a de ustedes debe hacer una lista de cinco mujeres que ocupan puestos importantes en países hispanos o en su país. Hablen sobre estas mujeres, basándose en los siguientes puntos:

1. puesto que ocupan y responsabilidades que tienen
2. su personalidad y rasgos (*traits*) de carácter
3. obstáculos que cada una ha tenido que superar en su área de trabajo

SEGUNDA FASE. Ahora, comenten lo siguiente.

1. ¿Qué tipo de personalidad y rasgos de carácter tienen en común estas mujeres?
2. ¿Hacen estas mujeres trabajos tradicionalmente femeninos, o han incursionado en el mundo laboral típicamente masculino?
3. ¿Hay semejanzas entre los obstáculos que estas mujeres han tenido que superar? ¿Cuáles son? ¿Cómo han logrado superarlos?

**14-6 Los tiempos cambian.** Conversen sobre los logros de la mujer en este siglo y el pasado. Hagan una lista de los cambios que han afectado a la mujer en las siguientes áreas en los últimos 50 años.

1. la familia
2. el trabajo
3. la casa
4. el gobierno/la política
5. la educación

# Temas de hoy: los jóvenes y la emigración

El **desplazamiento** de personas de un país a otro es algo muy común en los últimos tiempos. En general, los jóvenes que emigran de sus países lo hacen por motivos económicos o políticos. Muchos tienen la esperanza de mejorar sus condiciones de vida. Entre los países hispanos, Chile y España son los que más **emigrantes** reciben.

En Chile, los argentinos y los peruanos son los dos grupos de extranjeros más numerosos. En España también las comunidades peruana y argentina son muy numerosas, sólo superadas por los inmigrantes de origen ecuatoriano. La ventaja de estas **migraciones** inter-hispanas es que todos hablan la misma lengua y esto hace que las dificultades de **adaptación** sean menores.

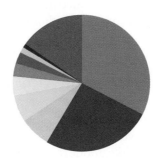

- ■ Argentina
- ■ Perú
- ■ Ecuador
- ■ Bolivia
- ■ Brasil
- ■ Venezuela
- ■ Colombia
- ■ Uruguay
- ■ Paraguay
- ■ Otros

Muchos hispanoamericanos, especialmente mexicanos y caribeños, prefieren emigrar a Estados Unidos **en vez de** a Europa en busca de oportunidades económicas y una mayor **proximidad** con sus países. Los jóvenes por lo general se adaptan más fácilmente que sus padres porque aprenden inglés rápidamente. Además, hoy en día las ventajas de ser bilingüe en EE.UU. son evidentes.

**14-7 Los emigrantes.** Complete las siguientes ideas con la forma correcta de las palabras de la lista.

| | | |
|---|---|---|
| bilingüismo | emigración | habitante |
| condición | emigrante | proximidad |

1. En España hay muchos _____ de nacionalidad ecuatoriana.
2. Una ventaja para los caribeños que emigran a Estados Unidos es la _____ a los países del Caribe.
3. El _____ es útil para los jóvenes hispanos que buscan trabajo.
4. Frecuentemente las personas se desplazan para mejorar sus _____ de vida.
5. La _____ es un fenómeno de nuestros días que está relacionada con la globalización.
6. Chile es uno de los países de Hispanoamérica que más _____ recibe.

**14-8 Los habitantes de su comunidad.** Preparen preguntas para entrevistar a un compañero/una compañera sobre sus orígenes y las costumbres de su comunidad o grupo étnico. Usen los puntos a continuación como guía para elaborar su cuestionario.

MODELO:    E1:   *¿Cuál es el origen de tu familia?*
           E2:   *Mis abuelos eran italianos.*
           E1:   *¿Cuándo emigraron a este país?*
           E2:   *Emigraron cuando mi padre tenía cinco años.*

1. origen de tu apellido
2. grupo(s) étnico(s) que asocias con tu familia
3. número de habitantes de ese grupo étnico o comunidad
4. área de concentración en Estados Unidos
5. costumbres e idioma
6. fiestas o celebraciones
7. productos que consumen
8. comida típica

**CD 6**
**Track 14** **14-9 La mujer en los países hispanos.** You will listen to a conversation between a reporter and a Professor of Sociology at the University of Santiago de Chile about the status of women in the Hispanic world. Before you listen, write two questions the reporter may ask the professor and the answers that you think she may provide.

As you listen, focus on the main ideas of what is said. Circle the appropriate ending to each statement.

1. La doctora Gómez dice que la situación de la mujer ha mejorado porque...
   **a.** más mujeres son jefas de empresas.
   **b.** ahora hay más leyes que las protegen.
   **c.** hay muchas mujeres que no tienen hijos.
2. Según la doctora Gómez, en comparación con los hombres, las mujeres...
   **a.** no tienen que trabajar tanto.
   **b.** tienen que estar mejor preparadas.
   **c.** no estudian tanto.
3. Las mujeres hispanas ganan...
   **a.** más dinero que los hombres.
   **b.** tanto dinero como los hombres.
   **c.** menos dinero que los hombres.
4. En los hogares hispanos, el trabajo de la casa y la crianza de los hijos...
   **a.** están principalmente en manos de las mujeres.
   **b.** son compartidos por todos los miembros de la familia.
   **c.** son la responsabilidad de los empleados domésticos.

## EN ACCIÓN

### Diarios de bicicleta: Elecciones "presidenciales"

#### Antes de ver

**14-10** Marque (✓) las características que usted considera más importantes en un líder y añada una más.

| | | |
|---|---|---|
| ___ activo/a | ___ culto/a | ___ popular |
| ___ atractivo/a | ___ decidido/a | ___ progresista |
| ___ autoritario/a | ___ diplomático/a | ___ razonable |
| ___ compasivo/a | ___ egoista | ___ responsable |
| ___ conservador/a | ___ generoso/a | ___ solidario/a |

#### Mientras ve

**14-11** Escriba los temas que Luciana dice que va a tratar como presidenta.

#### Después de ver

**14-12** Al final de este segmento, nos damos cuenta de que Luciana es candidata a la presidencia del equipo de natación. ¿Cree usted que Luciana ganará las elecciones? ¿Tiene ella las características necesarias para ocupar este puesto? ¿Cree usted que Gabi ganará las elecciones? ¿Por qué? ¿Alguna vez ha sido nominado/a usted para un puesto en alguna elección? Explique.

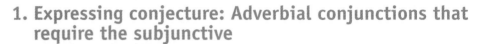

# FUNCIONES Y FORMAS

## 1. Expressing conjecture: Adverbial conjunctions that require the subjunctive

Estos inmigrantes cosechan cebollas en Texas. Según la ley, pueden trabajar en Estados Unidos **con tal de que** tengan estatus legal en el país. Muchos inmigrantes mandan dinero a su familia **para que** sus hijos vivan mejor. Muchos vuelven a su país, **a menos que** su familia pueda venir a Estados Unidos también.

**Piénselo.** Escoja en la columna de la derecha el significado de las palabras en negrita.

1. _A_ Pueden trabajar en Estados Unidos **con tal de que** tengan estatus.
2. _D_ Mandan dinero a su familia **para que** sus hijos vivan mejor.
3. _C_ Volverán a su país **a menos que** su familia pueda venir a Estados Unidos.
4. _C_ Para muchos inmigrantes es difícil conseguir trabajo **sin que** sus amigos los ayuden.
5. _B_ Los hijos de algunos inmigrantes pasan muchos años con sólo su madre **antes de que** su padre vuelva a casa.

a. si
b. anterioridad de tiempo
c. si... no
d. con la intención

■ Conjunctions are words or phrases that function as connectors in sentences. Some conjunctions introduce dependent clauses known as adverbial clauses, which communicate how, why, when, and where an action takes place.

■ Some conjunctions always require the subjunctive when followed by a dependent clause.

| | | | |
|---|---|---|---|
| a menos que | *unless* | para que | *so that* |
| antes (de) que | *before* | sin que | *without* |
| con tal (de) que | *provided that* | | |

Las mujeres tendrán una reunión **antes de que** sus representantes **hablen** con los oficiales.

*The women are having a meeting before their representatives speak with the officials.*

Las mujeres votarán por los oficiales **con tal de que** ellos **implementen** los cambios mencionados en la petición.

*The women will vote for the officials provided that they implement the changes mentioned in the petition.*

Las representantes negocian con los oficiales **para que** todos los niños **tengan** acceso a servicios médicos.

*The representatives negotiate with the officials so that all children have access to medical services.*

■ Use an infinitive after the prepositions **antes de, para,** and **sin** when there is no change of subject.

Las comunidades ofrecen clases **para que** los inmigrantes **aprendan** inglés.

*Communities offer classes so that immigrants can learn English.*

Los inmigrantes estudian inglés **para aprender** la lengua rápidamente.

*Immigrants study English to learn the language quickly.*

**14-13 En el futuro.** PRIMERA FASE. Túrnense para leer la primera parte de cada oración y después busquen el final apropiado a la derecha. Deben fijarse (*take note*) en el contexto y también en la forma verbal correcta.

1. \_\_\_ Muchos empleados trabajarán en casa sin…

2. \_\_\_ Las compañías de limpieza programarán los robots para que…

3. \_\_\_ Podremos jubilarnos (*retire*) antes de…

4. \_\_\_ Casi todos los cursos universitarios se ofrecerán en Internet sin que…

5. \_\_\_ Los jóvenes no tendrán que trabajar a menos que…

6. \_\_\_ Habrá computadoras de uso gratis en muchos lugares públicos para…

7. \_\_\_ Los empleados de las compañías multinacionales podrán comunicarse fácilmente con tal de que…

8. \_\_\_ Después de nacer sus hijos, los padres no volverán a trabajar antes de que los niños…

a. los profesores ni los alumnos tengan que ir a la universidad.

b. tengan aparatos de interpretación simultánea.

c. tener que comunicarse con los clientes o colegas en persona.

d. facilitar la comunicación entre las personas.

e. cumplan 5 años de edad.

f. limpien los edificios sin intervención de los seres humanos.

g. les interese hacer trabajo de voluntariado.

h. los 50 años.

SEGUNDA FASE. Ahora escojan dos de las oraciones de la izquierda y complétenlas de acuerdo con sus propias ideas. Después comparen sus respuestas con las de otra pareja.

**14-14 Una ingeniera se entrevista.** La ingeniera industrial María Victoria Martín se entrevista hoy con Sanofi Aventis, una compañía que fabrica medicinas. Para saber qué pasó en la entrevista, llene los espacios en blanco con la forma correcta del verbo apropiado: **decir, hacer, ofrecer, pasar,** o **saber.**

María Victoria llega temprano a la cita con la directora, y la secretaria le pide que espere unos minutos antes de (1) _____ a su oficina. María Victoria trata de tranquilizarse para que nadie (2) _____ que está muy nerviosa. Piensa que podrá dar una buena impresión con tal de que la directora le (3) _____ preguntas relevantes a su experiencia. Finalmente la directora se presenta y la invita a entrar en su oficina sin que María Victoria (4) _____ una palabra. Al final de la entrevista la directora le ofrece el puesto. María Victoria dice que no puede aceptar la oferta a menos que la compañía le (5) _____ seguro médico. La directora acepta esta condición.

**14-15 ¿Estudio en Chile o no?** Usted está considerando la posibilidad de estudiar en Chile el próximo semestre. Indique lo que piensa sobre esta posibilidad, usando las expresiones adverbiales de la lista. Su compañero/a va a responder de forma lógica.

a menos que    antes (de) que    con tal (de) que    para que    sin que

MODELO:       el programa sea muy caro
        E1:  *Voy a estudiar en Chile, a menos que el programa sea muy caro.*
        E2:  *No participes en el programa a menos que te den una beca.*

1. el semestre termine para el 1 de junio
2. mis amigos y yo aprendamos mucho español
3. viva con una familia amable
4. mi familia me visite durante el semestre
5. haya oportunidades de viajar o otros países
6. mi amigo/a también participe en el programa
7. conozca la cultura mapuche
8. pasemos las vacaciones esquiando en los Andes

## SITUACIONES

1. **Role A.** You are a Chilean exchange student who recently arrived in the United States. Ask a friend a) what his/her family does to help him/her attend college; b) if in big lecture classes students can use their cell phones and read e-mail without their professors' knowledge; and c) what your friend hopes to accomplish before graduating.

   **Role B.** Your Chilean friend is new to the United States. Answer his/her questions about university life here and ask about university life there.

2. **Role A.** You are a lawyer informing a client that he/she is going to inherit (**heredar**) a million dollars from a distant relative (**pariente lejano/a**), provided that he/she a) give one third (**la tercera parte**) to four low-income families so that they can send their children to college; and b) wait five years before spending another third. He/She can spend the remaining third now.

   **Role B.** Your lawyer calls with some surprising news about an inheritance (**herencia**). Ask about the conditions of the will (**testamento**).

## 2. Expressing conjecture or certainty: Adverbial conjunctions that take the subjunctive or indicative

SRA. LÓPEZ: ¿Qué le interesa hacer **cuando se gradúe**?

VICENTE: **Después de terminar** mis estudios, me gustaría trabajar en otro país para una organización sin fines de lucro (*non-profit*).

SRA. LÓPEZ: Muy bien. **Tan pronto como terminemos** de hablar, le mandaré una lista de organizaciones. No espere **hasta que se gradúe** para empezar a buscar trabajo. Familiarícese con las posiblidades ahora, **mientras es** estudiante.

Sra. López     Vicente

**Piénselo.** Indique si la persona que habla se refiere al presente (**P**) o al futuro (**F**).

1. ____ ¿Qué le interesa hacer **cuando se gradúe**?
2. ____ **Tan pronto como terminemos** de hablar, le mandaré una lista de organizaciones.
3. ____ No espere **hasta que se gradúe** para empezar a buscar trabajo.
4. ____ Familiarícese con las posibilidades ahora, **mientras es** estudiante.
5. ____ Vicente va a buscar trabajo en una organización sin fines de lucro, **aunque gane** poco dinero.
6. ____ Estas organizaciones siempre apoyan a las comunidades aun (*even*) **después de que** las comunidades **terminan** el proyecto.

■ Earlier in this chapter you learned about conjunctions that are always followed by the subjunctive. Here you will practice using conjunctions that are followed by a verb in either the subjunctive or indicative, depending on whether the event in the adverbial clause has occurred or not, or whether it is factual or unknown.

| | | | |
|---|---|---|---|
| **aunque** | *although, even though, even if* | **en cuanto** | *as soon as* |
| | | **hasta que** | *until* |
| **cuando** | *when* | **mientras** | *while* |
| **después (de) que** | *after* | **según** | *according to, as* |
| **donde** | *where, wherever* | **tan pronto (como)** | *as soon as* |

■ These conjunctions require the subjunctive when the event in the adverbial clause has not yet taken place. Note that the main clause expresses future time.

Va a luchar **hasta que** la comunidad **ofrezca** clases gratis para los inmigrantes nuevos.
*She is going to fight until the community offers free classes for new immigrants.*

Nos reuniremos **después de que comiencen** las clases.
*We will meet after classes start.*

Me llamará **tan pronto reciba** la aprobación del alcalde.
*She will call me as soon as she receives approval from the mayor.*

■ These conjunctions require the indicative when the event in the adverbial clause has already taken place, is taking place, or usually takes place.

Nos reunimos **después de que comenzaron** las clases.
*We met after classes started.*

Me llamó **tan pronto recibió** la aprobación del alcalde.
*She called me as soon as she received approval from the mayor.*

La organización apoya a los inmigrantes **hasta que se establecen** en la comunidad.
*The organization supports the immigrants until they become established in the community.*

■ **Donde** and **según** require the indicative when they refer to something definite or known, and the subjunctive when they refer to something indefinite or unknown.

Vamos a reunirnos **donde** ella **dice**.
*We are going to meet where she says.* (She has already announced the place.)

Vamos a reunirnos **donde** ella **diga**.
*We are going to meet wherever she says.* (She has not yet announced the place.)

Llena el formulario **según dice** el consejero.
*Fill out the form according to what the adviser says.* (Instructions have already been given.)

Vamos a seguir el procedimiento **según diga** el alcalde.
*We will follow the procedure in accordance with whatever the mayor says.* (Instructions have not yet been given.)

■ **Aunque** also requires the subjunctive when it introduces a condition not regarded as fact.

Lo compro **aunque es** caro.            *I will buy it, although it is expensive.*
Lo compro **aunque sea** caro.           *I will buy it, although it may (turn out to) be expensive.*

## Lengua

You learned that in Spanish, the subject is normally placed after the verb when asking a question: **¿Les dio instrucciones el alcalde?** (*Did the mayor give them instructions?*) You may also place the subject after the verb in statements, especially when you wish to emphasize the subject: **Les habló el alcalde.** (*The mayor talked to them.*) To avoid misinterpreting statements with this structure, you should locate the subject first, and not assume that the first noun or pronoun in the sentence is the subject.

**14-16 ¿Cuáles serán los cambios?** Escoja la forma verbal correcta para completar las siguientes afirmaciones.

1. No se permite que un inmigrante sea presidente de este país a menos de que cambia/cambie la Constitución.
2. Las leyes de los impuestos cambiaron según lo que pidieron/pidan los miembros de la comisión.
3. Las familias que tenían pocos hijos protestaron cuando se aprobaron/se aprueben las nuevas leyes.
4. Como resultado, el gobierno quiere disminuirles los impuestos a las familias numerosas para que las mujeres tienen/tengan más hijos.
5. Muchas personas dicen que no creerán en esta disminución de los impuestos hasta que la ven/vean.

**14-17 La educación a distancia.** Ustedes toman un curso en Internet sobre la historia de Chile por medio del programa VirtualU de la Universidad de Chile. Todo lo hacen en la computadora y se comunican por mensajes de texto y correo electrónico. Digan lo que van a hacer, terminando las oraciones abajo con una frase apropiada de la lista a continuación.

ser las 12:00
tener tiempo
ser muy tarde
tener sus horas de consulta
llegar el día del examen final
escribirme mi compañero virtual
leer unos mensajes electrónicos de la profesora
terminar de leer sobre los regímenes dictatoriales

MODELO:     Voy a trabajar en la computadora hasta que… empezar las
            noticias/ser la hora de cenar
    E1:     *Voy a trabajar en la computadora hasta que empiecen las noticias.*
    E2:     *Y yo voy a trabajar hasta que sea la hora de cenar.*

1. Voy a hablar con la profesora en cuanto…
2. Comeré después de que…
3. Voy a comprobar los datos tan pronto como…
4. Haré la mayoría del trabajo en nuestro ensayo hasta que…
5. Voy a estudiar el tema de la inmigración chilena esta noche aunque…
6. Le mandaré mi informe sobre las últimas lecturas a la profesora antes de que…

**14-18 Después de que termine el año escolar. PRIMERA FASE.** Usted quiere descansar y divertirse después de que terminen las clases, pero también quiere hacer algo por su comunidad. Complete dos de las opciones que más le interesen en cada columna y añada una más para expresar sus propias ideas. Después comparta sus planes con su compañero/a.

| DIVERSIÓN | AYUDA COMUNITARIA |
|---|---|
| 1. Quiero dormir hasta que… | 1. Trabajaré de voluntario donde… |
| 2. No voy a abrir los libros aunque… | 2. Ayudaré en la biblioteca después de que… |
| 3. Haré un crucero por… tan pronto como… | 3. Les serviré comida a los desamparados (*homeless*) mientras… |
| 4. Iré a la playa todos los días a menos que… | 4. Organizaré juegos infantiles en el parque para que… |
| 5. … | 5. … |

**SEGUNDA FASE.** Preparen un plan para ayudar a su comunidad. En su plan deben indicar lo siguiente:

1. sector de la comunidad
2. tipo de ayuda
3. frecuencia de su participación
4. medios que van a usar
5. resultados que esperan obtener

**14-19 El hombre y la mujer en la sociedad. PRIMERA FASE.** Indique (✓) si, según usted, las situaciones presentadas en las siguientes afirmaciones existen o no existen hoy en día.

| LOS HOMBRES Y LAS MUJERES... | SÍ | NO |
|---|---|---|
| 1. reciben la misma educación | | |
| 2. son tratados de la misma forma en el trabajo. | | |
| 3. ganan el mismo sueldo por el mismo trabajo. | | |
| 4. tienen las mismas oportunidades. | | |
| 5. hacen las mismas tareas domésticas. | | |
| 6. tienen los mismos derechos en un divorcio. | | |
| 7. sufren las mismas consecuencias cuando violan una norma moral, por ejemplo, si son infieles. | | |

**SEGUNDA FASE.** Ahora compare sus respuestas con las de su compañero/a. Defienda sus opiniones negativas y diga cuándo o bajo qué condiciones usted cree que los cambios necesarios ocurrirán.

MODELO:  E1:  *Los hombres y las mujeres ocupan más o menos el mismo número de puestos importantes.*

E2:  *No estoy de acuerdo. Los hombres ocupan la mayoría de los puestos importantes en las compañías y en el gobierno. Esto va a cambiar cuando las generaciones jóvenes puedan tomar más decisiones.*

---

### En directo

To make a polite request or a proposal:

**Quiero/Queremos proponer (que)...**

**Sugiero/Sugerimos (que)...**

---

## SITUACIONES

1. **Role A.** As the employee representative for your company, you meet with the president to ask that a yoga class be held for employees who are experiencing neck and back pain from working at their computers. Explain their needs and the advantages of yoga. Stress that the employees are willing to take the class wherever and whenever the president wishes.

   **Role B.** As president of a large company, you meet with an employee representative who wants the company to offer a yoga class during the work day. Ask a) how many employees would be interested; b) who would teach the class; and c) when and where it would take place. Say that you have no problem with the idea, provided that the board of directors (**junta directiva**) is in favor of it.

2. **Role A.** You make a presentation to the city council (**concejo municipal**) about starting an adult literacy program. Explain how the lives of participants will improve when they know how to read and write well. In response to questions, say that you will a) organize the program; b) hold classes wherever the council says; and c) decide on class schedules according to the needs of the participants.

   **Role B.** You are the president of the city council (**concejo municipal**). After listening to a presentation by a specialist in adult literacy who wants to start a program in the community, ask a) where and when the classes will be held; and b) who will pay for the program.

## 3. Talking about the past from a past perspective: The past perfect

VIOLETA: Oye, mamá, mi profesora habló un poco de Gabriela Mistral. ¿Tú sabes algo de ella?

MADRE: ¡Uf! Gabriela Mistral fue una gran poeta chilena que ganó el Premio Nobel de literatura en 1945. Pero antes de recibir el premio, Gabriela ya **había hecho** muchas cosas importantes.

VIOLETA: ¿Qué **había hecho**? Yo no sé nada de ella.

MADRE: Antes de ser famosa, Gabriela **había tenido** una vida muy dura. Su padre **había abandonado** a la familia cuando ella tenía tres años.

VIOLETA: ¡Qué triste la vida de Gabriela, mamá!

MADRE: Sí y no. Ella utilizó su sufrimiento positivamente para lograr mucho. Por ejemplo, a los 15 años, ya **había escrito** sus primeras poesías y **se había graduado** de profesora. Además, antes de ella, ningún escritor latinoamericano **había ganado** el Premio Nobel.

**Piénselo.** Indique si las siguientes experiencias de Gabriela Mistral y su madre se refieren a un momento cronológicamente anterior (**A**) al momento cuando Gabriela se hizo internacionalmente famosa.

1. \_\_\_\_ Gabriela ya **había hecho** muchas cosas importantes.
2. \_\_\_\_ Su madre y ella **habían tenido** una vida muy dura.
3. \_\_\_\_ **Ganó** el Premio Nobel en l945.
4. \_\_\_\_ Su padre **había abandonado** a Gabriela y a su madre.
5. \_\_\_\_ **Había escrito** poesías antes de cumplir los 15 años.
6. \_\_\_\_ Ningún escritor latinoamericano **había ganado** el Premio Nobel.

■ Use the past perfect to refer to a past event, action or condition that occurred prior to another past event, action or state.

*ya, antes, nunca, todavía*

| | |
|---|---|
| Ningún escritor latinoamericano **había ganado** el Premio Nobel de Literatura antes de Mistral. | *No Latin American writer had won the Nobel Prize for Literature before Mistral.* |
| Otros escritores **habían sido** nominados para el premio, pero ella lo recibió. | *Other writers had been nominated for the award, but she received it.* |

■ Form the past perfect with the imperfect tense of **haber** and the past participle of the main verb.

| IMPERFECT OF *HABER* | | PAST PARTICIPLE |
|---|---|---|
| yo | había | |
| tú | habías | |
| Ud., él, ella | había | hablado |
| nosotros/as | habíamos | comido |
| vosotros/as | habíais | vivido |
| Uds., ellos/as | habían | |

**14-20 ¡Recuerdos!** PRIMERA FASE. Para cada afirmación, ponga un círculo alrededor de la acción que ocurrió primero.

MODELO: Cuando yo cumplí diez años, ya había escuchado discusiones políticas.

1. Cuando cumplimos diecisiete años, mis amigos y yo ya nos habíamos inscrito en un partido político.
2. Cuando terminé la escuela secundaria, mis padres ya me habían comprado un carro.
3. Yo ya había trabajado y había ahorrado (*saved*) algún dinero cuando empecé la universidad.
4. Cuando pasó el primer mes de clases en la universidad, yo ya me había acostumbrado a todo el trabajo que tenía que hacer.
5. Mis padres ya sospechaban que yo me había hecho más independiente cuando los visité después de algunos meses.

SEGUNDA FASE. ¿Cuáles de las acciones de la *Primera fase* concuerdan (*agree*) con su experiencia personal? Comparta sus respuestas con las de su compañero/a.

**14-21 Una investigación.** PRIMERA FASE. Marque (✓) sus respuestas en la columna correspondiente y dígale a su compañero/a si usted o miembros de su familia ya habían hecho estas cosas antes del año 2005.

MODELO: buscar trabajo en Internet antes del año 2005

|  | SÍ | NO | ¿QUIÉNES? |
|---|---|---|---|
| E1: *Mi hermano y yo ya habíamos buscado trabajo en Internet. En 2004 los dos conseguimos trabajo por Internet.* | ✓ | | *Mi hermano y yo* |
| E2: *Pues, yo nunca había usado Internet para buscar trabajo. En 2004 yo era muy joven.* | | | |

|  | SÍ | NO | ¿QUIÉNES? |
|---|---|---|---|
| 1. manejar un carro híbrido | | | |
| 2. hacer trabajo voluntario | | | |
| 3. votar en las elecciones presidenciales | | | |
| 4. leer el periódico | | | |
| 5. comunicarse con los amigos por correo electrónico | | | |
| 6. comprar un iPod | | | |
| 7. diseñar una página web | | | |
| 8. dejar comentarios sobre una foto en Facebook de un amigo/una amiga | | | |

SEGUNDA FASE. Hagan una encuesta para averiguar qué tres actividades de la *Primera fase* marcaron más personas del grupo. Determinen si más hombres o más mujeres hicieron cada una de las tres actividades.

**14-22 ¡Una familia organizada!** Los señores Rosales salieron temprano para el trabajo hoy, pero cuando volvieron por la noche notaron que sus hijos Carlos, Eduardo y Magdalena habían hecho todo el trabajo doméstico. Túrnense para conjeturar qué había hecho cada uno.

MODELO: Al salir, les dijeron a sus hijos que iban a llegar un poco tarde y que no tendrían tiempo para cocinar. *Al volver, vieron que Eduardo había cocinado unos espaguetis para toda la familia.*

1. Después del desayuno dejaron los platos sucios en el lavaplatos.
2. Antes de irse a la oficina, la señora Rosales vio que había un montón de libros de la biblioteca en la mesa del comedor.
3. Cuando salía de casa el señor Rosales notó que el garaje estaba sucio.
4. Los dormitorios de sus hijos estaban desordenados; había ropa y libros en el piso.
5. Como tenía prisa, la señora Rosales olvidó mandar por correo unas cuentas importantes.
6. No llevaron a la tintorería (*dry cleaner*) una ropa que querían lavar en seco (*dry clean*).

# SITUACIONES

1. **Role A.** You are the founder of a company that conducts opinion polls (**encuestas de opinión**). Answer the questions that a reporter asks. Give detailed information on how you think polls will be conducted in the future.

   **Role B.** You are a reporter interviewing the founder of a company that conducts opinion polls (**encuestas de opinión**). Ask a) the date he/she started the company; b) what he/she had done before starting the company (studies, positions held, places of residence); and c) his/her ideas on how opinion polls will be conducted in the future.

2. **Role A.** You are interviewing a Chilean student for your campus newspaper. Ask a) what he/she had studied in Chile before deciding to study here; b) what U.S. schools he/she had considered before choosing this one; and c) how his/her experience has been different from what he/she had expected.

   **Role B.** You are an exchange student from Chile who is being interviewed for the campus newspaper. Provide as much information to the reporter as possible, including your expectations (**lo que había pensado**) while still in Chile and the reality you found when you started to live in the United States and study at this school.

## 4. Expressing actions: The infinitive as subject or object

LAURA: Mamá, ¿viste la marcha en la tele? Yo también estaba allí con todos mis compañeros de la clase de sociología.

MAMÁ: **Luchar** por la igualdad entre los sexos es tiempo perdido, hija. No hemos avanzado mucho. Mira, yo continúo trabajando en casa, pero no me importa.

LAURA: Pero **quedarse** de brazos cruzados tampoco es una opción para mí, mamá.

MAMÁ: **Trabajar** duro es lo que debemos hacer. Ninguna protesta nos ayudará.

LAURA: Mamá, ¿cómo puedes pensar así? **Guardar** silencio es **hacerse** cómplice de la injusticia. **Exigir** igualdad y respeto por nuestra dignidad es nuestro derecho.

**Piénselo.** Indique si usted cree que las siguientes acciones representan las opiniones de Laura (**L**) o las de su madre (**M**).

1. ___ **Trabajar** en casa no es un problema para la mujer.
2. ___ **Protestar** nos ayudará a cambiar la sociedad.
3. ___ No **resignarse** al trato desigual es fundamental para conseguir el cambio.
4. ___ **Mantenerse** de brazos cruzados significa aceptar la desigualdad y la injusticia.

■ The infinitive is the only verb form that may be used as the subject of a sentence. As the subject, it corresponds to the English -ing form.

| | |
|---|---|
| **Dialogar** es necesario para lograr cambios. | *Talking is necessary for changes to occur.* |
| **Hacer** comentarios negativos no es bueno para nuestras negociaciones. | *Making negative pronouncements is not good for our negotiations.* |

■ Use an infinitive after a preposition.

| | |
|---|---|
| Llama **antes de ir.** | *Call before going.* |
| No trates de argumentar **sin prepararte.** | *Do not try to argue without preparing yourself.* |

■ **Al** + *infinitive* is the equivalent of **cuando** + *verb.*

| | |
|---|---|
| **Al recibir** su carta de despido, llamó al director. | *Upon receiving his pink slip, he called the director.* |
| **Cuando recibió** su carta de despido, llamó al director. | *When he received his pink slip, he called the director.* |

■ When used in signs and instructions, the infinitive functions as a command.

| | |
|---|---|
| No **comer** en clase. | *No eating in class. (Lit. Don't eat in class)* |
| **Hablar** en voz baja. | *Speak softly.* |

**14-23 Ciudadanos (*Citizens*) responsables.** Asocie lógicamente las opciones de la columna de la izquierda con las ideas de la columna de la derecha.

1. _b_ Educarse…
2. _d_ Estudiar idiomas…
3. _a_ Votar en las elecciones…
4. _c_ Aceptar a los inmigrantes…

   a. es importante para mantener la democracia.
   b. es vital para conseguir un buen trabajo.
   c. es la mejor manera de aprender sobre otras culturas.
   d. es indispensable para una convivencia sana dentro de una comunidad.

**14-24 Opiniones.** PRIMERA FASE. Indique si las siguientes actividades son necesarias, opcionales o inaceptables. Después, compare sus respuestas con las de su compañero/a y explíquele las razones de sus respuestas.

| ACTIVIDAD | OPINIÓN |
|---|---|
| 1. ofrecer seguro de salud para todos | |
| 2. informarse sobre lo que pasa en el mundo | |
| 3. prohibir la proliferación de armas nucleares | |
| 4. hacer investigación sobre células troncales (*stem cell*) | |
| 5. discriminar a algunas personas por su etnia (*ethnicity*) | |

SEGUNDA FASE. Escojan el tema más importante para ustedes en la *Primera fase*. Expliquen por qué es importante y qué es necesario hacer para captar la atención de la gente.

**14-25 Interpretar los mensajes.** PRIMERA FASE. Observen los siguientes letreros y escriban una nota bajo cada uno de ellos.

1. _____    2. _____

3. _____    4. _____

SEGUNDA FASE. Preparen su propio letrero. Otra pareja tiene que decir dónde sería bueno ponerlo y por qué.

# MOSAICOS

## A escuchar

### ESTRATEGIA

**Identify the speaker's point of view**

When you listen to someone or see someone talk you may identify the speaker's intention and point of view by paying attention to the verbal and non-verbal cues such as tone, word choice, organization of ideas discussed, pitch, posture, and gestures. Identifying the speaker's point of view will help you understand his/her position on the issues.

### Antes de escuchar

**14-26 Preparación.** Dos mujeres mayores conversan sobre los cambios que han ocurrido en las sociedades hispanas. Antes de escuchar, escriba un cambio que cree que mencionarán en cada una de estas áreas: los quehaceres de casa y la crianza de los hijos.

### Escuchar

**14-27 ¿Comprende usted?** First read the statements below and then listen to Sonia and Vilma talk about the changes in the Hispanic family that have occurred during their lifetime. As you listen, indicate if each statement reflects Sonia's (**S**) point of view or Vilma's (**V**). Finally, check (✓) the clues that helped you identify Vilma's point of view and that of Sonia.

CD 6
Track 15

| | WORD CHOICE | ORGANIZATION OF IDEAS |
|---|---|---|
| 1. ___ Los cambios que han ocurrido en la sociedad han sido positivos. | | |
| 2. ___ Ahora nadie se ocupa de los quehaceres de casa. | | |
| 3. ___ No era bueno el papel secundario que tenía la mujer en la casa. | | |
| 4. ___ Los abuelos han perdido la importancia que tenían en la familia. | | |
| 5. ___ La mujer debe desarrollarse profesional e intelectualmente. | | |

### Después de escuchar

**14-28 Ahora usted.** Expliquen su punto de vista sobre los siguientes asuntos.

1. ¿Es necesario que uno de los padres se quede en casa mientras los hijos son pequeños?
2. Si ambos padres trabajan fuera de casa, ¿cómo se podría resolver la cuestión de la educación de los hijos?

# A conversar

## Antes de conversar

**14-29 Preparación.** Indiquen y expliquen por lo menos un problema (local, nacional o mundial) en cada una de las siguientes áreas.

MODELO: **Área:** seguridad

**Problema:** *terrorismo*

**Explicación del problema:** *Hoy existen grupos terroristas que atacan y crean caos en el mundo. Nadie se siente seguro.*

ÁREA

1. economía
2. igualdad
3. educación
4. salud

## Conversar

**14-30 Entre nosotros.** Conversen sobre los problemas que ustedes identificaron en **14-29.** Hagan lo siguiente:

1. Digan cuál de los problemas que identificaron en **14-29** es más serio. Expliquen por qué.
2. Luego, háganse preguntas relacionadas con ese problema. Utilicen en sus respuestas las expresiones indicadas en *En directo* y tomen notas de las respuestas del grupo.

MODELO: la falta de seguridad en las escuelas
E1: *¿Creen que haya solución al problema de la falta de seguridad en las escuelas?*
E2: *Sí, la solución es tener/establecer más comunicación con los padres, para que controlen mejor a sus hijos.*
E3: *A mí me parece que la solución es instalar máquinas en las entradas de las escuelas que registren a todas las personas que quieran entrar en la escuela.*
3. Lleguen a una conclusión entre todos sobre cuándo y cómo se solucionará el problema. Usen las siguientes expresiones: *después de que, tan pronto como, en cuanto, cuando.*

## Después de conversar

**14-31 Un poco más.** Preséntenle a la clase la información y conclusión a la que llegaron en la actividad **14-30.** Prepárense para defender su posición.

*En directo*

To present a group's conclusion:

**Después de hablar sobre el tema, hemos llegado a la siguiente conclusión. Nuestro grupo cree/piensa que...**

**A nuestro grupo le parece que...**

**Para nosotros, el problema más serio es...**

To support a group's view or position:

**No tenemos duda de que sea... el problema más serio porque...**

**Si miramos/observamos... nos damos cuenta de que...**

**Las estadísticas/La opinión de los expertos apoya(n) nuestra conclusión.**

## ESTRATEGIA

## A leer

**Identify the tone of a text**

Identifying the tone of a text is a task usually associated with works of literature. But expository and argumentative texts also use tone to present a point of view. Even a text that appears to be objective owes that tone to the choices in vocabulary and phrasing made by the author.

## Antes de leer

**14-32 Preparación.** Lea el título del artículo y examine la foto. Luego responda a las preguntas.

1. ¿Cuál puede ser el tema principal de la narrativa? Seleccione los temas posibles.
   a. la deserción escolar de los jóvenes hispanos
   b. por qué muchos estudiantes hispanos no asisten a la universidad
   c. programas en las universidades para ayudar a estudiantes minoritarios
2. ¿Cuáles cree que son los temas secundarios?
   a. Se incluye información demográfica.
   b. Se presentan los casos de estudiantes específicos.
   c. Se cita (*quote*) la opinión de unos expertos.

## Leer

### Alumnos hispanos preparados que no pueden acceder a la universidad

Cada vez son más los jóvenes hispanos con la preparación académica adecuada para entrar a la universidad, pero por falta de recursos económicos no pueden hacerlo, de acuerdo con un informe reciente. El informe preparado por la Junta de Regentes del Sistema de Universidades de Colorado indica que hay más alumnos de grupos minoritarios en la universidad hoy que en el pasado, pero todavía queda mucho por hacer.

Los administradores de estas universidades dicen que el aumento en el número de estudiantes minoritarios

Cada vez más hispanos se gradúan de las escuelas secundarias y aspiran a asistir a la universidad.

probablemente se debe al crecimiento del número de hispanos en el estado, sobre todo en el sur. Es decir, el aumento del número de alumnos hispanos que se gradúan de la escuela secundaria se debe simplemente a cambios demográficos, no al éxito de los programas de promoción universitarios.

Según un comentario del canciller de la Universidad de Colorado en Denver, el número de latinos y de otras minorías que estudian en su universidad ahora llega al 22 por ciento y pronto subirá al 38 por ciento. Parte del aumento se debe a un acuerdo entre la universidad en Denver y el Departamento de Educación de EE.UU. para promover los estudios universitarios en las escuelas secundarias locales.

A pesar de estos proyectos, aún es pequeño el número de estudiantes hispanos y de otras minorías que llega a la universidad.

El reporte de los regentes indica que sólo el 40 por ciento de los estudiantes minoritarios de las escuelas públicas de Colorado que pueden ir a la universidad lo hacen, debido al costo. Por ejemplo, según la organización CollegeInColorado, durante el año 2006-2007, el costo promedio para un estudiante de tiempo completo en la Universidad de Colorado o en la Escuela de Minería era de $9.000 dólares por año, sin incluir otros gastos como alojamiento, libros, transporte y seguro médico. En comparación, durante ese mismo período el costo de la matrícula para estudiantes de tiempo completo en instituciones de educación de nivel terciario[1] fue de $3.800 dólares al año.

Por ley, los alumnos que se gradúan de las escuelas secundarias de Colorado reciben un subsidio de hasta $2.670 dólares al año, sin importar la situación financiera de la familia del estudiante. Pero aun con esa ayuda, el costo promedio de seguir estudiando después de la educación secundaria oscila entre los $1.800 y los $7.800 dólares, para instituciones de educación de nivel terciario o grandes universidades, respectivamente.

Para muchos latinos, de acuerdo con CollegeInColorado, el costo se incrementa porque al llegar a la universidad, descubren que necesitan clases de recuperación, especialmente en matemáticas, lectura y escritura. Esas clases no se cuentan entre los cursos necesarios para obtener un título, pero cuestan como promedio $77 dólares por hora de crédito, y retrasan el inicio de los estudios universitarios.

[1] *community* colleges

**14-33 Primera mirada.** Indique si las siguientes afirmaciones relacionadas con el artículo son ciertas (**C**) o falsas (**F**). Si son falsas, corríjalas.

1. ___ El artículo trata de la educación de los hispanos en el estado de Colorado.
2. ___ Menos estudiantes hispanos se gradúan de las escuelas secundarias ahora que en el pasado.
3. ___ La población hispana en el estado está creciendo.
4. ___ Los programas para atraer a más estudiantes minoritarios a la universidad han tenido éxito.
5. ___ El número de hispanos en la Universidad de Colorado en Denver está creciendo.
6. ___ Muchos estudiantes hispanos muy calificados para hacer estudios universitarios asisten a universidades en otros estados.
7. ___ Hay diferencias grandes en el costo de los estudios universitarios, dependiendo del tipo de universidad.
8. ___ Las clases de recuperación son gratis para los estudiantes que las toman por obligación.

**14-34 Segunda mirada.** Indique si las oraciones representan un problema (**PB**) o progreso (**PG**) para la educación de los hispanos en Colorado.

1. ___ Cada vez son más los jóvenes hispanos con la preparación académica para entrar a la universidad, pero por falta de recursos económicos no pueden hacerlo.
2. ___ Según un comentario del canciller de la Universidad de Colorado en Denver, el número de latinos y de otras minorías que estudian en su universidad ahora llega al 22 por ciento y pronto subirá al 38 por ciento.
3. ___ Para muchos latinos, el costo se incrementa debido a que, una vez que llegan a la universidad, descubren que necesitan clases de recuperación, especialmente en matemáticas, lectura y escritura.
4. ___ Esas clases no se cuentan entre los cursos necesarios para obtener un título.

## Después de leer

**14-35 Ampliación.** Comenten en parejas el siguiente tema y prepárense para compartir las respuestas con la clase.

1. Según el artículo, el costo de asistir a la Universidad de Colorado es mucho mayor que el costo de asistir a una institución de educación de nivel terciario.

   ■ ¿Es justo que existan estas diferencias en el costo de la matrícula?

   ■ ¿Debería costar lo mismo la matrícula en todas las universidades públicas del estado?

# A escribir

ESTRATEGIA

## Use language to express emotions

Emotions have a psychological and social function in communication. We express emotions for various reasons and with different purposes. For example, we may express anger to complain about a computer malfunction or appreciation to thank someone for a gift.

Poetry is a genre well suited to the expression of emotions. Writing a poem may enable us to describe artistically feelings of heroism, beauty, love, sadness, loss, or injustice, or to celebrate a special event. To compose an effective poem, it is important to think carefully about the feelings we want to convey and our purpose in writing it.

Remember that poetry is a reflection of human experience, and in that sense, anyone can write poetry!

## Antes de escribir

**14-36 Preparación.** PRIMERA FASE. Lea el siguiente poema que alude a las emociones de una persona en una relación tradicional en la sociedad.

### Hombre pequeñito

de Alfonsina Storni

Hombre pequeñito, hombre pequeñito,
Suelta a tu canario, que quiere volar...
Yo soy el canario, hombre pequeñito,
Déjame saltar.
Estuve en tu jaula, hombre pequeñito,
Hombre pequeñito que jaula me das,
Digo pequeñito porque no me entiendes,
Ni me entenderás.
Tampoco te entiendo, pero mientras tanto
Ábreme la jaula que quiero escapar;
Hombre pequeñito, te amé media hora.
No me pidas más.

SEGUNDA FASE. Indique si las siguientes afirmaciones interpretan el poema correcta (**C**) o incorrectamente (**I**) .

1. ___ El poema tiene un tono alegre.
2. ___ La persona que habla en este poema es un hombre.
3. ___ La voz del poema expresa su sentimiento de disgusto por la opresión en la que ha vivido.
4. ___ La persona expresa la esperanza de que su pareja lo/la comprenda en el futuro.
5. ___ Al usar la palabra *pequeñito* la voz del poema expresa irónicamente su desprecio por su pareja.
6. ___ La voz del poema quiere continuar viviendo con su compañero/a.
7. ___ La voz del poema desea expresarle amor a su pareja.

## A escribir

**14-37 Manos a la obra.** PRIMERA FASE. Prepárese para expresar sus sentimientos y emociones en su propio poema, siguiendo el modelo del poema de la actividad **14-36**. Haga lo siguiente:

1. Determine el tono (alegre, triste, nostálgico, etc.) y el propósito de su poema:
2. Decida a quién le va a escribir el poema: ¿a una mujer o a un hombre?
3. Escriba una o dos palabras que describan a esta persona:
4. Escoja un objeto, un animal, u otro elemento que simbolice sus sentimientos sobre la relación que usted tiene con esa persona:
5. Escriba tres o cuatro cosas que usted le pediría a esta persona hacer por usted:
6. Indique un lugar que usted asocia con esta relación:
7. Mencione una o dos cosas que usted le pediría a la persona no hacer.

SEGUNDA FASE. Ahora, complete su poema, siguiendo el poema en **14-36**. No se olvide de darle un título que exprese sus sentimientos.

Título: _____ Autor: _____
_____, _____,
_____ a tu _____, que quiere _____…
Yo soy _____, _____,
_____.
_____, _____,
_____ que _____ me das.
Digo _____ porque no _____,
Ni _____.
Tampoco te _____, pero mientras tanto
_____ que quiero _____;
_____, te _____ media hora.
No me _____ más.

## Después de escribir

**14-38 Revisión.** PRIMERA FASE. Lea su poema una vez más y responda a estas preguntas.

1. ¿Está usted satisfecho/a con el mensaje de su poema?
2. ¿Son comprensibles y coherentes las ideas?
3. ¿Tendrá el efecto que usted quiere?

SEGUNDA FASE. Ahora, revise si...

1. el vocabulario es apropiado para describir a esta persona y los sentimientos que usted tiene por él/ella.
2. la ortografía, puntuación, acentuación, etc. son apropiadas.

Finalmente, déle el poema a un compañero/una compañera para que lo lea y lo disfrute.

# ENFOQUE CULTURAL

## La compleja vida política de América Latina

Una de las actividades que más apasiona a muchos latinoamericanos es la política. Desde la independencia, la política ha despertado intensas pasiones en el continente, y muchos países han sufrido guerras civiles o conflictos de fronteras con países vecinos. El interés por la política y el deseo de solucionar los problemas sociales se entienden fácilmente en una región donde hay muchas diferencias entre la ciudad y el campo, entre las clases educadas y las que no tienen acceso a la educación, o entre las clases más ricas y las más pobres.

Dentro de este contexto, la vida política de Chile ofrece ejemplos de grandes triunfos democráticos, al igual que ejemplos de algunos de los grandes problemas que

caracterizan la política en América Latina. A finales del siglo XIX, por ejemplo, Chile vivió un conflicto de fronteras con Bolivia y Perú. Esta guerra, que ocurrió entre 1879 y 1884 y que se conoce como La Guerra del Pacífico, enfrentó a estos países por los derechos sobre el desierto de Atacama. Este desierto es rico en minerales, especialmente en salitre, que es un mineral usado como fertilizante y también en la fabricación de explosivos. Como resultado de esta guerra, Perú y Bolivia perdieron parte de su territorio, que hoy pertenece a Chile.

Durante la década de 1930, varios países latinoamericanos tuvieron guerras con países vecinos y así, por ejemplo, entre 1932 y 1935, Bolivia y Paraguay se vieron envueltos en la Guerra del Chaco. Este conflicto se considera el más violento del siglo XX en América Latina. También en 1933, Colombia y Perú lucharon por problemas de fronteras.

Todos los países latinoamericanos han buscado un camino para conseguir la democracia, aunque en algunos momentos ese ideal ha sido difícil de alcanzar. Las dictaduras militares que se han instalado en varios países han ocasionado episodios muy problemáticos en la región. Una de las dictaduras más violentas de los últimos tiempos fue la de Augusto Pinochet en Chile, que duró desde 1973 hasta 1990. El 11 de septiembre de 1973, Pinochet dirigió un golpe militar contra el gobierno del Presidente Salvador

Allende. Durante los diecisiete años de la dictadura de Pinochet, miles de personas fueron detenidas, torturadas y miles de ellas desaparecieron. Esas escenas de violencia y violaciones de los derechos humanos fueron representadas en la película *Missing*, del director Constantín Costa-Gavras. Una de las víctimas más simbólicas de esta dictadura fue el cantautor Víctor Jara, asesinado en un estadio de Santiago.

Esta arpillera representa a las madres de detenidos desaparecidos durante la dictadura de Pinochet.

Por la misma época, Argentina también se encontraba gobernada por una dictadura militar. Se dice que la dictadura argentina hizo desparecer a 30.000 personas durante esos años. Las madres de los desaparecidos formaron un grupo llamado Las Madres de Plaza de Mayo para protestar ante la Casa Rosada, la oficina del presidente en Buenos Aires, por la desaparición de sus hijos e hijas. El problema de los desaparecidos en Argentina también fue motivo de una película muy famosa, *La historia oficial*, del director Luis Puenzo.

Los esfuerzos de muchas personas en América Latina por construir una democracia sólida y estable han dado muy buenos resultados en Chile, ya que este país acaba de terminar una transición de la dictadura militar de Pinochet a un sistema de gobierno civil. Durante casi veinte años el pueblo chileno ha luchado para acercarse cada vez más al ideal político de la democracia. En

2006, Michelle Bachelet fue elegida como la primera presidenta de Chile, y la octava mujer en ocupar un cargo semejante en América Latina, después de Isabel Martínez de Perón en Argentina, Lidia Gueiler Tejada en Bolivia, Violeta Chamorro en Nicaragua, Ertha Pascal Troullot en Haití, Mireya Moscoso en Panamá, Janet Jagan en Guyana y Rosalía Arteaga en Ecuador. Para los chilenos, desde la década de los 90 en adelante, cuando empezó la transición, han sido años difíciles, y muchas de esas dificultades han sido retratadas en otra película, *Fiesta patria*, del director Luis Vera. Esta película presenta una reflexión sobre el estado social del Chile de hoy.

**14-39** PRIMERA FASE. **Reconocimiento de palabras clave.** Encuentre en el texto la palabra o expresión que mejor expresa el significado de las siguientes ideas.

1. border conflicts _____
2. neighboring countries _____
3. fertilizer _____
4. human rights _____
5. good results _____
6. portrayed _____

SEGUNDA FASE. **Oraciones importantes.** Subraye las afirmaciones que contienen ideas que se encuentran en el texto. Luego indique en qué parte del texto están.

1. Politics has caused many Latin Americans to fall in love.
2. Many Latin American countries have suffered through civil wars and border conflicts.
3. Latin American societies are divided in many different ways. Among these divisions are the division between urban and rural areas and between the rich and the poor.
4. Chile fought Bolivia and Peru over the Atacama Desert.
5. Peru and Colombia went to war over their common border with Chile.
6. Michelle Bachelet is the first woman to become president of a Latin American country.
7. Military dictatorships are the cause of some of the most difficult times in Latin American political history.
8. Argentina was under military rule while Chile was under the Pinochet dictatorship.

TERCERA FASE. **Ideas principales.** Escriba un párrafo breve en español resumiendo las ideas principales expresadas en el texto.

 **14-40 Use la información.** Prepare un afiche sobre un desaparecido/una desaparecida. Presente la información sobre esta persona, incluyendo su nombre, el país y la fecha de su desaparición y otra información que usted crea importante. Para ayudarse en esta actividad, visite la página web de *Mosaicos* y use los enlaces útiles para preparar su presentación.

# VOCABULARIO

**La sociedad** — *Society*

| | |
|---|---|
| la adaptación | *adjustment, adaptation* |
| al analfabetismo | *illiteracy* |
| el cambio | *change* |
| la confianza | *trust* |
| la democracia | *democracy* |
| el derecho | *right* |
| el desempleo | *unemployment* |
| el desplazamiento | *movement, displacement* |
| la diversificación | *diversification* |
| la eficiencia | *efficiency* |
| la elección | *election* |
| la emigración | *emigration* |
| la esperanza de vida | *life expectancy* |
| la exportación | *export* |
| la honestidad | *honesty* |
| la igualdad | *equality* |
| la inmigración | *immigration* |
| la lucha | *fight* |
| la migración | *migration* |
| la mortalidad | *mortality* |
| la pobreza | *poverty* |
| la proximidad | *proximity* |
| el régimen | *regime* |
| el tráfico de drogas | *drug trafficking* |

**Las encuestas** — *Surveys/Polls*

| | |
|---|---|
| los datos | *data* |
| la mayoría | *majority* |
| el porcentaje | *percentage* |
| el promedio | *average* |
| la tasa | *rate* |

**Las personas** — *People*

| | |
|---|---|
| el/la emigrante | *emigrant* |
| el/la habitante | *inhabitant* |
| la población | *population* |
| el presidente/la presidenta | *president* |

**Las descripciones** — *Descriptions*

| | |
|---|---|
| actual | *present, current* |
| amplio/a | *ample* |
| analfabeto/a | *illiterate* |
| dictatorial | *dictatorial* |
| enérgico/a | *energetic* |
| infantil | *children's* |
| políglota | *polyglot, multilingual* |

**Verbos** — *Verbs*

| | |
|---|---|
| destacarse | *to stand out* |
| elegir (i, i) | *to choose, to elect* |
| gobernar (ie) | *to govern* |
| mejorar | *to improve* |
| preceder | *to precede* |
| realizar (c) | *to carry out* |

**Palabras y expresiones útiles** — *Useful words and expressions*

| | |
|---|---|
| el nivel | *level* |
| en vez de | *instead of* |
| la sucursal | *branch (business)* |

See pages 474 and 477 for a list of adverbial conjunctions.

CAPÍTULO

15

# Hacia el futuro

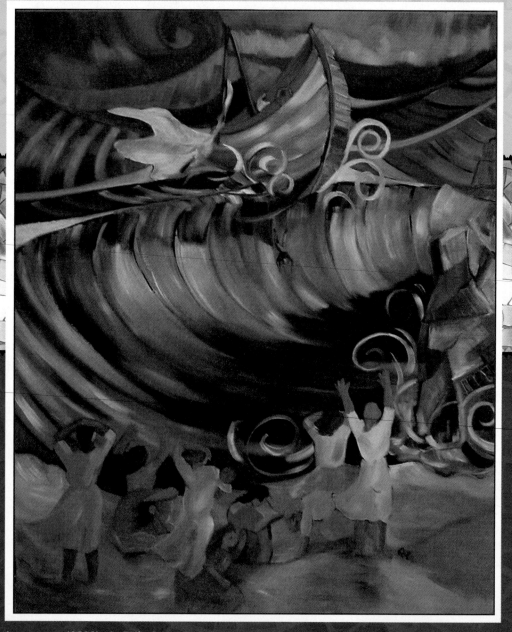

*La tormenta* (2000), de Zulia Gotay de Anderson, pintora puertorriqueña

# In this chapter you will learn how to:

- talk about advances in science and technology
- express wishes and recommendations in the past
- hypothesize about the present and the future
- express unexpected occurrences

## Cultural focus: **Puerto Rico**

PUERTO RICO

*OCÉANO ATLÁNTICO*

Calles de El Viejo San Juan

Arecibo

Observatorio astronómico
de Arecibo

**PUERTO RICO**

Manati

Bayamón
Guaynabo

San Juan

*Parque Nacional
de El Yunque*

Carolina

La cascada La Coca

**Mayagüez**

*Cerro de Punta* ▲

*CORDILLERA
CENTRAL*

Trujillo Alto
Caguas

Humacao

*Isla de
Culebra*

San Germán

Ponce

Guayama

Arroyo

El coquí, la rana nativa
de Puerto Rico

*Isla de
Vieques*

*Cabo Rojo*

*Mar Caribe*

El Carnaval
de Ponce

**A vista de pájaro.** Complete las siguientes oraciones con información de
Puerto Rico que usted sabe.

1. Una comida típica de Puerto Rico es _____.
2. Un animal típico de Puerto Rico es _____.
3. Muchos puertorriqueños hablan dos idiomas, el _____ y el
   _____.
4. El deporte más popular en Puerto Rico es _____.
5. El clima de Puerto Rico es _____.
6. El Yunque es _____.

## ◀)) La ciencia y la tecnología en el mundo de hoy

CD 6
Track 22

Antes de salir para la universidad Ángel, un joven puertorriqueño, **enciende** su computadora, abre Internet y **se conecta** con sus amigos. Entra en Facebook, le da un *poke* a Laura y le manda un *hug* a Carmen. Luego mira su correo electrónico por si tiene algún *podcast* para su clase *online* y le envía a su profesor de ciencias naturales un **mensaje** con un **documento adjunto**.

Entonces, Lorena, la hermana de Ángel, le pide que le **baje** una canción de Internet para **meterla** en su *mp3*. Por último, entra en el *blog* de su amigo Juanjo para leer las últimas novedades sobre sus **videojuegos** preferidos. Allí encuentra un **enlace** que le interesa.

Actualmente, la ciencia y la tecnología **contribuyen** a **unificar** algunas de las diferencias culturales que existen entre los pueblos. Los jóvenes de Europa e Hispanoamérica tienen muchas cosas en común con los de Asia, África o Estados Unidos. El **acceso** a Internet y a los teléfonos celulares hacen más fluida la comunicación y el **intercambio** de información.

Hace unos años se creó en Puerto Rico el Instituto de la Ciencia y la Tecnología para **difundir** noticias relacionadas con estas materias en América Latina. Pero el ICLT no es un instituto tradicional, sino una **biblioteca virtual**. Hoy en día las bibliotecas virtuales y los **buscadores** son una importante **fuente** de **recursos** y **diseminación** de **conocimientos**.

498

**15-1 ¿Para qué lo usamos?** En las siguientes afirmaciones relacionadas con diversos usos de tecnología, marque (✓) el uso que *no* corresponde.

1. Internet sirve para…
   a. acceder a información sobre muchas disciplinas.
   b. ver películas.
   c. enviar felicitaciones.
   d. calentar el café del desayuno.

2. El correo electrónico se usa para…
   a. comunicarse con los amigos.
   b. hacer fotografías.
   c. enviar un documento adjunto.
   d. recibir mensajes.

3. La biblioteca virtual se utiliza para…
   a. saludar a los profesores de la universidad.
   b. encontrar enlaces.
   c. bajar artículos.
   d. identificar documentación.

4. Los videojuegos sirven para…
   a. divertirse con los amigos.
   b. practicar deportes al aire libre.
   c. diseminar ciertos conocimientos.
   d. intercambiar información.

 **15-2 Usen la tecnología.** PRIMERA FASE. Visiten la página web de *Mosaicos* y usen la tecnología para preparar una presentación con *PowerPoint* sobre Puerto Rico que incluya lo siguiente:

1. localización de un lugar en un mapa
2. descripción y tres datos que se refieran a las características físicas del lugar, la gente del lugar y una costumbre del lugar
3. fotos

SEGUNDA FASE. Compartan la información con la clase, incluyendo una descripción de los recursos tecnológicos que utilizaron.

 **15-3 Una noticia.** PRIMERA FASE. Visite la página web de *Mosaicos* y busque una noticia que le interese en un periódico virtual de Puerto Rico. Léala y tome apuntes sobre lo esencial de la noticia.

 SEGUNDA FASE. Mande un correo electrónico a tres personas de la clase, incluyendo un resumen de la noticia y su opinión sobre la noticia.

# �))) La conservación del medio ambiente

CD 6
Track 23

La contribución de América Latina a la ciencia **se ha enfocado** principalmente en la biología, **debido a** la riqueza de la flora y la fauna, la **conservación** de la **naturaleza**, la agricultura y la medicina. Aunque a veces las **infraestructuras** y los recursos son insuficientes, algunos científicos de esta región han hecho **descubrimientos** importantes. Esta es una foto de El Yunque, en Puerto Rico, una de las muchas **reservas naturales** de Hispanoamérica.

¡TODAVÍA ESTAMOS A TIEMPO!

La reserva de la biosfera es nuestra oportunidad

La reserva de la biosfera del Alto Golfo de California y del delta del río Colorado puede ser la salvación de nuestra cultura pesquera. Juntos vamos a desarrollar un plan que nos permita manejar la reproducción y recuperación de los recursos naturales y de esta manera, asegurar nuestro bienestar y el de nuestros hijos.
¡El éxito depende de su participación!

La **cuenca** del río Amazonas cubre un área de más de siete millones de kilómetros cuadrados, región comparable en extensión a dos terceras partes del territorio continental de Estados Unidos. Debido a su densa vegetación selvática, esta área es conocida como el "pulmón" del **planeta**. Hoy en día, miles de campesinos llegan a la selva **en busca de tierra** para cultivar. La **deforestación** de nuestros **bosques** se considera una **pérdida** irreparable para el **medio ambiente**.

**15-4 Amigos de la tierra.** PRIMERA FASE. Indiquen cuáles de los siguientes problemas se asocian con la industria pesquera (**IP**), con los bosques tropicales (**BT**) o con los dos.

1. _____ la construcción de carreteras
2. _____ la desertización
3. _____ la erosión
4. _____ la exterminación de especies animales
5. _____ la tala (*felling*) de árboles
6. _____ la contaminación provocada por aguas residuales (*sewage*) y substancias químicas
7. _____ la disminución de la capa de ozono
8. _____ la pesca indiscriminada

SEGUNDA FASE. Den ideas para resolver cada problema.

**15-5 Los adelantos (*Advances*) científicos.** PRIMERA FASE. Haga una lista de tres adelantos científicos y tres cambios sociales que usted espera que se realicen en las próximas décadas.

| ADELANTOS CIENTÍFICOS | CAMBIOS SOCIALES |
|---|---|
| _____ | _____ |
| _____ | _____ |
| _____ | _____ |

SEGUNDA FASE. Comparen sus listas y justifiquen la razón de los cambios que indicaron en la *Primera fase.* ¿Por qué ocurrirán? ¿Son cambios necesarios?

**15-6 Organizaciones ecologistas.** Busquen información en Internet sobre organizaciones como Greenpeace o el Club Sierra, cuyo propósito es la protección del medio ambiente. Escojan una de esas organizaciones y preparen un breve informe oral con la siguiente información:

1. ¿Qué objetivos tiene la organización?
2. ¿Cómo se financia?
3. ¿Quiénes trabajan o hacen voluntariado en ella?
4. ¿Cuál fue una de sus campañas recientes?
5. ¿Qué objetivos tenía la campaña?
6. ¿Cómo la realizaron?
7. ¿Cuál fue el resultado de la campaña?
8. ¿En qué capacidad cree usted que podría ayudar?

# ◄)) Otros retos del futuro

## LAS CIUDADES

- Se **construirán** ciudades verticales con edificios **climatizados** por medio de **energía solar**. Algunas se construirán sobre el mar.

- El 90% de la población vivirá en las ciudades.

- Todas las basuras urbanas serán **recicladas**.

## EL MAR

- El nivel del mar subirá por los **deshielos** debido al **calentamiento** de la atmósfera y causará **inundaciones** y **la desaparición** de algunas costas.

- La contaminación de los mares provocará la **extinción** de los **bancos de peces**.

## LA ATMÓSFERA

- El agujero de la **capa de ozono** hará aumentar el número de enfermos de cáncer de piel.

- Se cultivarán plantas que mejoren la calidad del aire.

## LAS VIVIENDAS

- Todos los hogares estarán conectados a Internet. Las compras se harán siempre **virtualmente**.

- Las puertas y los aparatos electrónicos serán activados por la voz o con sensores que reconocerán a cada individuo.

- Habrá **robots** que se ocuparán de hacer la limpieza.

### EL TRANSPORTE

■ Los trenes de alta velocidad conectarán las grandes ciudades y circularán por **rieles** suspendidos a la altura de los edificios.

■ Los coches combinarán la energía eléctrica y la energía solar. Serán pequeñas **cápsulas voladoras** que podrán **despegar** y **aterrizar** verticalmente como los helicópteros.

■ El tráfico aéreo será controlado por satélite.

### LA CIENCIA Y LA TECNOLOGÍA

■ Habrá **clonaciones** de animales **extinguidos**.

■ Los embriones humanos se seleccionarán **genéticamente**.

■ Todos los teléfonos móviles tendrán una computadora incorporada.

■ Se explorarán energías alternativas.

■ Se **repoblarán** los bosques con técnicas avanzadas para eliminar la desertización.

**15-7 Un futuro mejor. PRIMERA FASE.** Comparen el mundo de hoy con el del futuro basándose en las fotos anteriores. Consideren por lo menos dos de los siguientes temas: uso de ciencia-tecnología, medio ambiente, transporte, calidad de vida, criminalidad, delincuencia, consumismo, salud.

**SEGUNDA FASE.** Ahora hablen sobre dos problemas específicos que existen en la ciudad contemporánea. Hagan una lista de dos aspectos de cada problema que les gustaría mejorar. Luego, compartan sus ideas con el resto de la clase.

**MODELO:** *En la ciudad del presente hay poca seguridad física. Cualquier persona puede tener un arma y matar a quien quiera. Nos gustaría proponer una ley para limitar el uso de las armas de fuego (firearms).*

**15-8 El reto más serio de hoy.** Preparen un informe oral sobre el reto más serio que enfrentan el mundo y el ser humano hoy, según su opinión. Describan detalladamente el problema y ofrezcan algunas soluciones.

**15-9 ¡El futuro es hoy!** Primero, individualmente hagan una lista de cinco cosas (aparatos, sistemas de comunicación, transporte, etc.) que existen hoy y que no existían cuando sus padres tenían la edad de usted. Luego, comparen su lista entre ustedes y expliquen el impacto y las consecuencias de estas nuevas cosas en sus vidas.

**15-10 Los OVNIS (Objetos Voladores No Identificados).** Lean la tira cómica de Mafalda. Imagínense que han visto una nave espacial de otro planeta. Describan todo lo que vieron, comentando las semejanzas y las diferencias entre ustedes y los visitantes desconocidos.

 **15-11 ¿Vamos al planeta Marte?** ¿Creen ustedes que, durante su vida, será posible viajar al planeta Marte? Planeen el viaje y expliquen con quiénes irán, qué llevarán, cuánto tiempo tardarán en llegar, qué verán allí y cómo se sentirán física y emocionalmente en este nuevo ambiente. Compartan su plan con otros astronautas (sus compañeros/as) para formular el mejor plan posible.

**15-12 El problema de la alimentación.** You will listen to a short talk about the problem of feeding the world's population. Before you listen, list two problems you think the speaker may mention and two solutions you think she may provide.

CD 6
Track 25

First, read the following incomplete ideas. Then, as you listen, pay attention to the general idea of what is said and mark (✓) the appropriate ending to each statement.

1. Los gobiernos tienen que solucionar el problema de...
   ___ la agricultura tradicional.
   ___ la falta de alimentos para la población.
   ___ las pocas variedades de productos.
2. La tecnología y los científicos...
   ___ pueden ayudar a solucionar este problema.
   ___ trabajan en las Islas Filipinas.
   ___ desarrollan computadoras de mucha utilidad.
3. Si se aumenta la producción del arroz, los gobiernos pueden...
   ___ exportarlo y ganar más dinero.
   ___ alimentar a más personas.
   ___ obtener variedades más nutritivas.
4. Hay que aprovechar los avances de la tecnología, pero también es necesario...
   ___ aumentar la productividad en un 70%.
   ___ conseguir alimentos básicos.
   ___ preservar el medio ambiente.

# EN ACCIÓN

## Diarios de bicicleta: La despedida

### Antes de ver

**15-13** En el siguiente segmento, Javier graba (*tapes*) a sus amigos hablando de sí mismos. ¿De qué cree usted que podrían hablar?

### Mientras ve

**15-14** Indique si las siguientes afirmaciones son ciertas (**C**) o falsas (**F**), según lo que dicen los personajes.

**Luciana**
1. ____ Conocí a Javier en un concierto.
2. ____ Si no fuera por Javier, no sabría nada de Colombia, Panamá ni Costa Rica.
3. ____ El Distrito Federal es una de las ciudades más grandes del planeta.

**Gabi**
4. ____ Estudio teatro y danza en la universidad.
5. ____ No soy de México sino de Medellín.

**Daniel**
6. ____ Vengo de Oaxaca y estudio computación.
7. ____ Espero ir a España algún día.

### Después de ver

**15-15 PRIMERA FASE.** Mire sus respuestas en *Antes de ver* y subraye los temas de los que los personajes hablaron.

**SEGUNDA FASE.** Complete las siguientes frases:
1. Si Gabi viajara en bicicleta por Centroamérica _____.
2. Si Daniel fuera a Colombia _____.
3. Si (yo) conociera a Javier, _____.

# FUNCIONES Y FORMAS

## 1. Expressing wishes and recommendations in the past: The imperfect subjunctive

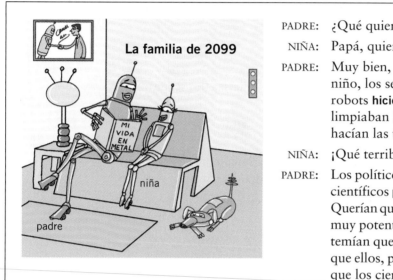

**La familia de 2099**

padre

niña

MI VIDA EN METAL

PADRE: ¿Qué quieres que **hagamos** ahora?

NIÑA: Papá, quiero que me **cuentes** un cuento.

PADRE: Muy bien, hija. Cuando mi abuelo era niño, los seres humanos querían que los robots **hicieran** todo su trabajo. Mis abuelos limpiaban la casa, preparaban las comidas, hacían las tareas de los niños...

NIÑA: ¡Qué terrible, papá! Pero luego, ¿qué pasó?

PADRE: Los políticos recomendaron que los científicos **produjeran** robots más complejos. Querían que los robots **tuvieran** computadoras muy potentes (*powerful*). Los científicos temían que los robots **fueran** más inteligentes que ellos, pero los políticos insistieron en que los científicos los **construyeran** con más capacidad intelectual. Entonces...

**Piénselo.** Indique (✔) si las siguientes oraciones se refieren al presente/al futuro o al pasado.

|  | PRESENT/FUTURO | PASADO |
|---|---|---|
| 1. ¿Qué quieres que **hagamos** ahora? | ___ | ___ |
| 2. Quiero que me **cuentes** un cuento. | ___ | ___ |
| 3. Los seres humanos querían que los robots **hicieran** todo su trabajo. | ___ | ___ |
| 4. Los políticos recomendaron que los científicos **produjeran** robots más complejos. | ___ | ___ |
| 5. Querían que los robots **tuvieran** computadoras muy potentes. | ___ | ___ |
| 6. Los científicos temían que los robots **fueran** más inteligentes que ellos. | ___ | ___ |
| 7. Los políticos insistieron en que los **construyeran** con más capacidad intelectual. | ___ | ___ |

■ In previous chapters, you studied the forms and uses of the present subjunctive. Now you will study the past subjunctive, also called the imperfect subjunctive. All regular and irregular past subjunctive verb forms are based on the **ustedes/ellos/ellas** form of the preterit. Drop the **-on** preterit ending and substitute the past subjunctive endings. Note the written accent on the **nosotros/as** forms.

| PAST OR IMPERFECT SUBJUNCTIVE | | | | |
|---|---|---|---|---|
| | **HABLAR** | **COMER** | **VIVIR** | **ESTAR** |
| | (hablar~~on~~) | (comier~~on~~) | (vivier~~on~~) | (estuvier~~on~~) |
| yo | habl**ara** | com**iera** | viv**iera** | estuv**iera** |
| tú | habl**aras** | com**ieras** | viv**ieras** | estuv**ieras** |
| Ud., él, ella | habl**ara** | com**iera** | viv**iera** | estuv**iera** |
| nosotros/as | habl**áramos** | com**iéramos** | viv**iéramos** | estuv**iéramos** |
| vosotros/as | habl**arais** | com**ierais** | viv**ierais** | estuv**ierais** |
| Uds., ellos/as | habl**aran** | com**ieran** | viv**ieran** | estuv**ieran** |

■ The present subjunctive is oriented to the present or future, whereas the past subjunctive focuses on the past. In general, the same rules that determine the use of the present subjunctive also apply to the past subjunctive.

HOY O MAÑANA ➔ PRESENT SUBJUNCTIVE

Sandra quiere comprar una computadora portátil que **sea** ligera.
*Sandra wants to buy a laptop that is lightweight.*

Hablará con sus amigos para que le **den** unas recomendaciones.
*She will talk to her friends so that they will give her some recommendations.*

AYER ➔ PAST SUBJUNCTIVE

Sandra quería una computadora portátil que **fuera** ligera.
*Sandra wanted a laptop that was lightweight.*

Habló con sus amigos para que le **dieran** unas recomendaciones.
*She talked to her friends so that they would give her some recommendations.*

■ Always use the past subjunctive after **como si** (*as if, as though*).

Gastan dinero en aparatos electrónicos **como si fueran** millonarios.
*They spend money on electronic gadgets as though they were millionaires.*

Hablaba con la científica **como si entendiera** el problema.
*He talked with the scientist as if he understood the problem.*

**15-16 Cuando era niño/a. PRIMERA FASE.** Marque (✓) lo que sus padres querían o no querían que usted hiciera cuando era niño/a. Después compare sus respuestas con las de su compañero/a.

_____ **1.** Querían que yo comiera muchos vegetales y frutas.
_____ **2.** Querían que yo estudiara ciencias.
_____ **3.** No querían que yo viera programas violentos en la televisión.
_____ **4.** Querían que yo cuidara el medio ambiente.
_____ **5.** Querían que yo leyera sobre el programa espacial y los astronautas.
_____ **6.** No querían que yo estuviera sin hacer nada.

**SEGUNDA FASE.** Ahora, marque con un círculo lo que usted quería que sus padres hicieran cuando era niño/a. Luego, compare sus respuestas con las de su compañero/a. Añada otra opción, si es necesario.

1. Para divertirme con la tecnología…
   **a.** yo quería que mis padres me llevaran a ver una nave espacial.
   **b.** deseaba que mis padres me permitieran jugar a videojuegos muchas horas.
2. Para estar con mis amigos…
   **a.** yo quería que mis padres me llevaran al parque los fines de semana.
   **b.** les pedía a mis padres que me permitieran jugar en las casas de ellos.
3. Para pasarlo bien los fines de semana…
   **a.** yo quería que mis padres me dieran más dinero.
   **b.** insistía en que mis padres me permitieran tener fiestas en casa.
4. Para celebrar mi cumpleaños…
   **a.** siempre quería que mis padres me regalaran juguetes electrónicos.
   **b.** prefería que mis padres me compraran ropa.

**15-17 En el laboratorio.** Miguel es un estudiante muy inteligente, pero muy distraído. Hoy hizo unos experimentos con su profesor de química en el laboratorio. ¿Qué le dijo el profesor en estas situaciones? Túrnense para dar respuestas lógicas.

**MODELO:** Miguel no se puso los guantes para hacer el experimento.
_El profesor le dijo que se pusiera los guantes._

1. Llegó tarde al laboratorio.
2. Escuchaba música mientras hacía un experimento.
3. Dejó una botella de alcohol cerca de una estufa.
4. No esterilizó unos instrumentos.
5. Recibió una llamada en su celular.
6. La mesa donde Miguel trabajaba estaba muy desordenada.
7. No comparó sus resultados con los del estudiante graduado del profesor.
8. Salió del laboratorio durante un experimento para conversar con su novia.

**En otras palabras**

For cell phones both **teléfonos móviles** and **teléfonos celulares** are used. The phrases are usually shortened to **móvil** and **celular**.

**15-18 Alguien que no nos cae bien.** PRIMERA FASE. Imagínense que ustedes conocen a una persona arrogante que se cree mejor que nadie. Digan cómo se comporta esta persona en los siguientes aspectos de su vida. Pueden usar los verbos que aparecen más abajo u otros.

MODELO: cuando va de un lugar a otro a pie
*Camina como si fuera la única persona en la calle.*

| | |
|---|---|
| cambiar | manejar |
| caminar | usar |
| discutir | vestirse |
| gastar | vivir |

1. cuando quiere comprar algo
2. cuando se prepara para salir con un grupo de amigos
3. cuando habla con otras personas
4. cuando sube a (*gets into*) su automóvil

SEGUNDA FASE. Ahora respondan a las siguientes preguntas.

1. ¿Conoce usted a alguna persona que sea arrogante?
2. ¿Qué hábito o comportamiento de esa persona le molesta a usted? ¿Por qué?
3. ¿Le gustaría a usted que esta persona cambiara? Si es así, ¿qué costumbre o comportamiento le gustaría que cambiara?

# SITUACIONES

1. **Role A.** You belong to an organization that wants to reduce pollution and the deterioration of the environment. You are disappointed that the organization has not accomplished more. Tell your partner a) what activities you hoped the group would organize; b) what impact you wanted those activities to have on the community; and c) what the group has accomplished up to now. Explain how you feel as a member of the group.

   **Role B.** Your partner tells you about an ecological organization to which he/she belongs. After listening to a description of the group and its activities, ask about members' duties, meetings, and so on. Say that you have some ideas to make the group more effective, and find out the date and time of the next meeting.

2. **Role A.** You are unhappy with your new laptop. You go back to the store where you bought it and tell the manager that a) you hoped the laptop would be lightweight, but it isn't; b) you were looking for a computer that had graphics applications (**aplicaciones gráficas**), but this one doesn't; and c) you would like to return (**devolver**) it.

   **Role B.** You are the manager of the computer department of an electronics store. A customer is unhappy with a recent laptop purchase and tells you why. Explain that a) the store does not give refunds (**devolver el dinero**); b) you would be glad to exchange the laptop for a different one; and c) you hope that the customer will like the new laptop.

## 2. Hypothesizing about the present and the future: *If*-clauses

MATEO: Oye, Lucía. ¿Has visto el nuevo teléfono celular cámara? ¡Es increíble! **Si** la tecnología **continúa** avanzando así, pronto **producirán** un automóvil-tanque.

LUCÍA: **Si** lo **hicieran**, no me **sorprendería**. Pero **si** la ciencia **avanza** tan rápidamente, ¿por qué no **podemos** conseguir la paz? Yo no quiero que se perfeccione la tecnología para matar a la gente.

MATEO: Buen punto, Lucía. **Si** los jóvenes no **hacemos** nada para controlar los usos de la tecnología, no **tendremos** un mañana.

**Piénselo.** Indique si las siguientes afirmaciones hechas por Mateo y Lucía indican una condición relacionada con el presente (**P**), con el futuro (**F**) o si indican una condición que es improbable (**I**) que se cumpla (*fulfill*).

1. \_\_\_\_ **Si** la tecnología **continúa** avanzando así, pronto **producirán** un automóvil-tanque.
2. \_\_\_\_ **Si** lo **hicieran**, no me **sorprendería**.
3. \_\_\_\_ Pero **si** la ciencia **avanza** tan rápidamente, ¿por qué no **podemos** conseguir la paz?
4. \_\_\_\_ **Si** los jóvenes no **hacemos** nada para controlar los usos de la tecnología, no **tendremos** un mañana.

■ To express what happens or will happen *if* certain conditions are met, use the present or future indicative in the main clause and the present indicative in the *if*-clause.

Si **continuamos** cortando árboles, los bosques **van a** desaparecer.
*If we continue cutting down trees, forests will disappear.*

Si **creamos** tecnología para cuidar los recursos naturales, las generaciones futuras **tendrán** una vida mejor.
*If we create technology to protect the natural resources, future generations will have a better life.*

**Puedes** obtener información sobre las últimas novedades tecnológicas si la **buscas** en Internet.
*You can get information on the latest technology if you look for it on the Internet.*

■ To express a condition that is unlikely or contrary to fact, use the imperfect subjunctive in the *if*-clause. Use the conditional in the main clause.

Si le **dieran** más dinero al aeropuerto, el tráfico aéreo **podría** mejorar.
*If they gave more money to the airport, air traffic could improve.*

Si **usáramos** la energía solar en las casas, **ahorraríamos** mucho petróleo.
*If we used solar energy in our homes, we would save a lot of oil.*

**15-19 El mundo que todos queremos.** Complete cada idea de la izquierda con una de las conclusiones de la derecha. En algunos casos, puede haber más de una respuesta lógica. Luego compare sus respuestas con las de su compañero/a.

1. ____ Si tuviéramos más dinero en las escuelas,…
2. ____ Si hubiera menos armas de fuego en manos de la gente,…
3. ____ Si cuidáramos más nuestro planeta,…
4. ____ Tendríamos un mundo mejor,…
5. ____ Si hubiera trenes de alta velocidad,…
6. ____ Gastaríamos menos gasolina,…

a. no contaminaríamos tanto el medio ambiente.
b. todos los alumnos tendrían acceso a los laboratorios para hacer investigación.
c. si todos nos respetáramos y dialogáramos en vez de pelear.
d. las personas manejarían menos en las carreteras.
e. habría menos homicidios en la sociedad.
f. si usáramos el transporte público.

**15-20 ¿Qué pasa si… ?** Túrnense para decir qué resultados se pueden obtener si se hacen ciertas cosas.

**MODELO:** leer los periódicos
*Si todos leen los periódicos regularmente, sabrán qué está pasando en el mundo.*

1. usar solamente tecnología para aprender otra lengua
2. inventar aparatos electrónicos desechables (*disposable*)
3. proteger los recursos naturales
4. legalizar las drogas
5. comunicarse solamente por correo electrónico
6. construir más estaciones espaciales

**15-21 ¿Cómo sería el mundo?** Den sus razones para explicar cómo sería el mundo si se dieran las siguientes circunstancias. Después, compartan sus ideas con otros/as estudiantes.

1. si no hubiera televisión
2. si los seres humanos viviéramos más de 150 años
3. si la clonación fuera legal
4. si no existieran fronteras entre los países
5. si pudiéramos viajar en autos supersónicos a todas partes
6. si toda la educación se hiciera por Internet

## En directo

To ask that people request the floor before speaking:

**Por favor, no interrumpa(n) sin pedir la palabra.**
*Please don't interrupt without requesting the floor.*

**Pida(n) la palabra.**
*Request the floor.*

To request the floor:

**Yo quisiera decir/añadir/ explicar algo.**
*I would like to say/add/explain something.*

**¿Podría añadir/agregar algo?**
*Could I add something?*

To give the floor to someone:

**X tiene la palabra.**
*X has the floor.*

**Dinos lo que tú piensas.**
*Tell us what you think.*

**15-22 Cambios. PRIMERA FASE.** Identifique un problema serio en cada una de las siguientes áreas en la vida de su comunidad, de su país o del mundo. Tome notas de por qué lo considera un problema serio.

1. la seguridad personal y/o colectiva
2. el consumo excesivo de alcohol por los jóvenes
3. el transporte público
4. el costo de las necesidades básicas, como la comida y la gasolina

**SEGUNDA FASE.** Ahora compartan el problema más serio en cada área, según ustedes. Explíquenles a sus compañeros por qué lo consideran serio. ¿Qué harían para eliminar cada problema si pudieran?

MODELO: **Área:** el medio ambiente

**Problema serio:** *la contaminación del aire y el agua*

**Razón:** *El mal uso y el descuido (neglect) de los recursos naturales como el petróleo han causado el calentamiento del planeta. Todos usamos carros que contaminan el aire. Además, las industrias ponen sus desperdicios (waste) en los ríos. Contaminan el agua que todos bebemos.*

**Plan hipotético:** *Crearíamos incentivos para usar el transporte público y pondríamos multas (fines) muy altas a las compañías que tiran desperdicios en los ríos.*

## SITUACIONES

1. **Role A.** You are the coordinator of your university's new and very strict recycling program. At a meeting with the Student Council, you explain that a) if the publicity campaign (**campaña de publicidad**) starts soon, students and faculty can volunteer to help; b) there will be fines if people don't cooperate; and c) if everyone collaborates, the program will be successful.

   **Role B.** You are at a meeting of the Student Council at which a new and very strict recycling program is being discussed. Listen to the presentation of the coordinator of the program (your classmate) and ask a) when it will go into effect (**ponerse en marcha**) and b) what will happen if people don't want to cooperate with such a strict program.

2. **Role A.** You are a multi-millionaire who believes that higher education should be radically different in the future. Offer the president of your local college twenty million dollars to implement these innovations: a) there would be no required courses; students could choose all their own courses; b) there would be no exams, only projects and papers; and c) students would tell the faculty what courses should be taught. Respond to the reaction of the college president.

   **Role B.** You are a college president. A multi-millionaire (your classmate) wants to donate twenty million dollars to your institution to realize his/her vision of an ideal education. Listen and respond with your hypotheses of what would happen if there were no requirements or final exams, and if professors had to create new courses every semester according to students' interests.

## 3. Expressing the unexpected: *Se* for unplanned occurrences

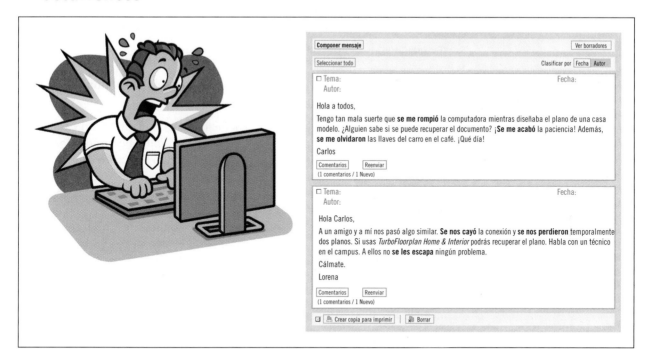

**Piénselo.** Indique si en las siguientes afirmaciones se pone énfasis en el evento (**E**) o en la persona responsable del evento (**PR**).

1. \_\_\_\_ **Se me rompió** la computadora.
2. \_\_\_\_ **Rompí** la computadora.
3. \_\_\_\_ **Olvidé** las llaves del carro en el café.
4. \_\_\_\_ **Se me olvidaron** las llaves del carro en el café.
5. \_\_\_\_ **Se nos perdieron** temporalmente dos planos.
6. \_\_\_\_ **Perdimos** temporalmente dos planos.

■ Use **se** + *indirect object* + *verb* to express unplanned or accidental events. This construction puts the focus on the unexpected nature of the event rather than on personal responsibility for its occurrence. Some verbs often used with this construction include **olvidar** (*to forget*), **apagar** (*to turn off*), **acabar** (*to run out of something*), **romper** (*to break, to tear*), and **quedar** (*to leave something behind*).

| | |
|---|---|
| **Se les apagaron** las luces del carro. | *The headlights of their car went out.* |
| A él **se le acabó** el dinero. | *He ran out of money.* |
| **Se nos olvidó** el código. | *We forgot the code.* |
| **Se te rompió** la chaqueta. | *Your jacket got torn.* |

■ Use an indirect object pronoun (**me, te, le, nos, os, les**) to indicate whom the unplanned event affects. Place the pronoun between **se** and the verb. If what is lost, forgotten, and so on, is plural, the verb also must be plural.

| | |
|---|---|
| **Se me quedó** el DVD en la computadora. | *I left the DVD in the computer.* |
| **Se me quedaron** los cables en casa. | *I left the cables at home.* |

**15-23 ¿Qué les pasó?** Termine lógicamente las ideas de la columna de la izquierda, usando las ideas de la columna de la derecha.

1. ____ Hablaron con el plomero porque…
2. ____ Tuve que usar la tarjeta de crédito porque…
3. ____ No pude llamarte por el celular porque…
4. ____ Tuvieron que llamar al electricista porque…
5. ____ Tuvimos que llamar al técnico porque…
6. ____ Llegué tarde a casa de mi novia porque…

**a.** se me quedó el dinero en casa.
**b.** se nos rompió la computadora.
**c.** se me olvidó tu nuevo número de teléfono.
**d.** se me perdió la llave del coche.
**e.** se les inundó el baño.
**f.** se les apagaron las luces en la casa.

**15-24 Problemas.** Usted trabaja en un laboratorio de ingeniería genética. Ayer hubo muchos problemas técnicos. Explique qué pasó. Seleccione su respuesta entre las opciones de la lista u otras propias.

MODELO:   El investigador no pudo completar el experimento.
          *Se le olvidó la fórmula.*

| | |
|---|---|
| perder las llaves | romper la computadora |
| acabarse la gasolina | escapar el perro en el parque |
| enfermarse un hijo | perder unos datos importantes |
| romper el microscopio | quedar documentos confidenciales en un café |

1. Los técnicos estaban preocupados después de empezar a observar algunas bacterias.
2. El director nunca falta al trabajo, pero ayer no fue a trabajar.
3. Los ayudantes llegaron tarde de un viaje a un laboratorio en otra ciudad.
4. La doctora Milán no pudo entrar en el laboratorio durante el fin de semana.
5. El subdirector no recibió un correo electrónico importante.
6. El presidente de la compañía estaba histérico cuando llegó a la oficina y se dio cuenta de lo que le había ocurrido.

**15-25 Momentos difíciles.** Miren los dibujos y túrnense para contestar las preguntas que siguen.

a.

b.

1. ¿Qué les pasó a las personas en los dos dibujos? Inventen un cuento para cada situación: ¿Cuándo y dónde pasó, cómo se sintieron las personas y qué hicieron después?
2. ¿Les ha pasado a ustedes una situación semejante? Cuéntense la historia de su problema y cómo lo resolvió cada uno de ustedes.
3. Si usted viviera una experiencia semejante otra vez, ¿haría algo diferente esta vez? ¿Su respuesta es similar o diferente a la de su compañero/a?

## SITUACIONES

1. **Role A.** You are driving too fast in a school zone. A police officer stops you. Explain that you left your license at home. Try to politely talk your way out of the situation.

   **Role B.** You are a police officer who is looking for speeders in a school zone. You stop a driver who is going too fast and ask a) what speed must be maintained in a school zone; b) at what speed he/she was driving; and c) if you can see his/her driver's license. Finally, say that if he/she is driving without a license, you will have to give him/her a fine.

2. **Role A.** You have had a bad day and you call your friend to vent. Say that a) you forgot to set your alarm clock so you got up late and missed your first class; b) you ran out of gas on the highway; c) you left your homework for your Spanish class at home; and d) in the cafeteria you accidentally dropped your soup and salad on your friend's backpack.

   **Role B.** Your friend calls to complain about his/her day. Commiserate with him/her and describe what happened to you last night: a) there was a big storm in your city and the lights went out so you could not watch your favorite TV show; b) you decided to drive to your parents' house, but when were leaving your apartment, both of your cats accidentally escaped; and c) when you were walking in the dark (**oscuridad**), you accidentally dropped your wallet and could not find it.

**En directo**

To talk about traffic violations:

**¿Podría ver su permiso/carnet de conducir?**
*May I see your driver's license?*

**Tengo que ponerle/darle una multa.**
*I have to give you a fine/ticket.*

# MOSAICOS

## A escuchar

### Antes de escuchar

**ESTRATEGIA**

**Identify the speaker's intention through the main idea and specific information**

To understand accurately what a speaker says, it is necessary to use a number of strategies. To identify the main idea, anticipate key concepts that may be associated with the topic, and focus on transitional phrases that signal the presentation of the main idea. Keep track of the speaker's specific information by organizing it mentally. Pay attention to the speaker's verbal and nonverbal cues, such as word choice, tone, and gestures.

**15-26 Preparación.** Usted escuchará una breve presentación sobre el futuro de la tecnología en la medicina. Antes de escuchar, escriba dos avances tecnológicos o médicos que, según usted, ayudarán a los pacientes del futuro.

### Escuchar

🔊 **15-27 ¿Comprende usted?** PRIMERA FASE. Read the statements below and then listen to the presentation. As you listen, circle the statement(s) that reflect the main idea and the supporting details.

CD 6
Track 26

| | IDEA PRINCIPAL | DETALLES |
|---|---|---|
| 1. El marcapasos... | **a.** se usa para ayudar a los corredores. <br> **b.** les ha salvado la vida a muchas personas. <br> **c.** es un tipo de tecnología obsoleta. | **a.** regula los latidos del corazón. <br> **b.** se inventó hace diez años. <br> **c.** es una microcomputadora. |
| 2. Con el implante en el oído... | **a.** los sonidos suenan como una lengua extranjera. <br> **b.** los sordos pueden oír muy pocos sonidos. <br> **c.** los sordos no sufren de dolor de oídos. | **a.** el aparato se pone en la parte externa del oído. <br> **b.** el aparato aumenta el volumen. <br> **c.** el aparato se coloca en el oído interno. |

SEGUNDA FASE. What is the speaker's intention in sharing this information?

**a.** aliviar a los pacientes
**b.** informar al público
**c.** entretener a la familia de los pacientes

### Después de escuchar

 **15-28 Ahora usted.** Compartan sus respuestas a las siguientes preguntas.

1. Según ustedes, ¿de qué otra forma la tecnología puede ayudar a la medicina?
2. ¿En qué otras áreas, puede ayudar la tecnología? Expliquen.

# A conversar

**Use drama and humor in telling a personal anecdote**

You learned in *Capítulo 12* to keep your listeners interested in your story by inserting remarks to draw their attention to moments that are particularly funny, frightening, or surprising. You can use these remarks, called *evaluations*, to make your story humorous or to heighten the drama. You can also increase the drama by strategically using descriptive details to slow down the pace and thus create suspense.

## Antes de conversar

**15-29 Preparación.** PRIMERA FASE. Lea las siguientes anécdotas que les ocurrieron a dos celebridades.

"Hace dos años, una amiga mía vino a San Francisco para visitarme. Como era su cumpleaños, el sábado por la noche fuimos a un restaurante francés muy elegante y caro para celebrarlo. Después de comer muy bien y beber el mejor champán que tenían, me trajeron la cuenta. La cantidad era enorme, pero no había problema, porque mis películas siempre tenían mucho éxito y me pagaban bien. Llevé la mano al bolsillo de mi chaqueta y me di cuenta de que la billetera estaba en mi casa, no en mi chaqueta. Llamé al camarero y le expliqué la situación. Incluso le dije quién era. Con una mirada irónica y un tono más frío que la Antártida en invierno, el camarero me dijo: Si usted es… , yo soy Brad Pitt. Por favor, no me cuente historias."

"Una tarde de verano mi esposo y yo decidimos ir de incógnito a Manhattan. Íbamos a pasar unas horas comprando, y luego íbamos a ver una película. Después de viajar como veinte minutos por la carretera, se nos descompuso el Jag. ¡Qué feo! Había mucho tráfico y hacía un calor insoportable. Bajamos del carro y mi esposo, que tiene talento para eso, levantó el capó y revisó lo que había allí dentro. Como aparentemente no había ningún problema mecánico, volvimos al carro. De repente, mi esposo se acordó de que el marcador de gasolina no funcionaba, y que ¡se le había olvidado llenar el tanque! En ese momento llegaron dos policías y nos preguntaron cuál era el problema. Les contamos la historia, pero no nos creyeron y nos pusieron una multa altísima. ¡Claro, estábamos en Nueva York, donde todo es carísimo!"

### Lengua

Spanish has several expressions with **se** that speakers use daily. Read the following and think of possible situations in which they may be used.

**Se me puso la piel de gallina.**
*I got goosebumps.*

**Se me fue el alma a los pies.**
*My heart sank.*

**Se me fue la lengua.**
*I gave myself away.*

**Se me congeló la pantalla.**
*The screen froze up on me.*

**SEGUNDA FASE.** Ahora piense en una experiencia real suya semejante (trágica, cómica, tragicómica) a la de los relatos de la *Primera fase*. Tome nota de los siguientes detalles para compartir con su compañero/a.

1. Quién(es) estaba(n) presente(s).
2. Cuándo y dónde ocurrió. Escriba algunas palabras (adjetivos, verbos, adverbios) que describan el escenario.
3. Qué ocurrió, qué hicieron y cómo reaccionaron usted y la(s) otra(s) persona(s).
4. Cómo terminó la situación.
5. Qué haría usted si esto ocurriera otra vez.

En el recuadro hay algunas ideas que lo/la pueden ayudar.

> Se le quedó algo importante en un lugar que ya estaba cerrado.
>
> Se le rompió algo de mucho valor: una joya, un jarrón de cristal, un espejo fino...
>
> Al regresar de un viaje, se da cuenta de que se le quedó algo indispensable en el hotel.

## Conversar

**15-30 Entre nosotros.** Comparta su experiencia con el grupo. Use las expresiones de *En directo* para que su anécdota tenga humor y un tono dramático. Cada miembro del grupo debe hacerle preguntas y consultar el segundo recuadro de *En directo* para expresar sus reacciones efectivamente. Finalmente, el grupo debe señalar los aspectos de cada anécdota que la hicieron graciosa (*funny*) o dramática.

## Después de conversar

**15-31 Un poco más.** Un miembro de cada grupo de la actividad anterior debe compartir con la clase la anécdota más dramática o graciosa de su grupo. Al final, todos deben votar por la anécdota favorita de la clase. Finalmente, la persona que tuvo esta experiencia responderá a las preguntas o reaccionará a los comentarios de sus compañeros/as.

# A leer

**Identify the narrator's perspective**

A narrative can be told by a narrator from one of several perspectives. Two important points of view are the perspective of a protagonist (someone who tells his/her own experiences: I, we) and that of a witness (someone who tells what he/she sees or witnesses: he, she, they). Therefore, to identify the perspective of the narrator, the following questions will help you: Who witnesses the event? Who is speaking? Who is responding?

## Antes de leer

**15-32 Preparación. PRIMERA FASE.** De la siguiente lista, marquen (✓) las máquinas, aparatos o servicios que ustedes esperarían encontrar en una sociedad donde se usa una tecnología avanzada.

___ **1.** automóviles voladores
___ **2.** electricidad generada por la energía eólica (energía del viento)
___ **3.** servicio postal automatizado
___ **4.** computadoras nanomecánicas
___ **5.** impresoras que escanean, faxean y fotocopian
___ **6.** aviones de pasajeros sin pilotos

**SEGUNDA FASE.** Lea el título del cuento a continuación y luego ponga en un círculo la respuesta a cada pregunta, basándose en su conocimiento de la tecnología.

1. ¿Qué ideas o conceptos asocia usted con la palabra *apocalipsis*? Hay más de una respuesta lógica.
   a. el nacimiento
   b. la muerte
   c. la destrucción
   d. la vida

2. Pensando en el título, ¿cuál de las frases podría ser el tema del cuento?
   a. Un científico usa la tecnología para destruirse a sí mismo.
   b. Los seres humanos usan la tecnología para hacer la vida más fácil.
   c. La tecnología tiene dos caras, una constructiva y la otra destructiva.

3. Ahora, lea por encima (*skim*) el cuento. Anote por lo menos dos palabras que apoyen sus respuestas a las preguntas 1 y 2.

### Cultura

Marco Denevi (1922-1998), escritor argentino, escribió novelas, obras de teatro y cuentos cortos (entre ellos, cuentos muy cortos o *microcuentos*). También fue abogado y periodista. Tanto en su ficción como en sus escritos periodísticos expresó su preocupación por los problemas políticos y sociales de su tiempo.

## Leer

**15-33 Primera mirada.** Lea el siguiente microcuento escrito por Marco
Denevi, un conocido escritor argentino, y luego siga las instrucciones.

### Apocalipsis I

La extinción de la raza de los hombres se sitúa
aproximadamente a fines del siglo XXXI. La cosa
sucedió así: las máquinas habían alcanzado tal
perfección que los hombres no necesitaban comer,
ni dormir, ni leer, ni escribir, ni siquiera pensar. Les
bastaba apretar botones y las máquinas lo hacían
todo por ellos.

Gradualmente fueron desapareciendo las mesas, los
teléfonos, los Leonardo da Vinci, las rosas de té,
las tiendas de antigüedades, los discos con las
nueve sinfonías de Beethoven, el vino de Burdeos[1],
las golondrinas, los cuadros de Salvador Dalí[2], los
relojes, los sellos postales, los alfileres[3], el Museo
del Prado, la sopa de cebolla, los transatlánticos,
las pirámides de Egipto, las Obras Completas de
don Benito Pérez Galdós.[4] Sólo había máquinas.

Después los hombres empezaron a notar que ellos
mismos iban desapareciendo paulatinamente[5] y que
en cambio las máquinas se multiplicaban. Bastó
poco tiempo para que el número de los hombres
quedase reducido a la mitad y el de las máquinas
aumentase al doble y luego al décuplo.[6] Las
máquinas terminaron por ocupar todo el espacio
disponible. Nadie podía dar un paso, hacer un
simple ademán[7] sin tropezarse[8] con una de ellas.
Finalmente los hombres se extinguieron.

Como el último se olvidó de desconectar las
máquinas, desde entonces seguimos funcionando.

[1]región de Francia famosa por sus vinos  [2]famoso pintor y diseñador español conocido por su estilo surrealista y su excentricidad
[3]*pins*  [4]famoso novelista español (1843–1920)  [5]*gradualmente*  [6]*tenfold*  [7]*gesture*  [8]*stumble*

Marque (✓) la información relacionada con la perspectiva del narrador.

1. ___ El narrador habla de una experiencia que le contaron.
2. ___ El narrador habla de una experiencia que ha vivido.

Marque (✓) la información relacionada con el narrador.
3. ___ Al final del cuento descubrimos quién es el narrador.
4. ___ El narrador habla desde la perspectiva del tiempo futuro.
5. ___ El narrador es una máquina.

Marque (✓) la información relacionada con la trama de esta historia.
6. ___ El ser humano, según el narrador, se dio cuenta de que las máquinas lo
estaban controlando, y las destruyó.
7. ___ Al final del cuento, ya no había seres humanos, sino solamente
máquinas.

## Después de leer

**15-34 Segunda mirada y ampliación.** Respondan a las preguntas y apunten
las ideas que salgan en su discusión. Estén listos para presentar sus respuestas y
justificaciones a la clase.

1. ¿Cuál es el significado del título de este cuento? Explíquenlo.
2. ¿Hace un comentario social este cuento? ¿Cuál es el mensaje?
3. ¿Están ustedes de acuerdo con el mensaje? Expliquen sus ideas.

# A escribir

**Use imagination and humor in writing a narrative**

In creative writing you can use your imagination to invent events and characters that would be impossible in real life. You can use fantasy and humor to exaggerate events and characters' behaviors in order to entertain your readers. To write an imaginative and humorous story, consider the following tips:

■ Create situations or behaviors that differ from people's expectations.
■ Use contradictions within a character to create humor. The humor will be apparent when you poke fun at the contradictions.
■ Base your humor on situations and characterizations that will be familiar to your audience.

## Antes de escribir

**15-35 Preparación.** Imagínese que usted es una de las máquinas que quedaron funcionando después de la desaparición de los seres humanos.

1. Escriba algunas ideas que describan la existencia de las máquinas después de la desaparición del ser humano: ¿Es su existencia semejante o diferente a la del pasado? ¿Es más o menos divertida? ¿Qué hacía usted antes que ya no hace hoy o viceversa?
2. Mencione tres errores cometidos por el ser humano que, según usted, tuvieron relación directa con su desaparición y explique por qué.

## Escribir

**15-36 Manos a la obra.** Ahora, en el papel de una de las máquinas que sobrevivió la desaparición del ser humano, escriba una narración. Use la información que preparó en **15-35**.

1. Describa su existencia antes y después de la desaparición de los seres humanos. Use humor para captar la atención de su lector.
2. Indique con humor algunos aspectos de su interacción y trabajo cotidianos con los humanos que usted extraña con nostalgia.
3. Especule sobre algunos errores que, según usted, provocaron la extinción de la raza humana.

## Después de escribir

**15-37 Revisión.** Recuerde que su texto va a ser leído por otras máquinas de inteligencia superior a la humana que disfrutan del humor, pero que no toleran errores ni imprecisiones de ningún tipo.

1. ¿Usó ideas y situaciones originales y absurdas para captar la atención del lector? ¿Exageró las situaciones o los comportamientos?
2. ¿Hay un orden lógico y claro?
3. ¿Usó vocabulario apropiado? ¿Revisó la concordancia, el tiempo y los modos? ¿Utilizó la puntuación y ortografía correctas?

# ENFOQUE CULTURAL

## La ciencia y la tecnología

**M**uchos científicos latinoamericanos y españoles se han distinguido por sus descubrimientos e inventos, como se verá en una actividad posterior en esta sección. Un gran número de investigadores hispanos forma parte de equipos científicos en universidades de Estados Unidos y Europa. Sin embargo, la mayoría de los países latinoamericanos no son productores de ciencia y tecnología. La razón de esto es que los inventos y descubrimientos modernos por lo general son el resultado del trabajo de equipos humanos especializados y de laboratorios muy costosos y estos países tienen que dedicar sus recursos a otras necesidades urgentes, como por ejemplo, desarrollar la infraestructura de

El Observatorio Interamericano de Cerro Tololo en Chile es un ejemplo de la cooperación internacional para el desarrollo de la ciencia en América Latina.

comunicaciones o mejorar la salud de sus ciudadanos. En la actualidad los cambios tecnológicos se producen más rápidamente que nunca. Y la distancia entre los países que usan más tecnología y los que usan menos aumenta más rápidamente que nunca.

Algunos países hispanos se han asociado con universidades o con instituciones científicas de Estados Unidos o de Europa para construir centros de investigación científica dentro de su territorio. Un ejemplo sobresaliente de esta cooperación es el observatorio astronómico de Cerro Tololo en Chile. Este centro de investigación es administrado por un consorcio de universidades de varios países llamado AURA (Asociación de Universidades para la Investigación en Astronomía). El observatorio está situado a más de 2.000 metros sobre el nivel del mar, en un lugar que tiene excelentes condiciones de clima para la observación de las estrellas. Cerro Tololo es utilizado por un gran número de astrónomos de todo el mundo durante un promedio de unos 300 días al año para la observación y el estudio de las estrellas del hemisferio sur.

El Radiotelescopio de Arecibo, Puerto Rico, es uno de los centros científicos más importantes de América Latina.

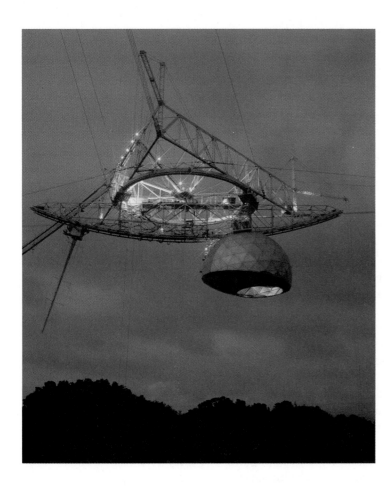

La antena esférica de Arecibo fue hasta hace muy pocos años la más grande del mundo.

Otro ejemplo de la cooperación internacional para el desarrollo de la ciencia y la tecnología en los países hispanos es el Radiotelescopio de Arecibo, situado en la ciudad puertorriqueña de ese mismo nombre. Este telescopio tiene la segunda antena esférica más grande del mundo y fue construido entre 1960 y 1963. A diferencia del observatorio de Cerro Tololo, Arecibo funciona mediante un receptor de ondas de radio. En Arecibo se han realizado importantes observaciones astronómicas, como por ejemplo, la de los primeros planetas descubiertos fuera de nuestro sistema solar.

A pesar de su importancia científica, muchas personas conocen este observatorio porque ha aparecido en varias películas de ciencia ficción y en alguna de las series de James Bond. Otras personas asocian Arecibo principalmente con el famoso "Mensaje de Arecibo", un texto codificado que se envió desde este radiotelescopio a una zona muy lejana del universo con una descripción del sistema solar, la Tierra y el ADN de los seres humanos. La idea de enviar un mensaje de radio con la esperanza de que los habitantes de una región lejana del universo puedan entenderlo ha fascinado a la imaginación de los humanos, pero a pesar de ello, nadie está esperando una respuesta, ya que el mensaje tardará más de 20.000 años en llegar a su destino.

**15-38 Comprensión.** PRIMERA FASE. **Reconocimiento de palabras clave.** Encuentre en el texto la palabra o expresión que mejor expresa el significado de las siguientes ideas.

1. teams      _____
2. to develop      _____
3. outstanding      _____
4. sea level      _____
5. average      _____
6. radio waves      _____
7. hope      _____

SEGUNDA FASE. **Oraciones importantes.** Subraye las afirmaciones que contienen ideas que se encuentran en el texto. Luego indique en qué parte del texto están.

1. Modern science requires expensive human teams and laboratories.
2. Partnerships with foreign universities and institutions have helped some Hispanic countries develop important research centers.
3. Although Cerro Tololo is located very high up in the mountains, the humidity of the region produces heavy clouds that often cover the sky.
4. Because of adverse weather conditions, Cerro Tololo is open only five months a year.
5. Scientists at the observatory in Arecibo were the first to view planets from outside our solar system.
6. The telescope in Arecibo works with a combination of laser and gamma rays.
7. The Arecibo Message contains an English text that describes the most important achievements of the human race.

TERCERA FASE. **Ideas principales.** Escriba un párrafo breve en español resumiendo las ideas principales expresadas en el texto.

 **15-39 Use la información.** Escriba una breve biografía de un científico/una científica o inventor/inventora del mundo hispano. Explique de qué país proviene y en qué época vivió, donde estudió, cuál fue su contribución más importante a la ciencia o la tecnología, qué premios importantes recibió, y otros datos de interés que usted encuentre. Para preparar esta actividad, visite la página web de *Mosaicos* y siga los enlaces útiles.

# VOCABULARIO

## La ciencia y la tecnología — *Science and technology*

| | |
|---|---|
| el acceso | *access* |
| el adelanto | *advance* |
| la biblioteca virtual | *virtual library* |
| el buscador | *search engine* |
| la cápsula | *capsule* |
| la clonación | *cloning* |
| el conocimiento | *knowledge* |
| el descubrimiento | *discovery* |
| la diseminación | *dispersal, dissemination* |
| el documento adjunto | *attachment, attached document* |
| la energía solar | *solar energy* |
| el enlace | *link* |
| la fuente | *source* |
| la infraestructura | *infrastructure* |
| el intercambio | *exchange* |
| el mensaje | *message* |
| el reto | *challenge* |
| el riel | *rail* |
| el robot | *robot* |
| el videojuego | *video game* |

## El medio ambiente — *Environment*

| | |
|---|---|
| el banco de peces | *shoal; school of fish* |
| el bosque | *forest* |
| el bosque tropical | *rain forest* |
| el calentamiento | *warming* |
| la capa de ozono | *ozone layer* |
| la conservación | *preservation* |
| la cuenca | *(river) basin* |
| la deforestación | *deforestation* |
| la desaparición | *disappearance* |
| el deshielo | *thaw, thawing* |
| la extinción | *extinction* |
| la inundación | *flood* |
| la naturaleza | *nature* |
| la pérdida | *loss* |
| el planeta | *planet* |
| los recursos | *resources* |
| la reserva natural | *nature preserve* |
| la tierra | *land, soil* |

## Las descripciones — *Descriptions*

| | |
|---|---|
| climatizado/a | *air-conditioned* |
| extinguido/a | *extinguished* |
| reciclado/a | *recycled* |
| volador/a | *flying* |

## Verbos — *Verbs*

| | |
|---|---|
| aterrizar (c) | *to land* |
| bajar | *to download* |
| conectarse | *to connect* |
| construir (y) | *to build* |
| contribuir (y) | *to contribute* |
| despegar (u) | *to take off (airplane)* |
| difundir | *to spread, to disseminate* |
| encender (ie) | *to turn on* |
| enfocarse (qu) | *to focus* |
| meter | *to insert* |
| repoblar | *to reforest* |
| unificar (qu) | *to unify* |

## Palabras y expresiones útiles — *Useful words and expressions*

| | |
|---|---|
| debido a | *due to* |
| en busca de | *in search of* |
| genéticamente | *genetically* |
| virtualmente | *virtually* |

# Expansión gramatical

This grammatical supplement includes structures often considered optional for the introductory level, because the functions and forms presented here are far beyond the performance level of most first-year students. Many instructors choose to present them for recognition only, if at all. The *vosotros* command forms are included in this section for the instructors who use them to address their students.

The explanation and activities in this section use the same format as the grammatical material throughout *Mosaicos* in order to facilitate their incorporation into the core lessons of the program or their addition as another chapter in the book.

## Funciones y formas

1. Giving informal orders or commands to two or more people (in Spain): *Vosotros* commands
2. Expressing an indirect wish that a third party do something: Indirect commands
3. Suggesting that someone and the speaker do something: The Spanish equivalents of English *let's*
4. Reacting to a past occurrence or event: The present perfect subjunctive
5. Hypothesizing about an occurrence or event in the past: The conditional perfect and the pluperfect subjunctive
6. Expressing contrary-to-fact conditions in the past: *If*-clauses (using the perfect tense)
7. Emphasizing a fact resulting from an action by someone or something: The passive voice

## 1. Giving informal orders or commands to two or more people (in Spain): *Vosotros* commands

|  | AFFIRMATIVE | NEGATIVE |
|---|---|---|
| hablar | habla**d** | no **habléis** |
| comer | come**d** | no **comáis** |
| escribir | escribi**d** | no **escribáis** |

■ To use the affirmative **vosotros** command, change the final **-r** of the infinitive to **-d**.

■ Use the **vosotros** form of the present subjunctive for the **vosotros** negative command.

■ For the affirmative **vosotros** command of reflexive verbs, drop the final **-d** and add the pronoun **os: levantad + os = levantaos.** The verb **irse** is an exception: **idos.**

**EG-1 Buenos consejos.** Usted quiere que sus mejores amigos cambien sus hábitos y vivan una vida más sana. Dígales qué deben hacer.

**MODELO:**   caminar dos kilómetros todos los días
*Caminad dos kilómetros todos los días.*

**1.** comer muchas frutas y vegetales
**2.** empezar un programa de ejercicios
**3.** no respirar por la boca
**4.** no cansarse mucho los primeros días
**5.** relajarse para evitar el estrés
**6.** dormir no menos de ocho horas

**EG-2 Órdenes en grupo.** Cada uno/a de ustedes va a hacer el papel de profesor/a de educación física y le va a dar una orden a los otros estudiantes del grupo. Los estudiantes deben hacer lo que el/la profesor/a les indica.

**MODELO:**   *Levantad los brazos y las piernas.*

## SITUACIONES

You and your partner have rented a cabin in the mountains for a month. Some of your friends are going to use the cabin part of the time and you would like to give them some rules to make sure they leave everything in order. Write the rules and then compare them with those of another couple.

## 2. Expressing an indirect wish that a third party do something: Indirect commands

You have used commands directly to tell others to do something: **Salga/Salgan ahora.** Now you are going to use indirect commands to say what someone else should do: **Que salga Berta.** Note that this indirect command is equivalent to saying **Quiero que Berta salga,** but without expressing the main verb **quiero.**

■ The word **que** introduces the indirect command. The subject, if stated, normally follows the verb.

| | |
|---|---|
| **Que cocine** Roberto. | *Let Roberto cook.* |
| **Que descanse** María. | *Let María rest.* |

■ Reflexive and object pronouns always precede the verb.

| | |
|---|---|
| Que **se siente** a la mesa. | *Let him sit at the table.* |
| Que **le sirvan** la cena. | *Let them serve him dinner.* |
| Que **se la sirvan** ahora. | *Let them serve it to him now.* |

 **EG-3 Una clase de cocina.** Un chef muy conocido ha accedido a dar una clase de cocina con el fin de recaudar (*raise*) dinero para una obra social. Usted y su compañero/a forman parte del comité que organiza la clase. Su compañero/a tiene la lista de las personas que desean ayudar y usted tiene la lista de las tareas pendientes. Háganse preguntas y contéstense con la información que cada uno/a tiene.

MODELO:    *Eduardo, Alicia y Pedro preparar los anuncios, comprar los refrescos*
    E1:  *¿Quién va a preparar los anuncios?*
    E2:  *Que los preparen Alicia y Pedro. ¿Y qué va a hacer Eduardo?*
    E1:  *Que compre los refrescos.*

### Personas

Beatriz
Alberto y Rubén
Miguel
Elena y Amanda
Ana María
Emilio
Un camarero

### Tareas

traer los platos
tener los ingredientes listos
buscar las sillas
copiar las recetas
servir el vino
recibir a las personas
ayudar al chef

**EG-4 Una fiesta hispana.** PRIMERA FASE. Para celebrar el final de curso ustedes han decidido organizar una fiesta en el departamento de español. Hagan una lista de todo lo que necesitan y otra lista de todas las personas que van a invitar, además de sus compañeros/as de clase.

SEGUNDA FASE. Decidan qué otras personas de la clase pueden encargarse de cada sección y por qué. Su compañero/a, que está de acuerdo con usted, le dará algunas ideas.

MODELO: E1: *Que se encargue Juan de comprar las invitaciones porque tiene que ir al supermercado esta tarde.*

E2: *Sí, pero que las escriban María y Pedro que escriben mejor.*

---

### En directo

To negotiate politely:

**Esperamos que...**

**Es mejor que...**

**Proponemos que...**

To show agreement:

**¡Claro!**

**¡Por supuesto!**

**¡Cómo no!**

**¡Desde luego!**

---

## SITUACIONES

**Role A.** You are a new manager for the Student Union who wants to improve the food and the service at the cafeteria. In a meeting with the cafeteria manager, say a) that it is important that students receive a better service, b) inform the manager of the type of food you would like to find in the cafeteria and of the ways in which the service could be improved, and c) say that you hope the prices will not increase (**subir**) this semester.

**Role B.** You are the cafeteria manager. Agree with the Student Union manager and tell him/her a) that you have a good team and you want everyone to do a good job, b) that you will be happy to meet with a student committee and have students suggest (**sugerir**) menus, and c) that you will do your best (**hacer lo posible**) to convince your team to incorporate your suggestions.

### 3. Suggesting that someone and the speaker do something: The Spanish equivalents of English *let's*

In Spanish, you may suggest that two or more people, including yourself, do something together in the following ways.

■ **Vamos + a +** *infinitive* is commonly used in Spanish to express English *let's* **+** *verb*.

| | |
|---|---|
| **Vamos a llamar** al doctor. | *Let's call the doctor.* |

■ Use **vamos** by itself to mean *let's go*. The negative *let's not go* is **no vayamos**.

| | |
|---|---|
| **Vamos** al hospital. | *Let's go to the hospital.* |
| **No vayamos** al hospital. | *Let's not go to the hospital.* |

■ Another equivalent for *let's* **+** *verb* is the **nosotros** form of the present subjunctive.

| | |
|---|---|
| **Hablemos** con el médico. | *Let's talk to the doctor.* |
| **No hablemos** con la enfermera. | *Let's not talk to the nurse.* |

■ The final **-s** of reflexive affirmative commands is dropped when the pronoun **nos** is attached. Note the additional written accent.

| | | |
|---|---|---|
| **Levantemos + nos** | → | **Levantémonos.** |
| **Sirvamos + nos** | → | **Sirvámonos.** |

■ Placement of object and reflexive pronouns is the same as with **usted(es)** commands.

| | |
|---|---|
| **Comprémosla.** | *Let's buy it.* |
| **No la compremos.** | *Let's not buy it.* |

 **EG-5 ¿Qué debemos hacer?** Usted y un/a compañero/a están estudiando y cuidando a su hermanito al mismo tiempo. El niño les dice que se siente mal. Cada uno/a de ustedes debe escoger tres de las siguientes opciones y decirle a su compañero/a lo que deben o no deben hacer.

**MODELO:** llevarlo a su cuarto      llamar a tus padres
E1: *Llevémoslo a su cuarto.*      E2: *Llamemos a tus padres.*

1. darle agua
2. llevarlo al parque
3. comprarle juguetes
4. ponerle el termómetro
5. llamar al médico
6. preguntarle qué le duele
7. prepararle una hamburguesa
8. explicarle los síntomas al doctor
9. ponerle la televisión
10. acostarlo

**EG-6 Resoluciones.** Usted y su compañero/a deciden llevar una vida más sana. Túrnense para decir lo que piensan hacer. Su compañero/a va a decirle si está de acuerdo o no con su sugerencia.

**MODELO:**         comer más verduras
         E1: *Vamos a comer más verduras.*
         E2: *Sí, comamos más verduras./No, (no comamos más verduras,) comamos más frutas.*

1. tomar vitaminas y minerales
2. caminar tres kilómetros diariamente
3. beber ocho vasos de agua todos los días
4. acostarse más temprano
5. dormir ocho horas todas las noches
6. ...

**EG-7 Los preparativos para un beneficio.** En pequeños grupos, decidan qué actividades van a hacer para recaudar (*collect*) fondos a beneficio de un hospital. Deben mencionar cinco actividades.

**MODELO:**     *Organicemos un partido del equipo de basquetbol.*

## SITUACIONES

You and your partner are planning to visit a classmate who is in the hospital. Decide a) when you will visit him/her, b) what you are going to take him/her, and c) what you can do for your classmate after he/she leaves the hospital. Then, exchange this information with another pair of students.

### 4. Reacting to a past occurrence or event: The present perfect subjunctive

Use the present perfect subjunctive to react to a past occurrence, event or condition. The present perfect subjunctive is formed with the present subjunctive of the verb **haber** + *past participle*.

| PRESENT SUBJUNCTIVE OF *HABER* + *PAST PARTICIPLE* | | |
|---|---|---|
| yo | haya | |
| yú | hayas | |
| Ud., él/ella | haya | hablado |
| nosotros/as | hayamos | comido |
| vosotros/as | hayáis | vivido |
| Uds., ellos/as | hayan | |

Note that the dependent clause using the present perfect subjunctive describes what has happened before the time expressed or implied in the main clause, which is the present. Its English equivalent is normally *has/have* + *past participle*, but it may vary according to the context.

Your friend tells you:

Mis hijos volvieron de sus vacaciones. →

Your reaction to this past event:

Me alegro de que **hayan llegado**. *I'm glad they arrived early.*

Your secretary informs you:

El gerente de ventas no vino a trabajar ayer. } →

Your reaction to this past news:

Es posible que **haya estado** enfermo. *It's possible that he may have been sick.*

 **EG-8 ¿Qué espera usted?** Escoja la oración que complete lógicamente las siguientes situaciones. Compare sus respuestas con las de su compañero/a.

1. Su computadora no estaba funcionando bien y usted se la dio a un técnico para que la reparara. Usted espera que...
   **a.** la haya vendido.
   **b.** haya destruido sus programas.
   **c.** haya encontrado el problema.
2. Su amigo acaba de regresar de Puerto Rico, donde fue a pasar sus vacaciones. Usted le dice: "Espero que...
   **a.** hayas visitado el Viejo San Juan".
   **b.** te hayas aburrido mucho".
   **c.** hayas perdido todo tu dinero".
3. Uno de sus compañeros ha estado muy grave en el hospital, pero ya está en la casa. Usted le habla y le dice: "Siento mucho que...
   **a.** hayas vendido la casa".
   **b.** hayas estado tan mal".
   **c.** hayas salido del hospital".

4. Usted llama por teléfono a un amigo para invitarlo a cenar, pero nadie contesta el teléfono. Es probable que su amigo…
   **a.** haya cenado ya.
   **b.** haya salido de su casa.
   **c.** haya cambiado su teléfono.
5. Uno de sus parientes dijo una mentira (*lie*). Como es natural, a usted le molesta mucho que no…
   **a.** haya dicho la verdad.
   **b.** haya dicho nada.
   **c.** haya hablado con sus parientes.

**EG-9 Un viaje.** Uno de sus amigos pasó un semestre en Los Ángeles. Túrnese con su compañero/a para decirle lo que esperan que haya hecho en su visita.

**MODELO:**      ir a Beverly Hills / visitar la Biblioteca Huntington
          E1: *Espero que hayas ido a Beverly Hills.*
          E2: *Y yo espero que hayas visitado la Biblioteca Huntington.*

1. ver las Torres de Watts
2. ir a los Estudios Universal
3. caminar por la calle Olvera
4. comer comida mexicana
5. manejar hasta el observatorio del Monte Wilson
6. asistir al Desfile de las Rosas

**EG-10 Los adelantos científicos.** Usted y su compañero/a trabajan con otros científicos en un laboratorio de ingeniería genética. Háganse preguntas para saber qué han logrado o no en sus investigaciones.

**MODELO:**      aislar el nuevo virus / es posible que
          E1: *¿Han aislado el nuevo virus?*
          E2: *Es posible que lo hayamos / hayan aislado.*

1. cambiar la estructura de la célula / dudar
2. no hacer implantes nuevos / es una lástima
3. duplicar órganos / no creer que
4. regular el ritmo del corazón / esperar
5. reactivar los músculos atrofiados / es probable que
6. modificar los genes / es importante que

---

### En directo

To express that you remember or recognize someone in a photo:

**Mira, mira, este/esta es…**
*Look, this is . . .*

**Te equivocas**
*You are wrong.*

**Pero, ¿no ves que es…/ Tiene/lleva…**
*But, don't you see it is . . .* (a person's name)

**¿Has visto a…?**

---

## SITUACIONES

You and your classmate graduated years ago and are remembering the times when you were at the university. You have found a group photo of your Spanish class. Talk about each of your classmates saying a) what you know they have done in their lives, b) what you hope they have done, and c) what you doubt they have done. Use your imagination and the expressions in the box to sound more natural.

### 5. Hypothesizing about an occurrence or event in the past: The conditional perfect and the pluperfect subjunctive

In this section you will study two new verb tenses: the conditional perfect and the pluperfect subjunctive. Use this tense to hypothesize about an occurrence or event in the past.

■ Use the conditional of **haber** + *past participle* to form the conditional perfect.

| CONDITIONAL PERFECT | | |
|---|---|---|
| yo | habría | |
| tú | habrías | |
| Ud., él, ella | habría | hablado |
| nosotros/as | habríamos | comido |
| vosotros/as | habríais | vivido |
| Uds., ellos/as | habrían | |

■ The conditional perfect usually corresponds to English *would have + past participle*.

| | |
|---|---|
| Sé que le **habría gustado** esta casa. | *I know you/he/she would have liked this house.* |

■ Use the past subjunctive of **haber** + *past participle* to form the pluperfect subjunctive.

| PLUPERFECT SUBJUNCTIVE | | |
|---|---|---|
| yo | hubiera | |
| tú | hubieras | |
| Ud., él, ella | hubiera | hablado |
| nosotros/as | hubiéramos | comido |
| vosotros/as | hubierais | vivido |
| Uds., ellos/as | hubieran | |

■ The pluperfect subjunctive corresponds to English *might have, would have,* or *had + past participle*. It is used in constructions where the subjunctive is normally required.

| | |
|---|---|
| Dudaba que **hubiera venido** temprano. | *I doubted that he had/would have come early.* |
| Esperaba que **hubieran comido** en casa. | *I was hoping that they would have eaten at home.* |
| Ojalá que **hubieran visto** ese letrero. | *I wish they had seen that sign.* |

**EG-11 ¿Qué habría hecho en estas situaciones?** PRIMERA FASE. Digan qué habría hecho cada uno/a de ustedes en las siguientes situaciones. Después escojan la respuesta que les parezca mejor para cada situación.

MODELO:     Usted recibió una invitación para una recepción en la Casa Blanca.
    E1: *Se lo habría dicho a todos mis compañeros.*
    E2: *Habría leído la invitación varias veces porque habría pensado que era una broma.*

1. En el aeropuerto le dijeron que podía viajar en primera clase todo el año sin pagar.
2. Le pidieron sugerencias para mejorar la situación de los vuelos y los aeropuertos.
3. La NASA lo/la llamó para ver si le interesaba vivir tres meses en una estación espacial.
4. Le dijeron que organizara la fiesta de fin de curso de su clase.
5. Le pidieron que revisara los programas en su universidad y sugiriera los cambios necesarios.

SEGUNDA FASE. Comparen las respuestas que escogieron con las de otra pareja y decidan cuál es la mejor. Después compartan sus respuestas con el resto de la clase.

**EG-12 Nuestras esperanzas.** Usted y su compañero/a esperaban que el nuevo gobierno hiciera muchas cosas en beneficio de la sociedad. Se lograron algunas cosas, pero otras no. Túrnense para decir qué esperaban que el nuevo gobierno y su gabinete hubieran hecho y si lo han hecho o no.

MODELO:     subir el sueldo mínimo / mejorar el sistema de educación
    E1: *Esperaba que hubieran subido el sueldo mínimo y (no) lo han hecho.*
    E2: *Y yo esperaba que hubieran mejorado el sistema de educación y (no) lo han hecho.*

1. bajar los impuestos (*taxes*)
2. mejorar el transporte público
3. terminar con la corrupción
4. construir viviendas (*housing*) para familias pobres
5. ofrecer mejores planes de salud
6. proteger el medio ambiente
7. ...

## SITUACIONES

**Role A.** You had an argument (**pelea**) with your significant other. Explain to your best friend what happened and ask him/her what he/she would have done in your place. Then tell him/her what you intend to do.

**Role B.** Your best friend explains to you that he/she had an argument (**pelea**) with his/her significant other. Ask questions to obtain some details. Then a) tell him/her what you would have done in the same situation, b) ask him/her what he/she intends to do and c) give him/her your advice.

## 6. Expressing contrary-to-fact conditions in the past: *If*-clauses (using the perfect tenses)

The conditional perfect and pluperfect subjunctive are used in contrary-to-fact if-statements which refer to actions, events, experiences related to the past.

Si **hubieras venido**, te **habría**      *If you had come (which you did not),*
  **gustado** la conferencia.      *you would have liked the lecture.*

**EG-13 La vida sería diferente.** Con su compañero/a, diga cuáles habrían sido las consecuencias si…

**MODELO:**      no se hubieran inventado los aviones
       E1: *Habríamos viajado en barco, en tren o en autobús.*
       E2: *Habríamos contaminado menos la atmósfera.*

**1.** no se hubiera inventado la bomba atómica
**2.** no se hubieran deforestado los bosques
**3.** los ingleses hubieran descubierto América
**4.** las mujeres hubieran tenido siempre las mismas oportunidades que los hombres
**5.** no se hubieran creado las vacunas (*vaccination*)
**6.** los jóvenes hubieran gobernado el mundo

**EG-14 Unas excusas.** ¿Qué excusas darían ustedes en las siguientes situaciones?

**MODELO:**      Un amigo le pidió que participara en un experimento.
       E1: *Si mis padres me lo hubieran permitido, habría participado.*
       E2: *Si hubiera tenido tiempo, habría participado.*

**1.** Una organización quería que usted donara botellas y papeles para reciclar.
**2.** Le pidieron su coche para llevar unas ratas al laboratorio.
**3.** Lo/La necesitaban de voluntario/a para probar una vacuna contra el catarro.
**4.** Un/a compañero/a quería venderle su computadora portátil.
**5.** Una compañía necesitaba probar unos paracaídas (*parachutes*) y buscaba personas interesadas en las pruebas.
**6.** Alquilaban un robot para que hiciera las tareas domésticas.

**EG-15 Volver a vivir.** Piense en una experiencia negativa que usted haya tenido. Cuéntele a su compañero/a qué le pasó y dígale qué habría hecho si hubiera sabido en ese momento lo que sabe hoy. Después, su compañero/a debe hacer lo mismo.

## SITUACIONES

**Role A.** You attended a conference/lecture about the city of the future. Tell your classmate a) where and when the conference/lecture took place, b) that he/she would have found it very interesting, and c) the things that he/she would have learned if he/she had attended.

**Role B.** Your classmate has attended a conference/lecture about the city of the future. Ask him/her questions to find out more about the things he/she learned.

## 7. Emphasizing a fact resulting from an action by someone or something: The passive voice

The passive voice emphasizes a fact resulting from the action by someone or something.

■ The passive voice in Spanish is formed with the verb **ser** + *past participle*; the passive voice is most commonly used in the preterit, though at times you may see it used in other tenses.

| | |
|---|---|
| La planta nuclear **fue construida** en 1980. | *The nuclear plant was built in 1980.* |

■ Use the preposition **por** when indicating who or what performs the action.

| | |
|---|---|
| El bosque **fue destruido**. (Who or what did it is not expressed.) | *The forest was destroyed.* |
| El bosque **fue destruido por** el fuego. (The fire did it.) | *The forest was destroyed by the fire.* |

■ The past participle functions as an adjective and therefore agrees in gender and number with the subject.

| | |
|---|---|
| Los árboles fueron **destruidos** por la lluvia ácida. | *The trees were destroyed by acid rain.* |
| La cura fue **descubierta** el año pasado. | *The cure was discovered last year.* |

■ You'll most often find the passive voice in written Spanish, especially in newspapers and formal writing. However, in conversation, Spanish speakers normally use two different constructions that you have already studied—a third person plural verb or a **se** construction.

| | |
|---|---|
| **Vendieron** el laboratorio. | *They sold the laboratory.* |
| **Se vendió** el edificio. | *The building was sold.* |

 **EG-16 La comunicación oral.** Túrnense para decir lo que pasó en una reunión del presidente y los ministros. ¿Cómo lo dirían los periódicos? ¿Cómo lo dirían ustedes en una conversación?

MODELO:      ministros / recibir / el presidente
          E1: *Los ministros fueron recibidos por el presidente.*
          E2: *El presidente recibió a los ministros.*

1. la agenda / preparar / el secretario
2. la agenda / aprobar / todos
3. el proyecto para disminuir la contaminación / escribir / el Sr. Sosa
4. el proyecto / presentar / la Ministra de Salud
5. unos comentarios / leer / el presidente
6. las preguntas / contestar / el ministro

**EG-17 Dos reporteros.** Túrnense para decir cómo escribirían las siguientes noticias para un periódico.

MODELO: la lluvia ácida dañó las cosechas
*Las cosechas fueron dañadas por la lluvia ácida.*

1. La zona del Amazonas se conoce como el "pulmón" del planeta.
2. Los campesinos deforestaron la selva.
3. Los campesinos cultivaron la tierra.
4. Estos grupos cortaron muchos árboles.
5. La invasión de los seres humanos exterminó muchas especies de animales.
6. El gobierno plantará mil árboles para mejorar la situación.

## SITUACIONES

You and your classmate are TV newscasters. You must write and give a piece of news to your viewers on a great discovery. Inform them that a) some very secret plans have been discovered by the CIA, b) that important security measures have been taken, c) that politicians are now deliberating on how to respond to a possible threat (**peligro**) to the population, d) that public transport has been interrupted in major cities, e) that the situation is under control and f) that nobody should be afraid.

# Appendix 1

## Stress and Written Accents in Spanish

### Rules for Written Accents

The following rules are based on pronunciation.

1. If a word ends in *n*, *s*, or a vowel, the penultimate (second-to-last) syllable is usually stressed.

    Examples:    cami**na**n
    **mu**chos
    **si**lla

2. If a word ends in a consonant other than *n* or *s*, the last syllable is stressed.

    Example:    fa**tal**

3. Words that are exceptions to the preceding rules have an accent mark on the stressed vowel.

    Examples:    sar**tén**
    **lá**pices
    ma**má**
    **fá**cil

4. **Separation of diphthongs.** When *i* or *u* are combined with another vowel, they are pronounced as one sound (a diphthong). When each vowel sound is pronounced separately, a written accent mark is placed over the stressed vowel (either the *i* or the *u*).

    Example:    gracias   día

Because the written accents in the following examples are not determined by pronunciation, the accent mark must be memorized as part of the spelling of the words as they are learned.

5. **Homonyms.** When two words are spelled the same, but have different meanings, a written accent is used to distinguish and differentiate meaning.

    | Examples: | de | *of* | dé | *give* (formal command) |
    |---|---|---|---|---|
    | | el | *the* | él | *he* |
    | | mas | *but* | más | *more* |
    | | mi | my | mí | me |
    | | se | *him/herself,* *(to) him/her/them* | sé | *I know, be* (formal command) |
    | | si | *if* | sí | *yes* |
    | | te | *(to) you* | té | *tea* |
    | | tu | *your* | tú | *you* |

6. **Interrogatives and exclamations.** In questions (direct and indirect) and exclamations, a written accent is placed over the following words: **dónde, cómo, cuándo, cuál(es), quién(es), cuánto(s)/cuánta(s),** and **qué.**

# Word Formation in Spanish

Recognizing certain patterns in Spanish word formation can be a big help in deciphering meaning. Use the following information about word formation to help you as you read.

■ **Prefixes.** Spanish and English share a number of prefixes that shade the meaning of the word to which they are attached: **inter-** (between, among); **intro/a-** (within); **ex-** (former, toward the outside); **en-/em-** (the state of becoming); **in-/a-** (not, without), among others.

| | |
|---|---|
| **inter-** | interdisciplinario, interacción |
| **intro/a-** | introvertido, introspección |
| **ex-** | exponer (*expose*) |
| **en-/em-** | enrojecer (*to turn red*), empobrecer (*to become poor*) |
| **in-/a-** | inmoral, incompleto, amoral, asexual |

■ **Suffixes.** Suffixes and, in general, word endings will help you identify various aspects of words such as part of speech, gender, meaning, degree, etc. Common Spanish suffixes are **-ría, -za, -miento, -dad/tad, -ura, -oso/a, -izo/a, -(c)ito/a,** and **-mente.**

| | |
|---|---|
| **-ría** | place where something is made and/or bought: **panadería, zapatería** (*shoe store*), **librería.** |
| **-za** | feminine, abstract noun: **pobreza** (*poverty*), **riqueza** (*wealth, richness*). |
| **-miento** | masculine, abstract noun: **empobrecimiento** (*impoverishment*), **entrenamiento** (*training*). |
| **-dad/tad** | feminine noun: **ciudad** (*city*), **libertad** (*liberty, freedom*) |
| **-ura** | feminine noun: **verdura, locura** (*craziness*). |
| **-oso/a** | adjective meaning having the characteristics of the noun to which it's attached: **montañoso, lluvioso** (*rainy*). |
| **-izo/a** | adjective meaning having the characteristics of the noun to which it's attached: **rojizo** (*reddish*), **enfermizo** (*sickly*). |
| **-(c)ito/a** | diminutive form of noun or adjective: **Juanito, mesita** (*little table*), **Carmencita.** |
| **-mente** | attached to the feminine form of adjective to form an adverb: **rápidamente, felizmente** (*happily*). |

■ **Compounds.** Compounds are made up of two words (e.g., *mailman*), each of which has meaning in and of itself: **altavoz** (*loudspeaker*) from **alto/a** and **voz; sacacorchos** (*corkscrew*) from **sacar** and **corcho.** Your knowledge of the root words will help you recognize the compound; and likewise, learning compounds can help you to learn the root words. What do you think **sacar** means?

■ **Spanish-English associations.** Learning to associate aspects of word formation in Spanish with aspects of word formation in English can be very helpful. Look at the associations below.

| SPANISH | ENGLISH |
|---|---|
| **es/ex +** consonant | *s* + consonant |
|   **esclerosis, extraño** |   *sclerosis, strange* |
| **gu-** | *w-* |
|   **guerra, Guillermo** |   *war, William* |
| **-tad/dad** | *-ty* |
|   **libertad, calidad** |   *liberty, quality* |
| **-sión/-ción** | *-sion/-tion* |
|   **tensión, emoción** |   *tension, emotion* |

# Appendix 2

## Verb Charts

### Regular Verbs: Simple Tenses

| Infinitive Present Participle Past Participle | Indicative | | | | | Subjunctive | | Imperative |
|---|---|---|---|---|---|---|---|---|
| | Present | Imperfect | Preterit | Future | Conditional | Present | Imperfect | Commands |
| hablar hablando hablado | hablo hablas habla hablamos habláis hablan | hablaba hablabas hablaba hablábamos hablabais hablaban | hablé hablaste habló hablamos hablasteis hablaron | hablaré hablarás hablará hablaremos hablaréis hablarán | hablaría hablarías hablaría hablaríamos hablaríais hablarían | hable hables hable hablemos habléis hablen | hablara hablaras hablara habláramos hablarais hablaran | habla (tú), no hables hable (usted) hablemos hablad (vosotros), no habléis hablen (Uds.) |
| comer comiendo comido | como comes come comemos coméis comen | comía comías comía comíamos comíais comían | comí comiste comió comimos comisteis comieron | comeré comerás comerá comeremos comeréis comerán | comería comerías comería comeríamos comeríais comerían | coma comas coma comamos comáis coman | comiera comieras comiera comiéramos comierais comieran | come (tú), no comas coma (usted) comamos comed (vosotros), no comáis coman (Uds.) |
| vivir viviendo vivido | vivo vives vive vivimos vivís viven | vivía vivías vivía vivíamos vivíais vivían | viví viviste vivió vivimos vivisteis vivieron | viviré vivirás vivirá viviremos viviréis vivirán | viviría vivirías viviría viviríamos viviríais vivirían | viva vivas viva vivamos viváis vivan | viviera vivieras viviera viviéramos vivierais vivieran | vive (tú), no vivas viva (usted) vivamos vivid (vosotros), no viváis vivan (Uds.) |

# Regular Verbs: Perfect Tenses

| | Indicative | | | | | Subjunctive | |
|---|---|---|---|---|---|---|---|
| | Present Perfect | Past Perfect | Preterit Perfect | Future Perfect | Conditional Perfect | Present Perfect | Past Perfect |
| | he | había | hube | habré | habría | haya | hubiera |
| | has | habías | hubiste | habrás | habrías | hayas | hubieras |
| | ha hablado | había hablado | hubo hablado | habrá hablado | habría hablado | haya hablado | hubiera hablado |
| | hemos comido | habíamos comido | hubimos comido | habremos comido | habríamos comido | hayamos comido | hubiéramos comido |
| | habéis vivido | habíais vivido | hubisteis vivido | habréis vivido | habríais vivido | hayáis vivido | hubierais vivido |
| | han | habían | hubieron | habrán | habrían | hayan | hubieran |

# Irregular Verbs

| Infinitive / Present Participle / Past Participle | Indicative | | | | | Subjunctive | | Imperative |
|---|---|---|---|---|---|---|---|---|
| | Present | Imperfect | Preterit | Future | Conditional | Present | Imperfect | Commands |
| andar andando andado | ando andas anda andamos andáis andan | andaba andabas andaba andábamos andabais andaban | anduve anduviste anduvo anduvimos anduvisteis anduvieron | andaré andarás andará andaremos andaréis andarán | andaría andarías andaría andaríamos andaríais andarían | ande andes ande andemos andéis anden | anduviera anduvieras anduviera anduviéramos anduvierais anduvieran | anda (tú), no andes ande (usted) andemos andad (vosotros), no andéis anden (Uds.) |
| caer cayendo caído | caigo caes cae caemos caéis caen | caía caías caía caíamos caíais caían | caí caíste cayó caímos caísteis cayeron | caeré caerás caerá caeremos caeréis caerán | caería caerías caería caeríamos caeríais caerían | caiga caigas caiga caigamos caigáis caigan | cayera cayeras cayera cayéramos cayerais cayeran | cae (tú), no caigas caiga (usted) caigamos caed (vosotros), no caigáis caigan (Uds.) |
| dar dando dado | doy das da damos dais dan | daba dabas daba dábamos dabais daban | di diste dio dimos disteis dieron | daré darás dará daremos daréis darán | daría darías daría daríamos daríais darían | dé des dé demos deis den | diera dieras diera diéramos dierais dieran | da (tú), no des dé (usted) demos dad (vosotros), no deis den (Uds.) |
| decir diciendo dicho | digo dices dice decimos decís dicen | decía decías decía decíamos decíais decían | dije dijiste dijo dijimos dijisteis dijeron | diré dirás dirá diremos diréis dirán | diría dirías diría diríamos diríais dirían | diga digas diga digamos digáis digan | dijera dijeras dijera dijéramos dijerais dijeran | di (tú), no digas diga (usted) digamos decid (vosotros), no digáis digan (Uds.) |

# Irregular Verbs (continued)

| Infinitive Present Participle Past Participle | Indicative |||||| Subjunctive || Imperative |
| --- | --- | --- | --- | --- | --- | --- | --- | --- | --- |
| | Present | Imperfect | Preterit | Future | Conditional | Present | Imperfect | Commands |
| estar estando estado | estoy estás está estamos estáis están | estaba estabas estaba estábamos estabais estaban | estuve estuviste estuvo estuvimos estuvisteis estuvieron | estaré estarás estará estaremos estaréis estarán | estaría estarías estaría estaríamos estaríais estarían | esté estés esté estemos estéis estén | estuviera estuvieras estuviera estuviéramos estuvierais estuvieran | está (tú), no estés esté (usted) estemos estad (vosotros), no estéis estén (Uds.) |
| haber habiendo habido | he has ha hemos habéis han | había habías había habíamos habíais habían | hube hubiste hubo hubimos hubisteis hubieron | habré habrás habrá habremos habréis habrán | habría habrías habría habríamos habríais habrían | haya hayas haya hayamos hayáis hayan | hubiera hubieras hubiera hubiéramos hubierais hubieran | |
| hacer haciendo hecho | hago haces hace hacemos hacéis hacen | hacía hacías hacía hacíamos hacíais hacían | hice hiciste hizo hicimos hicisteis hicieron | haré harás hará haremos haréis harán | haría harías haría haríamos haríais harían | haga hagas haga hagamos hagáis hagan | hiciera hicieras hiciera hiciéramos hicierais hicieran | haz (tú), no hagas haga (usted) hagamos haced (vosotros), no hagáis hagan (Uds.) |
| ir yendo ido | voy vas va vamos vais van | iba ibas iba íbamos ibais iban | fui fuiste fue fuimos fuisteis fueron | iré irás irá iremos iréis irán | iría irías iría iríamos iríais irían | vaya vayas vaya vayamos vayáis vayan | fuera fueras fuera fuéramos fuerais fueran | ve (tú), no vayas vaya (usted) vamos, no vayamos id (vosotros), no vayáis vayan (Uds.) |
| oír oyendo oído | oigo oyes oye oímos oís oyen | oía oías oía oíamos oíais oían | oí oíste oyó oímos oísteis oyeron | oiré oirás oirá oiremos oiréis oirán | oiría oirías oiría oiríamos oiríais oirían | oiga oigas oiga oigamos oigáis oigan | oyera oyeras oyera oyéramos oyerais oyeran | oye (tú), no oigas oiga (usted) oigamos oíd (vosotros), no oigáis oigan (Uds.) |

## Irregular Verbs (continued)

| Infinitive Present Participle Past Participle | Indicative | | | | | | Subjunctive | | Imperative |
|---|---|---|---|---|---|---|---|---|---|
| | Present | Imperfect | Preterit | Future | Conditional | | Present | Imperfect | Commands |
| poder pudiendo podido | puedo puedes puede podemos podéis pueden | podía podías podía podíamos podíais podían | pude pudiste pudo pudimos pudisteis pudieron | podré podrás podrá podremos podréis podrán | podría podrías podría podríamos podríais podrían | | pueda puedas pueda podamos podáis puedan | pudiera pudieras pudiera pudiéramos pudierais pudieran | |
| poner poniendo puesto | pongo pones pone ponemos ponéis ponen | ponía ponías ponía poníamos poníais ponían | puse pusiste puso pusimos pusisteis pusieron | pondré pondrás pondrá pondremos pondréis pondrán | pondría pondrías pondría pondríamos pondríais pondrían | | ponga pongas ponga pongamos pongáis pongan | pusiera pusieras pusiera pusiéramos pusierais pusieran | pon (tú), no pongas ponga (usted) pongamos poned (vosotros), no pongáis pongan (Uds.) |
| querer queriendo querido | quiero quieres quiere queremos queréis quieren | quería querías quería queríamos queríais querían | quise quisiste quiso quisimos quisisteis quisieron | querré querrás querrá querremos querréis querrán | querría querrías querría querríamos querríais querrían | | quiera quieras quiera queramos queráis quieran | quisiera quisieras quisiera quisiéramos quisierais quisieran | quiere (tú), no quieras quiera (usted) queramos quered (vosotros), no queráis quieran (Uds.) |
| saber sabiendo sabido | sé sabes sabe sabemos sabéis saben | sabía sabías sabía sabíamos sabíais sabían | supe supiste supo supimos supisteis supieron | sabré sabrás sabrá sabremos sabréis sabrán | sabría sabrías sabría sabríamos sabríais sabrían | | sepa sepas sepa sepamos sepáis sepan | supiera supieras supiera supiéramos supierais supieran | sabe (tú), no sepas sepa (usted) sepamos sabed (vosotros), no sepáis sepan (Uds.) |
| salir saliendo salido | salgo sales sale salimos salís salen | salía salías salía salíamos salíais salían | salí saliste salió salimos salisteis salieron | saldré saldrás saldrá saldremos saldréis saldrán | saldría saldrías saldría saldríamos saldríais saldrían | | salga salgas salga salgamos salgáis salgan | saliera salieras saliera saliéramos salierais salieran | sal (tú), no salgas salga (usted) salgamos salid (vosotros), no salgáis salgan (Uds.) |

# Irregular Verbs (continued)

| Infinitive Present Participle Past Participle | Indicative | | | | | Subjunctive | | Imperative |
|---|---|---|---|---|---|---|---|---|
| | Present | Imperfect | Preterit | Future | Conditional | Present | Imperfect | Commands |
| ser siendo sido | soy eres es somos sois son | era eras era éramos erais eran | fui fuiste fue fuimos fuisteis fueron | seré serás será seremos seréis serán | sería serías sería seríamos seríais serían | sea seas sea seamos seáis sean | fuera fueras fuera fuéramos fuerais fueran | sé (tú), no seas sea (usted) seamos sed (vosotros), no seáis sean (Uds.) |
| tener teniendo tenido | tengo tienes tiene tenemos tenéis tienen | tenía tenías tenía teníamos teníais tenían | tuve tuviste tuvo tuvimos tuvisteis tuvieron | tendré tendrás tendrá tendremos tendréis tendrán | tendría tendrías tendría tendríamos tendríais tendrían | tenga tengas tenga tengamos tengáis tengan | tuviera tuvieras tuviera tuviéramos tuvierais tuvieran | ten (tú), no tengas tenga (usted) tengamos tened (vosotros), no tengáis tengan (Uds.) |
| traer trayendo traído | traigo traes trae traemos traéis traen | traía traías traía traíamos traíais traían | traje trajiste trajo trajimos trajisteis trajeron | traeré traerás traerá traeremos traeréis traerán | traería traerías traería traeríamos traeríais traerían | traiga traigas traiga traigamos traigáis traigan | trajera trajeras trajera trajéramos trajerais trajeran | trae (tú), no traigas traiga (usted) traigamos traed (vosotros), no traigáis traigan (Uds.) |
| venir viniendo venido | vengo vienes viene venimos venís vienen | venía venías venía veníamos veníais venían | vine viniste vino vinimos vinisteis vinieron | vendré vendrás vendrá vendremos vendréis vendrán | vendría vendrías vendría vendríamos vendríais vendrían | venga vengas venga vengamos vengáis vengan | viniera vinieras viniera viniéramos vinierais vinieran | ven (tú), no vengas venga (usted) vengamos venid (vosotros), no vengáis vengan (Uds.) |
| ver viendo visto | veo ves ve vemos veis ven | veía veías veía veíamos veíais veían | vi viste vio vimos visteis vieron | veré verás verá veremos veréis verán | vería verías vería veríamos veríais verían | vea veas vea veamos veáis vean | viera vieras viera viéramos vierais vieran | ve (tú), no veas vea (usted) veamos ved (vosotros), no veáis vean (Uds.) |

# Stem-Changing and Orthographic-Changing Verbs

| Infinitive / Present Participle / Past Participle | Indicative Present | Imperfect | Preterit | Future | Conditional | Subjunctive Present | Imperfect | Imperative Commands |
|---|---|---|---|---|---|---|---|---|
| almorzar (z, c) almorzando almorzado | almuerzo almuerzas almuerza almorzamos almorzáis almuerzan | almorzaba almorzabas almorzaba almorzábamos almorzabais almorzaban | almorcé almorzaste almorzó almorzamos almorzasteis almorzaron | almorzaré almorzarás almorzará almorzaremos almorzaréis almorzarán | almorzaría almorzarías almorzaría almorzaríamos almorzaríais almorzarían | almuerce almuerces almuerce almorcemos almorcéis almuercen | almorzara almorzaras almorzara almorzáramos almorzarais almorzaran | almuerza (tú) no almuerces almuerce (usted) almorcemos almorzad (vosotros) no almorcéis almuercen (Uds.) |
| buscar (c, qu) buscando buscado | busco buscas busca buscamos buscáis buscan | buscaba buscabas buscaba buscábamos buscabais buscaban | busqué buscaste buscó buscamos buscasteis buscaron | buscaré buscarás buscará buscaremos buscaréis buscarán | buscaría buscarías buscaría buscaríamos buscaríais buscarían | busque busques busque busquemos busquéis busquen | buscara buscaras buscara buscáramos buscarais buscaran | busca (tú) no busques busque (usted) busquemos buscad (vosotros) no busquéis busquen (Uds.) |
| corregir (g, j) corrigiendo corregido | corrijo corriges corrige corregimos corregís corrigen | corregía corregías corregía corregíamos corregíais corregían | corregí corregiste corrigió corregimos corregisteis corrigieron | corregiré corregirás corregirá corregiremos corregiréis corregirán | corregiría corregirías corregiría corregiríamos corregiríais corregirían | corrija corrijas corrija corrijamos corrijáis corrijan | corrigiera corrigieras corrigiera corrigiéramos corrigierais corrigieran | corrige (tú) no corrijas corrija (usted) corrijamos corregid (vosotros) no corrijáis corrijan (Uds.) |
| dormir (ue, u) durmiendo dormido | duermo duermes duerme dormimos dormís duermen | dormía dormías dormía dormíamos dormíais dormían | dormí dormiste durmió dormimos dormisteis durmieron | dormiré dormirás dormirá dormiremos dormiréis dormirán | dormiría dormirías dormiría dormiríamos dormiríais dormirían | duerma duermas duerma durmamos durmáis duerman | durmiera durmieras durmiera durmiéramos durmierais durmieran | duerme (tú), no duermas duerma (usted) durmamos dormid (vosotros), no dormáis duerman (Uds.) |
| incluir (y) incluyendo incluido | incluyo incluyes incluye incluimos incluís incluyen | incluía incluías incluía incluíamos incluíais incluían | incluí incluiste incluyó incluimos incluisteis incluyeron | incluiré incluirás incluirá incluiremos incluiréis incluirán | incluiría incluirías incluiría incluiríamos incluiríais incluirían | incluya incluyas incluya incluyamos incluyáis incluyan | incluyera incluyeras incluyera incluyéramos incluyerais incluyeran | incluye (tú), no incluyas incluya (usted) incluyamos incluid (vosotros), no incluyáis incluyan (Uds.) |

## Stem-Changing and Orthographic-Changing Verbs (continued)

| Infinitive / Present Participle / Past Participle | Indicative Present | Indicative Imperfect | Indicative Preterit | Indicative Future | Indicative Conditional | Subjunctive Present | Subjunctive Imperfect | Imperative Commands |
|---|---|---|---|---|---|---|---|---|
| llegar (g, gu)<br>llegando<br>llegado | llego<br>llegas<br>llega<br>llegamos<br>llegáis<br>llegan | llegaba<br>llegabas<br>llegaba<br>llegábamos<br>llegabais<br>llegaban | llegué<br>llegaste<br>llegó<br>llegamos<br>llegasteis<br>llegaron | llegaré<br>llegarás<br>llegará<br>llegaremos<br>llegaréis<br>llegarán | llegaría<br>llegarías<br>llegaría<br>llegaríamos<br>llegaríais<br>llegarían | llegue<br>llegues<br>llegue<br>lleguemos<br>lleguéis<br>lleguen | llegara<br>llegaras<br>llegara<br>llegáramos<br>llegarais<br>llegaran | llega (tú)<br>no llegues<br>llegue (usted)<br>lleguemos<br>llegad (vosotros)<br>no lleguéis<br>lleguen (Uds.) |
| pedir (i, i)<br>pidiendo<br>pedido | pido<br>pides<br>pide<br>pedimos<br>pedís<br>piden | pedía<br>pedías<br>pedía<br>pedíamos<br>pedíais<br>pedían | pedí<br>pediste<br>pidió<br>pedimos<br>pedisteis<br>pidieron | pediré<br>pedirás<br>pedirá<br>pediremos<br>pediréis<br>pedirán | pediría<br>pedirías<br>pediría<br>pediríamos<br>pediríais<br>pedirían | pida<br>pidas<br>pida<br>pidamos<br>pidáis<br>pidan | pidiera<br>pidieras<br>pidiera<br>pidiéramos<br>pidierais<br>pidieran | pide (tú),<br>no pidas<br>pida (usted)<br>pidamos<br>pedid (vosotros),<br>no pidáis<br>pidan (Uds.) |
| pensar (ie)<br>pensando<br>pensado | pienso<br>piensas<br>piensa<br>pensamos<br>pensáis<br>piensan | pensaba<br>pensabas<br>pensaba<br>pensábamos<br>pensabais<br>pensaban | pensé<br>pensaste<br>pensó<br>pensamos<br>pensasteis<br>pensaron | pensaré<br>pensarás<br>pensará<br>pensaremos<br>pensaréis<br>pensarán | pensaría<br>pensarías<br>pensaría<br>pensaríamos<br>pensaríais<br>pensarían | piense<br>pienses<br>piense<br>pensemos<br>penséis<br>piensen | pensara<br>pensaras<br>pensara<br>pensáramos<br>pensarais<br>pensaran | piensa (tú),<br>no pienses<br>piense (usted)<br>pensemos<br>pensad (vosotros),<br>no penséis<br>piensen (Uds.) |
| producir (zc)<br>produciendo<br>producido | produzco<br>produces<br>produce<br>producimos<br>producís<br>producen | producía<br>producías<br>producía<br>producíamos<br>producíais<br>producían | produje<br>produjiste<br>produjo<br>produjimos<br>produjisteis<br>produjeron | produciré<br>producirás<br>producirá<br>produciremos<br>produciréis<br>producirán | produciría<br>producirías<br>produciría<br>produciríamos<br>produciríais<br>producirían | produzca<br>produzcas<br>produzca<br>produzcamos<br>produzcáis<br>produzcan | produjera<br>produjeras<br>produjera<br>produjéramos<br>produjerais<br>produjeran | produce (tú),<br>no produzcas<br>produzca (usted)<br>produzcamos<br>prucucid (vosotros), no produzcáis<br>produzcan (Uds.) |
| reír (i, i)<br>riendo<br>reído | río<br>ríes<br>ríe<br>reímos<br>reís<br>ríen | reía<br>reías<br>reía<br>reíamos<br>reíais<br>reían | reí<br>reíste<br>rio<br>reímos<br>reísteis<br>rieron | reiré<br>reirás<br>reirá<br>reiremos<br>reiréis<br>reirán | reiría<br>reirías<br>reiría<br>reiríamos<br>reiríais<br>reirían | ría<br>rías<br>ría<br>riamos<br>riáis<br>rían | riera<br>rieras<br>riera<br>riéramos<br>rierais<br>rieran | ríe (tú),<br>no rías<br>ría (usted)<br>riamos<br>reíd (vosotros),<br>no riáis<br>rían (Uds.) |

## Stem-Changing and Orthographic-Changing Verbs (continued)

| Infinitive Present Participle Past Participle | Indicative | | | | | Subjunctive | | Imperative |
|---|---|---|---|---|---|---|---|---|
| | Present | Imperfect | Preterit | Future | Conditional | Present | Imperfect | Commands |
| seguir (i, i) (ga) siguiendo seguido | sigo sigues sigue seguimos seguís siguen | seguía seguías seguía seguíamos seguíais seguían | seguí seguiste siguió seguimos seguisteis siguieron | seguiré seguirás seguirá seguiremos seguiréis seguirán | seguiría seguirías seguiría seguiríamos seguiríais seguirían | siga sigas siga sigamos sigáis sigan | siguiera siguieras siguiera siguiéramos siguierais siguieran | sigue (tú), no sigas siga (usted) sigamos seguid (vosotros), no sigáis sigan (Uds.) |
| sentir (ie, i) sintiendo sentido | siento sientes siente sentimos sentís sienten | sentía sentías sentía sentíamos sentíais sentían | sentí sentiste sintió sentimos sentisteis sintieron | sentiré sentirás sentirá sentiremos sentiréis sentirán | sentiría sentirías sentiría sentiríamos sentiríais sentirían | sienta sientas sienta sintamos sintáis sientan | sintiera sintieras sintiera sintiéramos sintierais sintieran | siente (tú), no sientas sienta (usted) sintamos sentid (vosotros), no sintáis sientan (Uds.) |
| volver (ue) volviendo vuelto | vuelvo vuelves vuelve volvemos volvéis vuelven | volvía volvías volvía volvíamos volvíais volvían | volví volviste volvió volvimos volvisteis volvieron | volveré volverás volverá volveremos volveréis volverán | volvería volverías volvería volveríamos volveríais volverían | vuelva vuelvas vuelva volvamos volváis vuelvan | volviera volvieras volviera volviéramos volvierais volvieran | vuelve (tú), no vuelvas vuelva (usted) volvamos volved (vosotros), no volváis vuelvan (Uds.) |

# Appendix 3

## Spanish to English Glossary

This vocabulary includes all words presented in the text, except for proper nouns spelled the same in English and Spanish, diminutives with a literal meaning, typical expressions of the Hispanic countries presented in the *Enfoque cultural,* and cardinal numbers (found on page 14). Other cognates and words easily recognized because of the context are not included either.

The number following each entry corresponds to the **capítulo** in which the word was first introduced. Numbers followed by "r" signal that the item was presented for recognition rather than as active vocabulary.

## A

**a**   *at, to* P
**abajo**   *below, under* 4r
**el/la abogado/a**   *lawyer* 9
**abordar**   *to board* 12r
**abrazar(se) (c)**   *to embrace* 13
**el abrazo**   *hug* 4r
**el abrigo**   *coat robe* 6
**abril**   *April* Pr
**abrir**   *to open* 12r
**la abuela**   *grandmother* 4
**el abuelo**   *grandfather* 4
**abundar**   *to abound* 13
**aburrido/a**   *bored* 6r; *boring* 1
**acabar(se)**   *to complete, to finish; to run out of* 9r
**el acceso**   *access* 15
**el accesorio**   *accessory* 5
**el aceite**   *oil* 10
**la aceituna**   *olive* 3r
**el achiote**   *paprika* 10r
**acompañar**   *to accompany* 8
**aconsejable**   *advisable* 11r
**aconsejar**   *to advise* 5r
**el acontecimiento**   *event* 13r
**acostar(se) (ue)**   *to put to bed; to go to bed* 4
**la actividad**   *activity* 1r
**activo/a**   *active* Pr
**el actor/la actriz**   *actor/actress* 9
**actual**   *present, current* 14
**actualmente**   *at the present time* 9
**actuar**   *to act* 13
**la adaptación**   *adjustment, adaptation* 14
**adaptar**   *to adapt* 11r

**Adelante.**   *Come in.* 5r
**el adelanto**   *advance* 15, 15r
**adelgazar**   *to lose weight* 10r
**el ademán**   *gesture* 15r
**además**   *besides* 11r
**el aderezo**   *salad dressing* 10
**adinerado/a**   *well-off* 8r
**adiós**   *good-bye* Pr
**adivinar**   *to guess* 6r
**adornado/a**   *decorated* 8
**la aduana**   *customs* 12
**la aerolínea/línea aérea el asiento**   *airline seat* 12
**el/la aeromozo**   *flight attendant* 12r
**el aeropuerto**   *airport* 12
**afeitar(se)**   *to shave; to shave (oneself)* 4
**el afiche**   *poster* 4r
**afirmar**   *to affirm* 7r
**afortunadamente**   *fortunately* 4r
**afuera**   *outside* 4r
**las afueras**   *outskirts* 5
**la agencia de viajes**   *travel agency* 12
**el/la agente de viajes**   *travel agent* 12
**agosto**   *August* Pr
**agradable**   *agreeable* 11r; *nice* 2
**agregar**   *to add* 10
**el/la agricultor/a**   *farmer* 9
**agrio/a**   *sour* 10
**el aguacate**   *avocado* 10, 10r
**agudo/a**   *sharp, acute* 11r
**el águila**   *eagle* 14r
**el/la ahijado/a**   *godchild* 4
**ahora**   *now* 1
**ahorrar**   *to save* 6r
**los ahorros**   *savings* 9r

**el aire acondicionado**   *air conditioning* 5
**el ají**   *chile pepper* 10r
**el ajo**   *garlic* 10, 10r
**al**   *to the (contraction of a+el)* 3
**la alacridad**   *alacrity* 13r
**al aire libre**   *outdoors* 3
**la alberca**   *swimming pool* 5r
**el albergue juvenil**   *youth hostel* 13r
**el alcalde**   *mayor* 14r
**la alcoba**   *bedroom* 5r
**al lado (de)**   *next to* P
**alegrarse (de)**   *to be glad (about)* 11; *to be happy* 4r
**alegre**   *happy, glad* 2
**alegremente**   *happily* 4r
**la alegría**   *joy* 8
**alemán/alemana**   *German* 2
**alérgico/a**   *allergic* 11r
**el alfiler**   *pin* 15r
**la alfombra**   *carpet, rug* 5
**al fondo**   *at the back, in the rear* 13
**la álgebra**   *algebra* 11r
**algo**   *anything* 13r; *something* 1
**alguien**   *everyone* 13r; *someone* 13r
**algún/alguno(s)/alguna(s)**   *any* 13r; *any, some* Pr; *several* 13r
**algunas veces**   *sometimes* 13r
**alguna vez**   *ever* 13r; *sometime* 13r
**aliviar**   *to relieve* 12r
**el alivio**   *relief* 15r
**allí**   *there* 4r
**el alma**   *soul* 15r
**el almacén**   *department store; warehouse* 6
**la almeja**   *clam* 10r

la almohada *pillow* 5
almorzar (ue) *to have lunch* 4
el almuerzo *lunch* 3, Pr
¿Aló? *Hello? (on the telephone)* 3r
el alojamiento *lodging* 11r, 12
el alquiler *rent* 5
alquilar *to rent* 3
alternativo/a *alternative* 1r
alto *loudly* Pr
alto/a *tall* 2
el/la alumno/a *student* 1
el ama/o de casa *housewife, homemaker* 9
amarillo/a *yellow* 2
ambicioso/a *ambitious* Pr
a menos que *unless* 14r
el/la amigo/a *friend* P
la amistad *friendship* 13, 13r
el amor *love* 13
amplio/a *ample* 14
añadir *to add* 10
el analfabetismo *illiteracy* 14
analfabeto/a *illiterate* 14
anaranjado/a *orange* 2
la anatomía *anatomy* 1r
ancho/a *wide* 6
andar *to go* 14r
el anillo *ring* 6
animado/a *lively* 8
el año *year* P
anoche *last night* 6r
el Año Nuevo *New Year's Day* 8r
el año pasado *last year* 6r
la ansiedad *anxiety* 12r
ante(a)noche *night before last* 6r
anteayer *day before yesterday* 6r
el antepasado *ancestor* 8
antes *before* 6r, 8
antes (de) que *before* 14r
el antibiótico *antibiotic* 11
antiguo/a *old* 1
antipático/a *unpleasant* 2
la antropología *anthropology* 1
el anuncio *ad, advertisement* 9
apagar *to extinguish, to turn off* 9
el apagón *blackout* 8r
el apartamento *apartment* 5
a petición *on demand* 5r
el apio *celery* 10r
la aplicación *application* 15r
apoyar *to support* 7r
aprender *to learn* 1
apropiado/a *appropriate* 6r
aprovechar *to take advantage* 7
el apunte *note* 1

aquel/aquella *that (over there)* 5r
el árbitro *umpire, referee* 7
el árbol *tree* 7
el arete *earring* 6
argentino/a *Argentinian* 2
el armario *cabinet* 5r; *closet, armoire* 5
el aro *earring* 6r
el arpa *harp* 13r
el/la arquitecto/a *architect* 9, 9r
la arquitectura *architecture* 1, 5
arrepentirse (ie) *to regret* 7r
arrogante *arrogant* Pr
el arroz *rice* 3
el arte *art* 1r
la artesanía *handicrafts* 6
el/la artesano/a *craftsman/woman* 9; *craftsperson* 9
los artes plásticas *plastic arts* 1r
el artículo de belleza *beauty item* 11
el/la artista *artist* 9r
asar *to roast* 10r
asegurar *to assure* 7r
el aserrín *sawdust* 8
el asiento *seat* 12
el asiento de pasillo *aisle seat* 12
el asiento de ventanilla *window seat* 12
asistir *to attend* 1
la aspiradora *vacuum cleaner* 5
el astronomía *astronomy* 1r
asumir *to assume* 12r
asustado/a *scared* 12r
atar *to bind* 13r
aterrizar (c) *to land* 15
el ático *attic* 5r
atlético/a *athletic* Pr
la atmósfera *atmosphere* 7
atractivo/a *attractive* Pr
atrás *back, behind, backwards* 6r
a través de *through* 13
atreverse *to dare* 7r
aun *event* 14r
aunque *although* 14r; *even if* 14r; *even though* 14r
el auto *car* 2
el autobús/bus *bus* 12
la autopista *freeway* 12
el autorretrato *self-portrait* 13
el/la auxiliar de vuelo *flight attendant* 12, 12r
avanzar *to advance* 15r
a veces *sometimes* 1r; *at times* 13r
la avenida *avenue* Pr

a la venta *for sale* 6r
averiguar *to find out* 5r
las aves *poultry, fowl* 10
el avión *plane* 12
ayer *yesterday* 6r
ayudar *to help* 5, 5r
la azafata *flight attendant* 12r
el azar *chance* 13r
el/la azúcar *sugar* 10
azul *blue* 2

# B

el bailarín/la bailarina *dancer* 13
bailar *to dance* 1
la bajada *slope* 7r
bajar *to download* 15
bajo/a *short (in stature)* 2
el balón *ball* 7r
el baloncesto/el básquetbol *basketball* 7
la bañadera *bathtub* 5r
la banana *banana, plantain* 10
el banano *banana, plantain* 10r
bañar(se) *to bathe; to take a bath* 4
el banco *bank* 9
el banco de peces *shoal; school of fish* 15
la banda ancha *broadband* 5r
la bandeja *tray* 10
la bañera *bathtub* 5, 5r
el baño *bathroom* 5
barato/a *inexpensive, cheap* 6
la barbacoa *barbecue pit; barbecue (event)* 5
el barco *ship/boat* 12
barrer *to sweep* 5
el barrio *neighborhood* 5
basar *to base* 13r
básicamente *basically* 4r
el básquetbol *basketball* 7
bastante *enough* Pr; *rather* P
la basura *garbage, trash* 5
la bata *robe* 6
el bate *bat* 7
el batido *milkshake, smoothie* 10r
batir *to beat* 10, 10r
el baúl *trunk* 12
el bautizo *baptism, christening* 4
beber *to drink* 1
la bebida *drink* 3
el béisbol *baseball* 7
las bellas artes *fine arts* 1r
beneficiar *to benefit* 6r
besar *to kiss* 11r

el **beso** *kiss* 4r
la **biblioteca** *library* 1; *library cafe,
coffee shop cafeteria* 1
el/la **bibliotecario/a** *librarian* 9, 9r
la **biblioteca virtual** *virtual library* 15
la **bicicleta** *bicycle* 3r
**bien** *well* P
**bienes raíces** *real estate* 5r
**bien parecido** *good-looking* 2r
**bilingüe** *bilingual* 2
el **billete** *ticket (Spain)* 12r
la **billetera** *wallet* 6
la **bioquímica** *biochemistry* 1r
el **bisonte** *bison* 13r
el **bistec** *steak* 3
**blando/a** *soft* 13
la **blusa** *blouse* 6
**blanco/a** *white* 2
la **boca** *mouth* 11
la **boda** *wedding* 3
la **bodega** *wine cellar* 5
la **bola** *bowling ball* 7r
el **boleto** *ticket* 12r
el **boliche** *bowling* 7r
el **bolígrafo** *ballpoint pen* P
**boliviano/a** *Bolivian* 2
el **bolo** *bowling ball* 7r
la **bolsa/el bolso** *purse* 6
el/la **bombero/a** *firefighter* 9
**bonito/a** *pretty* 2
el **laboratorio** *laboratory* 1, Pr
el **borrador** *eraser* P
el **bosque** *forest* 15
el **bosque tropical** *rain forest* 15
la **bota** *boot* 6
la **botella** *bottle* 10
el **bowling** *bowling* 7r
el **brazo** *arm* 6r, 11
la **broma** *joke* 10r
**brujo/a** *broke* 2r
el **buceo** *snorkeling* 12r
**buenas noches** *good evening* P
**buenas tardes** *good afternoon* P
**¡Buena suerte!** *Good luck!* 1
**buen mozo** *good-looking guy* 2r
**¡Bueno!** *Hello? (on the telephone)* 3r
**bueno/a** *good* 1; *well (health);
physically attractive* 6r
**buenos días** *good morning* P
la **bufanda** *scarf* 6, 6r
el **burgués** *middle class* 13r
el **bus** *bus (Puerto Rico, Cuba)* 12r
el **buscador** *search engine* 15
**buscar** *to look for* 1
la **butaca** *armchair* 5, 7r

# C

el **cabello** *hair* 11
la **cabeza** *head* 6r, 11
la **cabuya** *ammunition* 2r
**cada** *each* 7
**cada... horas** *every . . . hours* 11
la **cadera** *hip* 11
**caer** *to drop* 8r
**caer bien** *to like* 6r
**caer mal** *to dislike* 6r
**caer(se)** *to fall* 11
**café** *brown* 2r
el **café** *cafe, coffee shop* 1;
*coffee* 3
la **cafetería** *cafeteria* 1
**caigue** *lazy (Bolivia)* 13r
la **caja** *box* 6r
la **caja fuerte** *safe* 12
el/la **cajero/a** *cashier* 9
el/la **cajero/a** *cashier* 9r
el **cajero automático** *ATM* 12
el **calcetín** *sock* 6
el **calcio** *calcium* 10r
la **calculadora** *calculator* P
el **cálculo** *calculus* 1r
**callado/a** *quiet* 2
la **calefacción** *heating* 5
el **calendario** *calendar* Pr
el **calentamiento** *warming* 15
la **calidad** *quality* 6r, 13
**caliente** *hot* 3
**callarse** *to keep quiet* 14r
la **calle** *street* 5, Pr
**calmar** *to calm, alleviate* 11r
el **calor** *heat* 5r
el **calzado** *footwear* 6r
**calzar** *to wear a shoe size* 6r
el **calzoncillo** *boxer shorts* 6
la **cama** *bed* 5
la **cámara** *camera* 9r
el **camarero/la camarera** *server,
waiter/waitress* 3
el **camarón** *shrimp* 10
**cambiar** *to change, to exchange* 6
el **cambio** *change* 4r, 14
el **cambur** *banana, plantain* 10r
**caminar** *to walk* 1; *walk* 3r
el **camino** *road; way* 8
el **camión** *bus (Mexico)* 12r
la **camioneta** *bus (Guatemala)* 9r
la **camisa** *shirt* 6
la **camisa de manga corta** *short-
sleeved shirt* 6r
la **camiseta** *T-shirt* 6

el **camisón** *nightgown* 6
la **campaña de publicidad** *publicity
campaign* 15r
el **campeonato** *championship* 7;
*tournament* 7r
el **campeón/la campeona** *champion* 7
el/la **campesino/a** *peasant* 10
el **campo** *countryside* 9
**canadiense** *Canadian* 2
el **canal** *channel* 7r
**cancelar** *to cancel* 12
el **cáncer** *cancer* 11
la **canción** *song* 3
la **canela** *cinnamon* 10r
el **cangrejo** *crab* 10r
**cansado/a** *tired* 2
**cantar** *to sing* 3
la **cantidad** *quantity* 9r
la **capa de ozono** *ozone layer* 15
el **capitán** *captain* 3r
la **capitanía general** *administrative
unit of the Spanish
Empire* 3r
el **capó** *hood* 12
la **cápsula** *capsule* 15
la **cara** *face* 4r, 11; *expression* 15r
el **cargador de celular (del móvil)** *cell
phone charger* 5r
**cariños** *love (closing)* 3r
**caritativo/a** *charitable* 13r
**carmelita** *brown* 2r
el **carnaval** *carnival* 8
la **carne** *meat* 10
la **carne de res** *beef/steak* 10
la **carne molida/picada** *ground
meat* 10
el **carnet de conducir** *driver's
license* 15r
**caro/a** *expensive* 6, 6r
el/la **carpintero/a** *carpenter* 9
la **carrera** *major* 1r; *race* 7
la **carreta** *cart, wagon* 8
la **carretera** *highway* 12
el **carro** *car* 2
la **carroza** *float (in a parade)* 8
el **cartero/la cartera** *mail
carrier* 12
la **casa** *house, home* 1
**casado/a** *married* 2
la **casa editorial** *editorial
house* 13r
**casar(se)** *to get married* 4
**castaño/a** *brown* 2r
el **catarro** *cold* 11
la **cebolla** *onion* 10

la ceja   *eyebrow* 11

la celebración   *celebration* 3

celebrar   *to celebrate* 3

el cementerio   *cemetery* 8

la cena   *dinner, supper* 3

cenar   *to have dinner* 3

el centro   *downtown, center* 5

el centro comercial   *shopping center* 6

el centro de entrenamiento   *training resort* 7r

el centro de salud   *hospital* 11

el/la ceramista   *potter* 9

cerca   *near* 3r

cerca de   *close to, near* 3

el cerdo   *pork* 10

el cereal   *cereal* 3

el cerebro   *brain* 11

la cereza   *cherry* 10

cerrar (ie)   *to close* 4r

la certeza   *certainty* 13r

la cerveza   *beer* 1r, 3

el césped   *lawn* 5

el cesto   *wastebasket* P

el cesto/la cesta   *basket, hoop* 7

el ceviche   *dish of marinated raw fish* 3

las chanclas   *flip-flops* 9r

la chancona   *nerd (Peru)* 3r

chao   *good-bye* Pr

la chaqueta   *jacket* 6

chau   *good-bye* Pr

el/la chef   *chef* 9

el cheque   *check* 9r

el/la chico/a   *boy/girl* P

el chile   *chile pepper* 10r

chileno/a   *Chilean* 2

la chimenea   *fireplace* 5

la chivita   *bus* 1r; *bus (Colombia)* 12r

el choclo   *corn* 10r

el/la chofer (chófer)   *driver; chauffeur* 9

la chuleta   *chop* 10

el chunche   *thing (Costa Rica)* 12r

los churros   *fried dough* 10

el ciclismo   *cycling* 7

el/la ciclista   *cyclist* 7, 7r

la ciencia   *science* 1

las ciencias políticas   *political science* 1

cien/ciento   *hundred* 3r

el/la científico/a   *scientist* 9, 9r

cierto/a   *true* Pr

el cilantro   *cilantro* 10r

el cine   *cinema* 13r; *movies* 1r, 3

el/la cineasta   *filmmaker* 13r

la cintura   *waist* 11

el cinturón   *belt* 6

el/la cirujano/a   *surgeon* 11r

la cita   *date* 6r

citar   *to quote* 14r

la cita textual   *quotation* 7r

la ciudad   *city* 3

el ciudadano   *citizen* 14r

clarear el día   *dawn* 13r

¡claro!   *of course!* 3

la clase turista   *coach class* 12r; *tourist class* 12

el/la cliente/clienta   *client* 6r, 9

climatizado/a   *air-conditioned* 15

la clínica, el centro   *clinic* 11

la clonación   *cloning* 15

el clóset   *closet* 5r

la cobija   *blanket* 5r

el coche   *car* 2

cocido/a   *cooked* 3r

la cocina   *kitchen* 5; *stove* 5r

la cocina fusión   *fusion cuisine* 10r

cocinar   *to cook* 5

el/la cocinero/a   *cook* 5r

codiciado/a   *sought after* 13r

el código   *code* 15r

el codo   *elbow* 11

el cognado   *cognate* Pr

colapsar   *to collapse* 9r

el colectivo   *bus (Argentina)* 12r

el colesterol   *cholesterol* 10r

colocar   *to place* 5r

colombiano/a   *Colombian* 2

los colores   *colors* 2

el collar   *necklace* 6

el comedor   *dining room* 5, 5r

comenzar (ie)   *to begin* 8

comer   *to eat* 1

cómico/a   *comic* Pr

la comida   *food; meal; dinner, supper* 3

la comida chatarra   *junk food* 10r

el comienzo   *beginning* 7r, 8

el comino   *cumin* 10r

¿cómo?   *how/what?* 1r

la cómoda   *dresser* 5

cómodo/a   *comfortable* 9r

¿Cómo es?   *What is he/she/it like?* P

¿Cómo está?   *How are you (formal)?* P

¿Cómo estás?   *How are you (informal)?* P

¡Cómo no!   *Of course!* 9

¿Cómo se dice... ?   *How do you say . . . ?* Pr

¿Cómo se escribe... ?   *How do you spell . . . ?* Pr

¿Cómo se llama usted?   *What's your name? (formal)* P

¿Cómo te llamas?   *What's your name? (familiar)* P

¿Cómo te va?   *How is it going?* 1

el/la compañero/a   *partner, classmate* 1

la compañía de danza   *dance company* 13

la compañía de teatro   *theater company* 13

la compañía/empresa   *company* 9

la comparsa   *group dressed in similar costumes* 8

cómplice   *complicit* 14r

el comportamiento   *behavior* 9r

comprar   *to buy* 1

comprender   *to understand* 1

el compromiso   *engagement* 8r

la computación   *computer science* 1r

la computadora   *computer* P

la computadora portátil   *laptop* P

la comunicación   *communication* 1r

comunicar   *to communicate* 14r

comunicarse   *to reach out to* 14r

con   *with* 1

con cariño   *affectionately* 4r

el concejo municipal   *city council* 14r

la concha   *shell* 8r

la conclusión   *conclusion* 14r

la concordancia   *agreement* 6r

el concurso   *contest* 5r

el condimento   *seasoning* 10

conducir   *to drive* 15r

conectar   *to connect* 15r

conectarse   *to connect* 15

la conexión   *connection* 12r

la confianza   *trust* 14

el conflicto   *conflict* 1r

congelar(se)   *to freeze* 7

conmigo   *with me* 7

conocer (zc)   *to know* 3; *to meet* 13r

el conocimiento   *knowledge* 15

con permiso   *pardon me, excuse me* Pr

el/la consejero/a vocacional   *career counselor* 9r

el consenso   *consensus* 13r

la conservación *preservation* 15

construir (y) *to build* 15; *to construct* 12r

el consultorio *office (of doctor, dentist, etc.)* 9

consumir *to consume* 10r

la contabilidad *accounting* 1r

el/la contable *accountant* 9r

el/la contador/a *accountant* 9r

con tal (de) que *provided that* 14r

contaminado/a *polluted, contaminated* 7

contar *to count* 6r; *to tell* 7r

contemporáneo/a *contemporary* 1r

contento/a *happy, glad* 2

contestar *to answer* Pr

contigo *with you (familiar)* 7

continuar *to continue* 15r

contraer *to contract* 11r

contrario/a *opposing* 7, 7r

el contraste *contrast* 4r

el/la contratista *contractor* 9

contribuir (y) *to contribute* 15

conversador/a *talkative* 2

conversar *to talk, to converse* 1

la copa *(stemmed) glass* 10

la Copa Mundial *World Cup* 7r

el corazón *heart* 11, 11r

la corbata *tie* 6

el cordero *lamb* 10

el coroto *thing (Venezuela)* 6r

el correo *mail* 12

correr *to run* 1

la correspondencia *correspondence* 9r

la corrida (de toros) *bullfight* 8

cortar *to cut; to mow (lawn)* 5

la cortina *curtain* 5

corto/a *short (in length)* 2

la cosa *thing* 6

cosechar *to harvest* 9

costarricense *Costa Rican* 2

costar (ue) *to cost* 4

la costilla *rib* 10

la costumbre *custom* 8

creativo/a *creative* Pr

creer *to believe* 5

la crema *cream* 10

claro *of course* 4r

el crucero *cruise* 12

la clase *class* Pr

el cuaderno *notebook* P

la cuadra *city block* 12

el cuadro *picture, painting* 5

¿cuál(es)? *which?* 1r

¿Cuál es la fecha? *What is the date?* Pr

cuando *when* 14r

¿cuándo? *when?* 1r

¿cuánto/a? *how much?* 1r

¿Cuánto cuesta? *How much is it?* 1

¿cuántos/as? *how many?* 1r

el cuarto *bedroom* 5r; *room; bedroom* 5

el/la cuate *friend (Mexico)* 8r

cubano/a *Cuban* 2

cubista *cubist* 13

la cuchara *spoon* 10

la cucharada *spoonful* 10r

la cucharita *teaspoon* 10

el cuello *neck* 11

la cuenca *river basin* 15

la cuenta corriente *checking account* 9r

el cuento *story* 13

el cuero *leather* 6r

el cuerpo *body* 6r

el cuidado *care* 5r

cuidadosamente *carefully* 4r

cuidar(se) (de) *to take care of* 11

el culantro *cilantro* 10r

el cumpleaños *birthday* 3

cumplir *to fulfill* 7r

curar *to cure* 11

la curiosidad *curiosity* 12r

el currículum *résumé* 9

# D

dañino/a *harmful* 10r

la danza *dance* 13r

dar *to give, to hand* 6

dar de comer *to feed* 9r

dar un paseo *to take a walk* 8

los datos *data* 14

de *of, from* 2

debajo (de) *under* P

deber *should* 1

debido a *due to* 15

débil *weak* 2

decepcionado/a *disappointed* 6r

decir (g, i) *to say, to tell* 4

la decisión *decision* 13r

el dedo *finger* 11

de estatura mediana *average, medium (height)* 2

la deforestación *deforestation* 15

de ida y vuelta *round trip* 12

dejar *to leave* 9

del *of the (contraction of de + el)* 2

delgado/a *thin* 2

la democracia *democracy* 14

de moda *stylish* 6r

de nada *you're welcome* Pr

denunciar *to denounce* 13

el departamento *apartment* 5r

el dependiente/la dependienta *salesperson* 1

el deporte *sport* 7

el/la deportista *athlete* 7r

la depresión *depression* 1r

deprimido/a *depressed* 11

¿de quién? *whose?* 2

la derecha *right* 4

el derecho *right* 14

derecho *straight* 12r

derretir *to melt* 10r

desamparado/a *homeless* 14r

la desaparición *disappearence* 15

desarmar *to disassemble* 9r

desarrollar(se) *to develop* 8r

el desarrollo *development* 13

desayunar *to have breakfast* 4

el desayuno *breakfast* 3

descansar *to rest* 3

descomponer(se) *to break* 9r

describir *to describe* 6r

la descripción *description* 1

el descubrimiento *discovery* 15

descuidado/a *careless* 9r

desde *since* 13

desear *to desire* 5r; *to wish, to want* 2

desechable *disposable* 15r

el desempleo *unemployment* 14

el desfile *parade* 8

el deshielo *thaw, thawing* 15

despacio *slowly* Pr

la despedida *closing* 4r

despedir (i) *to fire* 9r

despedir(se) (i) *to say goodbye* 7r

despegar (u) *to take off (airplane)* 15

despertar(se) (ie) *to wake (someone up)* 4

la despidida *farewell* Pr

el desplazamiento *movement, displacement* 14

después *after, later* 3

después (de) que *after* 14r

destacado/a *outstanding* 13

destacarse *to stand out* 14

el destino *destination* 12r

la desventaja *disadvantage* 5

el **detalle**   *detail* 12r
**detener**   *to stop* 9r
**detrás (de)**   *behind* P
**devolver**   *to return* 6r, 15r
el **día**   *day* P
**diabético/a**   *diabetic* 11r
el **Día del Amor y la Amistad**   *Valentine's Day* 8r
el **Día de Acción de Gracias**   *Thanksgiving* 8r
el **Día de la Independencia**   *Independence Day* 8r
el **Día de la Independencia de México**   *Mexican Independence Day* 8r
el **Día de las Brujas**   *Halloween* 8r
el **Día de los Enamorados**   *Valentine's Day* 8r
el **Día de los Muertos**   *Day of the Dead* 8r
el **Día de la Madre**   *Mother's Day* 8r
el **Día del Padre**   *Father's Day* 8r
el **día feriado**   *legal holiday* 8
el **día festivo**   *holiday* 8
**dialogar**   *to talk* 14r
el **diccionario**   *dictionary* 1
**diciembre**   *December* Pr
**dictatorial**   *dictatorial* 14
el **diente**   *tooth* 10r, 11
el **diente de ajo**   *clove of garlic* 10r
la **dieta**   *diet* 3r
**difícil**   *difficult* 1
**difícilmente**   *difficultly* 4r
**difundir**   *to spread, to disseminate* 15
**difunto/a**   *dead* 8
**¿Diga?, ¿Dígame?**   *Hello? (on the telephone)* 3r
**digitalmente**   *digitally* 13r
**dinámico/a**   *dynamic* Pr
el **dinero en efectivo**   *money in cash* 6
**dirigir (j)**   *to direct* 13
**dirigirse (j)**   *to address* 4r
la **discoteca**   *dance club* 1
**disculparse**   *to apologize* 7r
**discutir**   *to argue* 7
la **diseminación**   *dispersal, dissemination* 15
el **diseñador**   *designer* 5r
el **diseño**   *design* 1r
el **diseño gráfico**   *graphic design* 1r
**disfrazarse**   *to wear a costume* 8
**disfrutar**   *to enjoy* 10
**disponible**   *available* 5r
el **dispositivo**   *device* 5r
**distinguir**   *to distinguish* 13
la **distribución**   *layout* 5r

la **diversificación**   *diversification* 14
las **diversiones**   *leisure activities* 3
**divertido/a**   *fun, funny* 1r; *funny, amusing* 2
**divertirse (ie, i)**   *to have a good time* 8
**divorciado/a**   *divorced* 4
el **lado**   *side* 4r
**doblar**   *to turn* 12
**doblar**   *to fold* 5, 5r
el **documento adjunto**   *attached document* 15; *attachment* 15
el **dólar**   *dollar* 3r
**doler (ue)**   *to hurt, ache* 11
el **dolor**   *pain* 11
**doméstico/a**   *domestic* 5r
el **domingo**   *Sunday* Pr
**dominicano/a**   *Dominican* 2
**dónde**   *where?* Pr
**¿Dónde está... ?**   *Where is . . . ?* P
**dorar**   *to brown* 10r
**dormir(se) (ue)**   *to sleep; to fall asleep* 4
**dormir (ue) la siesta**   *to take a nap* 4
el **dormitorio**   *bedroom* 5r
el **drama**   *drama* 1r
la **droga**   *drug* 1r
la **ducha**   *shower* 5
**duchar(se)**   *to give a shower to; (to take a shower)* 4
la **duda**   *doubt* 13r
**dudoso/a**   *doubtful* 13r
el **dulce**   *candy/sweets* 10
**duplicar**   *to double* 10r
**durante**   *during* 3; *for (time)* 3r
**durar**   *to last* 7
el **durazno**   *peach* 10r
el **DVD**   *DVD; DVD player* P

# E

la **economía**   *economics* 1
**económicamente**   *economically* 5r
**ecuatoriano/a**   *Ecuadorian* 2
el **edificio**   *building* 5
**eficaz**   *efficient* 12r
la **eficiencia**   *efficiency* 14
**eficiente**   *efficient* Pr
el/la **ejecutivo/a**   *executive* 9
el **ejercicio aeróbico**   *aerobic exercise* 11r
**él**   *he* P
**elaborar**   *to produce* 9
la **elección**   *election* 14r
el/la **electricista**   *electrician* 9r
el **electrodoméstico**   *appliance* 5

**elegante**   *elegant* Pr
**elegir (i, i)**   *to choose, to elect* 14
**ellos/ellas**   *they* 1
el **elote**   *corn* 10r
el/la **tenista**   *tennis player* 7
el **embarque**   *departure* 12r
la **emergencia**   *emergency* 9r
la **emigración**   *emigration* 14
el/la **emigrante**   *emigrant* 14
**emigrar**   *to emigrate* 9
**empezar (ie)**   *to begin, to start* 4
el/la **empleado/a**   *employee* 9
**en**   *in* P
**en la actualidad**   *at the present time* 13
**en busca de**   *in search of* 15
el **encaje**   *lace* 13r
**en cambio**   *on the other hand* 4r
**encantado/a**   *pleased/nice to meet you* P
**encantar**   *to delight, to love* 6
**encargar**   *to order* 9r
**encauzar**   *to channel* 7
**encender (ie)**   *to turn on* 15
**encerrar (ie)**   *to lock up* 8
**encontrar (ue)**   *to find* 6
**en contraste**   *in contraste* 4r
**en cuanto**   *as soon as* 14r
la **encuesta**   *Surveys/Polls* 14
la **encuesta de opinión**   *opinion poll* 14r
la **energía solar**   *solar energy* 15
**enérgico/a**   *energetic* 14
**enero**   *January* Pr
**enfadarse**   *to get angry* 7
**enfermarse**   *to become sick* 11
la **enfermedad**   *illness* 11
el/la **enfermero/a**   *nurse* 9
**enfermo/a**   *sick* 11
**enfocarse (qu)**   *to focus* 15
**enfrente (de)**   *in front of* P
el **enlace**   *link* 15
**enojado/a**   *angry* 2
**enojar(se)**   *to get angry* 7r
**¿En qué puedo servirle(s)?**   *How may I help you?* 6
**en realidad**   *in fact, really* 9
la **ensalada**   *salad* 3
**enseguida**   *immediately* 6
**entender (ie)**   *to understand* 4
**enterar**   *to find out* 7r
**enterrar**   *to bury* 8r
**entonces**   *then* 8

entrar (en)  *to go in, to enter* 6
entre  *between, among* P
entregar  *to deliver* 5r
el entrenador/la entrenadora  *coach* 7
el entrenamiento  *training* 7r
entretenerse  *to have fun* 5r
la entrevista  *interview* 9
entrevistar  *to interview* 7r
en vez de  *instead of* 14
enviar  *to send* 9
el equipaje  *luggage* 12
el equipo  *team; equipment* 7
el equipo deportivo  *sports equipment* 7
eres  *you are (familiar)* P
la ermita  *hermitage* 8r
es  *you are (formal), he/she is* P
la escala  *stopover* 12
la escalera  *stairs* 5
el escaparate  *store window* 6
la escena  *scene* 13
la escena retrospectiva  *flashback* 13r
escribir  *to write* 1, 6r, Pr
el escritorio  *desk* P
el escritor/la escritora  *writer* 13
escuchar  *to listen (to)* 1
la escuela  *school* 6r
el escultor/la escultora  *sculptor* 13
ese/a  *that (adjective)* P
el eslogan  *motto* 12r
eso  *that* 5r
los espaguetis  *spaghetti* 3
la espalda  *back* 11
el español  *Spanish* Pr
español/a  *Spanish* 2
la especialidad  *specialty* 9
el/la especialista  *specialist* 11r
las especias  *spices* 10
el espejo  *mirror* 5
el espejo retrovisor  *rearview mirror* 12
la esperanza de vida  *life expectancy* 14
esperar  *to wait for* 9
las espinacas  *spinach* 10
el espíritu  *spirit* 8r
la esposa  *wife* 4
el esposo  *husband* 4
el esquí  *skiing, ski* 7
esquiar  *to ski* 7
la esquina  *corner* 12, 12r
está  *he/she is, you are (formal)* P
está despejado  *it's clear* 7
el estadio  *stadium* 7r
la estadística  *statistics* 1

el estado de ánimo  *mood* 5r
Estados Unidos  *United States* 2r
estadounidense  *U.S. citizen* 2
esta noche  *tonight* 3r
está nublado  *it's cloudy* 7
estar  *to be* 1, Pr
estar de acuerdo  *to agree* 11r
estar de moda  *to be fashionable* 6
estar en forma  *to keep in shape* 7r
estás  *you are (familiar)* P
este/a  *this* 1
el estilo  *style* 5, 5r
Estimado/a  *Dear* 3r
esto  *this* 5r
el estómago  *stomach* 11
estornudar  *to sneeze* 11
estrecho/a  *narrow, tight* 6
la estrella  *star* 13
la estructura  *structure* 1r
el/la estudiante  *student* P
estudiar  *to study* 1
el estudio  *to show* 7r
estudioso/a  *studious* 1
la estufa  *stove* 5
estupendo/a  *fabulous* 3; *stupendous, marvelous* 10r
el evento  *event* 7
evidente  *evident* 12r
evitar  *to avoid* 10r
el examen  *test* 1
examinar  *to examine* 11
excelente  *excellent* 1
la excentricidad  *eccentricity* 15r
exigir  *to demand, exact, require* 14r
el éxito  *success* 10r, 13, Pr
la experiencia  *experience* 9
el experto  *expert* 7r
explicar  *to explain* 6r, 15r
exponer (g)  *to exhibit* 13
la exportación  *export* 14
la exposición  *exhibit* 12r
expresion  *expression* P
la extinción  *extinction* 15
extinguido/a  *extinct* 15r; *extinguished* 15
extrovertido/a  *extroverted* Pr

## F

fabuloso/a  *fabulous, great* 3
fácil  *easy* 1
fácilmente  *easily* 4r
facturar  *to check in (luggage)* 12

la facultad  *school, department* 1
la falda  *skirt* 6
falso/a  *false* Pr
la falta  *lack* 4r
la familia  *The family* 4
famoso/a  *famous* 10r
el/la farmacéutico/a  *pharmacist* 11
la farmacia  *pharmacy* 1r, 11
fascinar  *to fascinate, to be pleasing to* 6
favorito/a  *favorite* 1
febrero  *February* Pr
la fecha  *date* Pr
felicidades  *congratulations* 3
las felicitaciones  *congratulations* 11r
felicitar  *to congratulate* 11r
feo/a  *ugly* 2
el festival  *festival* 8
la festividad  *festivity; holiday* 8
la fibra  *fiber* 10r
la ficha  *note card* 7r
la fiebre  *fever* 11
la fiesta  *celebration* 8; *party* 3, 7r
la figura de autoridad  *authority figure* 6r
fijarse  *to check out* 3r; *to take note* 14r
¡Fíjate qué noticia!  *How about that!* 3r
la filología  *philology* 1r
la filosofía  *philosophy* 1r
finalmente  *finally, at last* 6r
el Fin de Año  *New Year's Eve* 8r
el fin de semana  *weekend* 1
firmar  *to sign* 9r
la física  *physics* Pr
la fisiología  *physiology* 1r
la flor  *flower* 2
fluir  *to flow* 10r
fomentar  *to encourage* 13r
el fondo  *background* 8r
el/la fontanero/a  *plumber* 9
la forma  *shape, form* 13
la foto(grafía)  *photo(graph)* 4
el fracaso  *failure* 13
fracturar(se)  *to fracture, to break* 11
francés/francesa  *French* 2
la frazada  *blanket* 5r
frecuentemente  *frequently* 4r
el fregadero  *kitchen sink* 5
freír (i)  *to fry* 10, 10r

la frente  *forehead* 11
la fresa  *strawberry* 10
el frijol  *bean* 3
el frío  *cold* 5r
frío/a  *cold* 3
frito/a  *fried* 3, 3r
la fruta  *fruit* 3, 10
el fruto de pasión  *passion fruit* 10r
la fuente  *bowl* 10r; *source* 15
fuerte  *strong* 2
fumar  *to smoke* 11
la fundación  *founding* 13
el fútbol  *soccer* 7
el fútbol americano  *football* 7r

# G

las gafas  *glasses* 13r
las gafas de sol  *sunglasses* 6r
la galleta  *cookie* 10
la gamba  *shrimp* 10
el ganado  *cattle* 10r
el ganador  *winner* 5r
ganar  *to win* 5r, 7
la ganga  *bargain* 6r
el garaje  *garage* 5
la garganta  *throat* 11
gastar  *to spend* 6
gemelo/a  *twin* 4, 4r
generalmente  *generally* 4r
generoso/a  *generous* Pr
genéticamente  *genetically* 15, 15r
la gente  *people* 8
la geografía  *geography* 1
el/la gerente (de ventas)  *(sales) manager* 9
el gimnasio  *gymnasium* 1
globalizar  *to globalize* 11r
la gobernación  *administrative unit of the Spanish Empire* 3r
el gobernador  *governor* 3r
gobernar (ie)  *to govern* 14
el gobierno  *government* 11
el gol  *goal* 7
el golf  *golf* 7
golpear  *to knock* 7r
gordo/a  *fat* 2
la gorra  *cap* 6, 6r
grabar  *to record* 13r
gracias  *thanks, thank you* Pr
gracioso/a  *funny* 15r
gradualmente  *gradually* 15r

graduarse  *to graduate* 14r
gráfico/a  *graphic* 15r
grande  *big* 1
la grasa  *fat* 10r
grave  *serious* 11; *seriously ill* 6r
la gripe  *flu* 11
gris  *gray* 2
el grupo  *group* 14r
la guagua  *bus (Puerto Rico, Cuba)* 12r
el guajolote  *turkey* 10r
el guante  *glove* 6
la guantera  *glove compartment* 12
guapo/a  *good-looking, handsome* 2
guardar silencio  *to keep silent* 14r
guatemalteco/a  *Guatemalan* 2
la guía  *guide* 6r
la guitarra  *guitar* 3, 8r
el/la guitarrista  *guitar player* 13
gustar (le)  *to be pleasing to, to like* 6; *to like* 2r

# H

la habitación  *bedroom, room* 5
la habitación doble/sencilla  *double/single room* 12
el/la habitante  *inhabitant* 14
hablar  *to speak* 1
hace  *ago* 4r; *since* 6r
hace fresco  *it's cool* 7
hacer  *to do, to make* 3r
hacer cola  *to stand in line* 12, 12r
hacer la cama  *to make the bed* 3
hacerse  *to become* 14r
Hace sol.  *It's sunny.* Pr
el hacha  *hachet* 13r
la hambre  *hunger* 5r
la hamburguesa  *hamburger* 3
la harina  *flour* 10
hasta  *including; until* 13
Hasta luego.  *See you later.* Pr
Hasta mañana.  *See you tomorrow.* Pr
Hasta pronto.  *See you soon.* Pr
hasta que  *until* 14r
hay  *there is, there are* P
el hecho  *fact* 6r
la heladería  *ice creamery* 6r
el helado  *ice cream* 3, 6r
heredar  *to inherit* 14r
el/la herencia  *inheritance* 14r

la herida  *wound* 11r
el/la herido/a  *injured person* 9r
herido/a  *wounded, injured* 9r
la hermana  *sister* 4
la hermanastra  *stepsister* 4
el hermanastro  *stepbrother* 4
el hermano  *brother* 4
el herrero  *blacksmith; ironworker* 9
hervir (ie, i)  *to boil* 10
el hielo  *ice* 7
la hierba  *herb* 10
el higo  *fig* 10r
la hija  *daughter* 4
el hijo  *son* 4
el hijo único/ la hija única  *only child* 4
hinchar  *to swell* 11r
la hinchazón  *swelling* 11r
la hipótesis  *hypothesis* 13r
hispano/a  *Hispanic* 2
la historia  *history* 1
hola  *hi, hello* P
el hogar  *home* 4r
la hoja  *leaf* 5
el hombre  *man* 3
el hombre/la mujer de negocios  *businessman/woman* 9
el hombro  *shoulder* 11
hondureño/a  *Honduran* 2
la honestidad  *honesty* 14
la hora  *time; hour* Pr
el horario  *schedule* Pr
hornear  *to bake, to microwave* 10r
el (horno) microondas  *microwave (oven)* 5
horrible  *horrible* 15r
el hospital  *hospital* 11
el hotel  *hotel* 12
hoy  *today* P
hoy en día  *nowadays* 8
Hoy es...  *Today is . . .* Pr
el hueso  *bone* 11
el huevo  *egg* 3
las humanidades  *humanities* 1
humano/a  *human* 11

# I

la idea  *idea* 10r
idealista  *idealistic* Pr

la iglesia   *church* 8
la igualdad   *equality* 14
igualmente   *likewise* P
imaginar   *imagine* 3r
el imperfecto   *imperfect* 6r
el impermeable   *raincoat* 6
implementar   *to implement* 14r
importante   *important* Pr
imposible   *impossible* 6r
la impresora   *printer* 5r
impulsivo/a   *impulsive* Pr
inapropiado/a   *inappropriate* 6r
el incendio   *fire* 9
increíble   *incredible* 4r
independiente   *independent* Pr
indicar   *to indicate* 7r
la infancia   *childhood* 6r
infantil   *children's* 14
la infección   *infection* 11
influir   *to influence* 13r
la información   *information* 7r
la informática   *computer science* 1
la infraestructura   *infrastructure* 15
el/la ingeniero/a   *engineer* 9
el iniciado   *apprentice* 13r
la inmigración   *immigration* 14
el inodoro   *toilet* 5
inolvidable   *unforgettable* 13
el inspector   *inspector* 12r
la instrucción   *instruction* 14r
el instrumento   *instrument* 3
inteligente   *intelligent* Pr
el intercambio   *exchange* 15
interesante   *interesting* 1, Pr
interesar   *to interest* 6
internacional   *international* 7r
el/la intérprete   *interpreter* 9; performer, artist 13
la intimidad   *intimacy* 4r
introvertido/a   *introverted* Pr
la inundación   *flood* 15
la investigación   *research* 7r
investigar   *to study, research* 11r
el invierno   *winter* 6r
la invitación   *invitation* 3r, 8
invitar   *to invite* 8
la inyección   *injection* 11
el ipod   *iPod* 5r
ir   *to go* 3r, Pr
ir de compras   *to go shopping* 6
ir de tapas   *to go out for tapas* 1r

ir(se)   *to go away, to leave* 7
la izquierda   *left* 4

## J

el jabón   *soap* 5
jamás   *never* 13r; *(not) ever* 13r
el jamón   *ham* 3
japonés/japonesa   *Japanese* 2
el jardín   *garden* 5
los jeans   *jeans* 6
el jefe/la jefa   *boss* 9
joven   *young* 2, 8r
el/la joven   *young man/woman* 3
la joya   *piece of jewelry* 6
el/la joyero/a   *jeweller* 9
jubilarse   *to retire* 14r
el juego/partido   *game* 7
el jueves   *Thursday* Pr
el/la juez   *judge* 9
el jugador/la jugadora   *player* 7
jugar (ue)   *to play (a game, sport)* 4
jugar (ue) a los bolos   *to bowl* 7
el jugo   *juice* 3
el juguete   *toy* 5r, 6
julio   *July* Pr
junio   *June* Pr
la junta directiva   *board of directors* 14r
juntos/as   *together* 4
el juramento   *oath* 13r

## L

ella   *she* P
el labio   *lip* 11
laboral   *labor-related* 13r
la consola   *game station* 5r
lácteo/a   *dairy (product)* 10
el lago   *lake* 7
lamentar   *to be sorry* 11r
la lana   *wool* 6r
la langosta   *lobster* 10
lanzar   *to throw* 7r
el lápiz   *pencil* P
el lavabo   *bathroom sink* 5
la lavadora   *washer* 5
la lavandería   *dry cleaner* 6r
lavar en seco   *dry clean* 6r
la lección   *lesson* 1r
la leche   *milk* 3
la leche de coco   *coconut milk* 10
la lechuga   *lettuce* 3

la lectura   *reading* Pr
leer   *to read* 1, 7r, Pr
leer por encima   *to skim* 15r
las legumbres   *legumes* 10
lejano/a   *distant* 14r
lejos (de)   *far; (far from)* 3r, 5
la lengua   *language* 1r; tongue 15r
lentamente   *slowly* 4r
las lentejas   *lentils* 10
los lentes de contacto   *contact lenses* 2
levantar   *to raise* Pr
levantar la mano   *to raise one's hand* Pr
levantar(se)   *to raise; to get up* 4
la librería   *bookstore* 1
el libro   *book* 1r, 6r, P
la licuadora   *blender* 10r
ligero/a   *lightweight* 15r
el limón   *lemon* 10
el limpiaparabrisas   *windshield wiper* 12
limpiar   *to clean; to tidy up* 5
lindo/a   *pretty, attractive* 2r
el lío   *mess* 3r
la lista   *list* 10r
listo/a   *clever* 6r; *smart; ready* 2
la literatura   *literature* 1, 13r
el living   *living room* 5r
llamar   *to call* 7r
la llanta   *tire* 12
la llave   *key* 12
la llegada   *arrival* 12r
llegar   *to arrive* 1
llenar   *to fill (out)* 9
lleno/a   *full* 12
llevar   *to wear, to take* 6
llevarse bien   *to get along well* 13r
llover (ue)   *to rain* 7
la lluvia   *rain* 7
la lluvia de ideas   *brainstorming* 7r
loco/a   *crazy* 11r
el/la locutor/a   *radio announcer* 9
lógicamente   *logically* 4r
lograr   *to achieve* 4r
el logro   *achievement* 4r
lo importante   *the important thing* 9
Lo siento.   *I'm sorry (to hear that).* Pr
lo siguiente   *the following* 13r

los recursos  *resources* 15
Lo vamos a pasar muy bien.  *We are going to have a good time.* 3r
la lucha  *fight* 14
luchar  *to fight* 14r
el lucro  *non-profit* 14r
luego  *later* 3; *then* 4r
el lugar  *place* 1
el lujo  *luxury* 12r
el lunes  *Monday* Pr

# M

machacar  *to crush* 10r
la madera  *wood* 9
la madrastra  *stepmother* 4
la madre  *mother* 4
la madrina  *godmother* 4
magnífico/a  *great* 6
el maíz  *corn* 10
mal  *bad* P
la maleta  *suitcase* 12, 12r
el maletero  *trunk* 12
el maletín  *briefcase* 12r
malo/a  *bad* 1; *ill* 6r
la mamá  *mom* 4
la mañana  *morning* P, Pr
mañana  *tomorrow* P
mandar  *to send* 9
mandar saludos  *to say hello* 5r
el mandato  *command* 9r
manejar  *to drive* 12
la mano  *hand* 6r, 11, Pr
la manta  *blanket* 5, 5r
la manteca/la mantequilla  *butter* 10
el mantel  *tablecloth* 10
mantener (g, ie)  *to maintain* 8
mantenerse en contacto  *to stay in touch* 5r
la manzana  *apple* 10
la manzanilla  *chamomile* 11r
el mapa  *map* P
maquillar(se)  *to put makeup on (someone);* 4
el mar  *sea* 3
el maracuyá  *passion fruit* 10
la maravilla  *marvel* 3r
maravilloso/a  *marvelous* 8
la marca  *brand* 7r
el marcador  *highlighter* 5r; *marker* P
la margarina  *margarine* 10
los mariscos  *shellfish* 10
marrón  *brown* 2, 2r
marroquí  *Moroccan* 2

el martes  *Tuesday* Pr
marzo  *March* Pr
más  *more* Pr
más o menos  *more or less* P
más tarde  *later* 3r; *much later* 4r
las matemáticas  *mathematics* Pr
el material  *material* 6r
mayo  *May* Pr
la mayonesa  *mayonnaise* 10
mayor  *old* 2
la mayoría  *majority* 14
el/la mecánico/a  *mechanic* 9r
el médano  *dune* 7r
el/la mediador  *mediator* 13r
la media hermana  *half-sister* 4
las medias  *stockings* 6r
la medicina  *medicine* 1, 11
el/la médico/a  *medical doctor* 9
la medida  *measure* 12r
el medio ambiente  *environment* 15
el medio hermano  *half-brother* 4
los medios de transporte  *means of transportation* 12
me gusta(n)  *I like* 2
Me gustaría...  *I would like . . .* 6
la mejilla  *cheek* 11
mejor  *better* 11r
mejorar  *to improve* 14
el melocotón  *peach* 10r
la melodía  *melody* 8, 13
el melón  *melon* 10
los menonitas  *Mennonites* 13r
el/la menor  *the youngest* 4
menos  *minus* Pr
el mensaje  *message* 14r, 15
mentir  *to lie* 11r
la mentira  *lie* 7r
el menú  *menu* 3r
el mercado  *market* 6
el mes  *month* P
la mesa  *table* 10, P
metal  *metal* 2r
meter  *to insert* 15
meter un gol  *to score a goal* 7
el metro  *subway* 12
el metro cuadrado  *square meter* 5r
mexicano/a  *Mexican* 2
mi amor  *my love (term of endearment)* 3r
mi cielo  *term of endearment* 3r
el micro  *bus (Chile)* 12r
el miedo  *fear* 5r
mientras  *while* 3, 8

el miércoles  *Wednesday* Pr
la migración  *migration* 14
migrar  *to migrate* 11r
mil  *thousand* 3r
mil gracias  *many thanks* 7r
el/la millonario/a  *millionaire* 15r
millón  *million* 3r
mirar  *to look (at)* 1
mi(s)  *my* P
mi vida  *my life (term of endearment)* 3r
la mochila  *backpack* P
moderno/a  *modern* 1r, Pr
módico/a  *moderate* 12r
molestar(le)  *to bother* 11
molido/a  *ground* 10
montar (en bicicleta)  *to ride (a bicycle)* 1
morado/a  *purple* 2
moreno/a  *brunette* 2
morir  *to die* 6r
la mortalidad  *mortality* 14
la mostaza  *mustard* 10
el mostrador  *counter* 12, 12r
mostrar (ue)  *to show* 6
el motor  *motor* 12
mover (ue)  *to move* 11r
muchas veces  *often* 1r
mucho  *much, a lot (adv.)* 2
mucho/a  *many (adj.)* 2
mucho gusto  *pleased/nice to meet you* P
mudarse  *to move* 5r
los muebles  *furniture* 5
muerto/a  *dead* 8; *dead (atmosphere); deceased* 6r
la mujer  *woman* 3
la mujer de negocios  *businesswoman* 9
la multa  *fine/ticket* 15r
mundial  *world, worldwide* 7
la muñeca  *wrist* 11
el mural  *mural* 13
el/la muralista  *muralist* 1r, 13
el músculo  *muscle* 11
el museo  *museum* 12r
la música  *music* 1r, 3; *Music* 8
muy  *very* P

# N

el nacimiento  *birth* 7r
nacional  *national* 7r
las nacionalidades  *Nationalities* 2

**nada** *nothing* 13r
**nadar** *to swim* 3
**nadie** *nobody, no one* 13r
**la naranja** *orange* 3
**naranja** *orange (color)* 2r
**la nariz** *nose* 11
**natal** *native* 10r
**la naturaleza** *nature* 15
**la nave** *ship* 15r
**la Navidad** *Christmas* 8r
**necesario/a** *necessary* 11r
**el negocio** *business* 1r
**negrita** *bold* 4r
**negro/a** *black* 2
**el nervio** *nerve* 11
**nervioso/a** *nervous* 2, Pr
**nevar (ie)** *to snow* 7
**la nevera** *refrigerator* 5r
**ni... ni** *neither . . . nor* 13r
**nicaragüense** *Nicaraguan* 2
**la nieta** *granddaughter* 4
**el nieto** *grandson* 4
**la nieve** *snow* 6r, 7
**nigeriano/a** *Nigerian* 2
**ningún/ninguno/ninguna** *no; no one; not any* 13r
**el niño/a** *child* 4
**el nivel** *level* 14
**no** *no* Pr
**la noche** *night* Pr
**la Nochebuena** *Christmas Eve* 8r
**la Nochevieja** *New Year's Eve* 8r
**No comprendo.** *I don't understand* Pr
**¡No me digas!** *Really!* 4r
**nominar** *to nominate* 13
**no obstante** *however* 11r
**normalmente** *normally* 4r
**norteamericano/a** *North American* 1
**No sé.** *I don't know* Pr
**nosotros/nosotras** *we* 1
**nostálgico** *nostalgic* 14r
**la nota** *note* 1
**la noticia** *news* 3r, 4
**la novela** *novel* 13
**el/la novelista** *novelist* 13, 15r
**la novia** *fiancée, girlfriend* 4
**noviembre** *November* Pr
**el novio** *fiancé, boyfriend* 4
**nuevo/a** *new* 2

**el número** *size* 6r
**nunca** *never* 1r; *(not) ever* 13r

**O**

**o** *or* 13r
**o... o** *either . . . or* 13r
**el objeto** *object* 6r
**la obra** *work* 13
**el/la obrero/a** *worker, laborer* 9r
**obtener** *to obtain* 10r
**obvio/a** *obvious* 13r
**el ocio** *free time* 11r
**octubre** *October* Pr
**la ocupación** *occupation* 9r
**ocupado/a** *busy* 4
**ocurrir** *to occur* 10r
**odiar** *to hate* 8r
**la oficina** *office* 1, Pr
**ofrecer (zc)** *to offer* 9
**el oído** *(inner) ear* 11
**Oiga, por favor.** *Listen, please.* 1r
**¡Oigo!** *Hello? (on the telephone)* 3r
**oír** *to hear* 3r; *to listen* 1r
**oír hablar** *to hear about* 7r
**ojalá que...** *I/we hope that . . .* 11r
**el ojo** *eye* 2
**las Olimpiadas** *Olympics* 7r
**olvidar** *to forget* 10r
**el ómnibus** *bus (Peru)* 12r
**la operación** *surgery* 11r
**la opinión** *opinion* 14r
**optimista** *optimistic* Pr
**el ordenador** *computer* 1r
**ordenar** *to clean* 5
**la oreja** *ear* 6r; *(outer) ear* 11
**la organización** *organization* 14r
**organizar** *to organize* 7r
**oro** *gold* 2r
**la orquesta** *orchestra* 8
**la oscuridad** *dark* 15r
**oscuro/a** *dark* 2
**el otoño** *fall, autumn* 6r
**otra cosa** *something else* 6r
**otra vez** *again* Pr
**otro/a** *other* 4r; *other, another* 3
**la oveja** *sheep* 10
**el OVNI** *UFO* 15r
**¡Oye!** *Listen!* 1r

**P**

**palabra** *word* P
**el/la paciente** *patient* 11
**paciente** *patient (adj.)* Pr
**el padrastro** *stepfather* 4
**el padre** *father* 4
**los padres** *parents* 4
**el padrino** *godfather* 4
**pagar** *to pay (for)* 6
**la página** *page* Pr
**el país** *country, nation* 3
**el paisaje** *landscape* 13
**la palabra** *word* 6r
**la palabra clave** *key word* 6r
**el paladar** *palate* 13r
**el palo** *golf club* 7
**las palomitas de maíz** *popcorn* 10r
**la palta** *avocado* 10r
**el pan** *bread* 3
**la panadería** *bakery* 6r
**panameño/a** *Panamanian* 2
**el pan dulce** *bun, small cake* 10
**la pantalla** *screen* P
**los pantalones** *pants* 6
**los pantalones cortos** *shorts* 6
**las pantimedias** *pantyhose* 6
**el pan tostado** *toast* 3
**el pañuelo** *handkerchief* 6
**el papá** *dad* 4
**la papa** *potato* 3
**las papas fritas** *French Fries* 3
**el penalti** *penalty* 7r
**el pendiente** *earring* 6r
**la pendiente** *slope* 7r
**pensar de** *to think of/about (opinion)* 4r
**pensar en** *to think of/about* 4r
**pensar (ie)** *to plan to* 4; *to think* 4
**el pepino** *cucumber* 10
**pequeño/a** *small* 1
**la pera** *pear* 10
**perder (ie)** *to lose* 7
**perderse (ie)** *to get lost* 12
**la pérdida** *loss* 15
**perdón** *pardon me, excuse me* Pr
**el perejil** *parsley* 10r
**perezoso/a** *lazy* 2
**perfeccionista** *perfectionistic* Pr
**perfectamente** *perfectly* 4r
**perfecto/a** *perfect* 10r

el periódico   *newspaper* 3; *periodical, newspaper* 1r
el/la periodista   *journalist* 9, 9r
el permiso de conducir   *driver's license* 15r
pero   *but* 1
el perro   *dog* 4, 11r
la persona   *person* P
el personaje principal   *main character* 13
la perspectiva   *perspective* 11r
las pertenencias   *belongings* 12r
peruano/a   *Peruvian* 2
la pesa   *weight* 10r
la pesadilla   *nightmare* 12r
el pescado   *fish* 3, 10
pesimista   *pessimistic* Pr
la pestaña   *eyelash* 11
el petróleo   *petroleum* 15r
picado/a   *chopped* 10r; *ground* 10
picar   *to chop* 10r
picar(se)   *to itch* 11r
el pie   *foot* 2r, 5r, 11
la piel   *skin* 10r
la piel de gallina   *goosebumps* 15r
la pierna   *leg* 2r, 6r, 11
el/la piyama   *pajamas* 6
la pileta   *swimming pool* 5r
el pimentón   *paprika* 10r
la pimienta   *pepper* 10
la pimienta roja   *red pepper* 10r
el pimiento (verde)   *(green) pepper* 10
la piña   *pineapple* 10
el pintor/la pintora   *painter* 13
la pintura   *painting* 13
la piscina   *swimming pool* 5, 5r
el piso   *floor; apartment* 5
pitar   *to whistle* 7
la pizarra   *chalkboard* P
la placa   *license plate* 12
el placer   *pleasure* 7r
el plan   *plan* 7r
el planeta   *planet* 15
plástico   *plastic* 2r
el plátano   *banana, plantain* 10
el plato   *plate, dish* 10
la plaza   *city square* 13r
el/la plomero/a   *plumber* 9
planchar   *to iron* 5
la planta baja   *first floor, ground floor* 5
la población   *population* 14
pobre   *poor* 2

la pobreza   *poverty* 14
poco   *few, little* 4r; *a little* 4r
polaco/a   *Polish* 2
poco a poco   *little by little* 4r
poco después   *a little later* 4r
poder (ue)   *to be able to, can* 4
el poema   *poem* 13; *poema* 1r
la poesía   *poetry* 13
el/la poeta   *poet* 13
el/la policía   *policeman/woman* 9
políglota   *polyglot, multilingual* 14
el pollo   *chicken* 3
el pomelo   *grapefruit* 10
poner   *to put* 3r
poner la mesa   *to set the table* 3
ponerse en marcha   *to go into effect* 15r
ponerse (g)   *to become* 14r; *to put on (clothes)* 6r
popular   *popular* Pr
la popularidad   *popularity* 7r
popularizar (c)   *to popularize* 13
por   *by; for; along; through; in (time)* 3r
el porcentaje   *percentage* 14
por ciento   *percent* 3r
por cierto   *by the way* 9
por ejemplo   *for example* 3r
por eso   *that is why* 3r
por favor   *please* Pr
por fin   *finally, at last* 3r, 15r
por lo menos   *at least* 3r
por la mañana   *in the morning* 3r
por la noche   *in the evening* 3r
el poroto   *bean* 10r
por otro lado   *on the other hand* 4r
porque   *because* 1r
¿por qué?   *why?* 1r
por supuesto   *of course* 3r
por la tarde   *in the afternoon* 3r
por teléfono   *by telephone* 3r
portugués/portuguesa   *Portuguese* 2
por último   *finally, at last* 4r
por un lado   *on the one hand* 4r
posible   *possible* 13r
la posición   *position* P
potente   *powerful* 15r
practicar   *to practice* 1
preceder   *to precede* 14
el precio   *price* 6, 6r
precioso/a   *beautiful* 6
preferir (ie)   *to prefer* 4
la pregunta   *question* Pr
premiar   *to reward* 9r

el premio   *award, prize* 13
preocupar(se)   *to concern; to be concerned, worried* 11r
preparar   *to prepare* 5
el preparativo   *preparation* 8
la presentación   *introduction* P
presente   *here (present)* Pr
presidencial   *presidential* 14r
el presidente/la presidenta   *president* 14
prestar   *to lend* 6r
el pretérito   *preterit* 6r
prever   *to foresee, to predict* 13r
la primavera   *spring* 6r
la primera clase   *first class* 12, 12r
primero/a   *first* 4r
el primo/a   *cousin* 4
la prisa   *speed, haste* 5r
probable   *probable* 13r
probar   *to try* 10r
probarse (ue)   *to try on* 6
el problema   *problem* 1r, 13r
la procesión   *procession* 8
producir   *to produce* 15r
el producto   *product* 10
el profesor/la profesora   *professor, teacher* P
el programa   *program* 1r
el progreso   *progress* 14r
prohibir   *to prohibit* 11r
el promedio   *average* 8r, 14
prometedor/a   *promising* 13
promocionar   *to advertise* 6r
el pronóstico del tiempo   *weather forecast* 7r
propio/a   *own* 9
la propuesta   *proposal* 7r
la proteína   *protein* 10r
el proveedor de comida   *caterer* 9r
el proveedor de salud   *health care provider* 11
la proximidad   *proximity* 14
próximo/a   *next* 3r
la (p)sicología   *psychology* 1, Pr
el/la (p)sicólogo/a   *psychologist* 9
el/la (p)siquiatra   *psychiatrist* 11r
el plato   *dish, plate* 5
la publicidad   *publicity* 6r
el pueblo   *village* 5
la puerta   *door* P
la puerta (de salida)   *gate* 12
puertorriqueño/a   *Puerto Rican* 2
el puesto   *position* 9

**el pulmón**  *lung* 11
**la pulsera**  *bracelet* 6
**el punto culminante**  *climax* 13r
**el punto de vista**  *point of view* 11r
**el pupitre**  *student desk* P
**la playa**  *beach* 1
**la plaza**  *plaza, square* 1

# Q

**¿qué?**  *what?* 1r
**¡Qué bárbaro!**  *Great!* 7r
**¡Qué bien/bueno!**  *That's great!* 4r
**¡Qué casualidad!**  *What a suprise/coincidence!* 1r
**quedar**  *to arrange to meet* 8; *to fit; to be left over* 6
**¿Qué día es hoy?**  *What day is it?* Pr
**¿Qué fecha es hoy?**  *What is the date?* Pr
**¿Qué hay?**  *Hello? (on the telephone)* 3r
**¿Qué hora es?**  *What time is it?* Pr
**¡Qué increíble!**  *How incredible!* 1r
**la queja**  *complaint* 13r
**quejarse**  *to complain* 7r
**¡Qué lástima!**  *What a pity!* 1
**querer (ie)**  *to want* 4
**querido/a**  *dear* 3r
**Querido/a**  *Dear* 3r
**el queso**  *cheese* 3
**el queso crema**  *cream cheese* 10
**¿Qué tal?**  *What's up, What's new? (informal)* P
**¿Qué te/le(s) pasa?**  *What's wrong (with you/them)?* 11
**¿Qué te parece?**  *What do you think?* 3
**¿Qué tiempo hace?**  *What is the weather like?* Pr
**¿Quién es... ?**  *Who is . . . ?* P
**¿quién(es)?**  *who?* 1r
**la quijada**  *jawbone* 13r
**Quisiera...**  *I would like . . .* 6
**quitar(se)**  *to take away; to take off* 4

# R

**el radiador**  *radiator* 12
**el/la radio**  *radio* 5
**el/la radiólogo/a**  *radiologist* 11r
**rallar**  *to grate* 10r

**rápidamente**  *quickly* 4r
**rápido/a**  *fast* 3
**la raqueta**  *racquet* 7
**el rasgo**  *feature, trait* 12r
**la razón**  *reason* 5r
**la realidad**  *reality* 13r
**realizar (c)**  *to carry out* 14
**realmente**  *of course* 9; *in fact, really* 9; *really* 4r
**reaparecer**  *to reappear* 11r
**la rebaja**  *sale* 6
**rebajado/a**  *marked down* 6
**la recámara**  *bedroom* 5r
**la recepción**  *front desk* 12
**la receta**  *prescription* 11; *receipt* 10r; *recipe* 10
**recetar**  *to prescribe* 11
**recibir**  *to receive* 14r
**reciclado/a**  *recycled* 15
**reclamar**  *to claim* 12r
**recoger (j)**  *to pick up* 5
**la recomendación**  *recommendation* 15r
**recomendar (ie)**  *to recommend* 10
**recopilar**  *to compile* 14r
**recordar(se) (ue)**  *to remember* 4r, 8
**recorrer**  *to cover, to travel* 12; *to travel, to cover (distance)* 7
**el recuerdo**  *memory* 13; *souvenir* 6r
**la red**  *net* 7; *network* 5r
**reducir**  *to reduce* 11r
**reflejar**  *to reflect* 5r, 13
**el refrán**  *proverb* 12r
**el refresco**  *soda; soft drink* 3
**el refrigerador**  *refrigerator* 5, 5r
**regalar**  *to give (a present)* 6
**el regalo**  *gift* 3r; *present* 6
**regar (ie)**  *to water* 5
**regatear**  *to haggle* 6r
**el régimen**  *regime* 14
**la región**  *region* 15r
**regular**  *fair* Pr
**regularmente**  *regularly* 4r
**reír (i)**  *to laugh* 7r
**religioso/a**  *religious* Pr
**el relleno**  *filling* 10r
**relleno/a**  *filled* 3r
**el reloj**  *clock* P
**el remedio**  *remedy, medicine* 11
**el renacimiento**  *rebirth* 8r
**el rendimiento**  *performance* 9r
**repetir (i)**  *to repeat* 4r
**repoblar**  *to reforest* 15; *to repopulate* 15r
**el reproductor de CDs**  *CD player* 5r

**el reproductor de DVDs**  *DVD player* 5r
**la reputación**  *reputation* 7r
**la reseña**  *review* 13r
**la reserva natural**  *nature preserve* 15
**reservar**  *to make a reservation* 12
**respetar**  *to respect* 13r
**respirar**  *to breathe* 11
**responder**  *to respond* 15r
**responsable**  *responsible* Pr
**el restaurante**  *restaurant* 1r
**el resultado**  *the result* 7r
**resumir**  *to summarize* 4r
**relativamente**  *relatively* 4r
**el reto**  *challenge* 15
**retornar**  *to return* 11r
**retratar**  *to portray* 13
**la reunión**  *meeting, gathering* 3
**reunirse**  *to get together, to meet* 8
**revisar**  *to inspect* 12
**la revista**  *magazine* 3
**la revista de corazón**  *gossip magazine* 13
**el rey/la reina**  *king/queen* 8
**largo/a**  *long* 2
**el riachuelo**  *creek* 4r
**rico/a**  *delicious (food)* 6r; *rich, wealthy* 2, 6r
**el riel**  *rail* 15, 15r
**la risa**  *laughter* 12r
**el robo**  *robbery* 10r
**el robot**  *robot* 15
**rociar**  *to spray* 8r
**el rocoto**  *pepper* 3r
**rodear**  *to surround* 13
**la rodilla**  *knee* 11
**rojo/a**  *red* 2
**romántico/a**  *romantic* Pr
**romper**  *to break* 15r; *to tear* 15r
**la ropa**  *clothes* 6
**la ropa de estar en casa**  *loungewear* 6r
**la ropa deportiva**  *sportswear* 6r
**la ropa formal**  *formalwear* 6r
**la ropa informal**  *casualwear* 6r
**la ropa interior**  *underwear* 6, 6r
**rosa**  *pink* 2
**rosado/a**  *pink* 2
**el rotulador**  *marker* P
**rubio/a**  *blond* 2
**la ruda**  *rue (herb)* 11r
**la rueda**  *wheel* 12
**el ruido**  *noise* 5r, 8

las ruinas *ruins* 5
la rutina *routine* 3r

# S

la sala *living room* 5, 5r
el sábado *Saturday* Pr
la sábana *sheet* 5
saber *to know* 3r, Pr
sacar *to take out* 5
sacar buenas/malas notas *to get good/bad grades* 1
el saco *blazer, jacket* 6
la sala de espera *waiting area* 12r
la sal *salt* 10
la salida *departure* 12r
la salida de emergencia *emergency exit* 12
la salida del sol *sunrise* 13r
salir *to go out* 3r
el salón *living room* 5r
el salón de clase *classroom* P
la salsa con queso *nacho cheese sauce* 10r
la salsa de tomate *tomato sauce* 10
saltear *to sauté* 10r
la salud *Health* 11
saludable *healthy* 10r
el saludo *greeting* 1
salvadoreño/a *Salvadorian* 2
la sandalia *sandal* 6
el sándwich *sandwich* 1r, 3
el sanatorio *hospital* 11r
las compras *shopping* 6
la secadora *dryer* 5
secar(se) *to dry (oneself)* 4
la sed *thirst* 5r
sedentario/a *sedentary* 11r
seguir (i) *to follow, to go on* 4
seguir (i) derecho *to go straight* 12
según *as* 14r; *according to* 14r
seguramente *surely, certainly* 4r
la seguridad *security* 13r
seguro/a *certain* 13r
la semana *week* P, Pr
la semilla *seed* 8
el seminario *seminar* 1r
la señal *signal* 9
el senderista *hiker* 4r
la señora (Sra.) *Ms., Mrs.* P
la señorita (Srta.) *Ms, Miss* P
el señor (Sr.) *Mr.* P

sentarse (ie) *to sit down* 4
sentimental *sentimental* Pr
sentir(se) (ie, i) *to be sorry* 11r; *to feel* 4, 11
septiembre *September* Pr
ser *to be* 2, Pr
serio/a *serious* 11, Pr
la servilleta *napkin* 10
servir (i) *to serve* 4
si *if* 3
sí *yes* P
siempre *always* 1r
sigilosamente *discreetly* 13r
el significado *meaning* 4r
siguiente *following* 14r
la silla *chair* P
el silencio *silence* 14r
silvestre *wild* 10r
el símbolo *symbol* 13
simpático/a *friendly* 14r; *nice, charming* 2
simplemente *simply* 4r
sin *without* 7r
sincero/a *sincere* Pr
sin embargo *nevertheless* 9, 9r
sin que *without* 14r
el síntoma *symptom* 11
las medias *stockings, socks* 6
sobre *on, above* P
sobrevivir *to survive* 9
la sobrina *niece* 4
el sobrino *nephew* 4
sobrio/a *sober* 14r
social *social* 1r
la sociedad *Society* 14
la sociología *sociology* 1
el sofá *sofa* 5
sofreír *to fry lightly* 10r
el sol *sun* Pr
solicitar *to apply (for)* 9
la solicitud *application* 9
sólo *only (adv.)* 1
soltero/a *single* 2
el sombrero *hat* 6, 6r
son *equals* Pr
sonar *to sound* 7r
la sopa *soup* 3
la sorpresa *surprise* 7r
sorprender *to surprise* 12r
el sostén *bra* 6
el sótano *basement* 5r
soy *I am* P
suave *soft* 8
subir *to get into* 15r; *to go up* 10r

subrayar *to underline* 4r
subvencionar *subsidize* 13r
la sucursal *branch (business)* 14
la sudadera *sweatshirt; jogging suit* 6
el sueldo *salary* 9
el sueño *dream* 5r; *sleep* 5r
la suerte *luck* 3r, 5r
el suéter *sweater* 6
sugerir *to suggest* 14r
el supermercado *supermarket* 6, 10r
surgir (j) *to emerge* 13
surrealista *surrealist* 13
su(s) *his/her/their* P
sustentar *to support* 12r
el susto *fear* 12r

# T

la talla *size (clothes)* 6
el taller *workshop* 9
el tamal *tamale* 3r
el tamaño *size* 6r
también *also, too* 1
tampoco *neither; not* 13r
tan pronto (como) *as soon as* 14r
tanto/a... como *as much ... as* 8r
tapar *to cover* 10r
las tapas *tapas* 1r
la tarde *afternoon* Pr
tarde *late* 4
la tarea *chore, task* 5r; *homework* 1, Pr
la tarjeta de crédito *credit card* 6
la tarjeta de embarque *boarding pass* 12, 12r
la tarjeta magnética *key card* 12
la tarta *pie* 10r
la tasa *rate* 14
la tasa de cambio *exchange rate* 8r
la taza *cup* 10, 10r
la tela *fabric* 2r
el té *tea* 3
el teatro *theater* 8, 13r
el/la técnico/a *technician* 9
la tecnología *technology* 15
te gusta(n) *you (familiar) like* 2
el tejado *roof* 9r
el teléfono *telephone* 3
el teléfono celular/móvil *cell phone* 15r

la telenovela   *soap opera* 11r
el televisor   *television set* P
el tema   *theme* 13
temer   *to fear* 11
temprano   *early* 4
tender (ie)   *to hang (clothes)* 5
el tenedor   *fork* 10
tener (g, ie)   *to have* 4
tener... años   *to be . . . old* 5r
tener calor   *to be hot* 5r
tener cuidado   *to be careful* 5r
tener dolor de...   *to have a(n) . . . ache* 11
tener éxito   *to be successful* 10r, 13
tener frío   *to be cold* 5r
tener hambre   *to be hungry* 5r
tener mala cara   *to look terrible* 11
tener miedo   *to be afraid* 5r
tener prisa   *to be in a hurry, rush* 5r
tener que   *to have to* 4r
tener razón   *to be right, correct* 5r
tener sed   *to be thirsty* 5r
tener sueño   *to be sleepy* 5r
tener suerte   *to be lucky* 5r
Tengo... años.   *I am . . . years old.* 2
tengo/tienes   *I have/you have* 1
el tenis   *tennis* Pr
el/la tenista   *tennis player* 7r
la tensión (arterial)   *(blood) pressure* 11
la terapia   *therapy* 13r
tercero/a   *third* 5r
terminar   *to finish* 14r
el termómetro   *thermometer* 11
la terraza   *deck* 9r; *terrace* 5
el terrorismo   *terrorism* 14r
el testamento   *will* 14r
la tía   *aunt* 4
el tiempo   *time; weather* Pr; *weather* 7
el tiempo libre   *free time* 3
la tienda   *store* 6
tiene   *he/she has; you (formal) have* 2
la tierra   *land, soil* 15
tímido/a   *timid* Pr
la tina   *bathtub* 5r
la tintorería   *dry cleaner* 14r
el tío   *uncle* 4
típico/a   *typical* 3
titular(se)   *to be called* 13
el título   *motto* 12r; *title* 4r
la tiza   *chalk* P
la toalla   *towel* 5

el tobillo   *ankle* 11
tocar (un instrumento)   *to play (an instrument)* 3
todas las semanas   *every week* 1r
todavía   *still, yet* 10
todo   *everything* 13r
todo/a   *every* 1r
todos/as   *all* 13r; *everybody* 2, 13r
todos los días   *every day* 1r
todos los meses   *every month* 1r
tomar   *to take; to drink* 1
tomar apuntes/notas   *to take notes* 1
tomar asiento   *to take a seat* 9r
tomar el sol   *sunbathe* 1r; *to sunbathe* 3
el tomate   *tomato* 3
el tono   *tone* 14r
tonto/a   *silly, foolish* 2
torcer(se) (ue)   *to twist* 11
el torneo   *tournament* 7r
el toro   *bull* 8
la toronja   *grapefruit* 10
torpe   *clumsy* 6r
la tos   *cough* 11
toser   *to cough* 11
tostar   *to toast* 10r
la tostada   *toast* 10
tóxico/a   *toxic* 1r
trabajador/a   *hardworking* 2
trabajar   *to work* 1
el trabajo   *work* 5, 9
el trabajo de campo   *fieldwork* 13r
la tradición   *tradition* 8
tradicional   *traditional* Pr
tradicionalmente   *traditionally* 4r
traducir (zc)   *to translate* 7
traer   *to bring* 3
el tráfico   *traffic* 15r
el tráfico de drogas   *drug trafficking* 14
el traje   *suit* 6
el traje de baño   *bathing suit* 6
el traje de chaqueta   *suit* 6
el traje pantalón   *pantsuit* 6
tranquilo/a   *tranquil* Pr
tranquilamente   *tranquilly* 4r
transitar   *to cross; to move back and forth* 12r
el tratamiento médico   *medical treatment* 11
tratar   *to treat* 11; *to be about* 13; *to try* 5r
el trayecto   *route* 12
el tren   *train* 12

triste   *sad* 2, 14r
tropezarse   *to stumble* 15r
tú   *you (familiar)* P
tu(s)   *your (familiar)* P
último/a   *last* 8

# U

la uña de gata   *cat's claw (herb)* 11r
una semana atrás   *a week ago* 6r
una vez   *once* 12, 13r
unificar (qu)   *to unify* 15
la universidad   *university* 1
un poco   *a little* 4
un/una   *a, an* P
urgente   *urgent* 11r
uruguayo/a   *Uruguayan* 2
usar   *to use* 2
usted   *you (formal)* P
ustedes   *you (plural)* 1
útil   *useful* P
la uva   *grape* 10

# V

las vacaciones   *vacation* 3
la vacante   *opening* 9
vacío/a   *empty* 12
la vainilla   *vanilla* 10
valer   *to be worth* 6
los vaqueros/jeans   *jeans* 6
el vaso   *glass* 10
Vaya.   *Go.* Pr
la vecina   *neighbor* 5r
el/la vecino/a   *neighbor* 5r
el vegetal/la verdura   *vegetable* 3
vegetariano/a   *vegetarian* 12r
la velocidad   *speed* 12
la vena   *vein* 11
¡Ven/Anda, anímate!   *Come on, cheer up!* 3r
el/la vendedor/a   *salesperson,* 9; *seller* 6r
vender   *to sell* 6, 6r
venezolano/a   *Venezuelan* 2
venir (g, ie)   *to come* 4
la venta   *sale* 9r
la ventaja   *advantage* 5
la ventana   *window* 1r, P
la ventanilla   *window* 12r
el ventilador   *fan* 5
ver   *to see* 1
el verano   *summer* 6r
verbos   *verbs* P

¿**verdad?** *right?* 1
**verdad** *true* 13r
la **verdad** *truth* 7r
**verde** *green; not ripe* 2
la **verdura** *vegetable* 10
**ver(se)** *to look, appear* 11r
el **vestido** *dress* 6
el **vestido de verano** *summer dress* 6r
**vestir(se) (i)** *to dress; to get dressed* 4
el/la **veterinario/a** *veterinarian* 9r
**viajar** *to travel* 12
el **viaje** *trips* 12
el **videojuego** *video game* 15, 15r
el **vidrio** *glass* 2r
**viejo/a** *old* 2, 8r
el **viento** *wind* 7
el **viernes** *Friday* Pr
el **vinagre** *vinegar* 10
el **vino** *wine* 3

el **virreinato** *administrative unit of the Spanish Empire* 3r
**virtualmente** *virtually* 15
la **viruela** *smallpox* 11r
**visitar** *to visit* 4
la **vista** *view* 5
la **vitamina** *vitamin* 11r
la **vivienda** *dwelling; apartment* 5r; *housing* 5
**vivir** *to live* 1
**vivo/a** *alive* 6r; *lively (personality)* 6r
**volador/a** *flying* 15, 15r
el **volante** *steering wheel* 12
**volar (ue)** *to fly* 12
el **vóleibol** *volleyball* 7
el **volibol** *volleyball* 7r
**volver (ue)** *to return* 4
la **voz** *voice* 13
el **vuelo** *flight* 12

# Y

**y** *and* P; *plus* Pr
**ya** *already* 10
**yo** *I* P
el **yogur** *yogurt* 10
la **yuca** *yucca* 3r

# Z

la **zanahoria** *carrot* 10
las **zapatillas de deporte** *tennis shoes* 6
las **zapatillas** *slippers* 6
los **zapatos** *shoes* 6
los **zapatos de tacón** *high-heeled shoe* 6
el **zarcillo** *earring* 6r
la **zona** *area* 5
la **zona peatonal** *pedestrian area* 10r

# Appendix 4

## English to Spanish Glossary

### A

**a** un/una
**a little later** poco después
**a lot (of)** mucho/a (adj.); mucho (adv.)
**to abound** abundar
**above** sobre
**access** el acceso
**accessory** el accesorio
**to accompany** acompañar
**according to** según
**accountant** el/la contador/a (contable)
**accounting** la contabilidad
**to ache** doler (ue)
**to achieve** lograr
**achievement** el logro
**to act** actuar
**active** activo/a
**activity** la actividad
**actor** el actor
**actress** la actriz
**ad, advertisement** el anuncio
**to adapt** adaptar
**adaptation** la adaptación
**to add** agregar; añadir
**to address** dirigirse
**adjustment** la adaptación
**advance** el adelanto
**to advance** avanzar
**advantage** la ventaja
**to advertise** promocionar
**advisable** aconsejable
**to advise** aconsejar
**aerobic exercise** el ejercicio aeróbico
**affectionately** con cariño
**to affirm** afirmar
**after** después; después (de) que
**afternoon** la tarde
**again** otra vez
**ago** hace
**to agree** estar de acuerdo
**agreeable** agradable
**agreement** la concordancia
**air-conditioned** climatizado/a
**air conditioning** el aire acondicionado

**airline** la aerolínea/línea aérea
**airport** el aeropuerto
**aisle seat** el asiento de pasillo
**alacrity** la alacridad
**algebra** la álgebra
**alive** vivo/a
**all** todos/as
**allergic** alérgico/a
**to alleviate** calmar
**along** por
**already** ya
**also** también
**alternative** alternativo/a
**although** aunque
**always** siempre
**ambitious** ambicioso/a
**ammunition** la cabuya
**ample** amplio/a
**amusing** divertido/a
**anatomy** la anatomía
**ancestor** el antepasado
**and** y
**angry** enojado/a
**ankle** el tobillo
**to answer** contestar
**Antarctica** la Antártida
**antes** before
**antes (de) que** before
**anthropology** la antropología
**antibiotic** el antibiótico
**anxiety** la ansiedad
**any, some** algún/alguno/alguna
**anything** algo
**apartment** el apartamento; el departamento; el piso; la vivienda
**to apologize** disculparse
**apple** la manzana
**appliance** el electrodoméstico
**application** la aplicación; la solicitud
**to apply (for)** solicitar
**apprentice** el iniciado
**appropriate** apropiado/a
**April** abril
**architect** el/la arquitecto/a
**architecture** la arquitectura
**area** la zona
**Argentinian** argentino/a
**to argue** discutir

**arm** el brazo
**armchair** la butaca
**arrival** la llegada
**to arrive** llegar
**arrogant** arrogante
**art** el arte
**artist** el/la artista; el/la intérprete
**as** según
**as much . . . as** tanto … como
**as soon as** as en cuanto
**to ask for** pedir (i)
**to assist** ayudar
**to assume** asumir
**to assure** asegurar
**astronomy** el astronomía
**at** a
**at times** a veces
**athlete** el/la deportista
**athletic** atlético/a
**ATM** el cajero automático
**atmosphere** la atmósfera
**attached document** el documento adjunto
**to attend** asistir
**attic** el ático
**attractive** atractivo/a; bonito/a; bueno/a; guapo/a; lindo/a
**August** agosto
**aunt** la tía
**authority figure** la figura de autoridad
**available** disponible
**avenue** la avenida
**average** el promedio
**avocado** el aguacate; la palta
**to avoid** evitar
**award, prize** el premio

### B

**back** al fondo, atrás; la espalda
**background** el fondo
**backpack** la mochila
**backwards** atrás
**bad** mal; malo/a
**bakery** la panadería
**ball** el balón/la pelota
**ballpoint pen** el bolígrafo

**A40**

banana   el banano; el cambur; el plátano; la banana
bank   el banco
baptism, christening   el bautizo
barbecue pit; barbecue (event)   la barbacoa
bargain   la ganga
to base   basar
baseball   el béisbol
basement   el sótano
basically   básicamente
basket (hoop)   el/la cesto/a
basketball   el baloncesto/el básquetbol
bat   el bate
to bathe; to take a bath   bañar(se)
bathing suit   el traje de baño
bathroom   el baño
bathroom sink   el lavabo
bathtub   la bañera; la tina; la bañadera; la bañera
to be   estar; ser
to be able to, can   poder (ue)
to be afraid   tener miedo
to be called   titular(se)
to be careful   tener cuidado
to be cold   tener frío
to be crazy (Cuba)   estar trocá
to be fashionable   estar de moda
to be glad (about)   alegrarse (de)
to be happy   alegrarse
to be hot   tener calor
to be hungry   tener hambre
to be in a hurry (Colombia)   estar de afán
to be in a hurry, rush   tener prisa
to be lucky   tener suerte
to be . . . old   tener … años
to be pleasing to, to like   gustar
to be right, correct   tener razón
to be sleepy   tener sueño
to be sorry   lamentar; sentir(se) (ie, i)
to be successful   tener éxito
to be thirsty   tener sed
to be worth   valer
beach   la playa
bead   la cuenta
bean   el frijol; el poroto
to beat   batir
beautiful   precioso/a
beauty item   el artículo de belleza
beauty salon, barbershop   la peluquería
because   porque
to become   hacerse; poner(se)
to become sick   enfermarse
bed   la cama

bedroom   el cuarto; el dormitorio; la habitación; la alcoba; la recámara
beef/steak   la carne de res
beer   la cerveza
to begin   comenzar (ie)
to begin, to start   empezar (ie)
beginning   el comienzo
behavior   el comportamiento
behind   atrás; detrás (de)
to believe   creer
belongings   las pertenencias
below   abajo
belt   el cinturón
to benefit   beneficiar
besides   además
better   mejor
between, among   entre
bicycle   la bicicleta
big   grande
bilingual   bilingüe
to bind   atar
biochemistry   la bioquímica
birth   el nacimiento
birthday   el cumpleaños
bison   el bisonte
black   negro/a
blackout   el apagón
blacksmith; ironworker   el herrero
blanket   la manta; la cobija; la frazada
blazer, jacket   el saco
blender   la licuadora
blond   rubio/a
(blood) pressure   la tensión (arterial)
blouse   la blusa
blue   azul
to board   abordar
board of directors   la junta directiva
boarding pass   la tarjeta de embarque;
boat   el barco
body   el cuerpo
to boil   hervir (ie, i)
bold   negrita
Bolivian   boliviano/a
bone   el hueso
book   el libro
bookstore   la librería
boot   la bota
bored   aburrido/a
boring   aburrido/a
boss   el jefe/la jefa
to bother   molestar(le)
bottle   la botella
to bowl   jugar (ue) a los bolos
bowl   la fuente
bowling   el boliche; el bowling

bowling ball   el bolo; la bola
box   la caja
boxer shorts   el calzoncillo
boy   el chico
boyfriend   el novio
bra   el sostén
bracelet   la pulsera
brain   el cerebro
brainstorming   la lluvia de ideas
branch (business)   la sucursal
brand   la marca
bread   el pan
to break   descomponer(se); fracturar(se); romper
breakfast   el desayuno
to breathe   respirar
briefcase   el malctín
to bring   traer
broadband   la banda ancha
broke   brujo/a
brother   el hermano
to brown   dorar
brown   marrón
brunette   moreno/a
to build   construir (y)
building   el edificio
bull   el toro
bullfight   la corrida (de toros)
bumper   el parachoques
bun, small cake   el pan dulce
to bury   enterrar
bus   el autobús, el bus
business   el negocio
businessman/woman   el hombre/la mujer de negocios
busy   ocupado/a
but   pero
butter   la manteca/la mantequilla
to buy   comprar
by   por
by telephone   por teléfono
by the way   por cierto

# C

cabinet   el armario
cafe, coffee shop   el café
cafeteria   la cafetería
calcium   el calcio
calculator   la calculadora
calculus   el cálculo
calendar   el calendario
to call   llamar
to calm, alleviate   calmar
camera   la cámara
Canadian   canadiense
to cancel   cancelar

cancer   el cáncer
candy/sweets   el dulce
cap   la gorra
capsule   la cápsula
captain   el capítan
car   el auto; el carro; el coche
care   el cuidado
career counselor   el/la consejero/a
   vocacional
carefully   cuidadosamente
careless   descuidado/a
carnival   el carnaval
carpenter   el/la carpintero/a
carpet, rug   la alfombra
carrot   la zanahoria
to carry out   realizar (c)
cart, wagon   la carreta
cashier   el/la cajero/a
casualwear   la ropa informal
caterer   el/la proveedor/a de comida
cattle   el ganado
CD player   el reproductor de CDs
to celebrate   celebrar
celebration   la celebración; la fiesta
celery   el apio
cell phone   el teléfono celular; el
   teléfono móvil
cell phone charger   el cargador de
   celular; el cargador del móvil
cemetery   el cementerio
cereal   el cereal
certain   seguro/a
certainly   seguramente
certainty   la certeza
chair   la silla
chalk   la tiza
chalkboard   la pizarra
challenge   el reto
chamomile   la manzanilla
champion   el campeón/la campeona
championship   el campeonato
chance   el azar
to change   cambiar
change   el cambio
channel   el canal
charitable   caritativo/a
charming   simpático/a
chauffeur   el/la chofer (chófer)
cheap   barato/a
check   el cheque
to check in (luggage)   facturar
to check out   fijarse
checking account   la cuenta corriente
cheek   la mejilla
cheese   el queso
chef   el/la chef
cherry   la cereza

chest   el pecho
chicken   el pollo
chicken breast   la pechuga de pollo
child   el niño/ la niña
childhood   la infancia
children's   infantil
Chile   Chile
chile pepper   el ají; el chile
Chilean   chileno/a
cholesterol   el colesterol
to choose   elegir (i, i)
chop   la chuleta
to chop   picar
chopped   picado/a
chore   la tarea
Christmas   la Navidad
Christmas Eve   la Nochebuena
church   la iglesia
cilantro   el cilantro; el culantro
cinema   el cine
cinnamon   la canela
citizen   el ciudadano
city   la ciudad
city block   la cuadra
city council   el concejo municipal
city square   la plaza
to claim   reclamar
clam   la almeja
class   la clase
classmate   el/la compañero/a
classroom   el salón de clase
to clean   limpiar; ordenar
clever   listo/a
client   el/la cliente/clienta
climax   el punto culminante
clinic   la clínica, el centro
clock   el reloj
clone   la clonación
cloning   la clonación
to close   cerrar (ie)
close to, near   cerca de
closet   el armario; el clóset
closing   la despedida
clothes   la ropa
clove of garlic   el diente de ajo
clumsy   torpe
coach   el/la entrenador/a
coach class   la clase turista
coat   el abrigo
coconut milk   la leche de coco
code   el código
coffee   el café
cognate   el cognado
cold   el catarro; el frío; frío/a
to collapse   colapsar
Colombian   colombiano/a
colors   los colores

to comb (someone's hair)   peinar(se)
to come   venir (g, ie)
Come in.   Adelante.; Pase(n).
Come on, cheer up!   ¡Ven/Anda,
   anímate!
comfortable   cómodo/a
comic   cómico/a
command   el mandato
to communicate   comunicar
communication   la comunicación
company   la compañía/empresa
to compile   recopilar
to complain   quejarse
complaint   la queja
to complete, to finish; to run out of
   acabar(se)
complicit   cómplice
computer   la computadora; el
   ordenador
computer science   la informática; la
   computación
conclusion   la conclusión
conflict   el conflicto
to congratulate   felicitar
congratulations   las felicidades; las
   felicitaciones
to connect   conectar(se)
connection   la conexión
consensus   el consenso
to construct   construir
to consume   consumir
contact lenses   los lentes de
   contacto
contaminated   contaminado/a
contemporary   contemporáneo/a
contest   el concurso
to continue   continuar
to contract   contraer
contractor   el/la contratista
contrast   el contraste
to contribute   contribuir (y)
convenience store   la tienda de
   conveniencia
to converse   conversar
to cook   cocinar
cook   el/la cocinero/a
cooked   cocido/a
cookie   la galleta
corn   el choclo; el elote; el maíz
corner   la esquina
correspondence   la correspondencia
corridor, hall   el pasillo
to cost   costar (ue)
Costa Rican   costarricense
cough   la tos
to cough   toser
council   el concejo

**to count** contar
**counter** el mostrador
**country, nation** el país
**countryside** el campo
**cousin** el primo/la prima
**to cover** recorrer; tapar
**crab** el cangrejo
**craftsperson** el/la artesano/a
**crazy** loco/a
**cream** la crema
**cream cheese** el queso crema
**creative** creativo/a
**credit card** la tarjeta de crédito
**creek** el riachuelo
**to cross** cruzar; transitar
**cruise** el crucero
**to crush** machacar
**Cuban** cubano/a
**cubist** cubista
**cucumber** el pepino
**cumin** el comino
**cup** la taza
**to cure** curar
**curiosity** la curiosidad
**current** actual
**curtain** la cortina
**custom** la costumbre
**customs** la aduana
**to cut** cortar
**cycling** el ciclismo
**cyclist** el/la ciclista

# D

**dad** el papá
**dairy (product)** lácteo/a
**to dance** bailar
**dance** la danza
**dance club** la discoteca
**dance company** la compañía de danza
**dancer** el bailarín/la bailarina
**dangerous** peligroso/a
**to dare** atreverse
**dark** la oscuridad; oscuro/a
**data** los datos
**date** la fecha; la cita
**daughter** la hija
**dawn** clarear el día
**day** el día
**day after tomorrow** pasado mañana
**day before yesterday** anteayer
**Day of the Dead** el Día de los Muertos
**dead** difunto/a; muerto/a
**Dear** Estimado/a; Querido/a
**dear** querido/a

**December** diciembre
**decision** la decisión
**deck** la terraza
**decorated** adornado/a
**deforestation** la deforestación
**delicious** rico/a
**to delight** encantar
**to deliver** entregar
**to demand** exigir
**democracy** la democracia
**to denounce** denunciar
**department, school** la facultad
**department store** el almacén
**departure** la salida
**depressed** deprimido/a
**depression** la depresión
**to describe** describir
**description** a descripción
**design** el diseño
**designer** el diseñador
**to desire** desear
**desk** el escritorio
**destination** el destino
**detail** el detalle
**to develop** desarrollar(se)
**development** el desarrollo
**device** el dispositivo
**diabetic** diabético/a
**dictatorial** dictatorial
**dictionary** el diccionario
**to die** morir
**diet** la dieta
**difficult** difícil
**difficultly** dificilmente
**digitally** digitalmente
**dining room** el comedor
**dinner** la comida
**dinner, supper** la cena
**to direct** dirigir (j)
**disadvantage** la desventaja
**disappearence** la desaparición
**disappointed** decepcionado/a
**to disassemble** desarmar
**discovery** el descubrimiento
**discreetly** sigilosamente
**dish, plate** el plato
**dishwasher** el lavaplatos
**to dislike** caer mal
**dispersal, dissemination** la diseminación
**displacement** el desplazamiento
**disposable** desechable
**distant** lejano/a
**to distinguish** distinguir
**diversification** la diversificación
**divorced** divorciado/a
**to do** hacer

**dog** el perro
**dollar** el dólar
**domestic** doméstico/a
**Dominican** dominicano/a
**door** la puerta
**to double** duplicar
**double/single room** la habitación doble/sencilla
**doubt** la duda
**doubtful** dudoso/a
**to download** bajar
**downtown, center** el centro
**drama** el drama
**dream** el sueño
**dress** el vestido
**to dress; to get dressed** vestir(se) (i)
**dresser** la cómoda
**to drink** beber
**drink** la bebida
**to drink** tomar
**to drive** conducir; manejar
**driver** el/la chofer (chófer)
**driver's license** el carnet de conducir; el permiso de conducir
**to drop** caer
**drug** la droga
**drug trafficking** el tráfico de drogas
**dry clean** lavar en seco
**dry cleaner** la lavandería; la tintorería
**to dry (oneself)** secar(se)
**dryer** la secadora
**due to** debido a
**dune** el médano
**during** durante
**DVD** el DVD
**DVD player** el reproductor de DVDs
**dwelling** la vivienda
**dynamic** dinámico/a

# E

**each** cada
**eagle** el águila
**ear** el oído; la oreja; la oreja
**early** temprano
**earring** el arete
**easily** fácilmente
**Easter** la Pascua
**easy** fácil
**to eat** comer
**eccentricity** la excentricidad
**economically** económicamente
**economics** la economía
**Ecuadorian** ecuatoriano/a
**editorial house** la casa editorial
**efficiency** la eficiencia

**efficient**   eficaz; eficiente
**egg**   el huevo
**either . . . or**   o … o
**elbow**   el codo
**to elect**   elegir (i, j)
**election**   la elección
**electrician**   el/la electricista
**elegant**   elegante
**to embrace**   abrazar(se) (c)
**to emerge**   surgir (j)
**emergency**   la emergencia
**emergency exit**   la salida de emergencia
**emigrant**   el/la emigrante
**to emigrate**   emigrar
**emigration**   la emigración
**employee**   el/la empleado/a
**empty**   vacío/a
**to encourage**   fomentar
**energetic**   enérgico/a
**engagement**   el compromiso
**engineer**   el/la ingeniero/a
**to enjoy**   disfrutar
**enough**   bastante
**to enter**   entrar (en)
**entertainment**   la diversión
**environment**   el medio ambiente
**equality**   la igualdad
**equals**   son
**equipment**   el equipo
**eraser**   el borrador
**even if**   aunque
**even though**   aunque
**evening**   por la noche
**event**   el acontecimiento; aun; el evento
**ever**   alguna vez
**every**   todo/a
**every day**   todos los días
**every . . . hours**   cada … horas
**every month**   todos los meses
**every week**   todas las semanas
**everybody**   todos/as
**everyone**   alguien
**everything**   todo
**evident**   evidente
**to exact**   exigir
**to examine**   examinar
**excellent**   excelente
**to exchange**   cambiar
**exchange**   el intercambio
**exchange rate**   la tasa de cambio
**excuse me**   con permiso, perdón
**executive**   el/la ejecutivo/a
**to exert effort**   fajar(se)
**to exhibit**   exponer (g)
**exhibit**   la exposición

**expensive**   caro/a
**experience**   la experiencia
**expert**   el experto
**to explain**   explicar
**export**   la exportación
**expression**   la cara; expresion
**extinct**   extinguido/a
**extinction**   la extinción
**to extinguish, to turn off**   apagar
**extinguished**   extinguido/a
**extroverted**   extrovertido/a
**eye**   el ojo
**eyebrow**   la ceja
**eyelash**   la pestaña

## F

**fabric**   la tela
**fabulous**   fabuloso/a
**face**   la cara
**fact**   el hecho
**failure**   el fracaso
**fair**   regular
**to fall**   caer(se)
**fall**   el otoño
**false**   falso/a
**family**   la familia
**famous**   famoso/a
**fan**   el ventilador
**far (from)**   lejos (de)
**farewell**   la despedida
**farmer**   el/la agricultor/a
**to fascinate**   fascinar
**fast**   rápido/a
**fat**   gordo/a; la grasa
**father**   el padre
**Father's Day**   el Día del Padre
**favorite**   favorito/a
**fear**   el miedo; el susto
**to fear**   temer
**feature, trait**   el rasgo
**February**   febrero
**to feed**   dar de comer
**to feel**   sentir (se) (ie)
**festival**   el festival
**festivity; holiday**   la festividad
**fever**   la fiebre
**few**   poco
**fiancé(e)**   el/la novio/a
**fiber**   la fibra
**fieldwork**   el trabajo de campo
**fig**   el higo
**fight**   la lucha
**to fight**   luchar
**to fill (out)**   llenar
**filled**   relleno/a
**filling**   el relleno

**film**   la película
**filmmaker**   el/la cineasta
**finally, at last**   finalmente; por fin; por último
**to find**   encontrar (ue)
**to find out**   averiguar; enterar(se)
**fine arts**   las bellas artes
**fine/ticket**   la multa
**finger**   el dedo
**to finish**   terminar
**to fire**   despedir (i)
**fire**   el incendio
**firefighter**   el/la bombero/a
**fireplace**   la chimenea
**first**   primero/a
**first class**   la primera clase
**first floor**   la planta baja
**fish**   el pescado
**flashback**   la escena retrospectiva
**flight**   el vuelo
**flight attendant**   el/la auxiliar de vuelo; el/la aeromozo/a; la azafata
**flip-flops**   las chanclas
**float (in a parade)**   la carroza
**flood**   la inundación
**floor**   el piso; la planta
**flour**   la harina
**to flow**   fluir
**flower**   la flor
**flu**   la gripe
**to fly**   volar (ue)
**flying**   volador/a
**to focus**   enfocarse (qu)
**to fold**   doblar
**to follow**   seguir (i)
**following**   siguiente
**food**   la comida
**foot**   el pie
**football**   el fútbol americano
**footwear**   el calzado
**for**   durante (time); para; por
**for example**   por ejemplo
**for sale**   a la venta
**forehead**   la frente
**to foresee**   prever
**forest**   el bosque
**to forget**   olvidar
**fork**   el tenedor
**form**   la forma
**formalwear**   la ropa formal
**fortunately**   afortunadamente
**to fracture**   fracturar(se)
**free time**   el ocio; el tiempo libre
**freeway**   la autopista
**to freeze**   congelar(se)
**French**   francés/francesa

**French fries**   las papas fritas
**frequently**   frecuentemente
**Friday**   el viernes
**fried**   frito/a
**fried dough**   los churros
**friend**   el/la amigo/a
**friendly**   simpático/a
**friendship**   la amistad
**from**   de
**front desk**   la recepción
**fruit**   la fruta
**to fry**   freír (i)
**to fry lightly**   sofreír
**to fulfill**   cumplir
**full**   lleno/a
**fun**   divertido/a
**funny**   divertido/a; gracioso/a
**furniture**   los muebles
**furrier**   el/la peletero/a
**fusion cuisine**   la cocina fusión

## G

**game**   el juego; el partido
**game station**   la consola
**garage**   el garaje
**garbage**   la basura
**garden**   el jardín
**garlic**   el ajo
**gas station**   la tienda de gasolina
**gate**   la puerta (de salida)
**generally**   generalmente
**generous**   generoso/a
**genetically**   genéticamente
**geography**   la geografía
**German**   alemán/alemana
**gesture**   el ademán
**to get along well**   llevarse bien
**to get angry**   enfadarse; enojar(se)
**to get good/bad grades**   sacar
   buenas/malas notas
**to get into**   subir
**to get lost**   perderse (ie)
**to get married**   casar(se)
**to get together**   reunirse
**to get up**   levantar
**gift**   el regalo
**girl**   la chica; la chica
**girlfriend**   la novia
**to give**   dar
**to give (a present)**   regalar
**glad**   alegre; contento/a
**glass**   la copa; el vaso; el vidrio
**glasses**   las gafas
**to globalize**   globalizar
**glove**   el guante
**glove compartment**   la guantera
**to go**   andar; ir

**Go.**   Vaya.
**to go away**   ir(se)
**to go in**   entrar (en)
**to go into effect**   ponerse en marcha
**to go out**   salir
**to go shopping**   ir de compras
**to go straight**   seguir (i) derecho
**to go to bed**   acostarse
**to go up**   subir
**goal**   el gol
**godchild**   el/la ahijado/a
**godfather**   el padrino
**godmother**   la madrina
**gold**   oro
**golf**   el golf
**golf club**   el palo
**good**   bueno/a
**good afternoon**   buenas tardes
**good-bye**   adiós; chao; chau
**good evening**   buenas noches
**good-looking**   bien parecido
**good-looking**   guapo/a
**Good luck!**   ¡Buena suerte!
**good morning**   buenos días
**goosebumps**   la piel de gallina
**gossip magazine**   la revista de
   corazón
**to govern**   gobernar (ie)
**government**   el gobierno
**governor**   el gobernador
**gradually**   gradualmente
**to graduate**   graduarse
**granddaughter**   la nieta
**grandfather**   el abuelo
**grandmother**   la abuela
**grandson**   el nieto
**grape**   la uva
**grapefruit**   el pomelo; la toronja
**graphic**   gráfico/a
**graphic design**   el diseño gráfico
**to grate**   rallar
**gray**   gris
**Great!**   ¡Estupendo!
**great**   fabuloso/a; magnífico/a
**green**   verde
**green pepper**   el pimiento verde
**greeting**   el saludo
**grill**   la parrilla
**ground**   molido/a; picado/a
**ground floor**   la planta baja
**ground meat**   la carne molida/picada
**group**   el grupo
**Guatemalan**   guatemalteco/a
**to guess**   adivinar
**guide**   la guía
**guitar**   la guitarra
**guitar player**   el/la guitarrista
**gymnasium**   el gimnasio

## H

**hachet**   el hacha
**to haggle**   regatear
**hair**   el cabello; el pelo
**hairdresser**   el/la peluquero/a
**half-brother**   el medio hermano
**half-sister**   la media hermana
**Halloween**   el Día de las Brujas
**hallway**   el pasillo
**ham**   el jamón
**hamburger**   la hamburguesa
**to hand**   dar
**hand**   la mano; la mano; la mano
**handicrafts**   la artesanía
**handkerchief**   el pañuelo
**handsome**   guapo/a
**to hang (clothes)**   tender (ie)
**to happen**   pasar
**happily**   alegremente
**happy**   alegre; contento/a
**hardworking**   trabajador/a
**harmful**   dañino/a
**harp**   el arpa
**to harvest**   cosechar
**hat**   el sombrero
**to hate**   odiar
**to have**   tener (g, ie)
**to have a good time**   divertirse (ie, i);
   pasar bien
**to have a(n) . . . ache**   tener dolor de...
**to have breakfast**   desayunar
**to have dinner**   cenar
**to have fun**   divertirse (ie);
   entretenerse
**to have lunch**   almorzar (ue)
**to have to**   tener que
**he**   él
**he/she is**   es
**head**   la cabeza
**health**   la salud
**health care provider**   el proveedor de
   salud
**health center**   el centro de salud
**healthy**   saludable
**to hear**   oír
**to hear about**   oír hablar
**heart**   el corazón
**heat**   el calor
**heating**   la calefacción
**height**   la estatura
**hello**   hola
**Hello? (on the telephone)**   ¿Aló?;
   ¡Bueno!; ¿Diga?; ¿Dígame?;
   ¡Oigo!; ¿Qué hay?
**to help**   ayudar
**her**   su(s)
**herb**   la hierba

**here (present)** presente
**hi** hola
**high-heeled shoe** el zapato de tacón
**highlighter** el marcador
**highway** la carretera
**hiker** el senderista
**hip** la cadera
**his/her/their** su(s)
**Hispanic** hispano/a
**history** la historia
**holiday** el día festivo
**home** el hogar
**homeless** desamparado/a
**homemaker** el ama/o de casa
**homework** la tarea
**Honduran** hondureño/a
**honesty** la honestidad
**hood** el capó
**horrible** horrible
**hospital** el hospital; el sanitorio
**hot** caliente
**hotel** el hotel
**hour** la hora
**house, home** la casa
**housewife** el ama/o de casa
**housing** la vivienda
**How about that!** ¡Fíjate qué noticia!
**How are you (formal)?** ¿Cómo está?
**How are you (informal)?** ¿Cómo estás?
**How do you say . . . ?** ¿Cómo se dice ... ?
**How do you spell . . . ?** ¿Cómo se escribe ... ?
**How incredible!** ¡Qué increíble!
**How is it going?** ¿Cómo te va?
**how many?** ¿cuántos/as?
**How may I help you?** ¿En qué puedo servirle(s)?
**how much?** ¿cuánto/a?
**How much is it?** ¿Cuánto cuesta?
**how/what?** ¿cómo?
**however** no obstante
**hug** el abrazo
**human** humano/a
**humanities** las humanidades
**hundred** cien/ciento
**hunger** la hambre
**to hurt** doler (ue)
**husband** el esposo
**hypothesis** la hipótesis

# I

**I** yo
**I am** soy
**I am . . . years old.** Tengo ... años.
**I don't know** No sé.

**I don't understand** No comprendo.
**I have/you have** tengo/tienes
**I like** me gusta(n)
**I/we hope that . . .** ojalá que ...
**I would like . . .** Me gustaría ...
**I would like . . .** Quisiera ...
**ice** el hielo
**ice cream** el helado
**ice creamery** la heladería
**idea** la idea
**idealistic** idealista
**if** si
**ill** malo/a
**ill person** el/la enfermo/a
**illiteracy** al analfabetismo
**illiterate** analfabeto/a
**illness** la enfermedad
**I'm sorry (to hear that)** lo siento
**imagine** imaginar
**immediately** enseguida
**immigration** la inmigración
**imperfect** el imperfecto
**to implement** implementar
**important** importante
**impossible** imposible
**to improve** mejorar
**impulsive** impulsivo/a
**in boldface** en negrita
**in contrast** en contraste
**in fact** in en realidad/realmente
**in front of** enfrente (de)
**in search of** en busca de
**in (time)** por
**inappropriate** inapropiado/a
**including** hasta
**incredible** increíble
**Independence Day** el Día de la Independencia
**independent** independiente
**to indicate** indicar
**inexpensive** barato/a
**infection** la infección
**to influence** influir
**information** la información
**infrastructure** la infraestructura
**inhabitant** el/la habitante
**to inherit** heredar
**inheritance** el/la herencia
**injection** la inyección
**injured** herido/a
**injured person** el/la herido/a
**to insert** meter
**to inspect** revisar
**inspector** el inspector
**instead of** en vez de
**instruction** la instrucción
**intelligent** inteligente
**interesante** en

**to interest** interesar
**interesting** interesante
**international** internacional
**interpreter** el/la intérprete
**interview** la entrevista
**to interview** entrevistar
**intimacy** la intimidad
**introduction** la presentación
**introverted** introvertido/a
**invitation** la invitación
**to invite** invitar
**iPod** el ipod
**to iron** to planchar
**to itch** picar(se)
**it's clear** está despejado
**it's cloudy** está nublado
**it's cool** hace fresco
**It's sunny.** Hace sol.
**it's sunny** hace sol

# J

**jacket** la chaqueta
**January** enero
**Japanese** japonés/japonesa
**jawbone** la quijada
**jeans** los jeans; los vaqueros/jeans
**jeweller** el/la joyero/a
**jewelry, piece of** la joya
**job** el trabajo
**jogging suit** la sudadera
**joke** la broma
**journalist** el/la periodista
**joy** la alegría
**judge** el/la juez
**juice** el jugo
**July** julio
**June** junio
**junk food** la comida chatarra

# K

**to keep in shape** estar en forma
**to keep quiet** callarse
**to keep silent** guardar silencio
**key** la llave
**key card** la tarjeta magnética
**key word** la palabra clave
**king** el rey
**to kiss** besar
**kiss** el beso
**kitchen** la cocina
**kitchen sink** el fregadero
**knee** la rodilla
**to knock** golpear
**to know** conocer; saber
**knowledge** el conocimiento

# L

labor-related   laboral
laboratory   el laboratorio
laborer   el/la obrero/a
lace   el encaje
lack   la falta
lake   el lago
lamb   el cordero
to land   aterrizar (c)
land   la tierra
landscape   el paisaje
language   la lengua
laptop   la computadora portátil
to last   durar
last   último/a
last night   anoche
last year   el año pasado
late   tarde
later   después; luego; más tarde
to laugh   reír (i)
laughter   la risa
laundry room   la lavandería
lawn   el césped
lawyer   el/la abogado/a
layout   ladistribución
lazy   perezoso/a
leaf   la hoja
to learn   aprender
least   at por lo menos
leather   el cuero
to leave   dejar; ir(se)
left   la izquierda
leg   la pierna
leg (animal)   la pata
legal holiday   el día feriado
legumes   las legumbres
leisure activities   las diversiones
lemon   el limón
to lend   prestar
lentils   las lentejas
lesson   la lección
lettuce   la lechuga
level   el nivel
librarian   el/la bibliotecario/a
library   la biblioteca
license plate   la placa
to lie   mentir
lie   la mentira
life expectancy   la esperanza de vida
lightweight   ligero/a
to like   caer bien; gustar
likewise   igualmente
link   el enlace
lip   el labio
list   la lista
to listen   oír

Listen!   ¡Oye!
Listen, please.   Oiga, por favor.
to listen (to)   escuchar
literature   la literatura
little   a poco; poco; a un poco
little by little   poco a poco
to live   vivir
lively   animado/a; vivo/a
living room   el living; la sala; el salón
lobster   la langosta
to lock up   encerrar (ie)
lodging   el alojamiento
logically   lógicamente
long   largo/a
to look, appear   ver(se)
to look (at)   mirar
to look for   buscar
to look terrible   to tener mala cara
to lose   perder (ie)
to lose weight   adelgazar
loss   la pérdida
loudly   alto
loungewear   la ropa de estar en casa
love   el amor
Love (closing)   Cariños
luck   lasuerte
luggage   el equipaje
lunch   el almuerzo
lung   el pulmón
luxury   el lujo

# M

magazine   la revista
mail   el correo
mail carrier   el/la cartero/a
main character   el personaje principal
to maintain   mantener (g, ie)
major   la carrera
majority   la mayoría
to make   hacer
to make a reservation   reservar
to make the bed   to hacer la cama
man   el hombre
manager   el/la gerente
many   mucho/a (adj.)
many . . . as   as tanto(s)/a(s) … como
map   el mapa
March   marzo
margarine   la margarina
marked down   rebajado/a
marker   el marcador; el rotulador
market   el mercado
married   casado/a
marvel   la maravilla
marvelous   estupendo/a;
   maravilloso/a

material   el material
mathematics   las matemáticas
May   mayo
mayonnaise   la mayonesa
mayor   el alcalde
meal   la comida
meaning   el significado
means of transportation   los medios de
   transporte
measure   la medida
meat   la carne
mechanic   el/la mecánico/a
mediator   el/la mediador
medical doctor   el/la médico/a
medical treatment   el tratamiento
   médico
medicine   la medicina
to meet   conocerse; reunir(se)
meeting, gathering   la reunión
melody   la melodía
melon   el melón
to melt   derretir
memory   el recuerdo
Mennonites   los menonitas
menu   el menú
mess   el lío; el majarete
message   el mensaje
metal   metal
mexican   mexicano/a
Mexican   mexicano/a
Mexican Independence Day   el Día de
   la Independencia de México
to microwave   hornear
microwave (oven)   el (horno)
   microondas
middle class   el burgués
to migrate   migrar
migration   la migración
milk   la leche
milkshake, smoothie   el batido
million   millón
millionaire   el/la millonario/a
minus   menos
mirror   el espejo
moderate   módico/a
modern   moderno/a
mom   la mamá
Monday   el lunes
money in cash   el dinero en efectivo
month   el mes
mood   el estado de ánimo
more   más
more or less   más o menos
morning   la mañana
Moroccan   marroquí
mortality   la mortalidad
mother   la madre

**Mother's Day**   el Día de la Madre
**motor**   el motor
**motto**   el eslogan; el título
**mouth**   la boca
**to move**   mover; mudarse
**movement**   el desplazamiento
**movies**   el cine
**to mow (lawn)**   cortar
**Mr.**   el señor (Sr.)
**Ms, Miss**   la señorita (Srta.)
**Ms., Mrs.**   la señora (Sra.)
**much**   mucho/a (adj.); mucho (adv.)
**much later**   más tarde
**multilingual**   políglota
**mural**   el mural
**muralist**   el/la muralista
**muscle**   el músculo
**museum**   el museo
**music**   la música
**must**   tener que
**mustard**   la mostaza
**my**   mi(s)

# N

**napkin**   la servilleta
**narrow**   estrecho/a
**national**   nacional
**nationality**   las nacionalidad
**native**   natal
**nature**   la naturaleza
**nature preserve**   la reserva natural
**near**   cerca (de)
**necessary**   necesario/a
**neck**   el cuello
**necklace**   el collar
**neighbor**   el/la vecino/a
**neighborhood**   el barrio
**neither**   tampoco
**neither . . . nor**   ni … ni
**nephew**   el sobrino
**nerve**   el nervio
**nervous**   nervioso/a
**net**   la red
**network**   la red
**never**   jamás; nunca
**nevertheless**   sin embargo
**new**   nuevo/a
**New Year's Day**   el Año Nuevo
**New Year's Eve**   el Fin de Año; la
   Nochevieja
**news**   la noticia
**newspaper**   el periódico
**next to**   al lado (de); próximo/a
**Nicaraguan**   nicaragüense
**nice**   agradable; majo/a; simpático/a
**niece**   la sobrina

**Nigerian**   nigeriano/a
**night**   la noche
**night before last**   ante(a)noche
**nightgown**   el camisón
**nightmare**   la pesadilla
**no**   ningún/ninguno/ninguna; no
**no one**   nadie
**nobody**   nadie
**noise**   el ruido
**to nominate**   nominar
**none**   ningún/ninguno/ninguna
**normally**   normalmente
**North American**   norteamericano/a
**nose**   la nariz
**nostalgic**   nostálgico
**not**   tampoco
**not any**   ningún/ninguno/ninguna
**(not) ever**   jamás; nunca
**note card**   la ficha
**notebook**   el cuaderno
**nothing**   nada
**novel**   la novela
**novelist**   el/la novelista
**November**   noviembre
**now**   ahora
**nowadays**   hoy en día
**nurse**   el/la enfermero/a

# O

**oath**   el juramento
**object**   el objeto
**to obtain**   obtener
**obvious**   obvio/a
**occupation**   la ocupación
**to occur**   ocurrir
**October**   octubre
**of**   de
**of course**   claro; por supuesto;
   realmente; cómo no
**to offer**   ofrecer (zc)
**office**   la oficina
**office (of doctor, dentist, etc.)**   el
   consultorio
**often**   muchas veces
**oil**   el aceite
**old**   antiguo/a; mayor; viejo/a
**olive**   la aceituna
**Olympics**   las Olimpiadas
**on, above**   sobre
**on demand**   a petición
**once**   una vez
**one hand**   por un lado
**onion**   la cebolla
**only (adv.)**   sólo
**only child**   el hijo único/la hija única
**to open**   abrir

**opening**   la vacante
**opinion**   la opinión
**opinion poll**   la encuesta de opinión
**opposing**   contrario/a
**optimistic**   optimista
**or**   o
**orange**   anaranjado/a, naranja (adj.);
   la naranja
**orchestra**   la orquesta
**to order**   encargar; pedir (i)
**organization**   la organización
**to organize**   organizar
**other**   otro/a
**other, another**   otro/a
**other hand**   en cambio; por
   otro lado
**outdoors**   al aire libre
**outside**   afuera
**outskirts**   las afueras
**outstanding**   destacado/a
**own**   propio/a
**ozone layer**   la capa de ozono

# P

**package**   el paquete
**page**   la página
**pain**   el dolor
**painter**   el/la pintor/a
**painting**   el cuadro; la pintura
**pajamas**   el/la piyama
**palate**   el paladar
**Panamanian**   panameño/a
**pants**   los pantalones
**pantsuit**   el traje pantalón
**pantyhose**   las pantimedias
**papaya**   la papaya
**paprika**   el achiote; el pimentón
**parade**   el desfile
**Paraguayan**   paraguayo/a
**pardon me**   con permiso, perdón
**parents**   los padres
**parsley**   el perejil
**to participate**   participar
**partner**   el/la compañero/a
**party**   la fiesta
**passenger**   el/la pasajero/a
**passion fruit**   el fruto de pasión
**passive**   pasivo/a
**passport**   el pasaporte
**past**   pasado/a
**pastry**   el pastel
**patient**   paciente; el/la paciente
**patriotic**   patriótico/a
**to pay (for)**   pagar
**peach**   el durazno; el melocotón
**pear**   la pera

**peasant** el/la campesino/a
**pedestrian area** la zona peatonal
**pediatrician** el/la pediatra
**pen** el bolígrafo
**penalty** el penalti
**pencil** el lápiz
**people** la gente
**pepper** la pimienta
**percent** por ciento
**percentage** el porcentaje
**perfect** perfecto/a
**perfectionistic** perfeccionista
**perfectly** perfectamente
**performance** el rendimiento
**performer** el/la intérprete
**periodical** el periódico
**person** la persona; la persona
**perspective** la perspectiva
**Peruvian** peruano/a
**pessimistic** pesimista
**petroleum** el petróleo
**pharmacist** el/la farmacéutico/a
**pharmacy** la farmacia
**philology** la filología
**philosophy** la filosofía
**photo(graph)** la foto(grafía)
**physics** la física
**physiology** la fisiología
**to pick up** recoger (j)
**picture** el cuadro
**pie** la tarta
**pill** la pastilla
**pillow** la almohada
**pin** el alfiler
**pineapple** la piña
**pink** rosado/a, rosa
**to place** colocar
**place** el lugar
**plan** el plan
**to plan to** pensar (ie) + infinitive
**plane** el avión
**planet** el planeta
**plastic** plástico
**plastic arts** los artes plásticas
**plate, dish** el plato
**to play (a game, sport)** jugar (ue)
**to play (an instrument)** tocar (un instrumento)
**player** el/la jugador/a
**plaza** la plaza
**please** por favor
**pleased/nice to meet you**
    encantado/a; mucho gusto
**pleasure** el placer
**plumber** el/la plomero/a; el/la fontanero/a
**plus** y

**poem** el poema
**poet** el/la poeta
**poetry** la poesía
**point of view** el punto de vista
**policeman/woman** el/la policía
**Polish** polaco/a
**political science** las ciencias políticas
**poll** la encuesta
**polluted** contaminado/a
**poor** pobre
**popcorn** las palomitas de maíz
**popular** popular
**popularity** la popularidad
**to popularize** popularizar (c)
**population** la población
**pork** el cerdo
**port** el deportes
**to portray** retratar
**Portuguese** portugués/ portuguesa
**position** el puesto
**possible** posible
**poster** el afiche
**potato** la papa
**potter** el/la ceramista
**poultry, fowl** las aves
**poverty** la pobreza
**powerful** potente
**position** la posición
**to practice** practicar
**to precede** preceder
**to predict** prever
**to prefer** preferir (ie)
**preparation** el preparativo
**to prepare** preparar
**to prescribe** recetar
**prescription** la receta
**present** actual; el regalo
**present time** actualmente; en la actualidad
**preservation** la conservación
**president** el presidente/la presidenta
**presidential** presidencial
**preterit** el pretérito
**pretty** bonito/a; lindo/a
**price** el precio
**printer** la impresora
**prize** el premio
**probable** probable
**problem** el problema
**procession** la procesión
**to produce** elaborar; producir
**product** el producto
**professor** el/la profesor/a
**program** el programa

**progress** el progreso
**to prohibit** prohibir
**promising** prometedor/a
**proposal** la propuesta
**protein** la proteína
**proverb** el refrán
**provided that** con tal (de) que
**proximity** la proximidad
**psychiatrist** el/la (p)siquiatra
**psychologist** el/la (p)sicólogo/a
**psychology** la (p)sicología
**publicity** la publicidad
**publicity campaign** la campaña de publicidad
**Puerto Rican** puertorriqueño/a
**purple** morado/a
**purse** la bolsa/el bolso
**to put** poner (g)
**to put to bed** acostar
**to put makeup on oneself** maquillar(se)
**to put one's clothes on** poner(se) (g) la ropa

# Q

**quality** la calidad
**quantity** la cantidad
**queen** la reina
**question** la pregunta
**quickly** rápidamente
**quiet** callado/a
**quotation** la cita textual
**to quote** citar

# R

**race** la carrera
**racquet** la raqueta
**radiator** el radiador
**radio** el/la radio
**radio announcer** el/la locutor/a
**radiologist** el/la radiólogo/a
**rail** el riel
**to rain** llover (ue)
**rain** la lluvia
**rain forest** el bosque tropical
**raincoat** el impermeable
**to raise one's hand** levantar la mano
**rate** la tasa
**rather** bastante
**to reach out to** comunicarse
**to read** leer
**reading** la lectura
**ready** listo/a
**real estate** bienes raíces
**reality** la realidad
**really** in en realidad/realmente

**Really!** ¡No me digas!
**to reappear** reaparecer
**rearview mirror** el espejo retrovisor
**reason** la razón
**rebirth** el renacimiento
**receipt** la receta
**to receive** recibir
**recipe** la receta
**to recommend** recomendar (ie)
**recommendation** la recomendación
**to record** grabar
**recycled** reciclado/a
**red** rojo/a
**red pepper** la pimienta roja
**redhead** pelirrojo/a
**to reduce** reducir
**to reflect** reflejar
**to reforest** repoblar
**refrigerator** el refrigerador; la nevera
**regime** el régimen
**region** la región
**to regret** arrepentirse (ie)
**regularly** regularmente
**relative** el pariente; el/la pariente
**relatively** relativamente
**relief** el alivio
**to relieve** aliviar
**religious** religioso/a
**remedy, medicine** el remedio
**to remember** recordar(se) (ue)
**to rent** alquilar
**rent** el alquiler
**to repeat** repetir (i)
**to repopulate** repoblar
**reputation** la reputación
**to require** exigir
**to research** investigar
**research** la investigación
**resources** los recursos
**to respect** respetar
**to respond** responder
**responsible** responsable
**to rest** descansar
**restaurant** el restaurante
**result** el resultado
**résumé** el currículum
**to retire** jubilarse
**to return** devolver; retornar; volver (ue)
**review** la reseña
**to reward** premiar
**rib** la costilla
**rice** el arroz
**rich, wealthy** rico/a
**to ride (a bicycle)** montar (en bicicleta)
**right** el derecho; la derecha

**right?** ¿verdad?
**ring** el anillo
**river basin** la cuenca
**road** el camino
**to roast** asar
**robbery** el robo
**robe** la bata
**robot** el robot
**romantic** romántico/a
**roof** el tejado
**room** la habitación
**room; bedroom** el cuarto
**round trip** de ida y vuelta
**route** el trayecto
**routine** la rutina
**rug** la alfombra
**ruins** las ruinas
**to run** correr

# S

**sad** triste
**safe** la caja fuerte
**salad** la ensalada
**salad dressing** el aderezo
**salary** el sueldo
**sale** la rebaja; la venta
**(sales) manager** el/la gerente (de ventas)
**salesman, saleswoman** el/la vendedor/a
**salesperson** el dependiente/la dependienta
**salt** la sal
**Salvadorian** salvadoreño/a
**sandal** la sandalia
**sandwich** el sándwich
**Saturday** el sábado
**to sauté** saltear
**to save** ahorrar
**savings** los ahorros
**sawdust** el aserrín
**to say** decir (g, i)
**to say goodbye** despedir(se) (i)
**to say hello** mandar saludos
**scared** asustado/a
**scarf** la bufanda
**scene** la escena
**schedule** el horario
**school** la escuela
**school, department** la facultad
**science** la ciencia
**scientist** el/la científico/a
**to score a goal** meter un gol
**screen** la pantalla
**sculptor** el escultor/la escultora
**sea** el mar

**search engine** el buscador
**seasoning** el condimento
**seat** el asiento
**security** la seguridad
**sedentary** sedentario/a
**to see** ver
**see you later** hasta luego
**see you soon** hasta pronto
**see you tomorrow** hasta mañana
**seed** la semilla
**to seem** parecer (zc)
**self-portrait** el autorretrato
**to sell** vender
**seller** el/la vendedor/a
**seminar** el seminario
**to send** enviar; mandar
**sentimental** sentimental
**September** septiembre
**serious** grave; serio/a
**to serve** servir (i)
**server** el/la camarero/a
**to set the table** poner la mesa
**several** algún/alguno(s)/alguna(s)
**shape** la forma
**sharp** agudo/a
**to shave (oneself)** afeitar(se)
**she** ella
**sheep** la oveja
**sheet** la sábana
**shell** la concha
**shellfish** los mariscos
**ship** la nave, el barco
**shirt** la camisa
**shoe** el zapato
**shopping** las compras
**shopping center** el centro comercial
**short (in length)** corto/a
**short (in stature)** bajo/a; chaparro/a
**short-sleeved shirt** la camisa de manga corta
**shorts** los pantalones cortos
**should** deber
**shoulder** el hombro
**to show** mostrar (ue)
**shower** la ducha
**shrimp** el camarón; la gamba
**sick** enfermo/a
**side** el lado
**to sign** firmar
**signal** la señal
**significant other** la pareja
**silence** el silencio
**silly, foolish** tonto/a
**simply** simplemente
**since** desde; hace
**sincere** sincero/a
**to sing** cantar

single   soltero/a
sister   la hermana
to sit down   sentarse (ie)
size   el número; la talla; el tamaño
to skate   patinar
ski   el esquí
to ski   esquiar
skiing   el esquí
to skim   leer por encima
skin   la piel
skirt   la falda
sleep   el sueño
to sleep (to fall asleep)   dormir(se) (ue)
slipper   la zapatilla
slope   la bajada; la pendiente
slowly   despacio; lentamente
small   pequeño/a
smallpox   la viruela
smart   listo/a
to smoke   fumar
snack   la merienda
to sneeze   estornudar
snorkeling   el buceo
to snow   nevar (ie)
snow   la nieve
so that   para que
soap   el jabón
soap opera   la telenovela
sober   sobrio/a
soccer   el fútbol
social   social
society   la sociedad
sociology   la sociología
sock   el calcetín
soda   el refresco
sofa   el sofá
soft   blando/a; suave
soft drink   el refresco
soil   la tierra
some   algún/alguno(s)/alguna(s)
someone   alguien
something   algo
something else   otra cosa
something foolish   la babada
sometime   alguna vez
sometimes   algunas veces; a veces
son   el hijo
song   la canción
to soon as   as tan pronto (como)
sorcerer   el brujo
soul   el alma
to sound   sonar
soup   la sopa
sour   agrio/a
source   la fuente
souvenir   el recuerdo

spaghetti   los espaguetis
Spanish   español/a; el español
to speak   hablar
specialist   el/la especialista
specialty   la especialidad
speed   la velocidad
speed, haste   la prisa
to spend   gastar
to spend (time)   pasar
spice   la especie
spinach   las espinacas
spirit   el espíritu
to sponsor   patrocinar
spoon   la cuchara
spoonful   la cucharada
sports equipment   el equipo deportivo
sportswear   la ropa deportiva
to spray   rociar
to spread, to disseminate   difundir
spring   la primavera
square   la plaza
square meter   el metro cuadrado
stadium   el estadio
stairs   la escalera
to stand in line   hacer cola
to stand out   destacarse
star   la estrella
to start   empezar
statistics   las estadísticas
to stay in touch   mantenerse en contacto
steak   el bistec
steering wheel   el volante
step   el paso
stepbrother   el hermanastro
stepfather   el padrastro
stepmother   la madrastra
stepsister   la hermanastra
still   todavía
stockings   las medias
stomach   el estómago
to stop   detener
stopover   la escala
store   la tienda
store window   el escaparate
story   el cuento
stove   la cocina; la estufa
straight   derecho
strawberry   la fresa
street   la calle
to stroll   pasear
strong   fuerte
structure   la estructura
student   el alumno/a; el/la estudiante
student desk   el pupitre
studious   estudioso/a

to study   estudiar; investigar
to stumble   tropezarse
stupendous   estupendo/a
style   el estilo
stylish   de moda
subsidize   subvencionar
subway   el metro
success   el éxito
sugar   el/la azúcar
to suggest   sugerir (ie, i)
suit   el traje; el traje de chaqueta
suitcase   la maleta
to summarize   resumir
summer   el verano
sun   el sol
to sunbathe   tomar el sol
Sunday   el domingo
sunglasses   las gafas de sol
sunrise   la salida del sol
supermarket   el supermercado
supper   la comida
to support   apoyar; sustentar
surely, certainly   seguramente
surgeon   el/la cirujano/a
surgery   la operación
to surprise   sorprender
surprise   la sorpresa
surrealist   surrealista
to surround   rodear
survey   la encuesta
to survive   sobrevivir
sweater   el suéter
sweatshirt; jogging suit   la sudadera
to sweep   barrer
to swell   hinchar
swelling   la hinchazón
to swim   nadar
swimming pool   la piscina; la alberca
symbol   el símbolo
symptom   el síntoma

# T

T-shirt   la camiseta
table   la mesa
tablecloth   el mantel
to take   llevar; tomar
to take a nap   to dormir (ue) la siesta
to take a seat   tomar asiento
to take a walk   dar un paseo; pasear
to take advantage   aprovechar
to take away   quitar(se)
to take care of   cuidar; cuidar(se) (de)
to take note   fijarse
to take notes   tomar apuntes/notas
to take off   quitar(se)
to take off (airplane)   despegar (u)

**to take out**  sacar (qu)
**to talk**  conversar; dialogar
**talkative**  conversador/a
**tall**  alto/a
**tamale**  el tamale
**tapas**  las tapas
**task**  la tarea
**tea**  el té
**teacher**  el/la profesor/a
**team; equipment**  el equipo
**to tear**  romper
**teaspoon**  la cucharita
**technician**  el/la técnico/a
**technology**  la tecnología
**telephone**  el teléfono
**television set**  el televisor
**to tell**  contar (ue); decir (g, i)
**tennis**  el tenis
**tennis player**  el/la tenista
**tennis shoe**  la zapatilla de deporte
**terrace**  la terraza
**terrorism**  el terrorismo
**test**  el examen
**thanks, thank you**  gracias
**Thanksgiving**  el Día de Acción de Gracias
**that**  ese/a (adj.); eso (pron.)
**that is why**  por eso
**that (over there)**  aquel/aquella
**That's great!**  ¡Qué bien/bueno!
**thaw, thawing**  el deshielo
**theater**  el teatro
**theater company**  la compañía de teatro
**their**  su(s)
**theme**  el tema
**then**  entonces; luego
**therapy**  la terapia
**there**  allí
**there is, there are**  hay
**thermometer**  el termómetro
**they**  ellos/ellas
**thin**  delgado/a
**thing**  la cosa
**to think**  pensar (ie)
**to think of/about**  pensar en
**to think of/about (opinion)**  pensar de
**third**  tercero/a
**thirst**  la sed
**this**  este/a; esto
**thousand**  mil
**throat**  la garganta
**through**  por; a través de
**to throw**  lanzar
**Thursday**  el jueves
**ticket**  el billete; el boleto, el pasaje
**tie**  la corbata

**tight**  estrecho/a
**time**  la hora; el tiempo
**timid**  tímido/a
**tire**  la llanta
**tired**  cansado/a
**title**  el título
**to**  a; para
**toast**  el pan tostado/la tostada
**to toast**  tostar
**today**  hoy
**Today is . . .**  Hoy es …
**together**  juntos/as
**toilet**  el inodoro
**tomato**  el tomate
**tomato sauce**  la salsa de tomate
**tomorrow**  mañana
**tone**  el tono
**tongue**  la lengua
**tonight**  esta noche
**too**  también
**tooth**  el diente
**toothpaste**  la pasta de dientes
**tourist class**  la clase turista
**tournament**  el campeonato; el torneo
**toward**  para
**towel**  la toalla
**toxic**  tóxico/a
**toy**  el juguete
**tradition**  la tradición
**traditional**  tradicional
**traditionally**  tradicionalmente
**traffic**  el tráfico
**train**  el tren
**trainer**  el/la entrenador/a
**training**  el entrenamiento
**training resort**  el centro de entrenamiento
**tranquil**  tranquilo/a
**tranquilly**  tranquilamente
**to translate**  traducir (zc)
**trash**  la basura
**to travel**  viajar
**travel agency**  la agencia de viajes
**travel agent**  el/la agente de viajes
**tray**  la bandeja
**to treat**  tratar
**to treat, to be about**  tratar
**tree**  el árbol
**trips**  el viaje
**true**  cierto/a; verdad
**trunk**  el baúl; el maletero
**trust**  la confianza
**truth**  la verdad
**to try**  probar; tratar
**to try on**  probarse (ue)
**Tuesday**  el martes
**turkey**  el pavo

**to turn**  doblar
**to turn on**  encender (ie)
**twin**  gemelo/a
**to twist**  torcer(se) (ue)
**typical**  típico/a

# U

**UFO**  el OVNI
**ugly**  feo/a
**umbrella**  el paraguas
**umpire, referee**  el árbitro
**uncle**  el tío
**under**  abajo; debajo (de)
**to underline**  subrayar
**to understand**  comprender; entender (ie)
**underwear**  la ropa interior
**unemployment**  el desempleo
**unforgettable**  inolvidable
**to unify**  unificar (qu)
**United States**  Estados Unidos
**university**  la universidad
**unless**  a menos que
**unpleasant**  antipático/a
**until**  hasta que
**urgent**  urgente
**Uruguayan**  uruguayo/a
**U.S. citizen**  estadounidense
**to use**  usar
**useful**  útil

# V

**vacation**  las vacaciones
**to vacuum**  pasar la aspiradora
**vacuum cleaner**  la aspiradora
**Valentine's Day**  el Día de los Enamorados; el Día del Amor y la Amistad
**vanilla**  la vainilla
**vegetable**  el vegetal, la verdura
**vegetarian**  vegetariano/a
**vein**  la vena
**Venezuelan**  venezolano/a
**verbs**  verbos
**very**  muy
**veterinarian**  el/la veterinario/a
**video game**  el videojuego
**view**  la vista
**village**  el pueblo
**vinegar**  el vinagre
**virtual library**  la biblioteca virtual
**virtually**  virtualmente
**to visit**  visitar
**vitamin**  la vitamina
**voice**  la voz
**volleyball**  el vóleibol; el volibol

# W

waist   la cintura
to wait for   esperar
waiter/waitress   el/la camarero/a
waiting area   la sala de espera
to wake (someone up); to
   despertar(se) (ie)
to wake up   despertar(se)
to walk   caminar
wallet   la billetera
to want   querer (ie)
warehouse   el almacén
warming   el calentamiento
to wash (oneself)   lavar(se)
washer   la lavadora
wastebasket   el cesto
water   el agua
to water   regar (ie)
way   el camino
we   nosotros/nosotras
We are going to have a good time.   Lo
   vamos a pasar muy bien.
weak   débil
to wear   llevar
to wear a costume   disfrazarse
to wear a shoe size   calzar
weather   el tiempo; el tiempo
weather forecast   el pronóstico del
   tiempo
wedding   la boda
Wednesday   el miércoles
week   la semana
week ago   a una semana atrás
weekend   el fin de semana
weight   la pesa
well   bien; bueno/a
well-off   adinerado/a
what?   ¿qué?
What a pity!   ¡Qué lástima!
What a suprise/coincidence!   ¡Qué
   casualidad!
What day is it?   ¿Qué día es hoy?
What do you think?   ¿Qué te parece?

What for?   ¿para qué?
What is he/she/it like?   ¿Cómo es?
What is the date?   ¿Cuál es la fecha?;
   ¿Qué fecha es hoy?
What is the weather like?   ¿Qué
   tiempo hace?
What time is it?   ¿Qué hora es?
What's new?   ¿Qué tal?
What's up?   ¿Qué tal?
What's wrong (with you/them)?   ¿Qué
   te/le(s) pasa?
What's your name? (familiar)   ¿Cómo
   te llamas?
What's your name? (formal)   ¿Cómo se
   llama usted?
wheel   la rueda
when   cuando
when?   ¿cuándo?
where?   ¿dónde?
Where do we meet?   ¿Dónde
   quedamos?
Where is . . . ?   ¿Dónde está... ?
where (to)?   ¿adónde?
wherever   donde
which?   ¿cuál(es)?
while   mientras
to whistle   pitar
white   blanco/a
who?   ¿quién(es)?
Who is . . . ?   ¿Quién es... ?
whose?   ¿de quién?
why?   ¿para qué?; ¿por qué?
wide   ancho/a
wife   la esposa
wild   silvestre
will   el/la testamento
to win   ganar
wind   el viento
window   la ventana; la ventanilla
window seat   el asiento de
   ventanilla
windshield wiper   el limpiaparabrisas
wine   el vino
wine cellar   la bodega

winner   el ganador
winter   el invierno
to wish, to want   desear
with   con
without   sin; sin que
woman   la mujer
wood   la madera
wool   la lana
word   la palabra
work   la obra
to work   trabajar
work   el trabajo
worker   el/la obrero/a
workshop   el taller
World Cup   la Copa
   Mundial
world, worldwide   mundial
to worry   preocupar(se)
wound   la herida
wounded   herido/a
wrist   la muñeca
to write   escribir
writer   el escritor/la escritora

# Y

year   el año
yellow   amarillo/a
yes   sí
yesterday   ayer
yet   todavía
yogurt   el yogur
you are (familiar)   eres; estás
you are (formal)   es; estás
you (familiar)   tú (familiar); vos
   (Argentina)
you (formal)   usted (formal)
you (plural)   ustedes (plural)
young   joven
young man/woman   el/la joven
your (familiar)   tu(s)
you're welcome   de nada
youth hostel   el albergue juvenil
yucca   la yuca

# Credits

## Text Credits

**p. 48:** "Un buen repaso a la Universidad de Salamanca" reprinted with permission from Alberto López Nájera; **p. 73:** ® All Rights Reserved by World Editors, Inc.; **p. 434:** "Dame la mano" by Gabriela Minstral. La Orden Franciscana de Chile autoriza el uso de la obra de Gabriela Mistral. Lo equivalente a los derechos de autoría es entregado a la Orden Franciscana de Chile, para los niños de Montegrande, de conformidad a la voluntad de Gabriela Minstral.; **p. 457:** El Entnógrafo by Jorge Luis Borges. ©1995 by Jorge Luis Borges, permission of The Wylie Agency Inc.; **p. 490:** Hombre pequenito by Alfonsina Storni. Editorial Losada S.A., Buenos Aires, 1997. Herederos de Alfonsina Storni. Used with permission; **p. 504:** Mafalda (#1126 and #104) por Joaquín S. Lavado, de QUINO. Ediciones de la Flor, 1997. Reprinted with permission of Caminito S.a.s.; **p. 520:** "Apocalipsis" © Denevi, Marco, Falsificaciones, Buenos Aires, Corregidor, 2007. Used with permission.

## Photo Credits

**Cover Image:** Ferran Traite Soler/ IStockphoto.com: p. 2 © Jeff Greenberg/Alamy; p. 5 (top) Ian O'Leary/ Getty Images Inc.—Stone Allstock; p. 5 (center) Getty Images—Stockbyte, Royalty Free; p. 5 (bottom) Christina Kennedy/ PhotoEdit Inc.; p. 22 Dagli Orti (A)/Picture Desk, Inc./Kobal Collection; p. 23 (lower bottom center) Matt Trommer/Shutterstock; p. 23 (right) Pilar Echevarria/Shutterstock; p. 23 (top) Jarno gonzalez Zarraonandia/ Shutterstock; p. 23 (bottom) Rafael Ramirez Lee/Shutterstock; p. 23 (lower upper left) © Robert Frerck/Odyssey/Chicago; p. 24 (top) Grimberg, Marc/Getty Images Inc.—Image Bank; p. 24 (bottom) Goncharov Roman/ Shutterstock; p. 25 Embassy of Peru; Robert Frerck/Odyssey Productions, Inc.; p. 35 Richard Nowitz/National Geographic Image Collection; p. 44 Spencer Grant/PhotoEdit Inc.; p. 50 © Robert Fried/robertfriedphotography.com; p. 51 (top) Robert Fried/robertfriedphotography.com; p. 51 (bottom) Denis Doyle/AP Wideworld Photo; p. 54 © Cristena Cardenas; p. 55 (bottom) Robin Holden, Sr./Shutterstock; p. 55 (center) Graca Victoria/Shutterstock; p. 55 (center) April Turner/Shutterstock; p. 55 (top right) Aaron D. Settipane/ Shutterstock; p. 55 (right) Photo by Rico Torres © 2003 Miramax/ Columbia Pictures, All Rights Reserved, Kobal Collection—The Picture Desk; p. 56 (top left) © Jimmy Dorantes/Latin Focus.com; p. 56 (bottom right) Andresr/Shutterstock; p. 56 (top right) digitalskillet/Shutterstock; p. 56 (bottom left) Mira.com/Artist Name; p. 57 EyeWire Collection/Getty Images—Photodisc; p. 60 (left) Wallenrock/Shutterstock; p. 60 (center left) Dallas Events Inc./Shutterstock; p. 60 (center right) Laurence Gough/ Shutterstock; p. 60 (right) Yuri Arcurs/Shutterstock; p. 66 (top left) © Michael Germana/SSI Photo/Landov; p. 66 (top right) Jack Vartoogian/Front Row Photos; p. 66 (bottom right) © Steve Nesius/Reuters/ Landov; p. 66 (bottom left) © Ramon Espinosa/AP Wide World Photos; p. 67 Scott Harrison/Getty Images; p. 84 Courtesy of the Library of Congress; p. 84 Library of Congress; p. 85 (top) © 2008 Kendal Larson; p. 85 (bottom) Wikipedia, The Free Encyclopedia; Artist unknown. First wedding of Inca princess Nusta Beatriz to Spanish noble Martin de Loyola, 18th century; p. 88; © The Art Archive/Museo Pedro de Osma Lima/Mireille Vautier; p. 89 (center) Mike von Bergen/ Shutterstock; p. 89 (bottom) Marshall Bruce/Shutterstock; p. 89 (top left) Chris Howey/Shutterstock; p. 89 (bottom left) Paul Clarke/Shutterstock; p. 89 (top left) Nicholas Raymond/Shutterstock; p. 90 (top left) Todd B. Powell/Creative Eye/MIRA.com; p. 90 (top right) Nik Wheeler; p. 90 (center) Robert Frerck/Odyssey Productions, Inc.; p. 90 (bottom) © Bob Daemmrich/PhotoEdit; p. 94 Adalberto Rios Szalay/Sexto Sol/Getty Images, Inc.—Photodisc; p. 96 © John Van Hasselt/Sygma/ CORBIS; p. 103 (top) Getty Images, Inc.; p. 103 (top center) William Albert Allard/NGS Image Collection; p. 103 (bottom center) © Victor Englebert; p. 103 (bottom) Chad Ehlers/Stock Connection; p. 118 (top) © Scala/Art Resource; p. 118 (bottom) Dagli Orti/Picture Desk, Inc./Kobal Collection; p. 122 Fernando Botero, "En familia" (The Family). © Fernando Botero, courtesy of Marlborough Gallery, New York; p. 123 (center left) © Alejandro Velasquez; p. 123 (top) © Amra Pasic/Shutterstock; p. 123 (center right) © John Chang/Courtesy of www.istockphoto.com; p. 123 (bottom left) © Richard Gunion/Courtesy of www.istockphoto.com; p. 123 (bottom right) © Galyna Andrushko/Shutterstock; p. 124 (left) © Paloma Lapuerta; p. 124 (center) Tony Freeman/PhotoEdit Inc.; p. 124 (right) Michael Newman/PhotoEdit Inc.; p. 138 © Andre Schafer/Courtesy of www. istockphoto.com; p. 147 (top) Ellen Senisi; p. 147 (bottom) Bill Aron/PhotoEdit Inc.; p. 150 HERMANN BREHM/Nature Picture Library; p. 151 Colombia Information Service Tourist Office; p. 154 Mireille Vautier/ Woodfin Camp & Associates, Inc.; p. 155 (top) © Toon Possemiers/Courtesy of www.istockphoto. com; p. 155 (bottom left) Jeff Chevrier/Courtesy of www. istockphoto.com; p. 155 (bottom right) © Eli Coory/Fotolia; p. 155 (center right) Courtesy of www.istockphoto.com; p. 155 (center left) © Tatiana Popova/Shutterstock; p. 155 (center left) © Kmitu/Shutterstock; p. 155 (center left) © Valentyn Volkov/Shutterstock; p. 156 © Nik Wheeler/Alamy; p. 166 (top) Bruce Ayres/Getty Images.—Stone Allstock; p. 166 (bottom) AP Wide World Photos; p. 166 (right) Robert Frerck/Getty Images Inc.—Stone Allstock; p. 170 (left) Laura Dwight/PhotoEdit Inc.; p. 170 (center) Tony Freeman/PhotoEdit Inc.; p. 170 (right) Robert Fried/robertfriedphotography. com; p. 184 Brennan Linsley/AP Wide World Photos; p. 185 (top) © Bettmann/CORBIS All Rights Reserved; p. 185 (bottom) Luis Romero/ AP Wide World Photos; p. 188 Simon Bolivar (1783–1830) (chromolitho) by Artist Unknown (pre 20th cenutry). Private Collection/Archives Charmet/Bridgeman Art Library; p. 189 (center) Jos? Enrique Molina/ AGE Fotostock America, Inc.; p. 189 (bottom right) Mark Cosslett/National Geographic Image Collection; p. 189 (bottom left) Rhodes, Leonard L T/ Animals Animals/ Earth Scenes; p. 189 (top) © Kimberly White/Reuters/ CORBIS All Rights Reserved; p. 190 (top) Ulrike Welsch/PhotoEdit Inc.; p. 190 (center) Beryl Goldberg; p. 190 (bottom) Jeff Greenberg/PhotoEdit Inc.; p. 202 (left) David Welling/Nature Picture Library; p. 202 (center) © Patrick Keen/Courtesy of www.istockphoto. com; p. 202 (right) © Yann Arthus-Bertrand/Bettmann/ CORBIS; p. 202 (bottom) Silva, Juan/Getty Images Inc.— Image Bank; p. 208 (left) Getty Images, Inc.; p. 208 (center) AP Wide World Photos; p. 208 (right) AP Wide World Photos; p. 210 Gordon, Larry Dale/Getty Images Inc.—Image Bank; p. 211 (left) © Lluis Gene/AFP/ Getty; p. 211 (center) Getty Images; p. 211 (right) Courtesy of Marshall Field's; p. 218 © Michael Stokes/ Shutterstock; p. 219 (top) Joese Caruci/AP Wide World Photos; p. 219 (bottom) © Javier Galeano/AP Wide World; p. 222 Xul Solar (Argentina 1887–1963), "Jefa (Patroness)". 1923. Watercolor on paper, set on cardboard. 10"x 10" (25.4 x 25.4 cm); Framed: 21 3/4" x 21 3/4" (55.2 x 55.2 cm). The Museum of Fine Arts, Houston; Museum purchase with funds provided by the Latin American Experience Gala and Auction; p. 223 (center left) © Mariano Heluani/Shutterstock; p. 223 (bottom center) © Wolfgang Kaehler www.wkaehler.com; p. 223 (bottom) © Ivonne Wierink-vanWetten/Courtesy of www.istockphoto.com; p. 223 (mid-center right) Daniel Rivademar/Odyssey Productions, Inc.; p. 223 (top) © Galina Barskaya/Shutterstock; p. 224 (top) © Marcos Brindicci/ Reuters/CORBIS; p. 224 (center) Bill Bachmann/PhotoEdit Inc.; p. 224 (bottom) © Chen Wei Seng/Shutterstock; p. 226 (left) © James M. Phelps, Jr./Shutterstock; p. 226 (center) © Kanwarjit Singh Boparai/ Shutterstock; p. 226 (right) © Adrees Latif/ Reuters/CORBIS; p. 249 (left) CARL SCHNEIDER/ Getty Images, Inc.—Taxi; p. 249 (right) © Monique Rodriguez/Courtesy of www.istockphoto.com; p. 249 (bottom) Courtesy of www.istockphoto.com; p. 252 © Stuart Cohen/The Image Works; p. 253 (top) Geoff Brightling © Dorling Kindersley; p. 253 (bottom) Getty Images Inc.—Hulton Archive Photos; p. 256 Frida Kahlo, "Self-Portrait at the Border Between Mexico and the United States". 1932. Museo Nacional de Arte Moderno, © 2001 Banco de Mexico Diego Rivera & Frida Kahlo Museums Trust. Av. Cinco de Mayo No. 2, Col. Centro, Del. Cuauhtemoc 06059, Mexico, D.F. Reproduction authorized by the Instituto Nacional de Bellas Artes y Literatura. © Christie's Images/CORBIS All

**A54**

# Language Functions Index

# Subject Index

Mar Caribe

OCÉANO
ATLÁNTICO

Barranquilla
Cartagena
Maracaibo
Caracas
Barquisimeto

VENEZUELA

Georgetown
Paramaribo
Medellín
CORDILLERA DE LOS ANDES
GUYANA
SURINAM
Cayenne
GUAYANA
FRANCESA
(Francia)

Manizales
Bogotá
Salto
Ángel

Cali
COLOMBIA

Quito
ECUADOR
Ecuador

Islas
Galápagos
(Ec.)
Guayaquil
Cuenca
Iquitos
Manaus
Río Amazonas
Belém

Fortaleza

Cajamarca
Río Madeira
Trujillo
PERÚ
Río Branco
B R A S I L
Recife

Machu
Picchu
Lima
Ayacucho
Cuzco
BOLIVIA
Salvador

OCÉANO
PACÍFICO
Arequipa
Lago
Titicaca
La Paz
Brasília
Belo
Horizonte

I. Pinta
I. Marchena
I. Fernandina
I. San Salvador
Santa Cruz
I. Santa Cruz
I. Isabela
Puerto
Ayora
I. San
Cristóbal
Puerto
Villamil
Puerto
Baquerizo
Moreno
Arica
Iquique
Cochabamba
Sucre
Potosí
Santa Cruz
Río de Janeiro
São Paulo
Santos

ISLAS GALÁPAGOS
(ECUADOR)
Desierto de Atacama
PARAGUAY
Salto
Iguazú
Trópico de Capricornio

Antofagasta
Salta
Asunción

OCÉANO
PACÍFICO
CHILE
CORDILLERA DE LOS ANDES
San Miguel
de Tucumán

Cabo Norte
Volcán
Katiki
Coquimbo
ARGENTINA
Córdoba
Río Paraná
Río Uruguay
Rivera
Pôrto Alegre

Hanga Roa
Cabo
Cumming
Valparaíso
Mendoza
Rosario
URUGUAY
Mataveri
Santiago
Buenos Aires
Montevideo
La Plata
OCÉANO
ATLÁNTICO

ISLA DE PASCUA
(CHILE)
Concepción
Bahía Blanca
Río de la Plata

Puerto Montt

OCÉANO

PACÍFICO

Estrecho de
Magallanes
Islas
Malvinas
(Br.)

Punta Arenas
TIERRA DEL FUEGO
Cabo de Hornos

América del Sur